T0392773

POETRY IN BYZANTINE LITERATURE AND SOCIETY (1081–1204)

The twelfth century was one of the most fertile periods in Byzantine literary history and this volume is the first to focus exclusively on its abundant poetic production. It explores the broader socio-cultural tendencies that shaped twelfth-century literature in both prose and verse by examining the school as an important venue for the composition and use of texts written in verse, by shedding new light on the relationship between poetry, patronage and power, and by offering the first editions and interpretive studies of hitherto neglected works. In this way, it enhances our knowledge of the history of Byzantine literature and enables us to situate Medieval Greek poetry in the broader literary world of the medieval Mediterranean.

BAUKJE VAN DEN BERG is Associate Professor of Byzantine Studies at the Central European University. She is the author of *Homer the Rhetorician: Eustathios of Thessalonike on the Composition of the Iliad* (2022).

NIKOS ZAGKLAS is Assistant Professor of Byzantine Studies at the University of Vienna. His recent publications include *Theodoros Prodromos: Miscellaneous Poems. An Edition and Literary Study* (2023).

POETRY IN BYZANTINE LITERATURE AND SOCIETY (1081–1204)

New Texts, New Approaches

EDITED BY

BAUKJE VAN DEN BERG

Central European University, Vienna

NIKOS ZAGKLAS

University of Vienna, Austria

Shaftesbury Road, Cambridge CB2 8EA, United Kingdom

One Liberty Plaza, 20th Floor, New York, NY 10006, USA

477 Williamstown Road, Port Melbourne, VIC 3207, Australia

314–321, 3rd Floor, Plot 3, Splendor Forum, Jasola District Centre, New Delhi – 110025, India

103 Penang Road, #05–06/07, Visioncrest Commercial, Singapore 238467

Cambridge University Press is part of Cambridge University Press & Assessment, a department of the University of Cambridge.

We share the University's mission to contribute to society through the pursuit of education, learning and research at the highest international levels of excellence.

www.cambridge.org
Information on this title: www.cambridge.org/9781009467322

DOI: 10.1017/9781009467292

When citing this work, please include a reference to the DOI 10.1017/9781009467292

First published 2024

A catalogue record for this publication is available from the British Library.

A Cataloging-in-Publication data record for this book is available from the Library of Congress.

ISBN 978-1-009-46732-2 Hardback

To the Memory of Elizabeth Jeffreys

Contents

Figures

Tables

Contributors

PANAGIOTIS A. AGAPITOS is Emeritus Professor of Byzantine Literature at the University of Cyprus and currently Distinguished Fellow of the Gutenberg Research College of the University of Mainz (2021–6). His research interests focus on textual and literary criticism, with an emphasis on Byzantine rhetoric and its performance, poetics, the theory of genre, erotic fiction and the representation of death in Byzantine literature. Over the past thirty years, he has published some ninety scholarly papers and five single-authored studies. He is working on a narrative history of Byzantine literature (AD 300–1500).

FLORIS BERNARD is Assistant Professor of Ancient and Medieval Greek at Ghent University. His research interests include Byzantine poetry and epistolography. He is the author of *Writing and Reading Byzantine Secular Poetry, 1025–1081* (2014).

JULIÁN BÉRTOLA studied classical philology at the University of Buenos Aires and completed his PhD in 2021 at Ghent University as a member of the Database of Byzantine Book Epigrams project. He is now a postdoctoral fellow of the Research Foundation Flanders at Ghent University, studying the socio-cultural practices associated with Byzantine poetry and the material context of its textual transmission. In 2023, he was awarded a Hannah Seeger Davis Postdoctoral Research Fellowship in Hellenic Studies at Princeton University to write a monograph on verse marginalia in Byzantine manuscripts of historians.

EMMANUEL C. BOURBOUHAKIS is Associate Professor of Classics and the Stanley J. Seeger '52 Center for Hellenic Studies at Princeton University. His research interests range broadly over Byzantine literature, especially in the areas of rhetoric, epistolography, historiography and classical reception. He is the author of *Not Composed in a Chance Manner: The Epitaphios for Manuel I Komnenos by Eustathios of Thessalonike* (2017).

KONSTANTINOS CHRYSSOGELOS is Assistant Professor at the University of Patras (Department of Philology) in the Division of Byzantine and Modern Greek Studies. His research interests include Byzantine and Post-Byzantine literature (fourth–eighteenth centuries), and the reception of the Byzantine past in modern Greece (nineteenth–twenty-first centuries). His most recent book is the critical edition of Constantine Manasses' *Hodoiporikon* (2017).

GIULIA GERBI obtained her PhD in Ancient Heritage Studies at Ca' Foscari University of Venice and Sorbonne University (2021). Her thesis, soon to be published, consists of a critical edition with Italian translation and commentary of Nikephoros Basilakes' *Progymnasmata*. She is currently a postdoctoral researcher at Ca' Foscari University of Venice, as a member of the ERC-project PURA – Purism in Antiquity.

ELIZABETH JEFFREYS was Emeritus Bywater and Sotheby Professor of Byzantine and Modern Greek Language and Literature at the University of Oxford and Emeritus Fellow of Exeter College, Oxford. She has published widely on topics in Byzantine literature; recent publications include *Four Byzantine Novels* (2012) and 'A Constantinopolitan Poet Views Frankish Antioch', *Crusades* 14 (2015).

MICHAEL JEFFREYS studied classics at Cambridge (UK) and then completed a PhD on the border of Byzantine Studies and Modern Greek at the University of London. After postdoctoral work in the US and Greece, he was appointed Lecturer in Modern Greek at the University of Sydney, where he took part in the extraordinary flowering of Greek education there in the late 1970s and the 1980s, and was elected Sir Nicholas Laurantus Professor of Modern Greek at Sydney. After taking early retirement at the end of millennium he returned to the UK and has been doing research at Oxford, largely in Byzantine Studies.

MARKÉTA KULHÁNKOVÁ works as researcher at the Czech Academy of Sciences and as an Associate Professor at Masaryk University (Brno). Her research focuses mainly on Byzantine narrative, both in verse and in prose; currently she is working on a narratological commentary on the *Digenis Akritis* poem. She is also interested in the reception of Byzantium in modern culture and translates Byzantine and Modern Greek literature into Czech. She has published a monograph entitled *Das gottgefällige Abenteuer: Eine narratologische Analyse der byzantinischen erbaulichen Erzählungen* (2015).

MARC D. LAUXTERMANN holds the Stavros Niarchos Foundation – Bywater and Sotheby chair in Byzantine and Modern Greek Language and Literature at the University of Oxford, and he is a Fellow of Exeter College. His books include *The Spring of Rhythm: An Essay on the Political Verse and Other Byzantine Metres* (1999) and *Byzantine Poetry from Pisides to Geometres: Texts and Contexts* (2 vols, 2003–19). Recent publications focus on the Eugenian recension of *Stephanites and Ichnelates* as well as on grammars and dictionaries in early modern Europe.

PAUL MAGDALINO studied at Oxford and taught for thirty years at the University of St Andrews, in addition to which he has held teaching appointments at Harvard and Koç University (Istanbul), and fellowships in Germany, the United States and Australia. He has published widely on many aspects of Byzantine history, although his research has concentrated on the Middle Byzantine period, court culture, the city of Constantinople, and the place of astrology and prophecy in Byzantine culture. He has been a Fellow of the British Academy since 2002.

UGO MONDINI is a British Academy Postdoctoral Fellow at the University of Oxford. He researches Byzantine poetry (tenth–fifteenth centuries) and has produced an edition of the poems by John Mauropous and Michael Choniates, as well as of *The Metaphraseis of the Psalms* by Manuel Philes (with Anna Gioffreda and Andreas Rhoby; 2024). His current research focuses on the teaching of the Greek language in the Middle Ages; it aims at producing a study of early schedography (tenth–eleventh centuries).

AGLAE PIZZONE is a Byzantinist with a training in Classics. In her research she focuses on cultural history and history of the ideas. She is currently Professor of Ancient and Medieval Greek Literature at the University of Southern Denmark. She is interested in autography, self-commentaries in the Greek Middle Ages, as well as in the Byzantine commentaries on Hermogenes. She has discovered new autograph notes by John Tzetzes in the Voss. Gr. Q1. Recent publications include the volume *Emotions through Time: From Greece to Byzantium* (co-edited with Douglas Cairns, Martin Hinterberger and Matteo Zaccarini; 2022).

RACHELE RICCERI (PhD, University of Rome Tor Vergata–Ghent University 2013) is a postdoctoral researcher at Ghent University, where she is the content manager of the Database of Byzantine Book Epigrams. Her current research focuses on the reception of the Psalms in Byzantium, as well as on the study of paratextuality in Byzantine manuscripts.

BAUKJE VAN DEN BERG is Associate Professor of Byzantine Studies at Central European University, Vienna. Her research focuses on Byzantine scholarship, Byzantine education and the role of ancient literature in Byzantine culture. Recent publications include the monograph *Homer the Rhetorician: Eustathios of Thessalonike on the Composition of the Iliad* (2022) and the co-edited volumes *Emotions and Narrative in Ancient Literature and Beyond: Studies in Honour of Irene de Jong* (with Mathieu de Bakker and Jacqueline Klooster; 2022) and *Byzantine Commentaries on Ancient Greek Texts, 12th–15th Centuries* (with Divna Manolova and Przemysław Marciniak; 2022).

NIKOS ZAGKLAS is Assistant Professor of Byzantine Studies at the Department of Byzantine and Modern Greek Studies at the University of Vienna. His research activity lies at the intersection of traditional philology and literary interpretation with a special focus on issues of patronage, poetry and genre theory. His recent publications include *Theodoros Prodromos: Miscellaneous Poems. An Edition and Literary Study* (2023) and the co-edited thematic cluster 'Why Write Poetry? Transcultural Perspectives from the Later Medieval Period' (with Krystina Kubina; *Medieval Encounters*, 2024).

NEKTARIOS ZARRAS is a member of the teaching staff at the University of the Aegean, Department of Mediterranean Studies, where he teaches Byzantine art and archaeology. In 2013 he was awarded the 'Maria Theochari' Grant by the Christian Archaeological Society (Greece) for the publication of his doctoral thesis, 'Ο εικονογραφικός κύκλος των εωθινών ευαγγελίων στην παλαιολόγεια μνημειακή ζωγραφική των Βαλκανίων' (2011). In the summer of 2013 he was a Fellow at Dumbarton Oaks, and in the period 2016–2018 he was an Alexander von Humboldt Senior Research Fellow at the University of Münster working on identity and patronage in Byzantium. He is currently publishing his book *Ideology and Patronage in Byzantium: Dedicatory Inscriptions and Patron Images from Middle Byzantine Macedonia and Thrace* (2023). His research interests focus on Byzantine painting, epigraphic material (dedicatory inscriptions) and patronage.

Introduction

*Poetry in Byzantine Literature and Society (1081–1204)**

Nikos Zagklas and Baukje van den Berg

In his well-known *On his Own Verses*, Gregory of Nazianzos elucidates the advantages of writing in verse: the poetic form promotes moderation in writing, possesses significant pedagogical qualities, and follows the example of the Bible, which contains a good deal of poetry, with the Psalms of the poet-king David as the principal representatives of biblical verse.[1] Despite the abundance of poetic production in the centuries after Gregory, few Byzantine texts provide theoretical considerations about the special qualities associated with verse. Byzantine poets rarely speak about the reasons behind their choice of verse over prose or of a specific metre. Apart from commentaries on ancient poetry, we have no Byzantine *ars poetica* with programmatic reflections on the aesthetics and practice of poetic production, such as we find in the medieval West.[2] To understand the formal and social dynamics of Byzantine poetry, therefore, we need to study the texts themselves, along with their contexts of production and consumption. Continuing the trailblazing work of recent studies devoted to the Byzantine poetry of the seventh to eleventh centuries, which have forged new scholarly approaches to the poetic tradition of the Byzantines, the present volume is the first to focus exclusively on the poetry of the twelfth

* This volume is partly based on the conference 'Byzantine Poetry in the "Long" Twelfth Century (1081–1204): Perceptions, Motivations, and Functions' organized at the Austrian Academy of Sciences (13–15 June 2018) in the framework of the project 'Byzantine Poetry in the "Long" Twelfth Century (1081–1204)', P 28959–G25, funded by the Austrian Science Fund (FWF).

1 The relevant poem is Gregory of Nazianzos 2.1.39; on Gregory's arguments for writing verse, see Bernard and Demoen (2021: 373–4). On David as poet-king, see Ricceri in this volume.

2 See Conley (1995) and Bernard and Demoen (2021: 373). However, for reflections on the special qualities of political verse, see M. J. Jeffreys (1974). While Aristotle's *Poetics* seems not to have enjoyed a wide reception in Byzantium, Horace's *Ars poetica* continued to be studied in the medieval West. See e.g. Fredborg (2014) for the eleventh and twelfth centuries. During approximately the same period, Geoffrey of Vinsauf wrote his influential *Poetria nova* and Matthew of Vendôme produced his *Ars versificatoria*. Concerning these works, see the relevant chapters in Copeland and Sluiter (2009). On medieval *artes poeticae*, see also the foundational Faral (1924).

century, one of the most fertile periods in Byzantine literary history, not least when it comes to literature in verse.[3]

The volume of poetic production dating from the time of the Komnenian emperors is immense and even central texts are still awaiting (updated) editions. A comprehensive discussion of the poetry of this period therefore lies beyond the scope of a single volume. Instead, the present collection of fifteen contributions aims to advance our understanding of Byzantine poetic culture – and twelfth-century literature more broadly – by concentrating on texts that presently remain poorly studied, by offering the first editions of hitherto unpublished texts, by placing individual poems within their broader literary contexts, and by studying well-known texts from new perspectives. It explores the broader tendencies that shaped twelfth-century literature in both prose and verse (Part I); it examines the school as an important venue for the composition and use of texts written in verse (Part II); it sheds new light on the relationship between poetry, patronage and power by studying texts that have received little or no scholarly attention so far (Part III); and it offers the first editions and interpretive studies of unknown or neglected works (Part IV). By combining wide-ranging surveys and close readings, and by tying in with recent developments in the study of Byzantine literature, this volume takes an important step towards a better understanding of the abundant poetic production of the twelfth century. In this way, it will not only help to complete our knowledge of the history of Byzantine literature but will eventually enable us to situate Medieval Greek poetry in the broader literary world of the medieval Mediterranean. In-depth studies of individual traditions and texts are essential if we wish to make the poetry of the Byzantines part of cross-cultural Mediterranean or global perspectives.[4]

The Age of Poetry

This volume takes as its point of departure the period beginning from the moment that Alexios I Komnenos ascended the imperial throne in 1081 to the Latin sack of Constantinople during the Fourth Crusade in 1204. As Elizabeth Jeffreys has noted, 'one aspect of the literature produced in the

3 Lauxtermann (2003–19) for the seventh to tenth centuries; Bernard (2014) for the period of 1025–81. The poetry of the Palaiologan period (from the Fourth Crusade to the fall of Constantinople in 1453) is the focus of the project 'The Power of Poetry in Late Byzantium', led by Krystina Kubina at the Austrian Academy of Sciences.

4 For cross-cultural approaches to Mediterranean poetry and occasional literature in general, see the papers collected in Kubina and Zagklas (2024a) and Nilsson and Zagklas (2024).

twelfth century that is in marked contrast to either the eleventh or the thirteenth, is that there was a very great deal of writing in verse'.[5] A provisional estimate of the quantity of surviving poetry from this period amounts to *c.* 150,000 verses in various metres, a number that would expand even more if one took into account the large amount of anonymous poetry surviving in manuscripts or in the form of inscriptions on various objects. By contrast, the oeuvre of the three most important poets in the period between 1025 and 1081, Christopher of Mytilene, John Mauropous, and Michael Psellos, does not exceed 10,000 verses. Even though this comparison should not be taken in absolute terms, it demonstrates the popularity of poetry throughout this century and the tendency of many authors to opt for verse for much of their literary output. This remarkable development in the history of Byzantine literature denotes a change in the balance between prose and verse: even though prose continued to be the dominant mode of literary expression, there was an unprecedented increase in poetic production and poetry started to be used for purposes hitherto reserved for prose.[6] Around the same time, prose and poetry started to join forces more systematically than they had previously, with the composition of works in a mixed form as the result.[7] The boundaries between prose and poetry thus became more fluid than ever before and many authors embellished their prose writings with a poetic style, as Emmanuel Bourbouhakis argues in his contribution to this volume.

The premise that this period saw unprecedented growth in the production of poetry is based on the presumption that the years between 1081 and 1204 form a distinct phase in the history of Byzantine poetry and literature more broadly. In his study of eleventh-century poetry, Floris Bernard has argued that the timespan between 1025 and 1081 constitutes a distinct period on account of common sociohistorical tendencies, including a high degree of social mobility and the quick succession of many reigns, as well as the lack of a strong dynastic family, in sharp contrast with the preceding and subsequent periods, when the Macedonian and Komnenian dynasties, respectively, controlled the political landscape.[8] Even though the towering figure of Michael Psellos dominated intellectual life in the capital during much of this period, it is rather Psellos' contemporaries John Mauropous

5 E. M. Jeffreys (2009: 222).

6 One could therefore compare this period with the fifth century BC, when the prominent place of poetry in Athens was challenged by the emergence of oratorical prose; on this shift from poetry to prose, see e.g. Godzich and Kittay (1987), Russell (1989), Cole (1991), Goldhill (2002), Graff (2005).

7 See Zagklas (2017); see also Agapitos in this volume.

8 Bernard (2014: 10–17).

and Christopher of Mytilene who have been praised by modern scholars for the unique traits of their poetic craft.[9]

Approximately forty years before the publication of Bernard's book, Wolfram Hörandner chose the year 1118 as the bookend of his survey of eleventh-century poetry, a year marked by the death of the emperor Alexios I Komnenos and the succession to the throne of his son John II Komnenos.[10] The different time periods chosen by Bernard and Hörandner remind us that chronological boundaries are modern constructions, often following a political timeline that does not neatly map onto literary developments. Chronological bookends should thus not be taken as hard dividing lines that artificially separate one period from another but as permeable boundaries delimiting time periods with recognizable literary and social tendencies.[11] This volume therefore does not claim that the period between 1081 and 1204 is completely independent, as lacking strong ties to the periods before and after. Rather, it claims that this period features certain historical and social tendencies that shaped poetic production in distinct ways. It is exactly the distinct nature of twelfth-century poetry (and prose) on which the different studies in this volume shed new light.

For the poetry produced between 1081 and 1204, we lack a systematic study comparable to those written by Marc Lauxtermann on the poetry of the seventh to tenth centuries and Floris Bernard on that of the eleventh century. Recent decades have seen significant progress regarding the study of individual authors and works as well as specific clusters of poetry. For the ceremonial poetry of the twelfth century, for instance, Wolfram Hörandner's 2003 study remains the main point of departure.[12] Seminal studies by Ivan Drpić and Foteini Spingou have significantly advanced our understanding of the epigrammatic poetry of the period: while Drpić has shed new light on the ties between epigrams, art and self-representation from the beginning of the twelfth until the fifteenth century, Spingou has opened a new perspective onto the Komnenian epigrammatic poetry preserved in the codex Venice, Biblioteca Nazionale Marciana, gr. Z. 524 [Diktyon 69995] by addressing questions of authorship, performativity and transmission.[13] Ingela Nilsson's recent monograph on Constantine

9 Bernard (2019: 213). For the poetry of the eleventh century, see also Bernard and Demoen (2012) and Bernard and Livanos (2018).

10 Hörandner (1976).

11 On the periodization of Byzantine literature, see Agapitos (2012) and (2020).

12 Hörandner (2003: 75–85). For a focus on Theodore Prodromos, see Hörandner (1974: 79–109). For a study of ceremonial poetry of the earlier period, see Lauxtermann (2003-19: 2:49–56).

13 Drpić (2016); Spingou (2014) and (2021).

Manasses and his occasional writings, many of which are in verse, has moreover contributed a great deal to a better understanding of how an author commissioned by aristocratic patrons used poetry.[14]

Even so, we do not have many studies that provide a synthesis of the verse production of this period, with the exception of an article by Elizabeth Jeffreys entitled 'Why Produce Poetry in Twelfth-Century Constantinople?', published in a volume dealing with questions of poetry and poeticality in Byzantium, and a chapter by Nikos Zagklas that examines the different poetic trends and the ties between patronage and poetry during this period, published in Brill's *Companion to Byzantine Poetry*.[15] The former offers useful reflections on the question of what may have motivated twelfth-century authors to write poetry; the latter is the first study seeking to identify different phases in twelfth-century poetic production, attempting to recognize continuities and discontinuities in this long timespan. The present volume is an important step towards filling the gap that remains.

Such an endeavour is greatly helped by the many modern editions published since the 1970s, including those of Theodore Prodromos' 'historical poems' by Wolfram Hörandner and his 'miscellaneous poems' by Nikos Zagklas,[16] as well as editions of the poems of Nicholas Kallikles by Roberto Romano and the Ptochoprodromic poems by Hans Eideneier.[17] Again, however, much remains to be done. An important missing piece of the puzzle is the long-anticipated edition of the entire corpus of Manganeios Prodromos, of which Elizabeth and Michael Jeffreys offer a tantalizing foretaste in their contribution to this volume. We will not be able to shed light on the complete poetic production of this period without an edition of his entire oeuvre. Many other poems likewise remain either unpublished or accessible only in outdated and unreliable editions, such as the well-known astrological poems by Constantine Manasses.[18] The oeuvre of the prolific poet and teacher John Tzetzes is another good example: his *Allegories of the Iliad* may be read in Boissonade's outdated edition from the mid-nineteenth century;[19] his little-known didactic poem on Porphyry's *Eisagoge*, which runs to more than 1,700 dodecasyllabic verses, is still

14 Nilsson (2021a). On patronage in the twelfth century, see Mullett (1984). For Prodromos as a poet to commission, see Zagklas (2023: 31–70).

15 E. M. Jeffreys (2009); Zagklas (2019).

16 Hörandner (1974); Zagklas (2023). On Prodromos' historical poems, see also Ricceri in this volume.

17 Romano (1980); Eideneier (1991) and (2012). For Kallikles, see Gerbi in this volume; for Ptochoprodromos, see Kulhánková in this volume.

18 See Chryssogelos in this volume.

19 Boissonade (1851). For an English translation, see Goldwyn and Kokkini (2015). Alberto Ravani is currently preparing a partial critical edition of the text.

completely unedited;[20] and his extensive verse commentary on the Hermogenean corpus is only partially available in a modern edition.[21] With much editorial work still in progress, our understanding of twelfth-century poetic culture will gradually grow. The present volume contributes to this by including editions of completely unknown material. In addition to the *editio princeps* of a poem by Mangeneios Prodromos, Julián Bértola offers the first edition of an unedited cycle of book epigrams on Herodotus, while Aglae Pizzone shares completely new Tzetzean material from the important manuscript Leiden, Bibliotheek der Rijksuniversiteit, Vossianus Gr. Q1 [Diktyon 38108].

Poetry, Patronage and Power

In 1081 Alexios was proclaimed emperor, paving the way for the family of the Komnenoi to rule for more than 100 years and thus to become one of the longest-ruling imperial dynasties in Byzantium. By contrast, the next dynasty, that of the Angeloi, lasted a mere twenty years due to the events of 1204, which to some extent were the result of bad political decisions on the part of members of the Angeloi family themselves. Throughout these 120 years the social and bureaucratic structures of the capital were reformed in such a way as to foster a system of constant self-promotion for the ruling family. The historian Zonaras reports that the ascension of Alexios Komnenos to the throne was followed by the distribution of offices and state land to family members, making them the wealthiest and most powerful family in the empire.[22] These developments created a close connection between literature and patronage as the former came to serve the agenda of the new imperial family on various levels and occasions. The court became one of the main settings for the composition and consumption of poetry in many different genres.[23] Poetry became an important means for expressing

20 A critical edition of this text is currently under preparation by Rogelio Toledo Martin at the University of Vienna.

21 Elisabetta Barili, Aglae Pizzone and Baukje van den Berg are preparing a complete edition of Tzetzes' commentary on Hermogenes. Until now, only Tzetzes' commentary on *On Types of Style* has been edited; see Barili (2022). For an edition of some further excerpts of this work, see Cramer (1837: 1–138) and Walz (1832–6: 3:670–86).

22 Zonaras, *Chronicle* 767.2–10 ed. Büttner-Wobst (1897). The most authoritative study of this phenomenon remains Kazhdan and Franklin (1984); see also Magdalino (1993: 180–227) on what he terms the 'Komnenian system'.

23 The term 'court poetry' tends to be used for the production of ceremonial poetry, but it should rather be understood as an umbrella term for various kinds of poetry produced and consumed at the court, ranging from ceremonial and didactic to epigrammatic and epistolary poetry. For an example, see the rubric of Manganeios Prodromos' *Poem* 15 (edited by Elizabeth and Michael Jeffreys in this volume), which argues that Emperor Manuel I Komnenos had ordered the poet to compose his verses.

imperial policy and propaganda, as well as for fashioning the crucial role of poets in doing so, as the contributions by Rachele Ricceri and Elizabeth and Michael Jeffreys clearly demonstrate in the cases of Theodore Prodromos and Manganeios Prodromos, respectively.

Although the Komnenians monopolized most high-ranking positions, various prestigious offices were still open to those who did not belong to the imperial family by blood or marriage. Take, for example, the high-ranking bureaucrat and courtier Theodore Styppeiotes, who held a prominent position at the Komnenian court before he fell from grace in the mid-twelfth century.[24] Styppeiotes was a fervent admirer of the poetry written by his teacher Theodore Prodromos and was the recipient of various of his epistolary poems.[25] A number of other high-ranking officials produced their own poetry, such as the *logothete of the dromos* Michael Hagiotheodorites, who wrote a vivid verse *ekphrasis* of a horse race addressed to an unnamed friend.[26] Less eminent court positions were likewise occupied by learned individuals with an interest in poetry. A certain imperial secretary by the name of Gregory, for instance, was involved in a literary polemic with Tzetzes and criticized the poetic qualities of the latter's verse.[27] Poetry and the court were thus inextricably connected.

Other twelfth-century poets held church offices and teaching positions in the capital and provinces of the empire. Many of them started their careers as deacons and acquired teaching positions before moving to bishoprics outside the capital. For example, Constantine Stilbes (*c.* 1150–1225) became teacher of the Apostle before moving to Kyzikos to take up the city's bishopric.[28] His *Fire Poem* describing the devastating fire sweeping through Constantinople in 1197 counts among the most impressive works of the period.[29] Approximately a century earlier, Theophylaktos of Ohrid (*c.* 1050–after 1108) had been ordained as deacon at Hagia Sophia and obtained the coveted position of master of the rhetoricians before being appointed Archbishop of Bulgaria sometime after 1088. Despite its important position as a turning point between the era of Christopher of Mytilene and John Mauropous and the time of the Komnenians, his poetic production remains largely unstudied.[30] Niketas of Herakleia, who was

24 See Kresten (1978) and Koufopoulou (1989).
25 Hörandner (1974: 516–23). On epistolary poetry more broadly, see Kubina and Riehle (2021).
26 Ed. Horna (1906) and Papadimitriou (1911). For a literary analysis of the text, see Marciniak and Warcaba (2014); for an English translation and commentary, see Marciniak and Warcaba (2021).
27 See Zagklas (2021: 298) with bibliography.
28 Stilbes' death used to be dated to *c.* 1208; a new date (1225) is suggested in Kotzabassi (2009: 442).
29 Ed. Diethart and Hörandner. On Stilbes' poem, see Magdalino in this volume, with further bibliography.
30 For some introductory remarks, see Gautier (1980: 118–26) and Mullett (1997: 243–7).

born sometime in the mid-eleventh century, followed a career path similar to that of Theophylaktos: he was first appointed director of the school of Chalkoprateia and became a teacher of the Apostle sometime after 1088; he served as deacon in the church of Hagia Sophia and was promoted to the bishopric of Herakleia in 1117. During his time as a teacher he produced various didactic poems on topics of grammar, various unedited examples of which are discussed by Floris Bernard in his contribution to this volume in order to offer new insights into the characteristics of such poetry and its important role in preparing students for schedographical contests. The similar professional trajectories of these twelfth-century poets owe much to the so-called Patriarchal school, which offered successful teachers prominent positions in the educational and ecclesiastical establishment.[31] Others, however, did not follow this career path. Theodore Prodromos and John Tzetzes, for instance, two of the leading poets and grammarians of the period, continued to work independently, without official teaching posts or positions in the church hierarchy.

Poetry and Twelfth-Century Literary Culture: Between Court, School and *theatron*

The twelfth century saw various new developments in literary production, among the most significant of which is the use of the vernacular or the 'mixed language'.[32] The twelfth century has been described as containing the 'seeds of modern Greek literature', and some Neohellenists have even gone so far as to include some of the vernacular works of the period in discussions of modern Greek literature.[33] Various vernacular texts in metrical form date from this period, covering a wide variety of genres: the long narrative poem *Digenis Akritis*, a group of begging or petitionary poems by Ptochoprodromos alongside the so-called *Maiuri poem* or fifth Ptochoprodromic poem, a poem from prison by the historian and intellectual Michael Glykas and an admonitory poem with the title *Spaneas* addressed by an aristocratic father to his son.[34] Vernacular features, however, permeated

31 Browning (1977).

32 For an introduction to this issue, see Hinterberger (2019), with further bibliography. For a new approach to this phenomenon, see Kulhánková in this volume.

33 'Seeds of modern Greek literature': Bernard (2014: 4). See Agapitos (2017) for a detailed discussion of the birth of so-called 'Medieval Neohellenic' texts around 1830–60.

34 The most important studies of the mentioned works include E. M. Jeffreys (1998) for *Digenis*; see also Kulhánková (2021). Markéta Kulhánková is currently preparing a narratological commentary to *Digenis Akritis*. For the Ptochoprodromic poems, see Kulhánková in this volume, with further bibliography. On Glykas' prison poem, see Bourbouhakis (2007). For *Spaneas*, see Danezis (1987).

much of the textual production of this time and can be found in texts ranging from ceremonial works to didactic poems and *schede*.[35] Moreover, poems in the vernacular were probably presented together with highbrow poems to various imperial recipients, which illustrates the close connection between the different linguistic registers.[36] Switching between different registers was employed as a deliberate and sophisticated literary technique. In her contribution to this volume, Markéta Kulhánková explores this issue in detail by revisiting the Ptochoprodromic poems and other texts.

Much of the poetry produced during this period was written for ceremonial purposes, in parallel with an abundant production of imperial panegyric in prose.[37] Encomiastic and congratulatory poetry was composed to celebrate a wide range of occasions at the court, including imperial victories and triumphal processions, coronations, weddings and the birth of imperial offspring. Ceremonial poetry had not played such a central role since the reign of Emperor Herakleios and his court poet George of Pisidia in the early seventh century.[38] As pointed out above, the new imperial dynasty very much depended on this kind of literature for the propagation of their self-representation and political ideology. On the other hand, poets themselves benefited from the production of court poetry as it helped them to secure a position closer to the imperial family, the source of power and the distribution of wealth, even though such positions were often neither official nor permanent. The surviving evidence suggests that ceremonial poetry enjoyed its heyday in the second and third generations of the Komnenian dynasty, corresponding to the time of Theodore Prodromos (*c.* 1110–58), who was active from the early 1120s to the mid-1150s. Prodromos' use of political verse and of stanzas with the same number of verses is not only characteristic of court poetry more broadly, but especially of the ceremonial hymns dedicated to the demes, of which we encounter an example in Paul Magdalino's contribution to the present volume.[39] Prodromos' poetry shares much imperial imagery with other panegyrical literature from the period, including the analogies drawn between the emperor and the sun, between the emperor and various heroes of the ancient Greek

35 See the case of a *schedos* by Theodore Prodromos addressed to a *sebastokratorissa*, most probably the *sebastokratorissa* Irene. For the text, see Polemis (1995).

36 See Agapitos (2015: 23–37).

37 See e.g. Magdalino (1993: 413–88) on the panegyrical oratory in both prose and verse from the reign of Manuel I Komnenos and its imagery. For panegyrical oratory of the Palaiologan period, see, most recently, Leonte (2023).

38 For very few exceptions from the eleventh century, see Bernard (2014: 108–10).

39 On deme hymns, see Hörandner (2003) and Magdalino (2016: 60–2).

past and between the emperor and David or even Christ.[40] His contemporary Manganeios Prodromos (*c.* 1110–?) employed similar imagery, as the panegyrical poem in praise of Manuel I Komnenos in the chapter by Elizabeth and Michael Jeffreys demonstrates. These parallels demonstrate how poets and orators from the period shared a common grammar or vocabulary of praise tailored to the self-image of the ruling family.

The anonymous poet Manganeios Prodromos started composing ceremonial poetry for the Komnenian court in the early 1140s, frequently writing for the very same occasion as his colleague Theodore Prodromos. For example, both of them contributed to the celebrations held at Christmas in the year 1149, following the successful military campaigns of Manuel I, which included the recapture of Corfu from the Sicilian Normans and the emperor's triumphal return from Serbia.[41] Prodromos wrote a long encomiastic poem of 424 verses together with hymns for Christmas and for Epiphany, while Manganeios composed a panegyrical poem for Manuel that mocks the Serbians for their cowardice.[42] It has been argued that the rise of Manganeios Prodromos as court poet alongside Theodore Prodromos suggests a change in the tastes of contemporary recipients of ceremonial poetry, or that the former had lost the high regard as imperial rhetor that he had enjoyed during the reign of John Komnenos, but this remains a hypothesis which is not supported by other sources.[43] Manganeios himself praised Prodromos as the leading rhetor of his time, which points to the high esteem the latter continued to enjoy also after the appearance of Manganeios.[44] More than anything, the parallel poems of the two Prodromoi indicate that more than one rhetor performed his works during the same imperial celebration, whether joining forces to increase the sense of triumph or competing with one another for the appreciation of the imperial audience.[45]

The popularity of ceremonial poetry did not increase immediately following the ascension of the Komnenian family to the throne. Before the time of Theodore Prodromos we have very little poetry of this kind. The

40 Hörandner (1974: 89–108). For the parallel between John II and David, see Ricceri in this volume; for Manuel I and David, see Magdalino (1993: 447–50, 469). On Old Testament kings as models of kingship more generally, see e.g. Rapp (2010). For Manuel and Christ, see also Magdalino (1993: 434, 451, 469).

41 Magdalino (1993: 440).

42 Prodromos, *Historical Poems* 30, 31 and 32 ed. Hörandner (1974); Manganeios Prodromos, *Poem* 26 ed. Miller (1881: 761–3).

43 For these hypotheses, see Stanković (2007: 214–15).

44 Manganeios Prodromos, *Poem* 10.21–32 ed. Bernardinello (1972); English trans. in Alexiou (1999).

45 For a case of competition between rhetors, see Agapitos in this volume; for competition in a school context, see Gerbi in this volume. For the theatrical nature of imperial ceremonies, see also Magdalino in this volume.

physician-poet Nicholas Kallikles wrote for the court, but none of his poems cover ceremonial occasions, as is the case with the poems of the two Prodromoi. What survives from the reign of Alexios Komnenos are two works by a certain Stephanos Physopalamites, which include an encomiastic alphabet for the emperor and a poem celebrating the recapture of a settlement during Alexios' struggles against the Normans.[46] For reasons that remain unclear, most ceremonial poetry was produced during the second and third quarters of the twelfth century, during the reigns of John II and Manuel I. While the two Prodromoi are responsible for a large part of the ceremonial poetry of the period – and hence feature prominently in this volume – additional examples survive in the codex Venice, Biblioteca Nazionale Marciana, gr. Z. 524 [Diktyon 69995], which transmits a cycle of five decastichs celebrating a victory of Emperor Manuel I during a triumphal procession in the city and a cycle of hexastichs for the same emperor on the occasion of Easter.[47] Niketas Eugenianos and Niketas Choniates, moreover, wrote *epithalamia* to celebrate imperial weddings, which shows that not only 'court poets' but also other rhetors active in the capital employed verse for their praise of the imperial family.[48]

In addition to the court, schools were responsible for many verse compositions during the twelfth century, a period that saw a continued increase in the production of didactic poetry that had started in the eleventh century, with Michael Psellos as its most prolific representative.[49] Other teacher-poets in the last quarter of the eleventh century and the mid-twelfth century followed suit by producing verse treatises on various grammatical and theological topics: Niketas of Herakleia wrote various works on grammar, some of them composed in hymnographic metres;[50] Philip Monotropos wrote his theological-philosophical *Dioptra*, a didactic poem of over 7,000 political verses that originated in a monastic milieu and is structured as a dialogue between the body and soul;[51] the patriarch Nicholas III Grammatikos (1084–1111) produced a verse treatise on the

46 See Welz (1910).

47 For the texts of these poems, see Lampros (1911: 57–9 and 187–9); for this kind of poetry in stanzas, see Lauxtermann (2003–19: 2:376).

48 For these texts, see van Dieten (1972: 45–6) and Gallavotti (1935).

49 On the emergence of didactic poetry in the eleventh century, see Hörandner (1976). Psellos' didactic poems have been edited by Westerink (1992); for introductory remarks on Psellos' didactic poetry, see Hörandner (2012: 57–62) and (2019: 459–86); see also Bernard (2014: 229–40). On literature and education, see also Agapitos in this volume.

50 See Bernard in this volume.

51 Eirene Afentoulidou is preparing an edition of the entire text, which has been edited only in part; see Lavriotes (1920). For an overview of the work, see Afentoulidou and Fuchsbauer (2019), with previous literature.

canonical rules for fast days.[52] In the mid-twelfth century the production of didactic poetry is linked to the oeuvre of two authors in particular, John Tzetzes and Constantine Manasses.[53] Both Tzetzes and Manasses produced thousands of verses, mainly in the form of political verse, which aimed to impart knowledge to their recipients on a variety of subjects, including grammar, rhetoric, philosophy, history, mythology and astrology. Both therefore feature prominently in the present volume, in the contributions by Baukje van den Berg (Tzetzes' *Carmina Iliaca*), Aglae Pizzone (Tzetzes' verse commentary on Hermogenes) and Konstantinos Chryssogelos (Manasses' astrological poem).

The category of didactic poetry thus covers a wide variety of texts, in different forms and on different subjects. Some are edifying texts that aim at teaching Christian ethical rules (such as Monotropos' *Dioptra*), others have strong ties to grammatical and rhetorical education (such as various works by Niketas of Herakleia and verse treatises on ancient poetry by John Tzetzes). Some are paraphrases of and commentaries on earlier texts (such as Tzetzes' *Theogony* or his *Allegories of the Iliad* and *Allegories of the Odyssey*), others assume the form of a chronicle (such as Manasses' *Synopsis Chronike* and Tzetzes' unfinished world chronicle).[54] Some were written for anonymous addressees, probably students, such as the poetry of Niketas of Herakleia that Floris Bernard discusses in the present volume; others are addressed to powerful imperial patrons, including the *sebastokratorissa* Irene or Bertha von Sulzbach, such as various works by Tzetzes and Manasses.[55] The extant corpus suggests that each poet had his own specialization and was known among audiences for particular types of poetry: Manganeios and Theodore Prodromos wrote ceremonial poetry for the *sebastokratorissa* and left the didactic works to their colleagues. Indeed, when Prodromos was commissioned to write a work providing basic instruction in Greek grammar for the *sebastokratorissa*, he opted for prose instead of verse.[56]

Closely related to education is the practice of schedography, a type of school exercise that had become popular in the eleventh century and underwent significant transformations in the twelfth. Even if it has attracted little attention from modern scholars, schedography was the most popular

52 Ed. Koder (1970). On the poem, see also Afentoulidou (2012: 92–5).

53 For Tzetzes' didactic poetry, see e.g. van den Berg (2020); for Manasses, see Nilsson (2021a: *passim*).

54 On Tzetzes' *Theogony*, see Tomadaki (2022); on Tzetzes' *Allegories*, see e.g. Goldwyn (2017), Haubold (2021) and Ravani (2022); on Tzetzes' verse chronicle, see Hunger (1955) and Braccini (2022).

55 On the *sebastokratorissa* Irene as a patron, see e.g. E. M. Jeffreys (2014); on Tzetzes as a commissioned poet, see also Rhoby (2010). For Manasses, see Nilsson (2021a: *passim*).

56 For some introductory remarks on this work, see Zagklas (2011).

method for teaching grammar and rhetoric until the conquest of Constantinople by the Ottomans in 1453.[57] Some eleventh-century *schede* already combine prose and verse, but this practice became more popular towards the end of the eleventh century or the beginning of the twelfth. For example, during his tenure as director at the school of Chalkoprateia, Niketas of Herakleia wrote three *schede*, one on St John the Forerunner, one on the Epiphany and one consisting of a paraphrase of Gregory of Nyssa's encomium for the forty martyrs.[58] All of these are prose texts, except for the one on the Epiphany, which concludes with a line conforming to the basic rules of a dodecasyllable.[59] Around the same time, three out of four surviving *schede* by Nicholas Kallikles in Vatican City, Biblioteca Apostolica Vaticana, pal. gr. 92 [Diktyon 65825], a thirteenth-century manuscript copied in southern Italy, combine prose and verse, concluding with two or four iambic verses.[60] One of the most ardent adherents of this practice is Theodore Prodromos, who composed most of his *schede* in this mixed form.[61] In addition to Prodromos, Constantine Manasses and Niketas Eugenianos also wrote *schede* in a mixed form, while Vaticanus pal. gr. 92 contains 212 twelfth-century *schede*, with approximately half of them written in a mixed form.

The ways in which Byzantine *schede* combine prose and verse varies: the verse part can either open or close the *schedos*, while in some cases it does both. Consider, for example, a twelfth-century *schedos* from the same Vatican manuscript, which has a complex tripartite structure (verse-prose-verse).[62] The *schedos* was written by a certain Leo, a teacher at the Orphanotropheion of St Paul in Constantinople, who asks the director

57 On schedography, see Vassis (1993–4), Agapitos (2014) and Nousia (2016); see also Bernard in this volume.

58 The texts are still unedited; see Vassis (2002: nos. 36, 134 and 152). No. 36 is also preserved in Vatican City, Biblioteca Apostolica Vaticana, Reg. gr. PP Pio II 54 [Diktyon 66413], fols. 386v–387; for the dating of the *schede*, see Nesseris (2014: 74).

59 The *schedos* ends as follows: Πᾶσιν βραβεύων τοῖς πιστοῖς σωτηρίας.

60 See Kallikles 116 (an *ethopoiia* with 4 verses), 164 (an *ethopoiia* with 2 verses), 184, 188 (an *ekphrasis* with 2 verses). For the verse parts of these *schede*, see Vassis (2002).

61 For a list of Prodromos' *schede* and an edition of two of his works, see Vassis (1993–4). The remaining *schede* are edited in various studies: see Papadimitriou (1905: 422–4 and 429–35), Polemis (1995) and Nesseris (2014: 407). See also Agapitos (2015) and in this volume.

62 See the edition by Miller (2003: 14–16), which fails to signal that both the opening and ending of the *schedos* are written not in prose, but in iambic verse: Ἐπαχθὲς ἔργον πᾶσα διδασκαλία, | πολὺ πλέον δὲ παιδοδιδασκαλία, | τοῖς δὲ τριγηράσασιν εἰσέτι πλέον. | [approximately twenty lines of prose text] | Ἀνδρὸς τὸ λοιπὸν τληπαθοῦς ὑπερλάλει. | Τὸν Παῦλον ἕξεις τὸν μέγαν συνεργάτην, | ὃν πρέσβιν αὐτὸν ἀγαθαῖς ἐπ' ἐλπίσι | προσῆξα τῷ ῥηθέντι τὴν τόλμαν βλέπεις. | Τούτῳ δὲ καὶ σὲ σήμερον συνεισφέρω. | Καὶ γὰρ ὅσος μοι Παῦλος ἐν τοῖς ἁγίοις, | τοσοῦτον αὐτὸς ἐν βροτοῖς· ἔρρει φθόνος. Ioannis Vassis did note the metrical parts of the *schedos*; see Vassis (2002: 58–9).

of the school (the *Orphanotrophos*) to intercede with the patriarch on his behalf for a promotion and relief from his teaching responsibilities.[63] More research on schedography is required to better understand its formal and didactic dynamics, and thus to enhance our picture both of the poetry written during this period and of grammatical education more broadly, where it featured alongside the didactic poetry to which the contributions by Bernard and Van den Berg are dedicated.[64] Giulia Gerbi, moreover, studies a poem by Nicholas Kallikles that refers to schedographical contests and may be closely related to a still unedited *schedos* by Kallikles.

In addition to ceremonial and didactic texts, a third major part of twelfth-century poetry consists of stories narrated in verse form, another practice which came to prominence for the first time in the twelfth century.[65] Most of the novels written in the second quarter of the twelfth century are long poems in dodecasyllable or political verse, probably performed in the *theatra* or literary gatherings of the capital.[66] The composition of lengthy love stories in verse form is not only a feature of Medieval Greek literary production, but is also found in Georgian, Persian and French literature from around the same period, perhaps as the result of interactions between these four literary traditions in the contact zone of Anatolia during this time.[67] Be that as it may, Byzantine literature from the twelfth century displays a general interest in long narrative texts composed in verse. In addition to *Digenis Akritis* (see above) and the three novels (Prodromos' *Rhodanthe and Dosikles*, Manasses' *Aristandros and Kallithea* and Eugenianos' *Drosilla and Charikleas*), we know of a long self-referential poem written in southern Italy in the second quarter of the twelfth century, which features dozens of embedded stories from the biblical and Greco-Roman traditions.[68] Manasses' verse chronicle assembles stories in an episodic form to narrate a universal history; Tzetzes' *Histories*, conceived as a commentary on his own letters, collects historical, legendary and mythological tales referred to throughout his correspondence.[69] Other nar-

63 This teacher is most likely identifiable as Leo of Rhodes, who obtained the metropolitan see of Rhodes around 1166; Miller (2003: 10).

64 Ugo Mondini is currently conducting a research project on eleventh-century schedography at the University of Oxford.

65 As already noted in E. M. Jeffreys (2009: 224); on this aspect, see also Agapitos in this volume.

66 The Komnenian novels have received much attention in recent scholarship and therefore remain outside the focus of this volume. For an introduction, see Nilsson (2016); for an English translation of the novels, see E. M. Jeffreys (2012). See further Roilos (2005) and Nilsson (2014: 39–86); for later verse romances, see also Beaton (2019), with further references. On the *theatron*, see e.g. Marciniak (2007).

67 See Cross (2024).

68 See Lauxtermann (2014) and Cupane (2019: 357–64).

rative works in verse include Prodromos' *Katomyomachia* and *On Friendship's Departure*, the anonymous *Christos Paschon*, Haploucheir's so-called *Dramation*, and the *Hodoiporikon* or *Itinerary* by Constantine Manasses, as well as the *Fire Poem* by Constantine Stilbes.[70] The strong interest in storytelling in verse may tie in with the theatricality of much of the poetry of this period. Indeed, it is in this context that Paul Magdalino and Marc Lauxtermann discuss Stilbes' *Fire Poem* and Prodromos' *Katomyomachia* in their respective contributions to this volume. While Magdalino discusses Stilbes' poem alongside a coronation poem by Theodore Prodromos and the verse chronicle by Constantine Manasses to highlight the 'theatrical turn' in twelfth-century poetry, Lauxtermann focuses on the dramatic features of the *Katomyomachia* as a text intended for a school environment and demonstrates how it functioned both as a parody of earlier texts and as a piece of beast literature.

While the production of poetry for all these 'secular' ceremonial, didactic and theatrical purposes flourished, the composition of verse for liturgical purposes did not follow suit. There is only scant evidence of the production of hymns in this period: Eugenios of Palermo produced hymnographical works for the Mother of God and St Demetrios, while the lesser-known George Skylitzes authored a hymn on the *Translation of the Holy Stone*.[71] Even so, many poets took an interest in hymnographic poetry, and some of them, including Gregory Pardos and Theodore Prodromos, commented on the well-known hymns of John of Damascus and Kosmas of Jerusalem.[72] Many twelfth-century poets, moreover, composed iambic poetry that acquired a supplementary role during the church liturgy. Examples include the metrical prefaces that were intended to introduce the reading of a hagiographical work or a sermon as composed by Theodore Prodromos, Manganeios Prodromos, Nikephoros Chrysoberges and John Apokaukos.[73] Metrical calendars, too, may have played a role in the liturgy. Following the example of Christopher of Mytilene, Prodromos composed

69 Manasses' chronicle has been extensively studied by Ingela Nilsson: on its literary – and poetic – form, see e.g. Nilsson (2006), (2019) and (2021b). See also Magdalino in this volume. For Tzetzes' *Histories*, see e.g. Pizzone (2017).

70 On the *Christos Paschon*, see most recently Mullett (2022); on Haploucheir's poem, Marciniak (2020); on the *Hodoiporikon*, Chryssogelos (2017) and Nilsson (2021a: 46–54), all with references to previous bibliography.

71 For the respective works, see Luzzi (2016) and (2018); Antonopoulou (2013).

72 On twelfth-century commentaries on hymnography, see Demetracopoulos (1979), Giannouli (2007), Cesaretti and Ronchey (2014). On Byzantine hymnography in general, see Giannouli (2019) and Papaioannou (2021), with further references.

73 For an excellent overview of this type of poetry, see Antonopoulou (2010).

a metrical calendar in monostichs that once again illustrates the wide scope of Prodromos' poetic production.[74]

Even though this liturgical poetry remains largely outside the scope of the present volume, we do encounter religious sentiments in verse compositions of different kinds, most prominently perhaps in epigrammatic poetry. Epigrams with religious themes appear, for instance, on reliquaries and other objects, while dedicatory inscriptions in various Byzantine churches shed light not only on the dynamics of patronage but also on the patrons' devotional motivations for founding churches and other religious establishments.[75] In his contribution to this volume, Nektarios Zarras discusses some twelfth-century examples from Kastoria and elsewhere, which remain largely neglected in current scholarship. Ugo Mondini gives a detailed analysis of a poem with eschatological themes by Michael Choniates, whose poetic work has received little scholarly attention to date. Giulia Gerbi offers a close reading of Kallikles' celebration of spring, a poem that may have featured in the context of a school contest and draws parallels between the arrival of spring and the worldly renewal of Christian revelation. These and other texts may serve as an important reminder that the categories of 'religious' and 'secular' were not as clearly separated in the minds of the Byzantines as modern scholarship tends to suggest.

Geographical Distribution and Material Circulation

During the period between 1081 and 1204, the geographical scope of poetic production became broader than it had been in the eleventh century, and it would extend even further from the thirteenth century onwards due to the territorial fragmentation of the empire. Twelfth-century Constantinople continued to be the centre for the production of poetry written in Greek, which explains the dominance of Constantinopolitan poets in the present volume. A great deal of poetry, however, was written in regions far from the capital, as we can see in the examples from medieval Greece in Zarras' contribution. As mentioned above, many intellectuals acquired metropolitan sees across the empire and wrote some of their poetry there.

74 Acconcia Longo (1983). On Byzantine metrical calendars, see also Darrouzès (1958). For Christopher of Mytilene in particular, see Bernard (2019: 224, 229) with further bibliography.

75 For the connections between epigram, art and devotion in Byzantium, with a focus on the period 1100–1450, see Drpić (2016). Brad Hostetler is currently preparing a monograph entitled *Inscribing Sacred Matter in Medieval Byzantium* that aims at exploring the meaning of relics and reliquaries in Byzantine devotional practice through inscriptions. See in the meantime his unpublished doctoral dissertation (2016) and a dossier of examples collected in Hostetler (2022).

Theophylaktos, for example, addressed his poems 1 and 2 to individuals in Constantinople during his time in Ohrid. Similarly, Michael Choniates – who is the subject of Mondini's contribution – wrote most of his poems during his tenure in Athens, while John Apokaukos produced some of his poetic work as bishop of Naupaktos. However, all these individuals were trained in Constantinople; they had close ties to the cultural and literary milieu in the capital, and as a result their poetry closely follows the literary developments manifest in texts produced in Constantinople.

Slightly different is the case of southern Italy. In the twelfth century, Sicily became a hotspot for poetry written in Greek, with a number of poets active in the Greek-speaking circles both within and outside the Norman court.[76] An anonymous author addressed the above-mentioned narrative poem (approximately 4,000 verses) to the admiral George of Antioch;[77] Leo the grammarian wrote two hagiographical works in a prosimetric form;[78] and Eugenios of Palermo composed twenty-four poems on various themes and in a variety of genres, ranging from self-referential and epigrammatic poetry to epistolary and ceremonial poems.[79] In addition to these works, there are numerous metrical inscriptions for buildings and other objects.[80] To a large extent, the language, metre, imagery and generic features of many of these works are in keeping with the poetry composed in Constantinople; at the same time, however, they display peculiar traits of their own, often borrowed from the Latin and Arabic literary traditions with which they coexisted in Norman Sicily and southern Italy.[81] Even though poetry from this region is not featured in the present volume, it is important to keep in mind that Greek poetry was produced across the Mediterranean world, in places far away from Constantinople. The cultural and political history of the empire was closely interwoven with that of other regions, and the military struggles between the Byzantines and the Normans during this period find their way into the realm of literature, as the poem by Manganeios Prodromos discussed in the chapter by Elizabeth and Michael Jeffreys demonstrates.

76 See Cupane (2019); Kubina and Zagklas (2024b).

77 For the text, see Vassis and Polemis (2016); for introductory discussions of the text, see Lauxtermann (2014), Cupane (2019: 357–64) and Kubina and Zagklas (2024b).

78 See Halkin (1985–6) and Follieri (1987).

79 Ed. Gigante (1964); for a discussion of various of these poems, see Cupane (2011), (2013) and (2019: 366–70); see also Marciniak (2019), Roilos (2020) and Kubina and Zagklas (2024b).

80 Rhoby (2014: IT 22–33).

81 See Cupane (2019).

Despite the richness of the surviving material, much remains unclear about the ways in which twelfth-century poetry circulated within and beyond the borders of the empire. While collections or anthologies of contemporary poetry survive from other periods, the twelfth century offers only scant evidence. Master copies of Byzantine poetry written before the twelfth century circulated during this time, such as the poetic collection in Vatican City, Biblioteca Apostolica Vaticana, gr. 676 [Diktyon 67307], which most likely continued to be read by twelfth-century poets.[82] Some twelfth-century authors copied and possessed manuscripts with ancient Greek poetry: it has, for instance, been argued that Niketas of Herakleia copied Venice, Biblioteca Nazionale Marciana, gr. 476 [Diktyon 69947], a manuscript transmitting Lycophron's cryptic *Alexandra* as well as Aratus' *Phenomena* with scholia for didactic purposes.[83] Even so, most of the manuscripts of twelfth-century poetry date from the Palaiologan period.

The late thirteenth century, when a significant number of manuscripts was copied, was a turning point for the transmission of Komnenian poetry. Venice, Biblioteca Nazionale Marciana, gr. Z. 524 [Diktyon 69995] transmits a rich anthology of both anonymous and well-known authors;[84] Venice, Biblioteca Nazionale Marciana, gr. XI.22 [Diktyon 70658] includes most of the poetry by Manganeios Prodromos;[85] and Vatican City, Biblioteca Apostolica Vaticana, gr. 305 [Diktyon 66936] is the most important collection of Prodromos' poetry (as well as his prose works).[86] Many of these collections or anthologies may go back to twelfth-century manuscripts, even though we should also consider other channels of circulation and consumption of poetry in the twelfth century. In addition to oral circulation, the market for *logoi* fostered a dissemination of literature not only in manuscripts, but also in looser forms, such as leaflets or scrolls, which commonly preceded publication in book form. Indeed, some Byzantine authors mention these two stages of publication and the transition from one stage to the next. Psellos, for instance, notes in various places throughout his oeuvre that he only had drafts of his works, which consisted of loose sheets, small scrolls or rollable pieces of paper or parchment, which were kept in boxes before they were copied into a book – if they ever were turned into book form.[87] This practice is documented well before the

82 For a discussion of the manuscript, see Bianconi (2011) and Bernard (2014: 128–48).
83 Mioni (1985: 267–9); see Nesseris (2014: 77–9), with previous bibliography.
84 Spingou (2021: 13–22), with further bibliography.
85 Mioni (1970: 116–31).
86 Zagklas (2023: 122–30).
87 See e.g. Boissonade (1938: 116.13–25). The same passage has been discussed in Papaioannou (2019: xl).

time of Psellos: in the ninth century, Photios noted in his *Amphilochia* that many of his books were put together from drafts (σχεδάρια).[88] Psellos and Photios thus provide us with some rare insights into the materiality and practicalities of Byzantine literary production. We can add to their testimonies the various comments of John Tzetzes, who repeatedly refers to the publication process of his books and the many problems involved with it, as we see in Pizzone's contribution to the present volume.[89]

A type of poetry that particularly seems to have circulated in unbound quires and leaflets is that of invective, which attacked other individuals – often professional rivals – and was sent in epistolary form. The Pseudo-Psellian poem 68, an invective in political verse likely written by a twelfth-century poet, directly testifies to this kind of circulation. The anonymous poet recounts that at some point a page of text had arrived at his place: a letter filled with abuse and attacks sent by an intellectual adversary of his.[90] The anonymous poet cared so little about his rival's message that it was left forgotten in a corner of his home, only to be rediscovered much later, when he was searching for something else. He read it and immediately started laughing and clapping his hands at his enemy's lack of education. We may not have surviving poetry books with contemporary material, but this anonymous poem is a good example of the hidden aspects of the circulation and consumption of poetry in twelfth-century Byzantium, on which future research will undoubtedly shed further light.

***

The broader poetic context outlined in the previous pages forms the essential framework in which each of this volume's chapters finds its place and to which each of the contributions adds further detail and nuance. In her essay 'Why Produce Poetry in Twelfth-Century Constantinople?', Elizabeth Jeffreys argues that Komnenian authors wrote poetry in ancient and Byzantine metres for two sets of reasons: first, 'to demonstrate [their] credentials as a potential mandarin to future employers'; and second, 'to make sensible communication with an audience'.[91] These two reasons are of course inextricably connected: in order to impress patrons or peers, poets had to establish meaningful communication. Jeffreys' essay places a great deal of emphasis on the social aspects of poetry, in line with a

88 Photios, *Amphilochia* 148.40–2 ed. Westerink and Laourdas (1986): Ταῦτα μὲν ἀπὸ σχεδαρίων ὡς ἠδυνήθημεν μετεγράψαμεν, τὰ δὲ βιβλία, ὡς καὶ ἡ σὴ ἀρχιερατικὴ τελειότης συνεπίσταται.
89 See also Pizzone (2020).
90 Vv. 57–8 ed. Westerink (1993: 453); English translation in Bernard (2021: 195).
91 E. M. Jeffreys (2009: 228).

well-established tendency in modern scholarship. Indeed, the composition of verse in the twelfth century continued to serve social needs and practical demands, but it is important not to overlook the aesthetic qualities of poetry, its ability to provide (private) literary enjoyment and (public) theatrical entertainment, or its didactic and devotional dynamics. In addition to the social dimension of twelfth-century poetry, therefore, the contributions to the present volume focus on the literary aspects of Byzantine poetry beyond erudite self-fashioning and communicative functionality. Taken together, this volume explores the complex entanglements of poetry in the social and literary world of the time in order to enrich and bring nuance to the interpretation of the poetic production of a period that left behind an abundance of verse that still awaits a more systematic engagement. This volume is one step in that direction.

A Note on Style

Following a common practice in Byzantine Studies, we have adopted a mixed system of transliteration. Late antique and Byzantine names are generally transliterated or anglicized, following the *Oxford Dictionary of Byzantium.* Ancient names appear in their common Latinized or Anglicized form, following the *Oxford Classical Dictionary.* Titles of ancient and Byzantine texts are given in English or, where this is conventional, in Latin. Abbreviations of journal titles in chapter bibliographies follow those used in *L'Année Philologique.* All translations are by the authors unless otherwise stated.

Bibliography

Acconcia Longo, A. (ed.) (1983) *Il calendario giambico in monostici di Teodoro Prodromo*. Rome.

Afentoulidou, E. (2012) 'Philippos Monotropos' *Dioptra* and its Social Milieu: Niketas Stethatos, Nikollaos III Grammatikos and the Persecution of Bogomilism', *Parekbolai* 2: 85–107.

Afentoulidou, E., and J. Fuchsbauer (2019) 'Philippos Monotropos in Byzantium and in the Slavonic World', in Hörandner, Rhoby and Zagklas, 331–52.

Agapitos, P. A. (2012) 'Late Antique or Early Byzantine? The Shifting Beginnings of Byzantine Literature', *Rendiconti: Classe di Lettere e Scienze Morali e Storiche* 146: 3–38.

(2014) 'Grammar, Genre and Patronage in the Twelfth Century: Redefining a Scientific Paradigm in the History of Byzantine Literature', *JÖByz* 64: 1–22.

(2015) 'New Genres in the Twelfth Century: The *Schedourgia* of Theodore Prodromos', *MEG* 15: 1–41.

(2017) 'Dangerous Literary Liaisons: Byzantium and Neohellenism', *Byzantina* 35: 33–126.
(2020) 'The Insignificance of 1204 and 1453 for the History of Byzantine Literature', *MEG* 20: 1–56.
Alexiou, M. (1999) 'Ploys of Performance: Games and Play in the Ptochoprodromic Poems', *DOP* 53: 91–109.
Antonopoulou, T. (2010) 'On the Reception of Homilies and Hagiography in Byzantium: The Recited Metrical Prefaces', in *Imitatio–Aemulatio–Variatio: Akten des internationalen wissenschaftlichen Symposions zur byzantinischen Sprache und Literatur (Wien, 22.–25. Oktober 2008)*, ed. A. Rhoby and E. Schiffer, 57–80. Vienna.
(2013) 'George Skylitzes' Office on the Translation of the Holy Stone: A Study and Critical Edition', in *The Pantokrator Monastery in Constantinople*, ed. S. Kotzabassi, 109–41 and Plate 1. Berlin.
Barili, E. (2022) 'Building Rhetorical (Self-)awareness through Hermogenes: John Tzetzes' Commentary on Περὶ ἰδεῶν λόγου', PhD thesis, University of Southern Denmark.
Beaton, R. (2019) 'Byzantine Verse Romances', in Hörandner, Rhoby and Zagklas, 539–55.
Bernard, F. (2014) *Writing and Reading Byzantine Secular Poetry, 1025–1081*. Oxford.
(2019) 'The 11th Century: Michael Psellos and Contemporaries', in Hörandner, Rhoby and Zagklas, 212–36.
(2021) 'Pseudo-Psellos, Poem 68', in *Epistolary Poetry in Byzantium and Beyond: An Anthology with Critical Essays*, ed. K. Kubina and A. Riehle, 192–7 and 329–32. New York.
Bernard, F., and K. Demoen (eds.) (2012) *Poetry and its Contexts in Eleventh-Century Byzantium*. Farnham.
(2021) 'Poetry?', in *Oxford Handbook of Byzantine Literature*, ed. S. Papaioannou, 365–80. Oxford.
Bernard, F., and C. Livanos (2018) *The Poems of Christopher of Mytilene and John Mauropous*. Dumbarton Oaks Medieval Library 50. Cambridge, MA.
Bernardinello, S. (ed.) (1972) *Theodori Prodromi De Manganis*. Padua.
Bianconi, D. (2011) '"Piccolo assaggio di abbondante fragranza": Giovanni Mauropode e il Vat. gr. 676', *JÖByz* 61: 89–103.
Boissonade, J. F. (ed.) (1838) *Michael Psellus de operatione daemonum cum notis Gaulmini. Accedunt inedita opuscula Pselli*. Nuremberg (repr. Amsterdam 1964).
(1851) *Tzetzae allegoriae Iliadis accedunt Pselli allegoriae*. Paris (repr. Hildesheim 1967).
Bourbouhakis, E. C. (2007) '"Political" Personae: The Poem from Prison of Michael Glykas: Byzantine Literature between Fact and Fiction', *BMGS* 31.1: 53–75.
Braccini, T. (2022) 'A Neglected Manuscript of Tzetzes' *Allegories from the Verse-chronicle*: First Remarks', in *Τζετζικαὶ ἔρευναι*, ed. E. E. Prodi, 1–17. Eikasmos Studi Online 4. Bologna.

Browning, R. (1977) 'The Patriarchal School at Constantinople in the Twelfth Century', in *Studies on Byzantine History, Literature and Education*, 167–201 and 11–40 (no. X). London (originally published in 1962 and 1963).

Büttner-Wobst, T. (ed.) (1897) *Ioannes Zonarae epitomae historiarum libri XVIII*, vol. 3: *Libri XIII–XVIII*. Bonn.

Cesaretti, P., and S. Ronchey (eds.) (2014) *Eustathii Thessalonicensis exegesis in canonem iambicum pentecostalem*. Supplementa Byzantina 10. Berlin.

Chryssogelos, K. (2017) *Κωνσταντίνου Μανασσῆ Ὁδοιπορικόν: Κριτική ἔκδοση, μετάφραση, σχόλια*. Athens.

Cole, T. (1991) *The Origins of Rhetoric in Ancient Greece*. Baltimore.

Conley, T. (1995) 'Practice to Theory: Byzantine "Poetrics"', in *Greek Literary Theory after Aristotle: A Collection of Papers in Honour of D. M. Schenkeveld*, ed. J. G. J. Abbenes, S. R. Slings and I. Sluiter, 301–20. Amsterdam.

Copeland, R. and I. Sluiter (eds.) (2009) *Medieval Grammar and Rhetoric: Language Arts and Literary Theory, AD 300–1475*. Oxford.

Cramer, J. A. (ed.) (1837) *Anecdota Graeca e codd. Manuscriptis bibliothecarum Oxoniensium*, vol. 4. Oxford.

Cross, C. (2024) 'Poetic Alchemy: The Rise of Romance from a Persian Perspective', in *Why Write Poetry? Transcultural Perspectives from the Later Medieval Period*, ed. K. Kubina and N. Zagklas. *Medieval Encounters*.

Cupane, C. (2011) 'Fortune rota volvitur: Moira e Tyche nel carme nr. 1 di Eugenio da Palermo', *Nea Rhome* 8: 137–52.

(2013) 'Eugenios von Palermo: Rhetorik und Realität am normannischen Königshof im 12. Jahrhundert', in *Dulce Melos II: Lateinische und griechische Dichtung in Spätantike, Mittelalter und Neuzeit. Akten des fünften Internationalen Symposiums (Wien, 25.–27. November 2010)*, ed. V. Zimmerl-Panagl, 247–70. Pisa.

(2019) 'Byzantine Poetry at the Norman Court of Sicily (1130–*c.*1200)', in Hörandner, Rhoby and Zagklas, 353–78.

Danezis, G. (1987) *Spaneas: Vorlage, Quellen, Versionen*. Munich.

Darrouzès, J. (1958) 'Les calendriers byzantins en vers', *REByz* 16: 59–84.

Demetracopoulos, P. (1979) 'The Exegeses of the Canons in the Twelfth Century as School Texts', *Diptycha* 1: 143–57.

Diethart, J. and W. Hörandner (eds.) (2005) *Constantinus Stilbes: Poemata*. Munich.

Drpić, I. (2016) *Epigram, Art, and Devotion in Later Byzantium*. Cambridge.

Eideneier, H. (ed.) (1991) *Ptochoprodromos: Einführung, kritische Ausgabe, deutsche Übersetzung, Glossar*. Neograeca Medii Aevi 5. Cologne.

(ed.) (2012) *Πτωχοπρόδρομος: Κριτική ἔκδοση*. Heraklion.

Faral, E. (1924) *Les arts poétiques du XIIe et du XIIIe siècle: Recherches et documents sur la technique littéraire du Moyen Âge*. Paris.

Follieri, E. (1987) 'Per l'identificazione del grammatikòs Leone Siculo con Leone da Centirupe', *RSBN* 24: 127–41 (repr. as eadem, *Byzantina et Italograeca: Studi di filologia e di paleografia*, ed. A. Acconcia Longo, L. Perria and A. Luzzi, 399–411. Rome 1997).

Fredborg, K. M. (2014) 'The *Ars poetica* in the Eleventh and Twelfth Centuries: From the *Vienna Scholia* to the *Materia* Commentary', *Aevum* 88.2: 399–442.
Gallavotti, C. (1935) 'Novi Laurentiani codicis analecta', *Studi Bizantini e Neoellenici* 4: 203–36.
Gautier, P. (ed.) (1980) *Théophylacte d'Achrida: Discours, traités, poesies*. Thessalonike.
Giannouli, A. (2007) *Die beiden byzantinischen Kommentare zum Großen Kanon des Andreas von Kreta: Eine quellenkritische und literarhistorische Studie*. Vienna.
(2019) 'Hymn Writing in Byzantium: Forms and Writers', in Hörandner, Rhoby and Zagklas, 487–516.
Gigante, M. (ed.) (1964) *Eugenii Panormitani Versus Iambici*. Palermo.
Godzich, W., and J. Kittay (1987) *The Emergence of Prose: An Essay in Prosaics*. Minneapolis.
Goldhill, S. (2002) *The Invention of Prose*. Oxford.
Goldwyn, A. J. (2017) 'Theory and Method in John Tzetzes' *Allegories of the* Iliad and *Allegories of the* Odyssey', *Scandinavian Journal of Byzantine and Modern Greek Studies* 3: 141–71.
Goldwyn, A. J., and D. Kokkini (2015) *John Tzetzes: Allegories of the Iliad*. Dumbarton Oaks Medieval Library 37. Cambridge, MA.
Graff, R. (2005) 'Poetry in Early Greek Theories of Style', *Rhetorica* 23.4: 303–35.
Halkin, F. (1985–6) 'L'éloge du patriarche S. Nectaire par Léon de Sicile (BHG 2284)', *RSBN* 22–3: 171–89.
Haubold, J. (2021) 'The Scholiast as Poet: Tzetzes and his *Allegories of the Iliad*', *BICS* 64: 73–80.
Hinterberger, M. (2019) 'The Language of Byzantine Poetry: New Words, Alternative Forms, and "Mixed Language"', in Hörandner, Rhoby and Zagklas, 38–65.
Hörandner, W. (ed.) (1974) *Theodoros Prodromos: Historische Gedichte*. Wiener Byzantinistische Studien 11. Vienna.
(1976) 'La poésie profane au XIe siècle et la connaissance des auteurs anciens', *TM* 6: 245–63.
(2003) 'Court Poetry: Questions of Motifs, Structure and Function', in *Rhetoric in Byzantium: Papers from the Thirty-Fifth Spring Symposium of Byzantine Studies, University of Oxford, March 2001*, ed. E. M. Jeffreys, 75–85. Society for the Promotion of Byzantine Studies Publications 11. Aldershot.
(2012) 'The Byzantine Didactic Poem – A Neglected Literary Genre? A Survey with Special Reference to the Eleventh Century', in Bernard and Demoen, 55–67.
(2019) 'Teaching with Verse in Byzantium', in Hörandner, Rhoby and Zagklas, 459–86.
Hörandner, W., A. Rhoby and N. Zagklas (eds.) (2019) *A Companion to Byzantine Poetry*. Brill's Companions to the Byzantine World 4. Leiden.
Horna, K. (ed.) (1906), 'Eine unedierte Rede des Konstantin Manasses', *WS* 28: 194–7.
Hostetler, B. (2016) 'The Function of Text: Byzantine Reliquaries with Epigrams, 843–1204', PhD thesis, Florida State University.

(2022) 'Epigrams on Relics and Reliquaries', in *Sources for Byzantine Art History*, vol. 3.1: *The Visual Culture of Later Byzantium (c. 1081–c. 1350)*, ed. F. Spingou, 751–88. Cambridge.

Hunger, H. (1955) 'Johannes Tzetzes, Allegorien aus der Verschronik: Kommentierte Textausgabe', *Jahrbuch der Österreichischen Byzantinischen Gesellschaft* 4: 13–49.

Jeffreys, E. M. (ed.) (1998) *Digenis Akritis: The Grottaferrata and Escorial Versions.* Cambridge Medieval Classics 7. Cambridge.

(2009) 'Why Produce Verse in Twelfth-Century Constantinople?', in *'Doux remède…': Poésie et poétique à Byzance. Actes du IVe Colloque International Philologique 'EPMHNEIA', Paris, 23–24–25 février 2006, organisé par l'E.H.E.S.S. et l'Université de Chypre*, ed. P. Odorico, P. A. Agapitos and M. Hinterberger, 219–28. Dossiers Byzantins 9. Paris.

(2012) *Four Byzantine Novels.* Liverpool.

(2014) 'The *Sebastokratorissa* Irene as Patron', in *Female Founders in Byzantium and Beyond*, ed. L. Theis, M. Mullett, and M. Grünbart, with G. Fingarova and M. Savage, 177–94. Vienna.

Jeffreys, M. J. (1974) 'The Nature and Origins of Political Verse', *DOP* 28: 141–95.

Kazhdan, A. P., and S. Franklin (1984) *Studies on Byzantine Literature of the Eleventh and Twelfth Centuries.* Cambridge.

Kotzabassi, S. (2009) 'An Unknown Epigram of Constantine Stilbes', *Nea Rhome* 6: 441–4.

Koufopoulou, V. (1989) 'Δύο ἀνέκδοτα ποιήματα τοῦ Θεοδώρου Στυππειώτη', *Byzantina* 15: 351–67.

Koder, J. (1970) 'Das Fastengedicht des Patriarchen Nikolaos III. Grammatikos', *JÖByz* 19: 203–41.

Kresten, O. (1978) 'Zum Sturz des Theodoros Styppeiotes', *JÖByz* 27: 49–103.

Kubina, K., and A. Riehle (eds.) (2021) *Epistolary Poetry in Byzantium and Beyond: An Anthology with Critical Essays.* New York.

Kubina, K., and N. Zagklas (eds.) (2024a) *Why Write Poetry? Transcultural Perspectives from the Later Medieval Period. Medieval Encounters.*

(2024b) 'Greek Poetry in a Multicultural Society: Sicily and Salento in the Twelfth and Thirteenth Centuries', in *Why Write Poetry? Transcultural Perspectives from the Later Medieval Period*, ed. K. Kubina and N. Zagklas. *Medieval Encounters.*

Kulhánková, M. (2021) 'Narrative Coherence in Digenes Akrites (G)', *BMGS* 45.2: 184–98.

Lampros, S. P. (ed.) (1911) ''Ο Μαρκιανὸς κῶδιξ 523', *Νέος Ἑλληνομνήμων* 8: 3–192.

Lauxtermann, M. D. (2003–19) *Byzantine Poetry from Pisides to Geometres: Texts and Contexts*, 2 vols. Wiener Byzantinistische Studien 24. Vienna.

(2014) 'Tomi, Mljet, Malta: Critical Notes on a Twelfth-Century Southern Italian Poem of Exile', *JÖByz* 64: 155–76.

Lavriotes, S. (ed.) (1920) ''Η Διόπτρα: Ἔμμετρον ψυχοθεραπευτικόν', *Ho Athos* 1: 1–264.

Leonte, F. (2023) *Ethos, Logos, and Perspective: Studies in Late Byzantine Rhetoric*. Abingdon.
Luzzi, A. (2016) 'Hymnographica Eugeniana: Inediti giambici e ritmici in una interessante silloge italogreca tramandata nel ms Scorial. X.IV.8 (gr. 403)', in *Studi bizantini in onore di Maria Dora Spadaro*, ed. T. Creazzo, C. Crimi, R. Gentile and G. Strano, 215–35. Catania.
(2018) 'La silloge innografica del manoscritto italogreco Scorial. X.IV.8: Descrizione analitica', *Nea Rhome* 15: 107–36.
Magdalino, P. (1993) *The Empire of Manuel I Komnenos, 1143–1180*. Cambridge.
(2016) 'The Triumph of 1133', in *John II Komnenos, Emperor of Byzantium: In the Shadow of Father and Son*, ed. A. Bucossi and A. Rodriguez Suarez, 53–70. Abingdon.
Marciniak, P. (2007) 'Byzantine *Theatron* – A Place of Performance?', in *Theatron: Rhetorische Kultur in Spätantike und Mittelalter*, ed. M. Grünbart, 277–85. Millennium-Studien 13. Berlin.
(2019) 'The *Paradoxical Enkomion* and the Byzantine Reception of Lucian's *Praise of the Fly*', *MEG* 19: 141–50.
(2020) 'The *Dramation* by Michael Haplucheir: A Reappraisal', *SO* 94.1: 212–28.
Marciniak, P., and K. Warcaba (2014) 'Racing with Rhetoric: A Byzantine Ekphrasis of a Chariot Race', *ByzZ* 107.1: 97–112.
(2021) 'Michael Hagiotheodorites', in *Epistolary Poetry in Byzantium and Beyond: An Anthology with Critical Essays*, ed. K. Kubina and A. Riehle, 184–91 and 325–8. New York.
Miller, E. (ed.) (1881) *Recueil des historiens des Croisades. Historiens grecs*, vol. 2. Paris.
Miller, T. S. (2003) 'Two Teaching Texts from the Twelfth-Century Orphanotropheion', in *Byzantine Authors: Literary Activities and Preoccupations, Texts and Translations Dedicated to the Memory of Nicolas Oikonomides*, ed. J. W. Nesbitt, 9–22. Leiden.
Mioni, E. (1970) *Biblioteca Divi Marci Venetiarum codices graeci manuscripti*, vol. 3. Venice.
(1985) *Bibliothecae Divi Marci Venetiarum Codices Graeci Manuscripti, Thesaurus Antiquus*, vol. 2: *Codices 300–625*. Rome.
Mullett, M. (1984) 'Aristocracy and Patronage in the Literary Circles of Comnenian Constantinople', in *The Byzantine Aristocracy, IX to XIII Centuries*, ed. M. Angold, 173–201. Oxford.
(1997) *Theophylact of Ochrid: Reading the Letters of a Byzantine Archbishop*. Birmingham Byzantine and Ottoman Monographs 2. Birmingham.
(2022) 'Painting and Polyphony: The *Christos Paschon* as Commentary', in *Byzantine Commentaries on Ancient Greek Texts, 12th–15th Centuries*, ed. B. van den Berg, D. Manolova and P. Marciniak, 214–39. Cambridge.
Nesseris, I. C. (2014) 'Η παιδεία στην Κωνσταντινούπολη κατά τον 12ο αιώνα', 2 vols. PhD thesis, University of Ioannina.

Nilsson, I. (2006) 'Discovering Literariness in the Past: Literature vs. History in the *Synopsis Chronike* of Konstantinos Manasses', in *L'écriture de la mémoire: La littérarité de l'historiographie*, ed. P. Odorico, P. A. Agapitos and M. Hinterberger, 15–31. Paris.
(2014) *Raconter Byzance: La littérature au XIIe siècle.* Paris.
(2016) 'Romantic Love in Rhetorical Guise: The Byzantine Revival of the Twelfth Century', in *Fictional Storytelling in the Medieval Eastern Mediterranean and Beyond*, ed. C. Cupane and B. Krönung, 39–66. Leiden.
(2019) 'The Past as Poetry: Two Byzantine World Chronicles in Verse', in Hörandner, Rhoby and Zagklas, 517–38.
(2021a) *Writer and Occasion in Twelfth-Century Byzantium: The Authorial Voice of Constantine Manasses.* Cambridge.
(2021b) 'The Literary Voice of a Chronicler: The *Synopsis Chronike* of Constantine Manasses', *Scandinavian Journal for Byzantine and Modern Greek Studies* 7: 9–40.
Nilsson, I., and N. Zagklas (eds.) (2024) *Occasional Literature and Patronage: Cross-cultural Perspectives in Later Medieval and Early Modern Periods. Interfaces: A Journal of Medieval European Literature.*
Nousia, F. (2016) *Byzantine Textbooks of the Palaeologan Period.* Studi e Testi 505. Vatican City.
Papadimitriou, S. D. (1905) *Feodor Prodrom.* Odessa.
(ed.) (1911) 'Partii Ippodroma i dima v XII stoletie', in *Serta Borysthenica: Sbornik v čest' zaslužennago professora Imperatorskago universiteta sv. Vladimira Iuliana Andreeviča Kulakovskago*, 89–95. Kiev.
Papaioannou, S. (ed.) (2019) *Michael Psellus: Epistulae.* Berlin.
(2021) 'Sacred Song', in *Oxford Handbook of Byzantine Literature*, ed. idem, 430–63. Oxford.
Pizzone, A. (2017) 'The *Historiai* of John Tzetzes: A Byzantine "Book of Memory"?', *BMGS* 41.2: 182–207.
(2020) 'Self-authorization and Strategies of Autography in John Tzetzes: The *Logismoi* Rediscovered', *GRBS* 60: 652–90.
Polemis, I. D. (1995) 'Προβλήματα τῆς βυζαντινῆς σχεδογραφίας', *Ἑλληνικά* 45: 277–302.
Rapp, C. (2010) 'Old Testament Models for Emperors in Early Byzantium', in *The Old Testament in Byzantium*, ed. P. Magdalino and R. S. Nelson, 175–97. Washington, DC.
Ravani, A. (2022) '"And wishes also a paraphrase of Homer's verses": Structure and Composition of the *Prolegomena* to the *Allegories of the Iliad*', in *Τζετζικαὶ ἔρευναι*, ed. E. E. Prodi, 261–89. Eikasmos Studi Online 4. Bologna.
Rhoby, A. (2010) 'Ioannes Tzetzes als Auftragsdichter', *Graeco-Latina Brunensia* 15.2: 155–70.
(2014) *Byzantinische Epigramme auf Stein. Nebst Addenda zu den Bänden 1 und 2.* Vienna.
Roilos, P. (2005) *Amphoteroglossia: A Poetics of the Twelfth-Century Medieval Greek Novel.* Cambridge, MA.

(2020) 'Satirical Modulations in Twelfth-Century Greek literature', in *Satire in the Middle Byzantine Period: The Golden Age of Laughter?*, ed. P. Marciniak and I. Nilsson, 254–78. Explorations in Medieval Culture 12. Leiden.

Romano, R. (ed.) (1980) *Nicola Callicle: Carmi. Testo critico, introduzione, traduzione, commentario e lessico*. Byzantina et Neo-Hellenica Neapolitana 8. Naples.

Russell, D. A. (1989) *The Place of Poetry in Ancient Literature*. Oxford.

Spingou, F. (2014) 'The Anonymous Poets of the *Anthologia Marciana*: Questions of Collection and Authorship', in *The Author in Middle Byzantine Literature: Modes, Functions, and Identities*, ed. A. Pizzone, 137–50. Berlin.

(2021) *Words and Artworks in the Twelfth Century and Beyond: Twelfth-Century Poetry on Art from MS. Marcianus Gr. 524*. Tolworth.

Stanković, V. (2007) 'A Generation Gap or Political Enmity? Emperor Manuel Komnenos, Byzantine Intellectuals and the Struggle for Domination in Twelfth Century Byzantium', *ZRVI* 44: 209–26.

Tomadaki, M. (2022) 'Uncovering the Literary Sources of John Tzetzes' *Theogony*', in *Byzantine Commentaries on Ancient Greek Texts, 12th–15th Centuries*, ed. B. van den Berg, D. Manolova and P. Marciniak, 130–47. Cambridge.

van den Berg, B. (2020) 'John Tzetzes as Didactic Poet and Learned Grammarian', *DOP* 74: 285–302.

van Dieten, J. L. (ed.) (1972) *Nicetae Choniatae orationes et epistulae*. Berlin.

Vassis, I. (1993–4) 'Graeca sunt, non leguntur: Zu den schedographischen Spielereien des Theodoros Prodromos', *ByzZ* 86–7.1: 1–19.

(2002) 'Τῶν νέων φιλολόγων παλαίσματα: Ἡ συλλογή σχεδῶν τοῦ κώδικα Vaticanus Palatinus gr. 92', *Ἑλληνικά* 52: 37–68.

Vassis, I., and I. Polemis (eds.) (2016) *Ἕνας Ἕλληνας ἐξόριστος στὴ Μάλτα τοῦ δωδέκατου αἰώνα. Τὸ ποίημα τοῦ ἑλληνικοῦ κώδικα τῆς Ἐθνικῆς Βιβλιοθήκης τῆς Μαδρίτης 4577: Νέα κριτικὴ ἔκδοση μὲ μετάφραση καὶ σημειώσεις*. Athens.

Walz, C. (ed.) (1832–6) *Rhetores Graeci*, vol. 3. Stuttgart.

(ed.) (1910) *Analecta Byzantina: Carmina inedita Theodori Prodromi et Stephani Physopalamitae*. Leipzig.

Westerink, L. G. (ed.) (1992) *Michaelis Pselli Poemata*. Stuttgart.

Westerink, L. G., and B. Laourdas (eds.) (1986) *Photii Patriarchae Constantinopolitani Epistulae et Amphilochia*, vol. 5. Leipzig.

Zagklas, N. (2011) 'A Byzantine Grammar Treatise Attributed to Theodore Prodromos', *Graeco-Latina Brunensia* 16: 77–86.

(2017) 'Experimenting with Prose and Verse in Twelfth-Century Byzantium', *DOP* 71: 229–48.

(2019) '"How Many Verses Shall I Write and Say?": Poetry in the Komnenian Period', in Hörandner, Rhoby and Zagklas, 237–63.

(2021) 'Satire in the Komnenian Period: Poetry, Satirical Strands, and Intellectual Antagonism', in *Satire in the Middle Byzantine Period: The Golden Age of Laughter?*, ed. P. Marciniak and I. Nilsson, 279–303. Explorations in Medieval Culture 12. Leiden.

(2023) *Theodore Prodromos, Miscellaneous Poems: An Edition and Literary Study.* Oxford.

PART I

Poetry and Twelfth-Century Literary Culture

CHAPTER I

'The Force of Discourses'
*Literary Production in the Komnenian Era**

Panagiotis A. Agapitos

It was fifty-five years ago that Herbert Hunger published a paper attempting a re-evaluation of literature during the Komnenian era,[1] while only a few years later Hans-Georg Beck published an essay proposing ways to understand Byzantine textuality as a literary phenomenon.[2] During the same time, Alexander Kazhdan was publishing articles on authors of the eleventh and twelfth century wherein he interpreted their works as parts of an actual involvement with the real life of their times, and not just as an imitation of antiquity.[3] This broader re-evaluation of Byzantine literature, especially of the twelfth century, was seen as necessary by Hunger, Beck and Kazhdan – three great scholars of the same generation but with quite different views of Byzantium – given the criticism that had been expressed by Karl Krumbacher in his *History of Byzantine Literature*.[4] In the half

* This condensed overview is an experiment in its early stages with omissions, inconsistencies and even some debatable aspects in the organization of its contents. However, it is hoped that it will give the readers a first idea of how I intend to approach the writing of a narrative history of Byzantine literature; see also Agapitos (2015b) and (2023a). I wish to express my thanks to Paul Magdalino, Simos Paschalidis and Alexander Riehle for sending me their published and unpublished work, but also to Andreas Rhoby and Nikolaos Zagklas for insisting that I should write this overview. I am grateful to Nektarios Zarras for sharing with me the findings of his study on the Chora narthex mosaic cycle and Metochites' poems. Finally, I am indebted to Theodore Papanghelis for two stimulating conversations in Thessalonike on literary interpretation and the study of genre. The chapter does not aim at bibliographical completeness, nor does it provide information on the lives and works of individual authors. The interested reader will have to turn to the handbooks by Beck (1959) and (1971) and Hunger (1978), along with the brief entries in the *Tusculum Lexikon* (3rd ed., 1982) and the *Oxford Dictionary of Byzantium* (1991). The long-awaited handbook on Byzantine literature edited by Papaioannou (2021) appeared too late to be used here, and readers are asked to read through the chapters on topics that have been touched upon here, e.g. authorial personae, narrative, rhetoric, poetry, invective, book culture.

1 Hunger (1973), originally published in 1968.

2 Beck (1974), further developed in Beck (1978: 109–62).

3 These essays, originally published in the 1960s and 1970s in Russian, were translated and fully revised by Kazhdan and Franklin (1984).

4 Krumbacher (1897: 16–18); on the scholarly and political context of this criticism, see Agapitos (2015b: 20–2).

century that elapsed since 1968, Byzantine Studies progressed immensely concerning textual and literary criticism of Byzantine literature during the long twelfth century.[5] Despite this progress there are a few voices reacting against the theoretically informed literary analysis of Byzantine texts[6] and, in particular, against the idea of writing a comprehensive literary history of Byzantium. This latter objection reflects a certain tendency among Byzantinists to reject the idea of cohesion and self-consciousness in Byzantine literature because the Byzantines had no understanding of literary history and were supposedly not interested in the products of their own age.[7] At the same time, critical theory has rightly rejected essentialist or teleological approaches to literary history.[8] Such concerns, however, cannot hide the fact that some kind of history of Byzantine literature is needed to establish a common ground of understanding within the field, communicate with other disciplines in the broader context of medieval European literatures and teach to students of the twenty-first century Medieval Greek texts within their appropriate literary and historical framework, but also to elicit scholarly criticism about how to improve the production of research output.

The present chapter is a small contribution towards this direction though, obviously, Byzantine literature of the Komnenian era cannot be dealt with here in any kind of exhaustive manner. Rather, what I intend to do is to present an interpretive overview of this textual production by means of four broader themes. The four themes are 'education and literature', 'patronage and literary production', 'rhetoric and genre in prose and verse', 'narrative art from the enormous to the minute'. By way of conclusion, I will touch upon a question that concerns Byzantine literary history from the late tenth to the early fifteenth century and discuss, more specifically, how Komnenian textual production fits into the literary and cultural developments of these 450 years.

5 Unfortunately, there exists no bibliographical study of Byzantinist research for the Komnenian era since 1968. Besides Kazhdan and Franklin (1984) and Kazhdan and Wharton Epstein (1985), one should mention the important theoretical essays by Mullett (1990) and (2010). A brief presentation of developments in the field by Rapp (2023) practically does not touch the study of literature at all. A selection of literary overviews, interpretive studies and critical editions of various Komnenian texts will be referred to in the following notes.

6 Indicatively, see the opinions of Kaldellis and Siniossoglou (2017: 17–18) about what 'some philologists turned literary critics' are supposed to do with Byzantine literature.

7 See, for example, Lauxtermann (2002: 147–8) or, more recently, Kaldellis (2014: 1).

8 More generally, see the introduction by Borsa et al. (2015) in the first issue of *Interfaces*, dedicated to the topic 'Histories of Medieval European Literatures: New Patterns of Representation and Explanation'; for Byzantine literature in this context, see Agapitos (2015a: 62–72).

Education and Literature

Until recently, education in Byzantine Studies was examined from a historical perspective with the aim to reconstruct the 'system of Byzantine education'.[9] Recent studies, however, take a different approach by studying, on the one hand, the actual practice of teachers and, on the other, the interrelations between education and literature.[10] Here, I believe, lies a key theme for understanding textual production under the Komnenoi as a literary, cultural, social and even political phenomenon. Knowledge of language and discourse centred on three technical fields: vocabulary, grammar and rhetoric. For each of these fields eleventh- and twelfth-century teachers either invented a new tool of instruction or innovatively developed older tools. Thus, the composition of *schede* ('grammatical sketches')[11] and *progymnasmata* ('rhetorical exercises')[12] along with the memorization of *epimerismoi* (variously organized clusters of words and phrases)[13] supplied the solid basis for pupils to write and declaim various types of verse and prose texts. At the same time, this tripartite instruction prepared them for all kinds of civil and ecclesiastical careers in the public domain, and for this reason pupils and teachers had to present themselves to the public. Schedography, in particular, was an exceptionally important form of performative exercise within a public contest overseen by members of the aristocracy.[14] The discursive performance of teachers and pupils took on an even more complex and demanding form when, for example, on the Feast of Epiphany the 'senior professor of rhetoric' (μαΐστωρ τῶν ῥητόρων) delivered a speech in praise of the emperor sometimes accompanied by his students,[15] while on the Saturday of Lazarus he and his students delivered speeches in praise of the patriarch, as we know from

9 See the older studies by Fuchs (1926), Lemerle (1971) and (1986), Speck (1974), Browning (1977), along with the recent overviews by Markopoulos (2006) and (2014).

10 Katsaros (1988), Loukaki (2005) and Nesseris (2014) on school practice and literary production; Vassis (1993–4), Polemis (1995) and (1997), Silvano (2015) and Nousia (2016) on the practice of schedography; Gaul (2014) on networks of learning. It is indicative that language instruction is not discussed in overviews of the history of Greek in Byzantine times; see, for example, Horrocks (2010: 189–369) and Cupane (2016: 925–30). For an exception, see the brief essay by Giannouli (2014).

11 See Agapitos (2014) and Nousia (2016: 49–92).

12 See briefly Beneker and Gibson (2016: viii–xiii).

13 See Robins (1993: 125–48).

14 For some references to contests, see Nousia (2016: 74–7).

15 For a particular case, see the orations delivered by George Tornikes the Younger and his pupils Constantine Stilbes and Sergios Kolyvas at Epiphany 1193 in honour of Emperor Isaac II Angelos; for the editions, see Regel (1982: 254–80), Browning (1958) and Regel (1982: 280–300). On the identification of Stilbes as the author and Isaac II as addressee of the anonymously transmitted oration, see Darrouzès (1960: 184–7).

works of Eustathios of Thessalonike,[16] George Tornikes the Younger[17] and Nikephoros Chrysoberges.[18]

Thus, performative rhetorical production was intimately related with the schools. But such education and career advancement depended on strong network connections. We therefore find 'families' of teachers playing an important role in promoting their own socio-economic interests and textual products, as well as those of their pupils. It is a form of teacherly nepotism that we already find in the eleventh century, but by the twelfth century it becomes a prominent feature of Byzantine society. One needs only to think of the line from John Mauropous via Michael Psellos to Theophylaktos of Ohrid;[19] or of Prodromos' teacher-father, Prodromos' teachers Stephanos Skylitzes and Michael Italikos, and Prodromos' pupil Niketas Eugeneianos;[20] or of the line from Nicholas Kataphloron to Gregory Antiochos to Michael Anchialou to Eustathios of Thessalonike and his pupil Michael Choniates and to Choniates' nephews at the Laskarid court of Nicaea;[21] finally, one should recall the Tornikes clan whose members held high government offices and high educational or ecclesiastical posts.[22]

A further important aspect of the connections between education and literature is the commentary tradition.[23] We can fairly safely say that the production of commentary in the Komnenian era grows exponentially from the basic scholia and catenae into full textual commentaries of grand proportions. Not only is there a renewed interest in producing extensive biblical catenae and biblical commentaries, as testified by the massive productions of Niketas of Herakleia and Theophylaktos of Ohrid, but also a substantial renewal of the classical commentary by John Tzetzes and Eustathios (one only needs to take a look at the Aristophanic and Homeric commentaries respectively of the two teachers), as well as of the philosophical commentary by Eustratios of Nicaea and Michael of Ephesus. New as a type of juridical exegesis are the commentaries to the canons of the ecumenical councils by John Zonaras, Alexios Aristenos and Theodore

16 *Orations* 6 and 7; see Wirth (2000: 78–99 and 100–40).

17 Two orations by George and three further orations by three of his advanced pupils; for an edition of the whole dossier with French translation, see Loukaki and Jouanno (2005).

18 Edited by Browning (1989); on this twelfth-century institution to honour the patriarch, see Loukaki (2005).

19 See Agapitos (1998c) and Bernard (2017) on Psellos and Mauropous, Mullett (1997) on Psellos and Theophylaktos.

20 See Agapitos (2015d: 12–14 and 20–3).

21 See Loukaki (2000) and (2019) on Kataphloron, Agapitos (2015c) and van den Berg (2017) on Eustathios, F. Kolovou (1999) on Choniates, Agapitos (2021) on the Choniates family in Nicaea.

22 On this family, see Darrouzès (1968) and (1970).

23 On what follows in this paragraph, see now Agapitos (2022b) with full bibliography.

Balsamon. Also completely new are the philological commentaries on the hymnical canons of John of Damascus and Kosmas the Melode by John Zonaras, Prodromos, Gregory Pardos[24] and Eustathios.[25] In my opinion, their production is not related to the decrease of hymnical composition, but to a new system of governance in need of officials equally well educated in matters of the state and of the church.[26]

However, one aspect of Komnenian education appears surprising. Despite the agreement of scholars that the twelfth century represents a high moment in the reception of the classics and the performance of Hellenism,[27] the number of manuscripts of the classical canon and the accompanying critical texts and didactic manuals being copied is quite low.[28] For example, although so much epideictic oratory is written and although so many scholars (including myself) have pointed to the importance of Menander Rhetor as a handbook for the composition of such orations, there survives from the twelfth century only one codex transmitting in complete form the two Menandrian treatises and a further one preserving some extracts.[29] The Hermogenean corpus, along with various synopses and scholia, survives in only three twelfth-century manuscripts as opposed to six of the eleventh and further six of the thirteenth century.[30] This absence should make us aware that Komnenian classicizing textual production owes more to its own dynamics – a movement starting in the eleventh century – than to the towering authority of Late Roman handbooks of Greek rhetoric.[31]

Patronage and Literary Production

Rhetorical performativity owed much to the patrons who were active in soliciting textual products so as to enhance their public image. Prodromos, but also others, expressed this particular two-directional relation in

24 On these three authors, see briefly Giannouli (2007: 17–19) with the older bibliography.
25 See now Cesaretti and Ronchey (2014).
26 See the remarks by Ronchey (2017) with the older bibliography.
27 See, indicatively, Macrides and Magdalino (1992), Kaldellis (2007: 225–316) and (2009).
28 Unfortunately, there exists for Greek manuscripts no comprehensive study like the monumental work of Birger Munk Olsen for the Latin manuscripts of Roman authors in the eleventh and twelfth centuries; see Munk Olsen (1982–2014) as well as Munk Olsen (1991) on the classics in the school canon of the High Middle Ages.
29 See Russell and Wilson (1981: xl–xliv).
30 See Patillon (2008: vi–xi). To the two twelfth-century manuscripts listed by Patillon, we must now add the Leiden, Bibliotheek der Rijksuniversiteit, Vossianus Gr. Q1 [Diktyon 38108], a manuscript copied under the guidance of and corrected by John Tzetzes, as his autograph notes reveal; see Pizzone (2020).
31 This traditional opinion is still reflected in some recent overviews of rhetoric and literary criticism in Byzantium; see Bourbouhakis (2017a) and Papaioannou (2017).

economic terms. When addressing his patron, Prodromos states that if he died from hunger, the patron would lose the person who excels in praising him, so the patron would do best to pay the poet.[32] The socio-economic parameters of literary production under Komnenian patronage are encapsulated in the 'theatres of discourse' (λογικὰ θέατρα) of the twelfth-century aristocracy.[33] It is in such gatherings that patrons listened to progymnasmatic improvisations, letters, passages from novels and philosophical treatises by sponsored literati, some of whom, like Michael Italikos and Nikephoros Basilakes, took up important posts in state and church. It is in such *theatra* that Prodromos presented his schedographic innovations directing the taste of various patrons towards a lighter style of writing, and incurring the criticism of traditionalist teachers like John Tzetzes[34] or strict aristocrats like Anna Komnene.[35]

This open literary competition between peers and the promise of awards for the writers involved is one of the reasons why the Komnenian era boasts of so many and so varied authorial portraits, almost an obsession of writers with their own self-staging. It is possible that the autographic voice created by Michael Psellos (decisively modelled on Gregory of Nazianzos) was an inspiration for some Komnenian authors[36] but their insistence on self-representation is nevertheless extraordinary. Authors so different as Eustratios of Nicaea, Italikos, Basilakes, Prodromos, Tzetzes, Eustathios, Michael Choniates, Eugenios of Palermo and Neophytos the Recluse write about themselves, their writerly aspirations and choices, their successes and failures, so that the twelfth century could be called the 'era of the authorial voice'.[37] Even aristocrats are concerned with the public reception of their own writings; Isaac Komnenos, for example, insisted in the foundation charter of the Kosmosoteira (*c.* 1150) that the book with his selected works (letters, *ekphraseis* and poems in various metres) should be handed out to those members of his monastic community who wished to read it and be instructed.[38]

32 See *Historical Poem* 16.218–28 ed. Hörandner (1974: 284) to John II Komnenos (*c.* 1139) and *Ptochopr.* 2.101–14 ed. Eideneier (1991: 115) and (2012: 170–1) to the *sebastokrator* Isaac Komnenos (*c.* 1140–50), John's brother. See also Ricceri in this volume.

33 On Komnenian 'literary salons', see Mullett (1984) and Magdalino (1993: 335–56), along with Marciniak (2007) and Chryssogelos (2017: 67–70).

34 Agapitos (2017: 7–27).

35 Agapitos (2013).

36 As proposed by Papaioannou (2013: 232–49).

37 Indicatively, one might refer to the essays in Pizzone (2014b), although we still lack in-depth studies of the authorial voice of many of these writers; for a very recent study of one twelfth-century author from this perspective, see Nilsson (2021).

38 *Typikon* §106 ed. Petit (1908: 69); English translation by Patterson Ševčenko (2000: 884).

This materiality of the text as a tangible book leads me to one further aspect of manuscript production. There is little left of costly manuscripts transmitting Komnenian texts presented to patrons as offerings of their authors: the fine volume of Euthymios Zigabenos' *Armour of Dogma* (Vatican City, Biblioteca Apostolica Vaticana, gr. 666 [Diktyon 67297]),[39] two luxurious volumes with the homilies on the life of the Virgin by James of Kokkinobaphos (Vatican City, Biblioteca Apostolica Vaticana, gr. 1162 [Diktyon 67793] and Paris, Bibliothèque nationale de France, gr. 1208 [Diktyon 50813]),[40] Prodromos' *Grammar* for the *sebastokratorissa* Irene (Jerusalem, Patriarchike Bibliotheke, Timiou Staurou 52 [Diktyon 35289]),[41] Prodromos' lost dedication copy of his novel to the caesar Nikephoros Bryennios,[42] but also Eustathios' parchment manuscripts of his *Parekbolai to the Iliad* (Florence, Biblioteca Medicea Laurenziana, Plut. 59.2 and 59.3 [Diktyon 16453 and 16454])[43] and the *Parekbolai to the Odyssey* (Venice, Biblioteca Nazionale Marciana, gr. Z.460 [Diktyon 69931]).[44] Otherwise, most of the prose and verse texts produced for the imperial court and related *theatra* are preserved in relatively inexpensive, densely written paper manuscripts from the late twelfth or thirteenth centuries, usually anthologies like Venice, Biblioteca Nazionale Marciana gr. Z. 524 [Diktyon 69995], Venice, Biblioteca Nazionale Marciana, XI.22 [Diktyon 70658], El Escorial, Real Biblioteca, Y-II-10 [Diktyon 15478] or Vatican City, Biblioteca Apostolica Vaticana, Barb. gr. 240 [Diktyon 64786]. Rare is the case of a manuscript transmitting a collection of such rhetorical works by a single author, like the Basel, Universitätsbibliothek, A-III-20 [Diktyon 8892] with Eustathios' Thessalonian works or the Vatican City, Biblioteca Apostolica Vaticana, gr. 305 [Diktyon 66936] with a broad selection of Prodromos' works, both paper codices.[45] To these not so costly books we should add thirteenth-century manuscripts preserving schedographic collections, like Vatican City, Biblioteca Apostolica Vaticana, Pal. gr. 92 [Diktyon 65825], Munich, Bayerische Staatsbibliothek, gr. 201 [Diktyon 44647], and Paris, Bibliothèque nationale de France, gr. 2556 [Diktyon 52188].[46] In most instances, all these texts survive in only one

39 Parpulov (2017) with further bibliography.
40 Linardou (2017).
41 See Jeffreys (2011–12: 184) with further bibliography and Zagklas (2011).
42 Agapitos (2000).
43 See the detailed discussion by van der Valk (1971–87: 1:ix–xxxi).
44 On this manuscript, see now Cullhed (2016: 36*–48*).
45 On the Basel manuscript of Eustathios, see Schönauer (2006: *25–*27); on the Vatican manuscript of Prodromos, see Zagklas (2023: 122–30).
46 For bibliography on these manuscripts, see above nn. 10–11.

manuscript, a clear indication that it was not the patrons who were interested in the preservation of these utilitarian texts but the authors as teachers, their colleagues and their pupils.

Rhetoric and Genre in Prose and Poetry

Upon the return of Emperor John II from his Cilician campaign to Constantinople in the autumn of 1138, a series of feasts were organized to celebrate this victory. Basilakes and Italikos wrote substantial encomiastic orations,[47] while Prodromos composed a poem in fifteen-syllable 'city verses' (πολιτικοὶ στίχοι) for the demes.[48] The explicit references to rhetoric as performative practice in the three texts are overwhelming. The three authors use various combinations of motifs to express the impossibility of describing the heroic deeds of the emperor. Basilakes and Italikos, who were rivalling each other for the emperor's favour (Basilakes won at that point), present themselves as members of a group of rhetors and philosophers who use in a novel manner the encomiastic practice both in oral and in textual form.[49] Prodromos, however, follows a different line. He considers that 'the force of discourses' (τὸ τῶν λόγων κράτος) and 'the invincible pomp of oratory' (τὸν ἀήττητον τῆς ῥητορείας τῦφον) have been defeated by the emperor.[50] Therefore, he will borrow his praises from the musician prophet David in order to celebrate the invincible ruler in a hymnic manner.[51] At the end of the poem, Prodromos – not without a certain irony – suggests to John to pity the chroniclers (συγγραφεῖς) of his heroic deeds: 'Grant them, o emperor, some respite, until they will be able to recount your victories so far' (κἂν γοῦν ἐκείνους, βασιλεῦ, ἀνάπαυσον ὀλίγον, | μέχρις ἀπαριθμήσονται τὰς ἄχρι νῦν σου νίκας).[52]

47 Basilakes' oration has been edited with Italian summary by Maisano (1977: 89–132), the Greek text only by Garzya (1984: 48–74); Italikos' oration has been edited with French summary by Gautier (1972: 239–70).

48 *Historical Poem* 11 ed. Hörandner (1974: 253–9). On poetry for the demes, see also Magdalino in this volume.

49 See, for example, Italikos in Gautier (1972: 247 and 253); Basilakes, *Encomium on John* §2 and 4 in Maisano (1977: 90–1 and 93) and Garzya (1984: 50–1 and 51–2).

50 *Historical Poem* 11.11–20 ed. Hörandner (1974: 254). The phrase 'the force of discourses' that also figures in the present chapter's title appears fairly often in oratorical works of the twelfth century, a kind of code about the splendour of public oratory and of the orators themselves. The phrase was first coined by Gregory of Nazianzos (see *Or.* 4, §100 ed. Bernardi [1983: 248.12–15]) in his first speech against Julian, a famous model text of intellectual invective for all learned Byzantines.

51 *Historical Poem* 11.141–50 ed. Hörandner (1974: 257). On the poet as David, see also Ricceri in this volume.

52 *Historical Poem* 11.211–20 ed. Hörandner (1974: 259).

Various issues appear in this context that will allow us to take a broader look at rhetoric and its prose genres as theory and practice, and their relation to poetic practice. Despite much excellent work on Byzantine prose and poetry, we are far removed from a deeper understanding of the literary and socio-cultural mechanics and poetics of rhetoric.[53] More generally, I view rhetoric as a theoretical and practical tool for composition and performance – what the Byzantines often called the 'laws/rules' of a specific type, like the various orations of praise, or of the art of rhetoric and of speech writing more broadly.[54] I do not understand rhetoric as a 'super-genre' wherein prose and poetry are placed without any essential differentiation. In my opinion, therefore, epistolary poems are poetry using some of the devices of epistolography and the mechanics of rhetoric but these poems are not types of texts simply interchangeable with prose letters.[55]

But to return to the texts of the three writers just mentioned: Italikos and Basilakes use substantial terminology and specific imagery to define their encomiastic projects, even if they do so in different ways – Basilakes by affirming the power of rhetoric, Italikos by criticizing his rivals. Prodromos appears to reject 'the force of discourses' in favour of David's hymnic praise. In this attitude I see a rivalry of the poet with the rhetors and, thus, an effort to raise poetry to the level of oratory. However, in examining the three texts more closely, we will recognize that the *matière* of encomiastic rhetoric is fully shared between them, not as meaningless variation of commonplaces, but as meaningful expression of different, even conflicting, artistic and social agendas. Here, I believe, we can clearly see that the distinction of Komnenian literary production into the traditional genres of Hellenistic and Roman imperial school rhetoric fails to capture the fluid interfaces of genres in the twelfth century.

What the three texts certainly point our attention to is the mass of works produced for all kinds of festive occasions from private events to public celebrations. Moreover, the three texts indicate that writers during the Komnenian era were quite preoccupied with developing a metaliterary discourse

53 The volumes edited by Littlewood (1995) and E. M. Jeffreys (2003) clearly show the long way we have to go, as do the brief overviews by Bourbouhakis (2017a) and Papaioannou (2017).

54 See, for example, John Geometres, *Progymnasma* 2 in Littlewood (1972: 9.22–3, ῥητορεία, τέχνη καὶ νόμος); Psellos, *Address to Emperor Constantine Doukas* in Dennis (1994: 131.3, ἐγκωμίων νόμος); Eustathios, *Funeral Oration on Nicholas Hagiotheodorites* in Wirth (2000: 3.10, ἐπιταφίου νόμος); Eustathios, *Funeral Oration on Emperor Manuel Komnenos* §4 in Bourbouhakis (2017b: 4.9–10, νόμοι λογογραφίας, ῥητορικὸς νόμος).

55 On epistolary poetry, see now Kubina and Riehle (2021) and, for the twelfth century, Zagklas (2021a). On the relationship between prose and poetry in the twelfth century, see also Bourbouhakis in this volume.

serving the theorization and vindication of writerly activity, be it occasional rhetoric, all kinds of narratives, or poetry in its multifarious forms. Through his poetry, Prodromos, in particular, became a leading figure in this critical theorization, and it is unfortunate that no study has been devoted to Prodromos' comments on literary writing, its theory and practice.[56] It will be useful to point here to a few more prose texts: Nikephoros Basilakes' *Prologue* to a collection of his works,[57] Nicholas Kataphloron's preface to his oration praising a *megas doux*,[58] Michael Choniates' *Prologue* to a collection of his works and his 'writerly apology' *Against Display*,[59] John Tzetzes' prefaces, epilogues and marginal scholia to much of his output,[60] Eustathios' prefaces to his five commentaries,[61] and also the anonymous essay *Against Those Writing Monodies*.[62] This corpus of texts gives us unique insights into literary production of a specific era within a complex network of friendly or competitive relations among peers and within various areas of intellectual and social tensions, such as state and church politics.[63]

Though Classical and Medieval Studies have moved away from sustained debates about genre,[64] Byzantine Studies have not yet reached such a state of saturation because we still operate with conventional notions of what 'genre' in Greek literature is.[65] Yet the long twelfth century allows us to re-examine such notions and possibly find more adequate categories for understanding debates about genre in Byzantine literature.[66] Let me start

56 For some remarks within a presentation of Prodromos as teacher and poet, see Zagklas (2023: 32–42).

57 Garzya (1984: 1–9); see also Pizzone (2014a).

58 Edited and discussed by Loukaki (2000); edition of the full text with French translation by Loukaki (2019), reedited by Polemis (2020) with Modern Greek translation.

59 Lampros (1968: 1:3–5 and 7–23); on the latter work, see Bourbouhakis (2014).

60 This rich material composed in prose and verse also remains substantially unstudied; for some recent approaches, with the relevant bibliography, see Cullhed (2014: 58–67), Goldwyn and Kokkini (2015) and (2019), Pizzone (2017), Agapitos (2017), van den Berg (2020).

61 This is another rich dossier that still awaits full interpretation. For all relevant bibliography to the editions, see Schönauer (2006: 9*–10*) and Cesaretti and Ronchey (2014: 324*–7*). For some interpretive approaches, see van den Berg (2017) and G. E. Kolovou (2018), and now more broadly van den Berg (2022). For a varied, though far from exhaustive, approach to Eustathios, see the essays in Pontani, Katsaros and Sarris (2017).

62 See Sideras (2002: 48–61) for the Greek text with facing German translation.

63 It would be a splendid project to unite all of these texts into a two-volume edition with English translations, introductions and notes. For a similar, very successful, project on Michael Psellos' essays on literature and art, see now Barber and Papaioannou (2017).

64 For Classics, see the old but influential study by Kroll (1924) in conjunction with the critique expressed by Barchiesi (2001); for recent approaches, one might consult Farrel (2003), Papanghelis et al. (2013); for Medieval Studies, see Jauß (1977), as well as the relevant section 'What Is the Value of Genre in Medieval French Literature' in Gaunt and Kay (2008: 137–94) and the two issues of *Exemplaria* devoted to 'Medieval Genre' in Gayk and Nelson (2015).

65 See the critique and various proposals by Mullett (1992), Agapitos (1998a) and (2003), Nilsson (2003) and Constantinou (2004).

66 See now Agapitos (2023b).

with a type of text that only very recently has received some attention, and where prose and poetry coexist in a dynamic manner.[67] I call such texts compound diptychs or triptychs; they are essentially performative in character. The attribute 'compound' indicates the sequential connection of two or more texts, clearly distinguished from each other and yet forming a larger entity of structure and meaning. Two such diptychs are Prodromos' *Historical Poem* 24 and *Ptochoprodromos* 1 addressed to John II in 1141/2[68] and *Historical Poem* 71 to Manuel I via his secretary Theodore Styppeiotes and the *Maiuri poem* addressed directly to Manuel in 1150/1.[69] Both diptychs follow the same structure: a humorous yet discreet plea for financial assistance in a 'learned' idiom is followed by a burlesque and vociferous repetition of the plea in a 'vernacular' idiom. Various thematic, linguistic and chronological elements make it clear that the two poems of each set belong together. Tearing them apart in two handbooks or in two different editions cancels their intended performative and generic effect.[70]

Another type is the compound triptych written with a public performance in mind. For example, Prodromos composes a laudatory triptych on the jurist Alexios Aristenos, director of the imperial orphanage (ὀρφανοτρόφος), consisting of a prose encomium,[71] a *schedos*[72] and four poems as variations on the same theme in four different metres (iambic, hexametric, pentametric, anacreontic).[73] With absolute self-confidence, the poet explains his complex triptych creation in the iambic poem (*Historical Poem* 56a.4–33).[74] Niketas Eugeneianos, in imitation of his teacher Prodromos, produced a funerary triptych in the latter's honour, which consists of a prose monody,[75] a *schedos* (so far unedited)[76] and two funerary poems

67 On this coexistence in the twelfth century, see Zagklas (2017).
68 Hörandner (1974: 330–3); Eideneier (1991: 99–107) and (2012: 153–61).
69 Hörandner (1974: 516–19); Maiuri (1914–19: 398–400).
70 For some first thoughts on this diptych form, see Agapitos (2015d: 29–37); on the satirical aspects of such texts, see Zagklas (2021b) and Kulhánková (2021). On their language, see also Kulhánková in this volume.
71 It is no. 91 in the list of Prodromos' works; see Hörandner (1974: 42). It has been critically edited with French translation by Op de Coul (2023: 51–7); there is an older edition in *Patr. Gr.* 133: 1268–74, where it wrongly figures as letter no. 8.
72 See the differing opinions of Vassis (1993–4: 8) and Polemis (1997: 255–6) about an anonymous *schedos* on an anonymous *orphanotrophos* in Venice, Biblioteca Nazionale Marciana, gr. XI.31 [Diktyon 70672], fols. 277v–278r, edited by Polemis (1997: 258–9).
73 *Historical Poem* 61a–d ed. Hörandner (1974: 460–8).
74 For a detailed analysis of this triptych, see Agapitos (2015d: 16–20) with translations of the relevant passages; for this type of metrical multiformity, see Zagklas (2018).
75 Edited by Petit (1902: 452–63); unfortunately, the end of the text has been lost.
76 The *schedos* (τοῦ κυροῦ Νικήτου τοῦ Εὐγενειανοῦ), referring to the story of the prophet Jonah, is preserved in Paris, Bibliothèque nationale de France, gr. 2556 (early fourteenth century) [Diktyon 52188], fols. 79r–80r.

as variations on the same theme in iambs and hexameters.[77] In both these triptychs the audience is led through the verses attached to the end of the prose *schedos* – a typical formal element of many twelfth-century *schede* – to the poetic third part which is in itself a compound form. Given our current knowledge of such compound triptychs, it seems that Prodromos was the inventor of this type of performative 'supertext'.[78] Away from the circle of Prodromos, we find another version of the compound triptych, this one by the otherwise unknown Leo of Megistos (ὁ τοῦ Μεγίστου), secretary of the grand hetairiarch George Palaiologos: a prose monody on the death of his employer (spoken by Leo),[79] a so far unedited verse monody (spoken by George's widow)[80] and a dialogic prose consolatory composition (framed by Leo as narrator, wherein the widow and the city of Constantinople speak).[81] Any attempt at a conventional generic description of these triptychs must fail. As texts they are dynamic combinations of different elements (prose and poetry, larger and smaller entities, different genres), while they create hybrid forms on both a micro- and a macrostructural level. They can only be fully appreciated when heard or read in the sequence planned by their writers, while they also show that any attempt to place them in the taxonomic boxes of our handbooks destroys the artistic and socio-cultural reality of Komnenian literature.

Forms that were already perceived as performative in Antiquity resurface in the twelfth century with a particular force and expanded textual functions. On the one hand, we find a plethora of 'pagan' and 'Christian' dialogues, shaped in various ways: from Lucianic reconstructions (such as the expansive *Timarion*[82] and Prodromos' shorter *Amarantos*[83]) to larger theological texts, such as Andronikos Kamateros' highly complex *Sacred Arsenal*[84] or Mesarites' *Funeral Oration on his Brother John* with its encased

77 Edited by Galavotti (1935: 222–9); on the reconstruction of this triptych, see Agapitos (2015d: 22–3).
78 Inspired by the term 'supersystem' (a macrolevel system composed of individual subsystems), I have coined the term 'supertext' to describe this type of textual unit with individual textual components that have their own logic but function fully only when read within an encompassing frame.
79 Lampsidis (1999: 121–33).
80 The text is preserved in Munich, Bayerische Staatsbibliothek, gr. 525 [Diktyon 44974], fols. 117r–118v; see Lampsidis (1999: 116–17) and Hinterberger (2005).
81 Edited with German translation by Sideras (1997); on the dialogic composition of the third text, see Hörandner (2017b).
82 Edited with Italian translation by Romano (1974), only Greek text by Macleod (1987: 432–70); English translation by Baldwin (1984); revised Greek text and Italian translation by Romano (1999: 99–175). After the pioneering literary study of this dialogue by Alexiou (1982–3), see now the essays by Kaldellis (2012) and Krallis (2013) for a historicist approach, and Nilsson (2016) for a differentiated literary interpretation.
83 Edited by Migliorini (2007); on the work, see now Cullhed (2017).
84 The first part of this work has been recently edited by Bucossi (2014).

acts of a meeting between Greeks and Latins on theological and ecclesiastical matters that took place after 1204.[85] We also find staged 'judiciary' competitions like Michael Choniates' *Personified Dialogue of the Soul and the Body*.[86] Furthermore, we note a marked presence of 'dramatic' compositions, not only the 'Euripidean' *Passion of Christ*[87] and the 'Aristophanic' *Dramation* by Michael Haploucheir,[88] but also the Lycophronian poem of Andronikos Protekdikos about a case of cannibalism judged at the patriarchate.[89] Finally, there are the 'antiquarian' novels composed in the second quarter of the century by Eumathios Makrembolites, Theodore Prodromos, Constantine Manasses and Niketas Eugeneianos. The three novels that survive complete display a series of narrative characteristics that are rhetorical reconfigurations of tragedy as it was taught in the schools. Two of the four novels use the iambic dodecasyllable, the dramatic metre par excellence.[90] This last group of dramatic/narrative texts leads me to the fourth and last theme of the present chapter.

Narrative Art from the Enormous to the Minute

Despite some progress in recent years, we are far removed from having understood the system of narrative in Byzantine literature as a whole. Most narratological approaches concentrate on the novels and the romances as the obvious choice for such an analysis.[91] However, narrative can be found in many other places than 'fiction' since the organization of 'telling' and 'showing' concerns a very broad spectrum of textual production. The tools narratology has been developing over the past fifty years are of great

85 Edited by Heisenberg (1973), translated into English by Angold (2017: 134–92).

86 The available editions for this work are incomplete and do not present Choniates' original text; see, for example, Migne (1865: 1347–72), where the work is falsely ascribed to the fourteenth-century theologian Gregory Palamas. For a brief presentation of the work's editorial history, see F. Kolovou (1999: 31–2). The recent book on dialogue and debate in the twelfth century by Cameron (2016) is rather descriptive; she does not mention Choniates' *Prosopopoiia*.

87 Edited with French translation by Tuilier (1969), who supported the attribution of the manuscripts to Gregory of Nazianzos. The text is now generally accepted to be of the twelfth century though its author remains unknown; see now Mullett (2022).

88 Edited by Leone (1969: 268–73); Italian translation with facing Greek text by Romano (1999: 407–35).

89 Edited with an English translation by Macrides (1985). On the theatrical tendencies of Komnenian literature, see also Magdalino in this volume.

90 For some literary approaches to the Komnenian novels, see, very selectively, Alexiou (1977), Agapitos (1998b), the various essays in Agapitos and Reinsch (2000), Nilsson (2001), Roilos (2005), Agapitos (2012) and Nilsson (2014: 39–86), as well as the relevant chapters in Cupane and Krönung (2016) with good bibliographies; for English translations of the four texts, see E. M. Jeffreys (2012); for Italian translations with facing Greek text, see Conca (1994).

91 See, indicatively, Agapitos (1991) and Nilsson (2001).

assistance for interpreting Byzantine narratives because the structuralist and post-structuralist approaches to narrative are very much in tune with the postmodern character of Byzantine aesthetics.[92]

In this sense, we should begin by examining Byzantine narrative art under a different light in order to discover some of its own mechanics and poetics. The Komnenian novels with their rhetorical techniques of dramatic display are a case in point. So, of course, is the *Tale of Digenis Akritis* in the Grottaferrata and Escorial redactions,[93] a text that, despite so much noise about its importance, still awaits a deep and comprehensive narrative analysis.[94] And even if we are fortunate to have solid critical editions of some major historiographical works of the twelfth century, no single full-scale narrative interpretation has been offered up to date.[95] The variety and polymorphy of these enormous narratives are quite stunning, while the texts (from Zonaras' *Chronicle* to Choniates' *Chronological Account* via Anna Komnene's *Alexiad* and Kinnamos' *History*) are certainly an important part of Komnenian literary modernity.[96] That these narratives are used as sources for the reconstruction of Byzantine history should not obscure the fact that they are literary texts following, expanding, subverting or even rejecting the practices of the Komnenian 'force of discourses'. Just to mention one example, one might compare the narrative structure of three works by Constantine Manasses: the enormous *Synopsis Chronike* (a world chronicle in *c.* 6,600 city verses),[97] the middle-sized *Itinerary* (a narrative poem in *c.* 800 iambic verses)[98] and the small *Description of the Earth* (a rhetorical set piece in *c.* 225 lines of prose).[99] Their narrative framing system, the organization of sequences, the positioning of narrators

92 For some recent attempts at narratological approaches to texts other than the novels, see the chapters in Messis et al. (2018), as well as the narratological readings of monastic edifying tales by Kulhánková (2015) and (2017).

93 The most recent edition of the two redactions with English translation is by E. M. Jeffreys (1998), where also the older bibliography is to be found.

94 Markéta Kulhánková is currently preparing a narratological commentary on the Grottaferrata redaction of *Digenis.*

95 Even in the case of Psellos' *Chronographia*, the studies by Pietsch (2005) and Lauritzen (2013) are not narratological analyses proper. For a recent effort, see Protogirou (2014). The studies by Simpson (2013) and Neville (2016) on Niketas Choniates and Anna Komnene are focused more on studying the two authors as historical personalities, which they do from quite different perspectives.

96 On this concept, see Agapitos (2022b).

97 Edited by Lampsidis (1996) and translated by Lampsidis (2003) into Modern Greek; see now Paul and Rhoby (2019) and Yuretich (2020) for German and English translations, respectively.

98 Old edition by Horna (1904); new edition with Modern Greek translation and substantial introduction by Chryssogelos (2017); on the poem, see also Aerts (2003).

99 Edition by Lampsidis (1991), Modern Greek translation with facing Greek text by Agapitos and Hinterberger (2006); for a recent art-historical interpretation of this *ekphrasis*, see Foskolou (2018).

and characters, the use of description (*ekphrasis*), the mixture of abstraction and concreteness, finally, the focus on acoustic and rhythmical effects of style are in all three texts the same, and they certainly differ from what we can see in texts from the middle of the tenth to the middle of the eleventh century.[100] In my opinion, we catch here a glimpse of a narrative system that reflects a broader framework of socio-cultural communication. As a further comparison, one might look at the way in which the visual arts are able to create the same effect from the minute to the enormous through their narrative system. Take as an example the formal and structural features of the Dormition of the Virgin (*Koimesis*) as represented in three twelfth-century media: a large-scale fresco on the south wall of the Panaghia tou Arakos in Cyprus,[101] an illuminated lectionary from the Great Lavra Monastery on Mount Athos [Diktyon 26928][102] and a golden ring now kept at the Dumbarton Oaks Collection.[103] The organization of the visual and textual 'telling' and 'showing' is the same despite the difference in size and media: the core of a narrative scene remains stable through the tools of the *topos* (i.e. stereotypical meaning) and *typos* (i.e. stereotypical structure),[104] the expansion of the narrative scene takes place in a paratactic manner by adding 'layers' of action and meaning, and by compartmentalizing every such addition through visual or verbal frames. This manner of organization is the Komnenian variant of the Byzantine narrative system.[105]

The same pertains to the lives of saints and their extraordinary generic and narrative variations in the twelfth century,[106] for example, competitive variations in the case of the life of the eleventh-century Meletios by Nicholas of Methone and by Theodore Prodromos,[107] the highly intellectualized variation of the life of the tenth-century Photios the Thessalonian by no less than Eustathios of Thessalonike,[108] the gnomologic varia-

100 On this system and its difference to what is found in the textual production between 950 and 1050, see my scattered remarks in Agapitos (1998b: 148–56), (2003) and (2020: 19–33).
101 See Winfield and Winfield (2003: pl. 23).
102 Mount Athos, Megistes Lavras 1, fol. 134v; see Pelekanidis (1979: pl. 80).
103 Intaglio ring (no. 56.15); see Kalavrezou (2003).
104 On these concepts, see Agapitos (2004: 106–8).
105 I am currently preparing a book-length essay on this narrative/cultural system with the tentative title *The Aesthetics of Layering in Byzantine Art and Literature*.
106 For a recent overview of eleventh- and twelfth-century hagiography, see Paschalidis (2011). My notion of 'variation' for the generic and narrative analysis of hagiography is inspired by Constantinou (2004).
107 New critical edition of these two texts with Modern Greek translation by Polemis (2022); for an interpretive approach, see Messis (2004).
108 For the convincing identification of the anonymous author of BHG 1545 with Eustathios, see Paschalidis (2008), who is also preparing a critical edition of this work.

tion of the expansive life of the eleventh/twelfth-century Cyril Phileotes by Nicholas Kataskepenos[109] and, finally, the episcopal variation of the life of the twelfth-century Leontios of Jerusalem by Theodosios Goudeles.[110] But then, since the present volume focuses on Komnenian poetry, it might be useful to look at the astonishing expansion of exegetical, admonitory and autobiographic narratives in verse. As Prodromos expressed it, we are here truly faced with 'the force of metre' (τὸ τοῦ μέτρου κράτος, *Historical Poem* 56a.17). And this force is overpowering given that all kinds of different narrative poems are produced, from Philip Monotropos' *Dioptra*[111] down to Constantine Stilbes' *Fire Poem*[112] via the resignation poem of Nicholas Mouzalon,[113] the mythological poems of Tzetzes[114] and the anonymously preserved and recently edited exile poem from Malta.[115] Moreover, we also find enormous and minute narrative verse cycles which take on highly experimental shapes, from Prodromos' *tetrasticha* on the lives of the Three Hierarchs[116] to Tzetzes' unique *Histories* of approximately 12,000 city verses,[117] where fragmentation, compartmentalization, repetition and disruption are key features of the 'post-modernist' narrative.[118]

All these texts cannot be fitted into any conventional generic category, neither those derived from Plato (*Republic* 392c–394d) and Aristotle (*Poetics* §1), nor those based on Hermogenes' proposals in *On Types of Style* 2.10.[119] They are part of various trends in experimentation starting in the first half

109 Edited with French translation by Sargologos (1964); for an extended interpretation, see Mullett (2004).
110 Edited with an English translation by Tsougarakis (1993).
111 Incomplete edition by Lavriotes (1920); further see Afentoulidou-Leitgeb (2007) and (2012), who is preparing a critical edition of this complex text.
112 Edited by Diethart and Hörandner (2005: 8–51); for an English translation with facing Greek text and notes, see Layman (2015). On Stilbes' poem, see also Magdalino in this volume.
113 Edited with Italian translation by Strano (2012); see further Mullett (2009).
114 On the editions of these poems, see Agapitos (2017: 2–3); for a corrected text of the *Allegories of the Iliad* and *Allegories of the Odyssey* along with an English translation, see Goldwyn and Kokkini (2015) and (2019); on Tzetzes' allegorical method, see Goldwyn (2017) and Conca (2018).
115 New critical edition with Modern Greek translation by Vassis and Polemis (2016); on the text, see also Lauxtermann (2014).
116 D'Ambrosi (2008) edited only the cycle on Gregory of Nazianzos.
117 Edited by Leone (2007).
118 On Tzetzes' *Histories*, see Pizzone (2017). Unfortunately, the critical edition with English translation and commentary by Elizabeth and Michael Jeffreys of the vast poetic corpus by an anonymous poet (conventionally known as 'Manganeios Prodromos') and transmitted in Venice, Biblioteca Nazionale Marciana, gr. XI.22 [Diktyon 70658] is still in preparation and, thus, cannot be studied as a meaningful whole; see Jeffreys and Jeffreys (2021) and in this volume.
119 For the chapters on genres in *On Types of Style*, see the excellent critical edition with translation and commentary by Patillon (2012: 210–16).

of the eleventh century and expanding well into the twelfth century.[120] In my opinion, this polymorphous narrative poetry is not written because it was easy to compose twelve- or fifteen-syllable verses,[121] but because narrative as a mode of display within the Komnenian system of cultural and social reference had taken an unprecedented importance. This importance derived, on the one hand, from a new approach to writing as it was developed in the schools and, on the other, from the wish of aristocratic patrons as members of a 'family-run' government to appropriate the social value of the arts for their image building. We can see these two parameters most clearly in the letters written by prominent and not so prominent people such as Theophylaktos,[122] Italikos,[123] Tzetzes,[124] Prodromos (in prose and in verse),[125] Hierotheos of Kataskepe,[126] George Tornikes[127] and Eustathios.[128] But we can also see this new approach to writing in the *ekphraseis* that pervade so much of Komnenian performative textual production.[129] I already mentioned the three works of Manasses, but I would further point to such topics as war, death and love that are also presented through the kinetic descriptive mode of *enargeia* ('translucent discourse') in a generically variegated set of texts: descriptions of battles in Eustathios, Anna Komnene and Prodromos;[130] variously presented descriptions of death in Anna, Michael Choniates, Goudeles, Italikos, Nicholas Kallikles and many anonymous

120 For a forceful proposal that the eleventh century is crucial in these processes for poetry, see Magdalino (2012) along with Bernard (2014).

121 So Jeffreys (2009).

122 On his collection, see comprehensively Mullett (1997).

123 Edited with French summaries by Gautier (1972); an interpretive study of Italikos' letters remains a desideratum.

124 No extensive study of Tzetzes' letters is available, despite the critical edition by Leone (1972) and the fine Modern Greek translation by Grigoriadis (2001); for some socio-cultural remarks on the corpus, see Agapitos (2022a).

125 See Op de Coul (2023) for the prose letters and Zagklas (2021a) on the verse letters.

126 See Grünbart (2016), who is also preparing a critical edition of this practically unknown collection.

127 Edited by Darrouzès (1970).

128 See F. Kolovou (2006) for a critical edition with an interpretive introduction. For two brief overviews of Byzantine epistolography, see Grünbart (2004) and Mullett (2008), as well as the collective volume edited by Riehle (2020).

129 There exists no broader literary study of *ekphrasis* in the eleventh and twelfth century; see briefly Mitsi and Agapitos (2006) with substantial theoretical bibliography along with Nilsson (2014: 135–69), as well as Messis and Nilsson (2015) and (2019) on *ekphraseis* by Manasses. The study by Taxidis (2021) is a useful presentation of the ekphrastic output of the twelfth century.

130 Eustathios, *Lent Oration* 1.776–902 (Schönauer [2006: 38–42] and Wirth [2000: 41.72–45.18]) describing emperor Manuel's siege of Dorylaion; Anna Komnene, *Alexiad* 4 (Reinsch and Kambylis [2001: 120–40], along with the German translation by Reinsch [1996: 142–63]) describing the battle at Dyrrachion; Prodromos, *Rhodanthe and Dosikles* 6.1–146 (Marcovich [1992: 91–6] and English translation by E. M. Jeffreys [2012: 96–101]) describing a fictional naval battle between the fleets of a barbarian king and a pirate leader.

poems;[131] finally, descriptions of love and sexuality in Eugeneianos, Basilakes, Manganeios Prodromos and Leo of Megistos.[132]

A Concluding Question

Up to this point, we have seen the broad variety, the complex literariness and the manifold generic and stylistic experimentations used by so many authors of the Komnenian era to compose their works within a dynamic social nexus of 'producers and consumers' of literature and art. By way, then, of conclusion, I would like to ask if we can detect in Byzantine literature evidence of change.[133] The long twelfth century, where we do see some kind of consistent literary system in operation, is a good vantage point from which to look at textual production between the tenth and the fifteenth centuries by raising our head from the depths of close reading and opening our eyes to the broad surfaces of textual correlations and literary entanglement.

Let us start with dialogues. The Komnenian dialogic texts I mentioned above, such as *Timarion* or Mesarites' debates with the Latins, when read next to *Philopatris* from the tenth century[134] and *The Journey of Mazaris to Hades* from the early fifteenth century,[135] tell us a few things about change in Byzantine literature. Firstly, the styles of these four texts stand at a substantial distance from each other. More importantly, their approach to

131 Anna Komnene, *Alexiad* 15.11 (Reinsch and Kambylis [2001: 493–505], along with the German translation by Reinsch [1996: 548–59]) describing the death of her father Emperor Alexios; Choniates, *Monody on Eustathios* §49–50bis (Lampros [1968: 1:302.27–304.12]) describing the death of his teacher; Goudeles, *Life of Leontios* §100 (Tsougarakis [1993: 152]) describing the death of the saint; Italikos, *Monody on his Deceased Partridge* (Gautier [1972: 102–4]); many funerary poems by Kallikles on various deceased aristocratic men, women and their children (e.g. nos. 9–13, 21–2, 30–1, edited with Italian translation by Romano [1980]); an anonymous poet from the *Anthologia Marciana* (ed. Lampros [1911: 186, no. 368]) presenting in a funerary poem the death of a young pregnant mother.

132 Eugeneianos, *Drosilla and Charikles* 5.325–5.46 (ed. Conca [1990: 116–23] with the English translation by E. M. Jeffreys [2012: 396–400]) describing a tender love scene between the protagonist couple; Basilakes, *Progymnasma* 54 = VII, 25 (ed. Pignani [1983: 221–4] with the English translation by Beneker and Gibson [2016: 306–13]) presenting as a monologue Pasiphae's falling in love with the bull from the sea; Manganeios Prodromos, *On Eros* (ed. Polemis [1994], with critical remarks by M. J. Jeffreys [1995]); Leo, *Kalliope* (ed. Lampsidis [1997]) describing how the Muse of epic poetry undresses and presents her naked beauty to an imaginary spectator.

133 Lauxtermann (2002) hesitantly accepts change but does not describe theoretically how it would manifest itself; Magdalino (2012), starting from Kazhdan and Epstein (1985), is supportive of the notion of change but with a rather conventional approach to literary analysis.

134 Edited by Anastasi (1968) and Macleod (1987: 367–89), revised Greek text and Italian translation by Romano (1999: 23–65); on the date of this work, see Angelidi (1977) and Baldwin (1982); for some literary thoughts on the text, see Marciniak (2021).

135 Edited with English translation by Westerink et al. (1975), revised Greek text and Italian translation by Romano (1999: 467–573); for a positivist approach to the text, see Garland (2007).

mimesis and the overall aesthetic effect achieved is radically different, while the socio-political aims and perspectives are equally divergent. Mesarites' text is not a Lucianic dialogue, yet it is composed in a manner whereby its supposed documentary character is subverted by the schedographic complexity of its rhetorical fabric. And although *Philopatris*, *Timarion* and *Mazaris* are 'Lucianic', only *Philopatris* could be described as 'classicizing', whereas in *Timarion* and *Mazaris* the approach to Lucian, the narrative and thematic organization, the highly visible connectedness to contemporary history, politics and society are not in the least antiquarian, while their respective 'antiquities' are individual, historically determined readings and creative manipulations of a textualized (qua imaginary) ancient world. In the *Timarion* the Hellenic appearance of the dialogue's staging is maintained with care – a device severely criticized as 'pagan' by Constantine Akropolites in the late thirteenth century.[136] However, in the *Mazaris* all pretence of a staged Hellenic antiquity has been dropped, while the dialogue is followed by further four texts also forming a complex dialogic-epistolographic conversation between contemporary living and deceased persons – an extraordinary form of validating documentation for a fictive narrative.

Let us take a further look at authorial voices. If we compare Eustathios, Neophytos and Prodromos to each other – a high-class professor and archbishop, a monk living as an ascetic recluse far away from the centre of the empire, a middle-class grammarian and poet with some high connections – we will immediately detect obvious differences, such as the type of texts they wrote, their approach to genre, their patrons, their perspective to contemporary history. However, we will also discover some important similarities. These concern the insistence with which the three authors present their 'methods' of writing, their 'emotionality' as to the act of writing and the broad gamut of their writing style, even if these styles differ and are employed for different reasons. While Eustathios and Neophytos made a conscious effort to collect their works into a kind of a multivolume *Gesamtausgabe*,[137] the works of Prodromos survive only in various collections, none of which can be related to the author as editor of his own works.[138]

136 See his *ep*. 90, edited by Romano (1991: 180–3) and translated into English by Baldwin (1984: 24–6).

137 On Eustathios' *opera omnia* edition, which was partly copied out on parchment codices (the already mentioned Laurentianus and Marcianus for which see above nn. 43–4, but also the lost El Escorial, Real Biblioteca, Λ-II-11 [Diktyon 14774]), see Wirth (1980: 65–9); see further the detailed analysis of the Scorialensis in Cesaretti and Ronchey (2014: 253*–72*). On Neophytos' edition, see his own remarks and list of books in the *Testamentary Rules* to his monastic foundation (*Typike Diatheke* §12.3–4 ed. Stephanis [1998: 41.4–42.4]).

138 See Hörandner (1974: 135–65) and Zagklas (2023: 88–122).

If we place these three authors next to John Geometres (*c.* 935/40–1000) and Theodore Metochites (1270–1332) – a teacher/soldier and poet of good social standing[139] and a high government official of almost aristocratic background – we will immediately recognize the difference in the self-representation of these two writers to each other and to the three twelfth-century authors. Both Geometres and Metochites present themselves as highly classicizing authors, the former standing in a direct and textually obvious dialogue with his chosen poetic models (Gregory of Nazianzos, George of Pisidia and the *Greek Anthology*), the latter discussing philosophical, scientific and literary matters related to antiquity or composing orations and poems about his own concerns and the vicissitudes of his life in a rather loose imitation of his ancient models (Plutarch, Dio Chrysostom, Synesios and Gregory). But while Geometres presents his authorial voice through the generic *topoi* of his models as 'poetic truth' (rather close to hymnographical practices, I would suggest), Metochites creates an apparently highly personal authorial voice of 'essayistic reality'. The two authors – especially when one compares their hexametric poems where Gregory is the main model – stand very far apart as to their use of 'epic' Greek and the mimesis of Gregory. Thus, the classicizing effect apparent in their works has a very different aesthetic impact on us as readers: fully worked out, metaphoric, emotional but restrained, static and solid in Geometres;[140] improvised, figurative, passionate and unrestrained, dynamic and fluid in Metochites.[141] It should be noted that the narrative system of Geometres and Metochites[142] differs substantially from the one employed by the three Komnenian authors, but it conforms to the narrative system of art during their time. One needs only to compare the static *Deesis* depictions of the late tenth or early eleventh century with Geometres' grand supplicatory poem (no. 290, titled δέησις)[143] or the kinetic narrative cycle in the double narthex of Metochites' Chora Church (AD 1321) with his two long laudatory poems to God and the Virgin Mary about his life and the refounding

139 For a revision of the current biography of Geometres, see Papaioannou (2019a).
140 For some remarks on the place of Geometres' poetry in the late tenth century, see Lauxtermann (2003); for a broader appreciation of his poetic achievement, see van Opstall (2008: 21–66) and Tomadaki (2023).
141 For some brief remarks on Metochites' 'neo-excessive' writing, see Agapitos (2021).
142 Geometres' poems have not been studied from a narrative point of view; for some first remarks on Metochites, see Polemis (2015: xxix–xlv) and (2017c).
143 Edited with French translation and commentary by van Opstall (2008: 467–505), who points to the similarities of the poem to ivory triptychs of the period; see van Opstall (2008: 42 and plate 3).

of the Chora Monastery (nos. 1 and 2)[144] to grasp the immense distance between the two poets and the different position of the Komnenian authors in this textual landscape. Furthermore, while Geometres' works are preserved in two completely miscellaneous manuscripts,[145] Metochites' works are preserved in a luxury edition of parchment codices prepared by himself and his pupil Nikephoros Gregoras and written by two of the best scribes at the imperial chancellery.[146] Therefore, in the case of authorial voice we can also detect important changes between the tenth and the fourteenth/fifteenth centuries and this even concerns the materiality of the manuscripts that preserve the works of the five authors.[147]

As a last example of potential change, I would like to present a type of text that I shall label 'clerical invective'.[148] Since the middle of the eleventh century we find texts wherein an author directs his criticism against a member of the clergy. Three such poetic invectives from the middle of the eleventh century are Michael Grammatikos' *About the Bishop of Philomelion*,[149] Christopher of Mytilene's *To the Monk Andrew*[150] and Psellos' *Against the Sabbaitan Monk*.[151] The first poem is openly satirical, the second discreetly ironic, the third one excessively abusive. The three texts are composed in iambic verse that was, of course, the time-honoured metre for

144 Edited by Polemis (2015: 5–51 and 52–73); English translation by Polemis (2017b: 47–92 and 93–111). On the Chora cycle, its spatial organization and its relation to Metochites' works, see now Zarras (2021).

145 Paris, Bibliothèque nationale de France, Suppl. gr. 352 [Diktyon 53102] and Vatican City, Biblioteca Apostolica Vaticana, gr. 743 [Diktyon 67374]; see now van Opstall (2008: 99–114).

146 For the manuscripts of this *Gesamtausgabe*, see Agapitos, Hult and Smith (1996: 9–10) and Förstel (2011); for one of these scribes, see Lamberz (2000).

147 For further thoughts on the material aspect of the authorial voice and the gradual development of multi-volume authorial corpora, see Agapitos (2021: 28–9). Particularly interesting for this development is John Mauropous (*c.* 1000–85), who created an authorial persona in the paratexts of a collection of some of his works, edited by his secretary (Vatican City, Biblioteca Apostolica Vaticana, gr. 676 [Diktyon 67307]), and who clearly separated his 'rhetorical' works from his hymnographic production; see Agapitos (2015a: 81–4) and (2020: 29–31).

148 On verse invective in Byzantium, see Bernard (2021); on the ninth–tenth centuries, see Lauxtermann (2019: 119–44); on the eleventh century, see Bernard (2014: 266–99); on the twelfth century, see Zagklas (2021b) and Magdalino (2021).

149 *Poem* 4, edited by Mercati (1970: 128–31), translated by Lauritzen (2009) and commented upon by Magdalino (2012: 26–7); see also the analysis by Lauxtermann (2019: 137–44).

150 *Poem* 114, edited by De Groote (2012: 107–13); English translation with facing Greek text by Bernard and Livanos (2018: 240–51).

151 *Poem* 21, edited by Westerink (1992: 258–69); on the context of the poem, see Bernard (2014: 280–90). Sabbaites is not the monk's name (as can be read in recent publications), but his characterization as a person who was tonsured at the Monastery of Saint Sabbas in Jerusalem, similar to other such appellations, for example, Chrysostomites (from the Monastery of Saint John Chrysostom in Cyprus) or Hagiotessarakontites (from the Monastery of the Holy Forty Martyrs in Constantinople). Sabbaites makes a further appearance as a blasphemous and abusive monk in a letter of Psellos, ed. Papaioannou (2019b: 781–2, no. 374); see Bernard (2014: 281).

skomma and *komodia*, that is, poetry of humorous mockery and vitriolic invective.[152] In the later twelfth century we find another form of this invective. Eustathios wrote his *Monologue of the Monk Neophytos of Mokissos*,[153] while Mesarites produced a *Monologue of an Astrologer Bishop*.[154] In contrast to the iambic abuses, these two texts pick up the progymnasmatic practice of *ethopoiia*, a quasi-dramatic monologue that was systematically taught in schools and that helped students to learn how to present the thoughts and emotions of a fictive or a historical character.[155] Shortly after the fall of Constantinople in 1204, we find yet another invective, this time composed again in iambic verse; it is the recently published *Verses against a Foolish Bishop of Seleukeia* by Euthymios Tornikes.[156] In my opinion, there are visible intertextual connections between these texts. More specifically, Tornikes' invective looks back to Michael Grammatikos and Psellos, while also utilizing the satirical-abusive vocabulary of Tzetzes and his attacks against ignorant 'buffalo clerics'.[157] Under the category 'clerical invective' we find two different subgenres of satire – one poetical, one rhetorical – interacting with each other over a period of a good 150 years, where it is obvious that the authors use both the ancient tradition and the available Byzantine practice to enrich and change the substance of their satirical texts.

As this brief overview has shown, the long twelfth century offers us a broad variety of literary works where many and different forms of experimental redefinitions take place, be it in matters of language and style, generic transgression and hybridity, the exploration of narrative possibilities and the self-representation of authorial voices. It is an era dominated by education and teacher-authors as well as by aristocratic patrons, by a profound belief in the 'force of discourses and metre' and the private networks of relations, but also a growing disbelief in the efficacy of the state

152 See Agosti (2001) for the 'iambic concept' in late antique poetry, where Byzantine authors such as Gregory of Nazianzos played an important role.

153 Edited by Tafel (1964: 328–32).

154 Edited with French translation by Flusin (2002); English translation by Angold (2017: 297–305). On the intellectual context of this *ethopoiia* in the late twelfth century, see Magdalino (2015) in a discussion with two other anti-astrological satires – the dialogue *Anacharsis* (probably by Niketas Eugeneianos) and an anonymous poem in elegiac couplets; for the latter, see Zagklas (2016).

155 Important specimens of such *ethopoiiai* can be found among Basilakes' collection of *progymnasmata*, but also in the novels of Prodromos and Eugeneianos. On *ethopoiia* more broadly, see Hagen (1966) and the various contributions in Amato and Schamp (2005).

156 *Poem* 4, edited with German translation by Hörandner (2017a: 104–27); re-edited with a Modern Greek translation by Polemis (2020: 178–201).

157 Compare Tornikes' *Poem* 4.8 ὁ βούπαπας δὲ βουφάγος Σελευκείας ('But the buffalo-devouring buffalo-cleric of Seleukeia') with βουβαλόπαπας in Tzetzes' *Histories* 9.298.958 and 299.960 ed. Leone (2007); see also the comments in Agapitos (2017: 11, 24–7 and 32–4).

and the cohesion of society.[158] If literature has something to contribute in understanding this complex era, then Komnenian textual production has to be examined from a new and encompassing point of view. To paraphrase Euthymios Tornikes: 'By having thus acquired the force of discourses, we will have enriched ourselves with the great wealth of wisdom.'[159] This wisdom will indeed provide us with important insights into the workings of Byzantine culture and its literary history.

Bibliography

Aerts, W. J. (2003) 'A Byzantine Traveller to One of the Crusader States', in *East and West in the Crusader States: Contexts – Contacts – Confrontations III*, ed. K. Cigaar and H. Teule, 165–221. Leuven.

Afentoulidou-Leitgeb, E. (2007) 'Die *Dioptra* des Philippos Monotropos und ihr Kontext: Ein Beitrag zur Rezeptionsgeschichte', *Byzantion* 77: 9–31.

(2012) 'The *Dioptra* of Philippos Monotropos: Didactic Verses or Poetry?', in Bernard and Demoen, 181–91.

Agapitos, P. A. (1991) *Narrative Structure in the Byzantine Vernacular Romances: A Textual and Literary Study of Kallimachos, Belthandros and Libistros*. Miscellanea Byzantina Monacensia 34. Munich.

(1998a) 'Mischung der Gattungen und Überschreitung der Gesetze: Die Grabrede des Eustathios von Thessalonike auf Nikolaos Hagiotheodorites', *JÖByz* 48: 119–46.

(1998b) 'Narrative, Rhetoric and "Drama" Rediscovered: Scholars and Poets in Byzantium Interpret Heliodorus', in *Studies in Heliodorus*, ed. R. Hunter, 125–56. Cambridge Philological Society: Supplementary Volume 21. Cambridge.

(1998c) 'Teachers, Pupils and Imperial Power in Eleventh-Century Byzantium', in *Pedagogy and Power: Rhetorics of Classical Learning*, ed. N. Livingstone and Y. L. Too, 170–91. Ideas in Context 50. Cambridge.

(2000) 'Poets and Painters: Theodoros Prodromos' Dedicatory Verses of his Novel to an Anonymous Caesar', *JÖByz* 50: 173–85.

(2003) 'Ancient Models and Novel Mixtures: The Concept of Genre in Byzantine Funerary Literature from Patriarch Photios to Eustathios of Thessalonike', in *Modern Greek Literature: Critical Essays*, ed. G. Nagy and A. Stavrakopoulou, 5–23. New York.

(2004) 'Mortuary Typology in the Lives of Saints: Michael the Synkellos and Stephen the Younger', in Odorico and Agapitos (2004) 103–35.

(ed.) (2006) *Εἰκὼν καὶ Λόγος: Ἕξι βυζαντινὲς περιγραφὲς ἔργων τέχνης. Εἰσαγωγικὸ δοκίμιο, ἀνθολόγηση, μετάφραση καὶ σχολιασμός*. Athens.

158 On this issue, see, for example, the collective volume edited by Simpson (2015).

159 From the funeral oration on his brother Demetrios (ed. Darrouzès [1968: 97.17–18]): οὕτω γοῦν τὸ κράτος τῶν λόγων ἀναδησάμενος, τὸν μέγαν ὄλβον τῆς σοφίας πεπλούτηκεν.

(2012) 'In Rhomaian, Frankish and Persian Lands: Fiction and Fictionality in Byzantium and Beyond', in *Medieval Narratives between History and Fiction: From the Center to the Periphery of Europe (c. 1100–1400)*, ed. P. A. Agapitos and L. B. Mortensen, 235–367. Copenhagen.

(2013) 'Anna Komnene and the Politics of Schedographic Training and Colloquial Discourse', *Nea Rhome* 10: 89–107.

(2014) 'Grammar, Genre and Patronage in the Twelfth Century: Redefining a Scientific Paradigm in the History of Byzantine Literature', *JÖByz* 64: 1–22.

(2015a) 'Contesting Conceptual Boundaries: Byzantine Literature and its History', *Interfaces: A Journal of Medieval European Literatures* 1: 62–91. https://riviste.unimi.it/interfaces/ issue/view/1.

(2015b) 'Karl Krumbacher and the History of Byzantine Literature', *ByzZ* 108.1: 1–52.

(2015c) 'Literary *haute cuisine* and its Dangers: Eustathios of Thessalonike on Schedography and Everyday Language', *DOP* 69: 225–41.

(2015d) 'New Genres in the Twelfth Century: The *schedourgia* of Theodore Prodromos', *MEG* 15: 1–41.

(2017) 'John Tzetzes and the Blemish Examiners: A Byzantine Teacher on Schedography, Everyday Language and Writerly Disposition', *MEG* 17: 1–57.

(2020) 'The Insignificance of 1204 and 1453 for the History of Byzantine Literature', *MEG* 20: 1–56.

(2021) 'Literature and Education in Nicaea and Their legacy: An Interpretive Synthesis', *MEG* 21: 1–37.

(2022a) '"Middle-class" Ideology of Education and Language, and the "Bookish" Identity of John Tzetzes', in *Identities and Ideologies in the Medieval East Roman World*, ed. Y. Stouraitis, 146–63. Edinburgh Byzantine Studies 3. Edinburgh.

(2022b) 'The Politics and Practices of Commentary in Komnenian Byzantium', in Van den Berg, Manolova and Marciniak, 41–60.

(2023a) 'The Periodization of Byzantine Literature: From a Historical to a Literary Model', in *Anekdota Byzantina: Studien zur byzantinischen Geschichte und Kultur. Festschrift für Albrecht Berger anlässlich seines 65. Geburtstags*, ed. I. Grimm-Stadelmann, A. Riehle, R. Tocci and M. M. Vuĉetić, 1–20. Byzantinisches Archiv 46. Berlin.

(2023b) '"These Devices Are the Writer's Own Technique": Eustathios of Thessalonike and the Redefinition of Rhetorical Genres', in *Virtute vir tutus: Studi di letteratura greca, bizantina e umanistica offerti a Enrico V. Maltese*, ed. L. Silvano, A. M. Taragna and P. Veralda, 63–97. Ghent.

Agapitos, P. A., and M. Hinterberger (2006) 'Κωνσταντίνου Μανασσῆ Ἔκφρασις γῆς', in Agapitos (2006), 41–73 and 175–7.

Agapitos, P. A., K. Hult and O. L. Smith (eds.) (1996) *Theodoros Metochites on Philosophic Irony and Greek History: Miscellanea 8 and 93*. Nicosia.

Agapitos, P. A., and D. R. Reinsch (eds.) (2000) *Der Roman im Byzanz der Komnenenzeit*. Frankfurt am Main.

Agosti, G. (2001) 'Late Antique Iambics and *Iambikè Idéa*', in *Iambic Ideas: Essays on a Poetic Tradition from Archaic Greece to the Late Roman Empire*, ed. A. Cavarzere, A. Aloni and A. Barchiesi, 219–55. Lanham.

Alexiou, M. (1977) 'A Critical Reappraisal of Eustathios Makrembolites', *Hysmine and Hysminias*', *BMGS* 3.1: 23–43.

(1982–3) 'Literary Subversion and the Aristocracy in Twelfth-Century Byzantium: A Stylistic Analysis of the *Timarion* (ch. 6–10)', *BMGS* 8.1: 29–45.

Amato, E., and J. Schamp (eds.) (2005) *ΗΘΟΠΟΙΙΑ: La représentation de caractères entre fiction scolaire et réalité vivante à l'époque impériale et tardive*. Salerno.

Anastasi, R. (ed.) (1968) *Incerti auctoris Φιλόπατρις ἢ διδασκόμενος*. Messina.

Angelidi, C. G. (1977) 'Η χρονολόγηση και ο συγγραφέας του διαλόγου Φιλόπατρις', *Ἑλληνικά* 30: 34–50.

Angold, M. (2017) *Nicholas Mesarites: His Life and Works. Translated with Notes and Commentary*. Translated Texts for Byzantinists 4. Liverpool.

Baldwin, B. (1982) 'The Date and Purpose of the Philopatris', in *Later Greek Literature*, ed. J. J. Winkler and G. Williams, 321–43. Yale Classical Studies 27. Cambridge.

(1984) *Timarion: Translated with an Introduction and Commentary*. Detroit.

Barber, C., and S. Papaioannou (eds.) (2017) *Michael Psellos on Literature and Art: A Byzantine Perspective on Aesthetics*. Michael Psellos in Translation. Notre Dame.

Barchiesi, A. (2001) 'The Crossing', in *Texts, Ideas, and the Classics: Scholarship, Theory and Classical Literature*, ed. S. J. Harrison, 142–63. Oxford.

Beck, H.-G. (1959) *Kirche und theologische Literatur im byzantinischen Reich*. Handbuch der Altertumswissenschaft XII.2.1. Munich.

(1971) *Geschichte der byzantinischen Volksliteratur*. Handbuch der Altertumswissenschaft XII.2.3. Munich.

(1974) *Das literarische Schaffen der Byzantiner: Wege zu seinem Verständnis*. Sitzungsberichte der Österreichischen Akademie der Wissenschaften. Philosophisch-historische Klasse 294/4. Vienna.

(1978) *Das byzantinische Jahrtausend*. Munich.

Beneker, J., and C. A. Gibson (ed. and trans.) (2016) *The Rhetorical Exercises of Nikephoros Basilakes: Progymnasmata from Twelfth-Century Byzantium*. Dumbarton Oaks Medieval Library 43. Cambridge, MA.

Bernard, F. (2014) *Writing and Reading Byzantine Secular Poetry, 1025–1081*. Oxford.

(2017) 'Educational Networks in the Letters of Michael Psellos', in *The Letters of Michael Psellos: Cultural Networks and Historical Realities*, ed. M. J. Jeffreys and M. D. Lauxtermann, 13–41. Oxford.

(2021) 'Laughter, Derision, and Abuse in Byzantine Verse', in Marciniak and Nilsson, 39–61.

Bernard, F., and K. Demoen (eds.) (2012) *Poetry and its Contexts in Eleventh-Century Byzantium*. Farnham.

Bernard, F., and C. Livanos (2018) *The Poems of Christopher of Mytilene and John Mauropous*. Dumbarton Oaks Medieval Library 50. Cambridge, MA.

Bernardi, J. (ed.) (1983) *Grégoire de Nazianze: Discours 4–5 contre Julien. Introduction, texte critique, traduction et notes*. Sources Chrétiennes 309. Paris.
Borsa, P., C. Høgel, L. B. Mortensen and E. Tyler (2015) 'What Is Medieval European Literature', *Interfaces: A Journal of Medieval European Literatures* 1: 7–24. https://riviste.unimi.it/interfaces/ issue/view/1.
Bourbouhakis, E. C. (2014) 'The End of ἐπίδειξις: Authorial Identity and Authorial Intention in Michael Choniates' Πρὸς τοὺς αἰτιωμένους τὸ ἀφιλένδεικτον', in Pizzone (2014b), 201–24.
(2017a) 'Byzantine Literary Criticism and the Classical Heritage', in Kaldellis and Siniossoglou, 113–28.
(2017b) *Not Composed in a Chance Manner: The Epitaphios for Manuel I Komnenos by Eustathios of Thessalonike*. Studia Byzantina Upsaliensia 18. Uppsala.
Browning, R. (1958) 'An Anonymous βασιλικὸς λόγος addressed to Alexios I Comnenus', *Byzantion* 28: 31–50.
(1977) 'The Patriarchal School at Constantinople in the Twelfth Century', in *Studies on Byzantine History, Literature and Education*, 167–201 and 11–40 (no. x). London (originally published in 1962 and 1963).
(1989) 'An Unpublished Address of Nicephorus Chrysoberges to Patriach John X Kamateros', in *History, Language and Literature in the Byzantine World*, 37–68. London (originally published in 1978).
Bucossi, A. (ed.) (2014) *Andronici Camateri Sacrum Armamentarium: Pars Prima*. Corpus Christianorum: Series Graeca 75. Turnhout.
Cameron, A. (2016) *Arguing it Out: Discussion in Twelfth-Century Byzantium*. The Natalie Zemon Davis Lecture Series 9. Budapest and New York.
Cesaretti, P., and S. Ronchey (eds.) (2014) *Eustathii Thessalonicensis exegesis in canonem iambicum pentecostalem*. Supplementa Byzantina 10. Berlin.
Chryssogelos, K. (2017) *Κωνσταντίνου Μανασσῆ Οδοιπορικόν: Κριτική έκδοση, μετάφραση, σχόλια*. Athens.
Conca, F. (ed.) (1990) *Nicetas Eugenianus: De Drosillae et Chariclis amoribus*. Amsterdam.
(ed.) (1994) *Il romanzo bizantino del XII secolo: Teodoro Prodromo, Niceta Eugeniano, Eustazio Macrembolita, Constantino Manasse*. Turin.
(2018) 'L'esegesi di Tzetzes ai *Carmina Iliaca* fra tradizione e innovazione', *Koinonia* 42: 75–99.
Constantinou, S. (2004) 'Subgenre and Gender in Saints' Lives', in Odorico and Agapitos (2004), 411–23.
Cullhed, E. (2014) 'The Blind Bard and "I": Homeric Biography and Authorial Personas in the Twelfth Century', *BMGS* 38.1: 49–67.
(ed.) (2016) *Eustathios of Thessalonike: Commentary on Homer's Odyssey*, vol. 1: *On Rhapsodies A–B*. Studia Byzantina Upsaliensia 16. Uppsala.
(2017) 'Theodore Prodromos in the Garden of Epicurus: The *Amarantos*', in *Dialogues and Debates from Late Antiquity to Late Byzantium*, ed. A. Cameron and N. Gaul, 153–66. London.

Cupane, C. (2016) 'Sprache–Literatur', in *Byzanz: Historisch-Kulturwissenschaftliches Handbuch*, ed. F. Daim, 925–71. Der Neue Pauly: Supplemente 11. Stuttgart.
Cupane, C., and B. Krönung (eds.) (2016) *Fictional Storytelling in the Medieval Eastern Mediterranean and Beyond*. Brill's Companions to the Byzantine World 1. Leiden–Boston.
D'Ambrosi, M. (ed.) (2008) *Teodoro Prodromo: I tetrastici iambici ed esametrici sugli episodi principali di Gregorio Nazianzeno. Introduzione, edizione critica, traduzione e commento*. Testi e Studi Bizantino-Neoellenici 17. Rome.
Darrouzès, J. (1960) 'Notes de littérature et de critique', *REByz* 18: 179–94.
(ed.) (1968) 'Les discours d'Euthyme Tornikès (1200–1205)', *REByz* 26: 49–121.
(ed.) (1970) *Georges et Dèmètrios Tornikès: Lettres et discours. Introduction, texte, analyses, traduction et notes*. Paris.
De Groote, M. (ed.) (2012) *Christophori Mitylenaii Versuum variorum collectio Cryptensis*. Corpus Christianorum: Series Graeca 74. Turnhout.
Dennis, G. T. (ed.) (1994) *Michaelis Pselli Orationes panegyricae*. Stuttgart.
Diethart, J., and W. Hörandner (eds.) (2005) *Constantinus Stilbes: Poemata*. Munich.
Efthymiadis, S., C. Messis, P. Odorico and I. Polemis (eds.) (2015) *Pour une poètique de Byzance: Hommage à Vassilis Katsaros*. Dossiers byzantins 16. Paris.
Eideneier, H. (ed.) (1991) *Ptochoprodromos: Einführung, kritische Ausgabe, deutsche Übersetzung, Glossar*. Neograeca Medii Aevi 5. Cologne.
(ed.) (2012) *Πτωχοπρόδρομος: Κριτική ἔκδοση*. Heraklion.
Farrel, J. (2003) 'Classical Genre in Theory and Practice', *New Literary History* 34: 383–408.
Flusin, B. (2002) 'Nicholas Mésaritès: Éthopoée d'un astrologue qui ne put devenir patriarche', *T&MByz* 14: 234–41.
Förstel, C. (2011) 'Metochites and his Books between the Chora and the Renaissance', in *The Kariye Camii Reconsidered*, ed. H. A. Klein, R. Ousterhout and B. Pitarakis, 241–66. Istanbul.
Foskolou, V. (2018) 'Decoding Byzantine *Ekphraseis* on Works of Art: Constantine Manasses's *Description of Earth* and its Audience', *ByzZ* 111.1: 71–102 and pls. I–VIII.
Fuchs, F. (1926) *Die höheren Schulen von Konstantinopel im Mittelalter*. Byzantinisches Archiv 8. Leipzig.
Galavotti, C. (1935) 'Novi Laurentiani codicis analecta', *Studi Bizantini e Neoellenici* 4: 203–36.
Garland, L. (2007) 'Mazaris's Journey to Hades: Further Reflections and Reappraisal', *DOP* 61: 183–214.
Garzya, A. (1984) *Nicephori Basilacae orationes et epistolae*. Leipzig.
Gaul, N. (2014) 'Rising Elites and Institutionalization – Ethos/Mores – "Debts" and Drafts: Three Concluding Steps towards Comparing Networks of Learning in Byzantium and the "Latin" West, c. 1000–1200', in Steckel, Gaul and Grünbart, 235–80.

Gaunt, S., and S. Kay (eds.) (2008) *The Cambridge Companion to Medieval French Literature*. Cambridge.
Gautier, P. (1972) *Michel Italikos: Lettres et discours*. Archives de l'Orient Chrétien 14. Paris.
Gayk, S., and I. Nelson (eds.) (2015) 'New Approaches to Medieval Genre', *Exemplaria* 27, issues 1–2.
Giannouli, A. (2007) *Die beiden byzantinischen Kommentare zum Großen Kanon des Andreas von Kreta: Eine quellenkritische und literarhistorische Studie*. Wiener Byzantinistische Studien 26. Vienna.
Giannouli, A. (2014) 'Education and Literary Language in Byzantium', in *The Language of Byzantine Learned Literature*, ed. M. Hinterberger, 52–71. Byzantios: Studies in Byzantine History and Civilization 9. Turnhout.
Goldwyn, A. J. (2017) 'Theory and Method in John Tzetzes' *Allegories of the Iliad* and *Allegories of the Odyssey*', *Scandinavian Journal for Byzantine and Modern Greek Studies* 3: 141–71.
Goldwyn, A. J., and D. Kokkini (2015) *John Tzetzes: Allegories of the Iliad*. Dumbarton Oaks Medieval Library 37. Cambridge, MA.
(2019) *John Tzetzes: Allegories of the Odyssey*. Dumbarton Oaks Medieval Library 56. Cambridge, MA.
Grigoriadis, I. (2001) *Ἰωάννης Τζέτζης: Ἐπιστολαί. Εἰσαγωγή, μετάφραση, σχόλια*. Κείμενα Βυζαντινῆς Λογοτεχνίας 3. Athens.
Grünbart, M. (2004) 'L'epistolografia', in *Lo spazio letterario del Medioevo. 3: Le culture circostanti*. Volume 1: *La cultura bizantina*, ed. G. Cavallo, 345–78. Rome.
(2016) 'Exploring the Hinterland: The Letter Collection of Hierotheos the Monk (Twelfth Century)', in *Studi Bizantini in onore di Maria Dora Spadaro*, ed. T. Creazzo, C. Crimi and G. Strano, 235–43. Orpheus 2. Rome.
Hagen, H.-M. (1966) *Ἠθοποιία: Zur Geschichte eines rhetorischen Begriffs*. Erlangen.
Heisenberg, A. (1973) 'Neue Quellen zur Geschichte des lateinischen Kaisertums und der Kirchenunion. I: Der Epitaphios des Nikolaos Mesarites auf seinen Bruder Johannes', in *Quellen und Studien zur spätbyzantinischen Geschichte*, ed. H.-G. Beck, 3–75 (no. 11.1). London (originally published in 1922).
Hinterberger, M. (2005) 'Ο Ανδρέας Λιβαδηνός, συγγραφέας/γραφέας λογίων κειμένων, αναγνώστης/γραφέας δημωδών κειμένων: ο ελληνικός κώδικας 525 του Μονάχου', in *Κωδικογράφοι, συλλέκτες, διασκευαστές και εκδότες: Χειρόγραφα και εκδόσεις της όψιμης βυζαντινής και πρώιμης νεοελληνικής λογοτεχνίας*, ed. D. Holton et al., 25–42. Heraklion.
Hörandner, W. (ed.) (1974) *Theodoros Prodromos: Historische Gedichte*. Wiener Byzantinistische Studien 11. Vienna.
(ed.) (2017a) 'Dichtungen des Euthymios Tornikes in Cod. Gr. 508 der Rumänischen Akademie', in Hörandner (2017c), 91–140.
(2017b) 'Es war die Nachtigall: Zum Sprecherinnenwechsel in einer byzantinischen Totenklage', in Hörandner (2017c), 185–92 (originally published in 2001).

(2017c) *Facettes de la littérature byzantine: Contributions choisies*, ed. P. Odorico, A. Rhoby and E. Schiffer. Dossiers byzantins 17. Paris.

Hörandner, W., A. Rhoby and N. Zagklas (eds.) (2019) *A Companion to Byzantine Poetry*. Brill's Companions to the Byzantine World 4. Leiden.

Horna, K. (1904) 'Das Hodoiporikon des Konstantin Manasses', *ByzZ* 13.2: 313–55.

Horrocks, G. (2010) *Greek: A History of the Language and its Speakers*, second edition. Chichester.

Hunger, H. (1973) 'Die byzantinische Literatur der Komnenenzeit: Versuch einer Neubewertung', in *Byzantinische Grundlagenforschung: Gesammelte Aufsätze*, 59–76 (no. XVI). London (originally published in 1968).

(1978) *Die hochsprachliche profane Literatur der Byzantiner*, 2 vols. Handbuch der Altertumswissenschaft XII.5.1–2. Munich.

Jauß, H. R. (1977) 'Theorie der Gattungen und Literatur des Mittelalters', in *Alterität und Modernität der mittelalterlichen Literatur: Gesammelte Aufsätze 1956–1976*, 327–58. Munich (originally published in 1972).

Jeffreys, E. M. (ed.) (1998) *Digenis Akritis: The Grottaferrata and Escorial Versions*. Cambridge Medieval Classics 7. Cambridge.

(ed.) (2003) *Rhetoric in Byzantium: Papers from the Thirty-Fifth Spring Symposium of Byzantine Studies, University of Oxford, March 2001*. Society for the Promotion of Byzantine Studies Publications 11. Aldershot.

(2009) 'Why Produce Verse in Twelfth-Century Constantinople?', in *'Doux remède ...': Poésie et poétique à Byzance. Actes du IVe Colloque International Philologique 'EPMHNEIA', Paris, 23–24–25 février 2006, organisé par l'E.H.E.S.S. et l'Université de Chypre*, ed. P. Odorico, P. A. Agapitos and M. Hinterberger, 219–28. Dossiers byzantins 9. Paris.

(2011–12) 'The *Sebastokratorissa* Irene as Patron', in *Female Founders in Byzantium and Beyond*, ed. L. Theis, M. Mullett and M. Grünbart, with G. Fingarova and M. Savage, 177–94. Wiener Jahrbuch für Kunstgeschichte 60–1. Vienna.

(2012) *Four Byzantine Novels: Theodore Prodromos, Rhodanthe and Dosikles; Eumathios Makrembolites, Hysmine and Hysminias; Constantine Manasses, Aristandros and Kallithea; Niketas Eugenianos, Drosilla and Charikles. Translated with Introductions and Notes*. Translated Texts for Byzantinists 1. Liverpool.

Jeffreys, E. M., and M. J. Jeffreys (2021) 'Manganeios Prodromos', in Kubina and Riehle, 160–83 and 314–24.

Jeffreys, M. J. (1995) 'Manganeios Prodromos Poem 45 and the Hazards of Editing Texts', *Ἑλληνικά* 45: 357–9.

Kalavrezou, I. (2003) 'Intaglio Ring with Koimesis of the Virgin', in *Byzantine Women and Their World*, ed. I. Kalavrezou, 299 (no. 182). Cambridge, MA.

Kaldellis, A. (2007) *Hellenism in Byzantium: The Transformation of Greek Identity and the Reception of the Classical Tradition*. Cambridge.

(2009) 'Classical Scholarship in Twelfth-Century Byzantium', in *Medieval Greek Commentaries on the Nicomachean Ethics*, ed. C. Barber and D. Jenkins, 1–43. Studien und Texte zur Geistesgeschichte des Mittelalters 101. Leiden.

(2012) 'The *Timarion*: Toward a Literary Interpretation', in (2012) *La face cachée de la littérature byzantine: Le texte en tant que message immédiat. Actes du colloque international (Paris, juin 2008)*, ed. P. Odorico, 275–87. Dossiers byzantins 11. Paris.

(2014) 'The Emergence of Literary Fiction in Byzantium and the Paradox of Plausibility', in *Medieval Greek Storytelling: Fictionality and Narrative in Byzantium*, ed. P. Roilos, 115–29. Mainzer Veröffentlichungen zur Byzantinistik 12. Wiesbaden.

Kaldellis, A., and N. Siniossoglou (eds.) (2017) *The Cambridge Intellectual History of Byzantium*. Cambridge.

Katsaros, V. (1988) *Ἰωάννης Κασταμονίτης: Συμβολή στή μελέτη τοῦ βίου, τοῦ ἔργου καὶ τῆς ἐποχῆς του*. Βυζαντινὰ Κείμενα καὶ Μελέται 22. Thessalonike.

Kazhdan, A. P., and S. Franklin (1984) *Studies on Byzantine Literature of the Eleventh and Twelfth Centuries*. Cambridge.

Kazhdan, A. P., and A. Wharton Epstein (1985) *Change in Byzantine Culture in the Eleventh and Twelfth Centuries*. Berkeley.

Kolovou, F. (1999) *Μιχαήλ Χωνιάτης: Συμβολή στή μελέτη τοῦ βίου καὶ τοῦ ἔργου του. Τὸ corpus τῶν ἐπιστολῶν*. Ponemata 2. Athens.

(2006) *Die Briefe des Eustathios von Thessalonike: Einleitung, Regesten, Text, Indizes*. Beiträge zur Altertumswissenschaft 239. Munich.

Kolovou, G. E. (2018) 'Homère chez Eustathe de Thessalonique: la traduction des *Proèmes* sur l'*Iliade* et l'*Odyssée*', *CCO* 15: 71–118.

Krallis, D. (2013) 'Harmless Satire, Stinging Critique: Notes and Suggestions for Reading the Timarion', in *Power and Subversion in Byzantium: Papers from the 43rd Spring Symposium of Byzantine Studies (Birmingham, March 2010)*, ed. D. Angelov and M. Saxby, 221–45. Society for the Promotion of Byzantine Studies Publications 17. Farnham.

Kroll, W. (1924) 'Die Kreuzung der Gattungen', in *Studien zum Verständnis der römischen Literatur*, 202–24. Stuttgart.

Krumbacher, K. (1897) *Geschichte der byzantinischen Litteratur von Justinian bis zum Ende des Oströmischen Reiches (527–1453)*. Zweite Auflage, bearbeitet unter Mitwirkung von A. Erhard und H. Gelzer. Handbuch der Klassischen Altertumswissenschaft IX.1. Munich (reprinted New York 1970).

Kubina, K., and A. Riehle (eds.) (2021) *Epistolary Poetry in Byzantium and Beyond: An Anthology with Critical Essays*. New York.

Kulhánková, M. (2015) *Das gottgefällige Abenteuer: Eine narratologische Analyse der byzantinischen erbaulichen Erzählungen*. Pro Oriente 31. Červený Kostelec.

(2017) 'Scenic Narration in the *Daniel Sketiotes Dossier* of Spiritually Beneficial Tales', *Scandinavian Journal for Byzantine and Modern Greek Studies* 3: 61–79.

(2021) '"For Old Men Too Play, Albeit More Wisely So": The Game of Discourses in the *Ptochoprodromika*', in Marciniak and Nilsson, 304–23.

Lamberz, E. (2000) 'Das Geschenk des Kaisers Manuel II an das Kloster Saint-Denis und der "Metochitesschreiber" Michael Klostomalles', in *Λιθόστρωτον: Studien zur byzantinischen Kunst und Geschichte. Festschrift für Marcel Restle*, ed. B. Borkopp and T. Steppan, 155–65. Stuttgart.

Lampros, S. P. (ed.) (1911) ‘Ὁ Μαρκιανὸς κῶδιξ 524’, *Νέος Ἑλληνομνήμων* 8: 3–59 and 113–92.

(ed.) (1968) *Μιχαὴλ Ἀκομινάτου τοῦ Χωνιάτου τὰ Σωζόμενα*, 2 vols. Groningen (reprint of the original edition, Athens 1879–80).

(1991) ‘Der vollständige Text der Ἔκφρασις γῆς des Konstantinos Manasses’, *JÖByz* 41: 189–205.

(ed.) (1996) *Constantini Manassis Breviarium Chronicum*. Corpus Fontium Historiae Byzantinae 36. Athens.

(1997) ‘Die Entblößung der Muse Kalliope in einem byzantinischen Epigramm’, *JÖByz* 47: 107–10.

(1999) ‘Die Monodie von Leon Megistos auf Georgios Palaiologos Megas Hetaireiarches’, *JÖByz* 49: 113–42.

(2003) *Κωνσταντίνου Μανασσῆ Σύνοψις Χρονική*. Κείμενα Βυζαντινής Ιστοριογραφίας 11. Athens.

Lauritzen, F. (2009) ‘Michael the Grammarian’s Irony about Hypsilon’, *ByzSlav* 66: 161–8.

(2013) *The Depiction of Character in Psellos’ Chronographia*. Byzantios: Studies in Byzantine History and Civilization 8. Turnhout.

Lauxtermann, M. D. (2002) ‘Byzantine Poetry in Context’, in Odorico and Agapitos (2002), 139–51.

(2003) ‘Byzantine Poetry and the Paradox of Basil II’s Reign’, in *Byzantium in the Year 1000*, ed. P. Magdalino, 199–216. The Medieval Mediterranean 45. Leiden.

(2014) ‘Tomi, Mljet, Malta: Critical Notes on a Twelfth-Century Southern Italian Poem of Exile’, *JÖByz* 64: 155–76.

(2019) *Byzantine Poetry from Pisides to Geometres: Texts and Contexts*. Wiener Byzantinistische Studien 24/2. Vienna.

Lavriotes, S. (1920) ‘Ἡ Διόπτρα: Ἔμμετρον ψυχοθεραπευτικόν’, *Ho Athos* 1: 1–264.

Layman, T. (2015) *‘The Incineration of New Babylon’: The Fire Poem of Konstantinos Stilbes*. Geneva.

Lemerle, P. (1971) *Le premier humanisme byzantin: Notes et remarque sur enseignement et culture à Byzance des origines au Xe siècle*. Bibliothèque Byzantine: Études 6. Paris.

(1986) *Byzantine Humanism: The First Phase. Notes and Remarks on Education and Culture in Byzantium from its Origins to the 10th Century*, trans. H. Lindsay and A. Moffatt. Byzantina Australensia 3. Leiden–Boston.

Leone, P. L. M. (ed.) (1969) ‘Michaelis Hapluchiris versus cum excerptis’, *Byzantion* 39: 251–83.

(ed.) (1972) *Ioannis Tzetzae Epistulae*. Leipzig.

(ed.) (2007) *Ioannis Tzetzae Historiae*, 2nd ed. Galatina.

Linardou, K. (2017) ‘The Illustrated Homilies of the Kokkinobaphou Monastery’, in Tsamakda, 382–92.

Littlewood, A. R. (ed.) (1972) *The Progymnasmata of John Geometres*. Amsterdam.

(ed.) (1995) *Originality in Byzantine Literature, Art and Music: A Collection of Essays*. Oxbow Monographs 50. Oxford.

Loukaki, M. (2000) 'Τυμβωρύχοι και σκυλευτές νεκρών: Οι απόψεις του Νικολάου Καταφλώρον για τη ρητορική και τους ρήτορες στην Κωνσταντινούπολη του 12ου αιώνα', *Byzantina Symmeikta* 14: 143–66.

(2005) 'Le samedi du Lazare et les éloges annuels du patriarche de Constantinople', in *Κλητόριον εἰς μνήμην Νίκου Οἰκονομίδη*, ed. F. Evangelatou-Notara and T. Maniati-Kokkini, 327–45. Athens.

(ed.) (2019) *Les Grâces à Athènes: Éloge d'un gouverneur byzantin par Nikolaos Kataphlôron*. Byzantinisches Archiv 36. Berlin.

Loukaki, M., and C. Jouanno (ed.) (2005) *Discours annuels en l'honneur du patriarche Georges Xiphilin: Textes édités, commentés et traduits*. Centre de Recherche d'Histoire et Civilisation de Byzance: Monographies 18. Paris.

Macleod, M. D. (ed.) (1987) *Luciani opera. Tomus IV: Libelli 69–86*. Oxford.

Macrides, R. (1985) 'Poetic Justice in the Patriarchate – Murder and Cannibalism in the Provinces', in *Cupido Legum*, ed. L. Burgmann, M. T. Fögen and A. Schminck, 137–68. Frankfurt am Main.

Macrides, R., and P. Magdalino (1992) 'The Fourth Kingdom and the Rhetoric of Hellenism', in *The Perception of the Past in Twelfth-Century Europe*, ed. P. Magdalino, 117–56. London.

Magdalino, P. (1993) *The Empire of Manuel I Komnenos, 1143–1180*. Cambridge.

(2012) 'Cultural Change? The Context of Byzantine Poetry from Geometres to Prodromos', in Bernard and Demoen, 19–36.

(2015) 'Debunking Astrology in Twelfth-Century Constantinople', in Efthymiadis, Messis, Odorico and Polemis, 165–75.

(2021) 'Political Satire', in Marciniak and Nilsson, 104–26 and 331–5.

Maisano, R. (ed.) (1977) *Niceforo Basilace: Gli encomî per l'imperatore e per il patriarca*. Byzantina et Neo-Hellenica Neapolitana 5. Naples.

Maiuri, A. (ed.) (1914–9) 'Una nova poesia di Teodoro Prodromo in greco volgare', *ByzZ* 23.1: 397–407.

Marcovich, M. (ed.) (1992) *Theodori Prodromi De Rhodanthis et Dosiclis amoribus libri IX*. Stuttgart.

Marciniak, P. (2007) 'Byzantine *Theatron* – A Place of Performance?', in *Theatron: Rhetorische Kultur in Spätantike und Mittelalter*, ed. M. Grünbart, 277–85. Millennium-Studien 13. Berlin.

(2021) 'The Power of Old and New *Logoi*: The *Philopatris* Revisited', in Marciniak and Nilsson, 179–90.

Marciniak, P., and I. Nilsson (eds.) (2021) *Satire in the Middle Byzantine Period: The Golden Age of Laughter?* Explorations in Medieval Culture 12. Leiden.

Markopoulos, A. (2006) 'De la structure de l'école byzantine: Le maître, les livres et le processus éducatif', in *Lire et écrire à Byzance*, ed. B. Mondrain, 85–96. Centre de Recherche d'Histoire et Civilisation de Byzance: Monographies 19. Paris.

(2014) 'Teachers and Textbooks in Byzantium: Ninth to Eleventh Centuries', in Steckel, Gaul and Grünbart, 3–15.

Mercati, S. G. (ed.) (1970) 'Ancora intorno a Μιχαὴλ γραμματικὸς ὁ ἱερομόναχος', in *Collectanea Bizantina*, vol. 1, 121–35. Bari (originally published in 1917).

Messis, C. (2004) 'Deux versions de la même "verité": Les deux Vies d'*hosios* Mélétios au XIIe siècle', in Odorico and Agapitos (2004), 303–45.
Messis, C., M. Mullett and I. Nilsson (eds.) (2018) *Storytelling in Byzantium: Narratological Aprroaches to Byzantine Texts and Images*. Studia Byzantina Upsaliensia 19. Uppsala.
Messis, C., and I. Nilsson (2015) 'Constantin Manasses: La description d'un petit homme. Introduction, texte, traduction et commentaires', *JÖByz* 65: 169–94.
(2019) 'The Description of a Crane Hunt by Constantine Manasses: Introduction, Text and Translation', *Scandinavian Journal for Byzantine and Modern Greek Studies* 5: 9–89.
Migne, J-P. (1865) *Gregorii Palamae Thessalonicensis Archiepiscopi Opera omnia quae supersunt*. Patrologiae Graece Cursus Completus 150. Paris.
Migliorini, T. (2007) 'Theodoro Prodromo, *Amaranto*', *MEG* 7: 183–247.
Mitsi, E., and P. A. Agapitos (2006) 'Εἰκὼν καὶ Λόγος: Ἡ «ἔκφρασις» ἀπὸ τὴν ἀρχαία στὴ βυζαντινὴ λογοτεχνία', in Agapitos (2006), 15–38 and 165–74.
Mullett, M. (1984) 'Aristocracy and Patronage in the Literary Circles of Comnenian Constantinople', in *The Byzantine Aristocracy, IX to XIII Centuries*, ed. M. Angold, 173–201. Oxford (reprinted in Mullett [2007], no. VIII).
(1990) 'Dancing with Deconstructionists in the Gardens of the Muses: New Literary History vs?', *BMGS* 14.1: 258–75 (reprinted in Mullett [2007], no. XVI).
(1992) 'The Madness of Genre', *DOP* 46: 233–43 (reprinted in Mullett [2007], no. IX).
(1997) *Theophylact of Ochrid: Reading the Letters of a Byzantine Archbishop*. Birmingham Byzantine and Ottoman Monographs 2. Birmingham.
(2004) 'Literary Biography and Historical Genre in the *Life* of Cyril Phileotes by Nicholas Kataskepenos', in Odorico and Agapitos (2004), 387–409 (reprinted in Mullett [2007], no. XV).
(2007) *Letters, Literacy and Literature in Byzantium: Collected Papers*. Aldershot.
(2008) 'Epistolography', in *The Oxford Handbook of Byzantine Studies*, ed. E. M. Jeffreys, J. Haldon and R. Cormack, 882–93. Oxford.
(2009) 'The Poetics of Paraitesis: The Resignation Poems of Nicholas of Kerkyra and Nicholas Mouzalon', in Odorico, Agapitos and Hinterberger, 157–78.
(2010) 'No Drama, No Poetry, No Fiction, No Readership, No Literature', in *A Companion to Byzantium*, ed. L. James, 227–38. Chichester.
(2022) 'Painting and Polyphony: The *Christos Paschon* as Commentary', in Van den Berg, Manolova and Marciniak, 214–39.
Munk Olsen, B. (1982–2014) *L'étude des auteurs classiques latins au XIe et XIIe siècles*, 4 vols. Paris.
(1991) *I classici nel canone scolastico altomedievale*. Spoleto.
Nesseris, I. C. (2014) 'Η παιδεία στην Κωνσταντινούπολη κατά τον 12ο αιώνα', 2 vols. PhD thesis, University of Ioannina.

Neville, L. (2016) *Anna Komnene: The Life and Work of a Medieval Historian*. Onassis Series in Hellenic Culture 10. New York.

Nilsson, I. (2001) *Erotic Pathos, Rhetorical Pleasure: Narrative Technique and Mimesis in Eumathios Makrembolites' Hysmine & Hysminias*. Studia Byzantina Upsaliensia 7. Uppsala.

(2003) 'Archaists and Innovators: Byzantine "Classicism" and Experimentation with Genre in the Twelfth Century', in *Genres and their Problems: Theoretical and Historical Perspectives*, ed. B. Agrell and I. Nilsson, 413–24. Gothenburg.

(2014) *Raconter Byzance: La littérature au XIIe siècle*. Paris.

(2016) 'Poets and Teachers in the Underworld: From the Lucianic Katabasis to the *Timarion*', *SO* 90: 180–204.

(2021) *Writer and Occasion in Twelfth-Century Byzantium: The Authorial Voice of Constantine Manasses*. Cambridge.

Nousia, F. (2016) *Byzantine Textbooks of the Palaeologan Period*. Studi e Testi 505. Vatican City.

Odorico, P., and P. A. Agapitos (eds.) (2002) *Pour une 'nouvelle' histoire de la littérature byzantine: Problèmes, méthodes, approches, propositions. Actes du colloque international philologique (Nicosie, mai 2000)*. Dossiers byzantins 1. Paris.

(eds.) (2004) *Les Vies des Saints à Byzance: Genre littéraire ou biographie historique? Actes du IIe colloque international philologique* ΕΡΜΗΝΕΙΑ. *Paris, 6–8 juin 2002*. Dossiers byzantins 4. Paris.

Odorico, P., P. A. Agapitos and M. Hinterberger (eds.) (2009) *'Doux remède ...': Poésie et poétique à Byzance. Actes du IVe Colloque International Philologique* 'ΕΡΜΗΝΕΙΑ'. *Paris, 23–24–25 février 2006, organisé par l'E.H.E.S.S. et l'Université de Chypre*. Dossiers byzantins 9. Paris.

Op de Coul, M. D. J. (ed.) (2023) *Theodori Prodromi Epistulae et orations*. Corpus Christianorum: Series Graeca 81. Turnhout.

Papaioannou, S. (2013) *Michael Psellos: Rhetoric and Authorship in Byzantium*. Cambridge.

(2017) 'Rhetoric and Rhetorical Theory', in Kaldellis and Siniossoglou, 101–12.

(2019a) 'Ioannes Sikeliotes (and Ioannes Geometres) Re-Visited with an Appendix: Edition of Sikeliotes' Scholia on Aelius Aristides', *T&MByz* 23.1: 659–92.

(ed.) (2019b) *Michael Psellus: Epistulae*. Berlin.

Papaioannou, S. (ed.) (2021) *The Oxford Handbook of Byzantine Literature*. Oxford.

Papanghelis, T. D., S. J. Harrison and S. Frangoulidis (eds.) (2013) *Generic Interfaces in Latin Literature: Encounters, Interactions and Transformations*. Trends in Classics 20. Berlin.

Parpulov, G. R. (2017) 'The *Dogmatic Panoply*', in Tsamakda, 430–1.

Paschalidis, S. A. (2008) 'Τὸ ἀνώνυμο ἐγκώμιο στὸν Ὅσιο Φώτιο τὸν Θεσσαλὸ (BHG 1545): Ἕνα ἀκόμη ἔργο τοῦ Εὐσταθίου Θεσσαλονίκης;', *Byzantina* 28: 529–47.

(2011) 'The Hagiography of the Eleventh and Twelfth Centuries', in *The Ashgate Research Companion to Byzantine Hagiography*, vol. 1: *Periods and Places*, ed. S. Efthymiadis, 143–71. Farnham.

Patillon, M. (ed.) (2008) *Corpus rhetoricum, Tome I: Anonyme, Préambule à la Rhétorique. Aphthonios, Progymnasmata. En annexe: Pseudo-Hermogène, Progymnasmata*. Paris.

Patillon, M. (ed.) (2012) *Corpus rhetoricum, Tome IV: Prolégomènes au De Ideis. Hermogène, Le categories sytylistiques du discours (De Ideis). Synopses des exposés sur les Ideai*. Paris.

Patterson Ševčenko, N. (2000) '*Typikon* of the *Sebastokrator* Isaac Komnenos for the Monastery of the Mother of God *Kosmosoteira* near Bera', in *Byzantine Monastic Foundation Documents: A Complete Translation of the Surviving Founders' Typika and Testaments*, vol. 2, ed. J. Thomas and A. Constantinides Hero, 782–858. Washington, DC.

Paul, A., and A. Rhoby (2019) *Konstantinos Manasses: Verschronik (Synopsis Chronike)*. Bibliothek der griechischen Literatur 87. Stuttgart.

Pelekanidis, S. et al. (1979) *Οἱ θησαυροὶ τοῦ Ἁγίου Ὄρους*. Σειρὰ Α': *Εἰκονογραφημένα χειρόγραφα. Παραστάσεις-ἐπίτιτλα-ἀρχικὰ γράμματα*. Τόμος Γ': *Μ. Μεγίστης Λαύρας, Μ. Παντοκράτορος, Μ. Δοχειαρίου, Μ. Καρακάλου, Μ. Ἁγίου Παύλου*. Athens.

Petit, L. (1902) 'Monodie de Nicétas Eugénianos sur Théodore Prodrome', *Vizantijskij Vremennik* 9: 446–63.

Petit, L. (1908) 'Typikon du monastère de la Kosmosotira près d'Ænos (1152)', *Bulletin de l'Institut Archéologique Russe à Constantinople* 13: 17–75.

Pietsch, E. (2005) *Die Chronographia des Michael Psellos: Kaisergeschichte, Autobiographie und Apologie*. Serta Graeca 20. Wiesbaden.

Pignani, A. (ed.) (1983) *Niceforo Basilace: Progimnasmi e monodie. Testo critico, introduzione, traduzione*. Studia Byzantina et Neohellenica 10. Naples.

Pizzone, A. (2014a) 'Anonymity, Disposession and Reappropriation in the Prolog of Nikephoros Basilakes', in Pizzone (2014b), 225–43.

(ed.) (2014b) *The Author in Middle Byzantine Literature: Modes, Functions and Identities*. Byzantinisches Archiv 28. Munich.

(2017) 'The *Historiai* of John Tzetzes: A Byzantine "Book of Memory"?', *BMGS* 41.2: 182–207.

(2020) 'Self-authorization and Strategies of Autography in John Tzetzes: The *Logismoi* Rediscovered', *GRBS* 60: 652–90.

Polemis, I. D. (1994) 'Κριτικὲς καὶ ἑρμηνευτικὲς παρατηρήσεις σὲ βυζαντινὰ καὶ μεταβυζαντινὰ ποιήματα', *Ἑλληνικά* 44: 357–67.

(1995) 'Προβλήματα τῆς βυζαντινῆς σχεδογραφίας', *Ἑλληνικά* 45: 277–302.

(1997) 'Philologische und historische Probleme in der schedographischen Sammlung des Codex Marcianus gr. XI,34', *Byzantion* 67: 252–63.

(ed.) (2015) *Theodori Metochitae Carmina*. Corpus Christianorum: Series Graeca 83. Turnhout.

(2017a) 'Η φωνὴ τῆς ἐξουσίας: Ἡ δομὴ τῆς ἀφήγησης στὰ ποιήματα τοῦ Θεόδωρου Μετοχίτη', *Parekbolai* 7: 115–33. https://ejournals.lib.auth.gr/parekbolai/article/view/6001/5713.
(2017b) *Theodoros Metochites: Poems. Introduction, Translation and Notes*. Corpus Christianorum in Translation 26. Turnhout.
(ed.) (2020) *Κείμενα για την Ελλάδα στην περίοδο των Κομνηνών: Ένας λόγος του Νικολάου Καταφλώρον και δύο ποιήματα του Ευθυμίου Τορνίκη*. Athens.
(ed.) (2022) *Οἱ Βίοι τοῦ Ἁγίου Μελετίου τοῦ Νέου: Εἰσαγωγή, κριτικὴ ἔκδοση, μετάφραση, σημειώσεις*, 2nd ed. Athens.
Pontani, F., V. Katsaros and V. Sarris (eds.) (2017) *Reading Eustathios of Thessalonike*. Trends in Classics: Supplementary Volumes 46. Berlin.
Protogirou, S.-A. (2014) 'Ρητορική θεατρικότητα στο έργο του Μιχαήλ Ψελλού', PhD thesis, University of Cyprus. https://lekythos.library.ucy.ac.cy/handle/10797/14149.
Rapp, C. (2023) *Zerrspiegel, Streiflichter und Seitenblicke: Perspektiven der Byzantinistik heute*. Das mittelalterliche Jahrtausend 9. Göttingen.
Regel, W. (ed.) (1982) *Fontes rerum byzantinarum rhetorum saeculi XII: Orationes politicae. Mit einem wissenschaftsgeschichtlichen Vorwort von A. P. Kazhdan*. Subsidia Byzantina lucis ope iterata 5. Leipzig (reprint of the original 1892–1917 edition in two fascicules).
Reinsch, D. R. (1996) *Anna Komnene: Alexias. Übersetzt, eingeleitet und mit Anmerkungen versehen*. Cologne.
Reinsch, D. R., and A. Kambylis (eds.) (2001) *Annae Comnenae Alexias*. Corpus Fontium Historiae Byzantinae 40. Berlin.
Rhoby, A., and N. Zagklas (eds.) (2019) *Middle and Late Byzantine Poetry: Texts and Contexts*. Byzantios: Studies in Byzantine History and Civilization 14. Turnhout.
Riehle, A. (ed.) (2020) *A Companion to Byzantine Epistolography*. Brill's Companions to the Byzantine World 7. Leiden.
Robins, R. H. (1993) *The Byzantine Grammarians: Their Place in History*. Trends in Linguistics: Studies and Monographs 70. Berlin.
Roilos, P. (2005) *Amphoteroglossia: A Poetics of the Twelfth-Century Medieval Greek Novel*. Washington, DC.
Romano, R. (ed.) (1974) *Pseudo-Luciano: Timarione. Testo critico, introduzione, traduzione, commentario e lessico*. Byzantina et Neohellenica Neapolitana 2. Naples.
(ed.) (1980) *Nicola Callicle: Carmi. Testo critico, introduzione, traduzione, commentario e lessico*. Byzantina et Neo-Hellenica Neapolitana 8. Naples.
(ed.) (1991) *Constantino Acropolita: Epistole. Saggio introdutivo, testo critico, indici*. Naples.
(ed.) (1999) *La satira bizantina dei secoli XI–XV: Il patriota, Caridemo, Timarione, Cristoforo di Mitilene, Michele Psello, Teodoro Prodromo, Carmi ptocoprodromici, Michele Haplucheir, Giovanni Catrara, Mazaris, La messa del glabro, Sinassario del venerabile asino*. Turin.

Ronchey, S. (2017) 'Eustathios at Prodromos Petra? Some Remarks on the Manuscript Tradition of the *Exegesis in Canonem Iambicum Pentecostalem*', in Pontani, Katsaros and Sarris, 181–97.
Russell, D. A., and N. G. Wilson (eds.) (1981) *Menander Rhetor: Edited with Translation and Commentary*. Oxford.
Sargologos, E. (ed.) (1964) *La vie de Saint Cyrille le Philéote moine byzantin (†1110): Introduction, texte critique, traduction et notes*. Subsidia Hagiographica Graeca 39. Brussels.
Schönauer, S. (2006) *Eustathios von Thessalonike: Reden auf die große Quadragesima. Prolegomena, Text, Übersetzung, Kommentar, Indices*. Meletemata: Beiträge zur Byzantinistik und Neugriechischen Philologie 10. Frankfurt am Main.
Sideras, A. (1997) 'Eine unedierte byzantinische Totenklage', *JÖByz* 47: 111–56.
(2002) *Eine byzantinische Invektive gegen die Verfasser von Grabreden. Ἀνωνύμου μονῳδία εἰς μονῳδοῦντας. Erstmals herausgegeben und kommentiert, nebst einem Anhang über den rhythmischen Satzschluß*. Wiener Byzantinistische Studien 23. Vienna.
Silvano, L. (2015) 'Schedografia bizantina in Terra d'Otranto: Appunti su testi e contest didattici', in *Circolazione di testi e scambi culturali in Terra d'Otranto tra Tardoantico e Medioevo*, ed. A. Capone, 121–67. Vatican City.
Simpson, A. J. (2013) *Niketas Choniates: A Historiographical Study*. Oxford.
(ed.) (2015) *Byzantium, 1180–1204: 'The Sad Quarter of a Century'?* Athens.
Speck, P. (1974) *Die kaiserliche Universität von Konstantinopel: Präzisierungen zur Frage des höheren Schulwesens in Byzanz im 9. und 10. Jahrhundert*. Byzantinisches Archiv 14. Munich.
Steckel, S., N. Gaul and M. Grünbart (eds.) (2014) *Networks of Learning: Perspectives on Scholars in Byzantine East and Latin West, c. 1000–1200*. Byzantinische Studien und Texte 6. Zurich.
Stephanis, I. E. (ed.) (1998) 'Τυπικὴ Διαθήκη', in *Ἁγίου Νεοφύτου τοῦ Ἐγκλείστου Συγγράμματα. Τόμος Β': Τυπικὴ Διαθήκη – Βίβλος τῶν Κατηχήσεων*. Paphos.
Strano, G. (2012) *Nicola Muzalone: Carme apologetico. Introduzione, testo critico, traduzione e note*. La Gorgona 3. Rome.
Tafel, T. L. F. (ed.) (1964) *Eustathii metropolitae Thessalonicensis Opuscula*. Amsterdam (reprint of the original edition of 1832).
Taxidis, I. (2021) *The Ekphraseis in the Byzantine Literature of the 12th Century*. Hellenica 90. Alessandria.
Tomadaki, M. (ed.) (2023) *Iohannis Geometrae Carmina iambica*. Corpus Christianorum: Series Graeca 100. Turnhout.
Tsamakda, V. (ed.) (2017) *A Companion to Byzantine Illustrated Manuscripts*. Brill's Companions to the Byzantine World 2. Leiden.
Tsougarakis, D. (1993) *The Life of Leontios Patriarch of Jerusalem. Text, Translation, Commentary*. The Medieval Mediterranean 2. Leiden.
Tuilier, A. (ed.) (1969) *Grégoire de Nazianze: La Passion du Christ. Tragédie. Introduction, texte critique, traduction, notes et index*. Sources Chrétiennes 149. Paris.

van den Berg, B. (2017) 'The Wise Homer and his Erudite Commentator: Eustathios' Imagery in the Proem of the *Parekbolai on the Iliad*', *BMGS* 41.1: 30–44.

(2020) 'John Tzetzes as Didactic Poet and Learned Grammarian', *DOP* 74: 285–302.

(2022) *Homer the Rhetorician: Eustathios of Thessalonike on the Composition of the Iliad.* Oxford.

van den Berg, B., D. Manolova and P. Marciniak (ed.) (2022) *Byzantine Commentaries on Ancient Greek Texts, 12th–15th Centuries*. Cambridge.

van der Valk, M. (ed.) (1971–87) *Eustathii archiepiscopi Thessalonicensis Commentarii ad Homeri Iliadem pertinentes ad fidem codicis Laurentiani editi*, 4 vols. Leiden.

van Opstall, E. M. (ed.) (2008) *Jean Géomètre: Poèmes en hexamètres et en distiques élégiaques. Edition, traduction, commentaire*. The Medieval Mediterranean 75. Leiden.

Vassis, I. (1993–4) 'Graeca sunt, non leguntur: Zu den schedographischen Spielereien des Theodoros Prodromos', *ByzZ* 86–7.1: 1–19.

Vassis, I., and I. Polemis (eds.) (2016) *Ἕνας Ἕλληνας ἐξόριστος στὴ Μάλτα τοῦ δωδέκατου αἰώνα. Τὸ ποίημα τοῦ ἑλληνικοῦ κώδικα τῆς Ἐθνικῆς Βιβλιοθήκης τῆς Μαδρίτης 4577: Νέα κριτικὴ ἔκδοση μὲ μετάφραση καὶ σημειώσεις*. Athens.

Westerink, L. G. (ed.) (1992) *Michaelis Pselli Poemata*. Stuttgart.

Westerink, L. G. et al. (eds.) (1975) *Mazaris' Journey to Hades or Interviews with Dead Men about Certain Officials of the Imperial Court. Greek Text with Translation, Notes, Introduction and Index*. Arethusa Monographs 5. Buffalo, NY.

Winfield, D., and J. Winfield (2003) *The Church of the Panaghia tou Arakos at Lagoudhera, Cyprus: The Paintings and Their Painterly Significance*. Washington, DC.

Wirth, P. (1980) 'Spuren einer autorisierten mittelalterlichen Eustathiosedition', in *Eustathiana: Gesammelte Aufsätze zu Leben und Werk des Metropoliten Eustathios von Thessalonike*, 65–9. Amsterdam (originally published in 1972).

(2000) *Eustathii Thessalonicensis opera minora*. Corpus Fontium Historiae Byzantinae 32. Berlin.

Yuretich, L. (2020) *The Chronicle of Constantine Manasses: Translated with Commentary and Introduction*. Translated Texts for Byzantinists 6. Liverpool.

Zagklas, N. (2011) 'A Byzantine Grammar Treatise Attributed to Theodore Prodromos', *Graeco-Latina Brunensia* 16: 77–86.

(2016) 'Astrology, Piety and Poverty: Seven Anonymous Poems in Vaticanus gr. 743', *ByzZ* 109.2: 895–918.

(2017) 'Experimenting with Prose and Verse in Twelfth-Century Byzantium', *DOP* 71: 229–48.

(2018) 'Metrical *Polyeideia* and Generic Innovation in the Twelfth Century: The Multimetric Cycles of Occasional Poetry', in Rhoby and Zagklas, 43–70.

(2021a) 'Epistolarity in Twelfth-Century Byzantine Poetry: Singing Praises and Asking Favors *in Absentia*', in Kubina and Riehle, 64–77.
(2021b) 'Satire in the Komnenian Period: Poetry, Satirical Strands, and Intellectual Antagonism', in Marciniak and Nilsson, 279–303.
(2023) *Theodore Prodromos, Miscellaneous Poems: An Edition and Literary Study.* Oxford.
Zarras, N. (2021) 'Illness and Healing: The Ministry Cycle in the Chora Monastery and the Literary Œuvre of Theodore Metochites', *DOP* 75: 85–120.

CHAPTER 2

Poetry and Theatre in Twelfth-Century Constantinople

Paul Magdalino

We all know that twelfth-century Byzantine literature was special. But why do we think so? Over thirty years ago, I tried to define it in terms of three qualities that had come to the fore in the eleventh century, but intensified in the twelfth: Hellenism, humanism and authorial self-representation.[1] More recently, others, most notably Margaret Mullett and Ingela Nilsson, have focused on a particular literary aesthetic, that of narrativity or novelization.[2] Without denying or abandoning any of these criteria, I propose here to highlight another that I suggest is common to all of them, because it corresponds to the social and cultural context within which literary texts were published. To the best of our knowledge, *belles lettres*, which in Byzantium went under the general heading of rhetoric, were produced to be consumed at a combination of venue, occasion and social gathering known generically as a *theatron*, although its components could be defined in a variety of other ways.[3] Literary ambition, innovation, creativity and success may therefore be defined and measured in terms of a striving for theatrical effect, and what makes twelfth-century literature special is the enhanced theatricality of its texts. Theatricality was common to both prose and verse, but it had a particular affinity with verse, quite simply because verse was the most ancient medium of textual performance, in epic, drama and song, and its rhythms and cadences are expressive in themselves, creating a stage on which textual content can build its performance. Poetry had led the way in cultural innovation in the eleventh century, and thus had the momentum to play a dynamic role in the twelfth.[4]

1 Magdalino (1993: 398–404).

2 Mullett (2006), Nilsson (2014).

3 The literature is large and continues to grow. In addition to Magdalino (1993: 335–56), I cite the earliest and the latest studies of *theatron* in middle and late Byzantium: Mullett (1984) and Gaul (2018).

4 Magdalino (2012).

My chapter is concerned primarily with theatricality of textual content. I see this in terms of two kinds of expressive technique, which may or may not be combined in the same composition. One kind of expressiveness is that which explicitly calls attention and assigns roles to the persons who are actually or virtually involved in the performative occasion: the poet himself or the person whose voice he adopts, and the person with whom he and/or his adopted persona are in dialogue. Such demonstrative expression is to be found in all types of occasional poetry: acclamations, encomia, laments, ex-voto epigrams and meditations, as well as petitions, didactic and exegetical poems explicitly addressed to a patron. The other textual technique of theatrical expression consists in third-person description and narration, where the drama is achieved by the power of imagery, colourful and emotive vocabulary, direct speech, evoked action and character portrayal. Both types of dramatization between them characterize, indeed epitomize, the poetry of the long twelfth century. Most characteristic, and best known, are the long verse narratives composed around the middle of the century: the novels by Theodore Prodromos, Niketas Eugeneianos and Constantine Manasses,[5] as well as Manasses' *Synopsis Chronike* and *Itinerary* (*Hodoiporikon*).[6] But many other long poems, such as the *Dioptra* of Philip Monotropos,[7] Nicholas Mouzalon's apologia for his resignation from the archbishopric of Cyprus,[8] the vernacular verse petitions to John II and Manuel I by 'Ptochoprodromos'[9] and Michael Glykas,[10] the newly published invectives of Euthymios Tornikes,[11] along with many metrical encomia in high style addressed to emperors and other 'lords', by Theodore Prodromos,[12] Manganeios Prodromos[13] and others,[14] are remarkable for their use of dramatic language and technique. There is much theatrical posturing in the long metrical commentaries and exegeses of John Tzetzes.[15] And many short pieces of descriptive, admonitory and satirical verse are highly charged with emotional and sensual expression and portrayal.

5 Ed. Marcovich (1992), Conca (1990), Mazal (1967).
6 Ed. Lampsidis (1996), Chryssogelos (2017).
7 See Afentoulidou-Leitgeb (2012); Afentoulidou and Fuchsbauer (2019).
8 Ed. Strano (2012).
9 Ed. Eideneier (1991); cf. Alexiou (1999), Janssen and Lauxtermann (2018) and Kulhánková in this volume.
10 Ed. Tsolakis (1959); cf. Bourbouhakis (2007).
11 Ed. Hörandner (2017).
12 Ed. Hörandner (1974); see Magdalino (2016) for translation and analysis of one important piece.
13 M. J. Jeffreys (2003); E. M. Jeffreys and M. J. Jeffreys in this volume.
14 For example, Euthymios Tornikes, ed. Papadopoulos-Kerameus ([1913] 1976: 188–98).
15 Ed. Leone ([1968] 2007) and (2019), Boissonade (1851), Bekker (1842); see Agapitos (2017) and Pizzone (2017).

One thinks of the poems of Theophylaktos of Ohrid, a number of which are verse epistles,[16] the epigrams and epitaphs of Nicholas Kallikles[17] and Theodore Balsamon,[18] Michael Hagiotheodorites' description of a chariot race in the Hippodrome,[19] the verse satires of Theodore Prodromos,[20] the recently published anonymous urban fables that have been assigned to the twelfth century,[21] Michael Choniates' poetic evocation of a painting of ancient Athens[22] and many anonymous pieces in the codex Venice, Biblioteca Nazionale Marciana, gr. Z. 524 [Diktyon 69995].[23] Last but not least are the verse pieces that actually style themselves as dramas: Theodore Prodromos' *Katomyomachia*,[24] the *Dramation* of Michael Haploucheir,[25] the nun's confession told by the *protekdikos* Andronikos[26] and the lament on the great fire of 1197 by Constantine Stilbes.[27] This is not to mention the *Christos Paschon*, 'the only Byzantine tragedy', a Euripidean cento on the Passion of Christ, attributed by its manuscripts to Gregory of Nazianzos, but assigned by a consensus of modern scholarship to a twelfth-century author.[28] The dating and authorship are too uncertain for the work to merit consideration in this chapter, or indeed this volume, but it says a lot about twelfth-century Byzantine poetry that this is the context where the *Christos Paschon* is thought to belong.

Thus the twelfth century saw not merely the continuation of a 'performative turn' in textual delivery,[29] but also the culmination of a 'theatrical turn' in poetic composition. To get an idea of how poetic theatricality developed during the period, it is instructive to look at three compositions dating respectively from 1119, *c.* 1150 and 1197. These texts are: Prodromos' verses on the coronation of Alexios Komenos, son of John II, as co-emperor; the *Synopsis Chronike* of Constantine Manasses; and the *Fire Poem*, just mentioned, of Constantine Stilbes.

16 Ed. Gautier (1980: 346–77) and Zagklas (2021: 150–9).
17 Ed Romano (1980), especially nos. 24 and 25; cf. Magdalino and Nelson (1982: 124–30).
18 Ed. Horna (1903); cf. Magdalino and Nelson (1982: 152–60). On Kallikles, see also Gerbi in this volume.
19 See Marciniak and Warcaba (2014).
20 See Marciniak (2015), Kucharski and Marciniak (2017), Zagklas (2021).
21 Zagklas (2016).
22 Livanos (2006), Rhoby (2003: 29–33). On Choniates' poetry, see also Mondini in this volume.
23 Mostly edited by Lampros (1911); cf. Rhoby (2010), Spingou (2014).
24 Ed. Hunger (1968); see below and Lauxtermann in this volume.
25 Ed. Romano (1999: 414–27).
26 Ed. Macrides (1985).
27 Ed. Diethart and Hörandner (2005: 8–51); trans. with facing text Layman (2015).
28 Ed. Tuilier (1969); Mullett (2010: 228). On this text, see also Mullett (2022).
29 Marciniak (2014a).

Theodore Prodromos, *On the Crown-Wearing of Alexios Komnenos* (*Historical Poem* 1)

Theodore Prodromos was the most versatile and innovatory of the twelfth-century writers whose poetry survives. He has some claim to be considered the leading exponent of the 'theatrical turn'. While a number of his compositions could be used to illustrate his theatrical talent, the one chosen here deserves attention because it marks the debut not only of his literary career, but also of the 'new and interesting trends in Byzantine literature that had their origins during the reign of John II'.[30] The poem, in 155 lines of fifteen-syllable verse, is a 'first' in several respects.[31] It is Prodromos' earliest dateable surviving work, the earliest programmatic statement of Komnenian imperial ideology, and it is the earliest surviving piece of deme poetry written in celebration of a living emperor. In the present context, it deserves attention for the way in which it turns a traditional topos of ruler acclamation into a lively interplay between the imperial family, who perform the action of the ritual, and the poet, who performs the script as the official voice of the popular circus factions, the *demoi*, who represent the city. On one side of the stage, as it were, the poet faces the palace and calls upon the imperial family to rise and shine on their people, inviting the young heir to return in orbit to his father and receive the crown (ll. 1–17). He picks up the solar metaphor again, using it both to dramatize the dynamics of the senior emperor's rule (ll. 63–73) and to evoke the reflected glory of the empress; she is the moon to the emperor's sun, but nevertheless merits thirty-three lines of praise (ll. 57–62, 74–103). She is the vehicle for portraying the subservience of Western Christendom, echoed in a long list of western peoples (ll. 64–99), and she is the focus of the ceremonial action that the poem evokes on the imperial side: the poet brings in 'a choir of virtues, who dance around you, who applaud you, who dance around you like tender virgins, praising, singing, cheering, entwining their tender fingers in a rhythmic dance' (ll.79–83); later, she is led in procession by 'all the noble daughters of the kings', accompanied by the senate and the people (ll. 100–3). The image of procession is subsequently taken up to describe the cortege of illustrious ancestors who have preceded the emperor on the throne, thereby securing his right to the succession (ll. 130–5). Meanwhile, the narrative of the imperial performance has been interrupted by a number of passages in which the author

30 Jeffreys (2016: 120).
31 Ed. Hörandner (1974: 177–84); Magdalino and Macrides (2022).

turns the reader's and, at least notionally, the imperial family's attention to himself, and to the assembly of people, army, senate and clergy in whose presence he is writing. His interjections imply stage directions, which at first are addressed to the junior emperor – 'As from a distance, I the *demos* shout, "Let him come forth!"' (l. 11) – and then describe the gathering of the audience who also include the chorus:

> For we have assembled on the occasion of your crown-wearing, the demes and all the city with instruments of music, to celebrate in hymns the coronation feast, not just the army and the myriad populace, but the assembly of elders, the senatorial council, and the elect of the priesthood with the great chief shepherd, participating, approving, urging and bringing to fulfilment. (Prodromos, *Historical Poem* 1.18–24)

Thus the poet also signals the special participation of another actor among the chorus, the patriarch, who crosses over to join the imperial performance by blessing the coronation. Another distinguished participant is David, who as the author of the Psalms that are quoted, is invited to take part, because

> this brilliant coronation feast, taking place today on the acropolis of Rome, needs an equally brilliant rhetor and a sonorous tongue. We badly need a rhetor loudly to broadcast, with lofty proclamation in a herald's booming voice, 'Good men and Romans, gather eagerly, let us rejoice together, let us all celebrate fervently as one, as David the choirmaster leads the refrain with his lovely lyre moved by the Spirit ...' (Prodromos, *Historical Poem* 1.34–43)[32]

Homer too is discreetly but explicitly brought in with a quote towards the end of the poem (ll. 150–1). Thus, when we analyse the voicing, the actors and the stage directions, the text can be seen as a drama in which the imperial family are the actors, and the chorus is formed by the city (l. 110), led by the poet and his great biblical and classical predecessors.

The coronation poem by Prodromos is not the first piece of Byzantine poetry that evokes the choreography and movement of ceremonial occasions. This evocation is a feature of two well-known sixth-century hexameter texts, Paul the Silentiary's *Ekphrasis of Hagia Sophia*[33] and Corippus' *In Praise of Justin II*;[34] it also characterizes Leo Choirosphaktes' anacreontic

32 On the poet as David, see also Ricceri in this volume.
33 Ed. De Stefani (2011); cf. Whitby (1985), Macrides and Magdalino (1988).
34 A. M. Cameron (1976).

ekphrasis of the palace bath built by Leo VI, which, we can deduce from the content, was sung at the inauguration ceremony.[35] These texts show that the technique of built-in, allusive stage directions was well developed long before the twelfth century. Even so, Prodromos' poem appears to break new ground in the popular medium of its delivery and the demotic role of its performer. It also differs from the earlier examples in the greater prominence that it gives, spatially as well as thematically, to the performance of its own choral commentary on the main ceremonial action. Prodromos would go on to give other, more elaborate performances of this kind, notably his composition and delivery of multiple poems in connection with John II's revival in 1133 of the ceremony of the imperial victory parade.[36]

The *Synopsis Chronike* of Constantine Manasses

There can be no dispute about the innovative and theatrical quality of the second text to be reviewed here. In more than one way, the *Synopsis Chronike* of Constantine Manasses is a new and unprecedented type of history writing.[37] Along with his equally innovative novel *Aristandros and Kallithea*, it was written, like the poem of Prodromos we have just considered, in fifteen-syllable 'political' verse, and as in the case of that poem, the choice of metre was deliberately theatrical. Political verse had a pleasing rhythm and it was intellectually unpretentious, being by this time primarily the medium of Hippodrome songs and simplified teaching texts,[38] in addition to becoming 'the typical vehicle for fiction'.[39] True to this tradition, the *Synopsis Chronike* offers a 'pop' version of world history for the instruction and entertainment of an aristocratic lady, the *sebastokratorissa* Irene, sister-in-law of Manuel I and well-known patron of several twelfth-century literati.[40] The qualities that make it of doubtful value as a source of historical information give it prime importance as a piece of creative literature.[41] The *Synopsis Chronike* is not merely a novelization of the narrative of world and imperial history from the Creation to the eleventh century; it adapts this novelistic narrative for the Byzantine intellectual equivalent of the big

35 Magdalino (1988).
36 Magdalino (2016); for the practice of multiple poems in different metres for the same occasion, see Zagklas (2018) and Agapitos in this volume.
37 Ed. Lampsidis (1996).
38 See Nilsson (2019: 518–24) and bibliography; cf. also the recent observations of M. J. Jeffreys (2019).
39 Afentoulidou and Fuchsbauer (2019: 341–2).
40 E. M. Jeffreys (2011–12).
41 See Nilsson (2008) and (2020), Reinsch (2008), Nilsson and Nyström (2009), Papaioannou (2010: 19–20).

screen. In terms of twelfth-century chronicle writing, we might think of it like this: Kedrenos and Zonaras wrote the book; Manasses scripted and produced the movie. It would require a book-length study to analyse all the choices and techniques by which Manasses produces his cinematic effects. Suffice to say that he constantly plays on the senses and the emotions; he always goes for the story with anecdotal or dramatic potential; he invariably describes settings, situations and personalities in sensual and sensational language. He sets up contrasts and confrontations that are only implicit in his sources, and to do so, he uses the full rhetorical toolkit of *ekphrasis*, *ethopoiia*, *diegesis* and *synkrisis* to enliven and amplify his narrative. Not content with the dramatic and often melodramatic portrayal of real historical characters, Manasses gives personal identities and dramatic roles to the impersonal forces of change in human affairs: Fortune (Tyche), Envy/Jealousy (Phthonos/Baskania), Love (Eros) and Gold (Chryson) – a personification, which, as far as I know, he is the first to invent. He further dramatizes the ups and downs of historical change by recurrent reference to the Wheel of Fortune.[42]

To illustrate his narrative technique, here is just one of the passages in which he takes a simply reported fact from his sources and turns it into a lurid melodrama. The excerpt is from his account of the blinding of Constantine VI by his mother Irene:

> Alas, she shared her beastly intention with her attendants, and found them all amenable, not one was unreceptive. For what would those foul souls, her bedchamber eunuchs, not have done, perpetrators of all evil? She concocted the plot against her dearest son and suggested how they should do it. What happened then? The emperor slept, but a sleep of unending darkness, after which he would never see the beauty of the sun. They rushed in like eye-gouging crows, and blackened the brightness of his eyes. His eyeballs popped out of his eyelids, falling like hailstones made round by murder, and a stream of blood stained his garment, as he lay there convulsed with terrible suffering, a pitiable sight, alas, which would make stones weep. His eyes were cut out and his vision extinguished in the very place where he had first seen the sun's rays; they call that building the Porphyra.[43] Who ever heard of such intensely wrathful madness, the rage of a mother against her son? Such obsessive desire for power! No mother leopard rages thus against her cubs, no tigress, shark or rabid dog gets savage with her young like that. Only Medea, they say, laid hands on her children, and she was driven by Scythian savage-mindedness. (Manasses, *Synopsis Chronike* 4381–4405, ed. Lampsidis 1996)

42 See also Macrides and Magdalino (1992: 123–6), Magdalino (1997: 161–5).

43 The Porphyra was the birth chamber in the imperial palace, whose walls were lined with porphyry.

The *Fire Poem* of Constantine Stilbes

We come finally to a work in 937 twelve-syllable verses that bears the title *Iambic verses of Konstantinos Stilbes, magister and teacher, about a great conflagration sent by God that occurred in Constantinople on 25 July 1197.*[44] The *Fire Poem* of Constantine Stilbes resembles the *Synopsis Chronike* of Manasses in presenting a third-person narrative that achieves theatrical effect by feeding the imagination with sensual and sensational evocations. In keeping with the subject matter – the all-consuming destruction of a raging, uncontrollable blaze – the pace of the narrative is even more frenetic, the images are more violent, and the sympathy is more poignant; the style itself is explosive, with descriptive vignettes, metaphors, philosophical reflections, classical and biblical allusions being spat-out in rapid-fire succession. Yet at the same time as presenting a dramatic narrative, the poem is also a piece of occasional verse rhetoric in the sense that it presents itself as a lament and adopts the style and *topoi* of commemorative mourning. The description is shot through with woeful exclamations. The author frequently introduces himself as the chief mourner who is overcome by grief and cannot do justice to the terrible event. In this role of lamentation, he implicitly assumes the voice of an Old Testament prophet, and indeed the text is peppered with Old Testament allusions, including reminiscences of Sodom and Gomorrah, Babylon and the destruction of the Temple. Insofar as Stilbes has an ulterior purpose, as a man of the Church, this is to lament the fire as divine punishment for sin. Nevertheless, classical allusions abound, and the voice that the author *explicitly* adopts is that of tragic dramatist. He repeatedly refers to himself as a tragedian and to his work as a tragedy, and he reinforces the comparison with the imagery of classical drama. Thus the poem is not only a dramatic, technical recreation of the terrible fire; it is also self-consciously a theatrical composition.

Here are some excerpts that give the flavour of the work. First is a preliminary overview of the fire's movement.

> For you burned Byzantium in a moment, spanning the expanses like lightning flame with thunderbolt speed. For you rode on the wings of the winds, and being light, you were taken aloft even by the north-east wind. Oh fiery thunderbolt, albeit welling up from below, not from the clouds, but from dense matter. Oh woe, an earthbound hurricane, but which runs up and even shoots out from the land and the lower depths, continuing to

44 Trans. Layman (2015: 43); ed. Diethart and Hörandner (2005: 8): Τοῦ Κωνσταντίνου μαΐστωρος καὶ διδασκάλου τοῦ Στιλβῆ στίχοι ἰαμβικοὶ ἐπὶ τῷ συμβάντι ἐν Κωνσταντινουπόλει θεηλάτῳ μεγάλῳ ἐμπρησμῷ μηνὶ Ἰουλίῳ κε´ ἔτους ͵ϛψε´.

> maintain its shooting nature. For it runs sideways, burning all the more. It flows in every direction, expanding as it burns. Like lightning it thunders with whooshing noises; whenever it devours all by raging sideways, it feeds its natural urge to rise. It rises up to the highest rooftops, and sets fire to the loftiest halls. (Constantine Stilbes, *Fire Poem* 89–102 ed. Diethart and Hörandner; trans. after Layman [2015])
>
> ...
>
> I bring back my account, forcing out my words, to the painful beginning under baleful stars, and I will show you a prologue of the epilogue, a serpent's head worthy of its tail; I will show the rough dragging of its scaly hulk that I am not writing a satyr play, but putting together an entire tragedy. For the great stage had Furies with torches scaring, causing upheaval and bearing fire over all the expanse of Byzantion that was mapped out by the metrics of the fire. It takes a great house to contain the tragedy. (Constantine Stilbes, *Fire Poem* 129–40 ed. Diethart and Hörandner; trans. after Layman 2015)

Here the poet describes in greater detail, using serpentine and sea imagery, the advance of the fire from its origin in the granaries near the Droungarios Gate beside the Golden Horn.

> It was there that the serpent left Paradise, hissing and spilling out, undulating, it slithers and feasts on earth and stones; then having raised high its head, it ravages, alas, even three-story houses, and fire leapt into the air. The serpent crept up out of the sea, like a sea-monster or the mouth of Charybdis, and a beacon on the seaside, not a friendly one but one warning of rolling swells and seasickness. It washed over even the high roofs, like a rushing wave, like the tossing of the sea. For it carried itself with wavelike conceit and it washed over the coastal areas, like the water of the sea it poured forth across the expanse, and burst a greater wave upon the land. And a booming noise like the breaking of surf arose, and the fire sputtered out crashing noises like those of the sea. So both the booming and the glare of the fire completely wiped sleep from the eyes. (Constantine Stilbes, *Fire Poem* 180–99 ed. Diethart and Hörandner; trans. after Layman 2015)

Here Stilbes describes the impact of the fire on the residents, and the resulting effect on the senses:

> The infants, alas, break out crying together, frightened by the bogey-man sound of fire, seeking their fathers and mothers, from whom they have been torn apart by the sword of fire. For the fathers and mothers, the fire was twice the fuel of tears – both for the state of their children and for the flame. The maiden, having shed the colour of modesty, taking on a shade of green

> from the fear, sees her house's chambers as foes, wearing just one robe she ran into the streets, since this is all she snatched from the fire. A brother has been broken off from his siblings, for the fire conquers the flame of familial love. Then, a mixed shout arises. The mourning of women, the shouting of men, weeping of newborns, and the groaning of maidens, a unification of many components into a melody of wailing, a Telchine concert.[45] It was like a tragedy: the twirling of burning torches as on stage, and the fire's roaring and the wailing were thunderous applause. With noises from the nearby sea, the threefold booming burst upon the ears, and was an even more monstrous shock than the sight. The fire flashed, and the tumultuous din resounded. Such was the turmoil of the primary senses, the most spontaneous and physical perceptions [of sight and sound]. The seething of the fire then afflicted touch, and the foul-smelling smoke did the same to the inhaling nose. But the lips, not tasting fire, drank the bitterness of tears. And the blaze whirled about the entire pentad of senses, just like the fire of old burned the Pentapolis to ashes.[46] (Constantine Stilbes, *Fire Poem* 250–79 ed. Diethart and Hörandner; trans. after Layman 2015)

The 'tragedy' of the fire of 1197 marks a new departure in Byzantine poetry, although it is not entirely without parallel or precedent.[47] Of uncertain date within the long twelfth century, but quite possibly from its final decades, is the verse piece purporting to be a judicial decision by the penitential tribunal of Hagia Sophia, in which the *protekdikos* Andronikos reports the tragedy of a nun from south-western Anatolia who had confessed to killing and eating her daughter along with other corpses and unclean foods.[48] Of mid-twelfth-century date, if the attribution to Theodore Prodromos is correct, is the *Katomyomachia*, which has been characterized as 'a satire in the form of a parody of a tragedy', and more recently as a mock epic.[49] We may note in passing that all three 'dramas' are concerned with the theme of a monstrous, 'all-devouring' (παμφάγος) consumer, and all are transmitted in the poetic collection of a single manuscript, Venice, Biblioteca Nazionale Marciana, gr. 524. This suggests that the anonymous Byzantine compiler of the collection was himself aware of and interested in the 'theatrical turn' in twelfth-century poetry.

45 An allusion to the Telchines, mythical, malevolent goblins who in secular, classicizing literature of this period are the equivalent of evil demons in hagiographical texts.

46 The group of five cities to which Sodom and Gomorrah belonged (Gen 14, 19.24–5; Wisdom 10.6).

47 See Chryssogelos (2017: 47–51).

48 Ed. Macrides (1985).

49 Macrides (1985: 158), Marciniak and Warcaba (2018). See also Lauxtermann in this volume.

Social and Cultural Context

It remains to explain this theatrical turn: why did the theatricality that had always been present in Greek poetry get a new lease of life in the twelfth century, apparently becoming more pronounced and more explicit? A large part of the answer has been anticipated at the beginning of this chapter, and, before that, in studies dating back more than thirty years. The twelfth century was more theatrical because it showcased more and better rhetorical *theatra*, because it saw the proliferation and enhancement of the venues and occasions in which *belles lettres* were performed. However, the typology of these contexts has not been systematically explored, and its different strands have not been brought together, or looked at in the light of the cultural developments that favoured a greater appreciation of drama as a mode of rhetorical discourse.

Without attempting to supply this desideratum in the depth that it merits, I shall briefly outline the contributing factors. First, we should not overlook the continuing existence of one ancient theatre that was still going strong, the Hippodrome of Constantinople: 'this theatre here, the one of recreation, with the capacity to accommodate whole cities and tribes, in which competing horses race for our delight', as Constantine Manasses described it in his *Synopsis Chronike* (2243–5).[50] Chariot racing still generated much excitement in the twelfth century, to judge from the poem that Michael Hagiotheodorites wrote to describe one race,[51] and from the fact that one popular astrologer owed his reputation to his skill in predicting the winners – surely a sign that betting took place.[52] The races, as well as the other entertainments offered in the interludes, were presumably still organized by the four popular 'colour' factions – the Blues, Greens, Whites and Reds – that comprised the performing personnel, the ancillary staff and the supporter clubs.[53] It is unlikely that the Hippodrome shows contained much in the way of verbal performance, although Choniates tells us that one charioteer in the 1180s, Zinziphitzes, was famous for the wicked wit of his satirical verse.[54] In any case, the circus factions were still an integral part of public ceremonial, traditionally responsible not only for acclaiming the emperor when he presided over the games, but also for performing songs of praise and acclamation on festive occasions

50 Ed. Lampsidis (1996). On the Hippodrome, see in general Pitarakis (2010), Dagron (2011); for theatres in late antique Constantinople, see Magdalino (2023).
51 Marciniak and Warcaba (2014).
52 Wuilleumier (1927).
53 A. Cameron (1976), Roueché (2010).
54 Choniates, *History* ed. van Dieten (1975: 315).

such as imperial coronations, weddings and triumphs.[55] It presumably fell to the factions, as well, to compose and perform the mocking verses that were sung to boo emperors in public or to accompany the shame parades of convicted criminals.[56] We cannot be sure to what extent the surviving deme-hymns from the twelfth century represent a continuity, a revival or a transformation of the genre, but one important innovation seems clear: the texts were no longer composed and delivered by the deme poets in the separate employment of the Blue and the Green factions. The authors of the twelfth-century texts wrote for both factions, and the two authors whose names we know, Theodore Prodromos and Niketas Choniates, are best known for their work in a higher intellectual register and a higher social milieu.[57] In other words, the ceremonial poetry of the circus factions was now performed by learned men who enjoyed or aspired to the patronage of the court. It is a reasonable hypothesis, on the basis of the coronation poem of 1119, that this began with Prodromos and the reign of John II.

After the Hippodrome, the next best thing to a real theatre in Constantinople was the imperial palace. In addition to being a *theatron* for the recital of ceremonial texts, it was the main refuge of the mime shows that had been the staple of theatrical entertainment in late antiquity.[58] We may also recall the evidence, from the seventh to ninth centuries, for dances and chants performed by the Blues and the Greens at imperial banquets, and for the ballet (*saximon*) performed by all the members of the court on other occasions;[59] moreover, twelfth-century texts remind us that the Byzantine imperial court, like royal courts worldwide, was a place for the exhibition of *curiosa*, like the dwarf from Chios who was brought to the Palace of Manuel I,[60] and for the risqué jokes of court jesters, like Chalivoures who went too far at one dinner of Isaac II.[61] It is thus no accident that the court of John II, who enjoyed the occasional laugh according to Choniates, gave rise to the most innovative, theatrical

55 The poets and other personnel responsible for the acclamations are mentioned in ceremonial treatises of the ninth and tenth centuries: Philotheos, ed. Oikonomides (1972: 122–5, 160–1, 326); Constantine Porphyrogennetos, *De ceremoniis* 2:44–5, 2:142–3, 3:404–5 ed. Dagron and Flusin (2020).

56 Maas (1912: 35–6), Morgan (1954); Anna Komnene, *Alexiad* 12.6.5 ed. Reinsch and Kambylis (2001: 374–5). Cf. Magdalino (2007: 67–9) and (2021: 108–14), Lauxtermann (2019: 128–33).

57 Hörandner (2003); cf. Magdalino (2016: 60–2).

58 Webb (2009), Marciniak (2014b) and (2017), Roilos (2021: 275–8).

59 *De ceremoniis* 2:150–93, 4:425–34 ed. Dagron and Flusin (2020); Magdalino (2015: 175), Pitarakis (2013: 131–8).

60 Messis and Nilsson (2015).

61 Ed. van Dieten (1975: 441–2); cf. Marciniak (2014b: 140).

and entertaining verse texts of the period, the *Ptochoprodromika*, which combined literary novelty and comic entertainment in the framework of petitions to the emperor.[62] They are remarkable not only for their experimentation with literary vernacular, but also for their elevation of slapstick comedy to a literary level. Perhaps we should think of them as the textual metaphrasis of a mime show. But however we define their textual innovation, it is important to point out that they, like the court and deme poetry of the undisguised Theodore Prodromos, appeared at a time of unprecedented change in the social environment of the imperial court. From the reign of Alexios I, the imperial palace was no longer the only *theatron* for the performance of 'royal' entertainment and ceremonial.[63] Both the titled aristocracy and the flatterers who knocked at their doors and sang their praises in return for cash received an upgrade as a result of Alexios' restructuring of the imperial hierarchy.[64] Now the princes of the extended imperial family had the status, the resources, and the residential premises to create their own self-contained cultural establishments based on their palatial households. They held audiences at which they welcomed literary accolades, both for themselves and for the antique *objets d'art* in their possession;[65] it is no accident that the three authors who offer social comment on rhetorical *theatron* write of 'frequenting the houses of the great'.[66] The Komnenian aristocracy could offer job opportunities as well as occasional patronage, and could thus compete with the imperial court to attract the services, the talents and the loyalties of men of learning. This had serious implications when the princes in question also nurtured political ambitions and intellectual pretensions, as was the case in the generation that succeeded Alexios I.[67] We know that John II felt politically threatened by his sister Anna and brother Isaac.[68] Did he also feel disadvantaged by their intellectual profile and reputation? At any rate, it is surely revealing that Theodore Prodromos, the innovatory court poet of John II, also flirted with other patrons, including both Anna and Isaac *sebastokrator*, so that at the beginning of

62 Choniates, *History* ed. van Dieten (1975: 47); see above, n. 9 and E. M. Jeffreys (2016: 112, 118–19).

63 Magdalino (1993: 180–91, 342–56).

64 For the situation immediately before Alexios, see Michael Attaleiates, *History* ed. Pérez Martín (2002: 198).

65 Lampsidis (1997).

66 Nicholas Kataphloron, ed. Loukaki (2000: 152–6); Nikephoros Basilakes, ed. Garzya (1984: 5); Michael Choniates, ed. Lampros (1879: 10).

67 Magdalino (1993: 192–5).

68 Magdalino and Nelson (1982: 128–32), Hill (2000), Magdalino (2000: 18–23) and (2016: 62–5). On Isaac as cultural patron, see Linardou (2016).

Manuel's reign he felt obliged to issue a poetic statement of denial when seeking a renewal of his contract: no, he had not opportunistically played the field; no, he had not served any other lords than the emperor's father and grandmother.[69]

If there was competition among aristocratic *theatra* to attract the best performers, there was certainly competition among men of learning to pass the test of performance, for the *theatron* did not deal kindly with failures.[70] This competitiveness can be traced to the schools of grammar and rhetoric where the aspiring literati learned their craft. As Floris Bernard has shown for the eleventh century, the classroom itself was a trainee *theatron*, where some dramatically expressive poems originated as school exercises.[71] The agonistic atmosphere reflected not only the competition between students, but also the rivalry between teachers keen to advertise the superiority of their own teaching methods and to trash the work of others. From their comments and their teaching manuals, which have survived in some abundance, it is clear that they devoted considerable effort and ingenuity to the composition of model texts exemplifying the theatrical effects that make twelfth-century poetry so eminently readable. Nikephoros Basilakes, a contemporary of Theodore Prodromos, produced a set of rhetorical exercises (*progymnasmata*) that were obviously meant to provide a lively, alternative introduction to learning the rhetorical skills of evocative composition;[72] he no doubt used them to good effect in his four long verse satires, which he consigned to the flames when he decided on an ecclesiastical career.[73] But Basilakes was also proud of his innovations in the composition of *schede*, the grammatical exercises that were the preparation for the *progymnasmata*, and he was not alone in setting great store by this type of teaching tool, which predated the long twelfth century.[74] The two star poets of the twelfth century, and of this volume, Theodore Prodromos and Constantine Manasses, wrote *schede*.[75] The dismissive comments on *schedographia* by other twelfth-century authors – Anna Komnene, John Tzetzes and Eustathios of Thessalonike – were thus effectively backhanded

69 Ed. Maiuri (1914–19); see also Prodromos' *Historical Poem* 71.92 ed. Hörandner (1974: 514–21).

70 Both Nikephoros Basilakes (ed. Garzya [1984: 5]) and Michael Choniates (ed. Lampros [1879: 13]) cite negative peer reaction as a reason not to perform in the *theatron*. Cf. Magdalino (1993: 336–8), Bourbouhakis (2010: 178–9).

71 Bernard (2014: 222–9, 253–90). Gerbi in this volume argues for a similar agonistic school context for a poem by Nicholas Kallikles.

72 Ed. and trans. Beneker and Gibson (2016).

73 Ed. Garzya (1984: 4–5).

74 Ed. Garzya (1984: 3), Agapitos (2014: 8–10 and *passim*) and (2013).

75 Agapitos (2014: 14–19) and (2015c); for Manasses, see Polemis (1996).

compliments, reflecting the ubiquity and popularity of the genre.[76] They derive from the fact that *schede* were novel, original compositions, which obliged students to learn from the teacher's inventions rather than from the classics of ancient literature. *Schedographia* was indeed the exact opposite of what was long considered to have been the besetting sin of Byzantine literary education, namely its adherence to and imitation of classical models. It was, rather, an exercise in creative writing, if only for its teachers, but some of this creativity surely rubbed off on the students.[77]

At the same time, the critics of *schedographia*, particularly Tzetzes and Eustathios, reflect another trend in twelfth-century education that demonstrably enhanced the theatricality of contemporary poetry. This was the rediscovery and revaluation of Homer as the ultimate source of all rhetorical eloquence, and the ultimate inspiration for all literary techniques.[78] I do not mean to argue that the exegesis of Tzetzes and Eustathios resulted in greater imitation of the Homeric epics. If anything, it was the other way round: their commentaries reflected the increased exploitation of epic language and style that we can already see at work in Prodromos' hexameter encomia for John II.[79] I would merely suggest that the ever-increasing popularity of the epics as school texts was an incentive to use them as models of narrative technique for oral presentation, and to quote from them for dramatic effect, comic as well as tragic.[80] More generally, the pedagogical authority of Tzetzes, and especially of Eustathios, by whom we can assume that all the important writers of the late twelfth century had been taught, increased the moral and intellectual value of ancient poetry in the eyes of the educated public. Poetry was explained as teaching by entertainment, and this applied not only to Homer, as we can deduce from an under-exploited text of Eustathios, his sermon *On Hypocrisy*. Although directed at the hypocritical monks of Thessalonike, it begins with a discourse on the meaning of *hypokrisis* that Eustathios must have formulated in his lectures to his students in Constantinople. He points out that *hypokrisis* had originally referred to the noble art of dramatic impersonation:

> There was a time when actors gained praise and renown in theatres, by adorning themselves with wisdom, which the teachers of tragedy contrived

76 Agapitos (2013), (2015b) and (2017), van den Berg (2020: 296–301), Lovato (2022).

77 See also Agapitos (2015a) and in this volume.

78 In his *Allegories of the Iliad* (ed. Boissonade; trans. Goldwyn and Kokkini [2015]), Tzetzes repeatedly refers to Homer as a master rhetorician; for Eustathios, see Pizzone (2016), van den Berg (2017: 22–8) and (2022).

79 Ed. Hörandner (1974), poems 3, 6, 8.

80 A superb example of comic use is the anonymous satire on an astrologer, ed. Zagklas (2016: 897–901).

> by reaching back to ancient stories, full of edifying lessons, and as it were resuscitating the characters involved. The dramatists made them visible through men who could, so to speak, impersonate them in acting, both by the plausibility of rhetorical fiction and by character portrayal. In their emotions and words, as if in mirrors, they directed the people who saw and heard them towards the beauty of virtue. By such imaging (or one could say impersonation, or even simulation) they evoked the teachings in books by which our own life is still regulated.
>
> So people at that time, indeed even people today, could learn from this art about the whole mutability of fortune, the diversity of human character, and the inexpressible differences in the human condition. The misfortunes of kings, as recounted by the actors' art, taught and indeed still teach that one should not assume, trusting in a lofty position in life, that one will always remain on top, but one should watch out for the downfall.[81]

Eustathios stops short of recommending a revival of the ancient theatre as an antidote to the pernicious hypocrisy of contemporary monasticism, but this is where he is pointing by saying that ancient acting – comic as well as tragic – was a virtuous pursuit whose lessons are still valid in his own day.[82] It was not difficult for him, or for his students, to make a connection between ancient tragedy and the composition of new poems about tragic events. At least one person who made the connection was Constantine Stilbes, in his tragic lament on the fire of 1197; his debt to Eustathios, in addition to Tzetzes and Prodromos, has been highlighted in the recent study of his work.[83]

We do not know where Stilbes delivered his poem and before what audience. It is tempting to think that with this performance, the connection between poetry and rhetorical *theatron* was on the point of taking off into a revival of real theatre: an institution with multiple actors and material props to amplify the verbal performance. May we conclude that here, as in other areas of cultural life, a promising development was cut short by 1204? In this case, I do not think so. It seems to me that the trend all along had been towards a greater sophistication and illusionism of virtual, verbal theatre, rather than towards a crystallization of drama into a solid material, spatial reality that catered *directly* to all the senses. Apart from the spectacle of imperial ceremonial, where dialogue, choreography and musical instruments came into play, the whole point of rhetorical *theatron* had always been to maintain and develop a theatricality of pure *logos*, in

81 Cf. van den Berg (2017). The translation is my own, but indebted to van den Berg (2017: 20).
82 Cf. Metzler (2006: 89), Roilos (2021: 264–5), van den Berg (2021: 236–7).
83 Layman (2015: 10–16).

which all the action, all the sensational and sensual effects were intellectualized and verbalized in the vocal presentation of the solo performer. Byzantine *theatron* was a performance without accompaniment and props, which dematerialized the process of representation, by sublimating all sensory communication into the conception and reception of the written, sung and spoken word. In this, twelfth-century rhetorical practice may be thought to have followed the minimalist tendencies, both of ancient Greek epic and drama (which clearly appealed to Eustathios because of its intellectualism), and of Christian preaching and liturgy, which had always privileged the sacred word and the unaccompanied human voice, even when sanctioning, though not uncontroversially, the presence of sacred images and the elaboration of liturgical music. Twelfth-century Byzantium, while continuing to give icons their due and developing polyphonic chant, experimented and invested above all in the representational power of *logos*. In this, its ultimate inspiration lay perhaps in the eloquence of the fourth-century Church Fathers, notably that scourge of the theatre John Chrysostom.[84]

Conclusion

In any case, the precedent of Chrysostom stands as a reminder that if the virtual theatre of *logos* did, counterfactually, have a real future in Constantinople on the eve of 1204, this did not necessarily lie with poetry. In conclusion, I have to go with the prevailing drift of this volume and emphasize the close, interactive, egalitarian symbiosis between poetry and prose.[85] For both the teachers and the practitioners of Byzantine literature, poetry was a subdivision of rhetoric. The great poets of antiquity were revered as master rhetoricians, and Byzantine poetry was profoundly influenced by the construction of prose rhetoric.[86] The theatrical techniques of poetry were essentially the methods taught in rhetorical handbooks, which were written in prose primarily as guides to the composition of prose orations. Prose was not only the traditional medium of classical oratory; it was also the canonical medium of philosophy, the Bible and biblical exegesis, and the most common form of dramatization: the Platonic and Lucianic dialogue. For several reasons, therefore, by 1204 the theatrical turn in Byzantine literature was no longer being led by verse, in contrast to the middle

84 Webb (2017), Lugaresi (2017).
85 See also Zagklas (2017).
86 Lauxtermann (1998).

of the century, and in spite of Constantine Stilbes and his contemporaries who wrote fine poems, such as Michael Choniates and Euthymios Tornikes.[87] Eustathios himself put his creative energy into the composition of rhythmic prose.[88] Prose was the medium favoured by Nicholas Mesarites for his highly cinematic descriptions and narrations.[89] The work that surpassed the poem of Stilbes as a combination of tragic lament and Old Testament-style incrimination, the work that said the last word on the long twelfth century, was the *History* of Niketas Choniates.

Bibliography

Afentoulidou-Leitgeb, E. (2012) 'The *Dioptra* of Philippos Monotropos: Didactic Verses or Poetry?', in *Poetry and its Contexts in Eleventh-century Byzantium*, ed. F. Bernard and K. Demoen, 181–91. Farnham.

Afentoulidou, E., and J. Fuchsbauer (2019) 'Philippos Monotropos in Byzantium and the Slavonic World', in *A Companion to Byzantine Poetry*, ed. W. Hörandner, A. Rhoby and N. Zagklas, 332–52. Brill's Companions to the Byzantine World 4. Leiden.

Agapitos, P. A. (2013) 'Anna Komnene and the Politics of Schedographic Training and Colloquial Discourse', *Nea Rhome* 10: 89–107.

(2014) 'Grammar, Genre and Patronage in the Twelfth Century: A Scientific Paradigm and its Implications', *JÖByz* 64: 1–22.

(2015a) 'Learning to Read and Write a *schedos*: The Verse Dictionary of Par. gr. 400', in *Pour une poétique de Byzance: Hommage à Vassilis Katsaros*, ed. S. Efthymiadis, C. Messis, P. Odorico and I. Polemis, 11–28. Dossiers byzantins 16. Paris.

(2015b) 'Literary *Haute Cuisine* and its Dangers: Eustathios of Thessalonike on Schedography and Everyday Language', *DOP* 69: 225–41.

(2015c) 'New Genres in the Twelfth Century: The *Schedourgia* of Theodore Prodromos', *MEG* 15: 1–41.

(2017) 'John Tzetzes and the Blemish Examiners: A Byzantine Teacher on Schedography, Everyday Language and Writerly Disposition', *MEG* 17: 1–57.

Alexiou, M. (1999) 'Ploys of Performance: Games and Play in the Ptochoprodromic Poems', *DOP* 53: 91–109.

Bekker, I. (ed.) (1842), 'Die Theogonie des Johannes Tzetzes aus der Bibliotheca Casanatensis', *Abhandlungen der königlichen Akademie der Wissenschaften zu Berlin aus dem Jahr 1840: philosophische und historische Klasse*: 147–69.

87 Zagklas (2019: 249–51)
88 Bourbouhakis (2017).
89 Daskas (2012), Macrides (2019).

Beneker, J., and C. A. Gibson (ed. and trans.) (2016) *The Rhetorical Exercises of Nikephoros Basilakes: Progymnasmata from Twelfth-Century Byzantium.* Dumbarton Oaks Medieval Library 43. Cambridge, MA.

Bernard, F. (2014) *Writing and Reading Byzantine Secular Poetry, 1025–1081.* Oxford.

Boissonade, J. F. (ed.) (1851) *Tzetzae allegoriae Iliadis accedunt Pselli allegoriae.* Paris (repr. Hildesheim 1967).

Bourbouhakis, E. C. (2007) '"Political" Personae: The Poem from Prison of Michael Glykas: Byzantine Literature between Fact and Fiction', *BMGS* 31.1: 53–75.

(2010) 'Rhetoric and Performance', in *The Byzantine World*, ed. P. Stephenson, 175–87. Abingdon.

(2017) *Not Composed in a Chance Manner: The Epitaphios for Manuel I Komnenos by Eustathios of Thessalonike.* Studia Byzantina Upsaliensia 18. Uppsala.

Cameron, A. (1976) *Circus Factions.* Oxford.

Cameron, A. M. (ed.) (1976) *Flavius Cresconius Corippus, In laudem Iustini minoris libri quattuor.* London.

Chryssogelos, K. (ed.) (2017) *Κωσταντίνου Μανασσῆ Ὁδοιπορικόν.* Athens.

Conca, F. (ed.) (1990) *Nicetas Eugenianus, De Drosillae et Chariclis amoribus.* Amsterdam.

Dagron, G. (2011) *L'hippodrome de Constantinople: Jeux, people et politique.* Paris.

Dagron, G., and B. Flusin (eds.) (2020) *Constantin VII Porphyrogénète: Le Livre des cérémonies*, 4 vols. Paris.

Daskas, B. (2012) 'Images de la ville impériale dans les ἐκφραστικαὶ διηγήσεις de Nicolas Mésaritès: Le *Récit sur la révolution du Palais*', in *Villes de toute beauté: L'ekphrasis des cités dans les littératures byzantine et byzantino-slave*, ed. P. Odorico and C. Messis, 135–48. Dossiers byzantins 12. Paris.

De Stefani, C. (ed.) (2011) *Paulus Silentiarius, Descriptio Sanctae Sophiae, Descripto ambonis.* Berlin.

Diethart, J., and W. Hörandner (eds.) (2005) *Constantinus Stilbes, Poemata.* Munich.

Eideneier, H. (ed.) (1991) *Ptochoprodromos.* Neograeca Medii Aevi 5. Cologne.

Garzya, A. (ed.) (1984) *Nicephori Basilacae orationes et epistulae.* Leipzig.

Gautier, P. (ed.) (1980) *Théophylacte d'Achrida: Discours, traités, poesies.* Thessalonike.

Gaul, N. (2018) 'Performative Reading in the Late Byzantine *theatron*', in *Reading in the Byzantine Empire and Beyond*, ed. T. Shawcross and I. Toth, 215–33. Cambridge.

Goldwyn, A. J., and D. Kokkini (2015) *John Tzetzes: Allegories of the Iliad.* Dumbarton Oaks Medieval Library 37. Cambridge, MA.

Hill, B. (2000) 'Actions Speak Louder than Words: Anna Komnene's Attempted Usurpation', in *Anna Komnene and her Times*, ed. T. Gouma-Peterson, 45–62. New York.

Hörandner, W. (ed.) (1974) *Theodoros Prodromos: Historische Gedichte.* Wiener Byzantinistische Studien 11. Vienna.

(2003) 'Court Poetry: Questions of Motifs, Structure and Function', in *Rhetoric in Byzantium: Papers from the Thirty-Fifth Spring Symposium of Byzantine Studies, University of Oxford, March 2001*, ed. E. M. Jeffreys, 75–85. Society for the Promotion of Byzantine Studies Publications 11. Aldershot.

(ed.) (2017) 'Dichtungen des Euthymios Tornikes in Cod. Gr. 508 der Rumänischen Akademie', in *Facettes de la littérature byzantine: Contributions choisies*, 91–140. Paris.

Horna, K. (ed.) (1903) 'Die Epigramme des Theodoros Balsamon', *WS* 25: 165–217.

Hunger, H. (ed.) (1968) *Der byzantinische Katz-Mäuse-Krieg. Theodoros Prodromos, Katomyomachia: Einleitung, Text und Übersetzung*. Graz.

Janssen, M. C., and M. D. Lauxtermann (2018) 'Authorship Revisited: Language and Metre in the *Ptochodromika*', in *Reading in the Byzantine Empire and Beyond*, ed. T. Shawcross and I. Toth, 558–84. Cambridge.

Jeffreys, E. M. (2011–12) 'The *Sebastokratorissa* Irene as Patron', in *Female Founders in Byzantium and Beyond*, ed. L. Theis, M. Mullett and M. Grünbart, with G. Fingarova and M. Savage, 177–94. Wiener Jahrbuch für Kunstgeschichte 60–1. Vienna.

(2016) 'Literary Trends in the Constantinopolitan Courts in the 1120s and 1130s', in *John II Komnenos, Emperor of Byzantium: In the Shadow of Father and Son*, ed. A. Bucossi and A. Rodriguez Suarez, 110–20. Abingdon.

(2019) 'Byzantine Poetry and Rhetoric', in *A Companion to Byzantine Poetry*, ed. W. Hörandner, A. Rhoby and N. Zagklas, 92–112. Brill's Companions to the Byzantine World 4. Leiden.

Jeffreys, M. J. (2003) '"Rhetorical" texts', in *Rhetoric in Byzantium: Papers from the Thirty-Fifth Spring Symposium of Byzantine Studies, University of Oxford, March 2001*, ed. E. M. Jeffreys, 87–100. Society for the Promotion of Byzantine Studies Publications 11. Aldershot.

(2019) 'From Hexameters to Fifteen-Syllable Verse', in *A Companion to Byzantine Poetry*, ed. W. Hörandner, A. Rhoby and N. Zagklas, 66–91. Brill's Companions to the Byzantine World 4. Leiden.

Kucharski, J., and P. Marciniak (2017) 'The Beard and its Philosopher: Theodore Prodromos on the Philosopher's Beard in Byzantium', *BMGS* 41.1: 45–54.

Lampros, S. P. (ed.) (1879) *Μιχαὴλ Ἀκομινάτου τοῦ Χωνιάτου τὰ σωζόμενα*. Athens (repr. Groningen 1968).

(ed.) (1911) 'Ὁ Μαρκιανὸς κώδιξ 524', *Νέος Ἑλληνομνήμων* 8: 3–59, 113–92.

Lampsidis, O. (ed.) (1996) *Constantini Manassis Breviarium Chronicum*. Corpus Fontium Historiae Byzantinae 36. Athens.

(1997) 'Die Entblössung der Muse Kalliope in einem byzantinischen Epigramm', *JÖByz* 47: 107–10.

Lauxtermann, M. D. (1998) 'The Velocity of Pure Iambs: Byzantine Observations on the Metre and Rhythm of the Dodecasyllable', *JÖByz* 48: 9–33.

(2019) *Byzantine Poetry from Pisides to Geometres: Texts and Contexts*, vol. 2. Wiener Byzantinistische Studien 24/2. Vienna.

Layman, T. (2015) *'The Incineration of New Babylon': The Fire Poem of Konstantinos Stilbes*. Geneva.

Leone, P. L. M. (ed.) ([1968] 2007) *Ioannis Tzetzae Historiae*. Galatina.

(ed.) (2019) *Ioannis Tzetzae Theogonia*. Lecce.

Linardou, K. (2016) 'Imperial Impersonations: Disguised Portraits of a Komnenian Prince and his Father', in *John II Komnenos, Emperor of Byzantium: In the Shadow of Father and Son*, ed. A. Bucossi and A. Rodriguez Suarez, 155–82. Abingdon.

Livanos, C. (2006) 'Michael Choniates, Poet of Love and Knowledge', *BMGS* 30.2: 103–14.

Loukaki, M. (ed.) (2000) 'Τυμβώρυχοι και σκυλευτές νεκρών: Οι απόψεις του Νικολάου Καταφλῶρον για τη ρητορική και τους ρήτορες στη Κωνσταντινούπολη του 12ου αιώνα', *Byzantina Symmeikta* 14: 143–66.

Lovato, V. F. (2022). 'Odysseus the Schedographer', in *Byzantine Commentaries on Ancient Greek Texts, 12th–15th Centuries*, ed. B. van den Berg, D. Manolova and P. Marciniak, 148–68. Cambridge.

Lugaresi, L. (2017) 'Rhetoric against the Theatre and Theatre by Means of Rhetoric in John Chrysostom', in *Rhetorical Strategies in Late Antique Literature: Images, Metatexts and Interpretation*, ed. A. Quiroga Puertas, 117–48. Leiden.

Maas, P. (1912) 'Metrische Akklamationen der Byzantiner', *ByzZ* 21.1: 28–51.

Macrides, R. (1985) 'Poetic Justice in the Patriarchate: Murder and Cannibalism in the Provinces', in *Cupido Legum*, ed. L. Burgmann, M. T. Fögen and A. Schminck, 137–68. Frankfurt am Main. Reprinted in Macrides (1999), no. XI.

(1999) *Kinship and Justice in Byzantium, 11th–15th Centuries*. Aldershot.

(2019) 'The Logos of Nicholas Mesarites', in *The Holy Apostles: A Lost Monument, a Forgotten Project and the Presentness of the Past*, ed. M. Mullett and R. Ousterhout, 175–91. Washington, DC.

Macrides, R., and P. Magdalino (1988) 'The Architecture of *ekphrasis*: Construction and Context of Paul the Silentiary's Poem on Hagia Sophia', *BMGS* 12.1: 47–82.

(1992) 'The Fourth Kingdom and the Rhetoric of Hellenism', in *The Perception of the Past in Twelfth-Century Europe*, ed. P. Magdalino, 117–56. London.

Magdalino, P. (1988) 'The Bath of Leo the Wise and the "Macedonian Renaissance" Revisited: Topography, Iconography, Ceremonial, Ideology', *DOP* 42: 97–118.

(1993) *The Empire of Manuel I Komnenos, 1143–1180*. Cambridge.

(1997) 'In Search of the Byzantine Courtier: Leo Choirosphaktes and Constantine Manasses', in *Byzantine Court Culture from 829 to 1204*, ed. H. Maguire, 141–65. Washington, DC.

(2000) 'The Pen of the Aunt: Echoes of the Mid-Twelfth Century in the *Alexiad*', in *Anna Komnene and her Times*, ed. T. Gouma-Peterson, 15–43. New York.

(2007) 'Tourner en dérision à Byzance', in *La dérision au Moyen Âge*, ed. É. Crouzet-Pavan and J. Verger, 55–72. Paris.

(2012) 'Cultural Change? The Context of Byzantine Poetry from Geometres to Prodromos', in *Poetry and its Contexts in Eleventh-Century Byzantium*, ed. F. Bernard and K. Demoen, 19–36. Farnham.

(2015) 'The People and the Palace', in *The Emperor's House: Palaces from Augustus to the Age of Absolutism*, ed. M. Featherstone, J.-M. Spieser, G. Tanman and U. Wulf-Rheidt, 169–78. Berlin.

(2016) 'The Triumph of 1133', in *John II Komnenos, Emperor of Byzantium: In the Shadow of Father and Son*, ed. A. Bucossi and A. Rodriguez Suarez, 53–70. Abingdon.

(2021) 'Political Satire', in *Satire in the Middle Byzantine Period: The Golden Age of Laughter?*, ed. P. Marciniak and I. Nilsson, 104–26. Explorations in Medieval Culture 12. Leiden.

(2023) 'The Theatre of Byzantion-Constantinople', *Anekdota Byzantina: Studien zur byzantinischen Geschichte und Kultur. Festschrift für Albrecht Berger anlässlich seines 65. Geburtstags*, ed. I. Grimm-Stadelmann, A. Riehle, R. Tocci and M. M. Vuĉetić, 427–33. Byzantinisches Archiv 46. Berlin.

Magdalino, P., and R. Macrides (2022) 'Theodore Prodromos, *Carmina Historica*, I: Translation and Commentary', in *After the Text: Enquiries in Honour of Margaret Mullett*, ed. L. James, O. Nicholson and R. Scott, 29–40. London.

Magdalino, P., and R. Nelson (1982) 'The Emperor in Byzantine Art of the Twelfth Century', *ByzF* 8: 123–83.

Maiuri, A. (ed.) (1914–19) 'Una nova poesia di Teodoro Prodromo in Greco volgare', *ByzZ* 23.1: 397–407.

Marciniak, P. (2014a) 'The Byzantine Performative Turn', in *Within the Circle of Ancient Ideas and Virtues: Studies in Honour of Professor Maria Dzielska*, ed. K. Twardowska, M. Salamon, S. Sprawski, M. Stachura and S. Turlej, 423–30. Krakow.

(2014b) 'How to Entertain the Byzantines: Some Remarks on Mimes and Jesters in Byzantium', in *Medieval and Early Modern Performance in the Eastern Mediterranean*, ed. A. Öztürkmen and E. B. Vitz, 125–48. Turnhout.

(2017) 'Laughter on Display: Mimic Performances and the Danger of Laughing in Byzantium', in *Greek Laughter and Tears: Antiquity and After*, ed. M. Alexiou and D. Cairns, 232–42. Edinburgh.

(2015) 'Prodromos, Aristophanes and a Lustful Woman: A Byzantine Satire by Theodore Prodromos', *ByzSlav* 73: 23–34.

Marciniak, P., and K. Warcaba (2014) 'Racing with Rhetoric: A Byzantine Ekphrasis of a Chariot Race', *ByzZ* 107.1: 97–112.

(2018) 'Theodore Prodromos' *Katomyomachia* as a Byzantine Version of Mock Epic', in *Middle Byzantine Poetry: Texts and Contexts*, ed. A. Rhoby and N. Zagklas, 97–110. Byzantios: Studies in Byzantine History and Civilization 14. Turnhout.

Marcovich, M. (1992) *Theodori Prodromi, De Rhodanthes et Dosiklis amoribus libri IX*. Stuttgart.

Mazal, O. (1967) *Der Roman des Konstantinos Manasses*. Vienna.
Messis, C., and I. Nilsson (2015) 'Constantin Manassès, La description d'un petit homme', *JÖByz* 65: 169–94.
Metzler, K. (2006) *Eustathios von Thessalonike und das Mönchtum: Untersuchungen und Kommentar zur Schrift De emendanda vita monachica*. Berlin.
Morgan, G. (1954) 'A Byzantine Satirical Song', *ByzZ* 47.2: 292–7.
Mullett, M. (1984) 'Aristocracy and Patronage in the Literary Circles of Comnenian Constantinople', in *The Byzantine Aristocracy, IX–XIII Centuries*, ed. M. Angold, 173–201. Oxford.
(2006) 'Novelisation in Byzantium: Narrative after the Revival of Fiction', in *Byzantine Narrative: Papers in Honour of Roger Scott*, ed. J. Burke, 1–28. Melbourne.
(2010) 'No Drama, No Poetry, No Fiction, No Readership, No Literature', in *A Companion to Byzantium*, ed. L. James, 227–38. Chichester.
(2022) 'Painting and Polyphony: The *Christos Paschon* as Commentary', *Byzantine Commentaries on Ancient Greek Texts, 12th–15th Centuries*, ed. B. van den Berg, D. Manolova and P. Marciniak, 214–39. Cambridge.
Nilsson, I. (2008) 'Discovering Literariness in the Past: Literature vs. History in the *Synopsis Chronike* of Konstantinos Manasses', in *L'écriture de la mémoire: La littérarité de l'historiographie*, ed. P. Odorico, P. A. Agapitos and M. Hinterberger, 15–31. Dossiers byzantins 6. Paris.
(2014) *Raconter Byzance: La littérature au XIIe siècle*. Paris.
(2019) 'The Past as Poetry: Two Byzantine World Chronicles in Verse', in *A Companion to Byzantine Poetry*, ed. W. Hörandner, A. Rhoby and N. Zagklas, 517–38. Brill's Companions to the Byzantine World 4. Leiden.
(2020) *Writer and Occasion in Twelfth-Century Byzantium: The Authorial Voice of Constantine Manasses*. Cambridge.
Nilsson, I., and E. Nyström (2009) 'To Compose, Read and Use a Byzantine Text: Aspects of the Chronicle of Constantine Manasses', *BMGS* 33.1: 42–60.
Oikonomides, N. (ed.) (1972) *Les listes de préséance byzantines des IXe et Xe siècles*. Paris.
Papadopoulos-Kerameus, A. (ed.) ([1913] 1976) *Noctes Petropolitanae*. St. Petersburg.
Papaioannou, S. (2010) 'The Aesthetics of History: From Theophanes to Eustathios', in *History as Literature in Byzantium*, ed. R. Macrides, 3–21. Farnham.
Pérez Martín, I. (ed.) (2002) *Miguel Ataliates, Historia*. Madrid.
Pitarakis, B. (2013) 'From the Hippodrome to the Reception Halls of the Great Palace: Acclamations and Dances in the Service of Imperial Ideology', in *The Byzantine Court: Source of Power and Culture*, ed. A. Ödekan, N. Necipoğlu and E. Akyürek, 129–38. Istanbul.
(ed.) (2010) *The Hippodrome/Atmeydanı: A Stage for Istanbul's History*. Istanbul.
Pizzone, A. (2016) 'Audiences and Emotions in Eustathios of Thessalonike's Commentaries on Homer', *DOP* 70: 225–41.

(2017) 'The *Historiai* of John Tzetzes: A Byzantine "Book of Memory"?', *BMGS* 41.2: 182–207.

Polemis, I. (1996) 'Fünf unedierte Texte des Konstantinos Manasses', *RSBN* 33: 279–92.

Reinsch, D. R. (2008) 'Historia ancilla litterarum? Zum literarischen Geschmack in der Komnenenzeit: Das Beispiel der Σύνοψις Χρονική des Konstantinos Manasses', *L'écriture de la mémoire: la littérarité de l'historiographie*, ed. P. Odorico, P. A. Agapitos and M. Hinterberger, 81–94. Dossiers byzantins 6. Paris.

Reinsch, D. R., and A. Kambylis (eds.) (2001) *Annae Comnenae Alexias*. Corpus Fontium Historiae Byzantinae 40. Berlin.

Rhoby, A. (2003) *Reminiszenzen an antike Stätten in der mittel- und spätbyzantinischen Literatur: Eine Untersuchung zur Antikenrezeption in Byzanz*. Göttingen.

(2010) 'Zur Identifizierung von bekannten Autoren im Codex Marcianus Graecus 524', *MEG* 10: 167–204.

Roilos, P. (2021) 'Satirical Modulations in 12th-Century Greek Literature', in *Satire in the Middle Byzantine Period: The Golden Age of Laughter?*, ed. P. Marciniak and I. Nilsson, 254–78. Explorations in Medieval Culture 12. Leiden.

Romano, R. (ed.) (1980) *Nicola Callicle: Carmi. Testo critico, introduzione, traduzione, commentario e lessico*. Byzantina et Neo-Hellenica Neapolitana 8. Naples.

(1999) *La satira bizantina dei secoli XI–XV: Il patriota, Caridemo, Timarione, Cristoforo di Mitilene, Michele Psello, Teodoro Prodromo, Carmi ptocoprodromici, Michele Haplucheir, Giovanni Catrara, Mazaris, La messa del glabro, Sinassario del venerabile asino*. Turin.

Roueché, C. (2010) 'The Factions and Entertainment', in Pitarakis (2010), 50–64.

Spingou, F. (2014) 'The Anonymous Poets of the *Anthologia Marciana*: Questions of Collection and Authorship', in *The Author in Middle Byzantine Literature*, ed. A. Pizzone, 139–53. Boston.

Strano, G. (ed.) (2012) *Nicola Muzalone: Carme apologetico. Introduzione, testo critico, traduzione e note*. La Gorgona 3. Rome.

Tsolakis, E. T. (ed.) (1959) *Μιχαηλ Γλυκας: Στίχοι οὓς ἔγραψε καθ᾽ ὅν κατεσχέθη καιρόν*. Thessalonike.

Tuilier, A. (ed.) *La passion du Christ: Tragédie de Grégoire de Nazianze*. Paris.

van den Berg, B. (2017) '"The Excellent Man Lies Sometimes": Eustathios of Thessalonike on Good Hypocrisy, Praiseworthy Falsehood, and Rhetorical Plausibility in Ancient Poetry', *Scandinavian Journal of Byzantine and Modern Greek Studies* 3: 15–35.

(2020) 'John Tzetzes as Didactic Poet and Learned Grammarian', *DOP* 74: 285–302.

(2021) 'Playwright, Satirist, Atticist: The Reception of Aristophanes in 12th-Century Byzantium', in *Satire in the Middle Byzantine Period: The Golden Age of Laughter?*, ed. P. Marciniak and I. Nilsson, 227–53. Explorations in Medieval Culture 12. Leiden.

(2022) *Homer the Rhetorician: Eustathios of Thessalonike on the Composition of the Iliad.* Oxford.

van Dieten, J. L. (1975) *Nicetae Choniatae historia.* Corpus Fontium Historiae Byzantinae 11. Berlin.

Webb, R. (2009) *Demons and Dancers: Performance in Late Antiquity.* Cambridge, MA.

(2017) 'Virtual Sensations and Inner Visions: Words and the Senses in Late Antiquity and Byzantium', in *Knowing Bodies, Passionate Souls: Sense Perceptions in Byzantium*, ed. S. Ashbrook Harvey and M. Mullett, 261–9. Washington, DC.

Whitby, M. (1985) 'The Occasion of Paul the Silentiary's *ekphrasis* of St Sophia', *CQ* 35: 215–28.

Wuilleumier, P. (1927) 'Cirque et astrologie', *Mélanges d'archéologie et d'histoire de l'École française de Rome* 44: 184–209.

Zagklas, N. (ed.) (2016) 'Astrology, Piety and Poverty: Seven Anonymous Poems in Vaticanus gr. 743', *ByzZ* 109.2: 895–918.

(2017) 'Experimenting with Prose and Verse in Twelfth-Century Byzantium: A Preliminary Study', *DOP* 71: 229–48.

(2018) 'Metrical *Polyeideia* and Generic Innovation in Twelfth-Century Poetry: Multimetric Poetic Cycles of Occasional Poetry', in *Middle and Late Byzantine Poetry: Texts and Contexts*, ed. A. Rhoby and N. Zagklas, 43–70. Byzantios: Studies in Byzantine History and Civilization 14. Turnhout.

(2021) 'Satire in the Komnenian Period: Poetry, Satirical Strands and Intellectual Antagonism', in *Satire in the Middle Byzantine Period: The Golden Age of Laughter?*, ed. P Marciniak and I. Nilsson, 270–303. Explorations in Medieval Culture 12. Leiden.

CHAPTER 3

*Rethinking the Mixed Style in Twelfth-Century Poetry**

Markéta Kulhánková

Intense exploration of the literature of the twelfth century has borne fruit. We now know a great deal about the prominent status of poetry, literary experiments with both prose and verse, and the restoration of ancient genres and forms. We have started to better understand the phenomenon of schedography and appreciate the performativity of literature produced during this period. One still relatively obscure issue is the penetration of vernacular language into the literature of this period,[1] represented chiefly by the *Ptochoprodromika*,[2] a well-known and much-discussed collection of four (or five) supplicatory humorous poems;[3] the *Verses from Prison* by Michael Glykas;[4] and partly also the heroic poem *Digenis Akritis*,[5] although the situation with this work is even more complicated due to, above all, the unknown relationship between the known (later) versions and the original (lost) poem.

The aim of this chapter is to revisit scholarly opinions on the principles and functions of the switching between language registers in these works and to reconsider the issue from a narratological point of view.[6] I will explore whether we can determine certain principles for the changes in language levels that are more specific than the commonly mentioned vague distinction between 'more popular' and 'more learned'. I will suggest that

* This study is a result of the project 'A Narratological Commentary on the Byzantine Epos *Digenis Akritis*' funded by the Czech Science Foundation (19-05387S).

1 For a useful socio-linguistic approach to Byzantine diglossia and register variation, see Toufexis (2008).

2 Ed. Eideneier (1991); cf. also the revised version of both the edition and the introduction (in Greek) in Eideneier (2012), and the older edition by Hesseling and Pernot (1910).

3 Sometimes, and for good reasons, the so-called *Maiuri Poem* (ed. Maiuri ([1919]) is also attached to the *Ptochoprodromika*; cf. Eideneier (1991: 34–7), Hörandner (1993), Janssen and Lauxtermann (2018).

4 Ed. Tsolakis (1959).

5 Ed. Jeffreys (1998); see also the editions by Trapp (1971) and S. Alexiou (2006).

6 In addition to classical narratological concepts, chiefly those of Genette ([1972] 1980) and Bal (2009), I also draw on contemporary, post-classical approaches, especially of diachronic or medieval narratology; cf. Fludernik (2003) and especially von Contzen (2014).

there are chiefly two principles influencing the choice between the lower and higher registers: one is the narrative distance of the speaking voice from the narrated events, and the other is the deliberate use of different types of discourse.

Ptochoprodromika: Characteristics and Language

Fierce debates about the *Ptochoprodromika*, focusing especially on the authorship of the collection, took place during the last quarter of the twentieth century and then fell silent towards the turn of the millennium since neither the defenders nor opponents of Theodore Prodromos' authorship were able to propose persuasive direct evidence. Therefore, while the majority of scholars have, based on indirect evidence and more or less intuitively, tended to accept Prodromos' authorship, many of Hans Eideneier's arguments against it have never been convincingly rejected.[7] Of the numerous studies dedicated to the analysis of the *Ptochoprodromika*, I would like to recall here the analysis of the fourth poem[8] by Roderick Beaton, who suggested that the vernacular literary works of the twelfth century have to be read and perceived within the frame of Byzantine rhetoric and proposed seeing them as satirical rhetorical exercises; thus he considered the fourth poem a humorous rendering of the two most popular types of *progymnasmata*: the *ethopoiia* and the *enkomion*.[9] In other words, Beaton suggested that the speaking voice of the poem is nothing more than a literary persona, an aspect that Emmanuel Bourbouhakis further elaborated in his analysis of Glykas' *Verses from Prison*.[10]

The invitation to read and appreciate these works within the context of Byzantine rhetoric expressed by Beaton and Bourbouhakis largely concurs with Panagiotis Agapitos' recent attempt to put the *Ptochoprodromika* more properly within the literary context of the period. Agapitos directed attention to Prodromos' schedographic works and discovered noteworthy parallels with the *Ptochoprodromika*, especially in the combination of vernacular and learned language features, the humorous and moralizing character, the experimentation with literary forms and the predilection for forming various types of literary series or sequels.[11] Since all these features

7 E.g. the objections against Prodromos' authorship of the *Maiuri Poem*. For an overview of the scholarly discussions, see Kulhánková (2021a).

8 Numbering follows Eideneier (1991).

9 Beaton (1990); cf. also Beaton (1987).

10 Bourbouhakis (2007).

11 Agapitos (2015: 20); see also Agapitos (2014).

and techniques emerge in the context of school education, Agapitos calls them a 'teacherly style'.[12]

The language of the *Ptochoprodromika* is often labelled as a 'mixed' style. However, it is worth recalling that this term can refer to two quite different phenomena. First, it has been used for the combination of modern and conservative linguistic features which creates the vernacular parts of the poems,[13] and, second, the same term can indicate the shifting between this lower language register and a higher one within a single poem.[14] As Maria Karyolemou showed, the mixing of vernacular and archaizing features is more or less typical for all Byzantine literature. Karyolemou further argued that 'very often what differentiates two literary texts is not the presence of a classic/vernacular feature in one text as compared to the absence of the very same feature in another, but rather the frequency of use of each feature in each text'.[15] In the *Ptochoprodromika*, some archaizing and some vernacular features can be found throughout the poems in their entirety, but still, the tendency towards a more learned and more vernacular language respectively in some passages is perceptible enough. The explanation, however, that learned language is reserved for the proems and epilogues and the vernacular for the poems' cores is too simplistic,[16] and similarly simplistic and vague is Hans Eideneier's statement that the popular ('volkstümlich') scenes make use of the vernacular, while the non-popular passages use standard learned written language ('übliche gelehrte Schriftkoine').[17]

The most serious attempt so far at a complex insight into the collection's language has been Geoffrey Horrocks' brief exposition in his substantial survey of the history of the Greek language.[18] Horrocks, however, deals with the *Ptochoprodromika* within a chapter dedicated to the development of Byzantine spoken language, and thus takes into consideration only the 'vernacular' poems' cores. He assumes that in these parts 'the language [...] is based predominantly on the speech of the educated aristocracy, a variety

12 Agapitos (2015: 33). See also Marciniak and Warcaba (2018), who uncovered in Prodromos' *Katomyomachia* a similar manner of combining features of different genres and discourses to that which can be found in vernacular works.

13 Horrocks (2010: 341–2).

14 Eideneier (1991: 26).

15 Karyolemou (2014: 43–4); cf. also Trapp (1993). For the difficulty in making a clear distinction between the low and high registers, see also Toufexis (2008: 213–15): 'H and L represent two extreme points of a continuum'. For an account of some conservative linguistic features of the *Ptochoprodromika*, see Janssen and Lauxtermann (2018: 570).

16 Cf. e.g. Toufexis (2008: 216–17).

17 Eideneier (1991: 26).

18 See below for the new analysis of some linguistic peculiarities by Janssen and Lauxtermann (2018). For the overview of older studies, see ibid., p. 565, n. 31.

which is sometimes deliberately distorted in the mouths of the would-be upwardly mobile, and supplemented for comic effect with items of everyday vocabulary and urban slang or the very formal language of the court'.[19] Panagiotis Agapitos is more cautious regarding the relationship between the so-called vernacular language and the contemporary language spoken in the streets. He labels the register a 'poetic idiom' and a 'crafted style fitted for ambitious literary compositions'.[20] However, what Agapitos presents as opposite to this language level as a 'very good specimen of colloquial discourse',[21] a legal document full of orthographical mistakes and obviously both written and dictated by a person with very limited education, is still a testimony composed as a written text and as such necessarily influenced by the – although possibly limited – ideas of both the witness and the scribe about what a written legal document should look like. In my view, this text with a series of datives, infinitives, participial constructions and dependent clauses can be hardly considered a more authentic sample of colloquial discourse than what we read in the *Ptochoprodromika* or Glykas' verses.[22] That the idiom of the poems is indeed poetic and cannot be put on the same level as spoken language is beyond any doubt, but it is equally likely that it is based on contemporary spoken language.[23] I therefore concur with Martin Hinterberger's suggestion that spoken language ('demotic', as Hinterberger calls it) was initially used in literary texts to render direct speech and it gradually developed into the literary so-called vernacular, whereas the *Ptochoprodromika* 'mark a transitional period where the vernacular slowly transcends the confines of direct discourse'.[24] Furthermore, to the *Ptochoprodromika* we surely cannot wholly apply what Agapitos stated regarding Prodromos' *schede*, namely that the switching between the two language registers is 'fluid and unmarked'.[25]

19 Horrocks (2010: 338).
20 Agapitos (2015: 37).
21 Agapitos (2015: 38).
22 For the exposition of how little these language features correspond with the contemporary spoken language, see now the respective chapters in Holton et al. (2019).
23 Cf. also Hinterberger (2018: 40–1).
24 Hinterberger (2006: 8–9). Cf. Hinterberger (1993: 452) and (2016: 139–41); see also Trapp (1993: 117), who suggested that 'vernacular tendencies ... can be due to vivid narration, quotation of original sayings, or satiric intention'. A suitable parallel, after some simplification, is to be found in Greek literature some 700 years later, when vernacular language (*dimotiki*) penetrated into literary texts starting with direct discourse and followed by narrative passages, while the archaizing *katharevousa* was preserved longest in descriptions. However, concerning the relationship between spoken language and the written low register, see also Toufexis (2008), who explains why the parallel with the modern Greek diglossia is only partly fitting.
25 Agapitos (2015: 10).

My intention is to pursue the analysis of the switching of language registers more thoroughly. I will not offer a detailed linguistic treatment of the language of the *Ptochoprodromika*, however useful this would be,[26] and although especially now, when the long-awaited monumental *Cambridge Grammar of Medieval and Early Modern Greek* offers an excellent tool to describe more precisely the phonetic, morphological and syntactic specifics of a particular text,[27] such a task is no longer impossible. My ambition is much more modest: to suggest that there is a narrative-internal logic behind switching registers.

Switching Registers: Introductory Remarks

For a closer parallel to the register switching in the *Ptochoprodromika* let us first turn to a later literary work, namely the *Entertaining Tale of Quadrupeds*. Nick Nicholas and George Baloglou, in their introductory study to the English translation of this vernacular allegorical poem from the fourteenth century, suggested that the use of particular language registers in this work is influenced by the type of voice (direct speech – narration). They observed that the narrative parts are written in a 'more conventional discourse', which they explained as being due to the fact that 'the narrative voice needs to be distanced from the invective and vulgarity of the animals'.[28] At the same time, they pointed out that the narrative of the battle in the closing part of the poem is in language 'as straightforward as in the disputation', a fact they explained by the demands of the 'action-packed struggle'.[29] Influenced by these observations, Hans Eideneier in his last paper on the *Ptochoprodromika* undertook a quick analysis of the first poem and stated that the shifting of language registers here works on the same principle and that the internal dialogues fall into the same category of more vernacular language as direct speech.[30]

Nicholas and Baloglou used as criteria for distinguishing the higher register from the lower three distinct features: (1) the classical construction of the genitive absolute, (2) the dative and (3) adjectival participles

26 Recently, Marjolijne Janssen and Marc Lauxtermann have made first steps towards such an analysis with their study of one particular language phenomenon (conditional clauses) and one metrical phenomenon (synizesis and hiatus). They have indicated some differences in *Ptoch.* 4 and thus reopened the question of different authors for different poems: see Janssen and Lauxtermann (2018).

27 Holton et al. (2019).

28 Nicholas and Baloglou (2003: 119).

29 Nicholas and Baloglou (2003: 120).

30 Eideneier (2007: 65–6); cf. Horrocks (2010: 341–2).

of the active and passive aorist. Traditionally, the usage of the particle νά with subjunctive was considered a main sign of the vernacular.[31] With the support of the *Cambridge Grammar* and the recent study on some aspects of the language and metre of the *Ptochoprodromika* by Marjolijne Janssen and Marc Lauxtermann,[32] it is now possible to refine the criteria of the distinction between the 'learned' and the 'vernacular' passages in the poems.

I have chosen one or two features of each part of grammar which are, in my view, distinct enough to be perceptible for an audience of the period. Starting with phonology, the tendency to avoid hiatus by synizesis can be considered as one such feature. In his recent survey of the metre of Byzantine poetry, Marc Lauxtermann showed that synizesis is extremely rare in learned poetry.[33] In his particular study of synizesis and hiatus in the *Ptochoprodromika*, Lauxtermann does not comment on differences between the learned and the vernacular sections.[34] A closer look at this phenomenon proves that there is indeed hardly any synizesis in the prooimia and high-style passages of *Ptoch.* 1, 3 and 4,[35] and synizesis thus can be indeed considered the first distinct feature of the vernacular.[36]

Of the morphological and morphosyntactic features, the use of archaic possessive adjectives instead of weak forms of the genitive of the personal pronouns can be used as a distinct sign of more learned style,[37] and the privileging of the analytic future and subjunctive (νὰ + subjunctive and other analytic forms) over the synthetic as a sign of the opposite tendency.[38]

For the syntactic features, Nicholas and Baloglou can be followed in two of their three points: the use of the classical construction of the genitive absolute and the dative (both for nouns and pronouns) is characteristic of the passages in higher register. On the other hand, preference for parataxis instead of hypotaxis is one of the long-recognized signs of the vernacular. On the contrary, inflected participles and infinitives are used in the

31 Hinterberger (2006: 6–7).

32 Janssen and Lauxtermann (2018).

33 Lauxtermann (2019: 293).

34 Janssen and Lauxtermann (2018: 580–3; see esp. fig. 25.1).

35 Lauxtermann went through the first 100 verses of *Ptoch.* 1, where the first synizesis occurs in v. 28, after the end of the learned prooimion. For poems 3 and 4, he started counting from verses 56 and 38 respectively, after the prooimion. In my inquiry I have neglected *Ptoch.* 2 and the *Maiuri Poem*, where the prooimia are very short and the switches less clear, which would make the survey less convincing.

36 Cf. Holton et al. (2019: 98–110).

37 *Ptoch* 1.3: τὰς σὰς λαμπρὰς εὐεργεσίας; *Ptoch* 2.5: πρὸς τὸν ἐμὸν δεσπότην; *Ptoch.* 3.5: τῆς σῆς ἀνακτορίας. Cf. Holton et al. (2019: 914).

38 Cf. the chapter on morphosyntax in Holton et al. (2019: 1767–1857).

Ptochoprodromika in both lower and higher registers and either might have still been in use in spoken language at that time,[39] or maybe were one of the archaic specifics of the particular work.[40]

Although from a linguist's point of view these criteria may seem insufficiently scientific, I believe that for the purposes of narratological rather than linguistic analysis and for the sake of clarity this brief list of distinct features may suffice.

The Voices of *Ptochoprodromika*

Let us now turn to the narratological section. I will enlarge the list of the types of voice and consider, apart from direct speech (including internal monologues) and narration, also metanarrative, a type of voice which includes the narrator's remarks and comments regarding the story, the discourse and the process of narration and comprises a significant part of the poems (almost one fourth of the first poem and more than one third of the third).[41] In addition to the *Ptochoprodromika*, I will also briefly discuss the other contemporary poetic works where changing of language registers has been noted: Michael Glykas' *Verses from Prison* and both basic versions of the poem *Digenis Akritis*: the Grottaferrata and Escorial versions.

Let us have a closer look at the aforementioned three types of voice. Direct speech, which is frequent in the *Ptochoprodromika*, can be classified in most cases as vernacular/low register. This includes not only standard direct speech,[42] but also typical examples such as the hero's internal monologue from the first poem:

1 Διὰ τὴν ψυχήν σου, Πρόδρομε, καθίζου σιγηρός σου,
ὅσα κἂν λέγῃ βάσταζε καὶ φέρε τα γενναίως·
ἂν πλήξῃς γὰρ καὶ δώσῃς την πολλάκις νὰ πονέσῃ,
ὡς εἶσαι γέρων καὶ κοντὸς καὶ ὡσὰν ἀδυνατίζεις,
ἴσως νὰ ἁπλώσῃ ἐπάνω σου καὶ νὰ σὲ σύρῃ ἐμπρός της,
καὶ ἂν τύχῃ καὶ ἀποδείρῃ σε, νὰ σὲ ἐξεσφοντυλίσῃ. (*Ptochoprodromika* 1.158–63)

39 Cf. Horrocks (2010: 298, 341).
40 The same is also true in the case of e.g. the old active aorist imperative in -ον; cf. *Ptoch.* 1.14: ἄκουσον ἅπερ ὁ τάλας γράφω (learned passage) and 1.195: κατάλειψον τὴν δύναμιν (vernacular passage).
41 For the theoretical narratological background, see Genette ([1972] 1980: 161–268), von Contzen (2014: 184) and, specifically for the last category, Nünning (2004).
42 E.g. 1.193–7 and 3.164–5.

Prodromos, sit and hush, for thine soul's sake,
whatev'r she says endure and bravely bear,
if you shall strike and give her only pain,
yourself now aged and withered, short of breath,
against you she may rush and pull you close,
and she might flay you red and break thy neck.[43]

This extract contains several synizeses (καὶ ὡσὰν, νὰ ἁπλώσῃ, καὶ ἂν, καὶ ἀποδείρῃ, σὲ ἐξεσφοντυλίσῃ), weak forms of personal nouns (σου, την, σου, σέ) and exclusively analytic subjunctives (νὰ πονέσῃ, νὰ ἁπλώσῃ, νὰ σὲ σύρῃ, νὰ σὲ ἐξεσφοντυλίσῃ). On the other hand, no archaic features – possessive adjectives, synthetic future or subjunctive or genitive absolutes – occur. It is noteworthy that more or less the same register is also found in some narrative passages, such as:

2 Ἡ δὲ τὰς ἀποκρίσεις μου μὴ καταδεχομένη,
στήκει, τριχομαδίζεται, δέρει τὰ μάγουλά της·
συνάγει τὰ παιδία της, ἀπαίρει καὶ τὴν ρόκαν,
ἐμβαίνει εἰς τὸ κουβούκλιν της, κλείει σφικτὴν τὴν θύραν,
μουλλώνεται καὶ κρύπτεται, ἐμὲ δ' ἀφήνει ἔξω. (*Ptochoprodromika* 1.123–7)

Of my responses she accepted none,
she stands, she tears her hair, she claws her cheeks,
she gathers kids and takes the distaff out,
she enters in her room, locks sturdy door,
hiding, mute as a mule, she keeps me out.

The syntax is simple, paratactic, with no datives or absolute genitives; possessive adjectives are replaced by the weak form of genitive of personal nouns (τὰς ἀποκρίσεις μου, τὰ μάγουλά της, τὰ παιδία της, τὸ κουβούκλιν της); the first hemistich of verse 126 has to be read with synizesis to sustain the metre.[44]

43 This study deals with the language and style rather than with the content of the poems. I do not believe it is possible, at least in the present state of research, to represent the Greek properly in English translation. I have therefore decided to provide, instead of a standard philological translation, which would not contribute noticeably to my argument, an experimental poetic translation in blank verse that, on occasion, tries to emulate the shifts in register by freely mixing both archaic and modern English. The author of the translation is my dear colleague, classical philologist Juraj Franek, to whom I am immensely grateful that he found the time and energy to get to grips with the peculiar Byzantine language and its poetic ploys. We both hope that the reader will receive this small literary experiment kindly, as 'condiments' (as our hero would express it).

44 Cf. similar style in 3.120–7.

On the other hand, other narrative passages bear many characteristic features of the high register, as can be seen in the next example:

3 Ἀσχολουμένων τοιγαροῦν τῶν γυναικῶν καὶ πάντων
τῶν συνελθόντων ἐπ' αὐτῷ, ὡς φθάσας εἶπον ἄνω,
τοῦ βρέφους τῷ συμπτώματι καὶ τοῦ παιδὸς τῷ πάθει,
κρυπτῶς ἀπῆρα τὸ κλειδὶν καὶ ἤνοιξα τὸ ἀρμάριν·
φαγὼν εὐθύς τε καὶ πιὼν καὶ κορεσθεὶς ἐξαίφνης,
ἐξῆλθον ἔξωθεν κἀγὼ θρηνῶν σὺν τοῖς ἑτέροις. (*Ptochoprodromika* 1.213–18)

When women then and all those standing there
were engaged, as I mentioned just above,
with the babe's mishap, with the child's distress,
in secret, key I took, breached pantry's door.
I ate, I drank, got stuffed with no delay,
and went out joining others in lament.

In the second hemistich of verse 216 we find two hiatus which have to be pronounced if the metre is to be kept properly; moreover, there is a large construction with the genitive absolute (Ἀσχολουμένων τῶν γυναικῶν καὶ πάντων τῶν συνελθόντων) and two constructions with the dative (τοῦ βρέφους τῷ συμπτώματι καὶ τοῦ παιδὸς τῷ πάθει; σὺν τοῖς ἑτέροις).[45] I would like to suggest that the difference between examples 2 and 3 may lie in the use of present-tense vs past-tense narration. The hero, who is simultaneously the narrator,[46] uses a series of present tenses describing a *scene*: a passage of a narrative where events are told in great detail and the time of narration comes close to the real-time duration of the particular event.[47] The narrator-hero here submerges more into the narrated world than is the case with past-tense narration, and he presents himself, in that specific moment, more as a hero than as a narrator.[48]

The stylistic level of the metanarrative passages is similarly varied. Even within the proems, traditionally regarded as using high style, we encounter

45 Cf. stylistically similar passages: 3.255–63 and 4.625–32.

46 On the concept of narrator and its relation to the heroes in medieval literature, see von Contzen (2018).

47 There is abundant narratological literature on the present tense used in narrative. On this type of a series of presents describing an action, see, most illustratively, Fleischman (1990: 23–6 and 149–50), who calls this device visualizing present tense, and Fludernik (1991) and (1992). For a detailed account of the modern theory, see Philippowski (2018). This so-called mimetic present tense occurs frequently in the E version of *Digenis Akritis*, but is not to be found in the G version; see Dzurillová and Kulhánková (2022: 377–80).

48 Similarly, in the narrative of the battle in the *Entertaining Tale of Quadrupeds*, the present tense prevails over the past tense: see verses 1016ff. in Nicholas and Baloglou (2003).

both higher (example 4, see esp. the way the infinitive in verse 6 is substantivized and the generally more elevated syntax) and lower (example 5, see the analytic subjunctives) registers:

4 Πρό τινος ἤδη πρὸ καιροῦ καὶ πρὸ βραχέος χρόνου
οὐκ εἶχον οὖν ὁ δύστηνος τὸ τί προσαγαγεῖν σοι
κατάλληλον τῷ κράτει σου καὶ τῇ χρηστότητί σου
καὶ τῇ περηφανείᾳ σου καὶ χαριτότητί σου,
εἰ μή τινας πολιτικοὺς ἀμέτρους πάλιν στίχους,
συνεσταλμένους, παίζοντας, ἀλλ' οὐκ ἀναισχυντῶντας,
παίζουσι γὰρ καὶ γέροντες, ἀλλὰ σωφρονεστέρως.
(*Ptochoprodromika* 1.5–11)

It's been some time ago, not long before,
that poor old me had naught to offer you,
to match thy might and heart both good and kind,
and equal your noblesse and state of grace,
if not – again – some verses out of step,
political, low, playful, but not mean,
for greybeards, they play too, but wisely so.

5 καὶ κρεῖσσον εἶχον, δέσποτα, τὸ νὰ μὲ θάψουν ζῶντα
καὶ νὰ μὲ βάλουν εἰς τὴν γῆν καὶ νὰ μὲ περιχώσουν,
παρὰ νὰ μάθῃ τίποτε τῶν ἄρτι γραφομένων.
(*Ptochoprodromika* 1.30–2)

O Lord, they'd better bury me alive,
and lay me into earth and close the grave,
rather than she finds out what I just wrote.

The proems of the *Ptochoprodromika* have been much discussed, but usually separately from the poems' cores and not as an organic part of the poems with an important and specific narrative function.[49] However, as Margaret Alexiou noted, the structure of the *Ptochoprodromika* is deliberately 'episodic and discursive' and the poems are kept together and formed into an autonomous literary unit mainly by those passages Alexiou called 'transitional sections', precisely what is called metanarrative in narratology.[50] In other words, the proems are the most prominent – but by far not the only – metanarrative passages, comprising a substantial part of the poems, and their importance for our understanding of the poems is crucial. The cardinal function of the

49 See, symptomatically, Reinsch (2001).
50 Cf. M. Alexiou (1999: 95–102).

poems' metanarrative passages is, as Alexiou recognized, organizational, but they perform a wide range of other functions, referring to the story, the discourse and the process of narration. Many of the metanarrative passages in the *Ptochoprodromika* are oriented to the factual audience outside the literary text, as they contain a direct address to the emperor (or other sponsor).[51] I believe that a similar tendency to that which I suggested above for the narrative parts can be observed here: the more extra-diegetic and digressive a metanarrative passage is, the higher its language level is, as can be seen in example 4. In contrast, brief story-oriented comments that approach the diegetic level are often in the same lower register as standard narrative and direct speech passages. The two following excerpts can be compared. Example 6 in lower style, with the colloquial question τί μὲ λέγεις; consists of only one verse and the narration continues immediately, whereas in example 7 the first verse, with exactly the same meaning, but in higher register and the more learned variant of both the verb and the pronoun in dative, is followed by a short series of encomiastic verses, and thus the whole passage recedes significantly from the diegetic level:

6 Τὴν κεφαλήν σου, βασιλεῦ, πρὸς τοῦτο, τί μὲ λέγεις;
(*Ptochoprodromika* 3.108)

By heaven, King, what do you say to this?

7 Σὺ δὲ πρὸς τοῦτο, βασιλεῦ, τί μοι διακελεύεις;
Ἐλπίζω εἰς τὸ κράτος σου, ἵνα με ἐλεήσῃς,
καὶ πάλιν ἐκκλησιαστικὸς διάκονος νὰ γένω,
νὰ εὔχωμαι τὰ σκῆπτρα σου μέσης ἀπὸ καρδίας
σκῆπτρα κρατῆσαι κραταιῶς γῆς πάσης καὶ θαλάσσης.
(*Ptochoprodromika* 3.217–21)

What counsel, King, you give me as to this?
I trust your regal state to show me grace,
and once more make me deacon of the Church.
Your sceptres I shall praise in heart of hearts,
all-ruling sceptres, lords of land and sea.

Moving forward to the second factor influencing the choice of register, I would like to pay attention to parody. There have been several attempts to

51 For a discussion of the character of the metanarrative and a thorough classification of metanarrative comments, see Nünning (2003).

identify parody in the *Ptochoprodromika*. One of the passages that invite a parodic interpretation is the narrative about the combat of the hero-narrator with his wife (1.115–97), which most probably draws on an epic narrative scheme, turning it to parody by replacing a wild animal with the hero's wife.[52] Another type of parody can be found in imitations of the speech of various characters, as demonstrated by Geoffrey Horrocks:[53] one example is the shifts in vocabulary and morphology in *Ptochoprodromika* 3.56–77, the passage where a father exhorts his son to study by trying to upgrade his own language (at the beginning and end of this passage, he elevates his style notably, while in the central part the speaker slips into the lower register); another is 1.251–2, where the hero disguises himself as a begging monk of apparently Slavic origin. In all these passages the language register imitates the register of the object of parody.

Not everywhere is parody easily discernible and provable. An example of a shift to a higher register which could be motivated by a parodic intention is 1.206–22, the passage in which Roderick Beaton saw such a strong thematic link with Prodromos' genuine works, the novel *Rhodanthe and Dosikles* and the short dramatic parody *Battle of Cat and Mice* (*Katomyomachia*), that he used it as one of his arguments for identifying the author of the *Ptochoprodromika* as Theodore Prodromos.[54] Although Beaton interprets all the three passages in a somewhat misleading way and the affinity is, in my view, not close enough to be used as an argument for Prodromos' authorship, the style is indeed significantly elevated in comparison to the previous and following sections of the poem and probably could be seen, if not as parody, at least as an imitation of the high register used in contemporary learned literature.[55]

I have argued elsewhere that the main literary feature of the *Ptochoprodromika* lies in its play with various discourses.[56] I have identified four main discourses: laudatory, supplicatory, satiric and parodic. Parodic discourse, as we have seen, comprises elements of different styles: the epic, the learned and the spoken language. Like Prodromos' *schede* or his *Katomyomachia*, the *Ptochoprodromika* are an intentional amusing puzzle of genres

52 Cf. *Digenis Akritis* G, 4.112–45 ed. Jeffreys (1998). Margaret Alexiou (1999: 97) speaks about 'parodic treatment of the twin Byzantine concepts of heroism and warfare', while Elizabeth Jeffreys (2014: 147) sees in this passage a direct 'misogynic parody of Digenes' fight with a wild beast in his adolescent *aristeia*'. My own suggestion is slightly different: I do not consider the passage from the *Ptochoprodromika* necessarily a parody of this exact passage from *Digenis*, but a parodic use of a widespread epic schema: cf. Kulhánková (2021b).

53 Cf. Horrocks (2010: 342).

54 Beaton (1987: 24–5). On the *Katomyomachia*, see Lauxtermann in this volume.

55 Cf. e.g. 1.206 (Τοῦ γοῦν ἡλίου πρὸς δυσμὰς μέλλοντος ἤδη κλῖναι), with quite frequent passages describing the sunset in *Rhodanthe and Dosikles* ed. Marcovich (1992: 1.1–2, 1.86, 6.1–2, 7.72).

56 Kulhánková (2021a).

and discourses, which includes shifts in the language levels that are not haphazard but function according to a recognizable logic.

Glykas' *Verses from Prison* and *Digenis Akritis*

Let us now prove the suggestion about intended and well-motivated shifting of language register by turning briefly to the other two literary works connected with the 'diglossia' of the Komnenian period. What we find in Glykas' *Verses from Prison* is quite close to what we have just observed in the *Ptochoprodromika*. We can basically distinguish the hero-narrator's voice, which sometimes slips into an internal monologue (the addressee changes from the reader or listener to the narrator himself), direct speech and quotations. There are two basic categories of quotations and paraphrases, the language register of which corresponds to the respective sources: the language of biblical quotations and paraphrases is biblical,[57] while the passages quoting or paraphrasing folk proverbs are written in the low register.[58] Similarly, a distinguishably lower register is used in the last section of the poem, where direct speech is delivered by an anonymous voice (520–37, 574–81), while the language of the hero-narrator (both when he speaks to the addressee and during his internal monologue) could be characterized as middle register with the occasional use of vernacular elements. It is thus one more illustration of the process which Hinterberger has described as the use of demotic Greek to render direct speech (or quotation in this case) slowly transgressing these boundaries.[59] Glykas' use of the various registers is not as sophisticated as what we have seen in the *Ptochoprodromika*, but it goes in the same direction. It is worth noting that the changes in register are not as frequent and elaborated in all the poems of the *Ptochoprodromika* as they are in the examples we have seen above, mostly from the first and third poems. In the fourth poem, the shifts are rare and not as distinct (but it is important to mention that nearly the entire poem is in the present tense; the past-tense narration is limited to a few cases, one of them the aforementioned passage 4.625–32). Both the second poem of the *Ptochoprodromika* and the *Maiuri Poem* are closer to Agapitos' notion of the 'fluid and unmarked' mixture of various linguistic registers.[60]

57 See the list in Tsolakis (1959: 23–5).
58 See the list in Politis (1898).
59 Hinterberger (2006).
60 Agapitos (2015: 10). See e.g. 2.1–12.

A slightly different example of the same tendency is offered by *Digenis Akritis*. Martin Hinterberger has pointed to a linguistic differentiation between the direct speech and narrative passages in the G version of the *Digenis* poem.[61] A closer look at the G version proves Hinterberger's suggestion, although the differences in the language level of direct speech, narration and metanarrative are not as distinct as in the *Ptochoprodromika*: no stylistic differences between present-tense and past-tense narration emerge because the mimetic historical present tense in a scene is not used at all,[62] the genitive absolutes occur in both narrative passages and direct speech, the style of the metanarrative passages does not vary, and the narrative passages and the fifth and sixth books consisting of Digenis' first-person narration do not differ in language level from the other books. However, there are some less striking details that indeed prove that there is at least a slight tendency to differentiate direct speech from narrative passages: Hinterberger mentioned the copula ἔνι, but there is also vernacular vocabulary which occurs exclusively in direct discourse,[63] and the conjunctive or future formed with the particle να occurs predominantly in direct speech (only 5 of 47 occurrences are in narrative sections, and none in the metanarrative).

Roderick Beaton suggested that the lost original version of *Digenis* had the same fluctuation among different registers as the other early vernacular texts and that the editor of the different versions set out to regularize the original text into another style.[64] Geoffrey Horrocks showed that there occurs a blending of vernacular and learned elements in version E. In brief, he suggested that the passages which draw upon literary tradition, such as the well-known invocation of Eros (E 702–22), are composed in an obviously higher language register than those which originated from the oral epic songs.[65] Both of these suggestions would match quite well with the principle of discourses changing according to the source or object of imitation, as we have observed in the *Ptochoprodromika* and the *Verses from Prison*.

61 Hinterberger (2006: 9): 'This phenomenon we also observe in the Grottaferrata version of the *Digenis* poem where demotic features are concentrated in passages consisting of direct speech [...]. I don't see any differentiation of this kind in the later and purely vernacular Escorial version.'

62 The present tense used in the narration of *Digenis* G is the so-called diegetic present tense used as an optional replacement for the narrative aorist, i.e. within a series of verbs in the past tense there occurs one verb in the present tense which highlights a narrative turn. On the contrary, the passages of the *Ptochoprodromika* with the register shift have a series of actions narrated in the present tense in a scene, the so-called mimetic present tense, a device that does not occur in the G version of *Digenis* but is frequent in the E version; see Dzurillová and Kulhánková (2022).

63 E.g. κύρης 4.284, 442, 594; κύρκας 2.131, 4.439, 6.105; ψυχίτζα 2.129, 4.626, 778, 808; εὐγενικόπουλα 2.198 – cf. *Ptoch*. 4.467.

64 Beaton (1996: 48).

65 Horrocks (2010: 334). On the oral background of Byzantine popular poetry, see also Jeffreys and Jeffreys (1986).

Conclusion

I have argued for a twofold logic behind switching between or combining two language registers. The first principle can be described as follows: the smaller the narrative distance between the narrator and the narrated world, the closer his speech is to the speech of the characters. It is not a rule, only a tendency, but in some texts (especially *Ptochoprodromika* 1 and 3) it is quite clearly discernible. The other principle is the adaption of the language level to a pattern or source, for various purposes. The simplest is the mere imitation of the style of a particular text or discourse, another is the preservation of the prescripts of a rhetorical form or a genre, and yet another is the more sophisticated use of a language register associated with the object of a parody.

Adapting the language level and style of speech to a speaking character to different degrees according the narrative distance (direct speech – free indirect speech – indirect speech) is a phenomenon well known in modern literatures and familiar to narratologists,[66] and the same holds for the adaption of the language for the sake of imitation or parody.[67] Today, as in the Byzantine literature of the twelfth century, the technique can be more or less conscious and more or less elaborated.[68] However, if we bear in mind that combining features of different genres and discourses is also a favourite technique of Theodore Prodromos, as in his *schede* and *Katomyomachia*, the sophisticated play with shifting language levels we have observed especially in the first and third poems of the *Ptochoprodromika* is yet another argument for Prodromos' authorship of these peculiar poems, or at least some of them.[69]

Bibliography

Agapitos, P. A. (2014) 'Grammar, Genre and Patronage in the Twelfth Century: A Scientific Paradigm and its Implications', *JÖByz* 64: 1–22.

(2015) 'New Genres in the Twelfth Century: The *Schedourgia* of Theodore Prodromos', *MEG* 15: 1–41.

Alexiou, M. (1999) 'Ploys of Performance: Games and Play in the Ptochoprodromic Poems', *DOP* 53: 91–109.

66 Cf. Genette ([1972] 1980: 161–268), Bal (2009: 48–71) or Cohn (1978).

67 E.g. one of the most popular modern literary works for narratologists, Joyce's *Ulysses*, is a puzzle of different styles and linguistic registers.

68 But hardly fully unconscious as Hans Eideneier (1968: 9) wanted to see it.

69 The question of different authors for different poems of the *Ptochoprodromika* was recently raised again by Janssen and Lauxtermann (2018). They claim that there are some hints that the fourth poem could be a work of a different author from the remaining four (including the *Maiuri Poem*).

Alexiou, S. (ed.) (2006) *Βασίλειος Διγενής Ακρίτης (κατά το χειρόγραφο του Εσκοριάλ) και το άσμα του Αρμούρη*, 3rd ed. Athens.

Bal, M. (2009) *Narratology: Introduction to the Theory of Narrative*, 3rd ed. Toronto.

Beaton, R. (1987) 'The Rhetoric of Poverty: The Lives and Opinions of Theodore Prodromos', *BMGS* 11.1: 1–28.

(1990) 'Πτωχοπροδρομικά Γ: η ηθοποιία του άτακτου μοναχού', in *Μνήμη Σταμάτη Καρατζά: ερευνητικά προβλήματα νεοελληνικής φιλολογίας και γλωσσολογίας*, ed. A. Kechaglia-Lipouri and T. Petridis, 101–7. Thessalonike.

(1996) *The Medieval Greek Romance*, 2nd ed. London.

Bourbouhakis, E. C. (2007) '"Political" Personae: The Poem from Prison of Michael Glykas: Byzantine Literature between Fact and Fiction', *BMGS* 31.1: 53–75.

Cohn, D. (1978) *Transparent Minds: Narrative Modes for Presenting Consciousness in Fiction*. Princeton.

Dzurillová, Z., and M. Kulhánková (2022) 'The Historical Present in the Grottaferrata and Escorial Versions of Digenis Akritis: A Narratological Insight', *GRBS* 62: 365–84.

Eideneier, H. (1968) 'Zur Sprache des Michael Glykas', *ByzZ* 61.1: 5–9.

Eideneier, H. (ed.) (1991) *Ptochoprodromos: Einführung, kritische Ausgabe, deutsche Übersetzung, Glossar*. Neograeca Medii Aevi 5. Cologne.

(2007) 'Tou Ptochoprodromou', in *Byzantinische Sprachkunst*, ed. M. Hinterberger and E. Schiffer, 56–76. Berlin.

(ed.) (2012) *Πτωχοπρόδρομος: Κριτική έκδοση*. Heraklion.

Fleischman, Z. (1990) *Tense and Narrativity: From Medieval Performance to Modern Fiction*. Austin.

Fludernik, M. (1991) 'The Historical Present Tense Yet Again: Tense Switching and Narrative Dynamics in Oral and Quasi-Oral Storytelling', *Text* 11: 365–98.

Fludernik, M. (1992) 'The Historical Present Tense in English Literature: An Oral Pattern and its Literary Adaptation', *Language and Literature* 17: 77–107.

(2003) 'The Diachronization of Narratology', *Narrative* 11: 331–48.

Genette, G. ([1972] 1980) *Narrative Discourse: An Essay in Method,* trans. J. E. Lewin; foreword by J. Culler. Ithaca, NY.

Hesseling, D. C., and H. Pernot (eds.) (1910) *Poèmes prodromiques en grec vulgaire*. Amsterdam.

Hinterberger, M. (1993) Review of Eideneier's Ptochoprodromos, *JÖByz* 43: 451–4.

(2006) 'How Should We Define Vernacular Literature?', in *Unlocking the Potential of Texts: Interdisciplinary Perspectives on Medieval Greek*. Cambridge (https://www.mmll.cam.ac.uk/files/hinterberger.pdf).

(2016) 'Bemerkungen zur Sprache der Choniates-Metaphrase', in *Ὡς ἀθύρματα παῖδας: Festschrift für Hans Eideneier*, ed. U. Moennig, 135–55. Berlin.

Holton, D., G. Horrocks, T. Lendari, I. Manolessou and N. Toufexis (2019) *The Cambridge Grammar of Medieval and Early Modern Greek*. Cambridge.

Hörandner, W. (1993) 'Autor oder Genus? Diskussionsbeiträge zur "Prodromischen Frage" aus gegebenem Anlass', *ByzSlav* 54: 314–24.

Horrocks, G. (2010) *Greek: A History of the Language and its Speakers*, 2nd ed. London.

Janssen, M. C., and M. D. Lauxtermann (2018) 'Authorship Revisited: Language and Metre in the *Ptochoprodromika*', in *Reading in the Byzantine Empire and Beyond*, ed. T. Shawcross and I. Toth, 558–84. Cambridge.

Jeffreys, E. M. (ed.) (1998) *Digenis Akritis: The Grottaferrata and Escorial Versions.* Cambridge Medieval Classics 7. Cambridge.

(2014) 'The Afterlife of *Digenes Akrites*', in *Medieval Greek Storytelling: Fictionality and Narrative in Byzantium*, ed. P. Roilos, 141–61. Mainzer Veröffentlichungen zur Byzantinistik 12. Wiesbaden.

Jeffreys, E. M., and M. J. Jeffreys (1986) 'The Oral Background of Byzantine Popular Poetry', *Oral Tradition* 1: 504–47.

Karyolemou, M. (2014) 'What Can Sociolinguistics Tell Us about Learned Literary Languages?', in *The Language of Byzantine Learned Literature*, ed. M. Hinterberger, 34–51. Turnhout.

Kulhánková, M. (2021a) '"For Old Men Too Can Play, Albeit More Wisely So": The Game of Discourses in the *Ptochoprodromika*', in *Satire in the Middle Byzantine Period: The Golden Age of Laughter?*, ed. P. Marciniak and I. Nilsson, 304–23. Explorations in Medieval Culture 12. Leiden.

(2021b) 'Narrative Coherence in *Digenes Akrites* (G)', *BMGS* 45.2: 184–98.

Maiuri, A. (1919) 'Una nuova poesia di Theodoro Prodromo in greco volgare', *ByzZ* 23.1: 397–407.

Marciniak, P., and K. Warcaba (2018) 'Theodore Prodromos' *Katomyomachia* as a Byzantine Version of Mock-Heroic Epic', in *Middle and Late Byzantine Poetry: Texts and Contexts*, ed. A. Rhoby and N. Zagklas, 97–110. Byzantios: Studies in Byzantine History and Civilization 14. Turnhout.

Marcovich, M. (ed.) (1992) *Theodori Prodromi de Rhodanthes et Dosiclis amoribus libri ix*. Stuttgart.

Nicholas, N., and G. Baloglou (2003) *An Entertaining Tale of Quadrupeds: Translation and Commentary.* New York.

Nünning, A. (2004) 'Towards a Definition, a Typology and an Outline of the Functions of Metanarrative Commentary', in *The Dynamics of Narrative Form: Studies in Anglo-American Narratology*, ed. J. Pier, 11–57. Berlin.

Philippowski, K. (2018) 'Die deiktische Poetik des Präsens, oder: Wie das "jetzt" ein "hier" erschafft', in *Narratologie und mittelalterliches Erzählen*, ed. E. von Contzen and F. Kragl, 165–92. Berlin.

Politis, N. G. (1898) 'Δηώδεις παροιμίαι ἐν τοῖς Στίχοις τοῦ Μιχαὴλ Γλυκᾶ', *ByzZ* 7.1: 138–65.

Reinsch, D. R. (2001) 'Zu den Prooimia von (Ptocho-)Prodromos III und IV', *JÖByz* 51: 215–23.

Toufexis, N. (2008) 'Diglossia and Register Variation in Medieval Greek', *BMGS* 32.2: 203–17.

Trapp, E. (ed.) (1971) *Digenes Akrites: Synoptische Ausgabe der ältesten Versionen*. Wiener Byzantinistische Studien 8. Vienna.
(1993) 'Learned and Vernacular Literature in Byzantium: Dichotomy or Symbiosis?', *DOP* 47: 115–29.
Tsolakis, E. T. (ed.) (1959) *Μιχαὴλ Γλυκᾶς: Στίχοι οὓς ἔγραψε καθ' ὃν κατεσχέθη καιρόν*. Thessalonike.
von Contzen, E. (2014) 'Saints' Lives as Narrative Art? Towards a Pragma-Narratological Approach to the *Scottish Legendary*', in *Linguistics and Literary Studies: Interfaces, Encounters, Transfers*, ed. M. Fludernik and D. Jacob, 171–97. Berlin.
(2018) 'Narrative and Experience in Medieval Literature', in *Narratologie und mittelalterliches Erzählen*, ed. E. von Contzen and F. Kragl, 61–79. Berlin.

CHAPTER 4

'Wishing to Imitate the Poet' Prose and the Study of Ancient Poetry in the Twelfth Century

Emmanuel C. Bourbouhakis

I began my presentation at the conference which occasioned this volume with something of a confession of trespassing in a neighbouring field, or more precisely, a neighbouring *form*. After all, I had come to a gathering dedicated to poetry intending to talk about prose. I admitted that I had no insights to share about the nature of twelfth-century poetry *per se*. Instead, I hoped to draw on what I regard as the comparative advantage of poetry specialists in matters of close formal analysis and a general alertness to what the late and much missed Hayden White memorably called *the content of the form*.[1] I thus begged the indulgence of the audience and expressed the hope that I would not been seen as encroaching. To underline why a discussion of prose might be especially apt at such a conference, I offered the fact that what is arguably the single-most significant study of Medieval Greek prose form had come from the desk of the now late Wolfram Hörandner, the doyen of the study of Byzantine verse and in many ways the intellectual patron saint of this conference. I was referring, of course, to his seminal monograph, *Der Prosarhythmus in der rhetorischen Literatur der Byzantiner*.[2] Not having seen its equal in the study of prose in the interim, it made sense to come to a gathering of his many colleagues devoted to poetry in search of ideas. For even if we routinely segregate discussion of poetic and prose texts for what seem like good professional reasons, I remain unconvinced that such a partition accurately reflects Byzantine literary culture.[3]

Perhaps the most compelling reason for wishing to take part in a conference dedicated to poetry in the 'long' twelfth century was the opportunity to hear from colleagues accustomed to linking form to function and sense

1 White (1987).
2 Hörandner (1981).
3 Bernard (2014: 56) has made the point well: 'Byzantines only rarely divided the domain of *logoi* into prose and poetry, and even where they did the difference between the two is merely a question of form, with no further-reaching consequences.'

to structure. I do not think it would be unjust to the otherwise compelling studies of various Medieval Greek prose genres and individual texts to admit that when compared with poetry, the study of Byzantine prose poetics lags considerably behind. To illustrate this, I asked the audience to try to imagine convening an analogous conference entitled 'Prose in the Long Twelfth Century'. The implausibility of such a hypothesis speaks to the incommensurate perception of the two forms. While the one is deemed unmistakably the product of artifice, the other is widely assumed to be the default mode of verbal communication, akin to a natural state of language. No one, I think, would have trouble identifying which is which here.

Like everything else to do with language, this, too, has a long and complex history which we cannot recapitulate here. Suffice it to say that little about prose is 'natural', or at any rate more natural than verse. None of us are born speaking 'prose' and we only do so after sustained formal training. Prose had to be 'invented', to use Simon Goldhill's term, no less than poetry did.[4] This was recognized throughout Greco-Roman antiquity, which is credited with having fostered, then amplified, an art of prose, bequeathed and further elaborated by successors to this tradition, including the later Roman society of Byzantium, which continued to apply the lessons of antiquity in matters of language. And like their ancient forebears, highly literate Byzantines defined prose as the absence of metre, not the absence of art. It is with this in mind that Ingela Nilsson has made the point with reference to the once maligned twelfth-century versified chronicle *Synopsis Chronike* of Manasses that verse alone is not what makes a text 'literary' or 'poetic'.[5]

But whereas poetry *qua* metrically patterned expression suffices to bring together analyses of otherwise vastly different texts, prose has never served as a common formal attribute binding various Medieval Greek texts across genres. Things were not always thus, of course. A product of both occasional or ceremonial oratory and the many proliferating genres of written λόγος in antiquity, prose was regarded for most of history, and certainly in the period spanning from Greco-Roman times down to Byzantium, as a form of exacting and effective verbal artistry. True, its effectiveness, at times, derived precisely from its ability to disguise or distract from its own design. But both ancient and Byzantine authors and audiences of prose genres remained attuned to the artfulness of the form and could, as a result of their education, analyse it relatively independent of specific content.

4 Goldhill (2002).
5 Nilsson (2006).

The schools of rhetoric that emerged after the fifth century BC and became near-synonymous with advanced Greek education well into the Byzantine period taught proficiency in prose as a *learned* skill, in both senses of the word. Rhetorical instruction was premised on a view of prose as something achieved. Eventually, this joint Greco-Roman legacy was not only bequeathed to speakers of both Greek and Latin, but adapted to the vernaculars that gradually displaced Latin in much of Western Europe. It was not until the renunciation of 'rhetoric' as a curricular subject in many European and North American schools and universities after the nineteenth century, a shift which coincided with an avowed naturalism in literature, that a vocabulary to profile the formal design of prose receded from view, and along with it a widespread recognition of its inherent artfulness. Needless to say, writers continued to pay close attention to the many elements which went into creating a prose style. In English alone, in a little more than half a century, prose was marked by such striking variety as that displayed by Henry James, Virginia Woolf, James Joyce, William Faulkner and Ernest Hemingway. I mention this by way of offering some much-needed backstory to our inattention to prose form over and above the *index graecitatis* found in the appendices of critical editions.

To begin with, we must resist the tendency to regard prose texts in the various registers, but especially those in the uppermost reaches of the language, as an unvariegated mass. I know of no systematic argument that Byzantine prose did not undergo historical development from, say, the sixth to the sixteenth centuries; or that Greek prose did not manifest notable variety of styles, even within broad registers, as is sometimes assumed but almost never precisely articulated. Experience teaches us that, like any complex form of expression, prose over the course of the 'long' twelfth century could not remain unchanged over long periods, and not in spite of the pronounced cultural imperative of *mimesis* but precisely because ever new ways had to be found in order to accomplish the long-standing directive by authors in competition with one another to emulate authoritative models of artful expression.

Without wishing to discount either the scale or significance of twelfth-century verse, whose relative neglect this volume rightly seeks to redress, I would nevertheless venture that the arena with the highest formal stakes in this period was prose, if for no other reason than that it was the medium most closely associated with prestige genres, be it ceremonial addresses at the imperial court, occasional tributes such as *epitaphioi* or *monodiai*, or informal performances at élite-sponsored *theatra*.

The unprecedented prominence, then, of ancient poetry in this very period requires some explanation.

Earlier, I suggested by way of an answer to anyone questioning the place of prose at a conference on twelfth-century Byzantine poetry that recognition of the poetics of prose was more likely to come from a gathering of colleagues inclined to uphold the importance of formal structure to literature. The metrical scaffolding of verse and its consequences for poetic expression make us naturally attuned to the shape and, where recoverable, the sound of texts. This is more elusive in the case of prose. The combinations of prose are seemingly more plastic than those of poetry and definitions of what constitutes a prose style more controversial. But less obvious does not mean less important. However elusive, prose form – or style – does not fail to influence our reception of its contents. The twelfth century's stylistic sensibility in matters of prose may be gauged by its reputation for acute rhetorical self-consciousness, a reputation earned largely, though by no means exclusively, on account of its remarkable profusion of studiously crafted prose texts across a variety of genres. Indeed, few periods have produced so many works assigned the classification 'rhetorical', as if the point of the works were to showcase their virtuoso composition and little more. The underlying assumption is that verbal ingenuity and resourcefulness in the arrangement of the text were the author's overriding purpose. Somewhat ironically, it is in twelfth-century prose instead of verse that scholars have tended to see the triumph of form over content.

Not incidentally, the twelfth century's reputation for highly 'rhetorical', that is, patently (one is tempted to say 'proudly') stylized, prose was closely wedded to a highly resourceful and significantly expanding classicism. Fluency *per se* in Attic prose had by then become less an achievement than a basic requirement for any author wishing to make his mark. The successful revival of epideictic initiated in the ninth and tenth centuries subsequently raised the stylistic stakes.[6] Michael Psellos, in whose wake we may arguably date the start of the 'long' twelfth century, represents a notably increased mastery in the handling of Greek prose, including a newly confident Atticism. The next century sought to go beyond this. A rhetor aspiring to compose in an arresting style had to exhibit more than proficiency with Attic diction and inflection. There is a strong, albeit imprecisely understood, sense in which twelfth-century prose in the topmost registers feels more stylized, more formally ambitious than most prose had been until then. This is not to say that there were not highly accomplished, formally

6 Bourbouhakis (2024).

exacting, writers prior to the twelfth century. Arethas comes to mind, and not just because he seems to have felt it necessary to defend what some had characterized as his opaque and loquacious style.[7] And yet the 'long twelfth century' seems particularly deserving of its reputation as 'a period of experiment, innovation, and reassessment' in prose at least as much as in verse.[8]

The stylistic ambition of Byzantine authors in this period, their virtuosity in the handling of both the classicizing and demotic ends of the language, went hand in hand with what Robert Browning characterized as the 'developing self-confidence of Byzantine scholars'.[9] This, in turn, bore directly on the relation with ancient poetry, the study of which both expanded and deepened in this period. Many of these scholars, who also doubled as authors in their own right, devoted unprecedented energy to the systematic study of ancient poetry, beginning always with Homer, but extending to such canonical poets as Hesiod, Pindar, Aristophanes, as well as more outré authors, such as the decidedly esoteric Lycophron. The sheer scale of commentary – a term which can only imperfectly capture the range and variety of the exegetical modes brought to bear on ancient poetry, from the lexical to the allegorical – was unlike anything seen since the heyday of Alexandrian scholarship, the model for so much twelfth-century analysis of ancient Greek verse.[10]

***

It is a commonplace of what we use to call 'the Classical Tradition' that we owe the 'survival' of so much ancient Greek poetry to the Byzantine transmission of the received texts. What often goes unmentioned, however, are the motives which underwrote this sustained cultural campaign of classicism. For the one thing we may say with considerable certainty is that preservation *per se* was not the aim and that the investment in the Classics was not a project of cultural curation, for which we are wont to credit the Byzantines. Those who commissioned copies of ancient poetic texts, as well as those who produced commentaries and treatises about them, did not have 'transmission' to posterity in mind. Ancient Greek poetry, from Homeric epic to post-Hellenistic epigram, was copied by Byzantines because direct knowledge of it was deemed at once desirable and profitable. In short, being well versed in ancient poetry, if the pun may be said to be apt, had a purpose.

7 Arethas, *Opusc.* 17 ed. Westerink (1968–72: 1:186–91).
8 Browning (1992: 144).
9 Browning (1964).
10 Browning (1992). For Byzantine commentaries on ancient Greek texts, see now also the papers collected in van den Berg, Manolova and Marciniak (2022).

That purpose, contrary to the impression often given of Byzantine classicism, was neither constant nor unchanging. Like many cultural practices, it evolved over time. The reception and role assigned to ancient poetry is a case in point. As every student of Byzantine literary history knows, the ninth-century scholar-patriarch Photios conspicuously omitted all poetry from his prolific inventory of book profiles, the so-called *Bibliotheke* or *Myriobiblos*. To judge from the stylistic codas attached to many of the *Bibliotheke*'s entries, prose genres alone were deemed the most suitable source of instruction for how best to wed form to content in the sort of texts Photios expected his peers might wish to emulate. Had we but Photios to guide us as to the estimate of ancient poetry's instructive potential in this period of cultural restoration, we might conclude that its standing had suffered, at least in formal terms. But the reason we are puzzled by Photios' deliberate exclusion of poetry is that we know how prominently it continued to feature in the curriculum. Nevertheless, by the time of the later twelfth century, I would argue, the relative weight of literary *mimesis*, that long-standing imitative aesthetic imperative governing composition in the higher registers of the language, had shifted considerably in favour of poetry; to the point of eliciting inordinately detailed commentaries and other aids not just to comprehension but to instruction for aspiring Byzantine authors.[11]

Of course, Byzantine professors of rhetoric of the twelfth century were not the first to find the study of ancient poetry profitable. The abiding assumption that prose writers had much to learn from the canonical poets had its origins in antiquity, when the prose author's forerunner, the orator, looked to poetry as the precursor and wellspring of captivating and convincing public speech.[12] This is not surprising, given the shared aural sensibility of early sung verse and occasional oratory. Consequently, the early Sophists of the Classical period who first taught public speaking urged the study of the poets on the basis of a shared sensibility about the requirements of eloquence. Aristotle's testimony on this count is instructive because it anticipates, even as it takes a strong position on, the appropriate affinity of prose to poetry:

> ἐπεὶ δ᾽ οἱ ποιηταί, λέγοντες εὐήθη, διὰ τὴν λέξιν ἐδόκουν πορίσασθαι τὴν δόξαν, διὰ τοῦτο ποιητικὴ πρώτη ἐγένετο λέξις, οἷον ἡ Γοργίου, καὶ

11 On literary education through ancient poetry, see also van den Berg in this volume.

12 Eduard Norden was among the earliest to discern a distinctly poetic prose style (*poetische Prosa*) and his discussion of the reciprocal influence between poetry and rhetoric remains astute. See Norden (1909: 30–41, 883–908).

> νῦν ἔτι οἱ πολλοὶ τῶν ἀπαιδεύτων τοὺς τοιούτους οἴονται διαλέγεσθαι κάλλιστα. τοῦτο δ' οὐκ ἔστιν, ἀλλ' ἑτέρα λόγου καὶ ποιήσεως λέξις ἐστίν. (Aristotle, *Rhetoric* 1404a24–9 ed. Ross 1959)
>
> But since the poets, who expressed unsophisticated ideas, seemed to have acquired their reputation by means of their style, this was the reason that the first style was a poetic one, such as that of Gorgias, and even now most of the uneducated think that such persons express themselves most beautifully. Yet this is not the case, since the style of prose is different from that of poetry.

Aristotle's dissent from the implicit conventional view on matters of style would provide the counterpoint to the chorus which recommended poetry as a compass of eloquence.[13] His successors in this branch of criticism would continue to caution against excessive emulation of poetic style through the use of devices common to verse. What Aristotle was objecting to, as best as we can infer, were widespread efforts at mimicking the musical qualities of metre, especially efforts to endow oratory/prose with evident rhythmical effects, among other conspicuously poetic features. Prose could seek to approximate something of poetry's rhythmical quality and elevated diction but had to stop short of an overtly mannered expression, lest it smack of excessive artifice or obscurity, a point repeated by most Byzantine commentators.[14]

By the fourth century BC, Gorgianic oratory, with its notoriously 'dithyrambic' style, had become the foil for such calls for poetic restraint. Isocrates, whose orations and letters Photios included in his *Bibliotheke* as a paragon of prose style, had insisted on independence from poetic aesthetics, especially where figurative language and recherché diction were concerned. As an orator, however, Isocrates was not willing to forego rhythm, thereby ensuring that his medieval imitators would also seek the support of similarly acoustic scaffolding. Preferring to forego the verse-like *cola* of Gorgias, he opted instead for the controlled cadence of the long period, which prose could accommodate in ways metrically bound versified expression could not. Isocrates, it was said, rather ironically, wished to rival Pindar in order to produce on the hearer/reader a lyrical

13 In the *Poetics*, Aristotle acknowledges that poetry shares a number of devices with prose, which accounts for the numerous cross-references between the *Rhetoric* and the *Poetics*: e.g. *Rhetoric* 1372a2, 1404a39, 1404b7–8 and 28, 1405a6–7, 1419b6–7; cf. *Poetics* 1456a.

14 Aristotle, *Rhetoric* 1408b20ff. Cf. the analysis and description of the periodic style (1409a35ff.) and the description of the figures of thought and diction appropriate to prose (1405a28ff.).

effect similar to that of poetry.[15] More than one scholar has noted that eulogies and panegyrics, once the preserve of lyric poets such as Pindar, Simonides and Bacchylides, increasingly came to form the bread and butter of prose over the course of later antiquity. After the fourth century, in the words of Werner Jaeger, prose entered into 'frank competition with poetry, *in form as well as in content*' [italics mine].[16] Not coincidentally, I would argue, these epideictic rivals to poetry saw a great flowering in the long twelfth century.[17]

Aelius Aristides, whose place in the Byzantine prose canon was rivalled only by Demosthenes, had argued for the formal equality of prose and poetry.[18] In the *Hymn to Serapis*, a paean to prose as much as to the Greco-Egyptian god, Aristides questions the assumption that metre is indispensable for exalted subject matter.[19] Prose writers would henceforward seek to usurp the poets' mantle as 'teachers of Greece', a role which required them to fashion suitably arresting expression. For its part, poetry had gradually become defined less and less by reference to its ritual or other occasions and more and more by its didactic function. In due course, it would become a branch of rhetoric, thereby closing the gap with prose.[20] By the time of Hermogenes, a staple of rhetorical instruction throughout the Byzantine era, poetry was regarded by teachers of prose composition as akin to metrical epideictic.[21] 'Since Homer's is the best kind of poetry and Homer the best of poets', says Hermogenes, 'though

15 Isocrates, in the *Antidosis* (*Or.* 15.166), somewhat provocatively compares himself with Pindar. He was not to be the last prose specialist who would do so. Eustathios holds Pindar up as an exemplar of compositional techniques suited to the kind of occasional rhetoric he both practised and taught. See discussion below.

16 Jaeger (1959: 296).

17 It is worth recalling that of the roughly thirty sub-genres of epideictic found in Menander Rhetor, many had previously been the province of lyric or elegiac poetry, whether epithalamium, *epitaphios*, monody or hymns. See Menander Rhetor 333, 340, 393, 402, 437 (references are to page numbers of Spengel [1856], which are followed in the more recent edition of Russell and Wilson [1981]); for the use of models from lyric poetry, cf. Longinus 10 and 15, Dionysius of Halicarnassus, *On Composition* 22 and 23.

18 Aristides (*Or.* 32.21, 32) describes how devoted to poetry his own grammarian, Alexander of Kotyaion, had been. Many of the second-century Sophists, Aristides included, wrote poetry as well as discourses, and some of their extant works occupy a middle ground between prose and verse. This aspect of the Second Sophistic has generally been eclipsed by the prose works.

19 At times, Aristides' *Monody on Smyrna* and the *Hymn to the Aegean* both blur the dividing line between prose and verse.

20 It is worth recalling, for example, that we have Sappho's ode Φαίνεταί μοι because Longinus (10) cites it as a model for the selection and arrangement of detail in prose style, while Dionysius of Halicarnassus quotes her *Hymn to Aphrodite* as an example of the 'smooth' style in prose composition (*On Composition* 2.185–6).

21 Hermogenes, *On Types of Style* 2.10.30.7–8 ed. Patillon (2012).

were I to say [that he is the best] rhetor or prose writer, as well, I would perhaps be saying the same thing.'[22]

For its part, epideictic – understood as texts showcasing their compositional skill as much as their subject matter – became especially receptive to the qualities associated with verse, including rhythm and other markedly poetic devices.[23] What is more, the centrality of epideictic to Byzantine prose sensibility, especially in the upper registers, brought with it an abiding reliance on poetry as the enduring reservoir of arresting, nimble, uncommon expression.

We are so accustomed to associating such poeticization of prose primarily with diction or *lexis* that we tend to overlook Hermogenes' observations regarding effective syntax, as well: 'A pleasing word order, being the same as that which produces Beauty, is obviously one that comes rather close to rendering the passage metrical, for a sweet passage must give some pleasure to the ear by means of its syntax. That said, the metrical feet characteristic of Solemnity should predominate in such syntax.'[24] Hermogenes' syntactical prescriptions have generally received much less attention. To be sure, their application is less easily discernible since they admitted of considerable latitude by authors seeking to achieve the kind of pleasing syntax recommended by the late Roman doyen of rhetorical instruction. We nevertheless do well to bear in mind this broader dimension of composition because it helps to account for the prominence of poetry in a curriculum which largely envisaged prose writing. As we will see, such a recommendation was likely to be read by Byzantines of the twelfth century as encouraging a greater seamlessness between poetic and prosaic language.

This blurring of the purposes of poetry and prose would make it easier to draw lessons from the former and apply them to the latter. Most of the traffic, admittedly, went in one direction. Verse, after all, had the older, more venerable titles to its name. It was typical to come across comments such as that of Strabo, who writes that poetry is the ἀρχὴ καὶ πηγή, 'the fount and the source', of eloquence.[25] Stylistically ambitious prose would continue to labour in the shadow of poetry, seeking after its effects,

22 Hermogenes, *On Types of Style*, 2.10.30.10–12 ed. Patillon (2012): ἀρίστη τε γὰρ ποιήσεων ἡ Ὁμήρου, καὶ Ὅμηρος ποιητῶν ἄριστος, φαίην δ' ἂν ὅτι καὶ ῥητόρων καὶ λογογράφων, λέγω δ' ἴσως ταὐτόν.

23 On the enduring effect of ancient poetry on epideictic oratory, see Burgess (1902: 166–94).

24 Hermogenes, *On Types of Style* 2.4.32.1–5 ed. Patillon (2012): Συνθήκη δὲ ἡδεῖα, ἥπερ καὶ καλή, δηλονότι ἡ σφόδρα ἐγγὺς ἄγουσα τὸν λόγον τοῦ καὶ ἔμμετρον εἶναι·δεῖ γὰρ καὶ κατὰ τὴν συνθήκην προσβάλλειν τινὰ ἡδονὴν τῇ αἰσθήσει τὴν γλυκύτητα. πόδες μέντοι πλεονάζειν ἐν αὐτῇ ὀφείλουσιν οἱ τῆς σεμνότητος οἰκεῖοι.

25 Strabo 1.2.6. Cf. Kim (2007: 363–88).

and not a little of its prestige. And while it dispensed with overt metre, it retained many of the remaining features which Strabo characterizes as 'poetic'. This ancient tradition of identifying rhetorical figures, as well as diction or musical qualities, like rhythm, commonly used by both verse and prose, helped establish the continuum between ancient poetry and the broad class of epideictic which would form the core of Byzantine prose in centuries to come.

In all, the various instructional handbooks of Hermogenes, Menander Rhetor, Theon or Aphthonios speak variously to the role assigned ancient poetry in the composition of prose. A host of prose exercises thus came to draw on epic, lyric and tragedy, not simply recasting the mythical narratives found there but adapting stylistic features, as well. Among lyric poets, for example, Sappho, Alcaeus and Pindar were cast as authoritative models for aspiring rhetors. When Pindar was revived as a source of instruction in the twelfth century by Eustathios, it was largely by retracing the steps of this earlier tradition.[26] Of course, as would prove the case with the rhetorically conceived commentaries or *Parekbolai* to the Homeric epics, the utility of the poetry depended on the guidance and expertise of the Byzantine rhetor. In what would prove a lasting precedent for stylistically ambitious Byzantine prose, Greek rhetorical instruction continued to look to ancient poetry as the epitome of expressive attainment.

As one might expect, education continued to play an outsize role in systematizing the reading of poetry as a resource for prose. It was under the *grammatikos* that the student began the methodical study of poetry. He analysed each verse, plumbed its stylistic peculiarities and offered detailed commentary on matters of diction, figural speech, ambiguous or striking syntactical arrangements and anything else which lent the verse potency. Both Greek and Latin examples from this early but formative period (Dionysius Thrax 1.1, 10.9; Quintilian 1.8.13ff.) confirm that the parsing of a poem's constitutive elements, including its figural language or word ordering, were regarded as the aptest training for aspiring rhetors who anticipated composing mostly in prose. Besides the detailed formalist deconstruction of verse, there followed various *progymnasmata*, including the prose paraphrase of poetry, an exercise which sought at once to demarcate clearly the line between verse and prose but invariably also demonstrated their kinship by suggesting that they might aspire to similar effects.

26 This despite what appears to have been a fashionable dismissive attitude towards lyric, such as Cicero's rather ambiguous comment (ap. Seneca, *Ep.* 49.5) that if a man's life were twice as long as it is, it would still be too short for lyric poetry, and Dio Chrysostom's terse dismissal of lyric, together with elegiac, iambic and dithyrambic poetry, as useless to the orator (*Or.* 18.8).

The conservatism of the received late ancient curriculum, adhered to with remarkable tenacity by Byzantine education, made all this far less remote from the twelfth century than the time elapsed might suggest. It thus furnishes not so much a distant backdrop but an enduring warrant for the socio-cultural preoccupations which underwrote the remarkable flowering of Komnenian-era literature. It also provided much of the rationale for the unprecedented attention ancient poetry would receive in the course of what we are calling the 'long' twelfth century. After all, we should not take for granted that an education system intended to produce authors adept at sophisticated prose, making up the greater part of occasional or ceremonial composition, as well as a wide range of miscellaneous writings, would have necessarily devoted so much of its advanced curriculum and rhetorical instruction to the study of ancient poetry. Need this have been a given in Byzantine literary culture or the rhetorical apprenticeship that might lead to literary success? To be sure, there was an unmistakable propensity for hewing close to tradition, as I noted above. But under the inevitable pressure of changing circumstances, including rivalry among a growing body of writers such as the twelfth century could boast, declared conservatism could offer cover for significant, albeit subtle, shifts in aesthetics (as distinct from the sort of wholesale departures often sought by modern scholars in search of 'originality').[27] Thus, whereas oratory or prose composition had struggled to get out of poetry's illustrious shadow in the Classical and late Hellenistic eras (a late echo of which we still hear in Aristides' defence of prose), a little less than a millennium later, on the eve of the 'long' twelfth century, poetry had come to share, if it had not ceded, a good deal of its pride of place. In the words of Floris Bernard, 'verse was viewed as puerile', at least where rhetorical formation was concerned.[28] 'Contemporaries', as Bernard notes, 'looked with condescension upon this [early] "poetic" stage of education'.[29] The long-running campaign in later antiquity to win respect for prose as an art form had long ago achieved considerable success, if Photios' *Bibliotheke* may serve as a yardstick.

The eleventh-century scholar John Doxapatres offers a different kind of testimony when he reports anecdotally in his commentary on Aphthonios' *Progymnasmata* that students grew apprehensive in anticipation of graduating from the verse-based curriculum of ancient poetry to the more advanced study of prose rhetoric; an attitude perhaps indirectly confirmed by Michael

27 The classical exposition, taken up repeatedly and refined over time, is Kazhdan and Wharton Epstein (1985).
28 Bernard (2014: 209).
29 Bernard (2014: 213).

Psellos' telling remark when he writes that he wished to be 'delivered from hearing the poems', and looked forward to 'the art of words with grace'.[30] And yet, as Bernard observes, poetry was deemed 'a preparatory phase of the curriculum, decidedly inferior to rhetorical education'.[31] For Psellos' successors a little over a century later, however, ancient poetry had once more become synonymous with the highest rung of rhetorical training.

We probably have no better guide to the place of ancient poetry in the literary and rhetorical imagination of twelfth century audiences, especially in the second half of that century, than the abundance of surviving commentaries and treatises on ancient poets produced during this period. Some, like that which comes to us from the pen of Isaac Porphyrogennetos, seem to derive almost wholly from late Hellenistic treatises on Homeric poetry, such as the so-called Ps.-Plutarchan *On Homer*.[32] This late ancient work, especially well known in later Byzantium, to judge from its manuscript tradition, invoked rhythm and metre to explain poetry's ability to make the listener attentive to the message of a work.[33] No less importantly, however, it furnished lessons to prose authors, noting that the poet 'does not just elevate his subject matter and divert it from its customary course but also [elevates] the text':

> οὐ μόνον τὰ πράγματα μετεωρίζει καὶ ἐκτρέπει τῆς συνηθείας ἀλλὰ καὶ τοὺς λόγους. ὅτι δὲ ἀεὶ τὰ καινὰ καὶ ἔξω τοῦ προχείρου θαυμάζεται καὶ τὸν ἀκροατὴν ἐπάγεται, παντί που δῆλον. … καὶ πολλὰς ἀφορμὰς καὶ οἱονεὶ σπέρματα λόγων καὶ πράξεων παντοδαπῶν τοῖς μετ᾽ αὐτὸν παρεσχημένος, καὶ οὐ τοῖς ποιηταῖς μόνον ἀλλὰ καὶ τοῖς πεζῶν λόγων συνθέταις ἱστορικῶν τε καὶ θεωρηματικῶν. (Ps.-Plutarch, *On Homer* 6 ed. Kindstrand 1990; my emphasis)
>
> *He does not just elevate his subject matter and divert it from its customary course but also [elevates] the text.* It is clear to everyone that that which is new and outside of the everyday evokes wonder and captivates the imagination of the listener. … He provides the starting points and so to speak the seeds of all kinds of discourse and action to those who come after him, not only for the poets but for the writers of prose as well, both historical and speculative. (trans. after Keaney and Lamberton 1996; my emphasis)

30 Michael Psellos, *Funerary Oration for his Mother* 841–2 ed. Criscuolo (1989): ἄρτι τοῦ ποιημάτων ἀκούειν ἀπαλλαγεὶς καὶ παρακύψας εἰς τὴν τῶν λόγων τέχνην σὺν χάριτι. In one of his letters, Psellos urges attention to 'harmony' not just in song, but in 'both poetry and prose'. Psellos, *Ep.* 280.33–4 ed. Papaioannou (2019): Τήν γέ τοι ἁρμονίαν μὴ ἐν μέλεσι μόνον ἡγοῦ, ἀλλὰ καὶ ἐν ἔπεσι καὶ λόγῳ πεζῷ.

31 Bernard (2014: 215).

32 Isaac Porphyrogennetos, *Preface to Homer* ed. Kindstrand (1979).

33 Ps.-Plutarch, *On Homer* 6 ed. Kindstrand (1990). For the relevant analysis and its influence on Isaac's treatise, see Keaney and Lamberton (1996).

The author of this short treatise, in all likelihood intended for school use, traded on the assumption that poetry could not just supply memorable characters and situations but could also serve as a reservoir of arresting and persuasive expression. Isaac's unoriginal pamphlet speaks to a shift in perspective regarding poetry. The depth of that shift would be more fully plumbed by the prolific pens of John Tzetzes and Eustathios. Isaac's contribution nevertheless illustrates how widespread the perception of poetry's promise for prose had once more become that a relative dilettante like himself should take up the subject.

It is common enough to see *mimesis* invoked whenever the relation of ancient to medieval Greek literature is at issue. Less common is the exploration of *mimesis* across formal divides, such as that of verse and prose. Still, imitation and reproduction were not necessarily self-sustaining. Successive cultural phases of Hellenism, including that of the twelfth century, had to reaffirm and thus renegotiate their reverence for, and reliance on, ancient poetry. One way the twelfth century sought to do this was by making the mostly dormant, accumulated store of ancient scholarship newly relevant. There were important enabling antecedents, of course. The Venetus A manuscript of the *Iliad*, with its innovative and occasionally eclectic collation of the extant scholia in the tenth century, presupposes some degree of contemporary purpose beyond mere curation of the Homeric text. Offering a corrective to the mistaken impression that collections of scholia were simply copied out and mechanically collated, Nigel Wilson reminds us that 'every successive generation sought to adapt the traditional commentary on classical authors according to its own taste or to contemporary needs'.[34] More to the point here, Wilson cites as evidence the twelfth century's singularly flourishing exploitation of the ancient scholiastic tradition, a good deal of which had languished for nearly a millennium.

One of the tasks of a commentary was to render the ancient poetic text at once intelligible and *useful*. This latter purpose is mostly unfamiliar to modern scholars and students of ancient texts, who judge the Byzantine commentaries and various treatises according to their ability to help us reconstruct the original meaning of the work in question. No doubt, Byzantine scholars sometimes shared this aim, leading many to weigh these works according to this one common measure: interpretive or philological accuracy. In doing so, however, we neglect the second, and by no means lesser aim, of immediate utility. And while I would not want to reduce the study of any class of ancient texts in Byzantium to any single purpose, I

34 Wilson (1984: 91).

think it worthwhile to underline here the primacy of harnessing ancient poetry to contemporary composition, principally of prose texts defined as *logographia* (λογογραφία), spanning a broad gamut of occasions and genres, from imperial encomia to epistolography.

Somewhat paradoxically, perhaps, the focus by Byzantine scholars of ancient poetry on its lessons for prose was the result of so much medieval accentual verse becoming uncoupled from most quantitative metre. The study of ancient epic, lyric or iambic verse no longer lent itself to fluency in versification *per se* (except perhaps in the schools, where such exercises persisted). Even a work ostensibly dedicated to allegorical exegesis of the *Iliad* by John Tzetzes, an energetic author of didactic works about ancient poetry, ranging from Homeric epic to Lycophron's otherwise obscure Hellenistic-age *Alexandra*, invokes the value of such study for the attainment of outstanding prose:

> ὅς ἄν δὲ χρήζῃ μέθοδον δεινότητος μανθάνειν
> καὶ θέλῃ ῥήτορα δεινόν, καὶ θέλῃ λογογράφον
> καὶ μεταφράσει χρῆσθαι δέ, τῇ καὶ μεταποιήσει
> καί, λέγων πάλιν τὰ αὐτά, δοκεῖν ὡς ἄλλα λέγειν,
> τὸν Ὅμηρον ἐχέτω μοι παράδειγμα τῆς τέχνης.
> (Tzetzes, *Allegories of the Iliad* 15.37–41 ed. Boissonade 1851)

> <anyone> who needs to learn a vigorous rhetorical style,
> and wishes to become either a skilled orator or prose writer,
> and to make use of paraphrase, as well as adaptation,
> and though saying the same things once again, seems to say something else,
> let him have Homer as a model of his art.

Tzetzes makes explicit here the claim, found in nearly all twelfth-century commentaries on ancient poetry, that in order to learn to write better prose, one should study ancient verse, presumably with him.[35] Of course, it will be immediately pointed out that the *Allegories* do not fully illustrate the sort of formal analysis Tzetzes is advertising here. This is not surprising. As much as anything else, the 'published' scholarship was intended to serve as a means to market one's proficiency as an expert teacher. The mention of μετάφρασις and μεταποίησις (v. 39) suggest lessons that extend beyond apt citation or allusion and hearken back to the prose paraphrases taught by the *grammatistes* as far back as the late Hellenistic period. In this respect,

35 There are other, similar, pronouncements on the rhetorical lessons to be gleaned from the study of poetry: cf. *Allegories of the Iliad* 16.322, 16.333, 16.343; *Histories* 11.707–11 ed. Leone (2007).

Herbert Hunger's judgement that ancient verse had become 'poetry for the eye', while accurate as far as perceived prosody goes, should not be understood as foreclosing the appreciation of poetic structure or expression more broadly, whether in syntax or in grammar.[36]

As van der Valk, the modern editor of Eustathios' monumental commentary on the *Iliad*, the *Parekbolai*, repeatedly underlines, the enabling context of the twelfth-century commentary on ancient poetry was the composition lesson.[37] And *its* primary purpose was to train aspiring rhetors to compose memorably imposing prose in the tradition of epideictic, that is, formally accomplished *logos*, whether for a variety of ceremonial or informal occasions or for such highly wrought genres as historiography or epistolography. Van der Valk's landmark edition of the *Parekbolai to the Iliad* inventories the many instances in which Eustathios discerned in the poetry of Homer (as well as other ancient poets cited in the course of his analytical parsing) rhetorical figures familiar and applicable to prose writers. Van der Valk saw these as evidence that the commentary re-enacted the lessons of Eustathios' classroom, with a view to teaching students how to compose 'unfettered orations', that is, non-metrical, or prose, texts. The conclusion that Eustathios' mammoth study of Homeric poetry was aimed principally at prose composition has been further foregrounded in recent studies by Eric Cullhed and Baukje van den Berg.[38]

Van der Valk's point about the classroom is especially pertinent here because it places the locus of interest in the potential of ancient poetry stylistically to enhance prose squarely in the centre of rhetorical education and literary formation. And while Eustathios' labours were undoubtably unique in philological depth and breadth, there is good reason to think that the broad tenor of his work was in keeping with the rhetorical trends and literary sensibility which had built up over the course of the twelfth century. Eustathios' aim in compiling the commentary, van der Valk concluded, was to help its users become better 'rhetors', a purpose all but synonymous with becoming 'prose authors'.[39] If we limit such instruction to lexical borrowing or imitation, or the repurposing of whole or partial verses, as has been the case when looking at ancient poetry's contribution to prose, we are likely to pay insufficient attention to the less obvious, but potentially more significant, correlations of form between ancient verse

36 Hunger (1969/70: 33).
37 Van der Valk (1971–87: 1:xcii–c; 2:li–lxx).
38 See Cullhed (2016), van den Berg (2022).
39 Van der Valk (1971–87: 1:xcii): *Eustathius enim ... id ipsum studebat, ut discipuli discerent oratione soluta scribere, vel ut tunc temporis dicebant, rhetores fieri.*

and contemporary prose in this period, affecting such structural features as rhythm, syntax and grammar.

Eustathios' *Parekbolai* to the *Iliad* and *Odyssey*, easily the most comprehensive study of ancient Greek poetry in Byzantium, were created to provide what the one-time μαΐστωρ τῶν ῥητόρων or 'dean of the rhetors' assured his readers and former pupils would amount to πολλαὶ ἀφορμαὶ εἰς ῥητορείας δαψίλειαν, that is, 'many opportunities and materials for rhetorical amplification'. What were these 'opportunities and materials' for rhetorical abundance? In his bid to market the increasingly gargantuan opus, Eustathios promised to furnish aspiring authors of prose not just with apt lexical or mythical material, but also with:

> ἐννοίας εὐχρήστους τῷ καταλογάδην γράφοντι καὶ βουλομένῳ ῥητορικὰς ποιεῖν εὐκαίρως παραπλοκάς· μεθόδους, ἐξ ὧν καὶ ὠφελεῖταί τις μιμεῖσθαι θέλων καὶ τῆς εὐτεχνίας θαυμάζει τὸν ποιητήν· (Eustathios, *Parekbolai to the Iliad* 1.3.12–15 ed. van der Valk 1971–87; my emphasis)

> useful ideas for prose writers and those who wish to weave well-timed rhetorical effects; *techniques, from which one stands to gain who wishes to imitate <the poet> and admires the poet for his skill.*

Such claims may strike us as somewhat counter-intuitive, since ancient verse, whether Homeric hexameters or Pindaric lyric, another of Eustathios' commentary projects, would hardly seem to lend themselves as models for Byzantine prose, nor indeed do they seem *prima facie* to have much in common with it.

Byzantine prose, especially in the highest registers, has tended to be thought of as needlessly prolix and ponderous, lacking in precisely the discipline and economy of expression imposed on poetry by metre. But our perception of Byzantine prose is often clouded by a general misprision of its inner workings. By comparison with verse, Byzantine prose has seen little systematic profiling of its manifold formal features, other than a now routine pegging of texts along the familiar high-middle-low axis of style, usually by the extent of their archaizing vocabulary and vaguely 'Atticizing' grammar. Simply put, we lack the kind of precise taxonomy and closely calibrated analysis of Byzantine prose that would allow us to register the syntactical and other structural and semantic shifts adopted by authors in search of conspicuous and engaging formulations.

Because we have not studied the Byzantine prose of any period quite as methodically as we have catalogued Byzantine verse over the last few decades, it is difficult to talk about it in anything more than impressionistic terms.

It remains for us to develop a working vocabulary to describe Byzantine prose. One place to begin – I underline 'begin', lest there be any confusion about how far we have left to go – would be with what Byzantine rhetors themselves had to say about prose style. I have previously sketched instances of Eustathios' parsing of poetic style which exhibit what he characterized as *stryphnotes* (στρυφνότης), a deliberate economy of expression resulting in a notably 'astringent' or conspicuously *austere* effect.[40] Understanding this effect, to what degree it was sought and, no less important, to what degree it may have been achieved, in which genres and by whom – all of which are distinct questions – requires us to read a good deal of twelfth-century prose with an eye to the structural elements of composition, at the clausal and phrasal level even; as well as the larger periodic or other syntactical arrangements. This is not separate but nevertheless distinct from reading for meaning alone, already a challenge when making our way through some Byzantine prose texts. The example of στρυφνότης is telling of both the difficulty and the promise of understanding what Byzantine rhetors in this period may have seen in ancient poetry that they deemed patently imitable by prose authors.

Eustathios appears to have revived στρυφνότης as a critical term – famously applied by Dionysius of Halicarnassus to Thucydides on account of the historian's unwillingness to make concessions to a more 'flowing' and effortlessly accessible prose style – in order to designate syntax which disrupted the expected accumulation and disposition of a sentence's parts. Στρυφνότης was defined, in part, by contrast with *glykytes* (γλυκύτης), a mellifluous arrangement demanding little of the reader and leaving little ambiguity in its wake.[41] Broadly speaking, Eustathios invoked this label to designate a marked density of syntactic texture and an economy of expression. This flouted conventional expectations and could produce an appealing ambiguity born of a combination of stylistic 'astringency' and ellipsis.[42] Among the examples of στρυφνότης he gives is *Iliad* 1.258, where he transposes the text from its allegedly opaque compactness to a more conventionally prosaic elaboration:

> Ὅτι τελείων ἀνθρώπων ἔπαινος τὸ «οἳ περὶ μὲν βουλῇ Δαναῶν, περὶ δ' ἐστὲ μάχεσθαι». αὐξάνων δέ τις που τὸ ἐγκώμιον ἀντὶ τοῦ Δαναῶν πάντων ἐρεῖ ἢ ἄλλο τι τοιοῦτον· παραφράσας δὲ αὐτό, εἰ βούλεται, μεταγάγῃ ἐκ τῆς ποιητικῆς στρυφνότητος εἰς τοιαύτην τινὰ σαφήνειαν· οἳ περίεστε μὲν

40 Bourbouhakis (2017: 83*–103*).
41 It is interesting to compare this aesthetic imperative with that of Hermogenes, cited above, n. 24.
42 For elliptical phrasing, see e.g. *Parekbolai to the Iliad* 1.83.16ff., 4.597.13ff.

> πάντων τῇ βουλῇ περίεστε δὲ καὶ τῇ κατὰ πόλεμον δεξιότητι. (Eustathios, *Parekbolai to the Iliad* 1.155.21–6 ed. van der Valk 1971–87)
>
> The verse 'you, who surpass all Danaans in council, in fighting', amounts to praise of flawless people. But if one were to further amplify the encomium, instead of all the Danaans he would say something else similar to it; but if he should wish to paraphrase it, he might shift from poetic compendiousness to clarity along these lines: 'those of you who agree with the decision of the Danaans must also share in their prowess in war'.

We thus have a typical lesson in the appropriation of a Homeric line of verse, followed by its potential for rhetorical amplification through 'paraphrase' (παράφρασις), the age-old exercise taught in schools through the use of ancient poetry. Eustathios spells out the highly abridged sense by filling in individual verbs for the subject of each clause to achieve syntactical balance and greater clarity, admittedly at considerable cost to style. And that is exactly his point. Poetic style involves trade-offs, including a willingness to frustrate the audience's desire to grasp everything quickly and effortlessly (a desire and attendant frustration often shared by modern scholars of high-brow Byzantine prose). Παράφρασις here belongs to the same set of rhetorical techniques as μετάφρασις and μεταποίησις mentioned above.[43]

By noting the structural distance between the Homeric text and its prosaic equivalent, Eustathios marked for aspiring authors how poetic expression might be achieved. Στρυφνότης appears to describe the kind of synoptic phrasing encouraged by the metrical requirements of verse. But could a prose writer emulate this kind of economy on the clausal or larger syntactical scale? Eustathios suggests as much when he unfolds the meaning of another Homeric verse, *Iliad* 17.98 (ὁππότ' ἀνὴρ ἐθέλῃ πρὸς δαίμονα φωτὶ μάχεσθαι), which he analyses by offering a more prosaic explanation:

> Τὸ δὲ «πρὸς δαίμονα φωτὶ μάχεσθαι» ταὐτὸν μέν ἐστι τῷ διὰ μέσου φωτὸς θεοφιλοῦς δαιμονομαχεῖν, <u>στρυφνῶς δὲ καὶ συνεστραμμένως πέφρασται διὰ συντομίαν</u>. βούλεται δὲ λέγειν, ὅτι ὁ μαχόμενος ἀνδρί, ὃν δαίμων τιμᾷ, εἰ καὶ δοκεῖ ἁπλῶς ἀνθρώπῳ μάχεσθαι, ἀλλ' ἀληθῶς διὰ μέσου τοῦ τοιούτου δαίμονι μάχεται. (Eustathios, *Parekbolai to the Iliad* 4.21.2–6 ed. van der Valk 1971–87)
>
> «πρὸς δαίμονα φωτὶ μάχεσθαι» is the same thing as [saying] 'to battle demons by means of light from a favourable deity', *only expressed in a densely*

43 On metaphrasis, see also Ricceri in this volume.

> *abridged and intertwined way through brevity*. What he means to say is that anyone fighting with a man whom the daemon honours, even if he appears to be fighting only a man, nevertheless is in fact fighting with a spirit through this man.

The conciseness of expression and consequent abbreviation of meaning Eustathios appears to prize in poets such as Homer and Pindar was intended to serve as a model for prose writers of his day. To illustrate the point, Eustathios restores to some Homeric verses the στρυφνότης he claims is atypically missing:

> Ὅτι ἐν τῷ «τὼ δὲ μνησαμένω», ἤγουν οἱ δὲ ἀναμνησθέντες, «ὃ μὲν Ἕκτορος ἔκλαιεν ἀδινά, αὐτὰρ Ἀχιλλεὺς ἔκλαιεν ἑὸν πατέρα, ἄλλοτε δὲ Πάτροκλον» καινῶς διὰ σαφήνειαν ἐσχημάτισεν ὁ ποιητής. ἠδύνατο γὰρ ἄλλως τὸ ὅλον στρυφνῶς οὕτω φράσαι· μνησαμένω ὁ μὲν Ἕκτορος, Ἀχιλλεὺς δὲ πατρός, ἔκλαιον, ὃ δὴ καιρία λέξις. (Eustathios, *Parekbolai to the Iliad* 4.941.24–7 ed. van der Valk 1971–87)

> In the [verse] 'the two men bringing to mind', namely, those recalling, 'the one [thought] of Hector [and] cried uncontrollably, while Achilles wept for his own father, or in turn for Patroclus' the poet arranged [the words] with unusual clarity. Since he could have expressed the whole thing differently, in an austere manner: 'both men remembered, on the one hand Hector, on the other Achilles [recalled] his father, as they cried', which is the vital word here.

We see here an oblique lesson in composition. The point of this passage is to illustrate how one may introduce a 'poetic' turn to otherwise plain phrasing. By showing the discrepancy between the two styles, Eustathios was offering lessons in an expressive manner which engaged the reader's own capacity to bridge the elisions of unresolved meaning, a feature I would argue was striven for by some of the more accomplished writers of this period. It is revealing that Pindar, a difficult ancient poet, saw more formal analyses of his verses in precisely this century than he had seen since the Hellenistic age. Among the qualities which seem to have made Pindar's poetry a promising source of instruction for prose authors – there being fewer lessons here, perhaps, for accentual poetry – was the notoriously elaborate structure and frequently enigmatic meaning produced by his compressed style:

> Οὕτω δὲ στρυφνῶς φράζει ταῖς ἐννοίαις κατὰ πολύνοιαν, ὡς ἔργον εἶναι πολλαχοῦ μιᾷ τινι σταθερῶς ἐννοίᾳ ἐνευστοχῆσαι τὸν ἀναγινώσκοντα διὰ τὸ οὕτω καὶ οὕτω νοεῖσθαι αὐτὴν ... ἔστι δὲ δεινὸς καὶ οὐ μόνον τὸ

> ἓν ἐπεκτείνειν παραφράσεσι καὶ περιφράσεσι καί τισιν ἑτεροίαις μεθόδοις. (Eustathios, *Preface to the Commentary on Pindar* 20.19 ed. Kambylis 1991)
>
> And in this way he expresses ideas in a dense and ambiguous manner which produces multiple meanings, so that in many places the task of the reader is to accurately arrive at some stable meaning by understanding it in such and such a manner ... and [Pindar] is quite able not only to extend [the meaning] of one thing with paraphrases and circumlocutions and certain other means.

I draw attention here to this Eustathian lesson drawn from ancient lyric and epic poetry because it illustrates how such formal analysis was in fact aimed at prose style. This was distinct from the more oft-discussed exegetical approaches, which have garnered more attention, or the emphasis on purely lexical borrowings and apt citation, which are frequently found in the *apparatus fontium* and periodically serve as lessons in what we have come to call intertextuality.[44] But the poeticization of prose was not exhausted by the use of rarefied poetic vocabulary, which on its own would have no doubt sounded like a fragment of verse spolia inserted into a wall of prose. The question remains, then, why Eustathios would have decided to give new life to this otherwise obscure stylistic label. Or to frame it slightly more broadly, in keeping with the theme of this volume: what did the role assigned to poetry more generally in the twelfth century have to do with this shift in the study of ancient verse? Moreover, can we identify developments in Byzantine literature of this period that exemplify the recommended *poeticization* of prose?

In a eulogy he composed celebrating the great rhetor's accomplishments, Michael Choniates, perhaps Eustathios' most accomplished former student, credited his late teacher with having revived the study of rhetoric after it had grown moribund in previous generations. Making use of the language of pagan mystery rituals, Michael likens Eustathios to a 'hierophant of the rites of the arts of speech [for students] carrying poetry books under their arms' (ἐκείνῳ δ' ὅμως ἱεροφαντοῦντι τὰ λογικῶν τεχνῶν ὄργια ... τῶν φοιτώντων, πυκτίδα ποιητικὴν ὑπὸ μάλην φέρων).[45] The encomiastic licence of a funeral lament may have led Michael to exaggerate Eustathios' single-handed reform of twelfth-century rhetoric. But the image of students on their way to their lessons with books of poetry under

44 Bourbouhakis (2017: 177*–94*).
45 Michael Choniates, *Oration* 16, 288.21–6 ed. Lampros (1879).

their arms was not the product of panegyrical distortion. The brief vignette captures the traffic between poetry and prose at a formative stage.

In what remains a classic, albeit insufficient, assessment of the place of Homeric poetry in Byzantium, Robert Browning once observed that scholars needed to pursue 'not so much who could quote Homer, or even who read him, *but the purposes for which Homer was read … and the extent to which study of Homer led to results, which go beyond the pleasure of the immediate reader*'.[46] Browning could have been writing of ancient poetry in the twelfth century more generally. Scholars of the twelfth century had to reconcile the antiquity of the text with its direct bearing on the literary and rhetorical practice of their day, a practice their modern counterparts sometimes deem culpable for the frequent misreadings they find contained there. But as Felix Budelmann has astutely observed, Byzantine commentaries strike us as flawed precisely because we take the remoteness of the ancient text for granted, and expect a Byzantine commentary to do so as well.[47] What we find in the twelfth-century commentaries is at once a recognition of the distant origins of the text and its simultaneous formal relevance in the present.

It is doubtless difficult to trace direct and specific correspondences between passages of twelfth-century prose and the often broadly schematic lessons drawn from the formal study of ancient poetry. But I am not making a case here for direct imitation of recognizably poetic form drawn from ancient texts, something all rhetorical instruction, from Hermogenes to Eustathios, cautioned against. I am referring, instead, to an attempt by twelfth-century rhetors and authors to broaden the formal repertoire of prose, to seek additional variations of style through the close study of ancient poetry. We are helped, in some cases, by the authors and texts themselves. Byzantine writers did not share the late modern conviction that good prose style should be 'unobtrusive' and inconspicuous. They foregrounded the artifice of their text, its highly deliberate and constructed character. When viewed through the lens of formal attainment, the showcasing of style and surplus of rhetoric, long seen as a handicap by scholars, becomes more readily appreciated as a desire to explore the boundaries and possibilities of language, a long-recognized virtue of poetry, in any century, long or otherwise.

46 Browning (1975: 15; italics mine).
47 Budelman (2002).

Bibliography

Bernard, F. (2014) *Writing and Reading Byzantine Secular Poetry, 1025–1081*. Oxford.
Boissonade, J. F. (ed.) (1851) *Tzetzae allegoriae Iliadis accedunt Pselli allegoriae*. Paris (repr. Hildesheim 1967).
Bourbouhakis, E. C. (2017) *Not Composed in a Chance Manner: The Epitaphios for Manuel I Komnenos by Eustathios of Thessalonike*. Studia Byzantina Upsaliensia 18. Uppsala.
(2024) 'Continuing Influence of Late Classical Epideictic Tradition in Byzantium (9th–10th Cent.)', in *The Cambridge History of Rhetoric*, ed. R. Copeland and P. Mack. Cambridge.
Browning, R. (1964) 'Byzantine Scholarship', *P&P* 28: 3–20.
(1975) 'Homer in Byzantium', *Viator* 6: 15–33.
(1992) 'The Byzantines and Homer', in *Homer's Ancient Readers: The Hermeneutics of Greek Epic's Earliest Exegetes*, ed. R. Lamberton and J. J. Keaney, 134–48. Princeton.
Budelmann, F. (2002) 'Classical Commentary in Byzantium: John Tzetzes on Ancient Greek Literature', in *The Classical Commentary: Histories, Practices, Theory*, ed. G. Gibson and C. Shuttleworth Kraus, 141–69. Leiden.
Burgess, T. C. (1902) *Epideictic Literature*. Chicago.
Criscuolo, U. (1989) *Michele Psello, Autobiografia: Encomio per la madre*. Naples.
Cullhed, E. (ed.) (2016) *Eustathios of Thessalonike: Commentary on Homer's Odyssey*, vol. 1: *On Rhapsodies A–B*. Studia Byzantina Upsaliensia 16. Uppsala.
Goldhill, S. (2002) *The Invention of Prose*. Oxford.
Hörandner, W. (1981) *Der Prosarhythmus in der rhetorischen Literatur der Byzantiner*. Vienna.
Hunger, H. (1969/70) 'On the Imitation (ΜΙΜΗΣΙΣ) of Antiquity in Byzantine Literature', *DOP* 23/24: 15–38.
Jaeger, W. (1959) *Paideia: die Formung des griechischen Menschen*. Berlin.
Kambylis, A. (ed.) (1991) *Eustathios von Thessalonike, Prooimion zum Pindarkommentar*. Göttingen.
Kazhdan, A., and A. Wharton Epstein (1985) *Change in Byzantine Culture in the Eleventh and Twelfth Centuries*. Berkeley.
Keaney, J., and R. Lamberton (eds.) (1996) *Essay on the Life and Poetry of Homer*. Atlanta.
Kim, L. (2007) 'The Portrait of Homer in Strabo's *Geography*', *CPh* 102.4: 363–88.
Kindstrand, J. F. (ed.) (1979) *Praefatio in Homerum*. Uppsala.
(ed.) (1990) *[Plutarchi] De Homero*. Leipzig.
Lampros, S. P. (1879) *Μιχαὴλ Ἀκομινάτου τοῦ Χωνιάτου τὰ σωζόμενα*, vol. 1. Athens.
Leone, P. L. M. (ed.) (2007) *Ioannis Tzetzae Historiae*, 2nd ed. Galatina.
Nilsson, I. (2006) 'Discovering Literariness in the Past: Literature vs. History in the *Synopsis Chronike* of Konstantinos Manasses', in *L'écriture de la mémoire: La littérarité de l'historiographie. Actes du IIIe colloque international philologique. Nicosie, 6–7–8 mai 2004*, ed. P. Odorico, P. A. Agapitos and M. Hinterberger, 15–31. Dossiers byzantins 6. Paris.

Norden, E. (1909) *Die antike Kunstprosa vom VI. Jahrhundert v. Chr. bis in die Zeit der Renaissance*. Leipzig.

Papaioannou, S. (ed.) (2019) *Michael Psellus: Epistulae*. Berlin.

Patillon, M. (2012) *Corpus Rhetoricum*, vol. 4: *Prolégomènes au de ideis; Hermogène: Les catégories stylistiques du discours (de ideis); Synopses des exposés sur les ideai*. Paris.

Ross, W. D. (1959) *Aristotelis ars rhetorica*. Oxford.

Russell, D. A., and N. G. Wilson (1981) *Menander Rhetor*. Oxford.

Spengel, L. (ed.) (1956) *Rhetores Graeci*, vol. 3. Leipzig.

van den Berg, B. (2022) *Homer the Rhetorician: Eustathios of Thessalonike on the Composition of the Iliad*. Oxford.

van den Berg, B., D. Manolova and P. Marciniak (eds.) (2022) *Byzantine Commentaries on Ancient Greek Texts, 12th–15th Centuries*. Cambridge.

van der Valk, M. (ed.) (1971–87) *Eustathii archiepiscopi Thessalonicensis Commentarii ad Homeri Iliadem pertinentes ad fidem codicis Laurentiani editi*, 4 vols. Leiden.

Westerink, L. G. (ed.) (1968–72) *Arethae archiepiscopi Caesariensis scripta minora*, 2 vols. Leipzig.

White, H. (1987) *The Content of the Form: Narrative Discourse and Historical Representation*. Baltimore.

Wilson, N. G. (1984) 'Scoliasti e commentatori', *Studi Classici e Orientali* 33: 83–112.

PART II

Poetry and the School

CHAPTER 5

The Didactic Poetry of Niketas of Herakleia and the Use of Verse in Byzantine Teaching Practice

Floris Bernard

More than any other kind of poetry, didactic poetry forces us to come to terms with the question why to express something in metrical form, and not in prose. Binary oppositions which we customarily use, such as fiction versus non-fiction, literature vs *Gebrauchsliteratur*, prose vs poetry, will have to be reconsidered when we try to understand Byzantine didactic poetry.[1] But the genre was extremely popular: there are numerous poems that appear, in a rather strict sense, to 'teach'.[2] They impart instruction and information on the most divergent topics: Bible exegesis, law, medicine, rhetoric, diet, grammar, geometry, etc.[3] Judging on the basis of the relatively broad circulation of didactic poems in manuscripts, there was a huge demand to express and consume knowledge in verse.

Didactic poetry defies the frameworks and terminology with which we approach literature. The very concept of 'literature' falls apart, since for us the purpose of transmitting knowledge is alien to the goals of literature. The paratactic structure of these texts, geared towards a didactic exposition of the subject matter, runs counter to how we think literature should look like. And yet these texts employ a device that is for us eminently literary: metre. While we have come to see metre as totally opposed to factual statements, for the medieval mind the marriage between both was not problematic at all.

It would be interesting to investigate why verse was seen as an aid to transmit knowledge rather than an obstacle. This is not the occasion to tackle this question in full, but at least it may be helpful to point out that there is the well-known trope that poetry 'sweetens' discourse that would

1 For an excellent introduction to the genre of Byzantine didactic poetry (including an overview of themes, techniques and literary traditions), see Hörandner (2019). For its connection with definitions of 'poetry', see Lauxtermann (2009).

2 I define here 'didactic poetry' as poems that impart knowledge, in contrast to poems that aim to moralize, that is, to edify (and are also sometimes called 'didactic'). See Lauxtermann (2019: 201).

3 For a didactic poem on astrology by Constantine Manasses, see Chryssogelos in this volume.

otherwise be difficult to swallow. This trope is in some form or another ubiquitous in metapoetic statements that are found in didactic poems. Ancient texts (especially in the medical domain) imply that the metrical form was felt to be conducive to purely cognitive and informational goals such as memorization and precision.[4]

Viewing the genre in broad diachronic terms, we should acknowledge the differences between ancient and medieval didactic poetry, as well as the common features that unite didactic poetry of many periods and cultures.[5] Seen from this vantage point, it is striking that Byzantine didactic poetry seems to have no thematic layer beneath or beyond the transmission of knowledge. For all we can ascertain, these poems were written and consumed as they purported to be done: in order to instruct the reader about a given subject matter. This hypothesis warrants further study, but one important indication is telling: in the manuscripts transmitting them, didactic poems are often not grouped together with other poems, but rather with prose texts on the same subject.[6] We can assume that the poems were used in the same way as the texts surrounding them in the manuscripts: as sources of information and instruction. This rather pragmatic context of use contrasts with the more purely literary and aesthetical aims that are commonly associated with Hellenistic Greek and classical Latin didactic poetry. Also these poems purport to instruct, but this is often considered a playful 'fiction', a kind of smoke screen through which the poet achieves other, rather literary, goals.[7] One would be hard pressed to find similar procedures in Byzantine didactic poetry. Knowledge is all there is: no narrative, no descriptions, no double layers. And while playfulness is certainly present, as we will see, the purpose of instruction and the role of the poet as a teacher are no fiction.

This chapter will make a case for this rather concrete functional purpose of didactic poetry, using the example of the grammatical poems of Niketas of Herakleia, where the world of contemporary teaching is very much in evidence. Niketas' poems take a very practical approach towards the learning of grammar. Unlike many other didactic poems, these were not dedicated to emperors, but rather addressed to a large audience of pupils. And compared to other, previous, poems on grammar, such as the

4 Von Staden (1998) and Vogt (2005).

5 For intercultural common features, see for instance Schuler and Fitch (1983) and Kozodoy (2011). Byzantium is absent from these discussions.

6 Bernard (2014: 69–75).

7 For example, see Harder (2007: 43): 'the preservation and the transmission of knowledge are turned into a literary fiction'. See also Kneebone (2020).

one by Michael Psellos,[8] Niketas' poems do not intend to summarize the discipline, but rather to train students to follow very specific rules and guidelines when writing Greek. These features make his corpus particularly interesting for investigating the relationship between education and poetry.

Niketas, bishop of Herakleia, also identified as the nephew of Stephanos, the bishop of Serres, was probably born around 1060 and was active in the decades around the turn of the twelfth century.[9] He was *proximos* of the school of Chalkoprateia in Constantinople. Apart from his didactic poems, he is also known for his commentaries on biblical and theological texts. Niketas wrote an enormous body of didactic poems, many of which are unedited or edited unsatisfactorily.[10] Niketas' didactic poems mainly concern one field of knowledge: grammar.

The poems in hymnographic metres seem to form together a rather consistent[11] body of texts.[12] These poems follow the accentual pattern of a hymnographic *heirmos*, a melody of a liturgical tune known to all Byzantines.[13] Topics of some smaller hymnographic poems are the names for seas, rivers, stones, cities, and pagan gods.[14] Two long canons will be edited soon by Theodora Antonopoulou.[15] They treat the *antistoicha*, as also their title in some manuscripts indicates; that is, they discuss the vowels that in medieval Greek pronunciation sounded identical, but were written differently.[16] These two canons are effectively lists of words that provoke orthographical mistakes. They attempt to solve orthographical problems by formulating rules that often have no linguistic reality behind them, but serve as mnemonic clues.

The poems in dodecasyllables and *politikos stichos* are of various length and scope.[17] By far the longest (1,087 verses) is a poem *On Syntax*, dedicated

8 Michael Psellos, *Poem* 6 ed. Westerink (1992). On poetry in grammatical education, see also van den Berg in this volume.
9 On Niketas and his works, see Schneider (1999), Roosen (1999) and Antonopoulou (2003). For Niketas' place in the genre of Byzantine didactic poetry, see Hörandner (2012) and (2019).
10 A complete list can be found in Schneider (1999).
11 On this consistency, see Schneider (1999: 395) and Antonopoulou (2003: 178).
12 For these canons, see Antonopoulou (2003).
13 Mitsakis (1990).
14 For precise indications and references to existing editions, see Schneider (1999: 389–93).
15 The canons do in fact exist in printed form, in the periodical *Κέκροψ: σύγγραμμα περιοδικὸν τοῦ ἐν Κάιρῳ Ἑλληνικοῦ φιλεκπαιδευτικοῦ συλλόγου Ἡ Ἑνότης* 1.17–18 (1876), pp. 240–9, and 19–20 (1876), pp. 261–9. The (uncritical) 'edition' is not signed. This transcription is based on Alexandria, Bibliotheke tou Patriarcheiou, 364 [Diktyon 33251], fol. 211r–227v and 234r–242v (since the transcription mentions that the end of the second canon is mutilated, just as in the *Alexandrinus*). I thank Febe Schollaert for retrieving this edition online; see http://digital.lib.auth.gr/record/144809.
16 See Follieri (1986).
17 For precise indications, see Schneider (1999: 396–8), who counts seven poems.

to a 'respectable and noble child' (v. 1: πρὸς παῖδα σεμνὸν εὐγενῆ).[18] Despite the very general title 'Verses on Grammar' (στίχοι περὶ γραμματικῆς) in the manuscripts, the poem is chiefly concerned with the complement cases after verbs. The poem is supplemented by a similar poem dealing mainly with double constructions after certain verbs (i.e. verbs with several complement cases).[19] Other poems discuss various grammatical and orthographical problems, sometimes very specific ones.

While there has been no extensive study on the sources of Niketas, even a quick probe establishes that Niketas' poems are largely based on earlier grammatical literature, both in content and in method. The canons, for example, owe a lot to the orthographical rules of George Choiroboskos, and perhaps even more to Theognostos and the so-called epimerisms to Herodian. Also the transmission of Niketas' poems shows that Byzantine readers/users saw these texts as part of the tradition of orthographical treatises. Niketas' poems are chiefly to be found in manuscripts alongside various other (prose) grammatical works. In an even more telling example, the fourteenth-century manuscript Vienna, Österreichische Nationalbibliothek, theol. gr. 322 [Diktyon 71989], the scribe illustrated the (prose) grammatical treatises by interspersing verses taken from Niketas' poems (with his name duly attached to them).[20]

The Attractions of Metre

This makes our initial question perhaps even more relevant. What exactly is the difference between the prose texts on the same subject matter and the poems of Niketas? What are the distinctive features that urge the writer to put in all the effort to phrase knowledge in metre, and that make these poems so attractive to its readers?

A first set of answers is related to the formal features of metre itself. In the case of Niketas' hymnographic poetry, the choice of this metre has mostly been attributed to the need to memorize knowledge.[21] Since the pupils knew these tunes very well from liturgy, they could 'sing along'

18 *Poem on Syntax*, inc. πρὸς παῖδα σεμνόν, ed. Boissonade (1831: 340–93). The English titles I give to the poems in this article do not necessarily correspond to the titles in the manuscripts; I use them here for orientation of the reader. On the poem, see Tovar (1969).

19 This poem is unedited; Nina Vanhoutte is currently preparing an edition of the poem. I thank Nina Vanhoutte for sharing with me the preliminary text of the poem.

20 See Ludwich (1905: 6).

21 Antonopoulou (2003: 181). For a critical reassessment of this argument for Byzantine didactic poetry in general, see Hörandner (2019: 477–8).

with Niketas' poem, and this would enable them to remember these mnemonic orthographical clues better. The use of liturgical tunes for decidedly non-liturgical purposes is not so outlandish a phenomenon in Byzantium: liturgical tunes were used on a quite consistent basis for satire and instruction.[22]

But there is more to metre than just this. In the passages where Niketas discusses his choice of metre on a metapoetical level, he foregrounds a very traditional idea, namely that metre makes an otherwise unattractive or serious subject more palatable and playful.[23] The poem *On Second Aorist Verbs*, for example, begins like this (v. 1):[24]

> Φέρε μικρόν τι παίξωμεν πολιτικοῖς ἐν στίχοις
> τῆς νόσου παρηγόρημα καὶ τῆς μικροψυχίας.
>
> Come on, let us have a little fun in political verse
> as a consolation for sickness and faintheartedness.

And a very similar device is present in the poem *On Syntax* (v. 11):

> Σπουδὴν παιγνίῳ κεραννύς, πολιτικοῖς ἐν στίχοις
> ὡς ἔχῃς ταύτην ὅμηρον ἀγάπης διδασκάλου.
>
> Mingling earnestness with play, in political verse,
> so that you would have it as a pledge of your teacher's love.

In these two examples, the idea that metre adds an element of fun to an earnest subject seems to be associated with the use of the *politikos stichos*. They are perfectly comparable with other metapoetical statements about the motivations and contexts of the use of the *politikos stichos*, such as we find them in the didactic poems of Michael Psellos, for instance.[25] On top of that, Niketas' poem is presented as a gift from a teacher to his pupil (a 'pledge of his love'). Hence, the prologue sets the text firmly in a teacher–student relationship, which, as we will also see below, is a complex and rich relationship involving mutual affection and obligations.

But the idea of mixing earnestness with play in Byzantine poetry is not exclusively reserved for the *politikos stichos*. Remarkably, it is also

22 Mitsakis (1990).
23 See Hörandner (2019: 480–1).
24 *Poem on Second Aorist Verbs*, inc. Φέρε μικρόν τι παίξωμεν, line 1, ed. Lampros (1922: 192). Also quoted in Jeffreys (1974: 166).
25 As evident from the discussion in Jeffreys (1974).

foregrounded in one of Niketas' hymnographical poems, the canon B. This is its epilogue:[26]

> Παιγνία σεμνὰ τεθεικότες τοῖς φιλολόγοις μετὰ μέλους,
> ἔστι γὰρ καὶ παίζειν σωφρόνως·
> ὑμᾶς δ᾽αἰτοῦμαι ἀντιμισθίαν δοῦναι,
> ἀνθ᾽ὧνπερ ἐπονήσαμεν,
> τῆς σωτηρίας τὴν ἐξαίτησιν.
>
> I offer serious games with a melody, to lovers of learning,
> since it is possible to play in a thoughtful way.
> But from you I ask to give me a reward in exchange
> for the toils that I laboured,
> namely to pray for my salvation.

The idea is identical to the one expressed in the poems using *politikos stichos*. Metre (in general) makes discourse more attractive; it is playful, and also considered a 'precious gift' from a teacher to his pupils (similarly to the prologue to the *Poem on Syntax* quoted earlier). The only difference may be that Niketas highlights the 'melody' here, which of course refers to the fact that these poems were sung. Taking these statements together with similar ones for the *politikos stichos*, which was also a purely accentual metre, we can surmise that it is the accentual pattern that is associated with the attractiveness (or even playfulness) of the metre.

In the epilogue to the *Poem on Verbs with Double Constructions*, which is also written in *politikos stichos*, the element of play rather serves as a cover against criticisms for errors. Niketas hopes that he has written a useful piece of work, but if this would not be the case, it may be argued that this was just a play after all.[27] Niketas seems to assign poetic texts to a less respectable realm, where (allegedly) standards are less stringent. It can be related to the lower intellectual status of the *politikos stichos* in the discourse of intellectuals.[28]

26 Canon B, ode θ', strophe 26, as in Paris, Bibliothèque nationale de France, gr. 2558 [Diktyon 52190], fol. 65r, lines 13–15. In some other manuscripts, there are further *troparia* that can be considered 'book epigrams' or 'paratexts', but the poem proper seems to end with this *troparion*. Throughout this article, I will make use of manuscript reproductions because no reliable edition is available as of yet (as mentioned above, Theodora Antonopoulou is preparing one). For convenience, I based myself on the manuscript Paris. gr. 2558. By no means should this be seen as even a beginning of an edition. The manuscript reproductions are taken from https://gallica.bnf.fr/ark:/12148/btv1b8470442q (last accessed 17 April 2021). For a description of Niketas' works in this manuscript, see Schneider (1999: 399–400).

27 *Poem on Verbs with Double Constructions*, inc. τί δαὶ περὶ συντάξεων, lines 136–9, as in Paris. gr. 2558, fol. 85v, right column, lines 15–18.

28 About this tension, see Jeffreys (1974) and Agapitos (2017). See also Bernard (2014: 243–5).

Didactic Plot and Didactic Simultaneity

These features are all related to the formal qualities of metre. But to gauge why didactic poetry was a viable medium for knowledge transmission, we have to look for other more intrinsic features that set off these poems from the prose texts to which they are otherwise so similar.

To begin with, the text of each poem assumes throughout a communicative situation that is clearly pedagogical. In other words, in Niketas' didactic poems, there is a first person, the poet and teacher, who speaks and instructs, addressing a second person, who is represented as a pupil gradually introduced into the knowledge imparted by the text. This has been called the 'didactic plot',[29] since it effectively presupposes a narrative (step-by-step imparting of the knowledge), with certain fixed characters (teachers and pupil). It is common to a majority of didactic poetry, ancient and medieval, Greek and Latin, and probably beyond these languages as well. In doing this, the didactic poem establishes an impression of 'didactic simultaneity':[30] when we read it, we get the impression of an oral lesson unfolding temporally.

Niketas' poems are clearly built upon this didactic principle. At a very basic level, the imperative mood is a convenient tool to establish direct contact with the presupposed pupil. The *dativus ethicus* also enhances this impression of involvement of the addressee. One simple example: [31]

> ιος τὰ ὀξύτονα ἐκ τῶν εἰς ος μὴ γενόμενα μηδ' ὄντα ὀνόματα ποταμῶν βράχυνε ὡς τὰ ζῷα μοι κριὸν χαραδριόν τε etc.
>
> Write for me a short vowel [i.e. ι] in the oxytone words ending in -ιος that are not derived from words ending in -ος and that are no names of rivers, such as animals: κριόν and χαραδριόν.

Moreover, common imperative forms such as γραφέσθωσαν seem to suppose a pupil who in the future will have to 'write' these words.

The pupil is frequently addressed with a vocative, and this happens in both hymnographic and stichic poems. The address can be just βέλτιστε (in Canon B),[32] but also frequently a 'friend'. One poem begins right away with the address πεφιλμένε,[33] another one contains the addresses ὦ φίλος

29 Fowler (2000).
30 Volk (2002: 39–41) and *passim*.
31 Canon A, Ode α', strophe 3, ed. Cohn (1886: 662).
32 Canon B, Ode η', strophe 6, as in Paris, Bibliothèque nationale de France, gr. 2617 [Diktyon 52252], fol. 181r, col. 2, line 8.
33 *Poem inc. πέδον τιθηνόν,* line 1, as in Paris. gr. 2558, fol. 80v, col. 2, line 13.

and πεφιλμένος.[34] The poem *On Syntax* is not only in the prologue, but also throughout addressed to someone who is 'young' (νέε).[35] The *Poem on Noun Stems Ending in –ν* opens and closes with the address to his '(dearest) boys' (v. 2 and 98).[36]

In line with this 'didactic plot', the poems set up a communicative framework that is very typically pedagogical and constructs a little drama between teacher and pupil.[37] The teacher/poet urges the pupil to pay attention to specific parts of his 'lesson', with interjections such as 'and pay attention to these words',[38] or 'listen for me here, to those written with *eta*'.[39] Other passages emphasize that the pupil should not let his attention waver. Thus, the poem inc. πέδον τιθηνόν,[40] which as a whole contains frequent addresses to a 'friend', warns: 'do not pass by [this orthography]' (v. 2: μὴ παραδράμῃς), and (twice) 'let [this] not escape your notice' (v. 4: σὲ μὴ λανθανέτω, v. 5: μὴ σὲ φευγέτω).

Niketas peppers his grammatical rules and examples with many other devices that help to enliven the dry material. Some of them are already mentioned by earlier scholars.[41] Niketas has a habit, for example, of personifying his grammatical topics; he says for instance that certain verbs 'embrace' or 'dance with' a given orthography.

Moreover, Niketas' poems make use of typical structural pointers, announcing topics to be treated imminently, or concluding them. These pointers add a chronological dimension to the poems in time, enhancing the impression that they are oral lessons happening as we read. They also add a thematic structure to the text, dividing it into clearly delineated informational units, just as other informative texts would do.[42] Since the goal of didactic poetry is to transmit science, the poems employ a clear, transparent and often multilayered structure to present the topic at hand.[43] From beginning to end, the poem announces that it discusses the topics according to the logic that a didactic treatment of this topic imposes.

34 *Poem inc. ἔρον σμίκρυνε*, v.11 ὦ φίλος, and v. 80 πεφιλμένος, as in Paris. gr. 2558, fol. 81v, col. 2, line 26 and fol. 82v, col. 1, line 11.
35 *Poem on Syntax*, inc. πρὸς παῖδα σεμνόν, lines 14 and 109.
36 *Poem on Noun Stems Ending in -ν*, inc. καιρὸς μὲν ὕπνου, v. 2: παῖδες, and v. 98: παῖδες φίλτατοι.
37 For the dramatic element in didactic poetry, see also Pizzone (2022).
38 *Poem on Syntax*, inc. πρὸς παῖδα σεμνόν, line 82: καὶ σκόπει μοι τὸν λόγον.
39 Canon B, Ode ζ', strophe 26, as in Paris. gr. 2558, fol. 62r, line 10: τὰ δὲ δι' ἦτα δεῦρο μοι ἄκουε.
40 *Poem inc. πέδον τιθηνόν*, as in Paris. gr. 2558, fol. 80v, col. 2.
41 Schneider (1999: 405–9) and Antonopoulou (2003: 182).
42 For the same phenomenon in Tzetzes' didactic poetry, see van den Berg (2020).
43 This has also been remarked for medieval Latin didactic poetry: Haye (1997: 168–84).

One example out of the many: in the poem *On Syntax*, Niketas announces at a certain point that he will discuss the topic of prepositions.[44]

Τὰς δὲ προθέσεις σκόπει μοι, καὶ τὰς συντάξεις τούτων
ἐκ τῶν μονοσυλλάβων δὲ τῆς διδαχῆς ἀρκτέον.

Consider now the prepositions, and their constructions;
And let us start this lesson with the monosyllabic ones.

After this explanation of constructions with monosyllabic prepositions, Niketas marks the transition to the next subtopic.[45]

Περὶ τῶν δισυλλάβων δὲ καιρὸς ἀπάρτι λέγειν.

It is now time to give a full explanation of the disyllabic prepositions.

Also within this part, the explanation of each preposition is clearly structurally marked. One finds, for instance (in a line which is also a *leçon par l'exemple,* because it explains exactly the preposition μετά):[46]

Μετὰ δὲ ταῦτα πρόσεχε τῇ τῆς μετὰ συντάξει.

After that, pay attention to the construction of μετά.

These structural pointers thus add a three-level structure to the poem, with topic, subtopics, and concrete items within.

This pedagogical setting also includes (supposed) emotional reactions from the pupil, further enlivening the 'didactic drama'. Thus, the teacher sometimes shows concern that some part of the explanation has been going on for too long and may be boring, so it is time to put an end to it:[47]

Ὅσα τε εἰς -φων καταλήγει, καὶ τόνον ἔχει τὸν βαρυνόμενον, οὐ χρὴ γὰρ πλέον λέγειν τι· τοῦ κόρου φεύγοντες τὸ πλήσμιον

As for the nouns that end in -φων and have a barytone stress, we do not need to say more about them, avoiding the saturation of overload.

44 *Poem on Syntax,* inc. πρὸς παῖδα σεμνόν, lines 724–5.
45 *Poem on Syntax,* inc. πρὸς παῖδα σεμνόν, line 763.
46 *Poem on Syntax,* inc. πρὸς παῖδα σεμνόν, line 806.
47 *Canon B,* Ode θ', str. 15, as in Paris. gr. 2558, fol. 64v, lines 2–3.

This remark reminds us that didactic poems are not intended to treat the subject in exhaustive detail. They are summaries of knowledge for didactic consumption. Concision is indeed an important part of the didactic aesthetic. Time and again, didactic poems emphasize how they make knowledge more concise and easier to survey. Thus, in the introduction to the *Poem on Syntax*, which is nevertheless his longest, Niketas proudly states how he will attempt to teach syntax in 'a short treatise' (v. 10 τὴν σύνταξιν ... | συντόμῳ πειραθήσομαι μεθόδῳ παραδοῦναι). Yet, Niketas promises his pupil that his text will still transmit the full content of the topic (vv. 13–14):[48]

> Λέξεων τοίνυν πέφυκε παράθεσις ὁ λόγος
> σημαίνουσα διάνοιαν, ὦ νέε, πληρεστάτην.
>
> My text is a composition of words
> that nevertheless gives, my boy, a most complete meaning.

The poem *On Second Aorist Verbs* contains a long metatextual passage that focuses on the method Niketas uses (vv. 70–7):[49]

> Πλὴν ἀλλ' ὡς ἐν ὑφάσματι πάντα ἁρμοστέον
> κατὰ στοιχεῖον ἀπ' ἀρχῆς μέχρις αὐτοῦ τοῦ τέλους.
> δεῖ γὰρ τὸν πέπλον ἐντελῆ τοῦ λόγου προσυφαίνειν
> καὶ συντηρεῖν ἀκριβασμὸν τὸν τῆς ἀλληλουχίας
> καὶ καθ' εἱρμὸν καὶ σύνδεσμον τὰ λείποντα διδάσκειν,
> δεικνύντος τὴν ἀκρίβειαν τοῦ τεχνικοῦ κανόνος,
> πρὸς ὅνπερ ἀπευθύνοιτο ῥημάτων ἀρτιότης
> τὰ περιττὰ δὲ τέμνοιτο τοῦ λόγου τῇ μαχαίρᾳ.
>
> But just as in weaving, we have to fit everything together,
> one by one, from the beginning until the very end.
> For we need to weave the complete dress of words,
> preserve the requirements of consistency,
> teaching the lacunas according to tune and order.
> The precise method is shown by the art's rules,
> according to which the right proportion of words is defined,
> and the superfluous words are cut out with a knife.

Niketas is conscious here of his efforts to achieve a clearly structured, coherent whole, in which not a word too much is said, and where he cuts

48 *Poem on Syntax*, inc. πρὸς παῖδα σεμνόν, lines 13–14.
49 *Poem on Second Aorist Verbs*, inc. Φέρε μικρόν τι παίξωμεν, ed. Lampros (1922: 192).

out all unnecessary information. Concision, coherence and a clear logical structure are presented as major assets of the poems.

On a very basic level, this is what verse does: by forcing the author to put an end to his thought after a given number of syllables, he is automatically forced to express himself in a concise manner.[50] The idea of brevity, and especially, concision (being complete while using few words) is paramount in prologues and epilogues of didactic poems.[51] Thus, the verse format, by its very nature, provides structure to unwieldy material and makes it easy to survey. The prologue to the *Poem on Verbs with Double Constructions* uses a similar motif. Niketas avers that he wants to be brief, and wonders how he can best economize his words, so that still everything is being said, but that he avoids being boring or cumbersome (vv. 7–9).[52]

At times, the communicative setting becomes more concrete. The *Poem on Nouns Ending on -ια/εια* begins with the statement that a certain 'friend' named Michael had complained that this topic had been neglected.[53] Modern scholars assumed that Michael must have been a fellow teacher, because supposedly a pupil would not make such a brazen request.[54] But similar requests are also known from Psellos' letters, and there they certainly come from a pupil. We have to take into account that pupils were 'friends' (frequently called as thus by Niketas, as we have seen). They had a considerable say in the educational process. The poems are thus firmly anchored in the community of pupils under Niketas' care.

This brings us to another aspect of the didactic poetics of Niketas: his awareness that the marriage of 'unpoetic' content and metrical form is an extraordinary achievement.[55] In two instances, he compares his poetic enterprise with a horse race. In *The Poem on Second Aorist Verbs*, he specifically compares the 'horse race' (ἱππικὸς ἀγὼν) with the 'contest of words' (λογικὸς ἀγών):[56]

> Καὶ φέρε μυωπήσωμεν τὸν πῶλον πρὸς τὴν νύσσαν
> τὸν λογικὸν δραμοῦμενον ὡς ἱππικὸν ἀγῶνα
> καὶ τῇ τοῦ νοῦ μαστίξωμεν μάστιγι πρὸς τὸν δρόμον
> πετασθησόμενον εὐθὺς ὡς οἱ παρ' Ὁμήρῳ,

50 On concision and poetry, see Bernard and Demoen (2021).

51 For Tzetzes, see van den Berg (2020). For Psellos, see Bernard (2014: 238–40).

52 *Poem on Verbs with Double Constructions*, inc. τί δαί περὶ συντάξεων, lines 7–9, as in Paris. gr. 2558, fol. 84v, left column, lines 7–9.

53 Guglielmino (1974: 430): ἔφης, ὦ φίλε Μιχαήλ, μόνα με τῶν ἁπάντων | διὰ τῆς ιᾶ θηλυκὰ μὴ παραδεδωκέναι …

54 Schneider (1999: 413).

55 Haye (1997: 45–103).

56 *Poem on Second Aorist Verbs*, inc. φέρε μικρόν τι παίξωμεν, lines 85–93.

καὶ τοῦ διαύλου θεατὴς ὁ φιλόλογος ἔστω,
ᾧπερ καὶ παραινέσομεν χρήσιμους παρεμφάσεις,
αὐτὰ δὴ τὰ προκείμενα παράγοντες εἰς μέσον.
Μὴ τοὺς ἐμοὺς λυσιτελεῖς ἔρρειν ἀφήσεις λόγους,
ὡς ἀποβήσονται καλὰ τοῦ βίου σοῦ τὰ τέλη.

So, let us prod the horse towards the turning post,
so that it can run the contest of words like a horse race,
and let us whip it with the whip of our minds, towards the race,
so that it can rush forward as the horses of Homer.
And let the lover of words be the spectator of this course,
to whom I will give these useful pieces of advice,
putting forward these very words you are seeing.
Make sure to not leave my words to be for naught,
as they will turn out to be profitable life goals.

The race they are running is one of words, instead of horses. Niketas likens his enterprise to a horse that he wants to keep focused on the track. The spectators of his race are the 'philologists', his pupils, to whom he gives advice that will prove to be very useful in their lives. The pupils are the privileged audience of his poems, and also assess the performance of their teacher. This attributes a very theatrical aspect to the didactic poems (let us not forget that the hippodrome was the θέατρον par excellence for the Byzantines).

At the same time, Niketas shows himself very much aware of the extraordinary usefulness of his poem. Pupils will profit from it: the phrase τὰ τέλη τοῦ βίου quite unambiguously points to the professional prospects of the pupils. Displaying your brilliance in education was indeed in this time a viable means to climb the social ladder through bureaucratic functions, and spelling (as tested with the schedography contest) was the first of these prerequisites.

In the *Poem on Verbs with Double Constructions* the same imagery is used. In a long transitional passage, Niketas again compares his poetic enterprise to a horse who is riding a race.[57] Facing the sneers and taunts of the audience, Niketas spurs it on to the end. This idea may owe something to the context of competitions (see below), but it also shows his pride in his poetic achievement. Also in the prologue to the poem, Niketas mentions how the topic at hand (syntactic constructions) makes for a 'difficult enterprise',[58] which he will take on nevertheless.

57 *Poem on Verbs with Double Constructions*, lines 56–66; as quoted in Schneider (1999: 414).
58 *Poem on Verbs with Double Constructions*, line 2, πάνυ δύσεργον τὸ πόνημα, as quoted in Schneider (1999: 414).

While these passages do not refer specifically to the fact that Niketas wrote these texts in verse, one would be very hard pressed to find statements as this in prose texts. It is in poems that the didactic theatre, with its typical communicative situation and self-referentiality, comes to life. At the same time, as we have seen, verse made for a more playful, attractive performance.

Niketas was certainly proud of his poems: it is emphatically his own personal achievement. In the epilogue to Canon A, he is not shy of mentioning his full name and function of *proximos* of the Chalkoprateia school, adding that his poem is 'a very expedient piece of work' (φιλοτέχνημα πολυωφελέστατον).[59] In the following strophe, which in many manuscripts concludes the poem, Niketas (or a later scribe) states:[60]

> ὄνομα καλὸν καὶ σφόδρα θαυμάσιον ἡ βίβλος κτήσεται· μεγαλεμπορία γὰρ τοῖς φιλολόγοις, οἶδα, κληθήσεται, τοῖς ἀντιστοίχοις βρίθουσα καὶ πυκνουμένη καλῶς τοῖς κανόσιν.
>
> This book will acquire a beautiful and very wonderful name, for I know lovers of words will call it an 'advantageous affair', since it teems with homophones (*antistoicha*), and has a rich abundance of rules.

Once again, this strophe refers to the fact that students will reap benefit from the book. After having learnt it, they will be able to solve all orthographical problems, and this will propel them into a successful career.

The *Leçon par l'exemple* and the Didactic Setting

The didactic setting is not only in evidence in these brief metapoetical statements. It is also very much present in the content of Niketas' poems itself, especially in the examples with which he illustrates the grammatical and orthographical rules. For this, he makes use of a powerful pedagogical tool, namely the *leçon par l'exemple*. He illustrates knowledge by using an example, but these examples are not random: they have another meaning that is also relevant.[61] In other words, there is a double layer at work: ostensibly, the example illustrates a given grammatical or orthographical rule, say, a certain verb going together with a complement in a certain case,

59 Canon A, Ode θ', strophe 27, as quoted in Antonopoulou (2003: 182).
60 Canon A, Ode θ', strophe 28, here given according to Paris. gr. 2558, fol. 72r. See also Schneider (1999: 411–12).
61 Tzetzes, too, uses the *leçon par l'exemple* as a pedagogical strategy: see van den Berg in this volume.

but this example, if taken literally, also has a meaning in the teacher/pupil setting. In the verbs in the first person, it is the character of the teacher who is speaking, while in the second person, the actions are attributed to the pupil. The examples themselves often pertain to the world of education and/or contain a moral lesson.

The technique is present to some degree in all of Niketas' poems, but is used to great effect in the middle section of the long poem *On Syntax*, where Niketas embarks on a lengthy exposition of cases following verbs with various prefixes (v. 386–591). He introduces this section with the warning that this part of his discourse will contain some criticisms directed at the pupil, arguing that this is only the result of the pupil's sluggishness. Niketas also concludes the section with a justification why he has been so harsh on his pupil.

In between, there is a long series of model sentences that show the meaning of various verbs with various constructions. In them, the student is reproached for being lazy, careless, and contemptuous of his teacher, while the teacher goes out of his way to cater to the student's needs. The student is urged to put more effort. Here is an example from the section that deals with the syntactical construction of the verbs with the roots –ψεύδω and –τρέχω (lines 395–405).

ἐψεύσω, διεψεύσω με τῶν ἐλπισμῶν ὧν εἶχον. 395
ἐμοῦ καταψευσάμενος, συμψεύδῃ τοὺς ἐχθρούς μου·
ἐχθροὺς αὐτὸς γὰρ κέκτημαι τοὺς ἀμελεῖς τῶν νέων.
ἐν δόλοις ὑποτρέχειν με καὶ περιτρέχειν θέλεις,
τοῦς ῥᾳθυμοῦντας ἅπαντας ἀφρόνως ὑπερτρέχων·
οὐ διατρέχειν γὰρ φιλεῖς τοὺς διδασκάλων οἴκους 400
μισεῖς τοὺς λόγων ἔρωτας, τὰς βίβλους παρατρέχεις·
ἐκτρέχεις μου τῆς ὄψεως, καὶ φεύγων ἀποτρέχεις·
τῶν συναμιλλωμένων σοι προτρέχειν οὐκ ἐπείγῃ·
συντρέχειν οὐκ ἐπόθησας τοῖς φιλοπόνοις νέοις,
οὐδ' ἀντιτρέχειν ἔσπευσας τοῖς ἀντηγωνισμένοις. 405

You have lied, you have belied the hopes I had. 395
By accusing me falsely, you have joined the lies of my foes,
for the slothful among the youth, these are my own enemies.
You want stealthily to avoid and escape me,
mindlessly surpassing all the lazy ones.
For you don't desire to frequent the houses of the teacher. 400
You hate the love for words, you leave the books aside,
you run out of my sight, you flee away.
And you don't hurry to succour those who fight together with you,

for you didn't want to run the course with diligent youths,
neither did you strive to fight with your adversaries. 405

The passage paints a vivid picture of a teacher who goes out of his way to provide his pupils with the right knowledge, while the pupil is inclined to neglect books and words, and even avoids his teacher. In the three last lines of the passage quoted here, we also see references to 'contests'. The pupil's fellows, who are more diligent than him, valiantly take up 'fights' with adversaries – we will return to these.

The pupil is cast as a character who rather indulges in laziness or in horse riding (line 462). The teacher provides him with 'beneficial words' (line 488: λόγους ὠφελίμους, probably referring to this very poem),[62] but the pupil contradicts him (553: τὸ δ' ἀντιλέγειν μοι τολμᾷς) and even mocks him. It is only logical that this invokes the teacher's anger (548: θυμοῦ μοι ζέσαντος), and Niketas mentions frequently the whip as a tool to discipline him in vain (line 513: ταῖς διδασκάλων μάστιξιν; 500: μοι μαστίζοντι; 555: καταφρονεῖς μαστίγων). The examples also frequently bring up the theme of *agrypnia*: instead of being awake for the sake of study, the lazy pupil prefers to stay in bed (see line 420: ἐν κλίνῃ κατακείμενος οὐκ ἀγρυπνεῖν ἐθέλεις), he mocks those pupils who stay awake (467: τοὺς ἀγρυπνοῦντας παίζων), and he scorns the act of staying awake (512: τὸ δ' ἀγρυπνεῖν, ὡς ὑπνηλὸς, ὡς φαῦλον ἐξορχοῦμαι). His teacher, on the other hand, had completed this poem in one night (5: μικρὸς τῆς μιᾶς νυκτὸς πόνος). *Agrypnia* was indeed hailed by contemporary teachers as an ideal to live by: to devote a life to letters, one should be prepared to leave sleep behind, and study or write with the light of the oil lamp.[63]

The poem *On Noun Stems Ending in -ν* is completely built around the theme of *agrypnia*. The introduction, with a witty wordplay, goes as follows:[64]

καιρὸς μὲν ὕπνου, καὶ καθεύδειν ἦν δέον·
ἀλλ' οὖν δι' ὑμᾶς, παῖδες, ἀγρυπνητέον,
ἡ νὺξ δὲ τοῦ νῦ λῆξιν ἐξεταζέτω.

Yes, it is time to sleep, and we should go to bed.
But for your sake now, my boys, one should stay awake,
and let the night examine the stems ending in *-nu*.

62 *Poem on Syntax*, inc. πρὸς παῖδα σεμνόν, line 488.
63 For instance, Christopher of Mytilene, *Poem* 40, line 75, ed. De Groote (2012).
64 *Poem on Noun Stems Ending in -ν*, inc. καιρὸς μὲν ὕπνου, lines 1–3.

At the end of the poem, Niketas completes the joke, saying he will go off to sleep now (v. 96–7: ἀλλ' ὑπνωτέον. | Τὸ γὰρ πόνημα σὺν θεῷ τέλος φέρει; 'But now it's time to sleep, for the work, with the help of God, has come to an end'). His pupils, after learning this useful lesson, should also go to bed, mix the masculine with the feminine gender, and this way, they will beget the most accomplished words. Rather than just a tasteless joke,[65] Niketas cleverly combines the subject matter (the poem is about nouns that could be either masculine or feminine) with the well-known metaphor of begetting texts as children.

This is all quite playful of course, but it fits within a broader framework of texts where the social side of education comes very much into evidence. The poem constructs a teacher–student relationship that is quite typical for Byzantium, and can for instance also be compared to the letters of the Anonymous Professor,[66] or the short treatises of Michael Psellos addressed to his students.[67] These show a mixture of tender affection and censure and admonition: pupils are late, play truant, are inclined to lend their ear to other teachers as well, while the teacher forsakes even his sleep to provide the pupils with the best teaching materials.

Schedography

Let us go back to the passage quoted earlier, the long passage illustrating the various meanings of composite verbs when construed with different cases. As we have seen, these referred to 'fights' and 'alliances'. These 'contests' are of course nothing else than the famous *schedos* contests, which are so often mentioned in texts (especially poems) in the decades before and after Niketas.[68] These public contests pitted students from different schools against each other and tested their knowledge of grammar, especially the orthographical problem of *antistoicha*.[69] In the context of the contemporary didactic setting that Niketas evokes in his poems, it is only natural that the *schedos* contest, which was so vital to grammarians in eleventh- and twelfth-century Byzantium, is often mentioned.

65 Schneider (1999: 412).
66 As discussed in Markopoulos (2006).
67 Littlewood (1985), orations 21–4.
68 Before: Bernard (2014: 259–66). After (with connection to social context and literary culture): Agapitos (2014). On school contests, see also Gerbi in this volume.
69 On the *schedos*, see Vassis (1993–4), Polemis (1997), Agapitos (2013) and (2014), Nousia (2016: 49–92).

Continuing the plot line of the 'lazy pupil' censured in his syntactical examples, Niketas writes:[70]

> Καταπαλαίει σοῦ τὸν νοῦν ἡ φαύλη ῥᾳθυμία,
> καὶ συμπαλαίειν οὐ τολμᾷς ἀρίστοις σχεδογράφοις,
> ὅθεν ἀργὸς καθήμενος ταῖς ἄταις προσπαλαίεις.
>
> Evil laziness strikes down your brains,
> and you don't dare to fight with the best *schedos* writers,
> so that you sit there idle, wrestling with your delusions.

This fits with the image encountered in other poetry related to the *schedos*, or to the content of the *schede* themselves: pupils are continuously encouraged to fight a valiant fight and to not be so slothful.[71] The 'schedographers' are the fellow pupils who have to solve the *schede* at the specialized contests.[72]

Schedography is a constant theme in the *Poem on Syntax*. Already in the prologue, Niketas states (vv. 25–6) that the topic at hand is very relevant for '*schedos* writers such as you' (τοῖς σχεδογράφοις κατὰ σέ). In other words, Niketas will limit his poem to those issues that will be put to the students in the *schedos* contests. His didactic poem (perhaps his entire grammatical oeuvre) should thus be seen as a 'manual' for students to perform well at the *schedos* contests. Other references are to be found dispersed over the whole poem, in the examples Niketas uses to adumbrate his syntactical explanation. Thus, explaining verbs that are construed with a dative, Niketas has his pupil say: 'I delight and take pleasure in the study of *schede*' (v. 478: ἐνασμενίζω, φιληδῶ τῇ τῶν σχεδῶν μελέτῃ).

Niketas' poems contain hints not only at the present didactic situation, but also at future occasions where the orthographical skills of the pupils will be put to the test. Thus, in the canons Niketas at several occasions inserts remarks such as: 'You should write δριμύς, δριμεῖα and δρίον (an overgrown spot) with iota, and you will never be wrong.'[73] Even more relevant to the communal aspect of *schedos* contests is a remark such as 'When you write this with a diphthong, you will not betray my hope in

70 *Poem on Syntax*, inc. πρὸς παῖδα σεμνόν, lines 427–9.

71 For this theme in the texts of *schede* themselves, see especially the collection of *schede* edited in Vassis (2002).

72 *Schedos* writers (σχεδογράφοι) refer to the students solving the *schede*, not to teachers composing the *schede* (who are σχεδοπλόκοι or σχεδουργοί). See Vassis (1993–4: 9).

73 Canon B, Ode δ', strophe 16, as in Paris. gr. 2558, fol. 58r, line 23–4: δριμὺς, δριμεῖα, δρίον (τόπος σύμφυτος) ἰῶτα γραφέσθω σοι. καὶ οὐχ ἁμαρτήσεις οὐδέποτε. See also, very similarly, lines 11–12.

you.'[74] Niketas seems to imply that the poem prepares the pupil for future occasions, where he is expected to write correctly, and where the teacher anxiously watches his pupils' performances, hoping that they will do well.

A shorter poem on various orthographical problems, inc. πέδον τιθηνόν, is almost entirely written with the schedography contests in mind. The second person/pupil in this poem is called a 'schedographer' (v. 10: ἔκτεινε τὸν κώρυκον, ὦ σχεδογράφε), just as in the *Poem on Syntax*. In the examples, Niketas foresees that the orthographical problems will be put to the students in *schedos* contests. For example, he recommends: 'Write the word τυκαμή with an eta in the *schedos*',[75] or 'κίλιξ, Κίλικος and κιλίκιος are words that are angry with the *schedos* writer who makes mistakes against them.'[76] This last example implies that these words had been submitted to pupils in schedography contests and caused many of them to make errors. I even suspect that the very beginning of the poem is a typical schedographic problem: pupils will of course be inclined to hear rather παίδων than πέδον. The orthographical poem inc. ἔρον σμίκρυνε is similar. Niketas also here calls his pupil a 'schedographer',[77] and frequently recommends writing words in this or that way in the *schedos*.[78]

It is also in the context of *schedos* contests that we have to interpret a long and very interesting metapoetical passage in the poem *On Second Aorist Verbs*. The passage follows immediately upon the passage quoted earlier, where Niketas had likened his poem to a horse race, and where he had underlined the usefulness of his words. Niketas gives the following advice (while using as many asigmatic aorist and future conjugations as possible) (v. 94–105):[79]

> Ἂν γὰρ ἀνήσῃς τὴν πηγὴν τῶν φαύλων ῥᾳθυμίαν
> αἱρήσεις τε συμφοιτητὰς ἐν τῷ καιρῷ τῆς πάλης
> οὐκ ἂν εὐδοκιμήσεως τῆς φίλης ἁμαρτήσεις ...
> Ἂν δώσῃς δέ γε σεαυτὸν ἀνέσει καὶ ῥαστώνῃ
> οἱ δυσμενεῖς δυνήσονται βλάπτειν ἐκ τοῦ προχείρου

74 *Poem inc. πεδον τιθηνόν*, line 21, as in Paris. gr. 2558, fol. 81r, left column, line 3: Δίφθογγον ποιῶν οὐ σφαλεῖς τῆς ἐλπίδος.

75 *Poem inc. πεδον τιθηνόν*, line 41, as in Paris. gr. 2558, fol. 81r, left column, line 23: Τὸν τυκαμὴ τοῦ η τῷ σχέδει γράφε.

76 *Poem inc. πεδον τιθηνόν*, lines 69–70, as in Paris. gr. 2558, fol. 81r–v, last line and first line respectively: Κίλιξ Κίλικος καὶ κιλίκιος λόγος | προσώχθισαν πταίοντι τῷ σχεδοφράφῳ; also cited by Schneider (1999: 409).

77 *Poem inc. ἔρον σμίκρυνε*, lines 19–20, as in Paris. gr. 2558, fol. 82r, left column, lines 8–9.

78 A full list of references to schedography in these two poems is to be found in Schneider (1999: 416–17), who is primarily interested in the dating and coherence of Niketas' oeuvre.

79 See Lampros (1922: 195–6); adapted after viewing Paris. gr. 2558, fol. 83v.

ἡμεῖς δ᾽ οὐχ ἕξομεν ἰσχὺν ὥστε σοι προσαμύνειν,
εἰσόμεθα δ᾽ ὡς ἔσονται πάντες ὑπέρτεροί σου.

If you let go of slothfulness, that source of evil,
and if you side with your fellow students at the time of the contest,
then you will not miss the appreciation that you long for. …
But if you give yourself over to entertainment and laziness,
your enemies will be able to hurt you easily,
and I will not have the power to protect you,
knowing fully well that everyone will defeat you.

Again, the teacher exhorts the pupil to be diligent; only in this way can he, together with his classmates, face the adversaries in 'the contest', which can be nothing else than the schedography contest. If he gives in to laziness, his adversaries will ridicule him, and, Niketas adds, his teacher will then no longer be able to help him, and he will only suffer. This passage gives again an impression of the sense of community between teachers and students, solidified by solidarity and empathy. Moreover, in the passages that we have been quoting, students are often called φιλόλογοι, 'lovers of words', an enduring and endearing address that creates a common purpose among this tightly bonded group that would seek solidarity when engaging in the *schedos* contests.

In sum, Niketas' poems should be seen as poetic manuals preparing the students to be successful in the *schedos* contests. Contrary to earlier assessments, I would rather think that Niketas wrote these poems while still a *proximos* at the school of Chalkoprateia.[80] We know also from the poems of Christopher of Mytilene (poems 9–11) that this school was involved with schedography contests. But the poems are not only manuals: they encourage the students in the face of the *schedos* contests, and reiterate their teacher's trust in them. These texts strengthen the bonds among groups of students and between students and teachers.

Conclusion

These frequent references to *schedos* contests once more confirm that Niketas' didactic poetry is firmly rooted in the day-to-day practice of contemporary education. Rather than disseminating knowledge in general, Niketas' poems find their origins in the specific cultural and social characteristics of grammatical education at Constantinopolitan schools. Teachers operated independently, attempting to attract pupils, who were rather free to go from

80 For the earlier view, see Tovar (1969).

one teacher to the other. When it pertains to grammar and proper language teaching, the reputation of the teachers depended on their pupils' performance at the *schedos* contests. Hence, the most important task of a grammarian was to prepare students well for these typical problems. And if possible, a teacher would make sure his teaching material is easy to survey and finds an attractive place in classroom communication. That is exactly what the poems of Niketas do: they are poetic manuals preparing the students to be successful in the *schedos* contests. The teacher even holds up the favourable professional prospects for his pupils that result from this success.

In this way, the poems create a community regulated by ideals of intellectual friendship. In Byzantium, teacher–student relationships were defined in terms of friendship. In this framework, the teacher is utterly dedicated to the pursuit of grammar, as exemplified by *agrypnia*. He expects from his pupils the same, so they do not put him to shame in the schedography contests. In exchange for this, he produces poems that are on the one hand respectfully offered as tokens of affection, to be sung or declaimed together, but on the other hand he never ceases to urge them to alertness and zeal. The poems transmit a sense of community, more than turgid unrhythmical prose texts can do. Whereas those prose texts are rather reference works to be consulted in silence and alone, the poems evoke interaction and emotional response. Supposing that they are recited or sung collectively, we can see them as reinforcing a group culture, in a lively setting of communal bonds and competition.

Niketas' didactic poems share all the elements of didactic poetry in a large sense. But rather than a play of genre, the intratextual communicative situation is so specific that we should take historical circumstances into account. The writing of didactic poetry needs to be understood against the lively background of competitive school life in Constantinople. Niketas makes use of the means he has at his disposal (some innovative, some deeply ingrained in the didactic genre) to attain these goals. The communicative situation, the conscious structuring, the self-awareness of the poet/teacher, the typical 'plot' of teacher and pupil, complete with emotional overtones, can all be understood as traditional motives that are used and adapted by Niketas in his role as teacher/poet, which had a historical reality behind it.

Bibliography

Agapitos, P. A. (2013) 'Anna Komnene and the Politics of Schedographic Training and Colloquial Discourse', *Nea Rhome* 10: 89–107.

(2014) 'Grammar, Genre and Patronage in the Twelfth Century: A Scientific Paradigm and its Implications', *JÖByz* 64: 1–22.

(2017) 'John Tzetzes and the Blemish Examiners: A Byzantine Teacher on Schedography, Everyday Language and Writerly Disposition', *MEG* 17: 1–57.
Antonopoulou, T. (2003) 'The Orthographical Kanons of Nicetas of Heraclea', *JÖByz* 53: 171–85.
Bernard, F. (2014) *Writing and Reading Byzantine Secular Poetry, 1025–1081*. Oxford.
Bernard, F., and K. Demoen (2021) 'Poetry?', in *Oxford Handbook of Byzantine Literature*, ed. S. Papaioannou, 365–80. Oxford.
Boissonade, J. F. (ed.) (1831) *Anecdota Graeca*, vol. 3. Paris.
Cohn, L. (1886) 'Nicetae serrarum episcopi rhythmi de marium fluviorum lacuum montium urbium gentium lapidum nominibus', *Jahrbücher für classische Philologie* 133: 649–66.
De Groote, M. (ed.) (2012) *Christophori Mitylenaii Versuum variorum collectio Cryptensis*. Turnhout.
Follieri, E. (1986) 'Ἀντίστοιχα', *Diptycha* 4: 217–28.
Fowler, D. (2000) 'The Didactic Plot', in *Matrices of Genre: Authors, Canons, and Society*, ed. M. Depew and D. Obbink, 205–19. Cambridge, MA.
Guglielmino, A. M. (1974) 'Un maestro di grammatica a Bisanzio nell'XI secolo e l'epitafio per Niceta di Michele Psello', *Siculorum Gymnasium* 27: 421–63.
Harder, A. (2007) 'To Teach or Not to Teach ...? Some Aspects of the Genre of Didactic Poetry in Antiquity', in *Calliope's Classroom: Studies in Didactic Poetry from Antiquity to the Renaissance*, ed. A. Harder, A. MacDonald and G. J. Reinink, 23–47. Paris.
Haye, T. (1997) *Das lateinische Lehrgedicht im Mittelalter: Analyse einer Gattung*. Leiden.
Hörandner, W. (2012) 'The Byzantine Didactic Poem: A Neglected Literary Genre? A Survey with Special Reference to the Eleventh Century', in *Poetry and its Contexts in Eleventh-Century Byzantium*, ed. F. Bernard and K. Demoen, 55–67. Farnham.
(2019) 'Teaching with Verse in Byzantium', in *A Companion to Byzantine Poetry*, ed. W. Hörandner, A. Rhoby and N. Zagklas, 459–86. Brill's Companions to the Byzantine World 4. Leiden.
Jeffreys, M. J. (1974) 'The Nature and Origin of the Political Verse', *DOP* 28: 141–95.
Kneebone, E. (2020) *Oppian's Halieutica: Charting a Didactic Epic*. Cambridge.
Kozodoy, M. (2011) 'Medieval Hebrew Medical Poetry: Uses and Contexts', *Aleph* 11: 213–88.
Lampros, S. (1922) 'Ἰωάννου τοῦ Τζέτζου περὶ ῥημάτων αὐθυποτάκτων στίχοι πολιτικοί', *Νέος Ἑλληνομνήμων* 16: 191–7.
Lauxtermann, M. (2009) 'Byzantine Didactic Poetry and the Question of Poeticality', in *'Doux remède...': Poésie et poétique à Byzance. Actes du IVe Colloque International Philologique* 'ΕΡΜΗΝΕΙΑ', *Paris, 23–24–25 février 2006, organisé par l'E.H.E.S.S. et l'Université de Chypre*, ed. P. Odorico, P. A. Agapitos and M. Hinterberger, 37–46. Dossiers byzantins 9. Paris.
(2019) *Byzantine Poetry from Pisides to Geometres: Texts and Contexts*, vol. 2. Wiener Byzantinistische Studien 24/2. Vienna.

Littlewood, A. (ed.) (1985) *Michael Psellus: Oratoria minora*. Leipzig.
Ludwich, A. (1905) *Anekdota zur griechischen Orthographie*. Königsberg.
Markopoulos, A. (2006) 'De la structure de l'école byzantine: Le maître, les livres et le processus éducatif', in *Lire et écrire à Byzance*, ed. B. Mondrain, 85–96. Paris.
Mitsakis, K. (1990) 'Byzantine and Modern Greek Parahymnography', *Studies in Eastern Chant* 5: 9–76.
Nousia, F. (2016) *Byzantine Textbooks of the Palaeologan Period*. Studi e Testi 505. Vatican City.
Pizzone, A. (2022) 'Cultural Appropriation and the Performance of Exegesis in John Tzetzes' Scholia on Aristophanes', in *Byzantine Commentaries on Ancient Greek Texts, 12th–15th Centuries*, ed. B. van den Berg, D. Manolova and P. Marciniak, 100–29. Cambridge.
Polemis, I. (1997) 'Philologische und historische Probleme in der schedographischen Sammlung des Codex Marcianus gr. XI, 34', *Byzantion* 67: 252–63.
Roosen, B. (1999) 'The Works of Nicetas Heracleensis ὁ τοῦ Σερρῶν', *Byzantion* 69: 119–44.
Schneider, J. (1999) 'La poésie didactique à Byzance: Nicétas d'Héraclée', *BAGB* 58: 388–423.
Schuler, R. M., and J. G. Fitch (1983) 'Theory and Context of the Didactic Poem: Some Classical, Mediaeval, and Later Continuities', *Florilegium* 5: 1–43.
Tovar, A. (1969) 'Nicetas of Heraclea and Byzantine Grammatical Doctrine', in *Classical Studies Presented to Ben Edwin Perry*, 223–35. Urbana.
van den Berg, B. (2020) 'John Tzetzes as Didactic Poet and Learned Grammarian', *DOP* 74: 285–302.
Vassis, I. (1993–4) 'Graeca sunt, non leguntur: Zu den schedographischen Spielereien des Theodoros Prodromos', *ByzZ* 86–7.1: 1–19.
(2002) 'Των νέων φιλολόγων παλαίσματα: Η συλλογή σχέδων του κώδικα Vaticanus Palatinus Gr. 92', *Ἑλληνικά* 52: 37–68.
Vogt, S. (2005) '"... er schrieb in Versen, und er tat recht daran": Lehrdichtung im Urteil Galens', in *Antike Fachtexte / Ancient Technical Texts*, ed. T. Fögen, 51–78. Berlin.
Volk, K. (2002) *The Poetics of Latin Didactic: Lucretius, Vergil, Ovid, Manilius*. Oxford.
von Staden, H. (1998) 'Gattung und Gedächtnis: Galen über Wahrheit und Lehrdichtung', in *Gattungen wissenschaftlicher Literatur in der Antike*, ed. W. Kullmann, J. Althoff and M. Asper, 65–92. Tübingen.
Westerink, L. G. (ed.) (1992) *Michaelis Pselli Poemata*. Stuttgart.

CHAPTER 6

Teaching Grammar through Poetry
Tzetzes' Scholia on the Carmina Iliaca *in Context**

Baukje van den Berg

Poetry played an important role in Byzantine teaching of grammar: teachers used poetry, whether ancient or Byzantine, to instruct their students in the rules of grammar and to provide them with a wide variety of information on ancient Greek language, literature, history and mythology.[1] The many surviving texts related to grammatical education can therefore tell us much about Byzantine linguistic, literary and cultural thought. Twelfth-century scholars and teachers such as John Tzetzes, Eustathios of Thessalonike and Gregory of Corinth produced a large body of writings that, to a greater or lesser extent, were aimed at teaching grammar, often with ancient poetry as their point of departure.[2] This chapter will explore the topics and didactic strategies involved in teaching grammar through poetry in twelfth-century Byzantium. I will take the prolific grammarian John Tzetzes and his *Carmina Iliaca* as my case study, considering how he used his own poem to teach grammar.[3]

In characteristic fashion, Tzetzes furnished his poem with numerous explanatory scholia, the first of which expresses his didactic intentions: with the *Carmina Iliaca*, Tzetzes aimed to provide young students with a concise panorama of the Trojan War.[4] The poem relates the Trojan history

* I would like to thank Andrea Cuomo, Andreas Rhoby and Nikos Zagklas for their valuable comments on an earlier version of this chapter; I am also grateful to audiences in Vienna and Oxford for their useful feedback.

1 On poetry and (grammar) education, see e.g. Bernard (2014: 209–51). On Byzantine education in general, see e.g. Giannouli (2014), Markopoulos (2014) and Nesseris (2014), with references to further bibliography. See also Bernard in this volume for didactic poetry related to grammar teaching.

2 For an introduction to their scholarship, see Pontani (2020: 447–9 for Gregory, 452–9 for Tzetzes, 460–7 for Eustathios).

3 On Tzetzes as grammarian, see also van den Berg (2020); on didactic strategies in the *Carmina Iliaca*, see also Mondini (2022); for similar strategies in the *Theogony*, see Tomadaki (2022, esp. 138–42). On Tzetzes, see also Pizzone in this volume and Bértola in this volume.

4 Introductory scholion, p. 101 Leone (1995). References to and quotations from the text and scholia of the *Carmina Iliaca* are from the edition by Leone (1995). For an Italian translation of the *Carmina Iliaca*, see Leone (2005).

in about 1,700 hexameters, divided into three parts: (1) the *Antehomerica* deals with the events preceding Homer's *Iliad*, from Hecabe's dream anticipating the birth of Paris up to the death of Palamedes; (2) the *Homerica* presents a summary of the *Iliad*, with many deviations from the Homeric version of events; (3) the *Posthomerica* discusses the events after the *Iliad*, from the arrival of Penthesileia at Troy to the destruction of the city. Many of the scholia, however, demonstrate that the lessons Tzetzes intended to teach through his poem extended far beyond the history of the Trojan War. The scholia give us a glimpse into Tzetzes' teaching practice and illustrate how works of poetry – in this case Tzetzes' own, in other cases those of ancient poets such as Homer and Aristophanes – served as model texts in the classroom of a grammarian.[5]

I will study Tzetzes' scholia against the background of the *Art of Grammar* by Dionysius Thrax (*c.* 170–90 BC). Dionysius' treatise was central to the Byzantine study of grammar and as such provides a relevant framework for analysing the grammatical material in Tzetzes' scholia.[6] In later centuries, a large corpus of continuous commentaries and marginal scholia came to accompany Dionysius' brief treatise, which Tzetzes draws on in various places throughout his oeuvre.[7] After defining grammar as 'the acquaintance with the things poets and prose writers generally say', Dionysius divides the art into six parts, which, as one of the later scholiasts argues, represent the successive stages of grammatical instruction:[8] (1) skilful reading in accordance with prosody; (2) exegesis of the poetic tropes present in the text; (3) explanation of rare and dialectal words as well as histories; (4) discovery of etymologies; (5) consideration of analogies; (6) the critical appreciation of poems, 'which is the most beautiful of all the parts that make up the art of grammar'.[9]

5 On the *Carmina Iliaca* as 'erudita invenzione', see Braccini (2009–10); on the *Carmina Iliaca* as a poetic experiment and introduction to Homeric poetry, see Cardin (2018); cf. Kaldellis (2009: 26). See also Jeffreys (2009: 225–8).

6 On Dionysius' *Art of Grammar* in Byzantium, see Robins (1993: 41–86), Ronconi (2012: 72–80). The authorship of the treatise is much debated: see e.g. Callipo (2011: 28–34) and Pagani (2011: 30–8).

7 In the verse treatise *On Differences between Poets*, for instance, Tzetzes repeatedly draws on the scholia on Dionysius Thrax: see e.g. lines 25–50 ed. Koster (1975) and scholia on Dionysius Thrax 18.15–19.4; scholion on line 81 and scholia on Dionysius Thrax 19.4–11. The scholia and commentaries on Dionysius Thrax are collected in Hilgard (1901).

8 Scholia on Dionysius Thrax 453.25–31. On Dionysius' much-debated definition of grammar, see Wouters and Swiggers (2015: 522–8), with references to further bibliography.

9 Dionysius Thrax, *The Art of Grammar* 5.2–6.3 ed. Uhlig (1883): Γραμματική ἐστιν ἐμπειρία τῶν παρὰ ποιηταῖς τε καὶ συγγραφεῦσιν ὡς ἐπὶ τὸ πολὺ λεγομένων. Μέρη δὲ αὐτῆς ἐστιν ἕξ· πρῶτον ἀνάγνωσις ἐντριβὴς κατὰ προσῳδίαν, δεύτερον ἐξήγησις κατὰ τοὺς ἐνυπάρχοντας ποιητικοὺς τρόπους, τρίτον γλωσσῶν τε καὶ ἱστοριῶν πρόχειρος ἀπόδοσις, τέταρτον ἐτυμολογίας εὕρεσις, πέμπτον ἀναλογίας ἐκλογισμός, ἕκτον κρίσις ποιημάτων, ὃ δὴ κάλλιστόν ἐστι πάντων τῶν ἐν τῇ τέχνῃ.

In what follows, I will explore what was involved in teaching grammar in Byzantium by examining how Tzetzes uses the *Carmina Iliaca* to instruct his students in Dionysius' first four parts of grammar. How does he use his poem to teach general rules of prosody? How does he draw attention to poetic tropes and rhetorical figures in his own text as *leçons par l'exemple*? How does he teach linguistic competence as well as cultural knowledge by addressing obsolete and dialectal forms and providing miscellaneous background information? And how does etymology function as a didactic tool in the hands of a grammarian? I will consider Tzetzes' grammar lessons in the context of the various technical resources at his disposal and place his scholia into dialogue with the scholarly and didactic works of his contemporaries Eustathios of Thessalonike and Gregory of Corinth.

Reading in Accordance with Prosody: Learning the Rules of Grammar

One of Dionysius' scholiasts explains that the first thing one learns when arriving at the *grammatikos* is how to read well, with correct prosody, 'that is to say, according to accents, vowel length, breathings, and other diacritic signs'.[10] Failing to read with correct prosody, so another scholiast warns, may lead the listener astray, as a mistake in accentuation or aspiration can change the meaning of a word significantly (e.g. ὄρος, 'mountain' versus ὀρός, 'whey').[11] The scholia on the *Carmina Iliaca* demonstrate how Tzetzes uses his poem to teach general rules of prosody. He is very attentive to vowel length and the so-called dichronic vowels in particular, a topic of special interest to those who aspired to understand and use the ancient quantitative metres.[12] Leaving metre aside, however, I will focus here on aspiration as another aspect of prosody as defined by Dionysius' scholiasts. In the scholion on *Posthomerica* 120, for instance, Tzetzes explains the general rule behind the rough breathing of the form ἕηκεν occurring in the verse in question:

> τὸ ἕηκεν ἀντὶ τοῦ ἔπεμψεν δασύνεται. αἱ γὰρ λέξεις αἱ κατ' ἀρχὰς προσλαβοῦσαι φωνῆεν τὸ τοῦ πρωτοτύπου πνεῦμα φυλάττουσιν, εἴτε

10 Scholia on Dionysius Thrax 13.15–16: τουτέστι κατὰ τόνους, κατὰ χρόνους, κατὰ πνεύματα, κατὰ πάθη. Similar definitions are found in 16.12–13, 454.8–9, 567.17–20.

11 Scholia on Dionysius Thrax 170.33–171.6.

12 In *Commentary on Aristophanes' Wealth* 1098.35–69 ed. Massa Positano (1960), Tzetzes, however, argues that understanding the dichronic vowels is also crucial for prose writers. For the importance Tzetzes attaches to dichronic vowels, see Agapitos (2017: 11, 19), van den Berg (2020: 296–8, 301), Lauxtermann (2022).

> ψιλὸν ἢ εἴτε δασύ· ψιλὸν μὲν ὡς τὸ ἄγω τὸ κλῶ ἐάγη, κατεάγη καὶ τὰ ὅμοια, δασὺ δὲ ὡς τὸ ὁρῶ ἑώρων, ἧκεν ἀντὶ τοῦ ἔπεμψεν, ἕηκεν, ἐφέηκεν, ἥδω τὸ εὐφραίνομαι, ἡνδάνω, ἁνδάνω, ἑήνδανεν καὶ τὰ ὅμοια. ὅταν δὲ υ προσλάβωσιν ἐν τοῖς φωνήεσι ψιλοῦνται, κἂν τὸ πρωτότυπον αὐτῶν ἦν δασυνόμενον· ἕκηλος εὔκηλος, ὁρανὸς οὐρανὸς καὶ τὰ ὅμοια. (Tzetzes, scholion on *Carmina Iliaca* 3.120)
>
> ἕηκεν, i.e. 'she sent', has a rough breathing, because words that have taken on a vowel at the start keep the breathing of the original form, whether it is smooth or rough. Smooth, such as ἄγω, 'to break', ἐάγη, κατεάγη and similar examples; rough such as ὁρῶ ἑώρων, ἧκεν, i.e. 'he sent', ἕηκεν, ἐφέηκεν, ἥδω, 'to enjoy', ἡνδάνω, ἁνδάνω, ἑήνδανεν and similar examples. Whenever they take on an upsilon among the vowels, they are pronounced with a smooth breathing, even if their original form was pronounced with a rough breathing: ἕκηλος εὔκηλος, ὁρανὸς οὐρανὸς and similar examples.

Tzetzes first explains the meaning of ἕηκεν with the more common synonym ἔπεμψεν before elucidating the grammatical rule behind its aspiration: an augment preceding a vowel adopts the breathing of the unaugmented form.[13] According to the principle of analogy, which was common in grammar teaching and which Dionysius lists as the fifth part of grammar, Tzetzes gives various similar verbs to illustrate the validity of the rule.[14]

Tzetzes had at his disposal a large body of earlier treatises on different aspects of grammar, lexica of various kinds and ancient scholia on, for instance, Homer and Aristophanes. In the *Etymologicum Gudianum*, a lexicon compiled in the eleventh century, we find an entry that explains the same rule of aspiration and shares some examples with Tzetzes' scholion, with a reference to the second-century grammarian Herodian:

> Ἔειπεν <Β 156>· ψιλοῦται. τὸ ε πρὸ φωνήεντος πλεονάζον ψιλουμένου μὲν αὐτοῦ συμψιλοῦται, οἷον οἶκα ἔοικα, δασυνομένου δὲ <συνδασύνεται>, οἷον ὥρων ἑώρων. ὁ δὲ Ἡρωδιανός · "τὰ πλεονάσαντα φωνήεντα ἐν λέξεσι ταῖς ἀπὸ φωνήεντος δασυνομένου ἀρχομέναις μεταληπτικὰ γίνεται τοῦ δασέος πνεύματος, οἷον ἥνδανε<ν> ἑήνδανεν". (*Etymologicum Gudianum* ε 401.13–18 ed. De Stefani 1909–20)

13 Tzetzes repeats this rule in e.g. scholion on *Carmina Iliaca* 1.367.

14 See e.g. scholia on Dionysius Thrax 15.12–14: Τὸ οὖν πέμπτον μέρος ἐστὶν ἡ ἀκριβὴς τῶν ὁμοίων παράθεσις, δι' ἧς συνίστανται οἱ κανόνες τῶν γραμματικῶν, 'the fifth part, then, is the accurate juxtaposition of similar forms, which is the foundation of the grammarians' rules'. For similar definitions, see scholia on Dionysius Thrax 454.16–21, 470.11–20, 568.6–13. On analogy, see Pagani (2011) and (2015: 832–9), with further bibliography.

> Ἔειπεν [*Iliad* 2.156]: it is pronounced with a smooth breathing. The additional epsilon before a vowel that has a smooth breathing is also pronounced with a smooth breathing, such as οἶκα ἔοικα, but when the vowel has a rough breathing, the additional epsilon is also pronounced with a rough breathing, such as ὥρων ἑώρων. As Herodian [*On Prosody in General* 537.5 ed. Lentz 1867] says: the additional vowels in words that start with a rough vowel share the rough breathing, such as ἥνδανε<ν> ἑήνδανεν.

In a similar way, Eustathios draws on the technical texts at his disposal when explaining the smooth breathing of ἠέλιος in *Iliad* 1.601:

> Τὸ δὲ ἠέλιος δοκεῖ ἐκ τοῦ ἥλιος γενέσθαι κατὰ ἐπένθεσιν τοῦ ε. ψιλοῦται δὲ διὰ τὸν κανόνα τὸν λέγοντα, ὅτι τὸ η πρὸ φωνήεντος ὂν κατὰ διάστασιν ψιλοῦται, οἷον ἠΐθεος, ἤϊος ὁ τοξικός· οὕτως οὖν καὶ ἠέλιος.[15] (Eustathios, *Commentary on the Iliad* 1.248.23–5)

> Ἠέλιος seems to be derived from ἥλιος with an insertion of the epsilon. It has a smooth breathing because of the rule that says that an eta before a vowel, when it is not a diphthong, is pronounced with a smooth breathing, such as ἠΐθεος, ἤϊος 'the bowman'; the same then also applies to ἠέλιος.

Eustathios explains that the aspiration of ἠέλιος follows the general rule that an eta preceding another vowel, where the two do not form a diphthong, always has a smooth breathing; this is a rule we also find, for instance, in Herodian's influential treatise on prosody.[16] The point of these observations is not to trace back the words of our twelfth-century scholars to their sources but rather to illustrate how they appropriate the extensive technical material at their disposal to teach grammar by means of poetry.

In the above examples – of which there are many more – Tzetzes and Eustathios isolate a word from the text under discussion (in Tzetzes' case his own, in Eustathios' case the *Iliad*) to explain general rules of prosody. Such explanations are not particularly intended to help students comprehend the text but to teach them grammar via poetic model texts. The examples represent two ways of explaining aspiration that were common in ancient grammatical scholarship: either based on connections to related

15 The text of Eustathios' *Commentary on the Iliad* follows the edition by van der Valk (1971–87).
16 Herodian, *On Prosody in General* 539.9–11 ed. Lentz (1867): Τὸ α ι η ο πρὸ φωνήεντος ὄντα κατὰ διάστασιν ψιλοῦται, ἀάπτους, ἀήσυλα, ἀΐσσω, ἰάπτω, ἰατρός, ἠΐθεος, Ἠετίων, ἠέλιος, ὀΐω, ὀϊστός, 'α ι η ο before a vowel, where they do not form a diphthong, are pronounced with a smooth breathing, ἀάπτους, ἀήσυλα, ἀΐσσω, ἰάπτω, ἰατρός, ἠΐθεος, Ἠετίων, ἠέλιος, ὀΐω, ὀϊστός.' For Herodian and his treatise on prosody, see Dickey (2007: 75–7), Pagani (2015: 824–6).

words, as in Tzetzes' discussion of ἕηκεν, or based on the position of a vowel, as in Eustathios' explanation of ἠέλιος. In addition to this, ancient grammarians often cite etymology and the characteristics of the Greek dialects, such as the lack of rough breathings in Aeolic, a phenomenon repeatedly referred to by our twelfth-century scholars.[17] Tzetzes and Eustathios explain, for instance, that this Aeolic trait is the reason why the name Olympus has a smooth breathing despite its etymological derivation from ὁλολαμπός, 'shining all over': Olympus allegorically represents the heavens, which shine all over with stars.[18] The name underwent two other Aeolic sound changes, dropping the syllable -λα- (ὀλομπός) through syncope, and changing the ο into υ (Ὄλυμπος).[19] This form of analysis, which combines etymology, the idiosyncrasies of the Greek dialects and the explanation of aspiration, is frequent in Tzetzes' and Eustathios' grammatical teachings, as further examples below will illustrate.

Poetic Tropes and Rhetorical Figures in the *Carmina Iliaca* as *Leçons par l'exemple*

Dionysius defines the exegesis of poetic tropes as the second part of grammar. This is an important task of the grammarian, so Dionysius' scholiasts argue, as poetic tropes tend to obscure the meaning of the text.[20] Owing to this tendency towards obscurity (ἀσάφεια), such tropes are more suitable for poets than orators, as clarity (σαφήνεια) is one of the key virtues of oratory.[21] While Dionysius does not describe different poetic tropes, the grammatical tradition includes various treatises on poetic tropes and rhetorical figures, with Trypho's *On Tropes*, George Choiroboskos' *On Poetic Tropes*

17 See e.g. Tzetzes, *Commentary on Aristophanes' Clouds* 5a ed. Holwerda (1960), scholia on *Carmina Iliaca* 1.130; Eustathios, *Commentary on the Iliad* 1.357.11–14; Gregory of Corinth, *On Dialects* 5.3 ed. Schäfer (1811). On the ancient explanation of aspiration, see Probert (2015, esp. 928–9).

18 Tzetzes, *Exegesis of the Iliad* ad 1.18 (122.11–21 ed. Papathomopoulos 2007); *Scholia on Hesiod's Works and Days* ad 195 (128.5–17e ed. Gaisford [1823]); Eustathios, *Commentary on the Iliad* 1.44.29–45.2 (on *Iliad* 1.18). The same etymology is found in e.g. scholion D on *Iliad* 1.18 ed. van Thiel (2014), *Etymologicum Magnum* 623.6 ed. Gaisford (1848), *Etymologicum Gudianum* 426.25–6 ed. De Stefani (1909–20). It seems to go back to the Pseudo-Aristotelian *On the Universe* 400a7–8.

19 Gregory also lists this as a characteristic of the Aeolic dialect: see *On Dialects* 5.9 ed. Schäfer (1856).

20 See e.g. scholia on Dionysius Thrax 302.15–17, 456.8–14. See also *On Tropes* 191.20–2 ed. Spengel (1956), where Trypho argues that grammarians should explain everything poets say, both when they speak according to normal usage and when they use tropes.

21 See e.g. scholia on Dionysius Thrax 302.18–19, 456.14–17. Some tropes, however, are used by poets as well as orators (e.g. irony): see scholia on Dionysius Thrax 13.31–14.9 Cf. e.g. scholion on *Carmina Iliaca* 1.222, where Tzetzes points out that the figure in question has different names in poetical and rhetorical theory.

and Herodian's *On Figures* being prominent examples.[22] Rhetorical figures (σχήματα) are also part of Hermogenes' *On Types of Style*, where they are counted among the principal components of each style.[23] Following the example of ancient rhetoricians, most notably Hermogenes, Byzantine scholars such as Tzetzes and Eustathios considered all literary composition, whether prose or verse, to belong to the art of rhetoric. Rhetorical theory was therefore applicable to the analysis of both oratory and poetry, as Eustathios' rhetorical analysis of the Homeric epics demonstrates most clearly.[24] Tzetzes similarly draws attention to both poetic tropes and rhetorical figures in his scholia on the *Carmina Iliaca*.

Tzetzes discusses most tropes and figures only briefly, simply identifying them.[25] Occasionally, he describes the intended effect of the figure, often in terms of Hermogenes' theory of styles. For example, he draws attention to the figure of *epanalepsis*, resumption or repetition, in *Antehomerica* 124, where he concludes his flattering portrait of Helen with the summary 'such was the beauty of Tyndareus' daughter' (τοία μὲν ἦεν κάλλεϊ κούρη Τυνδαρεώνη).[26] In the corresponding scholion, Tzetzes explains that 'the figure is *epanalepsis*, which creates distinctness; distinctness and lucidity are types of style that produce clarity' (τὸ σχῆμα ἐπανάληψις, ὅπερ ἔργον εὐκρινείας· ἡ δὲ εὐκρίνεια καὶ καθαρότης ἰδέαι εἰσὶν ἐργαστικαὶ σαφηνείας).[27] Tzetzes here follows Hermogenes' stylistic handbook, where *epanalepsis* is defined as a resuming statement and is counted among the figures that produce distinctness, which, together with lucidity, is a substyle of clarity.[28] In this way, then, Tzetzes gives his students a first taste of Hermogenes' complex style theory, leaving a detailed discussion of the Hermogenean corpus to the teacher of rhetoric. In a similar vein, Eustathios repeatedly identifies the figure of *epanalepsis* in Homeric poetry, although most often according to the definition found in Pseudo-Hermogenes' *On the Method of Forcefulness*. Here *epanalepsis* is defined as the

22 On tropes and figures in Byzantine education and literary thought, see e.g. Conley (1986), Valiavitcharska (2021).

23 Hermogenes, *On Types of Style* 1.1.19 ed. Patillon (2012b); see also Lindberg (1977: 30–9).

24 See van den Berg (2022). On rhetorical theory as the literary theory of the Byzantines, see e.g. Katsaros (2002). On the relationship between (Byzantine) prose and (ancient) poetry, see also Bourbouhakis in this volume.

25 See e.g. scholia on *Carmina Iliaca* 1.57 (περίφρασις), 2.291b (περίφρασις), 3.461a (ἀστεϊσμός/χαριεντισμός). On Tzetzes' exegesis of words and figures in the scholia on the *Carmina Iliaca*, see also Conca (2018: 84–8).

26 On the portraits in the *Carmina Iliaca*, see Lovato (2017).

27 Scholion on *Carmina Iliaca* 1.124a. Tzetzes gives a similar explanation in scholion on *Carmina Iliaca* 2.160. For Tzetzes' commentary on Hermogenes, see Pizzone in this volume.

28 On *epanalepsis*, see Hermogenes, *On Types of Style* 1.4.14–16, 1.11.31 ed. Patillon (2012b).

literal repetition of words in consecutive verses or sentences, a figure designated as *epanastrophe* in *On Types of Style*.[29] Eustathios brings both treatises together in his commentary on *Iliad* 20.371–2, where Hector says 'Against him [sc. Achilles] I will go out, even if his hands are like fire | even if his hands are like fire and his fury like blazing iron (τοῦ δ' ἐγὼ ἀντίος εἶμι, καὶ εἰ πυρὶ χεῖρας ἔοικεν, | εἰ πυρὶ χεῖρας ἔοικε, μένος δ' αἴθωνι σιδήρῳ).[30] While these verses illustrate the figure of *epanalepsis* in Pseudo-Hermogenes' *On the Method of Forcefulness*, they serve as an example of *epanastrophe* in Hermogenes' *On Types of Style*. Eustathios thus attempts a synthesis of the Hermogenean corpus, teaching his readers that the same figure goes by two names. This is an explanation he repeats when commenting on *Iliad* 22.126–7, where he also states that *epanastrophe* is a figure of beauty (κάλλος), as Hermogenes explains in *On Types of Style*.[31]

Such explanations are part of Eustathios' general project systematically to reverse-engineer Homer's text 'so that the rhetorical choices of the poet could be laid open for aspiring Byzantine authors to adopt'.[32] In the same vein, Tzetzes lays open for his students the choices he made when composing the *Carmina Iliaca*.[33] In the scholion on *Antehomerica* 20, for example, he explains that at this point the *prodiegesis* (preliminary narration) ends and the *diegesis* (narration) begins:

> Ἤτοι μὲν Τροίῃ· ἐντεῦθεν ἄρχεται ἡ διήγησις ῥητορικωτάτη μετὰ μικρᾶς τῆς προδιηγήσεως. τὸ γὰρ ἀπ' αὐτῆς τῆς διηγήσεως ἄρχεσθαι ἀρητόρευτόν τε καὶ ἄτεχνον, τὸ δὲ πόρρωθεν ἄρχεσθαι καὶ μὴ συντόμως εἰσβάλλειν εἰς τὴν ὑπόθεσιν κακία ἐστὶ διηγήσεως· ἀσαφήνειαν γὰρ ἐμποιεῖ. ἀρεταὶ γὰρ διηγήσεως τέσσαρες· σαφήνεια, συντομία, πιθανότης καὶ ὁ τῶν ὀνομάτων ἑλληνισμός. (Tzetzes, scholion on *Carmina Iliaca* 1.20a)
>
> Troy, then: from here the rhetorical narration proper starts after the brief preliminary narration, because beginning from the narration itself would show a lack of rhetorical education and technique. To begin from a faraway point and not to introduce the subject matter briefly is a vice of narration.

29 Pseudo-Hermogenes, *On the Method of Forcefulness* 9 ed. Patillon (2014); Hermogenes, *On Types of Style* 1.12.28–30. *Epanalepsis* is defined in a similar way in George Choiroboskos, *On Poetic Tropes* 252.11–16 ed. Spengel (1956). See e.g. Eustathios, *Commentary on the Iliad* 1.159.4–6 (on *Iliad* 1.266–7).

30 The text of the *Iliad* follows the edition by Allen and Monro (1902–12); the translations are from Murray, rev. Wyatt (1999).

31 Eustathios, *Commentary on the Iliad* 4.418.9–13, 4.589.11–15. See also Lindberg (1977: 134, n. 7).

32 Bourbouhakis (2017: 124). Van den Berg (2022) studies Eustathios' 'reverse-engineering' of Homer's composition process.

33 Niketas of Herakleia similarly uses the *leçon par l'exemple* as a pedagogical strategy: see Bernard in this volume.

For it creates obscurity. For the virtues of narrative are four: clarity, brevity, plausibility and the correct use of words.[34]

Drawing on Pseudo-Hermogenes' *On Invention*,[35] Tzetzes' didactic and prescriptive scholion again introduces his students to basic rhetorical theory, using his own text as a model in the same way as he (and his colleagues) might use the works of ancient poets. Again, Tzetzes gives his students a first taste of rhetoric, preparing them for the next stage of their education.

Teaching Linguistic Competence and Cultural Knowledge: Dialects and Histories

Dionysius defines the explanation of *glossai* (γλῶσσαι), 'rare words and dialect forms', and *historiai* (ἱστορίαι), 'histories', as the third part of grammar, which suggests that the responsibilities of the grammarian extended far beyond teaching the basic rules of Greek grammar.

Proficiency in the Entirety of the Greek Language

Dionysius' scholiasts define γλῶσσαι as rare and uncommon words, in particular dialectal forms belonging to the main varieties of ancient Greek (Attic, Doric, Ionic, Aeolic).[36] They argue that, although grammarians can define regional words with more common synonyms, they must also be able to explain the general characteristics of each dialect.[37] Tzetzes uses both modes of explanation in the scholia on the *Carmina Iliaca* to elucidate uncommon forms in the poem. Numerous times, he explains the meaning of a rare poetic word by simply giving a more common, Attic synonym; this is a method he also employs, for instance, in his *Exegesis of the Iliad*, as does Eustathios in his Homeric commentaries. The sheer quantity of such explanations suggests that this was a much-used method to elucidate texts and familiarize students with dialect forms and Homeric diction, while at the same time expanding their vocabulary.[38] Technical resources again assisted our scholars in their didactic practice. Compare, for instance, Tzetzes' definition of the poetic form ἔρσε (*Antehomerica* 300)

34 For the virtues of narration, see e.g. Aphthonios, *Progymnasmata* 2.4 ed. Patillon (2008).

35 Pseudo-Hermogenes, *On Invention* 2.1 ed. Patillon (2012a).

36 See e.g. scholia on Dionysius Thrax 14.14–19, 169.13–15, 567.31–8.

37 See e.g. scholia on Dionysius Thrax 469.10–12, 470.14–25.

38 See also Van Rooy (2016) on Psellos' discussion of dialects in his poem on grammar (*Poem* 6 ed. Westerink [1992]). On Psellos' poem, see also Hörandner (2012: 60–1), Bernard (2014: 216–17, 248–50).

as ἀπέπνιξε ('he drowned', scholion on *Antehomerica* 300a) with the corresponding entry in Hesychios' lexicon (α 6332 ed. Latte 1953–66): ἀπόερσε· ἀπέπνιξε, τουτέστι ποταμοφόρητον ἐποίησεν ('he made him go under: he drowned him, i.e. he made him be carried away by a river').

In other scholia, Tzetzes proves that he is also familiar with the general characteristics of the different dialects, such as the Ionic tendency to change a long vowel into a short one, referred to as συστολή, 'shortening'. Tzetzes weaves two examples of Ionic shortening into verses 156–7 of the *Posthomerica:*

> καί νύ κε πάντα τέλεσσεν, ὅσα φρεσὶν ἔλπετο ᾖσιν·
> ἔνθε γὰρ Αἰνείας εἶχεν ἵππεον ἴλην,
> Δηΐφοβος δ' ἑτέρωθε λαὸν ἀσπιδιώτην· (Tzetzes, *Carmina Iliaca* 3.156–8)
>
> And now she [sc. Penthesileia] would have accomplished everything she hoped for in her heart; for from the one side Aeneas led a troop of cavalry, while from the other side Deïphobus led men equipped with shields.
>
> ἔλπετο· τὸ "ἔλπετο" καὶ "ἵππεον ἴλην" Ἰωνικαὶ συστολαί εἰσιν· ἤλπετο γὰρ καὶ ἵππειον ἴλην ὤφειλε τεθῆναι, ἀλλ' Ἴωνες, ὡς πολλάκις ἔφην, συσταλτικοί εἰσι καὶ οἱ πλείονες τῶν ποιητῶν Ἰωνικῶς γράφουσιν. (Tzetzes, scholion on *Carmina Iliaca* 3.156)
>
> ἔλπετο: ἔλπετο and ἵππεον ἴλην are Ionic shortenings. For ἤλπετο and ἵππειον ἴλην should have been used, but Ionians, as I have said many times,[39] tend to shorten vowels and the majority of the poets write in the Ionic dialect.

Tzetzes' formulation suggests that he takes the Attic dialect as his baseline: the forms should be ἤλπετο with an eta and ἵππειον with a diphthong. However, he has, of course, deliberately chosen these two Ionic forms for this Homerizing poem and uses them to illustrate the characteristic Ionic shortening.[40] A similar preference for the Attic dialect can be found in Eustathios' *Commentary on the Iliad.* He repeatedly gives the Attic equivalent of the words Homer uses, often with examples from the Athenian playwrights. In his commentary on *Iliad* 16.362, for instance, Eustathios explains that, unlike Homer, later Attic authors wrote the verbs γινώσκειν ('to recognize') and γίνεσθαι ('to happen') with a second gamma

39 See e.g. scholia on *Carmina Iliaca* 1.17, 1.78b, 1.141, 1.181, 2.419, 3.372.

40 On Ionic shortening, see also e.g. Eustathios, *Commentary on the Iliad* 2.240.4–5; Gregory of Corinth, *On Dialects* 4.24 ed. Schäfer (1811).

as γιγνώσκειν and γίγνεσθαι. He adds that 'Homer, however, in a more archaic manner, is ignorant of the second gamma in both verbs. Still, the form of the later authors is more accurate, even though Homer's form is more euphonic.'[41] In this way, Eustathios avoids challenging Homer's ultimate authority in all things linguistic, while teaching his readers – Byzantine prose authors – the preferred Attic form that they should use in their writings.[42]

Our twelfth-century scholars consider Homer's language a composite dialect with Ionic as its main component. In the introduction to his treatise *On Dialects*, Gregory of Corinth mentions Homer as the main representative of the Ionic dialect. Throughout the remainder of the work, however, he adduces Homeric examples for characteristics of all dialects.[43] Similarly, Eustathios recognizes that Homer writes mostly in the Ionic dialect, while simultaneously attributing to the poet a tendency to use forms from other dialects, for instance when these forms fit in better with the metre or when the poet is aiming for a certain stylistic effect.[44] In his commentary on *Iliad* 2.684 (Μυρμιδόνες δὲ καλεῦντο καὶ Ἕλληνες καὶ Ἀχαιοί, 'those who were called Myrmidons and Hellenes and Achaeans'), for example, Eustathios explains that Homer could have used the form ἐκαλοῦντο, in the *koine* dialect, which Eustathios considers to be clearer (σαφέστερον). The poet, however, 'deliberately avoided the *koine* dialect for the sake of stylistic loftiness by using the more poetic καλεῦντο' (ἐπετηδεύσατο ἐκφυγεῖν χάριν ὄγκου τὸ τῆς διαλέκτου κοινόν "καλεῦντο" εἰπὼν ποιητικώτερον).[45] Eustathios thus considers the poetic, Ionic form to be more elevated than the simple and mundane *koine*. Homer is not required to be consistent in his use of the Greek dialects: he can use the *koine* form ἔθηκε in one place (*Iliad* 24.531), while choosing the Ionic θῆκεν a few lines later (24.538), as 'he has much freedom to take pleasure in whichever dialect he wishes' (οἷα πολλὴν ἔχων ἄδειαν ἐγχορεύειν, αἷς ἂν διαλέκτοις βούλοιτο).[46] In

41 Eustathios, *Commentary on the Iliad* 3.862.9–14.

42 On the productive aim of the commentary, see p. 168 above; see also Cullhed (2016: 17*–25*). On the study of ancient poetry as facilitating the composition of prose, see also Bourbouhakis in this volume.

43 See e.g. *On Dialects* 2.4 ed. Schäfer (1811): the Attic habit of pronouncing ὁμοῖος with a circumflex on the penultimate syllable is illustrated with *Odyssey* 17.218; *On Dialects* 3.20: the Doric tendency to drop the final vowel of prepositions before words starting with a consonant is illustrated with *Iliad* 4.1; *On Dialects* 5.31: Homer's usage of Ἄρεος (*Iliad* 4.441, 19.47, *Odyssey* 8.267) with an omicron rather than an omega exemplifies the Aeolic spelling of the genitive of Ares' name.

44 See e.g. Eustathios, *Commentary on the Iliad* 1.340.16–18; cf. 2.260.5–8. For Eustathios' reflections on the dialect of Homeric poetry, see also van den Berg (2021: 123–4).

45 Eustathios, *Commentary on the Iliad* 1.499.29–500.2.

46 Eustathios, *Commentary on the Iliad* 4.949.12–13.

other words, Homer has the artistic liberty to move between the different dialects at will.

In line with Eustathios' general tendency to project his own didactic programme onto the poet and shape Homer in the image of the ideal twelfth-century author,[47] Homer's dialectal flexibility may represent an aesthetic ideal that Eustathios believed Byzantine authors should strive to achieve. After all, Homer's artistic use of the dialects does not altogether differ from Tzetzes' practice in the *Carmina Iliaca*. This means that the grammatical lessons on the idiosyncrasies of the dialects serve a practical purpose: knowledge of the dialects does not only enable students to appreciate ancient literature, but also allows them to use dialect forms in their own writings. Such a productive aim accords with the practical dimensions of Byzantine (grammar) education and the study of ancient literature: students were supposed to compose texts of their own, in prose as well as verse, following the example of ancient authors. As Ruth Webb has suggested for the grammatical glosses and scholia in Moschopoulos' commentary on Philostratus' *Eikones*, 'the discussions of the literary dialects ... can be read as prescriptive instructions for the formation of pseudo-dialect forms where required by the genre, rather than as accounts of historical phenomena'.[48] The works of Tzetzes, Eustathios and Gregory provide their students with the information required to gain proficiency in the entirety of the Greek language.

Towards Polymathy: historiai

The study of grammar also covered ἱστορίαι, which Dionysius' commentators define as 'accounts concerning the past'.[49] The grammarian was expected to explain and expand on historical allusions found in the text under discussion. The works of our twelfth-century scholars clearly testify to the responsibility of grammarians to expand the polymathy of their students. Tzetzes' scholia on the *Carmina Iliaca* contain much material that falls under the broad category of ἱστορίαι: a comparison of Diomedes' gleaming weapons to 'the Syracusan mirror' in the *Homerica* prompts a long discussion of the famous mirror of Archimedes in the scholia;[50] a

47 See esp. Cullhed (2016: 11*–12*).

48 Webb (1997: 16).

49 See e.g. scholia on Dionysius Thrax 303.4 (Ἱστορία δέ ἐστι παλαιῶν πράξεων ἀφήγησις), 454.34–5 (Ἱστορία δὲ ἡ τῶν παλαιῶν χρῆσις·), 567.40–2 (Ἱστορία δέ ἐστιν ἡ παλαιῶν πραγμάτων ἔχουσα ἀφήγησιν).

50 *Homerica* 46 with scholion 46ab. For Tzetzes and Archimedes' mirror, see Rance (2022).

scholion in the *Antehomerica* includes what Tzetzes calls 'an ἱστορία in verse by Tzetzes' (ἱστορία διὰ στίχων τοῦ Τζέτζου), which discusses in dodecasyllables the views of various ancient historians on a pre-Iliadic attack on Troy by the Amazons;[51] long summaries of Homeric battle scenes in the scholia compensate for details of the *Iliad* not included in Tzetzes' 'short sayings' or βραχυλογήματα, as he calls his own verses;[52] and, interestingly, the scholia include thirty-seven epitaphs of heroes, most of which are epigrams Tzetzes found in the sources at his disposal. For those heroes for whom the tradition did not transmit an epitaph, Tzetzes wrote one himself – the scholia contain eight such epigrams.[53] Again, we should not consider such historical accounts to be of purely antiquarian nature but rather to be an integral part of grammatical instruction, in line with Dionysius' third part of grammar. With such 'histories', the grammarian transmits the cultural knowledge that the educated man in Byzantium was expected to possess. This didactic role of the concept of ἱστορία may also shed light on the functionality of the *Histories*, in which Tzetzes explains, among other things, the historical and mythological allusions in his own letter collection.[54]

Eustathios' Homeric commentaries demonstrate a similar tendency to include a wealth of background information often only loosely related to the text under discussion: these monumental works present information on a wide variety of subjects – history, mythology, zoology, topography, medicine, etc. – that goes far beyond the explanation of the Homeric text.[55] In Eustathios' view, moreover, Homer himself included ἱστορίαι of various kinds in his poems. He repeatedly explains that the poet uses such 'histories' with information on, say, topography and genealogy at various places throughout his poems to avoid monotony.[56] An example of such a 'history' is found in the battle scene of *Iliad* 11, where Homer presents a

51 *Antehomerica* 22–3 with scholion 22c. Tzetzes uses the term ἱστορία in the same way in numerous places throughout his works on ancient poetry. In the *Prolegomena on Comedy*, for instance, Tzetzes symbolically refers to the virtues and graces of his own writings as Sappho, Gorgo and Peitho (39–42, p. 24 ed. Koster [1975]). Next, he adds three ἱστορίαι with information about the three women (44–65, pp. 24–5 ed. Koster [1975]).

52 Scholion on *Carmina Iliaca* 1.234b, 1.241b.

53 On these epigrams, see Martins de Jesus (2016), Conca (2018: 92–8).

54 Kaldellis (2009: 28–9) argues that the *Histories* are 'more "textbook" than "sources", and provide a pedagogy in grammar, composition, and classical knowledge'. Cardin (2018: 108) draws a connection between the *Histories* and the *Carmina Iliaca* and their scholia. On the functionality of the *Histories*, see also Pizzone (2017). On ἱστορία in Byzantine education, see also Papaioannou (2014).

55 On the encyclopedic character of Eustathios' Homeric commentaries, see also Cullhed (2016: 4*), van den Berg (2021: 119–20).

56 On Eustathios' discussion of Homeric ἱστορίαι, see van den Berg (2022: 79–81).

brief biography of the Trojan hero Iphidamas (vv. 221–31) moments before he is killed by Agamemnon. With this and similar histories, so Eustathios explains, Homer gives the audience a welcome relief from the intensity and monotony of the fighting.[57] Homer includes similar brief biographies of Trojan warriors who fall at the hands of the Greeks in the battle scene of *Iliad* 5. In addition to avoiding monotony, Eustathios identifies further reasons for the poet to include such histories:

> Ποιεῖ δὲ ταῦτα καὶ πυκναῖς ἱστορίαις ἀρτύει τὸν τόπον τοῦτον ἅμα καὶ τοὺς ἀκροατὰς ἐνάγων εἰς πολυμάθειαν, ὡς καὶ ἐν ἄλλοις τόποις, καὶ τοὺς ἀριστέας τῶν Ἀχαιῶν σεμνύνων, ὡς ἀξιολόγων Τρώων περιγινομένους, καὶ τὴν ποίησιν καταποικίλλων, καὶ τὸ ὕπτιον δὲ τῆς διηγήσεως ἀνιστῶν εἰς γοργότητα τῇ παρεμπλοκῇ τῶν ἱστοριῶν, καὶ ἑαυτὸν δὲ δεικνύων ἐν ἱστορίαις πολύϊδριν. τοῦτο δὲ καὶ ἀλλαχοῦ ποιήσει ἐν πολλοῖς τόποις διὰ τὰς αὐτὰς αἰτίας. (Eustathios, *Commentary on the Iliad* 2.24.9–15)

> He [sc. the poet] creates these things and seasons this passage with numerous historical narratives, while simultaneously introducing his listeners to much learning, as he often does, and exalting the chiefs of the Achaeans, because they prevailed over Trojans of note. He also varies his poem, turns the stagnancy of the narrative into rapidity by weaving in historical narratives and demonstrates that he is greatly knowledgeable in matters of history. He will do this in many other passages as well, and for the same reasons.

By alternating the potentially monotonous battle narrative with histories, the poet creates variation and saves his audience from boredom, while at the same time imparting much learning (πολυμάθεια), a practice that Eustathios ascribes to Homer in various places throughout his commentaries.[58] He also repeatedly attributes to Homer a desire to display his own erudition – Eustathios' presentation of Homer, then, seems to mirror the self-assertiveness and self-promotion common for authors in the competitive intellectual world of twelfth-century Byzantium.[59]

These statements are part of Eustathios' general presentation of Homer as a teacher of grammar and rhetoric: in a 'transhistorical mingling of didactic voices',[60] Eustathios projects his own didactic programme onto

57 Eustathios, *Commentary on the Iliad* 3.181.26–8.

58 On this passage, see also van den Berg (2017: 42–3) and (2022: 80–1). For another example, see e.g. *Commentary on the Iliad* 2.596.2. On Homer's desire to impart knowledge, see van den Berg (2022: 82–4).

59 In a similar vein, Eustathios repeatedly ascribes to Homer a desire to display his rhetorical prowess: see e.g. *Commentary on the Iliad* 2.493.5–16 and 3.258.4–7 with discussion in van den Berg (2022: 72 n. 78, 82).

60 Cullhed (2016: 12*).

the poet and presents the lessons he wishes to teach his Byzantine students as lessons inherent in the text and intended by the poet.[61] Homer and the Byzantine teachers share an ambition to encourage polymathy in their audience by providing information on topography, genealogy and other types of ἱστορία, in accordance with the third part of the art of grammar as defined by Dionysius. Just as Homer includes biographical and genealogical information in the *Iliad*, so does Eustathios in his commentaries.[62] Similarly, Tzetzes' scholia on the *Carmina Iliaca* provide genealogical information on heroes mentioned in the poem. A mention of Polydamas in the *Posthomerica*, for instance, prompts a scholion with information on the hero's parents as well as the genealogy of the descendants of Tros, the founder of Troy.[63] Following Homer's example, our twelfth-century teachers use ἱστορίαι to turn their students into the polymaths they need to be in order to become successful participants in the intellectual world of Byzantium, while at the same time offering them some relief from the more technical content.

Etymology as a Tool for Teaching

Many of the aspects of teaching grammar through poetry discussed above come together in the discovery of etymology, Dionysius' fourth part of grammar. One of Dionysius' scholiasts defines etymology as a statement that explains the meaning of a word or the reason behind proper names – ancient etymology should thus not be equated with the modern academic field of the same name.[64] Etymology was widespread in ancient thinking about language, and continued to be popular throughout the Byzantine period.[65] Like ancient scholars, Tzetzes uses etymology as a heuristic tool for assessing the semantics, orthography or prosody of a word.[66] In the scholia on the *Posthomerica*, for instance, Tzetzes uses etymology to explain the meaning of the words γωρυτός and φαρέτρα in line 61 (αὐτὰρ γωρυτὸς ὀσφύϊ καλὸς ἔην φαρέτρη τε, 'further, there was a beautiful bow-case on her [i.e. Penthesileia's] back and a quiver'):

61 For a similar tendency among ancient commentators, see Sluiter (1999, esp. 173–4, 176–9).

62 See e.g. *Commentary on the Odyssey* 1416.2–3 ed. Cullhed (2016).

63 Scholion on *Carmina Iliaca* 1.50a. Many similar examples can be found: see e.g. scholia on *Carmina Iliaca* 1.257a, 2.48b, 2.337, 3.632.

64 Scholia on Dionysius Thrax 470.29–31: Ἐτυμολογία ἐστὶ λόγος λέξεων ἔννοιαν ἐξηγούμενος, ἢ ὀνομάτων ἐξήγησις, καθ' ἣν αἰτίαν τὴν πρώτην ἔσχον προσηγορίαν. On ancient etymology, see Sluiter (2015) with references to further bibliography.

65 See also Pontani (2007: 577–9) on etymology in Isaac Porphyrogennetos' commentary on the *Iliad*.

66 Sluiter (2015: 919).

> γωρυτὸς· ἡ τοξοθήκη παρὰ τὸ γῶ τὸ χωρῶ καὶ τὸ ῥυτόν, ὃ δηλοῖ τὸ τόξον· φαρέτρα δὲ ἡ βελοθήκη παρὰ τὸ φέρειν τὰ τρῶντα ἤτοι τιτρώσκοντα. (Tzetzes, scholion on *Carmina Iliaca* 3.61)
>
> γωρυτὸς: bow-case, from γῶ, 'to contain', and ῥυτόν, which means 'bow'; φαρέτρα is a quiver, from φέρειν ['to carry'] τὰ τρῶντα, i.e. the things that wound.

Tzetzes first gives a synonym for the words in question before tracing them back to their original components to explain how they came to have their names. This example illustrates how etymological explanations are based on a semantic as well as a phonetic link between the *explanandum* and the *explanans.* A plausible etymological explanation requires some form of assonance, if only a slight one, between the word under discussion and its etymological derivation, as argued by Ineke Sluiter in her study of ancient etymology.[67]

In other cases, the etymological explanation serves to account for the prosodic features rather than the semantics of the word in question. In the *Exegesis of the Iliad*, for instance, Tzetzes explains that the word ἱερεύς ('priest') is pronounced with a rough breathing, as it derives from ἵημι ('to send'), and a priest is 'one who sends the streams of the sacrifices to the gods' (ὁ ἱεὶς τὰς ῥοὰς τῶν θυμάτων τοῖς θεοῖς).[68] These and many other examples in both Tzetzes' and Eustathios' scholarly and didactic works demonstrate that etymology was a much-used strategy to teach vocabulary and orthography based on specific words in a text, whether the teacher's own or that of an ancient poet. Moreover, as etymologies were often playful and easy to remember, they served as a mnemonic and pedagogic tool in the practice of a grammarian.[69]

When it comes to proper names, the etymological explanation is often related to the historical or mythological lore around the subject in question. In the scholia on the *Homerica*, for instance, Tzetzes presents the name Hector as deriving from ἐχέτωρ, 'holder', which he interprets as ruler (κρατητικός) and protector (φύλαξ) of the city.[70] He explains away the difference in breathing – ἐχέτωρ has a smooth breathing, Hector a rough – by referring back to the idiosyncrasies of the Attic dialect: Hector is aspirated because speakers of Attic pronounce the verb ἔχω with a

67 Sluiter (2015: 916).
68 Tzetzes, *Exegesis of the Iliad* 124.17–19 ed. Papathomopoulos (2007).
69 Sluiter (2015: 921–2).
70 Tzetzes, scholion on *Carmina Iliaca* 2.387.

rough breathing. He adduces the words ἀμφέχει (instead of ἀμπέχει) and ἐφίσης (instead of ἐπίσης) as proof of the Attic tendency to use aspiration where other dialects do not.[71] Like ancient etymologists, then, Tzetzes feels free to make use of any dialect to establish assonance between the name and its proposed etymology. Whether we find this etymology of 'Hector' valid or not, it clearly points to the status of names as vehicles of cultural information.

This becomes even clearer when we look at the etymologies of names of cities, regions, rivers, etc. The etymological explanations of such names often amount to narrating the historical or mythological event that gave the place its name and as such teach further ἱστορίαι. We find many examples of this practice in the introductory essay of Tzetzes' *Exegesis of the Iliad*, which includes a lengthy digression on name-giving and the names of places, such as the Icarian sea (after the unfortunate Icarus), the Atlas mountains and the Atlantic Ocean – the latter two are named after the Libyan mathematician Atlas, who lived on a mountain top to study the stars and the movements of the planets, and one day tripped and fell into the ocean below.[72] Etymology thus serves a function similar to the various types of ἱστορία mentioned before: it can be used to expand the cultural knowledge of the student or, as Ineke Sluiter argues, 'etymology, just like mythology and genealogy, may support cultural memory: in this mnemonic capacity, the words themselves are turned into repositories of cultural information'.[73] Byzantine scholars appropriated etymology as a tool for thinking about language, and the very persistence of this practice, despite the criticism that existed already in antiquity, testifies to how very useful it was considered to be.

Conclusion

If, according to one of Dionysios' scholiasts, a grammarian is 'someone who knows many poems' (ὁ πολλῶν ποιημάτων ἐπιστήμων), this chapter has explored what it means for a teacher of grammar to know a poem.[74] When read against Dionysius Thrax's *Art of Grammar*, Tzetzes' scholia on

71 Tzetzes discusses this Attic feature also in e.g. scholion on Hesiod's *Works and Days* 156bis, 450ter ed. Gaisford (1823); *Exegesis of the Iliad* ad 1.140, 216.9–15 ed. Papathomopoulos (2007). See also scholion on *Carmina Iliaca* 2.178.

72 Tzetzes, *Exegesis of the Iliad* 12.6–16 with scholia in 426.5–16 ed. Papathomopoulos (2007). Similar examples can be found in Eustathios; see e.g. *Commentary on the Odyssey* 1396.10–12 ed. Cullhed (2016).

73 Sluiter (2015: 918).

74 Scholia on Dionysius Thrax 164.4.

the *Carmina Iliaca* demonstrate how grammarians used poetry to teach the many things that students were expected to learn during the early stages of their literary education. Teachers of grammar intended, on the one hand, to give their students a perfect command of ancient Greek (in all its dialects) and, on the other hand, to expand their cultural knowledge and general polymathy. Tzetzes uses the *Carmina Iliaca* to teach linguistic and literary competence by setting forth general rules of prosody, drawing attention to poetic tropes and rhetorical figures in his poem, explaining the semantics of poetic words or dialect forms with synonyms, familiarizing his students with the general characteristics of the Greek dialects, and teaching semantics and orthography through etymology. In addition to this, he provides his students with cultural knowledge by means of etymological explanations and ἱστορίαι of various kinds. Parallels between the scholia on the *Carmina Iliaca* and Tzetzes' and Eustathios' works on the ancient poets suggest that teaching grammar by means of ancient poetry involved the same topics and pedagogical strategies. Parallels with ancient grammatical treatises and other technical works, furthermore, demonstrate how such texts formed the conceptual framework for Byzantine scholars' thinking on language and literature.

I have presented only a brief excursion into the mass of material available. Moreover, the dynamics behind the transmission of knowledge in Byzantium are more complex than I may have presented them here, without schools and classrooms in the modern sense; the intended use of works such as those by Tzetzes, Eustathios and Gregory reached beyond the earliest stages of education to their colleagues and other professional writers.[75] Closer study of, for instance, Tzetzes' scholia on the *Carmina Iliaca*, his *Exegesis of the Iliad*, Eustathios' Homeric commentaries and Gregory's *On Dialects* can further advance our understanding of how poetry, whether ancient or Byzantine, was used in grammar teaching and what the Byzantine student was expected to learn. This would shed light on the conceptual framework of Byzantine linguistic and literary thought: many of the technical texts constituting this framework remain understudied despite the large numbers of them and the wealth of information they contain. Grammatical instruction aimed to teach Byzantine authors how to engage creatively with ancient literature and, as such, forms an important background against which to appreciate Byzantine literature.

75 On these dynamics, see e.g. Markopoulos (2014).

Bibliography

Agapitos, P. A. (2017) 'John Tzetzes and the Blemish Examiners: A Byzantine Teacher on Schedography, Everyday Language and Writerly Disposition', *MEG* 17: 1–57.

Allen, T. W., and D. B. Monro (eds.) (1902–12) *Homeri opera*, 5 vols. Oxford.

Bernard, F. (2014) *Writing and Reading Byzantine Secular Poetry, 1025–1081*. Oxford.

Bourbouhakis, E. C. (2017) 'Byzantine Literary Criticism and the Classical Heritage', in *The Cambridge Intellectual History of Byzantium*, ed. A. Kaldellis and N. Siniossoglou, 113–28. Cambridge.

Braccini, T. (2009–10) 'Erudita invenzione: riflessioni sulla *Piccola grande Iliade* di Giovanni Tzetze', *Incontri triestini di filologia classica* 9: 153–73.

Callipo, M. (2011) *Dionisio Trace e la tradizione grammaticale*. Acireale.

Cardin, M. (2018) 'Teaching Homer through (Annotated) Poetry: John Tzetzes' *Carmina Iliaca*', in *Brill's Companion to Prequels, Sequels, and Retellings of Classical Epic*, ed. R. Simms, 90–114. Leiden.

Conca, F. (2018) 'L'esegesi di Tzetzes ai *Carmina Iliaca*, fra tradizione e innovazione', *ΚΟΙΝΩΝΙΑ* 42: 75–99.

Conley, T. M. (1986) 'Byzantine Teaching on Figures and Tropes: An Introduction', *Rhetorica* 4.4: 335–74.

Cullhed, E. (ed.) (2016) *Eustathios of Thessalonike: Commentary on Homer's Odyssey*, vol. 1: *On Rhapsodies A–B*. Studia Byzantina Upsaliensia 16. Uppsala.

De Stefani, E. L. (ed.) (1909–20) *Etymologicum Gudianum*, 2 vols. Leipzig.

Dickey, E. (2007) *Ancient Greek Scholarship: A Guide to Finding, Reading, and Understanding Scholia, Commentaries, Lexica, and Grammatical Treatises, from Their Beginnings to the Byzantine Period*. Oxford.

Gaisford, T. (ed.) (1823) *Poetae minores Graeci*, vol. 2. Leipzig.

(ed.) (1848) *Etymologicum Magnum*. Oxford (repr. Amsterdam 1976).

Giannouli, A. (2014) 'Education and Literary Language in Byzantium', in *The Language of Byzantine Learned Literature*, ed. M. Hinterberger, 52–71. Turnhout.

Hilgard, A. (ed.) (1901) *Scholia in Dionysii Thracis Artem Grammaticam*. Grammatici Graeci vol. 1.3. Leipzig.

Holwerda, D. (ed.) (1960) *Jo. Tzetzae Commentarii in Aristophanem, Fasc. II: Commentarium in Nubes*. Groningen.

Hörandner, W. (2012) 'The Byzantine Didactic Poem: A Neglected Literary Genre? A Survey with Special Reference to the Eleventh Century', in *Poetry and its Contexts in Eleventh-Century Byzantium*, ed. F. Bernard and K. Demoen, 55–67. Farnham.

Jeffreys, E. M. (2009) 'Why Produce Verse in Twelfth-Century Constantinople?', in *'Doux remède ...': Poésie et poétique à Byzance. Actes du IVe Colloque International Philologique 'ΕΡΜΗΝΕΙΑ', Paris, 23–24–25 février 2006, organisé par l'E.H.E.S.S. et l'Université de Chypre*, ed. P. Odorico, P. A. Agapitos and M. Hinterberger, 219–28. Dossiers byzantins 9. Paris.

Kaldellis, A. (2009) 'Classical Scholarship in Twelfth-Century Byzantium', in *Medieval Greek Commentaries on the Nicomachean Ethics*, ed. C. Barber and

D. Jenkins, 1–43. Studien und Texte zur Geistesgeschichte des Mittelalters 101. Leiden.
Katsaros, V. (2002) 'Η ρητορική ως 'θεωρία λογοτεχνίας' των Βυζαντινών', in *Pour une 'nouvelle' histoire de la littérature Byzantine. Actes du colloque international philologique, Nicosie, 2–28 mai 2000*, ed. P. Odorico and P. A. Agapitos, 95–106. Dossiers byzantins 1. Paris.
Koster, W. J. W. (ed.) (1975) *Prolegomena de comoedia. Scholia in Acharnenses, Equites, Nubes, fasc. I.I.a: Prolegomena de comoedia.* Groningen.
Latte, K. (ed.) (1953–66) *Hesychii Alexandrini lexicon*, 2 vols. Copenhagen.
Lauxtermann, M. D. (2022) 'Buffaloes and Bastards: Tzetzes on Metre', in *Τζετζικαὶ ἔρευναι*, ed. E. E. Prodi, 117–32. Eikasmos Studi Online 4. Bologna.
Lentz, A. (ed.) (1867) *Grammatici Graeci*, vol. 3.1. Leipzig (repr. Hildesheim 1965).
Leone, P. L. M. (ed.) (1995) *Ioannis Tzetzae Carmina Iliaca.* Catania.
(2005) *Giovanni Tzetzes, La leggenda troiana (Carmina Iliaca).* Lecce.
Lindberg, G. (1977) *Studies in Hermogenes and Eustathios: The Theory of Ideas and its Application in the Commentaries of Eustathios on the Epics of Homer.* Lund.
Lovato, V. F. (2017) 'Portrait de héros, portrait d'érudit: Jean Tzetzès et la tradition des *eikonismoi*', *MEG* 17: 137–56.
Markopoulos, A. (2014) 'Teachers and Textbooks in Byzantium, Ninth to Eleventh Centuries', in *Networks of Learning: Perspectives on Scholars in Byzantine East and Latin West, c. 1000–1200*, ed. S. Steckel, N. Gaul and M. Grünbart, 3–15. Byzantinische Studien und Texte 6. Zurich.
Martins de Jesus, C. A. (2016) 'John Tzetzes and the Pseudo-Aristotelian *Peplos* in Middle-Byzantium: The Testimony of the *Matritenses* gr. 4562 and 4621', *CFC: Estudios griegos e indoeuropeos* 26: 263–83.
Massa Positano, L. (ed.) (1960) *Jo. Tzetzae Commentarii in Aristophanem, Fasc. I: Prolegomena et commentarius in Plutum.* Groningen.
Mondini, U. (2022) 'John of All Trades: The Μικρομεγάλη Ἰλιάς and Tzetzes' "Didactic" Programme', in *Τζετζικαὶ ἔρευναι*, ed. E. E. Prodi, 237–59. Eikasmos Studi Online 4. Bologna.
Murray, A. T. (1999) *Homer: The Iliad*, 2 vols. Revised by W. F. Wyatt. Cambridge, MA.
Nesseris, I. C. (2014) 'Η Παιδεία στην Κωνσταντινούπολη κατά τον 12ο αιώνα', 2 vols. PhD thesis, University of Ioannina.
Pagani, L. (2011) 'Pioneers of Grammar: Hellenistic Scholarship and the Study of Language', in *From Scholars to Scholia: Chapters in the History of Ancient Greek Scholarship*, ed. F. Montanari and L. Pagani, 17–64. Berlin.
(2015) 'Language Correctness (*Hellenismos*) and its Criteria', in *Brill's Companion to Ancient Greek Scholarship*, vol. 2: *Between Theory and Practice*, ed. F. Montanari, S. Matthaios and A. Rengakos, 798–849. Leiden.
Papaioannou, S. (2014) 'Byzantine *historia*', in *Thinking, Recording, and Writing History in the Ancient World*, ed. K. A. Raaflaub, 297–313. Chichester.
Papathomopoulos, M. (ed.) (2007) *Ἐξήγησις Ἰωάννου Γραμματικοῦ τοῦ Τζέτζου εἰς τὴν Ὁμήρου Ἰλιάδα.* Athens.

Patillon, M. (ed.) (2008) *Corpus Rhetoricum, Tome I: Anonyme, Préambule à la rhétorique; Aphthonios, Progymnasmata. En annexe: Pseudo-Hermogène, Progymnasmata.* Paris.
(ed.) (2012a) *Corpus Rhetoricum, Tome III.2: Pseudo-Hermogène, L'Invention; Anonyme, Synopses des exordes.* Paris.
(ed.) (2012b) *Corpus Rhetoricum, Tome IV: Anonyme, Prolégomènes au 'De Ideis'; Hermogène, Les catégories stylistiques du discours (De Ideis); Anonyme, Synopses des exposés sur les 'Ideai'.* Paris.
(ed.) (2014) *Corpus Rhetoricum, Tome V: Pseudo-Hermogène, La méthode de l'habileté; Maxime, Les objections irréfutables; Anonyme, Méthode des discours d'adresse.* Paris.
Pontani, F. (2007) 'The First Byzantine Commentary on the *Iliad*: Isaac Porphyrogenitus and his Scholia', *ByzZ* 99.2: 551–96.
(2020) 'Scholarship in the Byzantine Empire (529–1453)', in *History of Ancient Greek Scholarship: From its Beginnings to the End of the Byzantine Age*, ed. F. Montanari, 373–529. Leiden.
Probert, P. (2015) 'Ancient Theory of Prosody', in *Brill's Companion to Ancient Greek Scholarship*, vol. 2: *Between Theory and Practice*, ed. F. Montanari, S. Matthaios and A. Rengakos, 923–48. Leiden.
Rance, P. (2022) 'Tzetzes and the *mechanographoi*: The Reception of Late Antique Scientific Texts in Byzantium', in *Τζετζικαὶ ἔρευναι*, ed. E. E. Prodi, 427–81. Eikasmos Studi Online 4. Bologna.
Robins, R. H. (1993) *The Byzantine Grammarians: Their Place in History.* Berlin.
Ronconi, F. (2012) 'Quelle grammaire à Byzance? La circulation des textes grammaticaux et son reflect dans les manuscrits', in *La produzione scritta tecnica e scientifica nel medioevo: libro e documento tra scuole e professioni*, ed. G. De Gregorio and M. Galante, 63–118. Spoleto.
Schäfer, G. H. (ed.) (1811) *Gregorii Corinthii et aliorum grammaticorum Graecorum libri de dialectis linguae Graecae.* Leipzig.
Sluiter, I. (1999) 'Commentaries and the Didactic Tradition', in *Commentaries = Kommentare*, ed. G. W. Most, 173–205. Aporemata: Kritische Studien zur Philologiegeschichte 4. Göttingen.
(2015) 'Ancient Etymology: A Tool for Thinking', in *Brill's Companion to Ancient Greek Scholarship*, vol. 2: *Between Theory and Practice*, ed. F. Montanari, S. Matthaios and A. Rengakos, 896–922. Leiden.
Spengel, L. (ed.) (1856) *Rhetores Graeci*, vol. 3. Leipzig.
Tomadaki, M. (2022) 'Uncovering the Literary Sources of John Tzetzes' *Theogony*', in *Byzantine Commentaries on Ancient Greek Texts, 12th–15th Centuries*, ed. B. van den Berg, D. Manolova and P. Marciniak, 130–47. Cambridge.
Valiavitcharska, V. (2021) 'Rhetorical Figures', in *The Oxford Handbook of Byzantine Literature*, ed. S. Papaioannou, 316–35. Oxford.
van den Berg, B. (2017) 'The Wise Homer and his Erudite Commentator: Eustathios' Imagery in the Proem of the *Parekbolai on the Iliad*', *BMGS* 41.1: 30–44.
(2020) 'John Tzetzes as Didactic Poet and Learned Grammarian', *DOP* 74: 285–302.

(2021) 'Eustathios' Homeric Commentaries: Translating Homer and Spoliating Ancient Traditions', in *Spoliation as Translation: Medieval Worlds in the Eastern Mediterranean. Convivium Supplementum*, ed. I. Jevtić and I. Nilsson, 116–31. Turnhout.

(2022) *Homer the Rhetorician: Eustathios of Thessalonike on the Composition of the Iliad.* Oxford.

van der Valk, M. (ed.) (1971–87) *Eustathii Archiepiscopi Thessalonicensis commentarii ad Homeri Iliadem pertinentes ad fidem codicis Laurentiani editi*, 4 vols. Leiden.

Van Rooy, R. (2016) 'Teaching Greek Grammar in 11th-century Constantinople: Michael Psellus on the Greek "Dialects"', *ByzZ* 109.1: 207–22.

van Thiel, H. (2014) *Scholia D in Iliadem, proecodisis aucta et correctior.* Cologne.

Webb, R. (1997) 'Greek Grammatical Glosses and Scholia: The Form and Function of a Late Byzantine Commentary', in *Medieval and Renaissance Scholarship*, ed. N. Mann and B. Munk Olsen, 1–18. Leiden.

Westerink, L. G. (ed.) (1992) *Michaelis Pselli Poemata.* Stuttgart.

Wouters, A., and P. Swiggers (2015) 'Definitions of Grammar', in *Brill's Companion to Ancient Greek Scholarship*, vol. 2: *Between Theory and Practice*, ed. F. Montanari, S. Matthaios and A. Rengakos, 515–44. Leiden.

Uhlig, G. (ed.) (1883) *Dionysii Thracis Ars Grammatica*, Grammatici Graeci vol. 1.1. Leipzig.

CHAPTER 7

Of Mice and Cat

The Katomyomachia *as Drama, Parody, School Text and Animal Tale**

Marc D. Lauxtermann

The *Katomyomachia* is a masterpiece of parody and wit.[1] And like so many other masterpieces of the Byzantine millennium (one may think of the *Akathistos Hymn*), it circulated mostly without ascription of authorship. Of the twenty manuscripts to have come down to us, it is only the oldest, the famous anthology in ms. Venice, Biblioteca Nazionale Marciana, gr. Z. 524 (late thirteenth century) [Diktyon 69995],[2] that preserves the name of its author: Theodore Prodromos; the other nineteen are silent on the matter, and so is the *editio princeps* produced by Arsenios Apostolis in Venice around 1495.[3] The reason why the *Katomyomachia* was transmitted in the manuscript tradition without a name attached to it was that it was used at school – and didactic materials in general have an unfortunate tendency to become anonymous.[4]

While the poem's anonymity is in itself unremarkable, the fact that it circulated in the oldest manuscripts without a title of its own is distinctly odd: there is no good explanation for this, although one could argue that the lack of a title leaves the work open to interpretation. The first editor, Arsenios Apostolis, faced with this problem, devised a title for it: *Galeomyomachia*, 'The Battle of Cat and Mice' (purloined, of course, from the

* An earlier and longer version of this chapter was published in Italian in Faraggiana di Sarzana and Funaioli (2021: 9–35).

1 Ed. Hunger (1968: 71–125). For excellent emendations, see Speck (1969) and Papatriandafyllou-Theodoridi (1999). The text has also been edited by Ahlborn (1968: 43–94): Ahlborn's edition is basically a reprint of Hercher (1873), including typographical errors and obvious mistakes. Kotłowska (2007–8) compares the two editions, but does not realize that Ahlborn's 'critical' edition in fact reproduces that of Hercher. The edition by García Romero (2003) combines readings from Ahlborn and Hunger. There is now a splendid new edition with facing translation in Italian by Faraggiana di Sarzana and Funaioli (2021): this edition is based on Hunger, with a number of important corrections and emendations. For a detailed study of the text tradition and a new collation of the manuscripts, see Ferreri (2021).

2 For the manuscript, see Spingou (2012: 9–50).

3 For the date of this extremely rare incunable, see Barker (1992: 17 and 52).

4 For didactic material becoming anonymous in later sources, see for example Vassis, Kotzabassi and Polemis (2019: 44–6).

pseudo-Homeric mock epic *Batrachomyomachia*, 'The Battle of Frogs and Mice').[5] The γαλῆ in Apostolis' made-up title owes its existence to a peculiarity of the manuscript tradition. In most manuscripts, including the exemplar used by Arsenios Apostolis for his edition, the medieval word for 'cat', κάτα, wherever it is used, has been emended to the pedantic and posh γαλῆ.[6] The title that we use nowadays, *Katomyomachia*, goes back to the first modern editor, Rudolph Hercher.[7] This title reintroduces the κάτα while retaining the second and third parts of Arsenios Apostolis' *Galeomyomachia*. To conclude, the poem has come down to us as a text without an author and a title.[8]

However, since the text deals with the heroic battle between mice and cat, there is nothing wrong with the modern title, nor with the attribution of the *Katomyomachia* to the famous twelfth-century author Theodore Prodromos. The ascription to Prodromos in Marc. gr. 524, though not corroborated by the rest of the manuscript tradition, is generally accepted. Not only does the anthology in Marc. gr. 524 offer a selection of Komnenian literature, including Prodromos,[9] the poem also clearly bears the imprint of his style and diction and can compete with the best of his works.[10]

The *Katomyomachia* as Drama

Typical of the Komnenian era are the rebranding of the novel as 'drama',[11] the development of dialogue as a means of creating a dramatic space (for example, Prodromos' satirical dialogues),[12] and the use of linguistic register as a means of bringing characters to life (for which see the *Ptochoprodromika*).[13] A brilliant example of the exploitation of dramatic means and the development of the histrionic voice is Constantine Manasses' *Hodoiporikon* or *Itinerary*, an account of an embassy to Palestine, which

5 All the manuscripts that have this title (including Oxford, Bodleian Library, Barocci 64 [Diktyon 47351], which does not date from the fifteenth century, as the editor states, but from the early sixteenth century: see Derron [1992: 11]), have borrowed it from the *editio princeps*.

6 In classical Greek, γαλῆ means 'weasel', but in later Greek it can mean 'cat' as it does up to the present day in *katharevousa* (the 'purified' form of Modern Greek).

7 Hercher (1873: 5).

8 For authorship and title, see Hunger (1968: 25–9).

9 For the anthology, see Spingou (2012).

10 Hunger (1968: 27–9).

11 See Agapitos (1998).

12 Ed. Migliorini (2010). For the *Bion Prasis*, see Marciniak (2013). For the *Amarantos*, see Migliorini (2007). See also Marciniak (2016: 218–21).

13 Ed. Eideneier (2012) and Maiuri (1920). On the disputed authorship of the *Ptochoprodromika*, see Janssen and Lauxtermann (2018) and Kulhánková (2021: 305–11). On the linguistic registers of the *Ptochoprodromika*, see Kulhánková in this volume.

the author transforms into a highly amusing text: it looks like an ego document, but it is in fact the dramatic monologue of a cantankerous intellectual who resents having to leave Constantinople with its literary *theatra* and, therefore, delivers his comments to himself, off-stage as it were.[14]

No better proof of this Komnenian interest in drama than the *Katomyomachia*. Firstly, to begin with the obvious, a text that has a *hypothesis* (a summary of the plot of a classical drama) and τὰ τοῦ δράματος πρόσωπα (*dramatis personae* in Latin, the protagonists of a play) at its beginning clearly positions itself as a drama. Secondly, a text that solely consists of dialogue, from beginning to end, and sometimes in the form of 'stichomythy' (verbal sparring in one-liners), immediately reminds one of the genre of drama. Thirdly, the presence of messenger speeches and the device of the *deus ex machina* at the end (the cat is killed by a beam that falls from the ceiling) are typical of ancient drama. And fourthly, as Hunger has shown, there are numerous allusions to Euripides and other tragedians in the *Katomyomachia*, especially in the second half, which reads as a parody of the *Persians* of Aeschylus.[15]

Hunger has also tried to divide the text into five acts (1–184, 185–239, 240–317, 318–33 and 334–84),[16] with little success it must be said: not only are these 'acts' breathtakingly short (16 lines for Act IV!), but there is also no Aristotelian unity of time because the plot takes place over two consecutive days. In fact, if there is a division, it is between day one (lines 1–184) and day two (lines 185–384): between the preparations for battle and the battle itself.[17]

The *Katomyomachia* belongs to a small group of versified texts that exhibit dialogue in some sort of theatrical setting, for which modern scholarship has coined the term *dramation* (short drama), though the Byzantines do not appear to have had a specific term for it.[18] It is generally assumed that these verse dialogues are not intended for the stage, but are meant to be read; they closely resemble the modern 'closet drama'.[19] This is what we have: *Susanna* by John of Damascus (lost except for two verses), *Verses on Adam* by Ignatios the Deacon, *Katomyomachia* by Theodore Prodromos, *Christos Paschon* (author unknown, but twelfth-century), *Verses on Fortune* by Michael Haploucheir and an untitled fragment by John Katrares. The

14 Ed. Chryssogelos (2017). See Lauxtermann (2004: 331–2). On the 'dramatic' or theatrical nature of Komnenian literature, see also Magdalino in this volume.
15 Hunger (1968: 44–7 and 52–5). For the parody of the *Persians*, see Popović (1991–2) and Aerts (1991).
16 Hunger (1968: 51).
17 See Meunier (2016: 196–9).
18 For the term 'dramation', see Leone (1969: 251–2).
19 See Marciniak (2004: 82).

first two date from the eighth–ninth centuries, the next three from the twelfth century, and the last one from the early fourteenth century.[20]

Typical of all these verse dialogues is the strong influence of Euripides: to quote Eustathios of Thessalonike, 'and a truly Euripidean style informed the plot of this play (John of Damascus' *Susanna*), because it showed Susanna tracing her own lineage and lamenting the prospect of encountering such evil in her own garden and being raped'.[21] Another common feature is the metre used in these verse dialogues: the dodecasyllable, the Byzantine equivalent of the iambic trimeter of the ancients. By using this metre, the authors of the verse dialogues strive after the literary effect of Euripidean drama.

Whereas *Susanna*, *Verses on Adam* and *Christos Paschon* are serious 'tragedies' based on biblical themes and the Katrares fragment is simply a pastiche of Euripides, Prodromos' *Katomyomachia* and Haploucheir's *Verses on Fortune* share a light-hearted sense of humour and tend, each in their own way, towards parody. Haploucheir makes fun of the plight of the typical Byzantine intellectual who, down on his luck, observes that upstarts without any formal training gain more money than he does, and therefore curses Lady Fortune for being blind and the Muses for not having taught him anything useful. There can be little doubt that Haploucheir's verse dialogue is a social satire. But what about the *Katomyomachia*?

The *Katomyomachia* as Parody and Palimpsest

The pseudo-Homeric *Batrachomyomachia* (first century BC) is widely regarded as the 'hypotext' for the *Katomyomachia* – or to put it differently, the latter constitutes the 'hypertext' of the former.[22] The relation that hypo- and hypertext entertain is one of literary imitation, or rivalry; and the chosen means of expression are citation, reference, allusion, parody, subtle subversion, deliberate misquotation or, the ultimate betrayal, embarrassed silence. Obliteration is what happens when one text is written upon another, the upper layer effacing what lies beneath, superimposing itself, foregrounding its own materiality. Byzantine literature is deeply palimpsestic in that it puts great stock in imitation (*mimesis*) and favours

20 See Lauxtermann (2019: 81–7).

21 Eustathios, *Commentary on the Iambic Canon for Pentecost*, Προοίμιον 86–9 ed. Cesaretti and Ronchey (2014: 11; cf. 132–3* and 141–2*): καὶ ἐσκευώρει τὴν διάθεσιν ἐκείνου τοῦ δράματος εὐριπίδειος αὐτόχρημα μέθοδος· ἐγενεαλόγει τε γὰρ ἑαυτὴν ἡ Σωσάννα καὶ ἀπεκλαίετο, εἰ περιπέσοι κακῷ τηλικούτῳ ἐντὸς κήπου καὶ βιασθείη.

22 For the concept of hypertextuality, see Genette (1982).

commentary over original thought. Writing in Byzantium is an act of rewriting; reading, an act of re-reading.

Since texts operate in a textual universe, each hypotext is also a hypertext, referring to earlier texts and superseding them, just as the hypertext in its turn will be superseded by a subsequent piece of literature and then inevitably become a hypotext.[23] The hypotext of the *Batrachomyomachia* is obviously Homer's *Iliad* and *Odyssey*: it refers to these two epics, plays with them, subverts them.[24] And this rewriting and re-reading of Homer is then passed on from text to text, in the intertextual chain that links the *Batrachomyomachia* and the *Katomyomachia*. Take lines 81–7 of the *Katomyomachia*:

> (Meaty Mouse) – Zeus appeared to me in my sleep and put courage in my heart. He said to me: 'Greetings, the victory is yours.' (Cheese-Pincher) – And what did he look like? Please tell me. (Meaty Mouse) – Like Cheese-Licker, our grey eminence. (Cheese-Pincher) – How come he hasn't shown up before? (Meaty Mouse) – My threats put the fear of God into him.

This passage alludes to the beginning of Book 2 of the *Iliad*, in which Zeus sends a deceptive dream to Agamemnon, the leader of the Greeks, and tells him that he will easily defeat the Trojans: the person who appears to Agamemnon in his dream and tells him to attack is Nestor, the elderly warrior famed for his wisdom.[25] The parody here is that famous old Nestor has turned into an old mouse who licks cheese and that mighty Zeus is mightily afraid of tiny Meaty Mouse. But there is also an ironic twist to it because whereas the dream Agamemnon sees is false, Meaty Mouse's dream will come true. Prodromos plays with the expectations of his audience, their knowledge of Homer, as a cat plays with the mouse it has caught, and then goes for the kill by turning the plot upside down.

Since the *Batrachomyomachia* was a very popular text with teachers and students alike, it has come down to us with many variants and many interpolations.[26] Some of these interpolations are clearly Byzantine for metrical reasons, such as lines 42–52, in which the leader of the mice, Crumb-Filcher, boasts that he has never flinched in battle and has always been the first to plunge straight into the fray, which immediately reminds one of

23 On the infinite possibilities of translating and transposing parodic elements into another language and thus creating a new hypertext, see Sarriu (2000: 171–9).
24 See, for example, Kelly (2009) and Hosty (2014).
25 See Meunier (2016: 183–4).
26 See Glei (1984: 39–45).

similar boasts of Meaty Mouse in Prodromos' *Katomyomachia*.[27] The two oldest manuscripts to offer these Byzantine interpolations are Florence, Biblioteca Medicea Laurenziana, 32.3 [Diktyon 16269] and El Escorial, Real Biblioteca, Ω. I. 12 (Andrés 513) [Diktyon 15062]: the former dates from around the year 1100, the latter is twelfth- or possibly thirteenth-century.[28] Given the date of Laur. 32.3, there can be little doubt that the direction of influence, if influence there was, ran from the interpolated version of the *Batrachomyomachia* to the *Katomyomachia*, and not the other way around.[29] However, vastly more important than the tedious question of who was first, is the fact that the *Batrachomyomachia* is a canvas on which to project ideas and forms, a palimpsest on which to develop new storylines, a text that generates a plurality of readings and writings.

In fact, Prodromos openly acknowledges his debt to the *Batrachomyomachia* (in whatever form the text may have come to him), but he does so with a twist. One of the mice reminds the other: 'Don't you remember how we once battled against the armies of the cats and the frogs and had multi-allied forces on our side?' (vv. 71–3). Mice and frogs fight valiantly in the *Batrachomyomachia*, but the cats are not involved in this heroic battle, though Pseudo-Homer does mention the γαλῆ (the weasel) as the arch-enemy of the mouse. Weasels were known in antiquity as able mouse-catchers:[30] it is because of their shared passion for mouse-catching that the word γαλῆ can denote both the weasel and the cat in post-classical Greek. So when the *Batrachomyomachia* begins by saying that one day a mouse had escaped the γαλῆ and went to the lake because it was thirsty, most Byzantine readers will have thought of the cat rather than the weasel. Similarly, when the mice single out mousetraps and γαλαῖ as their greatest danger, the Byzantines will have pictured felines rather than mustelids. The fact remains, however, that the mice are not battling against cats in the *Batrachomyomachia*, so Prodromos is deliberately rewriting its plot. He is turning it into a palimpsest for his own *Katomyomachia*.[31]

27 Hunger (1968: 58).

28 See Maniaci (2006: 233: Laur. 32.3) and (ibid., 222–3, n. 32: Esc. Ω. I. 12). Georgi Parpulov (*per litteras*) dates the Escorial manuscript to the twelfth century; Maniaci prefers the thirteenth century.

29 See Glei (1984: 129–30).

30 Contrary to popular belief, the ancients did not keep weasels as pets: see Schodde (2013). That is to say, texts that mention γαλέαι as pets, such as Theocritus 15.28, in fact refer to cats, not weasels.

31 Interestingly enough, the *Batrachomyomachia* in its turn appears to go back to another Hellenistic mock epic, the *Galeomyomachia*, fragments of which have been found on papyrus: see Schibli (1983). Both mock epics reflect an indigenous tradition in Egypt of depicting cats-and-mice battles in illustrated papyri and wall-paintings. As Brunner-Traut (1968: 29–33) points out, the Egyptian tale of the battle of the cats and the mice was turned into Arabic, probably via the intermediate stage of Coptic, in the early Islamic period and then became hugely popular in the Near East and the Levant. This oriental tradition is likely to have influenced Prodromos.

Although Pseudo-Homer's *Batrachomyomachia* undoubtedly serves as the main hypotext for the *Katomyomachia*, it parodies many more texts: Homer, the tragedians, Aristophanes, the New Testament, etc.[32] One may distinguish two types of parody: textual and structural. Textual parody is where source and target texts overlap and merge into one another, with ambiguity and double entendre as a result; structural parody operates on a higher level, that of thwarted generic expectations. A good example of textual parody is the opening passage of the *Katomyomachia* (lines 1–13), in which Prodromos alludes to one of the letters of Gregory of Nazianzos.[33] In the source text, Gregory tells his good friend, Basil the Great, that he has no wish to join him in his monastery in the Pontos region. Gregory jokingly calls this monastery a mouse-hole; so dark is the place, and so uninhabitable, that those who spend their lives there are worse off than the Cimmerians: the latter may not see the light for six months, but Basil and his fellow monks live constantly in the shadow of death.[34] In the target text, Prodromos' *Katomyomachia*, the mice are complaining that they cannot leave their mouse-holes on account of the cat: they live in eternal darkness, the shadow of death, 'just as legend has it that the murky Cimmerians, Pontian-wise, couldn't see a thing because they spent six months of the year in the dark' (the 'legend' is the *Odyssey*, 11.14–19 – yet another intertextual reference). The pun here is that mice are called ποντίκια (literally: 'Pontic mice') in vernacular Greek. So while Gregory of Nazianzos compares Basil's monastery in the Pontos to a mouse-hole and, by extension, the monks that live there to mice (probably because of the blackish colour of their habits), Prodromos calls the mice 'Pontian' and says that they suffer from poor eyesight because of their dark surroundings. A further intertextual link is with *Luke* 1.79 in which Zechariah predicts that John the Baptist will 'give light to those who sit in darkness and the shadow of death': it serves implicitly to reassure the mice that one day their life in obscurity while hiding from the hideous cat will end.

Structural parody is the deliberate violation of genre expectations for reasons of comedy. There is quite a lot of it in the *Katomyomachia*. To begin with, since the poem is patterned after the *Batrachomyomachia*, a mock epic, the reader would expect it to be a narrative text with dialogue interspersed, and preferably in dactylic hexameter. In fact, there is no narration

32 See Hunger (1968: *passim*), Popović (2008), Marciniak and Warcaba (2019). Meunier (2016) tends to identify literary parallels where there are none, such as the alleged parody of Pisides' panegyrics (pp. 247–66).

33 See Mercati (1923–4).

34 Ed. Gallay (1964–7: 1:3–4, letter 4). For this passage, see Crimi (2016: 154–8).

(only reported action), the form is that of drama, and the metre is the iamb. Another parody of genre are lines 319–32, in which the wife of Meaty Mouse and other female mice are mourning the death of Crumb-Filcher, who has been killed in battle. This is done in an antiphonal manner: mother-mouse utters a lament and the chorus responds either by repeating after her or slightly altering her words. As Margaret Alexiou has shown, refrains and antiphony are common features of the tradition of the ritual lament, both in antiquity and in modern times,[35] and there can be no doubt that in this passage Prodromos embeds the genre of the lament (or 'monody', to use the Byzantine term). The parody consists in the fact that the ritual lament is routinely performed by female mourners – not by mice.

Arguably by far the most impressive form of structural parody is to be found in the speech that Meaty Mouse delivers to his soldiers on the eve of the battle (lines 127–80). This falls into the category of the military harangue, a genre described in great detail by Syrianos and exemplified by two speeches of Constantine VII Porphyrogennetos.[36] A harangue is supposed to praise the soldiers for their courage and loyalty, to reassure them that the enemy they will face is weak and powerless, and to tell them that God is on their side: or to put it in the words of Cheese-Pincher, 'Right at the beginning start with a speech that will instil courage in the men' (vv. 116–17). In sharp contrast, Meaty Mouse reminds his soldiers that their fathers and forefathers had behaved in a cowardly manner because they feared the cat. The only reassurance he gives them is that they should follow his lead, for he, the great Meaty Mouse, descends from an illustrious family, is an expert in military affairs, has often proved his worth in battle, and is equal only to Zeus. This speech with all its boasting subverts the genre of the military harangue to such an extent that it will have prompted gales of laughter in the *theatron*.[37] In general, flaunting one's merits is allowed in Byzantium if one is setting oneself up as an exemplary model (as in the monastic *typika*) or if one has to defend oneself in public, in which case the autobiographical ego becomes a public persona.[38] But self-praise is otherwise frowned upon. The closest parallel to Meaty Mouse's deluded self-praise is a hilarious poem by Michael the Grammarian directed against the illiterate bishop of Philomelion: in it, the bishop himself delivers an auto-encomium without understanding that everything he says is damning

35 See Alexiou (1974: 131–60) and Marciniak (forthcoming).
36 For Syrianos, see Zuckermann (1990); for the harangues, see Markopoulos (2012).
37 See Hunger (1968: 57–8).
38 See Hinterberger (1999: 183–201 and 367–81).

evidence of his own incompetence.[39] Likewise, Meaty Mouse's speech is such a failure as a harangue that when he finally ends, he discovers that meanwhile all his soldiers have left (vv. 181–2): no need to listen to that kind of rhetoric!

Parody is often confused with satire. It is true that parody may be used as a means of social or political critique, but in most cases it has humorous intent only and does not aim at ridiculing individuals or denouncing social wrongs. And however hard I try, I fail to find any trace of political satire or sustained social critique in the *Katomyomachia*. However, others do. Hunger recognizes in Meaty Mouse the type of the bragging Byzantine generalissimo: a demagogue and a usurper;[40] Romano goes even further and identifies the mice as 'the kings and *condottieri* of this world';[41] and Cresci assumes that they represent the Komnenian emperors, those lovers of empty words and idle boasts.[42] Aerts avers that the mice are the Byzantines, and the cat Venice.[43] Hunger (again) views the mice as citizens who have to keep a low profile for political reasons;[44] and Kazhdan agrees, adding that the text 'may reflect the Byzantines' sense of political oppression'.[45] The latest attempt to read a message into the poem, and also the least convincing of all, is by Meunier, who portrays Prodromos as a free-thinker who in his *Katomyomachia* questions the tenets of Christianity and speaks out against the religious establishment.[46]

The *Katomyomachia* as Didactic Material

Almost all the Byzantine and post-Byzantine manuscripts that contain the *Katomyomachia* have a didactic character. A splendid example is ms. Naples, Biblioteca Nazionale 'Vittorio Emanuele III', II C 37 (fifteenth century) [Diktyon 46083] which contains grammatical materials, schedographic exercises, vocabularies and literary texts used at school, such as the *Sentences* of Pseudo-Phocylides, the *Golden Verses* of Pseudo-Pythagoras, the *Disticha* of Cato, the liturgical *kanons* of John of Damascus and Kosmas the Melode, and more.[47] Most of these didactic manuscripts present

39 See Amado Rodríguez and Ortega Villaro (2016: 369–76) and Lauxtermann (2019: 137–41).
40 Hunger (1968: 57–8).
41 Romano (1999: 234).
42 Cresci (2001: 203–4).
43 Aerts (1991: 205).
44 Hunger (1968: 56).
45 Kazhdan and Wharton Epstein (1985: 139).
46 Meunier (2016: *passim*); see the conclusion on pp. 371–80.
47 See Pierleoni (1962: 303–9).

the *Katomyomachia* with interlinear glosses, explaining the more unusual words to the students, and some have marginal notes that make the text more accessible to those struggling with the rules of Attic Greek.[48] Evidence for the continued use of the *Katomyomachia* at school can be found in post-Byzantine textbooks, the so-called μαθηματάρια, which may even tell that so-and-so gave a series of lectures on the text in the year so-and-so.[49]

The manuscripts quite often combine the *Katomyomachia* with the *Batrachomyomachia*: for instance, ms. Vienna, Österreichische Nationalbibliothek, Phil. gr. 293 (sixteenth century) [Diktyon 71407], which has just these two poems, both with interlinear glosses. There is plenty of evidence for the use of the *Batrachomyomachia* as didactic material: interlinear glosses and marginal commentaries; references to it as a school text in Byzantine sources; and oblique allusions to it, showing that the text must have been well known in Byzantine times.[50] There is every reason to believe that its companion piece, Prodromos' *Katomyomachia*, served a similar didactic purpose.[51] Arsenios Apostolis at least thought it did: in the prologue to the *editio princeps* he says that just as Homer wrote the *Batrachomyomachia* and other mock epics in order to educate the young, so too would the *Galeomyomachia* (= the *Katomyomachia*) satisfy the needs of diligent pupils.[52]

The many interpolations and variant readings in the manuscripts of the *Batrachomyomachia* and, to a lesser degree, the *Katomyomachia* clearly demonstrate that these two texts enjoyed an open text tradition in Byzantium. Because the classics have a canonical status, they are usually transmitted without deliberate alterations, omissions or additions. The *Batrachomyomachia* stands apart in this respect. The only other exception is Aesop. No literary genre lends itself more to *metaphrasis* (rewriting) than the fable, a genre that is in a constant process of transformation, from prose to verse and back again.[53] The main reason why we have so many different collections of fables is their continued use as didactic material, from Hellenistic times until the end of the Byzantine Empire and beyond.[54] Similarly, the reason why the *Batrachomyomachia* and the *Katomyomachia* lend themselves to change is the fact that they, like the Aesopic fables, are ideally suited for use at school.

48 None of these glosses and marginal notes have yet been edited; but see manuscript catalogues for descriptions of the manuscripts used by Hunger for his edition.
49 See Skarveli-Nikolopoulou (1993: 49–51).
50 See Wölke (1978: 33–41) and Carpinato (1988).
51 See Nesseris (2014: 86, n. 106).
52 Hunger (1968: 75).
53 For *metaphrasis* and the Aesopic tradition, see Lauxtermann (2019: 229–37).
54 For a useful overview of fables and fable collections in Byzantium, see van Dijk (2002).

Both texts are in fact free adaptations of fables. The *Batrachomyomachia* is loosely based on a fable Aesop told to the people of Delphi when they were about to kill him.[55] The beginning of the *Katomyomachia* is vaguely reminiscent of the Aesopic fable of the mice and the weasels/cats (γαλαῖ). The story goes that because they were always losing, the mice decided to be better organized and, therefore, appointed generals to lead them in battle, and that these generals, in order to distinguish themselves from the rank and file, put impressive horns on their heads. These horns may have looked nice, but when the mice were defeated in battle and fled to their nests, the generals did not fit through the hole and were all brutally killed.[56] Prodromos appears to have derived the idea of the cat-and-mice battle and the military organization of the mice from this fable; but all the rest is of course the product of his own fertile imagination.

There is another school text that shows remarkable similarities to the *Katomyomachia*. It is the *Schede tou Myos*,[57] commonly attributed to Prodromos, but in fact by Manasses.[58] This schedographic exercise consists of a diptych: the first part is a description of a mouse interested in the leftovers from a banquet, but afraid of being caught by the cat; the second part is a witty dialogue between the mouse and the cat. The bipartite structure of the *Schede tou Myos* occurs in other schedographic texts as well,[59] and one could argue that the *Katomyomachia* which is clearly divided into two parts, 1–184 (preparation for the battle) and 185–384 (the day of the battle), imitates this structure. The shared theme of cat-and-mouse rivalry is unlikely to be a mere coincidence: Manasses and Prodromos are clearly engaged in a game of one-upmanship and staking out their positions in the literary *theatron*.[60] In the *Schede tou Myos*, it is the cat who wins; in the *Katomyomachia*, the

55 *Vita Aesopi G*, §133 ed. Perry (1952: 75–6).

56 *Fable* 165 ed. Perry (1952: 385).

57 Ed. Papathomopoulos (1979).

58 Only one of the five manuscripts attributes the text to Prodromos; in the other four, the text is anonymous. Lines 9–22 of the *Schede tou Myos* are practically identical to another text by Manasses, the *Ekphrasis of the Earth*, lines 146–62 (ed. Lampsidis 1991: 200–1). As rightly argued by Horna (1905: 12–16), it is out of the question that Prodromos would copy Manasses in such an unimaginative way, or Manasses Prodromos, for that matter: they are both too good for that. And as seen by Hörandner (1981: 144–50), the prose rhythm of the *Schede tou Myos* is much closer to the practice of Manasses than that of Prodromos. In her recent discussion of the authorship of the *Schede*, Nilsson (2020: 134–8) fails to acknowledge the difference between literary imitation and downright plagiarism and downplays the significance of prose rhythm, though it is as unique to each writer as their writing style and choice of vocabulary.

59 See the text edited by Mercati (1927: 13–17).

60 As convincingly argued by Zagklas (2023: 53–70), the classroom and the literary *theatron* (the adult equivalent of the classroom) are not closed circuits: school texts, such as the *Schede tou Myos*, will also have been performed in the *theatron*.

mice win. Is Prodromos perhaps playing with his literary rival, subtly ridiculing his text, and turning it around to the amazement and amusement of the audience? As rightly observed by Marciniak, the purpose of the *Schede tou Myos* is to instruct the pupils in the art of *ekphrasis* (description) and *ethopoiia* (characterization through speech).[61] The stakes are much higher for the *Katomyomachia*: it serves the needs of more advanced students, eager to learn how to compose 'Euripidean' verses and write a proper dialogue. It is worth pointing out that right at the beginning of the *Schede tou Myos* there is a link with the *Batrachomyomachia* because the mouse is introduced as ἐμβασίχυτρος, 'pot-stalker', one of the characters of the pseudo-Homeric mock epic.[62] Regardless of who was first, Manasses or Prodromos, the common framework for these two school texts, the *Katomyomachia* and the *Schede tou Myos*, is the *Batrachomyomachia*.

The *Katomyomachia* as Beast Literature

There are four strands of beast literature in Byzantium: zoological (treatises on the properties of animals), allegorical (bestiaries: above all, the *Physiologos*) hexaemeral (homilies and hymns in praise of God's all-wise creation), and 'Aesopic' (texts with animals acting and speaking like humans). The last category encompasses many retellings of Aesopic fables (including original compositions passed off as 'Aesopic', but in fact clearly Byzantine), as well as a few other texts that in terms of genre do not count as fable, but still have much in common with the Aesopic tradition of story-telling.[63] These are, apart from the *Katomyomachia* and the *Schede tou Myos*, the following: (i) *Stephanites and Ichnelates* (late eleventh century, with later reworkings), a translation of the Arabic masterpiece *Kalīla wa-Dimna*, a collection of interwoven fables offering moral and political insights;[64] (ii) animal debates, highly abusive and highly amusing: *Entertaining Tale of Quadrupeds*, *Book of Birds* and *Book of Fish*, all three dating to the fourteenth century;[65] and (iii) *Synaxarion of the Honourable Donkey* (early fifteenth century), an absolutely brilliant animal tale.[66]

61 See Marciniak (2017: 516).

62 See Marciniak (2017: 518–22).

63 For beast literature in Byzantium, see Stewart (2015). For beast literature in Western Europe, see Ziolkowski (1993) and Mann (2009).

64 Ed. Puntoni (1889) and Sjöberg (1962). For a twelfth-century reworking of this text, see Lauxtermann (2018). On its reception in a poem by Michael Choniates, see Mondini in this volume.

65 For an edition, translation and commentary of the *Entertaining Tale* and information on the two other animal debates, see Nicholas and Baloglou (2003). See also Prinzing (2003) and Stewart (2019).

66 Ed. Moennig (2009). For the literary sources, see Lauxtermann and Janssen (2019).

These animal tales are too disparate and heterogeneous in composition and structure to form a genre of their own. Even texts produced in close proximity in time and space, and possibly responding to one another, such as the *Katomyomachia* and the *Schede tou Myos*, are far apart in terms of genre. What links them is the presence of talking animals. The use of talking animals as a literary stratagem ultimately derives from the genre of the Aesopic fable, and it is a skill the literati-to-be acquired at school, for in Byzantium education starts with Aesop. It is because of the connection with Aesop that Byzantine animal tales, though belonging to different genres, share common features.

The purpose of an Aesopic fable is twofold, functional and aesthetic: it aims to instruct and to amuse. Instruction may take the form of moral guidance or caustic satire; but whatever form it takes, positive or negative, the goal is invariably to persuade the audience by being witty and amusing. If animals are indeed 'good to think with' (as the phrase goes), then it is clear that for the Byzantines they make you laugh and can teach you a lesson. However, not all animal tales have an edifying purpose. As stated above, I do not think that the *Katomyomachia* has a particular message to convey: the same is true of the *Entertaining Tale of Quadrupeds*.[67] These texts restrict their remit to just being funny, and obviously there is nothing wrong with that. In fact, by refusing to express an opinion or pound home a message, these animal tales privilege humour over ridicule and seek to provoke laughter that is not directed at anyone in particular. Being just funny without any straightforward message or political agenda is actually the hardest thing to achieve.

The distinctive feature of the 'Aesopic' (fables and animal tales) is the anthropomorphic treatment of animals. The thoroughly humanized portrayal of the mice in the *Katomyomachia* is a case in point.[68] To give a few hilarious examples: mice that die an honourable death for family and home are remembered in the annals of history (vv. 50–4); like a Byzantine emperor, Meaty Mouse is acclaimed during triumphal processions (v. 138); like a true aristocrat, in his childhood he receives a military training and learns to ride horses (vv. 158–65); before going to battle, the mice sacrifice sheep and oxen to the gods (vv. 201–9); mother-mouse fears that if the cat were to win,

67 For various unconvincing interpretations of this poem, see Nicholas and Baloglou (2003: 431–47). The fact that oral poems very similar to the *Entertaining Tale of Quadrupeds* have been recorded in the twentieth century, without topical reference, demonstrates that animal debates do no need to have a political or social message to be entertaining: see ibid., pp. 475–81.

68 See Cresci (2001: 198–203).

she and her children would be taken as victory prizes and condemned to a life of servitude (vv. 232–9); etc. The mice are even complaining that they have to live in mouse-holes (vv. 1–13 and elsewhere)! Although the mice behave and speak like human beings, they do not identify themselves with us: Cheese-Pincher says that their enemy is called 'cat' by humans (v. 27). We will never know what the cat is called by the mice themselves.

In the anthropomorphized world of the 'Aesopic', animals do not have a solid identity: it is the story that gives them one.[69] The donkey is stupid, the donkey is clever; the fox wins, the fox loses. Either the mouse or the cat may be a monk, or they may be both monks. In the *Schede tou Myos*, the mouse pretends to be an abbot and the cat interrogates him about his monastic lifestyle.[70] In a fable recounted by Nikephoros Gregoras, it is the other way around: the cat has accidentally blackened up and the mice assume that he is wearing monastic garb and has renounced eating meat.[71] And in letter 116 (written not long after 1204), Michael Choniates is having it both ways. In this letter he expresses his fear that the newly appointed abbot of the monastery of St George, Kommolardos, would make a mess of things because that was his habit. And to hammer home his message that people do not change, he retells the Aesopic fable of the cat so much in love with her master that she prays to Aphrodite to become a girl. The miraculous metamorphosis takes place, but when the happy bride sees a mouse on her wedding day, she cannot resist her natural urge and jumps on it. Here the cat is the abbot Kommolardos and the mice are the poor monks of St George.[72]

And yet, despite endowing animals with human characteristics, 'Aesopic' beast literature emphasizes that their actions are ultimately dictated by nature. Cats and mice may speak and act like humans, and be whatever fiction wants them to be, but in the end it is the same old story: cats are predators, and mice their prey. The two have been at odds since time immemorial, each playing their role in the dialectics of eating and being eaten. In the *Stephanites and Ichnelates*, cat and mouse are both in danger and therefore help each other; but once the danger has passed, the mouse is once again suspicious of the cat.[73] In the *Entertaining Tale of Quadrupeds*,

69 Mann (2009: 29–31).
70 See Marciniak (2017: 521–2 and 525–7).
71 *Fable* 435 ed. Perry (1952: 493).
72 Ed. Kolovou (2001: 194.41–8; see also pp. 120–1). For the fable, see Perry (1952: 341, no. 50). For the fable's popularity in Byzantine times, see Papademetriou (1983: 125–7). The fable calls the animal/girl a γαλῆ: since weasels were not kept as pets (see above n. 30), this γαλῆ is almost certainly a cat.
73 Ed. Puntoni (1889: 270–5, VIII, §130).

cat and mouse are engaged in what can only be called unfriendly banter, accusing one another of absolutely disgusting behaviour.[74] The *Schede tou Myos* ends with the cat devouring the mouse: a menace ever present since the former caught the latter in the act of eating the leftovers from the banquet. In the *Katomyomachia*, the heroic battle of cat and mice is rather one-sided: until the moment he is struck by a piece of wood falling from the ceiling, the cat is killing all his opponents. As a medieval proverb succinctly puts it, 'the cat will thwart the mouse's ambitions'.[75]

Cats and mice exist also outside beast literature.[76] There are numerous references to these sworn enemies in letters, histories, commentaries, etc., and these shed light on the cultural assumptions regarding cats and mice. The *Oneirokritikon* of Achmet explains that if a person dreams of seeing a cat, it symbolically stands for a thief.[77] Symeon the New Theologian tells his monastic community that a good monk is like a cat that chases away the mouse (= the Devil) and does not steal.[78] And Ptochoprodromos recounts how the starving grammarian steals a piece of tenderloin and blames the poor cat.[79] But the cat is not only a thieving creature: it is also a pet. Empress Zoe lets her cat Mechlebe eat from golden plates, appoints special staff to take care of all his whims and interrupts meetings with senators to tell them that her cat has clearly had enough because he is yawning.[80] In the *Entertaining Tale of Quadrupeds*, the mouse has to admit, though grudgingly, that the thieving cat is dearly loved by humans.[81] And the *Synaxarion of the Honourable Donkey* has a moving story about an old lady and her beloved ginger cat, Parditsis.[82] The attitude towards mice is less friendly. They are generally seen as unclean animals and treated as pests that need to be eliminated either through cats (yes, them again) or mousetraps.[83] In the *Timarion*, the homonymous narrator discovers to his dismay that there are mice even in Hades: he had hoped that death would at least save him from their obnoxious presence.[84] In poem 103, Christopher of Mytilene complains that the mice are eating his papers and books;

74 Ed. Nicholas and Baloglou (2003: 166–9, lines 124–79).
75 Ed. Krumbacher (1893: 87, no. 40): ποντικοῦ βουλὰς κόψει κάτα.
76 For cats, see Kislinger (2011); for mice, see Carpinato (2005).
77 Ed. Drexl (1925: §278).
78 Ed. Koder (1971: hymn no. 21.403–7).
79 Ed. Eideneier (2012: 3.255–73).
80 See Tzetzes, *Histories* 5.12.524–40 ed. Leone (2007: 182).
81 Ed. Nicholas and Baloglou (2003: 168–9, lines 159–62).
82 Ed. Moennig (2009: 142–3, lines 169–89).
83 See, for instance, Christopher of Mytilene, poem 103 ed. Kurtz (1903), and Eustathios of Thessalonike, *ep.* 6 ed. Kolovou (2006).
84 Romano (1974: §18.476–84).

as luck would have it, the main manuscript of Christopher of Mytilene, Grottaferrata Z. α. XXIX (thirteenth century) [Diktyon 17975], has badly suffered from rodent damage.[85] It is doubly ironic, then, that Meaty Mouse claims to descend from the illustrious family of the Paper-Chewers (v. 156): Byzantine writers, such as Theodore Prodromos and the literary in-crowd gathered in the *theatron* to listen to the *Katomyomachia*, must have dreaded paper-devouring mice and what they could do to their writings.

The unexpected end of the *Katomyomachia* (vv. 371–8) is cartoonesque, with the cat crushed under a heavy beam, dead, and descending into the darkness of Hades where we found the mice at the beginning of this marvellous poem. It is the kind of humorous violence for which the *Tom and Jerry* cartoons are renowned. The difference, of course, is that the cat really dies whereas Tom and Jerry, whatever horrible things they may do to one another, always survive unscathed. One answer is that this is humour for advanced students, not small children. Another answer is that fictional beast literature (the 'Aesopic' category) creates its own discursive space in which death is just a way of ending the story. There is always a sequel (or a prequel). That is to say, the 'Aesopic' is in a state of perpetual motion: cat and mouse are at it, again and again and again. And they make us laugh, again and again. This is aptly summarized by a medieval proverb: κάτης καὶ ποντικὸς ἐμάχουντα καὶ ὁ βλέπων ἐγέλα, 'Cat and mouse were battling, and the onlooker was laughing.'[86] However sordid the cat-and-mouse game may be in reality, it is used to great comical effect in the world of the 'Aesopic'.

Bibliography

Aerts, W. J. (1991) 'A Tragedy in Fragments: The Cat-and-Mouse War', in *Fragmenta dramatica: Beiträge zur Interpretation der griechischen Tragikerfragmente und ihrer Wirkungsgeschichte*, ed. A. Harder and H. Hofmann, 203–18. Göttingen.

Agapitos, P. A. (1998) 'Narrative, Rhetoric, and "Drama" Rediscovered: Scholars and Poets in Byzantium Interpret Heliodorus', in *Studies in Heliodorus*, ed. R. Hunter, 125–56. Cambridge.

Ahlborn, H. (ed.) (1968) *Pseudo-Homer, Der Froschmäusekrieg – Theodoros Prodromos, Der Katzenmäusekrieg*. Berlin.

Alexiou, M. (1974) *The Ritual Lament in Greek Tradition.* Cambridge.

Amado Rodríguez, T., and B. Ortega Villaro (2016) *Poesía lúdico-satírica bizantina del siglo XI*. Madrid.

85 See Bernard (2014: 20).

86 Ed. Krumbacher (1893: 84, no. 28).

Barker, N. (1992) *Aldus Manutius and the Development of Greek Script and Type in the Fifteenth Century*. New York.
Bernard, F. (2014) *Writing and Reading Byzantine Secular Poetry, 1025–1081*. Oxford.
Brunner-Traut, E. (1968) *Altägyptische Tiergeschichte und Fabel: Gestalt und Strahlkraft*. Darmstadt.
Carpinato, C. (1988) 'La fortuna della Batrachomyomachia dal IX al XVI secolo: da testo scolastico a testo "politico"', in *La battaglia delle rane e dei topi: Batrachomyomachia*, ed. M. Fusillo, 137–48. Milan.
(2005) 'Topi nella letteratura greca medievale', in *Animali tra zoologia, mito e letteratura nella cultura classica e orientale*, ed. E. Cingano, A. Ghersetti and L. Milano, 175–92. Padua.
Cesaretti, P., and S. Ronchey (eds.) (2014) *Eustathii Thessalonicensis exegesis in canonem iambicum pentecostalem*. Supplementa Byzantina 10. Berlin.
Chryssogelos, K. (ed.) (2017) *Κωνσταντίνου Μανασσῆ Ὁδοιπορικόν: Κριτική ἔκδοση, μετάφραση, σχόλια*. Athens.
Cresci, L. R. (2001) 'Parodia e metafora nella Catomiomachia di Teodoro Prodromo', *Eikasmos* 12: 197–204.
Crimi, C. (2016) 'Da una frontiera all' altra: *eschatià* nei Padri cappadoci', in *Studi bizantini in onore di Maria Dora Spadaro*, ed. T. Creazzo, C. Crimi, R. Gentile and G. Strano, 145–61. Rome.
Derron, P. (1992) 'Inventaire des manuscrits des *Vers d'Or* pythagoriciens', *RHT* 22: 1–17.
Drexl, F. (ed.) (1925) *Achmetis Oneirocriticon*. Leipzig.
Eideneier, H. (ed.) (2012) *Πτωχοπρόδρομος: Κριτική ἔκδοση*. Heraklion.
Faraggiana di Sarzana, C., and M. P. Funaioli (eds.) (2021) *La battaglia della gatta e dei topi (Katomyomachia): Testo greco, traduzione e commento*. Rome.
Ferreri, L. (2021) *La tradizione manoscritta della Catomiomachia di Teodore Prodromo: Testo, traduzione e apparato delle varianti in appendice*. Trieste.
Gallay, P. (ed.) (1964–7) *Saint Grégoire de Nazianze: Lettres*, 2 vols. Paris.
García Romero, F. A. (ed.) (2003) *Teodoro Pródromo: La Catomiomaquia*. Jerez.
Genette, G. (1982) *Palimpsestes: La littérature au second degré*. Paris.
Glei, R. (ed.) (1984) *Die Batrachomyomachia: Synoptische Edition und Kommentar*. Frankfurt am Main.
Hercher, R. (ed.) (1873) *Catomyomachia*. Leipzig.
Hinterberger, M. (1999) *Autobiographische Traditionen in Byzanz*. Vienna.
Hörandner, W. (1981) *Der Prosarhythmus in der rhetorischen Literatur der Byzantiner*. Vienna.
Horna, K. (1905) 'Analekten zur byzantinischen Literatur', *Jahresbericht des k.k. Sophiengymnasiums in Wien*, 3–35. Vienna.
Hosty, M. (2014) 'The Mice of Ithaca: Homeric Models in the *Batrachomyomachia*', *Mnemosyne* 67: 1008–13.
Hunger, H (ed.) (1968) *Der byzantinische Katz-Mäuse-Krieg. Theodoros Prodromos, Katomyomachia: Einleitung, Text und Übersetzung*. Graz.

Janssen, M. C., and M. D. Lauxtermann (2018) 'Authorship Revisited: Language and Metre in the *Ptochoprodromika*', in *Reading in the Byzantine Empire and Beyond*, ed. T. Shawcross and I. Toth, 558–84. Cambridge.

Kazhdan, A., and A. Wharton Epstein (1985) *Change in Byzantine Culture in the Eleventh and Twelfth Centuries*. Berkeley.

Kelly, A. (2009) 'Parodic Inconsistency: Some Problems in the *Batrakhomyomakhia*', *JHS* 129: 45–51.

Kislinger, E. (2011) 'Byzantine Cats', in *Animals and Environment in Byzantium (7th–12th C.)*, ed. I. Anagnostakis, T. Kolias and E. Papadopoulou, 165–88. Athens.

Koder, J. (ed.) (1971) *Syméon le Nouveau Théologien: Hymnes*, vol. 2. Paris.

Kolovou, F. (ed.) (2001) *Michaelis Choniatae Epistulae*. Berlin.

(2006) *Die Briefe des Eustathios von Thessalonike: Einleitung, Regesten, Text, Indizes*. Beiträge zur Altertumswissenschaft 239. Munich.

Kotłowska, A. (2007–8) 'On the Two Critical Editions of *Cat and Mouse War* by Theodoros Prodromos', *Pomoerium* 6: 94–9.

Krumbacher, K. (ed.) (1893) 'Mittelgriechische Sprichwörter', *Sitzungsberichte der philosophisch-philologischen und der historischen Classe der köninglich bayerischen Akademie der Wissenschaften*, vol. 2. Munich (repr. Hildesheim, 1969).

Kurtz, E. (ed.) (1903) *Die Gedichte des Christophoros Mitylenaios*. Leipzig.

Kulhánková, M. (2021) '"For Old Men Too Can Play, Albeit More Wisely So": The Game of Discourses in the *Ptochoprodromika*', in *Satire in the Middle Byzantine Period: The Golden Age of Laughter?*, ed. P. Marciniak and I. Nilsson, 304–23. Explorations in Medieval Culture 12. Leiden.

Lampsidis, O. (ed.) (1991) 'Der vollständige Text der Ἔκφρασις τῆς γῆς des Konstantinos Manasses', *JÖByz* 41: 189–205.

Lauxtermann, M. D. (2004) 'La poesia', in *Lo spazio letterario del medioevo. 3: Le culture circostanti*, vol. 1: *La cultura bizantina*, ed. G. Cavallo, 301–43. Rome.

(2018) 'The Eugenian Recension of *Stephanites and Ichnelates*: Prologue and Paratexts', *Nea Rhome* 15: 55–106.

(2019) *Byzantine Poetry from Pisides to Geometres: Texts and Contexts*, vol. 2. Wiener Byzantinistische Studien 24/2. Vienna.

Lauxtermann, M. D., and M. C. Janssen (2019) 'Asinine Tales East and West: *The Ass's Confession* and *The Mule's Hoof*', *ByzZ* 112.1: 105–22.

Leone, P. L. M. (ed.) (1969) 'Michaelis Hapluchiris versus cum excerptis', *Byzantion* 39: 251–83.

(ed.) (2007) *Ioannis Tzetzae Historiae*, 2nd ed. Galatina.

Maiuri, A. (ed.) (1920) 'Una nuova poesia di Teodoro Prodromo in greco volgare', *ByzZ* 23.1: 397–407.

Maniaci, M. (2006) 'Problemi di mise en page dei monoscritti con commento a "cornice": l'esempio di alcuni testimoni dell'Iliade', *S&T* 4: 211–97.

Mann, J. (2009) *From Aesop to Reynard: Beast Literature in Medieval Britain*. Oxford.

Marciniak, P. (2004) *Greek Drama in Byzantine Times*. Katowice.

(2013) 'Theodore Prodromos' *Bion Prasis*: A Reappraisal', *GRBS* 53: 219–39.
(2016) 'Reinventing Lucian in Byzantium', *DOP* 70: 209–23.
(2017) 'A Pious Mouse and a Deadly Cat: The *Schede tou Myos*, Attributed to Theodore Prodromos', *GRBS* 57: 507–27.
(forthcoming) 'Living in the Mouse-Hole: Playing with the Conventions of Lament in Theodore Prodromos' *Katomyomachia*', in *Lament as Performance in Byzantium*, ed. N. Tsironi and T. Kampianaki. London.
Marciniak, P., and K. Warcaba (2019) 'Theodore Prodromos' *Katomyomachia* as a Byzantine Version of Mock-Epic', in *Middle and Late Byzantine Poetry: Texts and Contexts*, ed. A. Rhoby and N. Zagklas, 97–110. Byzantios: Studies in Byzantine History and Civilization 14. Turnhout.
Markopoulos, A. (2012) 'The Ideology of War in the Military Harangues of Constantine VII Porphyrogennetos', in *Byzantine War Ideology between Roman Imperial Concept and Christian Religion*, ed. J. Koder and I. Stouraitis, 47–56. Vienna.
Mercati, S. G. (1923–4) 'Il prologo della Catomyomachia di Teodoro Prodromo è imitato da Gregorio Nazianzeno, Epist. IV (Migne PG 37 col. 25B)', *ByzZ* 24.1: 28.
(1927) 'Intorno agli Σχέδη μυός', *Studi Bizantini* 2: 13–17.
Meunier, F. (2016) *Théodore Prodrome: Crime et châtiment chez les souris*. Paris.
Migliorini, T. (2007) 'Teodoro Prodromo, Amaranto', *MEG* 7: 183–247.
(ed.) (2010) 'Gli scritti satirici in greco letterario di Teodoro Prodromo: Introduzione, edizione, traduzione e commento', PhD thesis, Scuola Normale Superiore, Pisa.
Moennig, U. (ed.) (2009) 'Das Συναξάριον τοῦ τιμημένου Γαδάρου: Analyse, Ausgabe, Wörterverzeichnis', *ByzZ* 102.1: 109–66.
Nesseris, I. C. (2014) 'Η παιδεία στην Κωνσταντινούπολη κατά τον 12ο αιώνα', 2 vols. PhD thesis, University of Ioannina.
Nicholas, N., and G. Baloglou (2003) *An Entertaining Tale of Quadrupeds: Translation and Commentary*. New York.
Nilsson, I. (2020) *Writer and Occasion in Twelfth-Century Byzantium: The Authorial Voice of Constantine Manasses*. Cambridge.
Papademetriou, J.-T. (1983) 'Some Aesopic Fables in Byzantium and the Latin West: Tradition, Survival and Diffusion', *ICS* 8: 122–36.
Papathomopoulos, M. (ed.) (1979) 'Τοῦ σοφωτάτου κυροῦ Θεοδώρου τοῦ Προδρόμου τὰ Σχέδη τοῦ Μυός', *Parnassos* 21: 376–99.
Papatriandafyllou-Theodoridi, N. (1999) 'Παρατηρήσεις στην Κατομυομαχία', *EEThess(philos)* 8: 139–56.
Perry, B. E. (ed.) (1952) *Aesopica*. Urbana.
Pierleoni, G. (1962) *Catalogus codicum graecorum Bibliothecae Nationalis Neapolitanae*, vol. 1. Rome.
Popović, A. (1991–2) 'Prodromova *Katomiomahia* i Eschilovi *Persijanci*', *Zbornik Radova Vizantološkog Instituta* 29–30: 117–24.
(2008) 'Komička sredstva u spevu *Boi Mačke i miševa* Teodora Prodroma', in *Niš i Vizantija: Zbornik Radova VI*, ed. M. Rakocija, 379–91. Niš.

Prinzing, G. (2003) 'Zur byzantinischen Rangstreitliteratur in Prosa und Dichtung', *Römische historische Mitteilungen* 45: 241–86.
Puntoni, V. (ed.) (1889) *Στεφανίτης καὶ Ἰχνηλάτης: Quattro recensioni della versione greco del Kalīla wa-Dimna*. Florence.
Romano, R. (ed.) (1974) *Pseudo-Luciano: Timarione*. Naples.
(1999) *La satira bizantina dei secoli XI–XV: Il patriota, Caridemo, Timarione, Cristoforo di Mitilene, Michele Psello, Teodoro Prodromo, Carmi ptocoprodromici, Michele Haplucheir, Giovanni Catrara, Mazaris, La messa del glabro, Sinassario del venerabile asino*. Turin.
Sarriu, L. (2000) 'Parodia e traduzione: la *Catomiomachia* di Teodoro Prodromo', *AFLC* 55 (18 n.s.): 169–203.
Schibli, H. (ed.) (1983) 'Fragments of a Weasel and Mouse War', *ZPE* 53: 1–25.
Schodde, C. (2013) 'The Weasel in Antiquity: Pet or Pest?', at https://foundinantiquity.com/2013/10/28/the-weasel-in-antiquity-pet-or-pest/.
Sjöberg, L.-O. (ed.) (1962) *Stephanites und Ichnelates:* Überlieferungsgeschichte *und Text*. Uppsala.
Skarveli-Nikolopoulou, A. G. (1993) Μαθηματάρια των ελληνικών σχολείων κατά την Τουρκοκρατία. Athens.
Speck, P. (1969) 'Review of H. Hunger, *Der byzantinische Katz-Mäuse-Krieg*', Ἑλληνικά 22: 481–7.
Spingou, F. (2012) 'Words and Artworks in the Twelfth Century and Beyond: The Thirteenth-Century Manuscript Marc. gr. 524 and the Twelfth-Century Dedicatory Epigrams on Works of Art', PhD thesis, University of Oxford.
Stewart, K. L. (2015) 'Nature and Narratives: Landscapes, Plants and Animals in Palaiologan Vernacular Literature', PhD thesis, University of Oxford.
(2019) 'An Entertaining Tale of Quadrupeds: Animals and Insults in a Late Byzantine Poem', in *Impious Dogs, Haughty Foxes and Exquisite Fish: Evaluative Perception and Interpretation of Animals in Ancient and Medieval Mediterranean Thought*, ed. T. Schmidt and J. Pahlitzsch, 165–83. Berlin.
van Dijk, G. J. (2002) 'La fábula bizantina: panorama de su presencia en las colecciones y otros géneros literarios', in *'Y así dijo la zorra': La tradición fabulística en los pueblos del Mediterráneo*, ed. A. Pérez Jiménez and G. Cruz Andreotti, 141–83. Madrid.
Vassis, I., S. Kotzabassi and I. Polemis (2019) 'A Byzantine Textbook of the Palaeologan Period: The Schedographic Collection of Ms Laurentianus 56.17', *Parekbolai* 9: 33–182.
Wölke, H. (1978) *Untersuchungen zur Batrachomyomachia*. Meisenheim-am-Glan.
Ziolkowski, J. M. (1993) *Talking Animals: Medieval Latin Beast Poetry, 750–1150*. Philadelphia.
Zagklas, N. (2023) *Theodore Prodromos, Miscellaneous Poems: An Edition and Literary Study*. Oxford.
Zuckermann, C. (1990) 'The Military Compendium of Syrianus Magister', *JÖByz* 40: 209–24.

CHAPTER 8

On the Roses

*Reflections on a Neglected Poem by Nicholas Kallikles (*Carm. *29 Romano)**

Giulia Gerbi

Little is known about Nicholas Kallikles. The dates of his birth and death remain unknown, but it is certain that his life and career developed under the reign of the two great Komnenoi, Alexios I and John II, and that he was one of the most appreciated court physicians of his time.[1] The corpus of his works, published for the first time by Leon Sternbach (1903) and more recently by Roberto Romano (1980), consists of thirty-one poems,[2] the vast majority of which are ekphrastic, dedicatory and funerary texts.[3] All the surviving poems show his close relationship with the court aristocracy and the imperial family itself; several contemporary witnesses attest moreover to his important role at the court of the capital.[4]

Among the poems by Nicholas Kallikles, *Poem* 29, entitled Εἰς τὰ ῥόδα, 'On the Roses', stands out.[5] This poem is distinctive for its length (only poem 31, the epitaph for John II, is longer), its theme and some peculiar

* My gratitude goes to the conference's participants, who stimulated a fruitful debate for which I am truly thankful and whose comments and suggestions helped me to improve my work significantly. I would like to thank especially Panagiotis Agapitos, Emilie van Opstall, Nikos Zagklas and Baukje van den Berg. I also gratefully acknowledge Enrico Maltese and Thomas Coward for their valuable advice.

1 For the high esteem he enjoyed as court physician, see Anna Komnene, *Alexiad* 15.11.2 ed. Reinsch and Kambylis (2001) (T2 Romano); Theodore Prodromos, *Executioner or Physician* 21.17–22 ed. Podestà (T3a Romano), *Ptochoprodronika* 3(4).414–16 (T3b Romano).

2 Romano (1980) presents thirty-one poems as *Carmina genuina*, five as *dubia* and one as spurious.

3 Andriollo (2018: 4): 'this corpus can be roughly divided in two groups: a series of epitaphs and funerary poems, and a number of dedicatory poems for liturgical and profane artworks'. For recent studies on Kallikles' poetry, see Magnelli (2006) and Andriollo (2018).

4 See Anna Komnene, *Alexiad* 15.11.2–3 ed. Reinsch and Kambylis, which is perhaps the best-known witness to Kallikles' profession and his role at the court. Theophylaktos of Ohrid wrote two letters to him asking for help and protection: see *ep.* 93–4 ed. Gautier. The title of *ep.* 94 (τῷ αὐτῷ) identifies the recipient of the letter as Kallikles, but Gautier (1986: 70, 478) instead proposes the identification with another court physician of the period, Michael Pantechnes. For other witnesses and for further information about Kallikles' biography, see the *vetera testimonia* in Romano's edition (1980: 57–69), Gautier (1986: 69–73) and Andriollo (2018: 3–4).

5 The poem is preserved in Venice, Biblioteca Nazionale Marciana, gr. Z 524 = 318 [Diktyon 69995], fols. 101–2.

features. According to Romano,[6] Εἰς τὰ ῥόδα ought to be classified as a religious epigram due to its deep sensibility and personal inspiration, thus constituting an exception among the rest of Kallikles' poetic production.[7] Upon closer inspection, however, we can see how this poem resists this classification.

Text and Translation

Εἰς τὰ ῥόδα

Τοῦ Παρνασοῦ δὲ πρῶνας αἱ Βάκχαι πάλαι
κατεῖχον ὥσπερ οἶκον ἢ καινὴν πόλιν·
σύμμαχος αὐταῖς Διόνυσος ἦν τότε,
νεβρῶν δορὰς χιτῶνας ἐνδεδυμένος
5 καὶ ταῖν χεροῖν τὸν θύρσον ὡς σκῆπτρον φέρων·
εἶχον δὲ πεῦκαι τοῦδε τοὺς ἱπποδρόμους
καὶ πλατάνιστοι καὶ κυπαρίττων γένος,
καὶ Βακχικὸν σκιρτῶντος αὐτοῦ πολλάκις
τὸν Παρνασὸν κατεῖχεν ἐκ μύθων ἔαρ,
10 καὶ κύκνος ᾠδὰς εἶχεν ἐνθεεστέρας
τοῦ Πυθίου φθάσαντος εἰς Δελφοὺς πάλιν·
καὶ γὰρ μεθυσθεὶς ταῖς ὀδμαῖς τῶν ἀνθέων,
ἃς τοῦ θεοῦ φθάσαντος ἐν τῇ Πυθίᾳ
ἡ Δελφικὴ προὔπεμψεν εὐχερῶς πέτρα,
15 εὐθὺς μελῳδὸς ἦν ἑαυτοῦ βελτίων·
καὶ φοίνικες καὶ δένδρα πρὸς τῷ Λιβάνῳ
(ὁ Λίβανος δὲ τῆς Παλαιστίνης ὄρος)
ἤνθουν δι' Ἀστάρτην γε τὴν Σιδωνίαν,
κἂν μὴ παρῆν μάλιστα καιρὸς ἀνθέων.
20 Ὁρᾷς φυτουργὲ τῶν λογικῶν ἀνθέων,
πῶς καὶ θεοῖς ἔαρος ἡ χάρις φίλη;
Καὶ τί γράφω λειμῶνας ἐκ μύθων πλάνης,
βλέπων δι' αὐτῶν εἰς ἔαρ πεπλασμένον;
Τὸν Ἐμμανουήλ, τὸν θεάνθρωπον Λόγον,
25 παρῆξαν ἡμῖν μυστικώτεροι λόγοι
τρέφοντα τοὺς πεινῶντας Ἑβραίους πάλαι
ἅπαξ τε καὶ δὶς καὶ τρέφοντα πλουσίως·
ἀλλ' ἦν ὁ χόρτος τοῖς Ἰουδαίοις κλίνη
πολύς, χλοώδης, ἡδὺς ἐκ τῶν ἀνθέων

6 Romano (1980: 23–4).

7 Romano (1980: 23) points out that Kallikles' poetic work often lacks personal references, since, with the exception of *Poem* 29, it consists mainly of funerary poems and dedicatory epigrams for artworks commissioned by court personages.

30 καὶ τὴν ἁφὴν ἔθελγε τῇ κατακλίσει
καὶ τὴν ὅρασιν αὖθις ἐκ τῶν χρωμάτων,
ὀσφρήσεως δὲ ταῖς ὀδμαῖς ἐπεκράτει
καὶ παντοδαπὴν εἶχεν ἡ τροφὴ χάριν·
καὶ καινὸν οὐδὲν τοὺς Θεοῦ δαιτυμόνας
35 λαμπρῶς ἀριστᾶν ἀμφὶ τῷ χλόης τόπῳ
ἔαρος αὐτοῖς φαιδρύνοντος τὸν τόπον.
Κἀγώ σε λοιπὸν τοῖς ἐμοῖς τέρπων λόγοις
ἔαρ συνεργὸν εὗρον εἰς λόγου χάριν·
τὸ μὲν γὰρ ἁπλῶς στιβαρὸν τὸ τοῦ λόγου
40 καὶ πᾶν τὸ σεμνὸν καὶ τὸ συννοίας γέμον
οἱ σοὶ χορηγήσουσιν ἔνθεοι τρόποι,
ὡς ἀρετῆς δοχεῖον ὄντες ἐνθέου,
καὶ τοῖς λόγοις δώσουσιν εὐσθενῆ τόνον
πανεμβριθεῖς δεικνύντες ἐκ τῶν πραγμάτων·
45 τὸ μειδιῶν δὲ καὶ διακεχυμένον
ἢ καὶ γελῶν καὶ παῖζον ἐκ γλυκασμάτων
ἔαρος ἡμῖν ἐνσταλάξουσι δρόσοι,
ὑπὲρ 'μέλι γλυκάζον' ἐκκεχυμένου,[8]
ὑπὲρ μύρον πνέοντος ἐξ ἀρωμάτων,
50 ὃ τὴν 'κεφαλὴν Ἀαρὼν' διαβρέχει
τὸν ἱερατικόν τε πώγωνα βρέχει·
ἐαρινῆς χάριτος αἱ καλαὶ δρόσοι
καὶ τῆς Ἀερμὼν εἰσιν ἐγγύθεν δρόσου.
Τοὺς οὐρανούς τις εἶδε πρὶν ἀναστέρους,
55 τὸ τῆς σελήνης φέγγος ἐσκιαμάχει,
τὸν ἥλιον δὲ τῶν νεφῶν ἡ πυκνότης
ἐθαλάμευεν οἷα παρθένον νέαν·
ὑπὸ σκιὰν ἐζῶμεν ἡμεῖς ἀθλίως,
Νύμφας Ἁμαδρυάδας ἐζηλωκότες·
60 τανῦν δὲ πηγαὶ μυρίαι φαεσφόροι
ἐξ οὐρανοῦ βλύζουσιν ἄφθονον σέλας.
Τὸν Ἕσπερόν μοι καὶ τὸν Ἀρκτοῦρον σκόπει,
σκόπει τὸν Ὠρίωνα, τὸν Κύνα βλέπε
καὶ τὸν Βοώτην ἴδε σὺν τῷ Σειρίῳ·
65 φωτὸς φέρουσι πάντα λαμπρὰς λαμπάδας·
τὴν Ἄρκτον αὖθις καὶ τὰς Πλειάδας ἴδε
καὶ τὰς Ὑάδας, ἀστέρας φαεσφόρους·
εἴπω τὸ μεῖζον· χειμερινῆς ἡμέρας
ἐαρινὴ νὺξ πλεῖον ἐκστίλβει σέλας.
70 Τὴν γῆν δὲ τίς κατέσχε νῦν ἀταξία;
μὴ χιόνων τὸ πλῆθος ὡς ἄχθος φέρει;
μὴ πλῆθος ὄμβρων, μὴ χάλαζα πλησμία;

8 ἐκκεχυμένου, πνέοντος Sternbach, Romano : ἐκκεχυμένοι, πνέοντες **M** (Marc.gr. Z 524 = 318).

κρυμὸς μακρὰν ἀπῆλθεν, ἀνέμων βίαι.
Ποῦ νῦν παρ' ἡμῖν ἴχνος ἀργέστου Νότου;
75 Βορρᾶς δὲ Θρᾷξ ποῦ; ποῦ δὲ Λιβὸς ἡ βία;
τὸν Εὖρον οὐκ ἐφεῦρον, ἀργεῖ Καικίας,
ποιητικὸς Ζέφυρος ἡμῖν ἐμπνέει,
Ὅμηρος ὃν προεῖπεν εὐκραῆ πάλαι·
ἐλεύθερον μὲν τὸ πτερὸν τῶν ὀρνέων,
80 ἐλεύθερον βοῶσι, κοῦφος ὁ δρόμος,
ἠχοῦσιν οἱ τέττιγες ἀμφὶ τοῖς κλάδοις,
κίχλαι δὲ λαλαγοῦσιν ἀμφὶ ταῖς πόαις,
κράζουσι φάτται καὶ στένουσι τρυγόνες,
παίζουσιν ἀκανθίδες ἀμφὶ τοῖς ῥόδοις,
85 τοῖς ψιττακοῖς τὸ φθέγμα κλαγγῶδες πάλιν,
λαλίστερον μὲν ταῖς κορώναις τὸ στόμα
καὶ καλιὰν κολλῶσιν αἱ χελιδόνες·
ἔφθασεν ἡμᾶς ἡ καλὴ κωμῳδία
'ξουθὰς' ἀνυμνήσασα τὰς ἀηδόνας
90 'ἱππαλεκτρυόνας' τε τοὺς ἐν Περσίδι,
τὰς μὲν λαλοῦντα ζῶα καὶ ζῶσαν φύσιν,
τοὺς δ' ἐν πέπλοις μάλιστα κατεστιγμένους.
Τίς ζωγραφεῖ κοιλάδας ἢ πεδιάδας
ἐρυθρὸν ἄνθος μιγνύων τῇ πορφύρᾳ,
95 ξανθῷ κεραννὺς τὴν φύσιν τοῦ μηλίνου,
λευκοῖς ἁλουργές, κοκκίνοις πάλιν μέλαν;
Τίς ἐμβιβάζει μύρα τοῖς δρυμοῦ ξύλοις,
Τίς βαλσάμῳ τὸ πῖον εὐῶδες νέμει;
Χεὶρ ἡ Θεοῦ πλὴν εἰς ἔαρος ἡμέραν.
100 Ἀλλ' ὦ παρετράπημεν εἰς μακροὺς λόγους,
τὸν εὐθαλῆ σε κῆπον ἐκλελοιπότες,
ἀφ' οὗ τρυγῶμεν κρίνα, καὶ μᾶλλον ῥόδα,
νοῦν εὐγενῆ καὶ λέξιν εὐφραδεστέραν,
ἀφ' οὗ τὸ χρηστὸν ἦθος ὡς χρυσοῦν στάχυν
105 καλῶς ἀμῶμαι καὶ τρυφῶ βότρυν λόγου·
ὁ λωτὸς ἐν σοὶ καὶ φαγόντες οἱ νέοι
μένουσιν ἐν σοὶ πᾶν φίλον λελοιπότες·
ἐκ τῶν λόγων γεννᾷς με καὶ λόγοις τρέφεις
καὶ σπαργανοῖς λόγοις με καὶ λούεις λόγοις.
110 Ἀλλ' ὦ λόγου δοχεῖον ἐμψυχωμένον,
σφράγισμα λαμπρὸν ἠκριβωμένου βίου,
ἄναξον ἡμᾶς εἰς τέλος τῶν ἐλπίδων,
τόνωσον ἡμᾶς εἰς ἀνενδότους πόνους,
ῥίζωσον ἡμᾶς ἐν τόποις χλοηφόροις,
115 στόμωσον ἡμῖν τοῦ λογισμοῦ τὸ ξίφος,
ὡς ἂν φανῶμεν ἐν λόγοις νικηφόροι,
ἐκ σῶν πόνων φανέντες ἀσπιδηφόροι.

The Bacchae long ago took possession of Parnassus' heights as their home or new city; Dionysus, wearing a tunic of fawn skin and wielding the thyrsus as a sceptre in his hand, was then their ally. His pines, sycamores and cypress species occupied the racetracks, and while he often sprang about in a Bacchic dance, spring held sway on the Parnassus known from myths. And the swan of the Pythian engaged in more divine odes, after he had come to Delphi again: indeed, intoxicated by the scents of flowers that the Delphic stone cheerfully sent forth when the god came back to the Pythia, it suddenly became a better singer than it was. And palms and trees near the Lebanon (Lebanon the mountain of Palestine) flowered thanks to Sidonian Astarte, even if it was not the time for flowers. You see, sower of the flowers of discourse, how the grace of spring is cherished even by gods? But why do I write about meadows known from the deceit of myths, looking, through them, at a false spring?

[24] More sacred words brought to us the Emmanuel, the divine-human *Logos*, who long ago fed the starving Jews, feeding them once and then a second time, and abundantly so. The food was a banquet for the Jews, plentiful, grass-green, sweet-smelling from the flowers, and it enchanted the sense of touch through lying at the table, and the sight, in turn, with its colours; it conquered the sense of smell with the scents, and the food had all sorts of grace. And it was nothing new for God's guests to eat a splendid meal in the green pastures, while spring made the meadows bright for them. I, too, then, delighting you with my words, found spring as a helper for the grace of my words; its divinely inspired character, as if being a receptacle of divine virtue, will furnish for you the strength of my words in general and all dignity and the fullness of thought, and they will give the words a vigorous force, showing them entirely solemn through the subject matter. The spring dew will instil it in us to smile and relax, or even to laugh and play with sweetness, being more profuse than 'sweet honey' and, thanks to the aromatic herbs, more fragrant than the sweet myrrh that wets 'Aaron's head' and pours down the priestly beard. The beautiful dew of spring's grace is even near to Mt Hermon's dew.

[54] Earlier one saw starless skies, and the ray of the moon fought against shadows, and the thick clouds kept the sun locked up like a young maiden. We used to live pitifully under the shadows, begrudging the Hamadryad nymphs. Now countless light-bearing sources blaze forth a plentiful flame from the sky. Look at Hesperus and Arcturus, look at Orion, gaze at the Dog Star and behold Boötes together with Sirius: they bring all-bright torches of light. See, then, the Bear and the Pleiades, and the Hyades, light-bringing stars. Let me say what is better: a springtime night makes more brightness sparkle than a winter day. What disorder rules now the Earth? Does it no longer bear great burdens of snow? No longer a multitude of rainstorms? No longer an abundance of hail? The cold has gone far away, as has the strength of the winds. Where is now, with us, the track of the brightening Notos? Where is the Thracian Boreas? Where is the force of

the Libyan wind? I did not find the Euros, the north-east wind is at rest: for us blows the poetic Zephyr, which Homer once described as gentle in ancient times. Free is the wing of the birds, freely they sing, their course is easy, cicadas resound among the branches, the thrushes chirp in the grass; ringdoves cry, turtle-doves moan, goldfinches play between the roses, the shrill voice of parrots is there again, the mouth of crows is more talkative, and swallows build their nest: a beautiful comedy has come before us, which celebrates in song the 'chirruping' nightingales and the 'hippogriffs' in Persia, the former talking animals and living nature, the latter mostly marked on coats.

[93] Who paints valleys or plains, mixing the red flower with the purple, blending the nature of quince-yellow with the tawny, the purple with the white, the black again with the scarlet? Who places perfume in the woods of the forest? Who gives the sweet-smelling resin to the balsam-tree? The hand of God, but for a day of spring.

[100] But oh! We have turned aside towards long discourses, leaving you, the blooming garden from which we gather lilies, and especially roses, noble mind, and more elegant speech from which I collect rightly the good character like a golden ear of corn, and I feast on a bunch of words. The lotus is in you, and the young, eating it, remain in you, having left behind everything they love. Through words you beget me and with words you feed me, in words you swathe me, and with words you wash me. But O life-breathing receptacle of speech, bright seal of a perfect life, lead us to the completion of our hopes, strengthen us for unceasing toils, root us in grass-bearing meadows, harden the sword of our reason, so that we can appear victors in words, appearing as shield-bearers through your toils.

Poem 29 and the Tradition of Spring *ekphraseis*

Three sections can be identified in the poem (vv. 1–53, 54–99 and 100–17). The first (vv. 1–53) is a sketch of human history, following its development from the pagan to the Hebrew and Christian era. The poem starts on the heights of Parnassus and sketches the peaceful image of a flourishing pagan spring where Dionysus dances with the Maenads (1–9) and the Delphic swan sings beautifully, inebriated by the scent of flowers (10–15). The pagan era is portrayed as calm and bright, dominated by dance, music, flowers: even the *furor* of the Maenads is peacefully described as a spring-bringing dance. The mention of the goddess Astarte, who makes flowers grow, leads the poem eastwards, to the Hebrew milieu and to the wanderings of the Jews in the desert (24–36). The flowering meadows of the pagan spring correspond to the Manna sent to feed the Jews, a relief offered by a thoughtful and caring God to the people he loves. God's revelation embodies the greatest turning point in this sketch of human history, represented with a sense of continuity and harmony: spring is first described with mythical references, then is celebrated with biblical references and overtones.

The second sequence (54–99) is dedicated to the description of the world renewed by the hand of God, a cosmos which is depicted as a veritable *paradeisos*. Beauty dominates the scene with a triumph of peace and nature, and God is presented as an artist painting the world as a gigantic portrait, mixing colours to create the hues and the shades of nature, instilling scent and sweet oil into the trees (93–9). It is not hard to recognize in this passage (and, to varying degrees, in the whole poem) the marks of a specific tradition. Sure enough, *Poem* 29 inscribes itself in the tradition of spring *ekphraseis*, of which it shows several typical elements.[9]

Spring was considered one of the best themes for the progymnasmatic genre of *ekphrasis* in the handbooks of ancient rhetoric, its use being suggested by Aelius Theon,[10] Aphthonius of Antioch[11] and Ps.-Hermogenes.[12] Libanius' *ekphrasis* of spring is the progenitor of the tradition of spring *ekphraseis*,[13] where all the elements later to become *topoi* of the genre are present: light, warmth, sweet-smelling flowers,[14] chirping birds, men going joyfully back to their work after the winter pause, a deep sense of rebirth and freedom. After Libanius, spring remained one of the most widespread topics for poetry throughout the Byzantine era.[15] The spring *ekphrasis* genre is also represented in a discourse by Gregory of Nazianzos, *On New Sunday* (*Oration* 44),[16] where, due to the sense of rebirth and renaissance that spring embodies, the season is invested with a Christian meaning and becomes symbolic of Christ's resurrection. The tight bond between spring and Easter is later the subject of a poem by

9 Spring is central to such an extent that Leon Sternbach (1903: 342), *editor princeps* of the corpus, noted that it would have been better for the poem to be called Εἰς τὸ ἔαρ instead of Εἰς τὰ ῥόδα.

10 Theon, *Prog.* 67.21 ed. Patillon and Bolognesi (1997): χρόνων δὲ οἷον ἔαρος, θέρους, ἑορτῆς, καὶ τῶν τοιούτων, '(*ekphrasis*) about seasons such as spring, summer, festivities and the like'.

11 Aphthonius, *Prog.* 12.1 ed. Patillon (2008): Ἐκφραστέον … καιροὺς δὲ ὡς ἔαρ καὶ θέρος, φράζων ὁπόσα παρ'αὐτὰ προέρχεται τῶν ἀνθέων, 'One can describe … seasons such as spring and summer, telling how many flowers they bring'.

12 Ps.-Hermogenes, *Prog.* 10.2 ed. Patillon (2008), which repeats Theon's definition.

13 Libanius, *Prog.* 12.7 ed. Foerster (1963).

14 Here, the rose in particular has a significant role: in the final part of the poem the rose is presented as an essential part and a true symbol of spring. See Libanius, *Prog.* 12.7.9 ed. Foerster (1963).

15 For the spring *ekphrasis* in Byzantium, see Loukaki (2013).

16 Gregory, Libanius' contemporary, shows himself to be familiar with *Prog.* 12.7 and composes an *ekphrasis* in which all the precepts of ekphrastic composition are faithfully respected. In Gregory of Nazianzos, *Or.* 44.10 (CCSG 36, p. 617.30) a strong association is created between spring and Easter. See also the last part of the discourse, where the condition of universal rebirth that follows Christ's resurrection is presented as an all-encompassing spring: Gregory of Nazianzos, *Or.* 44.12 (CCSG 36, p. 621.1).

Arsenios, who worked as a teacher in Constantinople in the first half of the ninth century.[17] In the tenth century, the poem *On Spring* composed by John Geometres (*Poem* 300) constitutes the best surviving example of spring *ekphraseis*.[18]

Kallikles' *Poem* 29 constitutes a good twelfth-century example of this tradition, wholly fitting its *topoi*, and appears to have much in common with Geometres' *Poem* 300.[19] In the description of spring – developed in a very similar way in both poems – several typical elements of the genre's tradition are found: the contrast between winter and spring (Kallikles 68–9; Geometres 2), the mention of celestial bodies such as planets, stars and the moon (Kallikles 60–7; Geometres 13–23), the winds, the Zephyr in particular (Kallikles 73–8; Geometres 26, 56), the juxtaposition of the lily and the rose (Kallikles 102–3; Geometres 30–5) and the singing of birds and cicadas (Kallikles 79–92; Geometres 47–62, 72–3).[20] Kallikles follows the rules of the genre and uses all these elements of an ekphrastic description of spring, perfectly inserting himself into that tradition with the poem's bright and imaginative atmosphere and its exaltation of beauty, rebirth and joy. According to the precepts of the tradition, his *ekphrasis* proceeds from the general (the cosmological section) to the particular (the enumeration of flowers and birds). The ekphrastic section proper starts at verse 54, with the passage describing the change from the darkness to the brightness of the light. Nevertheless, the sense of joy and rebirth fills the whole poem, which is littered with references to the delights of spring. The first section of the poem makes explicit reference to spring more than once (9: ἔαρ, 21: ἔαρος ἡ χάρις φίλη, 23: ἔαρ πεπλασμένον, 36: ἔαρος αὐτοῖς φαιδρύνοντος τὸν τόπον, 38: ἔαρ συνεργὸν, 47: ἔαρος ... δρόσοι, 52: ἐαρινῆς χάριτος αἱ καλαὶ δρόσοι), and the element of sensation, which is of paramount importance, conveys a feeling of peacefulness

17 On Arsenios' poem on Holy Sunday, see Kaltsogianni (2010) and Crimi (2015).

18 John Geometres *Poem* 300 ed. van Opstall (2008). For the text, translation (French) and commentary, see van Opstall (2008: 514–50). In Geometres' poem, the hymnological section, which conveys a Christian message, is placed towards the end of the poem, after a long *ekphrasis* dedicated to the exaltation of spring (vv. 9–86) and to lamentation about the poet's unfortunate condition (vv. 87–113). For the similarities between Geometres' poem and another famous ekphrastic text, Meleager's *ekphrasis* of spring (*AP* IX 363), see van Opstall (2008: 546–8).

19 Of course, Kallikles' *Poem* 29 shows intriguing parallels with all the texts here mentioned. A further analogy with *Or.* 44 can be mentioned: in Gregory's oration the celebration of spring also comes after a portrayal of human history that, starting with the creation, culminates in Christ's resurrection.

20 Only a few elements appearing in Geometres' poem cannot be found in that of Kallikles: the human presence (pastors and sailors, vv. 64–71) and the bee (78–86). These two elements, which are typical of the ekphrastic tradition, are present in both Libanius (*Prog.* 17.7.7) and Gregory of Nazianzos (*Or.* 44.11).

and delight. The sense of sight is prominent,[21] but all the five senses take part in this ekphrastic construction and, furthermore, all the sensations acquired through the senses are positive. All the negative elements appearing in the poem are relegated to a faraway past, presented as definitively eradicated by the true Christian revelation and by the spring that God gifted to humans.[22]

Being ἐν λόγοις νικηφόροι: A Rhetorical Contest as a Possible Performative Occasion

What the poem Εἰς τὰ ῥόδα lacks is information about its social context, performance and dedicatee. In this respect, the third section (vv. 100–17) appears to be the most interesting, since it holds some clues. This concluding sequence addresses someone who is described by the speaker as the source of his inspiration and rhetorical strength. Romano has suggested identifying the recipient of the poem with God and thus interpreting its final section as a prayer invoking divine protection.[23] While this interpretation remains possible, a closer inspection of the poem's meaning, when combined with new perspectives offered by recent scholarship on the cultural milieu of the capital, suggests a different interpretation. The move at vv. 100–1, a sort of 'break-off formula' (*Abbruchsformel*) that announces a sudden change in topic and is used to move towards a conclusion, could constitute the first clue towards the identification of a concrete recipient. There is no doubt that the previous section (93–9) refers to God, since the poet clearly declares it.[24] However, after the praise of God's creation, the poet says he is diverting his path towards long discourses, neglecting the dedicatee (100–1). This *Abbruchsformel* may point to the passage from the divine to the human sphere: a turning point towards another subject seems not a mere rhetorical move but is concretely visible in the text. Two

21 An emphasis on seeing is typical of ekphrastic texts, since it recalls their visual dimension and their proximity to the image.

22 It is noteworthy that γέλος, 'laughter', is here depicted as a gift from God. Laughter is quite a typical element of the ekphrastic description of spring, though referring to the rejoicing of earth and nature and not to men (who are usually represented as resuming their work after the winter pause). Concerning the dismantlement of the theory according to which γέλος had a negative connotation in Byzantine world, see Pizzone (2017); on laughter in the twelfth century, see also the volume edited by Marciniak and Nilsson (2021).

23 Romano (1980: 24) has pointed to the sequence's heartfelt tone and biblical quotations and thus interpreted *Poem* 29 as a religious text, defining it as 'something more than a sacred epigram'.

24 See in particular v. 99: Χεὶρ ἡ Θεοῦ.

possibilities should be considered: either the move marks the passage to the praise of a human dedicatee (maybe a mentor or a patron), or the author addresses God again, asking for help before the *logikoi* contests. In any case, the distich marks the end of the long ekphrastic section and the beginning of the final part of the poem, which brings the text back to its performative occasion.

Throughout the verses of the final section, the crucial importance ascribed to rhetoric, learning and words immediately stands out. The themes of teaching and discourse are strongly emphasized in the whole poem, which is peppered with references to the importance of words and rhetoric.[25] In addition to the lexical stress on *logoi*, the cultural perspective of the poem is suggested by the sketching of global history itself. The choice to outline a path which passes through three stages – pagan era, Hebrew era, Christian era – makes more sense in a cultural perspective than in a historical or political one, since the pagan and the Hebrew traditions are the two complementary foundations on which Byzantine Christian culture is built, representing the classical heritage and the biblical substratum, respectively.

The importance attributed to education and learning is particularly evident in the two apostrophic sections of the poem (37–44 and 100–17), which might both help in the identification of the recipient and, particularly, the social and performative context of the poem. Of the two, the closing sequence is the more explicit, being a proper invocation for rhetorical strength and support. In this section, the speaker presents the achievement of rhetorical ability as the accomplishment of his hopes: a battle in the field of education and rhetoric appears to loom over him, making it necessary for him to take up sword and shield. The key role of culture, combined with the military imagery, suggests a context where cultural and rhetorical ability are put to the test. Recent scholarship has shown that such contexts of cultural competition, far from being rare in the learned and scholastic world of the twelfth century, were almost its bread and butter.

The competition which animated the cultural milieu of the capital is well known. Since schools were generally centred on a leading figure and were dependent on the number of their pupils, there was a strong competition between teachers to prove their teaching ability and obtain career benefits. This rivalry manifested itself not only in a harsh competitive envi-

25 The term λόγος with the meaning of 'word' occurs twenty times in the entire corpus by Kallikles: thirteen of these occurrences (65 per cent of the total number) can be found in *Poem* 29.

ronment between colleagues,[26] but also in formalized competitions.[27] These contests, referred to as λογικοὶ ἀγῶνες, οἱ τῶν λόγων ἀγῶνες or ἀγῶνες τοῦ λόγου ('rhetoric contests'), were aimed at proving rhetorical and literary ability (and, more generally, the range of skills that were acquired through education) and they probably took place in an inter-school context. The conduct of these contests is not fully understood but, based on the testimonies, we can assume that they were staged in a *theatron* and centred on the comparison between rival candidates (teachers or students) in front of an audience, and that performances were evaluated by a judge (*agonothetes*).[28] The language chosen to describe these contests can be traced back to the vocabulary of sporting competitions, to which words such as ἀγών ('competition'), θέατρον ('theatre', 'audience'), ἀγωνοθέτης ('judge in the contest'), ἀντεξετάζω ('to dispute with someone') clearly refer.[29]

A popular kind of contest was the ἀγών centred on schedography.[30] In the variegated world of schedography, a particular form of *schede* developed

26 Cases of fierce competition resulting in harsh mockery at the expense of colleagues and rivals are abundant in Byzantine literature. An example is the famous scoptic poem by Psellos against the Sabbaites (Psellos, *Poem* 21 ed. Westerink [1992]); see e.g. Bernard (2014: 254–9, 266–76). References to school rivalry, mutual mud-slinging and controversies between colleagues are also frequent in Tzetzes' work (see, for instance, the epistles connected with teaching controversies such as *ep.* 12, 17, 62–4 ed. Leone [1972], with their respective passages in the *Histories*, in particular *Histories* 298–9 ed. Leone [2007]). See also Agapitos (2017).

27 Michael Psellos mentions (or alludes to) rhetorical contests taking place in front of an audience several times in his work, for instance in his funeral oration for Xiphilinos (Psellos, *Or.* 3.9–11 ed. Polemis [2013]), where he dedicates a long section to his friendship with the patriarch and to their education during their youth. An English translation of the funeral oration for Xiphilinos can be found in Kaldellis and Polemis (2015: 180–228). On school contests, see also Bernard in this volume.

28 On these contests, see Lemerle (1977: 235–41) and Bernard (2014: 254–66).

29 See Bernard (2014: 254–9). On the concept of *theatron* and its socio-cultural contexts, see Mullett (1984), Magdalino (1993: 339), Marciniak (2007). On the theatrical character of twelfth-century literature, see Magdalino in this volume.

30 On schedography, see the lemma 'Schedographie' by I. Vassis in *Der Neue Pauly* 11 (2002: 152–3). For the typologies of exercises involved, see Schirò (1949), Browning (1976), Polemis (1995: 277–302), Vassis (1993–4: 9–12) and (2002: 37–44), Markopoulos (2006: 93–5), Agapitos (2013: 89–91) and (2017: 2–3, 7–8), Giannouli (2014: 62–5), Nousia (2016: 49–92); see also Introduction, pp. 12–14 and Bernard in this volume. For examples of *schede*, see Agapitos (2014), (2015a), (2015b) and (2015c) and Nousia (2016, Appendices II–III). After being regarded by earlier critics as a low-education phenomenon despised by the learned elite – see Agapitos (2013: 101–6) on Krumbacher's prejudice about it – schedography has recently attracted more objective attention and has been recognized as a crucial element of Byzantine education from the eleventh century onwards. A twelfth-century testimony on schedography which has often been glossed over is the statement of Nikephoros Basilakes about his role in the innovation of *schede* and the originality of his schedographic method (see Basilakes, *Prologue* 78–9 ed. Garzya [1984]). Basilakes' role in twelfth-century schedography has been the subject of an MA thesis: see Rothstein-Dowden (2015). Most of the information we have about *schede* competitions comes from poetic texts. Christopher of Mytilene's *Poems* 9, 10 and 11, focusing on education (and on schedography in particular), provide significant information about the rivalry existing between schools and the functioning of school practice, as well as of the relationship between teachers and students. See Bernard (2014: 261).

and diffused from the eleventh century onwards, which 'consisted of texts made up of unintelligible word groups from which the pupils had to extract the correct reading by applying alternative spelling and word breaks'.[31] *Schede* were not only challenging exercises to improve grammatical skills; they were the object of competitions in which the ability to decode grammatical difficulties was put to the test. On the battleground of *schede*, pupils were summoned to challenge rival students in order to prove not only their skills but also the quality of the teaching they had received and of the school to which they belonged.

A connection of *Εἰς τὰ ῥόδα* with the world of teaching and with school competitions has never been proposed; nevertheless, such a connection would explain and shed light on the passages for which the religious interpretation seems to be unsatisfactory. An analysis of some of the most significant passages of the poem, together with a comparison with texts dealing clearly with the milieu of school competitions, reveals substantial similarities.

The apostrophic sequence of vv. 37–44 defines the recipient of the apostrophe as a source of inspiration in a deeply educational sense. The inspiring power of the addressee is directed towards rhetorical prowess: its aim is to provide the speaker's words with strength (στιβαρὸν τὸ τοῦ λόγου, τοῖς λόγοις δώσουσιν εὐσθενῆ τόνον) and to prove them to be entirely solemn through their subject matter (πανεμβριθεῖς[32] δεικνύντες ἐκ τῶν πραγμάτων). The πράγματα which must prove the effectiveness of the speaker's words could consist of the competition itself, which is supposed to put to the test and to prove the student's ability during a performance.

The concluding sequence undoubtedly praises and invokes someone to whom the speaker is related in an educational context, through an intellectual bond alluded to with the imagery of nourishment (v. 106). The distich of vv. 108–9, ἐκ τῶν λόγων γεννᾷς με καὶ λόγοις τρέφεις | καὶ σπαργανοῖς λόγοις με καὶ λούεις λόγοις,[33] constitutes the most explicit praise of the value of culture and learning to occur in the poem. All the verbs employed referring to rhetorical ability (seen as something absolute and all-encompassing) relate to the care for infants: γεννάω ('to generate', 'to give birth'), τρέφω ('to nourish'), σπαργανόω ('to swathe'), λούω ('to wash'). Although the distich could easily refer to God, as in Romano's

31 Bernard (2014: 260) notes that this specific kind of *schede* must be the result of an innovation in the twelfth century, since all the relevant texts are from that era.

32 Note that πανεμβριθεῖς is a rare form.

33 Romano (1980: 24) defines these verses as the most representative of the personal dimension of Kallikles' poetry.

interpretation, this stress on the concept of *logoi* leads one to identify the recipient instead with a person who played a paramount role in education and in the world of learning and to connect the poem to a specific occasion. The distich would befit a patron who encourages and sustains the speaker's activity or a teacher who supports his education. The image of the teacher nourishing his students with knowledge is widespread and occurs, for instance, in *Poem* 10 by Christopher of Mytilene,[34] where the *maïstor* is said to pour wisdom around his pupils' ears and where students are described as nourished by the teacher's work, according to a popular and pervasive image. The final invocation (vv. 115–17: στόμωσον ἡμῖν τοῦ λογισμοῦ τὸ ξίφος, | ὡς ἂν φανῶμεν ἐν λόγοις νικηφόροι, | ἐκ σῶν πόνων φανέντες ἀσπιδηφόροι) is a prayer to obtain strength in eloquence and rhetoric and to be supported in the rhetorical milieu: the aim is to win a battle and to triumph in eloquence.[35] The invocation of *Poem* 29 refers to training in the use of the sword of reason (τοῦ λογισμοῦ τὸ ξίφος) in order to be victorious in words (ἐν λόγοις νικηφόροι) and includes the epithet 'shield-bearers' (ἀσπιδηφόροι). Thanks to the teacher's ability, pupils will be well-equipped and well-defended during the contest against another group. The military imagery (which is very widespread in both rhetoric and hagiography) is a typical feature of the description of school contests and finds a match in the lexicon adopted by Christopher of Mytilene in his poems about schools and contests.[36] Christopher describes pupils as the weapons of a teacher against his rival (9.8: ἔξεισι θαρρῶν τοῖς μαθηταῖς ὡς ὅπλοις) and speaks of a victory or a defeat in the *schedos* contests (9.4: ἧτταν δὲ δεινὴν οὔποτε σχέδους ἴδῃ; 10.15: τῶν πάντων κρατέουσι νέων σχεδέων ἐν ἀγῶσιν).

After examination of the similarities between these texts, a certain alignment between Kallikles' *Poem* 29 and texts related to the milieu of the school, competitions and *schede* seems to emerge. As a matter of

34 Christopher of Mytilene, *Poem* 10.7, 12–15 ed. Bernard and Livanos (2018): ἡδυεπῆ δὲ | Λέοντα πρόμον ποίησε ἀγητόν | … | ὃς ῥὰ ἑὸν στόμα βάψας Μουσῶν εἰς νόον ἄκρον | ῥοῦν ἐμέει σοφίης κούρων αἰεὶ περὶ ὦτα, | οἵ, λιπαινόμενοί τε καὶ εὐλογίην ξυνάγοντες, | τῶν πάντων κρατέουσι νέων σχεδέων ἐν ἀγῶσιν, 'And she made the sweet-tongued Leo its admirable leader … Having dipped his mouth in the Muses' deepest mind, he now spews forth a stream of wisdom around the ears of the young, who, nourishing themselves on it and gathering eloquence, are victorious over all other youths in the contests of *schede*' (trans. after Bernard and Livanos). See also Agapitos (2013: 99–100).

35 The theme of divine support for words can be found also in John Mauropous, *Poems* 89–90.

36 For the vocabulary of sporting events used to describe cultural contests and for the occurrence of military imagery, see Bernard (2014: 253–66). In Christopher of Mytilene, *Poem* 9.6, the verb στομόω (meaning 'to train', 'to strengthen') is used in a similar way, in the expression 'στομώσας τοὺς νέους' ('training the young'), which occurs in the context of a *schede* battle: see Bernard (2014: 261).

fact, the invocatory voice of *Εἰς τὰ ῥόδα* asks its recipient to accomplish exactly what the *maïstor* is said to do with his students: to provide rhetorical ability and victory in a cultural contest. Of course, *Εἰς τὰ ῥόδα* can in no way constitute a *schedos*, and neither can Christopher's poems. Bernard rightly wonders: 'how should we understand the exact purpose or signification of these poems within the context of *schedos* contests?'[37] If Christopher's poems may have been pronounced by the teacher before the contests in order to encourage his own students and influence the jury,[38] the speaking voice of *Poem* 29 suggests other possibilities.

The poem is likely to be intended as the opening of a contest taking place in the learned circles of the capital. The addressee could thus be either God, invoked to obtain rhetorical strength, a member of the court promoting cultural activities and contests, or a teacher. The rose could suggest a female addressee, perhaps a patroness,[39] but it is more likely that the central position of the spring theme and the insistence on the floral imagery are connected with the performative occasion, referring to the time of the year when the contest was held. *Εἰς τὰ ῥόδα* could have had an introductory function in the context of a school competition which was held in spring (presumably around Easter), being performed as a foreword to the contest. Following this path, it appears not too risky to assume that the final invocation of *Poem* 29 could be conceived as the invocation of a group of students to their teacher to praise his teaching ability (the 'infant care sequence' seems to express devotion and gratefulness) and to invoke his protection in order to defeat the other group and win the contest thanks to his teaching.[40] Several clues seem to support this interpretation. Beyond the strong connection which seems to exist between poetry and the world of contests and schedography (especially in the eleventh century) and the similarities of *Poem* 29 with *Poems* 9, 10 and 11 by Christopher of Mytilene, a link can be established between *Εἰς τὰ ῥόδα* and a particular *schedos*.

37 Bernard (2014: 266).
38 Bernard (2014: 266).
39 The image of the rose is also used to address a woman in Kallikles' *Poem* 22. The use of the word δοχεῖον (v. 112) could also be seen as a reference to the female womb.
40 The verbs and pronouns in the first-person plural in the final section of the poem, although they may indicate a singular meaning, most likely mirror the collective point of view of the group of students taking part in the contest. Therefore, the first-person plural has been maintained in the translation.

Nicholas Kallikles and the School Milieu: A *schedos* in Pal. gr. 92

Nicholas Kallikles is of course best known, beside his poetry, as a court physician. His only connection to the school milieu is the appellative of διδάσκαλος τῶν ἰατρῶν with which he is referred to by part of the manuscript tradition and which connects him to the teaching of medicine.[41] Nevertheless, he could have been involved in the educational environment to a greater extent than scholars have thought. Ms. Vatican City, Biblioteca Apostolica Vaticana, Pal. gr. 92 [Diktyon 65825], a Salentine collection of the late thirteenth century, preserves many school texts, and in particular *schede*, mostly unedited.[42] This manuscript contains, among others, four texts which are ascribed to a Kallikles ('τοῦ Καλλικλέος'):

- fols. 175r–176v: an *ethopoiia* entitled 'What would Phoenix, Achilles' instructor, say?' (116 ed. Vassis);
- fols. 210rv: an *ethopoiia* entitled 'What would Ajax say, while dying, to his own son?' (164 ed. Vassis);
- fols. 221v–222r: a eulogy followed by some grammatical notes (184 ed. Vassis);
- fols. 223v–224r: a *schedos* (188 ed. Vassis) which is also preserved in Florence, Biblioteca Medicea Laurenziana, conv. soppr. 2 [Diktyon 15778] at fol. 208r. With respect to a comparison with *Poem* 29, this last text is undoubtedly the most interesting. Vassis (2002: 61) describes it as Ἔκφρασις ἔαρος: its theme is indeed the rebirth of nature in spring, and we find in it the same themes and contents as those of *Poem* 29.

The attribution of these texts to Nicholas Kallikles would shed new light on his figure, connecting him more closely to the scholarly milieu and with non-medical teaching. Vassis rightly warns his readers against assigning the authorship on the basis of a schedographic collection, since it is not uncommon for the same *schedos* to circulate in different manuscripts with different attributions.[43] Nevertheless, the analogies between this short *schedos* and *Poem* 29, both circulating under Kallikles' name, are striking. The *schedos* is centred on spring and its good effects. In both manuscripts its *kephalaion*, namely the subject of the text,[44] is clearly stated as 'now everything is full of joy, while the spring-time light shines on us' (ἁπλῶς τὰ πάντα νῦν θυμηδίας γέμει ἐαρινοῦ φανέντος ἡμῖν φοσφόρου).

41 Romano (1980: 13–14).
42 The texts preserved in the manuscript are listed in Vassis (2002: 45–63).
43 Vassis (2002: 38–9, n. 11).
44 See the lemma 'Κεφάλαιον' in Berardi (2017: 182–6).

The ekphrastic *schedos* follows all the precepts stated in the rhetorical handbooks for ekphrastic composition and shows all the typical elements of the *ekphraseis* of spring, starting from the cosmological elements: the sky which becomes brilliant and clear (ὁ οὐρανὸς … διαυγέστερον δεικνύων τὸν ἑαυτοῦ πρόσωπον), the stars (κοσμῶν … καταστήματι), the golden rays of the sun (πας ἀκτὶς εἰς τὸ χρυσοειδέστερον μεταβάλλεται), the light (τοῦ φωσφόρου … λαμπρύνεται), the moon (ἀκριβῶς τὸν κύκλον φαιωότερον). After the cosmological section, the *schedos* mentions the blossoming of flowers (ἄνθη) and roses (ῥόδοις). Hereafter, the text directly addresses the student, promising him that snow and ice will not trouble him anymore by weighing down the earth and oppressing it (οὐκέτι σοι χιὼν ὦ νέε … οὐδὲ ὁ κρύσταλλος ἐνοχλήσει πείζων καὶ συσφρίγγων δεινῶς). After these elements, which are also found in *Poem* 29, the *schedos* deals with a *topos* of spring *ekphraseis* that does not appear in *Εἰς τὰ ῥόδα*: the return to work of sailors and farmers in the warm season. Sailors prepare their ships, no longer afraid of the winds (*νῦν* ὁ πλωτὴρ τὴν *ναῦν* εὐτρεπίζει … μὴ ὑποπτεύων ἀνέμων τὸ σφοδρὸν), and farmers (τὸν γεωργὸν) resume their work. The text ends with a praise of the positive effects of spring, where it is said to bring all sorts of good things (οὗτος παντοῖον ἀπ᾽ ἦρος ἔχω χρεστὸν).

This structure shows several similarities with the ekphrastic section of *Poem* 29, in particular in its first section. Both texts begin with the cosmological elements of the sky becoming brighter and the stars being visible. The image of the snow that weighs down the earth is common to both *Poem* 29 (v. 71: μὴ χιόνων τὸ πλῆθος ὡς ἄχθος φέρει;) and the *schedos* (πείζων καὶ συσφρίγγων δεινῶς). The image of the violence of the winds that has ceased also appears in both *Poem* 29 (v. 74–9, where the speaker asks where the strength and harshness of winds are) and the *schedos* (μὴ ὑποπτεύων ἀνέμων τὸ σφοδρὸν). The second sections of both texts, instead, show some differences. The *ekphrasis* in *Poem* 29 is centred on nature, focusing on the rebirth of flowers and plants and on the return of the animals. Several spring birds and insects are listed (cicadas, thrushes, ringdoves, parrots) and there is some insistence on their singing and their voices. In the *schedos*, flowers are only hinted at and there is no mention of animals but, on the other hand, there is some emphasis on the human figures returning to their occupations (a theme which is absent in *Poem* 29 but found in other spring *ekphraseis*).

Conclusion

The aim of this chapter was to shed new light on a rich and fascinating text, namely Kallikles' *Poem* 29, by investigating the socio-cultural context in which it was composed, its performative setting and its recipient. This text appears to resist the earlier assumption that it was a religious epigram. Since the invocation of rhetorical strength is well suited to a programmatic beginning of a poetic anthology, and since floral imagery is frequently used for poetic compilations, it could be seen as the introductory piece to an anthology composed by the author himself; it was certainly not unparalleled in the twelfth century for an author to prepare an edition of their own work for publication.[45] However, even if it is possible that the poem was used as a prologue to an anthology (for instance in a now-lost manuscript), there seems to be some justification for assuming that behind the composition of this text lies a specific performative occasion. First, the occasional nature of the text would be coherent with the oeuvre of Kallikles, whose poems were often intended to praise or commemorate members of the court or to serve as dedicatory epigrams for artworks. To assume that the occasion for which the poem was composed was a school contest does not appear too far-fetched. Since *logoi* are the core of the poem, it is reasonable to assume that the text was composed to be performed in a rhetorical contest and thus to be addressed to a patron or a teacher by virtue of his role in culture and education. Textual analysis has shown that the most ambiguous and fascinating sections of the poem have some features in common with texts related to school contests, and in particular with the *schede* competitions. Both the focus on learning and rhetorical strength and the use of military imagery seem to point in this direction. Contests among scholars were a solidly attested reality in twelfth-century Constantinople, involving to various extents the members of the school apparatus and of the court. It is not unlikely that Nicholas Kallikles, as an esteemed figure at the court, wrote a text intended to introduce a school contest, nor that he worked as a teacher of grammar and rhetoric for some time, composing *progymnasmata* and *schede*, as the manuscript Pal. gr. 92 suggests. Ultimately, the fact that among the very few texts which connect Nicholas Kallikles to the school milieu, two are centred on a spring *ekphrasis* and seem to feature some striking similarities, seems significant. The similarities that *Poem* 29 demonstrates with the spring *schedos* constitute an important clue in sup-

45 See for instance the prologue meant to introduce Nikephoros Basilakes' work, edited by Garzya (1984). On this text, see also Garzya (1969).

port of its connection to the performative context of school/intellectual ἀγῶνες, allowing us to discover some unprecedented traits of Kallikles' activity at the court and in the cultural milieu of the twelfth century.

Bibliography

Agapitos, P. A. (2013) 'Anna Komnene and the Politics of Schedographic Training and Colloquial Discourse', *Nea Rhome* 10: 89–107.

(2014) 'Grammar, Genre and Patronage in the Twelfth Century: A Scientific Paradigm and its Implications', *JÖByz* 64: 1–22.

(2015a) 'Learning to Read and Write a *Schedos*: The Verse Dictionary of Par. gr. 400', in *Pour une poètique de Byzance: Hommage à Vassilis Katsaros*, ed. Efthymiadis, C. Messis, P. Odorico and I. Polemis, 11–24. Dossiers byzantins 16. Paris.

(2015b) 'Literary *Haute Cuisine* and its Dangers: Eustathios of Thessalonike on Schedography and Everyday Language', *DOP* 69: 225–41.

(2015c) 'New Genres in the Twelfth Century: The *Schedourgia* of Theodore Prodromos', *MEG* 15: 1–41.

(2017) 'John Tzetzes and the Blemish Examiners: A Byzantine Teacher on Schedography, Everyday Language and Writerly Disposition', *MEG* 17: 1–57.

Andriollo, L. (2018) 'Nicholas Kallikles' Epitaph for the *sebastos* Roger: The Success of a Norman Chief at the Court of Alexios I Komnenos', *MEG* 18: 1–17.

Berardi, F. (2017) *La retorica degli esercizi preparatori: Glossario ragionato dei Progymnásmata*. Zurich.

Bernard, F. (2014) *Writing and Reading Byzantine Secular Poetry, 1025–1081*. Oxford.

Bernard, F., and C. Livanos (2018) *The Poems of Christopher of Mytilene and John Mauropous*. Dumbarton Oaks Medieval Library 50. Cambridge, MA.

Browning, R. (1976) 'Il codice Marciano Gr. XI.31 e la schedografia bizantina', in *Miscellanea marciana di studi bessarionei*, 21–34. Medioevo e Umanesimo 24. Padua.

Crimi, C. (2015) 'I "Versi per la domenica di Pasqua" di Arsenio: Testo, traduzione, commento', *RSBN* 52: 33–91.

Foerster, R. (ed.) (1963) *Libanii Opera*, vol. 3: *Progymnasmata, argumenta orationum demosthenicarum*. Hildesheim.

Garzya, A. (1969) 'Intorno al prologo di Niceforo Basilace', *JÖByz* 18: 55–71.

(ed.) (1984) *Nicephorus Basilaca, Orationes et Epistulae*. Leipzig.

Gautier, P. (ed.) (1986) *Théophilacte d'Achrida, Lettres*. Thessalonike.

Giannouli, A. (2014) 'Education and Literary Language in Byzantium', in *The Language of Byzantine Learned Literature*, ed. M. Hinterberger, 52–71. Turnhout.

Kaldellis, A., and I. Polemis (2015) *Psellos and the Patriarchs: Letters and Funeral Orations for Keroullarios, Leichoudes and Xiphilinos*. Michael Psellos in Translation. Notre Dame.

Kaltsogianni, E. (2010) 'A Byzantine Metrical Ekphrasis of Spring: On Arsenios' Verses on the Holy Sunday', *MEG* 10: 61–76.
Lemerle, P. (1977) *Cinq études sur le XIe siècle byzantin*. Paris.
Leone, P. L. M. (ed.) (1972) *Joannis Tzetzae Epistulae*. Leipzig.
(ed.) (2007) *Joannis Tzetzae Historiae*, 2nd ed. Galatina.
Loukaki, M. (2013) '*Ekphrasis Earos*: Le topos de la venue du printemps chez des auteurs byzantins', *Parekbolai* 3: 77–106.
Magdalino, P. (1993) *The Empire of Manuel I Komnenos, 1143–1180*. Cambridge.
Magnelli, E. (2006) 'Contributi ai carmi di Nicola *Callicle*', *MEG* 6: 149–57.
Marciniak, P. (2007) 'Byzantine *Theatron* – A Place of Performance?', in *Theatron: Rhetorische Kultur in Spätantike und Mittelalter*, ed. M. Grünbart, 277–85. Millennium-Studien 13. Berlin.
Marciniak, P., and I. Nilsson (eds.) (2021) *Satire in the Middle Byzantine Period: The Golden Age of Laughter?* Explorations in Medieval Culture 12. Leiden.
Markopoulos, A. (2006) 'De la structure de l'école byzantine: Le maître, les livres et le processus éducatif', in *Lire et écrire à Byzance*, ed. B. Mondrain, 85–96. Paris.
Mullett, M. (1984) 'Aristocracy and Patronage in the Literary Circles of Komnenian Constantinople', in *The Byzantine Aristocracy, IX to XIII Centuries*, ed. M. Angold, 173–201. Oxford.
Nousia, F. (2016) *Byzantine Textbooks of the Palaeologan Period*. Studi e Testi 505. Vatican City.
Patillon, M. (ed.) (2008) *Corpus Rhetoricum, Tome I: Anonyme: Préambule à la rhétorique; Aphthonios: Progymnasmata; En annexe: Pseudo-Hermogène: Progymnasmata*. Paris.
Patillon, M., and G. Bolognesi (eds.) (1997) *Aelius Théon, Progymnasmata*. Paris.
Pizzone, A. (2017) 'Towards a Byzantine Theory of the Comic?', in *Greek Laughter and Tears: Antiquity and After*, ed. M. Alexiou and D. Cairns, 146–65. Edinburgh Leventis Studies. Edinburgh.
Polemis I. (1995) 'Προβλήματα τῆς βυζαντινῆς σχεδογραφίας', *Ἑλληνικά* 45: 277–302.
Polemis, I. (ed.) (2013) *Michael Psellus, Orationes funebres*, vol. 1. Berlin.
Reinsch, D. R., and A. Kambylis (eds.) (2001) *Annae Comnenae Alexias*. Corpus Fontium Historiae Byzantinae 40. Berlin.
Romano, R. (ed.) (1980) *Nicola Callicle: Carmi. Testo critico, introduzione, traduzione, commentario e lessico*. Byzantina et Neo-Hellenica Neapolitana 8. Naples.
Rothstein-Dowden, Z. (2015) 'Unravelling the Cord: The Schedography of Nikephoros Basilakes', MA thesis, Central European University, Budapest.
Schirò, G. (1949) 'La schedografia a Bisanzio nei sec. XI–XII e la scuola dei SS. XL Martiri', *BBGG* 3–4: 11–29.
Sternbach, L. (ed.) (1903) 'Nicolai Calliclis carmina', *Rozprawy Akademii Umiejętności. Wydział Filologiczny*. Serya 2.21: 315–92.
van Opstall, E. M. (ed.) (2008) *Jean Géomètre: Poèmes en hexamètres et en distiques élégiaque. Edition, traduction, commentaire*. The Medieval Mediterranean 75. Leiden.

Vassis, I. (1993–4) 'Graeca sunt, non leguntur: Zu den schedographischen Spielereien des Theodoros Prodromos', *ByzZ* 86–7.1: 1–19.
(2002) 'Τῶν νέων φιλολόγων παλαίσματα: Ἡ συλλογή σχεδῶν τοῦ κώδικα Vaticanus Palatinus gr. 92', *Ἑλληνικά* 52: 37–68.
Westerink, L. G. (ed.) (1992) *Michaelis Pselli Poemata*. Stuttgart.

PART III

Poetry, Patronage and Power

CHAPTER 9

'Receiving Rich Gifts' *Negotiating Power in the Metrical Paratexts of the Vossianus Gr. Q1*

Aglae Pizzone

Before the composition of the *Histories*, Tzetzes' commentary on Aphthonios and Hermogenes in political verse, with its scope and sheer extension, was certainly meant to be the most representative among his mature work.[1] It is therefore no surprise that the ms. Leiden, Bibliotheek der Rijksuniversiteit, Vossianus Gr. Q1 [Diktyon 38108], a contemporary, 'bespoke' witness of the commentary, is equipped with a series of metrical and prose paratexts providing details on the genesis of this specific copy.[2] They are to be found at fol. 30r, after the end of the commentary on Aphthonios (six hexameters), and at fols. 211v–212r after the end of the commentary on the four Hermogenian treatises and before the section of the *Logismoi* preserved by the manuscript (respectively ten hexameters and twenty-four dodecasyllables). At fol. 212r there is also a prose note, detailing the problems encountered by Tzetzes after handing over the requested copy to its commissioners.[3] The longer hexametric poem provides us with information about the commissioner, one Nikephoros whose identity is not yet fully clarified.[4] It also describes Tzetzes in dialogue with the Muse, whom he persuades to dwell in the 'lower regions' of poetry in political verse.[5] This chapter focuses on the final iambic book epigram at fols. 211v–212r and on the hexametric poem at fol. 30r. While the text of latter – though not properly edited – is available in the catalogue of the Leiden University Library as well as in the Database of Byzantine Book Epigrams,[6] the former will be presented here in its first complete edition, accompanied by an English translation.

1 For a contextualization of the commentary and issues of chronology, see Pizzone (2020c: 658–62) and (2022).

2 For a description of the manuscript, see de Meyïer (1955: 91–3), Pizzone (2020b: 77–8) and (2020c: 654–8).

3 For text and translation, see Pizzone (2020c: 685–9).

4 Pizzone (2020c: 660–1).

5 See de Meyïer (1955: 93) and www.dbbe.ugent.be/occurrences/19742; edition and translation in Pizzone (2020c: 659–60).

6 de Meyïer (1955: 92) and www.dbbe.ugent.be/occurrences/19741.

My aim is to show that the paratexts in the Vossianus, in close dialogue with one another, form a conceptual frame around the manuscript and the texts it contains. They create a consistent web of cross-references which, besides clarifying the circumstances prompting that specific copy of the commentary, scaffold Tzetzes' authorial agency as well as his social role in a cultural economy based on patronage.[7] These paratexts also speak to the way Tzetzes exploits the inherent ambiguities of language and tradition. I would argue that they are examples of enacted *amphoteroglossia* (ἀμφοτερογλωσσία).[8] I will show that such ἀμφοτερογλωσσία rests on dialectic. The ability to exploit the capaciousness of language thus becomes a powerful means to negotiate power.

One Book Epigram and Five Labours

The twenty-four dodecasyllables stretching across fols. 211v–212r (Figures 9.1 and 9.2) take the shape of a dedicatory book epigram characterized by a few peculiar traits, as we shall see. Text and translation are as follows:

1 Ὦ τῶν μεγίστων ἐργεπεῖκτα σκαμμάτων, 211v
τὸν πρὶν ἐκεῖνον ζωγραφῶν Εὐρυσθέα,
κἂν οὐκ ἀμισθὶ τοὺς ἀγῶνας προτρέπῃς
– δώροις δὲ συχνοῖς νῦν ἐλαύνεις πρὸς πόνους –
5 δέξαι τὸν ἆθλον ἐντελῆ πεφηνότα·
ὁ σὸς γὰρ αὐτὸν Ἡρακλῆς, ὡς προὐτράπη,
δείκνυσι τανῦν ἐμφανῶς ἠνυσμένον.
Τρέσῃς δὲ μηδέν, μὴ προπέμψῃς Κοπρέα,
τούτου θεατήν – προστατοῦντα τῶν πόνων –
10 οὐ κάπρος ἐστὶν ἐνθαδί, ζῶν ἠγμένος,
ῥέγχων παρ᾽ὤμοις οὐ λέων πεπνιγμένος.
Ὕδρας κεφαλὰς νῦν οὐχ ὁρᾷς τετμημένας.
Οὐ νεβρὸς οὐδεὶς ἠνεμωμένος δρόμοις,
οὐδ᾽Ἀρκάδων ὄρνιθες ἐκφυὲς τέρας,
15 ὁμοῦ τε τόξον καὶ πτερὸν δὲ καὶ βέλος.
Οὐ ζῶμα, κόπρος, οὐδὲ ταῦρος πῦρ πνέων,
οὐ Θρᾷξ τὶς ἵππος αἷμα χόρτον ἐσθίων,
οὐ, φοίνιαι βοῦς, μῆλα, τρίκρανος κύων. 212r
Τοιοῦτον οὐδὲν ἐνθαδὶ καινὸν τέρας·

7 On patronage in the Komnenian period, see now Nilsson (2021: ch. 3), summarizing the developments in scholarship in the last thirty years; for Tzetzes in particular, see Zagklas (2019: 245–7).

8 See Roilos (2006: 53–6) and Agapitos (2017: 36).

20 πένταθλος ἐστὶ ῥητόρων ἠνυσμένος,
ὃν τερματώσας Ἡρακλῆς σὸς δεικνύει·
τῶν σῶν κελεύσει προσταγῶν πεπεισμένος.
Δέχου δὲ τοῦτον, καὶ παρὼν αὐτὸς, βλέπε˙
ῥήτωρ ἐλέγχων ῥητορεύοντας πόνους.

1 O taskmaster[9] of the greatest labours,[10]
by imitating that famous ancient Eurystheus,
even if you do not promote *agones* without compensation,
– with innumerable gifts you now exhort to labours –
5 please accept the feat that now appears to be completed.
Your Heracles, as he was urged to do,
shows it (to you) now as clearly accomplished.
Fear not and do not send forward Kopreus
to watch it, as a steward of the labours.
10 Here you won't find any boar dragged alive,
nor a strangled lion hissing on my shoulders,
you won't see the severed heads of the Hydra.
No, there won't be any doe carried by the wind in its run,
no Arcadian birds, extraordinary monsters,
15 and with them bow, arrow and spear.
No girdle, dung, not even a bull breathing fire,
no Thracian horse feeding on blood as if fodder,
no bloody cows, apples or three-headed dog.
There are no such novel monsters here:
20 a triumphant *pentathlos* of rhetors has been completed,
displayed and accomplished by your Heracles,
obeying the urge of your orders.
Take this, and being present yourself, look:
a rhetor putting to shame the labours of rhetors.

In the lengthy book epigram Tzetzes draws an analogy between himself and Heracles on the one hand, and between the commentary and the hero's labours on the other, while presenting the finished work to his patron/Eurystheus. Of the five roles identified by Bernard and Demoen as central to the communicative situation of book epigrams (author, patron, scribe, reader and text),[11] author, patron and text are clearly predominant. Tzetzes does not imply any other reader than the patron. Such exclusivity reflects the fact that the Vossianus is a commissioned bespoke copy, as declared by

9 The term usually occurs in contexts where waged and menial labour is addressed: see e.g. Eustathios, *Or*. 9.17.36 ed. Tafel (1832).
10 The word is literally connected with digging as shown e.g. by Pl. *Lg*. 845e.
11 Bernard and Demoen (2019: 416).

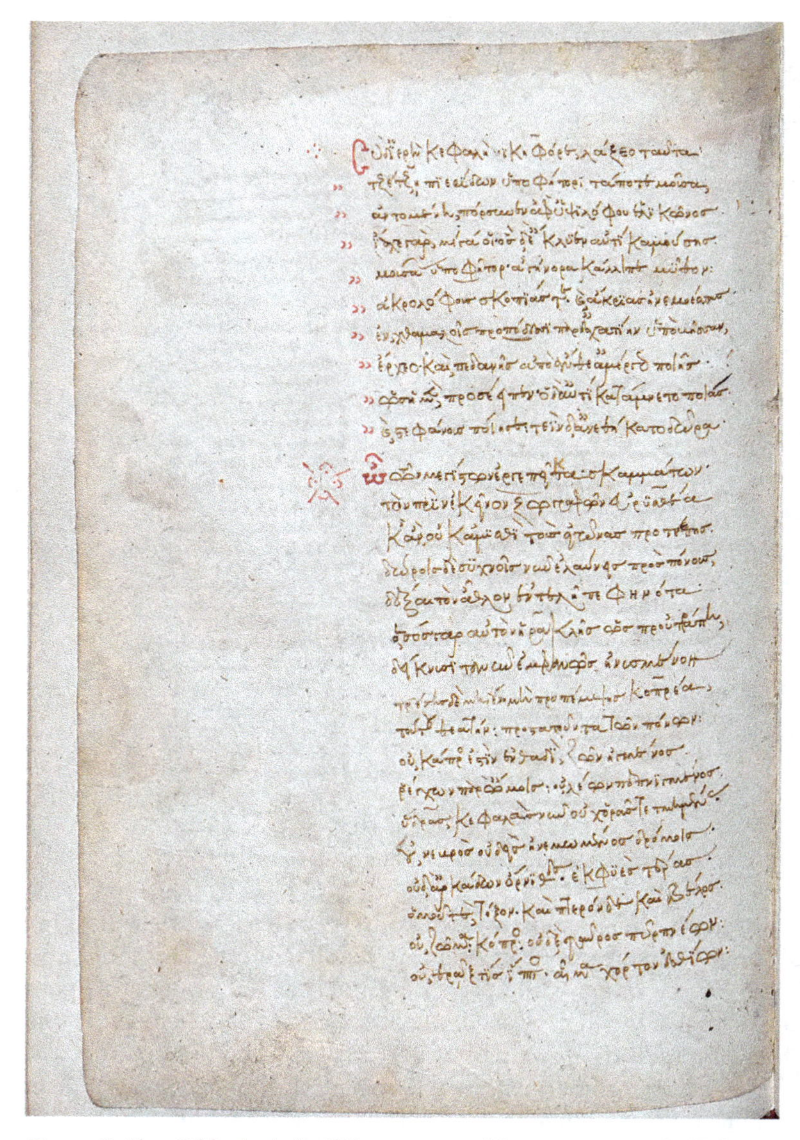

Fig 9.1 Leiden, Bibliotheek der Rijksuniversiteit, Vossianus graecus Q1 [Diktyon 38108], fol. 211v

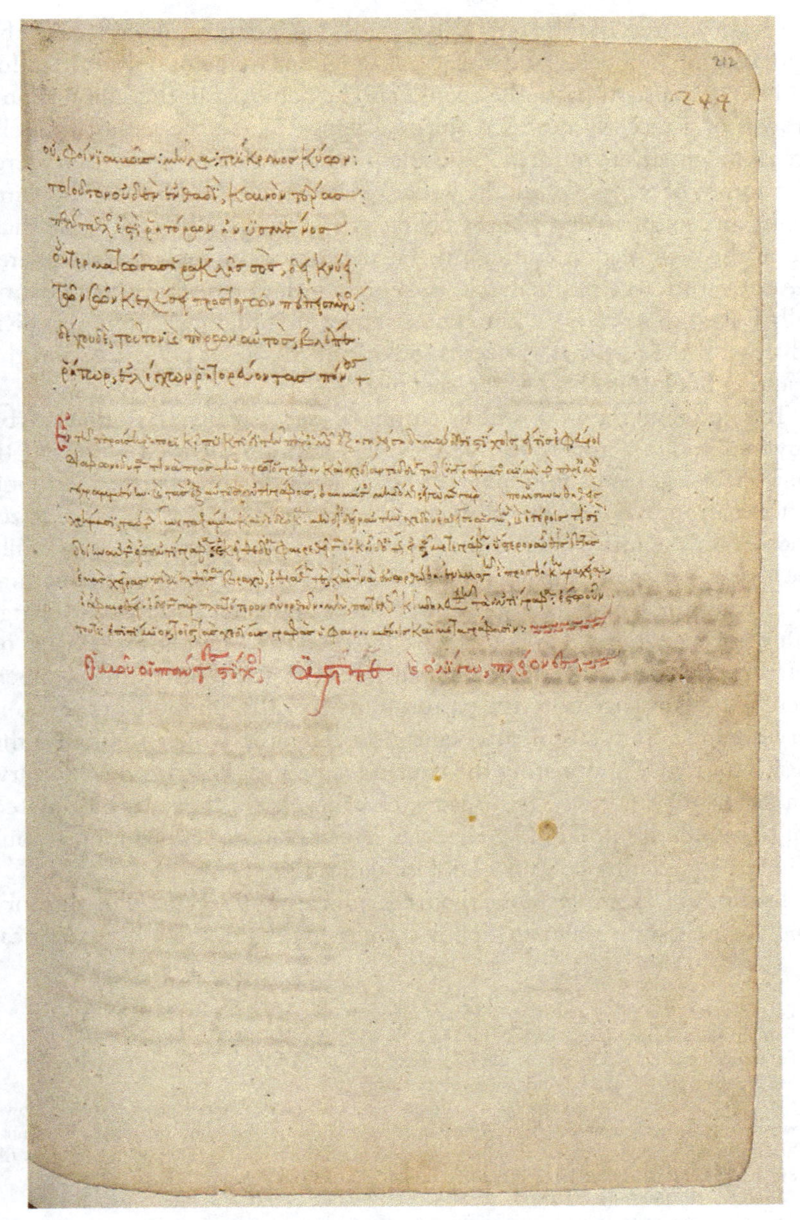

Fig 9.2 Leiden, Bibliotheek der Rijksuniversiteit, Vossianus graecus Q1 [Diktyon 38108], fol. 212r

the prose paratext of fol. 212r.[12] What is striking is that, while, as stressed by Bernard and Demoen, 'laudatory book epigrams were not only written for authors of a distant past. They could also be deployed in the canonization process of a recently deceased spiritual figure',[13] here the author himself, pretty much alive, appears to lead the process of canonization, as it were. The author of the work and the writer of the book epigram share the same voice, thus emphasizing Tzetzes' characteristic autography and, as we shall see in the next section, autonomy. Furthermore, although Tzetzes invites the patron to 'receive' the book, the epigram does not use verbs semantically linked to κτάομαι: the accent is rather on 'ordering', 'urging', which tallies with the fact that Tzetzes is looking at the act of patronage and the resulting book from his own perspective.[14]

The epigram shows a strong emphasis on visuality, as indicated by ζωγραφῶν (l. 2), πεφηνότα, ἐμφανῶς (l. 5 and l. 7), as well as θεατήν (l. 9). Tzetzes also seems to imply that he is physically offering the text/book to the patron, who in turn is urged to be present, παρών (l. 23). Tzetzes 'shows' and 'points' at his work (δείκνυσι l. 7 and δεικνύει l. 21), while the receiver is invited to 'look' at it (l. 23). Again, traditional structural patterns of book epigrams appear to be reversed here. If verbs of writing/painting are common in causative constructions (the patron 'makes' or 'lets' the copyist write/paint),[15] in our lines the act of 'picturing' – albeit mentally – falls back onto the patron himself.[16] The emotional tone too is very different from customary dedication epigrams, which emphasize the 'desire' and 'love' motivating the patron's requests.[17] Fear, on the contrary, is a dominant emotion here (Τρέσῃς δὲ μηδέν, l. 8). The patron is invited not to be afraid, since, unlike Heracles, Tzetzes has not tamed monstruous animals, completing instead a bookish enterprise.[18]

To sum up, Tzetzes exploits the rules informing the genre of dedicatory epigrams, twisting them to fit his own agenda and stress his exegetical

12 For a discussion of this paratext, see Pizzone (2020c: 656).

13 Bernard and Demoen (2019: 417).

14 See again Bernard and Demoen (2019: 418), based on Cavallo (1992).

15 See Bianconi (2013: 309), building on Iacobini (2007: 153).

16 On the representation of the scribes as painters, see Drpić (2013). Tzetzes often equates his own writing to the achievements of visual artists, playing with the ambiguity of γράφω. The most blatant – and unapologetically boastful – case comes from the last two lines of the *Theogony* (ll. 858–9), where he describes himself as the 'canon of Polycletus for writers'.

17 Bernard and Demoen (2019: 419).

18 Tzetzes' commentary exceeds by far that of other commentators, since he has managed to produce a commentary κατὰ λήμματα in political verse on *all* of the five treatises of the *corpus Hermogenianum*. See Jeffreys (2019: 94). Perhaps only John Doxapatres' engagement shows a scope comparable with Tzetzes': see Gibson (2009) and (2019).

achievement. In the next section I will show that this is not the only peculiarity of this text.

Heracles, Eurystheus and the Pitfalls of Patronage

The iambic dedication, by equating the commentary on Hermogenes to a Herculean task, prompts an obvious, broader analogy between the couples Heracles/Eurystheus and Tzetzes/Nikephoros. In this section I argue that Tzetzes exploits some aspects of the Heracles narrative to negotiate subordination and to make the balance of power tilt, at least within the space of this specific manuscript.[19]

A first point to be made is that Heracles features consistently in Tzetzes' work as one of his many proxies. When in the letter collection he addresses the Kamateroi, with whom he had a problematic relationship,[20] he tends to present himself as a new Heracles.[21] Equally, in the iambs appended to the second recension of the *Histories*,[22] he claims that he had to endure much more than Heracles, given, on the one hand, the lack of recognition for his work and, on the other, the general tendency of his time to honour questionable personalities. These lines also point to Eurystheus' malicious disposition, a detail on which I enlarge below:[23]

Αἰσχρῶν δὲ τιμὴν δυσμαθῶν τί μοι λέγεις;
Οὐ νῦν ἐπανθεῖ πρῶτον ἐν βίῳ τόδε·
ἀεὶ δὲ τιμὴ τῶν κακούργων ἦν βίῳ.
Οὐχ Ἡρακλῆς ἐκεῖνος ἦν πονῶν πόσα,
Εὐρυσθέως τρυφῶντος αὐτοῦ τοῖς πόνοις,
ἀνδρὸς πονηροῦ, μηδὲ ζῆν ἐπαξίου;
(Tzetzes, *Iambi* 2.230–5 ed. Leone 1969–70: 142)

19 That Tzetzes had often an uneasy relationship with his patrons is a well-known fact. The tip of the iceberg is represented by his dealings with Irene for the *Allegories of the Iliad*, but Tzetzes appears to be quite consistent in his attitude towards patrons. On this topic, besides the classic Rhoby (2010), see the more recent work of Savio (2020) (though with some problems as regards the way in which twelfth-century Constantinopolitan culture is understood); Lovato (2021) (discussed below) and (2022).

20 The trajectory of this relationship is retraced in Pizzone (2022).

21 Cf. above all *ep.* 87 to Theodore Kamateros, p. 127, ll. 15–20 ed. Leone (1972), to be read next to *Histories* 12.417.503–7 ed. Leone (2007). Tzetzes alludes here to the proverb 'born on the fourth day', used to describe people forced into the unlucky condition of labouring for others. Cf. Zenobios, *Epitome* 5.7 ed. Schneidewin and von Leutsch (1839); Hesychios T 613 ed. Cunningham and Hansen (2009); *Suda* T 388 ed. Adler (1928); Photios, *Lexicon* T 190 ed. Porson (1822), based on Philochoros fr. 328 F 85b ed. Jacoby; Eustathios, *Commentary on the Iliad* 1.469.3–4 ed. van der Valk (1971–87). See also the modern Greek translation in Grigoriadis (2001: 225, with n. 293 at p. 287). See Pizzone (2022: 24–6) with further bibliography.

22 See Leone (1969–70), D'Agostini and Pizzone (2021).

23 Eurystheus appears as a double-edged figure also in Eustathios, *Commentary on the Iliad* 3.379.1–4 ed. van der Valk (1971–87).

> Why do you say 'honour' among a shameful, ill-learned crowd?
> Not now for the first time do we see this in the world:
> honour has always dwelled among the criminals of the world.
> Did not that famous Heracles suffer such great labours,
> while Eurystheus was revelling in his labours,
> a cruel man, who did not deserve to live?

Such identification with Heracles is quite consistent throughout the years, as proven by the autograph notes appended to the Vossianus. At fol. 41v, for instance, we find one of Tzetzes' frequent rants against the copyist, who, through his mistakes, forces him to tackle disproportionately demanding labours (see Figure 9.3):

> ὁ μιαρὸς δὲ μεταγραφεὺς καὶ ἐχθρὸς τοῦ θεοῦ, μηδὲν ἐζημιωμένος, οὕτω πάντα παρελίμπανε, ἄθλους καὶ πόνους ὑπὲρ τοὺς ἡρακλείους πολλῷ ἀσυγκρίτως παρέχων τῷ γέροντι, εἰς τὴν τούτων ἀνόρθωσιν· ὅτι πόνημα ἦν ἡ βίβλος τοῦ γέροντος. Εἰ δεῖνος ἄλλου σύγγραμμα ἦν κἂν μυρία κεκαινοτόμηται πάνυ λεπτῶς, ἂν ταύτην κατατεμὼν πυρὶ κατετέφρωσα.

> The accursed copyist and enemy of God, without paying any penalty, thus overlooked everything, forcing the old man to face struggles and labours far exceeding those of Heracles, in order to correct this text. And this is only because the book was a labour of the old man. Had it been by anyone else, even acknowledging its innumerable and subtle novelties, I would have thrown it into the fire after tearing it apart.[24]

While in the Vossianus' book epigram the Herculean labour faced by Tzetzes relates to the content and the scope of the commentary, the autograph note is concerned with the material burden of purging the manuscript from mistakes and misunderstandings.[25] The dung to be cleaned up in this case finds material instantiation in the mistakes of the copyist: faecal imagery is quite common in the notes in the Vossianus.[26] The labels of πόνος or πόνημα often used for both the 'creative' content of books and the material work of copyists in book epigrams and subscriptions[27]

24 The note follows a long σημειῶσαι note added in the hand of Tzetzes and finds itself next to another autograph marginal gloss to Hermogenes. The whole page shows that Tzetzes has also added overlooked punctuation in several passages. If our note actually refers to the copyist forgetting to transcribe authorial marginal notes, this provides material proof that Tzetzes actually considered marginalia as integral to the discursive structure of his work.

25 Lovato (2017: 212) for Augias' labour, partly based on Luzzatto (1999: 25–8).

26 Cf. fol. 45v.

27 Cf. among the many possible examples www.dbbe.ugent.be/occurrences/23524 (scribe) and www.dbbe.ugent.be/occurrences/20967 (author).

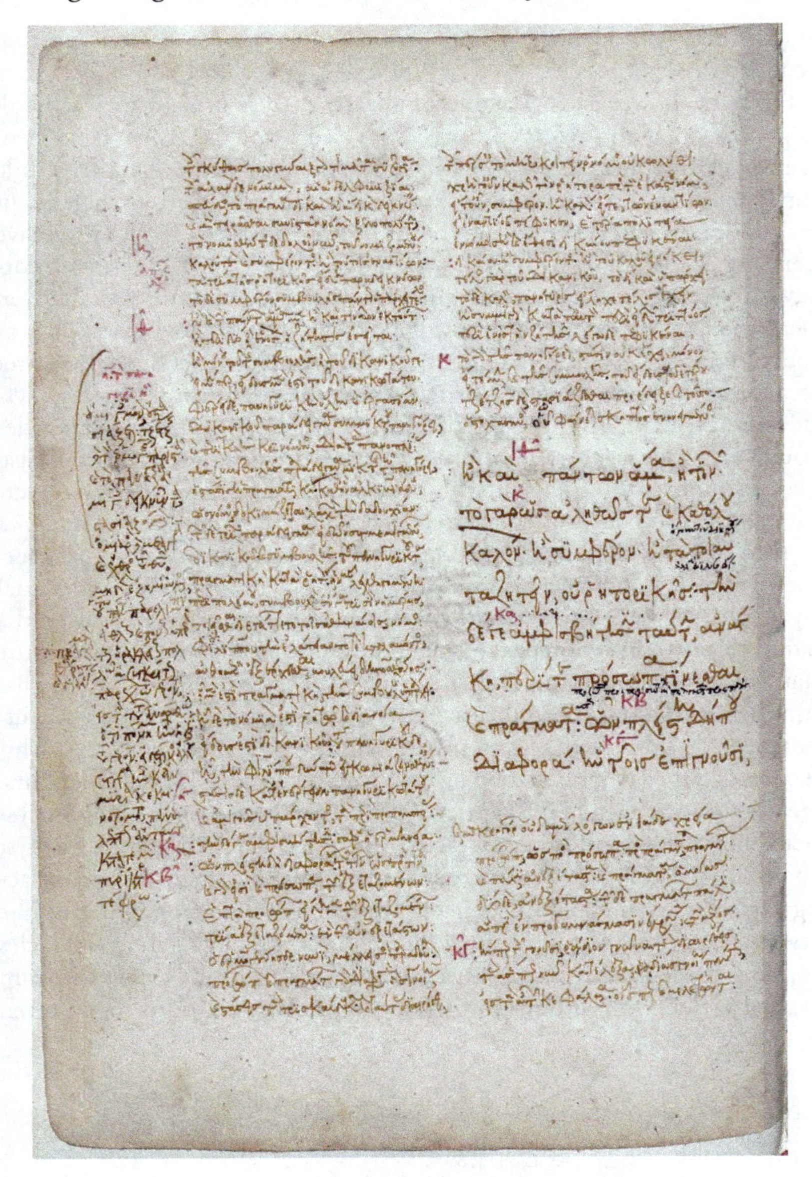

Fig 9.3 Leiden, Bibliotheek der Rijksuniversiteit, Vossianus graecus Q1 [Diktyon 38108], fol. 41v

conflate here with Heracles' labours, also described as πόνοι, thus creating a consistent set of images.

Heracles, however, is but one of the characters evoked in our book epigram, which also refers to Eurystheus and Kopreus. As we have seen, Tzetzes invites the patron to imitate Eurystheus. Although this simile might be taken at face value as rather standard and flattering, it is, in fact, double-edged. Several clues point in this direction. First, as we have seen, the iambs appended to the second recension of the *Histories* portray Eurystheus as a despicable figure. According to Eustathios, moreover, there were two ways to refer to Heracles in relation to Eurystheus: ὅς Εὐρυσθῆος ἀέθλων and ὅς Εὐρυσθῆος ἄνακτος. Homer chooses the latter because he did not want to κακολογῆσαι, that is to speak ill of Eurystheus, as if mentioning the unfair labours unjustly inflicted on Heracles would shed a derogatory light on his character.[28] Second, Eustathios also gives us important insights into how the power relationship between Heracles and Eurystheus was conceptualized. In the *Commentary on the Iliad* we read that the king's hierarchic superiority is only formal and that Heracles' voluntary subjugation to him is a sign of real greatness and actual royalty.[29] If we take into account this shade of meaning while reading the communicative situation of the epigram, we realize that, whereas it is true that Tzetzes subjects himself to the requests of his patron, such a submission, being voluntary, becomes actually a sign of superiority. Eurystheus, moreover, is portrayed as potentially afraid of Tzetzes' book/feat. This detail is again to be understood against the narrative of Heracles' labours. Tzetzes summarizes the relevant events in the *Histories*, describing Eurystheus' horrified reaction to Heracles returning victorious from his first labour. The victory was so unexpected that now Eurystheus, afraid of facing further unwanted consequences, prevents the hero from entering the city and asks him instead to show the spolia at the city's gates.[30] Heracles stopping at the gates of Mycenae is a powerful image, one that once again speaks to issues of in-group admission and gatekeeping featuring so often in Tzetzes' work.[31]

28 Eustathios, *Commentary on the Iliad* 3.779.27–30 ed. van der Valk (1971–87).

29 Eustathios, *Commentary on the Iliad* 4.284.15–19 ed. van der Valk (1971–87).

30 Tzetzes, *Histories* 2.36.235–9 ed. Leone (2007).

31 See for example the recurring reference to the κουστωδία (Luzzatto [1999: 50, 52 n. 54 and n. 103], D'Agostini and Pizzone [2021]), used for the 'band' of teachers literally gatekeeping cultural institutions in the capital. Again, we are to do with images that are not peculiar to Tzetzes alone but widely used in the parlance of Constantinopolitan intellectuals. As remarked by Loukaki (1996: 14 and n. 87), for instance, Gregory Antiochos uses the reference to E. *Rh.* 906 to describe his own position of 'watch of the doors' in a letter to Demetrios Tornikes.

The background story about Eurystheus also explains why Tzetzes introduces the figure of Kopreus, a minor character in the narrative, about whom we learn again from Eustathios.[32] Kopreus was sent forward by Eurystheus, who did not want to deal directly with Heracles anymore. Eustathios is struck by the etymology of the name Kopreus, which again evokes dung and faeces. Such an association makes sense to the way Tzetzes exploits the traditions regarding Heracles. In the narrative of the labours, Kopreus embodies the prototypical middleman and from Tzetzes' various notations we know that such middlemen intervening in producing copies of his work were often responsible for the βορβόροι defiling his oeuvre.[33]

Within Tzetzes' own poetics, moreover, Kopreus is associated with the double-tonguedness – on which I will enlarge later – of practices of praise and blame. When commenting on the *loci* of praise – lineage, education, training, age, nature of body and soul, inclinations, actions and status – mentioned in Hermogenes' *On Issues*,[34] Tzetzes offers his take on the subject, duly highlighted in the manuscript by a σημείωσαι note in the margin. He advances a model whereby the use of the *loci* is rather subtle – δεινότερον – as it makes the character's description more rounded and open to contradiction. This is where Kopreus comes into play as a character belonging into the rhetoric of blame. Tzetzes offers a mini-Homeric cento to showcase an example of praise capitalizing on potentially negative aspects, thus leaving room for a modicum of ambiguity (fol. 54v; see Figure 9.4):

> Ἐγὼ κἂν τοῖς τοιούτοις δὲ σύμπασι κεχρημένος,
> μᾶλλον ὡς Ὅμηρος ποιῶ δεινότερον τὸν λόγον·
> ἀπὸ τοιαύτης γὰρ φανεὶς οὗτος φημὶ πατρίδος
> καὶ τῶν λοιπῶν ὁμοίως δὲ τοιοῦτος ἐγεγόνει.
> Καὶ Ὅμηρος τὸν παῖδα γὰρ αἰνῶν τὸν τοῦ Κοπρέως
> ἀνθρώπου φαύλου σύρφακος οὕτω τὰ ἔπη λέγει·
> τοῦ γένετ' ἐκ πατρὸς πολὺ χείρονος υἱὸς ἀμείνων
> παῦροι τοι παῖδες ὁμοῖοι πατρὶ πέλονται
> οἱ πλέονες κακίους παῦροι δέ τε πατρὸς ἀρείους.

> Personally, while I have used all of them,
> I would rather make my speech more forceful, like Homer:
> 'This man – I say – appearing to be from such a land,
> and so on using the other *loci*, has proven himself such.'

32 Eustathios, *Commentary on the Iliad* 3.778.5–11 ed. van der Valk (1971–87).
33 See Agapitos (2017), Pizzone (2020c: 685–7) and (2020a) on the faecal imagery in Tzetzes.
34 *On Issues* 3.7–8 ed. Patillon (2009).

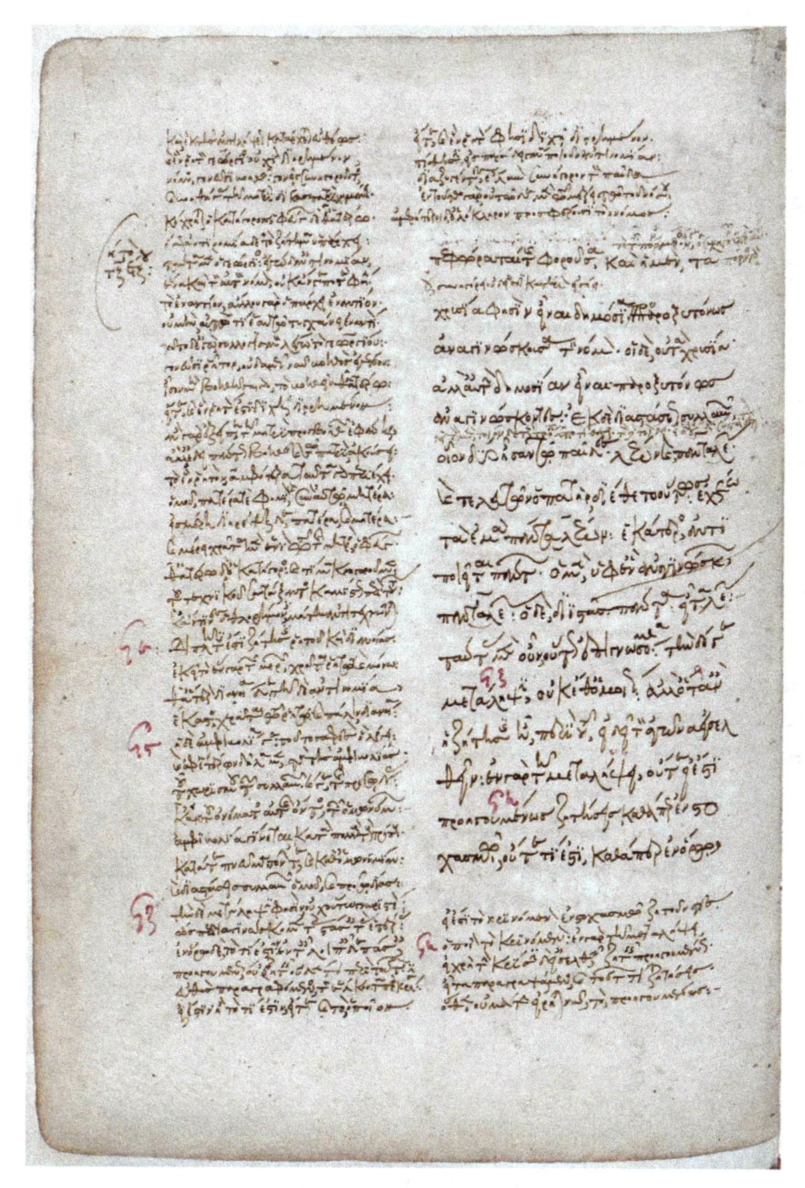

Fig 9.4 Leiden, Bibliotheek der Rijksuniversiteit, Vossianus graecus Q1 [Diktyon 38108], fol. 54v

For Homer too, in praising the son of Kopreus,
a pipsqueak from the populace, utters his lines as follows:
'Of him, a father baser by far, was begotten a better son [*Iliad* 15.641].
Few sons indeed are like their fathers;
most are worse, few better than the fathers [*Odyssey* 2.276–7].'

There is a further point made by Tzetzes in the dedication epigram, one that, as we shall see, resonates with the hexametric paratext of fol. 30r analysed in the next section: unlike Heracles', Tzetzes' challenge was rewarded with adequate compensation. Tzetzes refers here to the episode of Augeias' stables, as we gather again from Eustathios:

> Αὐγείας Ἡρακλεῖ τὴν τῶν αὐτοῦ βοῶν κόπρον καθήραντι οὐκ ἐδίδου ἀπαιτοῦντι τὸν μισθόν, ὃς ἦν δεκάτη τῶν βοῶν, λέγων οὐχ' ἑκόντα ποιῆσαι τὸ ἔργον, ἀλλ' ἐπιταγέντα ὑπὸ Εὐρυσθέως. (Eustathios, *Commentary on the Iliad* 3.309.8–10 ed. van der Valk 1971–87)
>
> Augeias did not give Heracles the requested compensation, after he cleaned the dung of his bulls, which was supposed to be a tenth of the cattle, arguing that he had not accomplished the feat of his own volition, but because he had been ordered to do so by Eurystheus.

Οὐχ' ἑκόντα, 'not of his own volition', is the key term here. In the epistle to Lachanas, opening the *Histories*, Tzetzes uses a quotation from Aeschylus' *Prometheus Bound* characterized by the reduplication of the adverb ἑκών to stress that even his proclaimed lower social status is not passively endured but actively chosen.[35] Equally, in our book epigram he uses the twelve labours narrative to stress that the compensation was earned precisely because, unlike Heracles, he was still at liberty to accept or refuse his patrons' requests. This attitude has to be understood against the backdrop of broader discourses of waged labour, as we shall see in the next section.

Wages, Books and Cultural Economy

In a recent paper, Valeria Lovato has stressed that the competing notions of μισθός ('wages') and δῶρον ('gift') both contribute to defining Tzetzes' position towards his patrons and his own creativity as well as his ἐλευθερία ('freedom').[36] In what follows I would like to add further considerations based on the Vossianus paratexts, contextualizing Tzetzes' attitude towards

35 Tzetzes, *Histories* 1.11.284 ed. Leone (2007). See on this passage Pizzone (2017: 205–6).
36 Lovato (2021) and (2022).

his commissioners within contemporary language of patronage – focused on but not confined to the arts.

As is well known, in Byzantium relationships of waged service between clients and patrons were conceptualized as δουλεία ('servitude') or θητεία ('hired service'), which stress the lack of agency of the client.[37] This is also how Tzetzes himself describes his own service under the *doux* of Berroia, Isaac, as shown by a famous passage in the *Carmina Iliaca*:[38]

> Οἷσι κἀμὲ καὶ ἄκων δειδίσκετο οὔλιος ἀνήρ,
> ᾧ πρὶν ἐγὼ θήτευσα, κατηφὼν Ἰσαάκιος,
> ἠδ' ἄλοχος κείνου περικερδής, ἀγκυλόβουλος,
> δειδιότες ἀμὴν ἀγέρωχον καλλιέπειαν.
> (Tzetzes, *Carmina Iliaca* 2.142–5 ed. Leone 1995)

> With such gifts, a baleful man, unwillingly, greeted me,
> a man whom I previously served, Isaac, who causes grief,
> and his greedy wife, mischievous,
> afraid as they were of my formidable, beautiful language.

Lovato has offered a detailed analysis of these lines,[39] showing how Tzetzes carefully projects his own self-representation and the struggles with patrons as well as rivals onto the figure of Ajax. This rhetorical strategy reflects broader twelfth-century discourses of patronage to be found throughout the work of Tzetzes, but also, as I argue, among his contemporaries. In this respect, mythical and literary parallels help make sense of reality as much as historical reality gives new meaning to traditional narratives. In the *Allegories of the Iliad* and in the *Exegesis of the Iliad*,[40] the very notion of θητεία is used by Tzetzes to frame the story of Poseidon and Apollo, when they are put to work 'for free' by Laomedon. The relationship between Heracles and Eurystheus fits the same rationale. In the twelfth century the figure of Heracles could serve as a model of ideal endurance in case of θήτεια gone awry, that is, of service ending up being 'unwaged', as in the cases related by John Kinnamos, Gregory Antiochos and Tzetzes himself.[41] Euthymios Malakes

37 See Loukaki (1996: 15, 21), with a focus on Gregory Antiochos, and Kazhdan (1985). A key source is Kinnamos, *Epitome* 6.8, 275.11–276.15 ed. Meineke (1836).

38 On this episode, see Braccini (2009–10: 154–5) and (2010: 99–101), Lovato (2022).

39 See Lovato (2017: 181–3).

40 Tzetzes, *Allegories of the Iliad* 15.72 ed. Boissonade (1851): ἔπαθον πρὶν θητείᾳ; *Exegesis of the Iliad* 350.21–351.1 ed. Papathomopoulos (2007): Ποσειδῶνα δὲ καὶ Ἀπόλλωνα τῷ Λαομέδοντι θητεύειν ἀπέσταλκε.

41 See above n. 37 for the relevant passages.

uses the reference to Eurystheus to this end. In letter 3 sent to a friend while stationed far from Constantinople – not unlike Tzetzes in Macedonia – Euthymios poignantly tells his correspondent how his hopes concerning his current appointment had been deluded. He should have known better: only the most debased souls are moved by a desire of riches after all. On the contrary, Heracles provides a viable model: τὸ δὲ προῖκα καὶ ἀμισθὶ ἄθλους Εὐρυσθείους διατελεῖν, ἀναλγήτου τοῦτο ψυχῆς καὶ γνώμης ἐστερημένης τῶν λογισμῶν ('to fully carry out the labours of Eurystheus, without compensation: now this is evidence of a soul insensible to pain and a spirit with no ulterior motives').[42] Accordingly, at the end of the epistle Euthymios asks for his friend's prayers, so that he might be able to come to the end of his service and return to the capital, 'a task worthy of Eurystheus'.[43]

Against this backdrop Tzetzes appears, once more, both conventional and particular in using established tropes. He resorts to a traditional set of images easily recognized by his audience in a way that helps him carve out his own personal space and emphasize his personal freedom. Rather than epitomizing service, wages become evidence of his free will and authorial autonomy. That is why, as I argue, across the paratexts of the Vossianus Tzetzes stresses, in (only) apparent contradiction with other passages from his work, the fact that this specific version of the commentary has been produced against compensation. Such compensation is referred to as μισθός ('wages') but also as δῶρα ('gifts'). However, unlike the unsatisfactory gifts received by the eparch and his wife, the δῶρα offered here appear to be adequate. The hexameters closing the commentary on Aphthonios at fol. 30r depict again a relationship with the sponsor in which the balance of power tilts in favour of the patronized author (see Figure 9.5):

στίχοι ἡρωικοί

1 Ἑρμείης ὅδ' ἔληξε διάκτορος Ἀφθονΐοιο
γῆρυν θεσπιέπειαν ἐπίδμονα ῥητροσυνάων
προφρονέως ἐρέων, ναετῆρος Ἀντιοχείης,
Τζέτζης ἣν τολύπευσεν, ἀριστοπόνοισιν ἀέθλοις·
5 ὄλβια δῶρα λαβὼν οὐ τηΰσίοις καμάτοισιν,
ὄλβια δῶρα λαβών, καὶ ἑταίρους ἀμφαγαπάζων.

Στί(χοι) σοδ καὶ ὁμοῦ ἡ τῆς ἐξηγέσ(εως) τῶν προγ(υμνασμά)τ(ων) στιχ(ομητρία) δψλθ καὶ ἡρωικοὶ ς καὶ ἕτεροι διαλαθόντες ὡς κε.

42 Euthymios Malakes, *ep.* 3.16 ed. Bonis (1937).
43 Euthymios Malakes, *ep.* 3.23–7 ed. Bonis.

Hexameters

1 This Hermes,[44] messenger of Aphthonios, ceased
from eagerly investigating his oracular voice versed[45] in rhetorical arts,
[Aphthonios], the inhabitant of Antioch,
[a voice] that Tzetzes unfolded through noble struggles,
5 receiving rich gifts for no idle labours,
receiving rich gifts and embracing with love his companions.

274 lines and overall the stichometry of the exegesis on the preparatory exercises 4,737 lines and 6 hexameters and other lines that escape notice around 25.

These hexameters – metapoetic in content as often in Tzetzes' work[46] – present the reader with the same set of metaphors encountered in the final book epigram sealing the commentary to the corpus. 'Enduring' Aphthonios might be an ἆθλος, but it is one met with ample compensation. Furthermore, such a task is accepted προφρονέως, that is, of Tzetzes' own will. The rich gifts obtained in exchange are but a consequence of the high, almost divine quality of his engagement with the text; they are not what prompted the work in the first place. Accordingly, Tzetzes presents himself as a new Hermes, that is to say, in twelfth-century terms, as an embodiment of *logos*. Such staging of his role as a commentator dovetails with the word play γῆρυν/ἐρέων. I will come back to the notions of 'voice' and 'tongue' in the last section of this contribution. Here I will confine myself to highlighting that ἐρέων could be derived from both λέγω ('to say') and ἐρέω ('to search', 'to enquire'). Tzetzes goes beyond the usual overlap between the commentator's and the commented author's voice.[47] By taking up the persona of Hermes/Logos he seems to suggest that his voice has in fact the power of validating Aphthonios. Aphthonios can be heard only as long as Tzetzes is willing (προφρονέως) to speak and to speak about him. Once more a trope familiar to the intellectual scene of the late Komnenian era is pushed to its limits.

44 Hermes is mentioned also in the book epigram introducing the commentary on Lycophron's *Alexandra* (p. 1.5 ed. Scheer 1881). On Hermes allegorized as *logos* by twelfth-century intellectuals, see van den Berg (2017: 132 and n. 18), with previous bibliography.

45 ἐπίδμων is apparently coined by Tzetzes, who uses it also in *Carmina Iliaca* 3.89 and 3.642.

46 See for instance the hexametric book epigram at the beginning of the exegesis on the *Iliad*, on which see p. 242 below.

47 See for instance Eustathios, *Commentary on Dionysius Periegetes*, introductory epistle 206.41–207.33 ed. Müller (1861) (on which see Cullhed [2016: 12*], D'Agostini [2021: 115–16]). Tzetzes customarily presents himself as a new Homer, as shown by Cullhed (2014: 58–61).

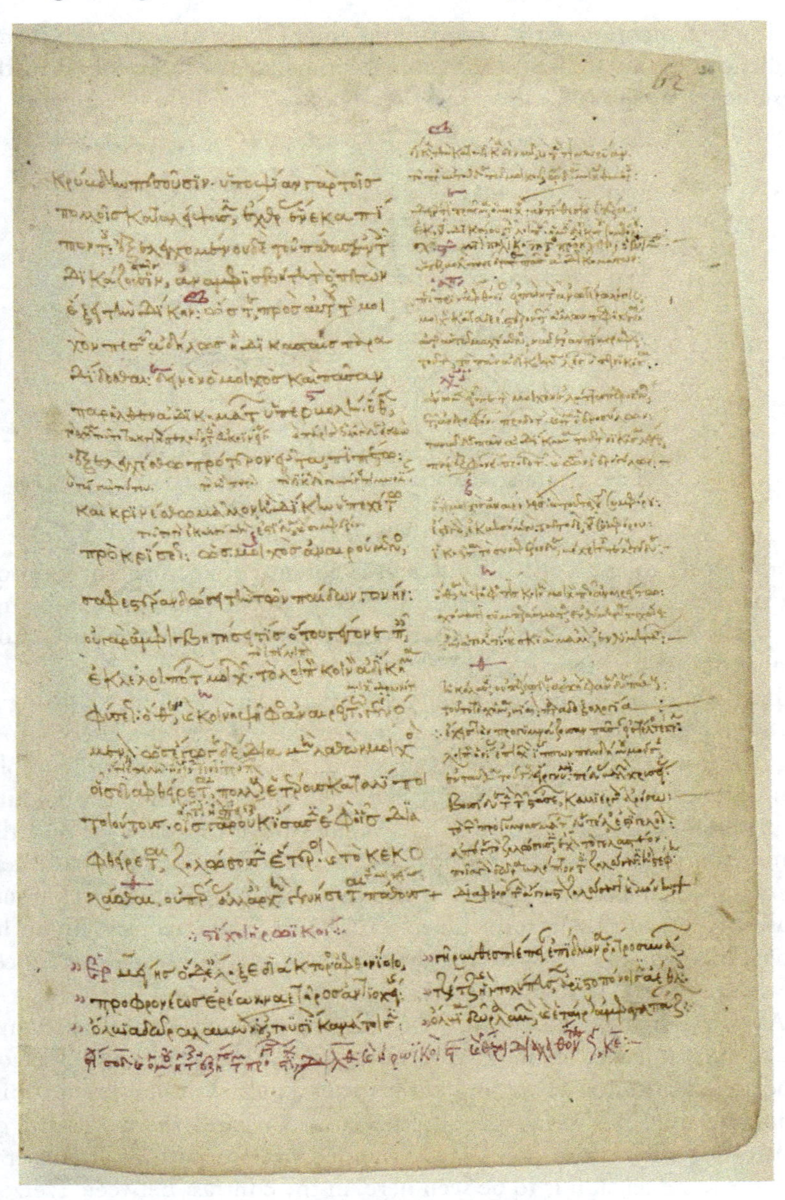

Fig 9.5 Leiden, Bibliotheek der Rijksuniversiteit, Vossianus graecus Q1 [Diktyon 38108], 30r

The final mention of the 'companions' might point to a selected, trusted audience or even students. Something comparable is to be found in the hexameters opening the *Exegesis of the Iliad*, with a striking similarity in vocabulary:

> Βίβλον ἑαῖς πραπίδεσσι γλαφυρολύτειραν Ὁμήρου
> τήνδε παραιφασίῃσιν ἐμῶν ἑτάρων τολυπεύσας,
> παισὶν Ὁμηριάδαις ἑρμήϊον ὤπασα δῶρον
> γραμματικὸς περίαλλα μογήσας Ἰωάννης,
> τὸν Τζέτζη καλέουσιν ἐπωνυμίην ἐρέοντες. (Tzetzes,
> *Exegesis of the Iliad* 3.1–5 ed. Papathomopoulos 2007)

> This book of Homer, elegantly explained for their heart,
> I unfolded at the instigation of my companions,
> preparing a gift worthy of Hermes to the children of Homer,
> I, John the grammarian, labouring at every single detail,
> the one whom they call by the name of Tzetzes.

With respect to the work as a gift, in the absence of an apparent sponsor, the pattern is reversed as compared to the hexameters on Aphthonios and Tzetzes' work is described as a gratuitous present, not unlike Eustathios' commentaries on Homer.

In the Vossianus, on the contrary, the stichometry is in direct dialogue with the preceding hexameters. It quantifies the scope of the ἆθλος, proving that it justifiably called for ὄλβια δῶρα. Since the Vossianus is acephalous, the stichometry is also particularly relevant to assessing the amount of material lost with the first quires. Besides the six hexameters and the commentary on Aphthonios proper, Tzetzes also mentions 25 lines interspersed in the text and 274 lines at the very beginning, which, as I argue, must have been the introduction to the whole commentary. There he probably provided further details about his patrons and the circumstances in which the texts were put together.

As I have mentioned above,[48] the metrical paratexts of the Vossianus are accompanied by a final prose note, showing that, despite Tzetzes' proclaimed autonomy, writing for patrons could prompt severe limitations to one's authorial agency, especially as regards the possibility of controlling the output after it was handed over to patrons. I contend that the same tension is to be seen here, in the contrast between Tzetzes'

48 See p. 225.

'free will' and the undeniable market value of his work, expressed by the detailed stichometry.

Such an attitude is consistent with Tzetzes' mixed feelings – to say the least – towards the commodification of books. Throughout Tzetzes' work, the book trade is seen as a troublesome practice as well as a source of anxiety. When Tzetzes' writings actually go on the market, it usually happens against his will.[49] To him, bookselling is directly related to loss of status and to withdrawal from the public sphere.[50]

The same attitude transpires in his treatment of Plato and of the fourth-century poet Philoxenus of Cythera.[51] Both guests of Dionysius of Syracuse,[52] Plato and Philoxenus displayed very different attitudes towards their patron, even though for both of them the relationship with the common patron did not end well. However, unlike Plato, Philoxenus, with whom Tzetzes identifies, stayed a free man, even if taken to Syracuse's stone quarries for forced labour.[53] Plato, by contrast, was sold and bought multiple times, ending up on the market square of Aegina, by then in war with Athens, before recovering his freedom.[54]

It surely is no coincidence that commodification of literature adds to Plato's moral failure in Tzetzes' eyes. Plato is depicted as heavily engaged in the book trade: both as a buyer and as a seller he did not refrain from dodgy practices, damaging others' authorship. Nor did Plato hesitate to sell his own work to the highest bidder, well beyond the acceptable boundaries of patronage etiquette.[55] He was also willing to have his dialogues circulated among anonymous readers, who could potentially appropriate

49 Cf. e.g. Tzetzes, *Histories* 6.40, introductory prose note (on which Pizzone [2020a: 54–5]).

50 Tzetzes, *Exegesis of the Iliad* 22.4–9 ed Papathomopoulos (2007). Cf. Braccini (2009–10: 160). Tzetzes retained only a book containing Plutarch's *Parallel Lives* and some technical treatises. Braccini takes for granted that the episode is to be connected to the falling out with Isaac, but the issue might need to be re-examined. The qualification of ἀβίβλης is probably to be connected to Tzetzes' mistrust of the book market: being without commodified books is turned into a badge of honour. Tzetzes becomes a walking and breathing library, self-sufficient and independent. See Pizzone (2017).

51 More broadly on Plato as an anti-Tzetzes, see Lovato (2022).

52 On Philoxenus, see LeVen (2014: ch. 3). On the traditions related to Plato's Sicilian 'adventure', see Swift Riginos (1976: 70–92).

53 See Tzetzes, *Histories* 10.358 ed. Leone (2007), and in particular 10.358.832–3: Ὁ δὲ σοφὸς Φιλόξενος, ὁ διθυραμβογράφος, | ἦν γένει μὲν Κυθήριος, ἐλεύθερος δὲ φύσιν, 'The wise Philoxenus, author of dithyrambs | was a Cypriot by family, but a free man by nature'. On this passage and the likely references to contemporary political and cultural events associated with Sicily and the Normans, see Rhoby and Zagklas (2011: 175–6) and Lovato (2022).

54 Several sources in Graeco-Roman times report this anecdote: Plu. *Demetr.* 5, D.L. 3.18, D.S. 15.6, Corn. Nep. *Dion* 2.

55 Tzetzes, *Histories* 10.355 ed. Leone (2007).

them,[56] selling them further. Finally, while selling his work, Plato kept also all the habits of a gift economy in its worst form, living off the goodwill of Dionysius at his Sicilian court.[57]

Not surprisingly, the commodification of Plato's body on the slave market mirrors the commodification of his dialogues and is a sort of retribution for disseminating the work of Pythagoreans against the authors' wishes.[58] Dionysius himself, according to Tzetzes' interpretation, was the first to sell or donate Plato as a slave.[59] From purchasing books, the next step to purchasing their very authors is a small one.

Inmaculada Pérez Martín has recently reviewed the book trade in Byzantium, arguing that 'there was no book trade as an activity independent of the book production process' and that books were always copied under commission.[60] This resonates with Tzetzes' anxiety about undue copying of his works, which he associates with unauthorized dissemination, and his tense relationship with copyists. However, the details he provides in the paratexts of the Vossianus, in the scholia on his letter collection and on the *Histories*, as well as in more desultory occasional poems, seem to suggest that texts could be copied and traded also without the author's consent.[61]

Unleashing the Tongue: Free Speech under Patrons

In this last section I will show how the communicative strategy at play in the paratexts of the Vossianus fits into the broader framework of Tzetzes' attempt to safeguard and centre his own voice. As seen above, in the

56 The source for Plato copying the dialogue format from Sophron is Timon of Phlius. In the *Silloi*, now lost, Timon made fun – using the first person and in dialogue with another philosopher Xenophanes – of the various philosophical schools. As pointed out by Massimo Di Marco (1989: 238), Tzetzes builds on fr. 54 by Timon, where it is said that Plato had bought a small and very expensive book, which he had then plagiarized to write the *Timaeus*. Di Marco does not believe that the more detailed information to be found in Tzetzes comes from Timon. However, since this is probably not the only passage where Tzetzes uses Timon and given that the *Silloi* are preserved only in scanty fragments, we cannot exclude the possibility that Tzetzes could rely on a more reliable source. But it is equally possible that he combined Timon with Diogenes Laertius (see n. 54 above), who, however, does not talk about plagiarism.

57 See Lovato (2022) on this point.

58 This view is further reinforced in *Histories* 10.362.988–1003 ed. Leone (2007), where Architas of Taranto, another Pythagorean, is introduced as one of Plato's buyers. This prompts Tzetzes to stress once again how Plato owed his best ideas to the books purchased for him by Dionysius in Syracuse. The main source is again Diogenes Laertius 3.9 and 18ff. combined with Plu. *Demetr.* 5.20.

59 Tzetzes, *Histories* 10.359.866 ed. Leone (2007).

60 Pérez Martín (2014: 39–40).

61 Scholion on the *Histories*, p. 159.8–23 ed. Leone (2007). The scholion, following the first letter to Epiphanios, is preserved by three manuscripts belonging to the second and later recension of the letters (b) and is printed in Leone's edition of the *Histories*.

hexameters at the end of the commentary on the *Progymnasmata*, Tzetzes depicts himself as the embodiment of *logos*, endowed with a voice that can validate (or not) Aphthonios' own voice. Emphasis on voice and tongue is in fact recurrent in Tzetzes' work. From the letter collection we learn that he had to face libel and slander early on in his career.[62] The prologue to the *Theogony* offers a compelling passage suggesting that Tzetzes had been somehow heavily silenced:

> οὕτω θαρρῶν ἐπεύχομαι καὶ λέγω παρρησίᾳ,
> σύν γε θεῷ δεσπόζοντι, κρατοῦντι τῶν ἁπάντων,
> κἂν νῦν ἀδίκων ὑπ' ἀνδρῶν, ἀνθρώπων ἀθεμίστων,
> ἄδικον ὀδυρόμενος ἀπάνθρωπον πενίαν,
> δεσμοῖς δεσμῶσαι σιωπῆς τὴν λαλιστάτην γλῶσσαν·
> καὶ παντελῶς ἂν ἄφωνος ἐκ τούτων ἐγενόμην,
> εἰ μή που σὺ διέρρηξας δεσμὰ τῆς ἀφωνίας,
> θερμῷ φαρμάκῳ τῷ χρυσῷ θάλπουσα τὴν πενίαν,
> ὑφ' ἧς τὰ κατατείνοντα νεῦρα περὶ τὴν γλῶτταν
> καταψυχθέντα περισσῶς τὴν μὲν φωνὴν ἐπεῖχον,
> δεινῶς δε τὸν ἐγκέφαλον ἠλιθιᾶν ἐποίουν·
> ἃ σὺ καλῶς ἐνθάλπουσα τοῖς τρόποις οἷσπερ εἶπον,
> δίδως μικρόν τι με λαλεῖν μηδ' ἠλιθιωθῆναι. (Tzetzes, *Theogony* 34–46 ed. Leone 2019)

> Thus I bravely vow and speak freely,
> with the help of God almighty, who rules over everything,
> even if, by the hand of unjust men, unlawful men,
> I mourn that unjust and inhuman poverty,
> to bind my most garrulous tongue with the bonds of silence;
> and I would have been made completely silent by those men,
> if you had not torn apart the bonds of silence,
> warming up with a hot balsam, the golden one, the poverty,
> which has made the nerves stretched around the tongue
> exceedingly cold, thus obstructing my speech,
> and making the brain terribly numb:
> but now you have warmed all this up nicely in the way I have said,
> allowing me to speak for a little bit instead of numbing away.[63]

62 See for instance *ep*. 63, p. 92 ed. Leone (1972).

63 Tzetzes stresses the short duration of his freedom of speech, as the *Theogony* is the result of an improvised performance, which only later – and if the patroness agrees to it – will be properly taken care of in writing and expanded on (see vv. 23–31). The title preserved by the manuscripts suggests that the text as we have it still reflects this first stage. For the manuscript tradition, see Leone (2019: v–xvi). Leone (2019: xiv) connects this passage with the episode of Berroia, given the reference to mischievous women we find at ll. 259ff. and to the malevolence of the Erinys at 418ff. On the *Theogony* and the relationship with the *sebastokratorissa* Irene, as well as with other poets working for her, such as Manasses, see Rhoby (2010: 166–9).

The tongue is very much present in its physicality in Tzetzes' conceptualization of free speech. His description combines social and anatomical/medical facts, resonating with the general interest for medicine shown by the intellectuals of the time.[64] These lines prove that Tzetzes' attitude towards patrons is not immutable but changes according to both his personal circumstances and the occasion as well as the genre of the work he is producing. The *Theogony* is a work of poetic improvisation. Therefore, the voice that Tzetzes is reclaiming for himself is a public one: it is literally the voice resounding in the physical space of the performance. It is a very different voice from the one 'unfolding' more steadily and at a slower pace (τολύπευσεν) on the pages of the Vossianus. In the *Theogony* as well, even if in a different way, Tzetzes deconstructs and reconstructs patronage as a space of freedom. Irene has given him a stage and his voice back. He is not afraid to use it, unapologetically and boastfully:

> κομπάζω τολμηρότερον καὶ λέγω παρρησίᾳ
> ὡς οὐδ' ἂν ἦσαν ἑκατὸν Ὅμηροι καὶ Μουσαῖοι,
> Ὀρφέες καὶ Ἡσίοδοι, Ἀντίμαχοι καὶ Λῖνοι
> καὶ πάντες ἄλλοι ποιηταὶ καὶ θεογονογράφοι,
> κρεῖττον ἂν ἔγραψαν ἐμοῦ τὰ περὶ τούτων πάντα.
> (Tzetzes, *Theogony* 27–31 ed. Leone 2019)

> I brag more daringly and I say freely
> that not even if there were hundreds of Homers and Musaei,
> Orphei and Hesiods, Antimachoi and Linoi,
> or even all the other poets and writers of theogonies,
> would they be able to write better than me on any of these matters.

Tzetzes' voice is very different from that of Manasses, who produced his chronicle for the same patroness. Manasses too mentions the authors and writers who came before him, but, unlike Tzetzes, he confines himself to 'selecting' (v. 24 ἡμεῖς προχειρισάμενοι) the most appropriate ones to fulfil the patroness' wishes.[65] Despite the overblown praise of Irene characterizing the first lines of the *Theogony*, Tzetzes does not point explicitly to any request of the patroness. It is only said that she has looked for the same content among other intellectuals (v. 20 πρὸς ἄλλοις ἐκζητεῖς). Tzetzes has the proactive role. Granted, Irene might or might not want to

64 See Magdalino ([1993] 2002: 361–4) with emphasis on the respect shown by Tzetzes for the medical profession.

65 Manasses, *Synopsis Chronike* ed. Lampsidis (1996); see Nilsson (2012: 179–80) and (2021: 146–7). On Tzetzes and his competitors, see Savio (2020) and Prodi (2022) with previous bibliography.

have everything explained better in writing after the performance (εἰ δέ ποτε θελήσειας μαθεῖν καὶ πλατυτέρως | κἀγώ σοι ταῦτα βουληθῶ μετὰ μελέτης γράφειν; 'Should you ever wish to learn these things at greater length, | I would write them for you with care'), but she appears as the passive receiver (v. 22) rather than the active force driving the poem.[66]

The emphasis on tongue and voice found in the *Theogony* shows that the well-known concept of ἀμφοτερογλωσσία, later developed by Tzetzes and usually translated as 'double-tonguedness' or 'ambivalence',[67] did not come out of the blue, nor was it simply a reworking of previous discursive traditions.[68] It is the result of a biographic trajectory with ups and downs, marked by a constant attempt to preserve his own voice in an environment that did not hesitate to react to aggression with aggression. Thus, ἀμφοτερογλωσσία is designed to meet challenges such as those described in the prologue of the *Theogony*. The notion is, for instance, crucial to Tzetzes' use of hermeneutics in the *Histories*. It provides the symbolic and linguistic space for self-commentary, and, at the same time, turns exegesis into a tool to negotiate power, with a mechanism that we also see at play in the book epigrams of the Vossianus.

But let us first examine the concept more closely. Tzetzes defines ἀμφοτερογλωσσία in a passage of the *Histories* that has received much attention from Byzantinists:[69]

> Σερβήλιος ἦν ὕπατος καὶ Καῖσαρ τῶν Ῥωμαίων.
> Μεθόδῳ δὲ δεινότητος ῥητορικῷ τῷ τρόπῳ,
> ἐκ Σερβηλίων τῆς γονῆς λέγω καὶ τὸν Σερβλίαν.
> Ὡς εἴπερ ἄλλος ἤθελε, Σέρβον Ἠλίαν εἶπεν.
> Τοῦτο γὰρ ῥήτορος ἀνδρὸς καὶ ἀμφοτερογλώσσου,
> καὶ πράγμασι καὶ κλήσεσι καὶ τοῖς λοιποῖς ὁμοίως
> πρὸς ἔπαινον καὶ ψόγον δε κεχρῆσθαι συμφερόντως.
> (Tzetzes, *Histories* 7.132.295–301 ed. Leone 2007)

> Servilius was a consul and Caesar of the Romans.
> By means of the technique of forcefulness, in a rhetorical way,

66 The tongue in the prologue of the *Theogony* is not severed – a customary punishment – but impeded. On the related symbolism, see Achmet 62.7–9 ed. Drexl (1909). On severing the tongue as mutilation, see Treadgold (1997: 310, 329, 339, 352, 392, 422).

67 Roilos (2006). In what follows, I will look at the notion from a different perspective. In fact, rather than to broader aesthetic concerns, I take *amphoteroglossia* as key to the way in which Tzetzes deals with the constraints of power.

68 Popular culture might again have played a role. The *Oneirocriticon* of Daniel (Oberhelman [2008: 73]) shows that dreaming of a double tongue was particularly welcome for lawyers and curators of big estates.

69 See Magdalino (1984: 61), Roilos (2006: 29–30), Agapitos (2017: 35–7), Alexiou (2018: 99).

> I declared Serblias to be of the family of the Servilii,
> just as someone else might wish to call him a Serbian Elias.
> For this is the talent of a man good in rhetoric and speaking in two ways,
> namely, to use situations and names and similar such things
> expediently for praise and for blame. (trans. Agapitos 2017)

These lines do not point so much to a generic ambiguity or hidden signification. Panagiotis Agapitos has argued that they play with the actual coexistence of two opposite but viable meanings, belonging in two different linguistic registers.[70] As aptly pointed out by Foteini Kolovou,[71] ἀμφοτερογλωσσία can refer broadly to rhetorical-linguistic practices, as in Tzetzes, but also more specifically to dialectic. Twelfth-century texts often emphasize – using ἀμφοτερογλώσσος among other terms – one's ability to sustain or refute an argument. This shade of meaning emerges in the praise speeches for the patriarch delivered by professors of rhetoric in the Patriarchal school during the Lazarus Saturday.[72] In praising the intellectual prowess of the Patriarch George Xiphilinos, George Tornikes presents dialectic, that is, ἀμφοτερογλωσσία, as his crowning virtue:

> καὶ πρό γε τούτων τὴν λαβυρινθώδη συλλογιστικὴν ἀνάλυσιν καὶ δυστέκμαρτον καὶ τὴν ἀμφοτερόγλωττον καὶ ἀντίστροφον τῇ ῥητορικῇ διαλεκτικὴν καὶ δικρόαν τὴν γλῶτταν προβεβλημένην ὀφιωδῶς, οὐ μικρὰν καὶ ταύτην εἰσφέρουσαν τὴν συντέλειαν εἰς τὴν τῆς ἀληθείας εὕρεσιν καὶ διάγνωσιν, εἰ μὴ καὶ μάλα μεγίστην εἰς ταύτην ἔχουσαν τὴν ῥοπήν. (George Tornikes, *Oration in Honour of George Xiphilinos* 2.9.205–10 ed. Loukaki 2005a)
>
> And above all, syllogistic analysis, which is like a labyrinth and is hard to disentangle, *and dialectic, which speaks both ways and is the counterpart of rhetoric* [Aristotle, *Rhetoric* 1354a] and, just like a snake, is characterized by a forked tongue; its contribution to the discovery and discernment of truth is not little, or perhaps it has even the greatest weight in it.

Along the same lines, a few years later, Nikephoros Chrysoberges praises John Kamateros' dialectics, referring to him as an ἀμφοτερογλώσσος.[73] Kamateros' ability becomes clear when he teaches or affirms theological principles, as well as when he refutes the forked tongues of his opponents.

70 Agapitos (2017: 35–7).
71 Kolovou (2006: 44–53).
72 See Loukaki (2005b).
73 Chrysoberges, *Oration on John Kamateros* 15.7 ed. Browning (1978: 119).

In these and other examples, ἀμφοτερογλωσσία has to do with maintaining an argument, as well as deploying the same weapons as one's opponent. Agapitos has shown that Tzetzes' use of the term differs slightly and is closer to rhetoric, understood as the practice of personal defence and attack, praise and blame. In the *Histories*, I argue, the notion of ἀμφοτερογλωσσία turns out to be intrinsically subversive as it paves the way for a kind of rhetorical hermeneutic that serves to negotiate power. In this respect it comes very close to the use of generic tropes we see at stake in the paratexts of the Vossianus.

At this point, I would like to examine more closely the passage from *Histories* 7. The lines quoted above come from the commentary on letter 18, addressed to the *mystikos* Nikephoros Serbilias around 1140. We do not know whether Nikephoros is the same person as the dedicatee of the Vossianus. This hypothesis cannot be proven beyond doubt.[74] The letter is an overblown plea for new accommodation, introduced by hyperbolic praise of the addressee.[75] Through a series of hyperbolic similes, Tzetzes embodies the persona of the destitute intellectual, framing himself as socially inferior to his patron. Yet, the cunning use of ἀμφοτερογλωσσία grants him a space to overturn this self-positioning. It is something more serious than a literary game revolving around the tool of rhetorical amplification.

On the one hand, the self-commentary exposes the rhetorical technique behind the hyperbolic genealogy of the *mystikos*, thus showing that Tzetzes' words ultimately have the power to aggrandize his prospective patron and shape his (social) reality. On the other hand, the self-commentary also uncovers the humble, possibly servile, origins of Nikephoros, thus reversing Tzetzes' own humiliating position. Here, ἀμφοτερογλωσσία has more to do with social pretence than dialectic sharpness. Through hermeneutic ingenuity, it offers a space and an opportunity of freedom for the (self-styled) marginalized intellectual.[76] Finally it also shows why Tzetzes' patrons might have had good reasons to be afraid of him, as hinted in the passages explored above.

Interestingly, the ambiguous meaning of ἀμφοτερογλωσσία as either 'dialectical sharpness' or 'pretence' was already inscribed in the word's origins, which accounts for its relevance to power relations. It was coined by Timon of Phlius in the third century BC to describe Zeno of Elea,

74 Scholia on the *Histories* pp. 31–4 ed. Leone (2007). See for a discussion Pizzone (2020c).
75 Tzetzes, *ep.* 18, 32.22–33.1 and 33.1–9 ed. Leone (1972).
76 It also raises once more serious questions regarding the face value of autobiographical statements.

traditionally regarded as the father of dialectic.[77] In Timon's usage, double-tonguedness is a term of faint praise, pointing both to Zeno's ability to argue for opposing conclusions and to his intrinsic deceitfulness. Given that Tzetzes knew and explicitly mentioned the work by Timon – the *Silloi* – that features the first recorded instance of ἀμφοτερογλώσσος, and that he had first-hand knowledge of Plutarch's *Parallel Lives*,[78] which also testify to Zeno's moniker, it is highly likely that these sources shaped his usage of the term.

Furthermore, in the late antique and early Byzantine tradition there is a slight but significant change in the way authors use Timon's description of Zeno. The sixth-century philosopher Olympiodoros interprets Zeno's ἀμφοτερογλωσσία as follows:

> Τοιοῦτος γὰρ ἦν ὁ Ζήνων, προσποιεῖσθαι ἱκανός, ὅς καὶ διὰ τοῦτο ἀμφοτερογλώσσος ἤκουεν, οὐχ ὅτι ἑκατέρῳ τῶν ἀντικειμένων συνηγόρει, ἀλλ' ὅτι προσεποιεῖτο. διὸ καί τινος τυράννου ἐρομένου αὐτὸν τοὺς σὺν αὐτῷ ἐπιβουλεύσαντας τῇ τυραννίδι τοὺς δορυφόρους αὐτοῦ ὑπέδειξεν, ὁ δὲ ἀνελὼν ἐκείνους ἑτοίμως ἀνῃρέθη. (Olympiodoros, *On Plato's Alcibiades* 140.12–16 ed. Westerink 1956)

> Such was Zeno, able to pretend, and therefore he was called *amphoteroglossos*, not because he could advocate two contrasting points of view, but because he was able to pretend. Therefore, when one tyrant asked him who had plotted together with him against tyranny, he indicated his bodyguards, and the tyrant immediately had them arrested and killed.

This story, reported by other sources as well, is a variation of an earlier anecdote told by Plutarch in which Zeno, caught plotting against the tyrant Demylus, spat his own tongue in the tyrant's face after biting it off himself.[79] The narrative shift is telling. The tongue, as conveyor of speech, grants the intellectuals freedom in the face of power. In Plutarch's story, it is severed to reassert independence. Zeno expresses his liberty by giving up the literal ability to speak, thus taking an overt position in contrast to power. However, in the late antique version of the anecdote, the tongue is symbolically duplicated. Zeno uses his verbal ability to negotiate the threats of a tyrannical power. While the story does not reveal whether Zeno had his life saved, sure enough, Zeno does not perform any act of

77 Fr. 45 Di Marco. The passage is quoted in Diogenes Laertius 9.25; cf. Plu. *Per.* 4.5. See Di Marco (1989: 212–14), with rich bibliography on the term.
78 See above, n. 50.
79 Plu. *ad Col.* 32.

clear and overt resistance. Power is fooled and secretly subverted rather than openly opposed. Equally the tongue is not severed but duplicated.

This more insidious approach to ἀμφοτερογλωσσία mirrors Tzetzes' attitude both in the *Histories* and in the book epigrams of the Vossianus. In the case of the *Histories* the duplication of his tongue is not just symbolic, since the organ materializes itself in the structure of the text, that is, in the text-commentary. Tzetzes has, quite literally, two voices, and therefore two tongues. Such an intrinsic ἀμφοτερογλωσσία grants him the opportunity to unveil the pretence of the letter collection,[80] the social conventions that are to be found in epistolary communication and the compromises faced by an intellectual struggling for patronage. The truth voiced by the prose text is contradicted by the voice of poetry.

Along the same lines, the paratexts of the Vossianus show a twofold double-tonguedness. On the one hand they reveal Tzetzes' freedom the very moment he expresses his gratitude towards his patrons. Through the couple Heracles–Eurystheus he reclaims superiority over the commissioner. Such a double-tonguedness is inherent in the text of the epigram. On the other hand, however, Tzetzes shows the same ambiguous attitude suspended between praise and blame also towards Aphthonios and Hermogenes. More than other Byzantine commentators, Tzetzes is highly critical of the rhetorical handbooks everyone in Byzantium read and used. In his commentaries we see the same discursive strategy sustaining the *Histories.* In the commentary on the *corpus Hermogenianum*, Tzetzes also comments in verse on a prosaic text, unpacking it, as it were, and pointing to its inherent contradictions. The hexameters at fol. 221v show beyond doubt that he positioned his exegesis in political verse to be within the sphere of poetic inspiration, so much so that he envisages the Muse climbing down to the lower regions of pentadecasyllables just for his sake.[81] The hexameters at fol. 30r, in turn, show the embodied *logos*, personified by Hermes the messenger, instantiating itself in the poetic text and heralding the prosaic voice of Aphthonios. Finally, metrical variety also contributes to challenging traditional expressive patterns: the more dignified heroic verse is here at the service of both prose and political verse. Semantic ambiguity, prose and verse, polymetry,[82] all build up ἀμφοτερογλωσσία and amplify Tzetzes' authorial voice.

80 Cf. Magdalino (1984: 61).
81 On Tzetzes as a poet and as a teacher, see van den Berg (2020).
82 On mixture of prose and verse as well as polymetry in this period, see Zagklas (2017) and (2018).

Bibliography

Adler, A. (ed.) (1928) *Suidae lexicon*, 4 vols. Leipzig.

Agapitos, P. A. (2017) 'John Tzetzes and the Blemish Examiners: A Byzantine Teacher on Schedography, Everyday Language and Writerly Disposition', *MEG* 17: 1–57.

Alexiou, M. (2018) *After Antiquity: Greek Language, Myth, and Metaphor*. Ithaca.

Bernard, F., and K. Demoen (2019) 'Book Epigrams', in *A Companion to Byzantine Poetry*, ed. W. Hörandner, A. Rhoby and N. Zagklas, 404–29. Brill's Companions to the Byzantine World 4. Leiden.

Bianconi, D. (2013) 'Libri e paratesti metrici a Bisanzio nell' XI secolo: In margine a una recente pubblicazione', *MEG* 13: 297–314.

Boissonade, J. F. (ed.) (1851) *Tzetzae allegoriae Iliadis accedunt Pselli allegoriae*. Paris (repr. Hildesheim 1967).

Bonis, K. (ed.) (1937) *Εὐθυμίου τοῦ Μαλάκη μητροπολίτου Νέων Πατρῶν Ὑπάτης τὰ σῳζόμενα*, 2 vols. Athens.

Braccini, T. (2009–10) 'Erudita invenzione: Riflessioni sulla *Piccola grande Iliade* di Giovanni Tzetze', *Incontri Triestini di Filologia Classica* 9: 153–73.

(2010) 'Mitografia e miturgia femminile a Bisanzio: Il caso di Giovanni Tzetze', *I Quaderni del Ramo d'Oro on-line* 3: 88–105.

Browning, R. (1978) 'An Unpublished Address of Nicephorus Chrysoberges to Patriarch John X Kamateros of 1202', *Études Byzantines* 5: 48–63.

Cavallo, G. (1992) *Libri, editori e pubblico nel mondo antico: Guida storica e critica*. Rome.

Cullhed, E. (2014) 'The Blind Bard and "I": Homeric Biography and Authorial Personas in the Twelfth Century', *BMGS* 38.1: 49–67.

(ed. and trans.) (2016) *Eustathios of Thessalonike: Commentary on Homer's Odyssey*, vol. 1: *On Rhapsodies* A–B. Studia Byzantina Upsaliensia 16. Uppsala.

Cunningham, I. C., and P. A. Hansen (ed.) (2009) *Hesychii Alexandrini lexicon*, vol. 4. Berlin.

D'Agostini, C. (2021) 'Mapping Empires: Re-appropriations of Ptolemy's *Geography* from the 12th to the 15th Century', PhD thesis, University of Southern Denmark.

D'Agostini, C., and A. Pizzone (2021) 'Clawing Rhetoric Back: Humor and Polemic in Tzetzes' Hexameters on the *Historiai*', *Parekbolai* 11: 123–38.

de Meyïer, K. A. (1955) *Codices Vossiani graeci et miscellanei*. Leiden.

Di Marco, M. (1989) *Timone di Fliunte: Silli*. Rome.

Drexl, F. X. (1909) *Achmets Traumbuch: Einleitung und Probe eines kritischen Textes*. Munich.

Drpić, I. (2013) 'Painter as Scribe: Artistic Identity and the *Arts* of *graphē* in Late *Byzantium*', *Word & Image* 29: 334–53.

Gibson, C. A. (2009) 'The Anonymous *Progymnasmata* in John Doxapatres' *Homiliae in Aphthonium*', *ByzZ* 102.1: 83–94.

(2019) 'Two Rhetorical Exercises on Ganymede in John Doxapatres' *Homiliae in Aphthonium*', *BMGS* 43.2: 181–93.

Grigoriadis, I. (2001) *Ιωάννης Τζέτζης· Επιστολαί. Μετάφραση*. Athens.

Iacobini, A. (2007) 'Il segno del possesso: committenti, destinatari, donatori nei manoscritti bizantini dell'età macedone', in *Bisanzio nell'età dei Macedoni: Forme della produzione letteraria e artistica. VIII Giornata di Studi Bizantini (Milano, 15–16 marzo 2005)*, ed. F. Conca and G. Fiaccadori, 151–94. Milan.

Jeffreys, E. M. (2019) 'Byzantine Poetry and Rhetoric', in *A Companion to Byzantine Poetry*, ed. W. Hörandner, A. Rhoby and N. Zagklas, 92–112. Brill's Companions to the Byzantine World 4. Leiden.

Kazhdan, A. P. (1985) 'The Concept of Freedom (eleutheria) and Slavery (duleia) in Byzantium', in *La notion de liberté au Moyen Age: Islam, Byzance, Occident*, ed. G. Makdisi, D. Sourdel and J. Sourdel-Thomine, 215–26. Paris.

Kolovou, F. (ed.) (2006) *Die Briefe des Eustathios von Thessalonike: Einleitung, Regesten, Text, Indizes*. Beiträge zur Altertumswissenschaft 239. Munich.

Lampsidis, O. (ed.) (1996) *Constantini Manassis Breviarium Chronicum*. Corpus Fontium Historiae Byzantinae 36. Athens.

Leone, P. L. M. (1969–70) 'Ioanni Tzetzae Iambi', *Rivista di Studi Bizantini e neoellenici* 6–7: 134–51.

(ed.) (1972) *Ioannis Tzetzae Epistulae*. Stuttgart.

(ed.) (1995) *Ioannis Tzetzae Carmina Iliaca*. Catania.

(ed.) (2007) *Ioannis Tzetzae Historiae*, 2nd ed. Galatina.

(ed.) (2019) *Ioannis Tzetzae Theogonia*. Lecce.

LeVen, P. A. (2014) *The Many-Headed Muse: Tradition and Innovation in Late Classical Greek Lyric Poetry*. Cambridge.

Loukaki, M. (ed.) (1996) *Grégoire Antiochos, Éloge du Patriarche Basile Kamatèros*. Paris.

(ed.) (2005a) *Discours annuels en l'honneur du patriarche Georges Xiphilin*. Monographies 18. Paris.

(2005b) 'Le samedi de Lazare et les éloges annuels du patriarche de Constantinople', in *Κλητόριον in Memory of Nikos Oikonomides*, ed. F. Evangelatou-Notara and T. Maniati-Kokkini, 327–46. Athens.

Lovato, V. F. (2017) 'La ricezione di Odisseo e di Omero presso Giovanni Tzetze e Eustazio di Tessalonica', PhD thesis, University of Turin–University of Lausanne.

(2021) 'Living by his Wit: Tzetzes' Aristophanic Variations on the Conundrums of a "Professional Writer"', *BMGS* 45.1: 25–41.

(2022) 'From Cato to Plato and back again: Friendship and Patronage in John Tzetzes' *Letters* and *Chiliades*', *C&M* 70: 59–98.

Luzzatto, M. J. (1999) *Tzetzes lettore di Tucidide: Note autografe sul Codice Heidelberg palatino greco 252*. Bari.

Magdalino, P. (1984) 'Byzantine Snobbery', in *The Byzantine Aristocracy, IX to XIII Centuries*, ed. M. Angold, 58–78. Oxford.

([1993] 2002) *The Empire of Manuel I Komnenos, 1143–1180*. Cambridge.

Meineke, A. (ed.) (1836) *Joannis Cinnami Epitome rerum ab Joanne et Alexio Comnenis gestarum*. Bonn.

Müller, K. (ed.) (1861) *Geographi Graeci minores*, vol. 2. Paris.

Nilsson, I. (2012) 'La douceur de dons abondants: Patronage et littérarité dans la Constantinople des Comnènes', in *La face caché de la littérature byzantine: Le texte en tant que message immédiat. Actes du colloque international, Paris 5–6–7 juin 2008*, ed. P. Odorico, 179–93. Dossiers byzantins 11. Paris.

Nilsson, I. (2021) *Writer and Occasion in Twelfth-Century Byzantium: The Authorial Voice of Constantine Manasses*. Cambridge.

Oberhelman, S. M. (2008) *Dreambooks in Byzantium: Six Oneirocritica in Translation, with Commentary and Introduction*. Aldershot.

Papathomopoulos, M. (ed.) (2007) *Εξήγησις Ιωάννου Γραμματικού του Τζέτζου εις την Ομήρου Ιλιάδα*. Athens.

Pérez Martín, I. (2014) 'Byzantine Books', in *The Cambridge Intellectual History of Byzantium*, ed. A. Kaldellis and N. Siniossoglou, 37–46. Cambridge.

Patillon, M. (ed.) (2009) *Corpus Rhetoricum, Tome II: Hermogène, Les états de cause*. Paris.

Pizzone, A. (2017) 'Tzetzes' *Historiai*: A Byzantine "Book of Memory"?', *BMGS* 41.2: 182–207.

(2020a) 'Bureaucratic Discourse, Signature and Authorship in John Tzetzes: A Comparative Perspective', *Acme* 73: 43–67.

(2020b) 'Saturno contro sul mare d'Ismaro: Una nuova fonte autobiografica per la vita di Giovanni Tzetze', in *Philoxenia: Viaggi e viaggiatori nella Grecia di ieri e di oggi*, ed. A. Capra, C. Nobili and S. Martinelli Tempesta, 75–94. Milan.

(2020c) 'Self-authorization and Strategies of Autography in John Tzetzes: The *Logismoi* Rediscovered', *GRBS* 60: 652–90.

(2022) 'Tzetzes and the *Prokatastasis*: A Tale of People, Manuscripts, and Performances', in *Τζετζικαὶ ἔρευναι*, ed. E. E. Prodi, 19–74. Eikasmos Studi Online 4. Bologna.

Porson, R. (ed.) (1822) *Φωτίου τοῦ πατριάρχου λέξεων συναγωγή*, vols. 1–2. Cambridge.

Prodi, E. E. (2022) 'Introduction: A Buffalo-eye View', in *Τζετζικαὶ ἔρευναι*, ed. E. E. Prodi, ix–xxxv. Eikasmos Studi Online 4. Bologna.

Rhoby, A. (2010) 'Ioannes Tzetzes als Auftragsdichter', *Graeco-Latina Bruniensia* 15: 155–70.

Rhoby, A., and N. Zagklas (2011) 'Zu einer möglichen Deutung von Πανιώτης', *JÖByz* 61: 171–7.

Roilos, P. (2006) *Amphoteroglossia: A Poetics of the Twelfth-Century Medieval Greek Novel*. Cambridge, MA.

Savio, M. (2020) *Screditare per valorizzare: Giovanni Tzetze e le sue fonti, i committenti e la concorrenza*. Rome.

Scheer, E. (ed.) (1881) *Lycophronis Alexandra*, 2 vols. Berlin.

Schneidewin, F. G., and E. L. von Leutsch (eds.) (1839) *Corpus paroemiographorum Graecorum*. Göttingen.

Swift Riginos, A. (1976) *Platonica: The Anecdotes Concerning the Life and Writings of Plato*. Leiden.

Tafel, T. L. F. (ed.) (1832) *Eustathii Metropolitae Thessalonicensis opuscula, accedunt Trapezuntinae historiae scriptores Panaretus et Eugenicus*. Frankfurt am Main.
Treadgold, W. (1997) *A History of the Byzantine State and Society*. Stanford, CA.
van den Berg, B. (2017) 'Eustathios on Homer's Narrative Art: The Homeric Gods and the Plot of the *Iliad*', in *Reading Eustathios of Thessalonike*, ed. F. Pontani, V. Katsaros and V. Sarris, 129–48. Berlin.
(2020) 'John Tzetzes as Didactic Poet and Learned Grammarian', *DOP* 74: 285–302.
van der Valk, M. (ed.) (1971–87) *Eustathii Archiepiscopi Thessalonicensis commentarii ad Homeri Iliadem pertinentes ad fidem codicis Laurentiani editi*, 4 vols. Leiden.
Westerink, G. L. (ed.) (1956) *Olympiodorus: Commentary on the First Alcibiades of Plato*. Amsterdam.
Zagklas, N. (2017) 'Experimenting with Prose and Verse in Twelfth-Century Byzantium: A Preliminary Study', *DOP* 71: 229–48.
(2018) 'Metrical *Polyeideia* and Generic Innovation in Twelfth Century: The Multimetric Cycles of Occasional Poetry', in *Middle and Late Byzantine Poetry: Texts and Contexts*, ed. A. Rhoby and N. Zagklas, 43–70. Byzantios: Studies in Byzantine History and Civilization 14. Turnhout.
(2019) '"How Many Verses Shall I Write and Say?": Poetry in the Komnenian Period (1081–1204)', in *A Companion to Byzantine Poetry*, ed. W. Hörandner, A. Rhoby and N. Zagklas, 237–63. Brill's Companions to the Byzantine World 4. Leiden.

CHAPTER 10

The Poetics of Patronage
*Constructing the Image of the Patron in Dedicatory Epigrams in Monumental Painting of the Komnenian Period in Greece**

Nektarios Zarras

Studying the epigrams which accompany donor representations in monumental painting from an art historical and archaeological perspective never ceases to fuel discussion. A key question relates to the patron and the way in which he/she is portrayed through text and image. The patron's decision to name himself and his family as *ktetors*, by using a poetic text, is frequently explained by scholars as being related to his educational level and social standing. This general assertion may help to explain the reasons for choosing to use a dedicatory epigram in the first place, but I do not think that it offers sufficient clues to explain the motives that influenced the content or to resolve other issues raised by research.[1] This chapter examines some of these issues through discussion of three characteristic dedicatory epigrams from central and northern Greece. First, the inscription from the Vytoumas monastery in Thessaly prompts consideration of the relationship between the text and the patron's image, and the *ktetoric* epigram is utilized to reconstruct the now-destroyed patronal representation. Second, the reappraisal of the *Deesis* epigram from the Vatopedi monastery on Mount Athos offers a new interpretation of the relationship of the persons mentioned in this text not only with the monastery, but also with the inscription itself. With respect to the third epigram, from the church

* I would like to express my thanks to the abbot of the Vatopedi monastery, Archimandrite Ephraim, for granting me permission to publish the photo from the *Mesonyktikon*. I am grateful to my colleague Ivan Drpić for his invaluable comments on an earlier version of the chapter. I thank also Stavros Mamaloukos, Maria Xenaki and Konstantinos Chryssogelos for their assistance. I am also indebted to Alexandra Doumas for editing the English text. The translations of the three dedicatory epigrams are mine.

1 For epigrammatic poetry in artworks and the role of the patron in dedicatory epigrams, in addition to the fundamental studies of Hörandner (2001), Lauxtermann (2003) and Rhoby (2009), (2010a) and (2014), see also Spingou (2012), Toth (2015), Drpić (2016a) and (2016b: 1–48), Drpić and Rhoby (2019).

of *Agioi Anargyroi* in Kastoria, the relationship between the poetic text, the symbolism of the space and the iconography is looked at as a whole. This research method for the Kastoria epigram, namely of examining the patron's views, the iconography and the space, which is applied here for the first time to the specific inscription, yields interesting evidence for the interaction between patron, poet and painter, while emphasis is placed on more personal aspects of the patronage. Furthermore, this third epigram offers an important insight into the deeper reasons for the patrons' choice of epigrammatic poetry.

Dedicatory Epigram and Patronal Iconography

The first epigram to be examined here is the dedicatory inscription from the Vytoumas monastery, which is located close to the town of Kalampaka in Thessaly. This monastery is dedicated to the Dormition of the Virgin and was founded in 1161.[2] Unfortunately, nothing remains of its Byzantine phase and the inscription itself is now lost, but its text is known to us from a seventeenth-century manuscript, kept in the monastery of the Transfiguration at Meteora:[3]

Τὸν ἀπερίγραπτόν σε τοῦ Π(ατ)ρ(ὸ)ς Λόγον
σὺν τῇ τεκούσῃ, παντάναξ, περιγράφω
τῇ κοσμοσώστῳ μητροπαρθένῳ κόρῃ·
ταύτῃ προσδείμ(ας) τόνδε τὸν δόμον πόθῳ
αἰτῶ θελήμων ὡς ἐνὸν λύσιν ὅπ(ως)
ἐν ἡμέρᾳ φεῦ κρίσε(ως) χρε(ῶν) λάβω
Ταρχανειώτης Κωνσταντῖνος ὁ λάτρης
σὺν τῇ συζύγῳ Ζωῇ δὲ τῇ κυρίᾳ
κλεινῷ σεβαστῷ λαμπρῷ τῷ Ἀνδρονίκῳ
εὐεργέτι<ν> τείνοντι χεῖρα μοι πάλαι.

You, the indescribable Logos of the Father,
Lord of all, along with your mother [lit. the one who gave birth to you],
the world-saving virgin-mother maiden, I depict.
After having erected this church for her with desire,
I ask with all my heart, as far as it is possible, that
on the Day of Judgement, alas, I may receive remission of my debts
– your servant Constantine Tarchaneiotes

2 Avraméa and Feissel (1987: 373–4). On the post-Byzantine monastery of Vytoumas, see Voyadjis (1998).
3 Rhoby (2009: 258–60).

along with my wife Lady Zoe
and with the glorious (and) brilliant *sebastos* Andronikos,
who offered me his beneficent hand in the past.[4]

This epigram is not only of interest in terms of *ktetoric* ideology, as it summarizes the expressive means of self-presentation of the patron and the way in which he is connected with his foundation, but also and primarily of iconographic interest. Here, we shall attempt to reconstruct the iconography of the donor representation in Vytoumas, on the basis of the epigram, which clearly accompanied the depiction of Tarchaneiotes or even of the other *ktetors*.

The *ktetor* Constantine Tarchaneiotes was most probably a member of the great Tarchaneiotes family, which is known mainly from lead seals.[5] He is the voice of the epigram, who is presented not only as founder but also as painter, which is a *topos* in dedicatory epigrams[6] and one of the principal elements of patronage, expressing the founder's profound relationship with his foundation. This relationship gives him the right to assume full responsibility for the monastery and to make decisions pertaining to it, such as engaging painters whose artistic activity in the foundation is projected through Tarchaneiotes and his patronage. In this way, the dedicatory epigram states within the space of the monastery the *ktetor*'s ownership of the foundation, and, through this relationship, defines the *ktetor*'s identity.

The question that arises at this point is: who is behind this portrait of the *ktetor*? In other words, who constructs the patron's image in the epigrams? In a discussion about the development of the metaphorical notion of the patron-narrator as painter-craftsman in dedicatory epigrams, it is essential to take one other important parameter into account, namely the poets, who very frequently adopt similar means to promote the works that they address to important persons.[7] Particularly illuminating are the cases of two leading twelfth-century poets. The first is Theodore Prodromos, who in his dedicatory epigrams for his novel *Rhodanthe and Dosikles*, dedicated to Nikephoros Bryennios, presents himself as a painter.[8] In this metaphorical scheme Prodromos is the painter who historiates the copy of the novel – he uses the verb ἐγράψατο ('he painted') – and calls upon Nikephoros to

4 Rhoby (2009: 258–70).
5 For Constantine Tarchaneiotes, see Leontiades (1998: 59–60).
6 Lauxtermann (2003: 162–6), Rhoby (2010b: 325–6), Spingou (2012: 178–228), Drpić (2014: 905–15) and (2016b: 71–117).
7 For the notion of the self-presentation of poets in the early Byzantine period, see Lauxtermann (2003: 37–9).
8 Agapitos (2000: 180), Jeffreys (2012).

judge his artistic product.[9] Equally important is the example of Eumathios Makrembolites, who compares his novel *Hysmine and Hysminias* to a painting and presents himself as the ὀψίγονος (late-born) painter who with his poetry erects a visual monument.[10] Since the poet himself compares his work to a painting and through a rhetorical device presents himself as painter, it is reasonable to assume that when he received the commission for a dedicatory epigram he transferred this promotion of self-portraiture to his client. This use of a common thought pattern and a rhetorical motif was applied systematically to the increasingly family-dominated aristocracy of the Komnenoi and the imperial propaganda they cultivated with regard to patronage.

The presentation of the patron as author of the text and painter of the accompanying image passed, via the poets, to another social class, that of the dignitaries who desired to be represented in public life not only as patrons but also as eloquent and artistic figures. The transfer of this multifarious role to the *ktetors* led to the composition of thousands of dedicatory epigrams, both for buildings and for portable artworks.[11] This development not only brought poets significant recognition for their contribution to shaping the patron's social images but also triggered changes in Byzantine society. The fact that state officials were presented as intellectuals and craftsmen of churches and sacred objects, which secured their salvation, gave, in my opinion, a huge impetus to patronage.

As the patron declares in the first lines of the Vytoumas inscription, he depicts a scene that includes Christ and the Virgin, and through the content of this image he expresses his desire for salvation on the Day of Judgement. As is often the case in dedicatory epigrams,[12] the text does not give a detailed description of an image but, occasioned by the epigram's soteriological content, a synoptic presentation of the figures in the representation. With the help of the poet's text, the state official, Tarchaneiotes, claims that he paints and offers his creation to God. What he really does is to express his faith through the status of dedicator and his hopes for the salvation of his soul.[13] The reference to the Second Coming in the sixth line

9 In this case the verb ἐγράψατο also means to write and has something of a double meaning. I thank Nikos Zagklas for this comment.

10 Agapitos (2000: 182–4). See also the *ekphrasis* of Manasses on the mosaic of the earth in the palace. See Lampsidis (1991: esp. 203–4).

11 Drpić (2016b: 67–117).

12 Lauxtermann (2003: 160).

13 These are the general ideas of reciprocation and anticipation, which are fundamental in devotional gift-giving and in dedicatory epigrams. On these principles in patronage, see Drpić (2016b: 244–61) with bibliography.

and the emphasis on the soteriological role of the Virgin, in combination with addressing Christ as Word of the Father (*Logos*), suggest an image of eschatological content, which is a structural element in donor epigrams.[14] Although the possibility of a depiction of the Virgin with the Christ-Child cannot be excluded, I propose that the most likely representation described in the Vytoumas inscription is that of the Virgin *Paraklesis* or *Eleousa* and Christ, in which the Mother of God converses and intercedes with her Son for the salvation of all mankind.[15] The intercessory and eschatological character of the Panagia *Paraklesis* explains why, from the time of its appearance in painting, it was used in donor compositions, since as text and image it expresses the *ktetor*'s deep desire for salvation.[16] Apart from the direct correlation of the *Paraklesis* with patronage iconography, the text on the scroll of the Virgin acquires, already from the eleventh–twelfth centuries, personal content expressing private devotion and often mentions the names of renowned individuals and patrons.[17]

The relationship between the Panagia *Paraklesis* scene and the donor inscription of the Vytoumas monastery is reinforced not only by the iconographic elements that emerge from the text, but also by the meaning and the vocabulary of the epigram.[18] The address to Christ as *Logos* (The Word), a clear reference to his divine nature, links the Vytoumas epigram to the dialogic text that is encountered constantly on the scroll of the Virgin *Paraklesis*.[19] Moreover, the word κοσμοσώστῳ in Vytoumas is fully attuned to the soteriological character of the *Deesis* of the Virgin,

14 Rhoby (2010b: esp. 319–25, 330–2).

15 See Djordjević and Marković (2000–1: 13–47) with bibliography. See also Drpić and Rhoby (2019: 430–55).

16 In monumental painting of this period the Virgin *Paraklesis* intercedes on behalf of the donors, either in direct relationship to them, as in the fresco in Saint George at Kurbinovo and the mosaic in the church of Saint Mary of the Admiral (1146–51) in Palermo (Martorana), or in relation to the dedicatory inscription, as in the Panagia of Arakas at Lagoudera (1192) in Cyprus. See Djordjević and Marković (2000–1: 18, fig. 9), Rhoby (2009: 323–30, 333, 391) with bibliography. See also Drpić (2016b: fig. 2.9), Konstantinidi (2018: 57–8, 69–70).

17 Cited as characteristic cases are the names of *ktetors* George of Antioch in Martorana and later Irene Petraliphina on the thirteenth-century revetment of the Spoleto icon originally dated to the eleventh century. See Drpić (2016b: 80–1), Djordjević and Marković (2000–1: 19, fig. 11a). In the Enkleistra of Saint Neophytos (1183) the homonymous *ktetor* is depicted below the scene of the *Deesis*. See Mango and Hawkins (1966: 180–2, figs. 95–7).

18 On the basis of the text of the fourth of the six epigrams on a scene, written by an unknown patrician, Lauxtermann (2003: 167–9) thinks that it describes the Virgin *Paraklesis* interceding on behalf of the donor Constantine VII.

19 As for example on the scroll of the Virgin *Paraklesis* in the church of *Agioi Anargyroi* in Kastoria. See Djordjević and Marković (2000–1: 19).

which refers either to the salvation of the world[20] or to the *ktetors* of monuments, as is the case in our epigram. Also of particular interest is the similarity between the phrase, rare for inscriptions, μητροπαρθένῳ κόρη and the phrase Λητὰς προσάγει μητρικὰς ἡ Παρθένος ('The Virgin offers her motherly entreaties'), which is written on the scroll of the Virgin *Eleousa*, represented in the narthex of the Panagia Phorbiotissa church on Cyprus.[21] The Virgin's scroll is visible on a layer of wall-paintings dated to 1322/3, but it is very possible that it copies the text that existed on the earlier Middle Byzantine layer. A similar phrase, which is linked directly to patronal iconography, is encountered in the Enkleistra of Saint Neophytos (1183). In the *Deesis* scene there, the text on the scroll, which is next to the kneeling figure of the *ktetor* Neophytos, opens with the phrase: Μ(ητ)ρικαὶς Χ(ριστ) ἐ λιταὶς ... ('with motherly entreaties, Christ, ...').[22] It could be argued that for the Vytoumas monastery, the *ktetor* Tarchaneiotes commissioned – very possibly in collaboration with the painter – the Panagia *Paraklesis* scene and that the author of the inscription, when writing the opening lines, was possibly inspired by this *Deesis* (?) scene and the text on the Virgin's scroll, as established in the iconography. This argument is based on the similarity observed in the vocabulary of the inscription to that of the text on the Virgin's scroll. As Andreas Rhoby has pointed out, the poem on the scroll of the Virgin is based on dialogic passages from the intercessory hymns of Orthodox liturgical poetry, which were read in monasteries.[23] It is therefore reasonable to argue that the dialogic text influenced the vocabulary of the inscription.

From the fourth line onwards, the content of the epigram changes completely in style and aims at stressing a different aspect of the *ktetor*'s personality, more spiritual; it discloses the motive for the patronage, which is Tarchaneiotes' desire for salvation. This difference in content, by promoting the *ktetor*'s activity and his faith as prerequisites for hope of eternal life, is the principal element in the structure of donor epigrams.[24] Tarchaneiotes' deep personal relationship with his foundation grants him, as founder, a dominant role in the text. In a strictly personal tone, denoted by the verbs

20 The meaning of the word is given by the phrase ΟΤΙ ΥΠΕΡ ΤΟΥ ΚΟCΜΟΥ ΔΕΟΜΑΙ on the scroll held by the Virgin in the mosaic representation with Saint Theodore, in the basilica of Saint Demetrios in Thessalonike. For the text, see Djordjević and Marković (2000–1: 17–18, fig. 8).

21 Rhoby (2009: 346–7), Ševčenko (2012: 85, fig. 3.12).

22 Mango and Hawkins (1966: 181–2), Rhoby (2009: 356–7).

23 Rhoby (2009: 329–31). See also Agapitos (2018: 94–6).

24 Rhoby (2010b: 318–19). Faith is also a prerequisite of the high standard of artistic creation, as is frequently the case in donor epigrams. See Hörandner (2001: 122).

in the first person singular αἰτῶ and λάβω, Tarchaneiotes expresses not only a petition for admission to heaven, but also his confidence that, because of his personal devotion and his high office, he will gain eternal life on the Day of Judgement.[25] Moreover, Tarchaneiotes sets himself apart from the other two *ktetors* by putting himself first, as well as by characterizing himself alone as *latres* (worshipper).[26] The idea of the individual salvation of Tarchaneiotes' soul is overt in lines 4–7 of the Vytoumas epigram and is linked directly to the same notion as is expressed in private monastic foundations.[27] By contrast, the salvation of the rest of the donors mentioned in epigrams, be they spouses and relatives or various kinds of peers, whose names follow, as in the case of Vytoumas, is referred to in summary manner at the end of the texts. The reference to Andronikos,[28] who must have been a renowned official, as denoted by the words κλεινῷ and λαμπρῷ, should also be interpreted in the sense of kinsman or close friend and colleague. The first adjective is rare in dedicatory inscriptions and is used to underscore the prestige of important religious and military dignitaries.[29]

On the basis of the descriptive epigram in the Vytoumas monastery, I suggest that the dedicatory representation would have included the Virgin, probably holding a scroll, and Christ-Logos, possibly enthroned or standing or within a *segmentum coeli*. The three donors, Tarchaneiotes, his wife Zoe and probably the *sebastos* Andronikos, would have completed the *Deesis* scene, according to the iconographic scheme of multi-figured dedicatory compositions, such as those surviving from the tenth and eleventh centuries in Cappadocia.[30] The continuation of this

25 Tarchaneiotes' confidence outdoes even that of the powerful dignitary Basil the Nothos, who, with the verb αἰτῶ, requests salvation. For Basil's request, see Lauxtermann (2003: 164–5).

26 The word is used for both male and female patrons; see Rhoby (2009: 162, 243) and (2014: 516, 576).

27 The same view on salvation is also expressed in *Typika* with the memorial services of the *ktetors* in their monastic foundations; see Thomas and Constantinides Hero (2000: 493, 544–6, 732, 742).

28 For an attempt to identify Andronikos with known persons of the period who bore the title *sebastos*, see Avraméa and Feissel (1987: 373).

29 The word κλεινῷ is used with this meaning in the Middle Byzantine period, both for bishops and military officers. See Rhoby (2010a: 369–70) and (2014: 225, 312). See also Drpić (2016a: 68).

30 Already by the tenth century Cappadocia was an important centre for early iconography of *ktetors*, with several examples of many-figured donor compositions, such as those in the so-called Grand Pigeonnier church (963–9), in Çavusin and the portraits in Karabaş kilise, in Aziözü and in Ayvali Köy. From the eleventh century on, donor iconography developed to a considerable degree, with representations of dignitaries, aristocrats and other officials playing a significant role in the iconographic programme of churches. In this period there is also an increase in donor compositions in which representations with one or more figures are depicted in *Deesis* scenes or in direct relation to the Virgin and Christ. I cite indicatively the Karanlik kilise (Göreme 23), Carikli kilise (Göreme 22), the Kale kilisesi, the church of dervis Akin and the church of Saint Basil (Göreme 18). For depictions of patrons in the above monuments, see Bernardini (1992), Ousterhout (1999: 72, fig. 9), Jolivet-Lévy (1998) and (2001: 55–90).

patronal iconography is obvious in many examples from the thirteenth and fourteenth centuries in Serbia.[31]

Of analogous interest for the relationship between image and text, as we saw in the Vytoumas epigram, is the dedicatory epigram surrounding the representation of the *Deesis* in the Vatopedi monastery on Mount Athos (Figure 10.1).[32] The *Deesis* is placed above the west entrance of the *Mesonyktikon*[33] of the *katholikon* and the epigram runs as follows:

Τὰ πρὶν ἀκαλλῆ καὶ ῥυέντα τῷ χρόνῳ
ψηφῖσι χρυσαῖς καὶ λαμπρῶς βεβαμμέναις
φαιδρῶς ἀγλαῶς κατεκοσμήθη λίαν
σπουδῇ πόνῳ τε καὶ πόθῳ διαπύρῳ
τοῦ ποιμενάρχου τῆσδε τῆς μονῆς, Λόγε,
Ἰωαννικίου τε τοῦ τρισολβίου
ᾧ καὶ παρέξοις σὴν βασιλείαν χάριν
ταῖς ἱκεσίαις πανάγνου καὶ Προδρόμου·
ταῦτα μοναχὸς Σωφρόνιος νῦν λέγει.

What earlier used to be deprived of beauty and decayed by time
was brightly and splendidly decorated
with golden and radiantly coloured stones
thanks to the effort, labour, and fiery desire
of the abbot of this convent, O Word,
Ioannikios the thrice-blessed
to whom may you grant your kingdom out of mercy
through the supplications of the All-Chaste (i.e. Virgin) and the Forerunner.
This is what the monk Sophronios says now.

The epigram has been discussed extensively,[34] but I would like to raise some new points regarding its interpretation and to re-examine the role of historical figures referred to in the text of the mosaic representation. The inscription starts with a reference to the destructive work of time, which the abbot Ioannikios ardently desires to rectify. The notion of destruction of man's works either by natural causes or hostile forces is a topos in the opening lines of dedicatory epigrams[35] and a rhetorical motif of clearly ideological orientation. The magnitude and ugliness of the destruction is

31 See Papamastorakis (1996: figs. 26–34).
32 On the text, see Millet, Pargoire and Petit (1904: 15), Mamaloukos (2001: 256–7), Rhoby (2009: 381–2) with bibliography.
33 Mamaloukos (2001: 51–2).
34 I cite indicatively Steppan (1994: 100–1), Tsigaridas (1996: 224, 226), Paul (2008: 65–6), Rhoby (2009: 381–5) with bibliography. See recently, Zarras (2019: 20), Kalopissi-Verti (2022).
35 See collected examples in Rhoby (2009: 383–5) and (2010b: 326–7) with bibliography.

Fig 10.1 Mount Athos, Vatopedi Monastery, *Deesis* (Vatopediou Monastery)

contrasted to the creative presence of the *ktetor*, who intervenes to stop the damage and to repair and restore the monument or works of smaller scale to their initial state and natural beauty, as emerges from the words ἀκαλλῆ and κατεκοσμήθη λίαν. These phrases refer to the decoration and hint very possibly at the representation that existed previously in the *Mesonyktikon* and which is related to the original phase of the monastery's construction.[36] In the Vatopedi epigram the rhetorical motif of the antithesis between destructive time, which has deprived the mosaic representation of its spiritual and material splendour, and the new construction with the beauty of the precious materials, places greater emphasis on justifying the abbot's patronage.[37]

Ioannikios' interest in decorating the church with mosaics emerges from the second and third lines of the inscription and mainly from the fourth line, where the abbot's overall responsibility for creating the representation is made apparent. The words πόθῳ διαπύρῳ declare his deep faith as precondition of the patronage and are quite common in dedicatory inscriptions.[38] The phrase σπουδῇ πόνῳ underlines the importance of organi-

36 Tsigaridas (1996: 226) argues that the representation pre-existing that of *Deesis* probably had the same subject. See also Mamaloukos (2001: 205–6).

37 See Rhoby (2010b: 316, 326–8). On references to the beauty, the quality and, indirectly, the cost of the materials, common in votive and secular epigrams, see Spingou (2012: 186–7).

38 Lauxtermann (2003: 163–4); Rhoby (2009: 162–5, 276, 318, 323, 342), (2010b: 317–18) and (2014: 233, 261, 316, 586, 674, 720); Drpić (2016b: 296–331).

zation in executing the donation, which is linked with Ioannikios' high office and role as abbot of the monastery and patron of its decoration. The emphasis on the patron's responsibility and effort for the decoration counterbalances what Ioannikios expects in return, namely his redemption from all sins and his salvation.[39] The personality, the aesthetic preferences and the spiritual perceptions of Ioannikios are expressed in the choice of the specific representation of the *Deesis* and the text of the inscription. In my opinion, the abbot made a decisive contribution to both the final content of the epigram and the imagery of the dedicatory mosaic.

In speaking about the abbot of the monastery, I take this opportunity to air some views that suggest a different interpretation of the epigram from that which prevails in current scholarly discussions. According to the interpretation I suggest, a new relationship between the inscription and the historical personages of the monastery emerges. It has been maintained that Ioannikios was dead at the time the decoration was executed and that the monk Sophronios, who wrote the epigram, as is declared in the last line, was abbot of the Vatopedi monastery after Ioannikios' death.[40] In my view, the epigram states explicitly that Sophronios is a monk, not an abbot, and leaves no leeway for misinterpretation that he is an abbot signing the dedicatory inscription as a monk, as an indication of humility. In dedicatory inscriptions there are other expressions that indicate an abbot's humility, such as humble, servant or suppliant.[41] My hypothesis that Sophronios was not the abbot at the time the decoration was executed is further supported by important pieces of evidence from textual sources. It is telling that in the list of abbots of the Vatopedi monastery there is no mention of a Sophronios, whereas, on the contrary, Ioannikios is referred to as abbot.[42] Furthermore, Ioannikios is also mentioned with the same status in the questionable information relating to the problem of the Vlachs on the Holy Mountain and as participant in an embassy of Athonite monks in 1094, during the reign of Emperor Alexios I Komnenos.[43] The view that Ioannikios was dead was based on the word τρισόλβιος (thrice-

39 The patron's donation through πόνος and μόχθος in return for his redemption is a topos in the structure of dedicatory epigrams. See Rhoby (2010b: 321–2).

40 Steppan (1994: 100–1).

41 As in the inscription in the church of Saint Mamas on Naxos and in several other examples; see Rhoby (2009: 383), (2010a: 144) and (2014: 294, 500). See also Spingou (2012: 203–5).

42 Bompaire et al. (2001: 51).

43 Millet, Pargoire and Petit (1904: 47), Mamaloukos (1996: 116), Tsigaridas (1996: 226), Müller (2005: 41–3), Rhoby (2009: 382). However, it has been pointed out in research that the specific information about the Vlachs is problematical from a historical standpoint. It is noteworthy that the abbacy of Ioannikios of the late eleventh and early twelfth centuries is also included in later lists of abbots of the Vatopedi monastery, which copy Byzantine lists. See Tsigaridas (1996: 336, n. 24).

blessed), which was regarded as being used only for deceased persons.[44] However, this is not unequivocally correct, because τρισόλβιος is also used in twelfth-century works addressed to individuals who are still alive. For example, it is used twice in the historical poems of Theodore Prodromos and indeed for cases totally opposite to the meaning of τρισόλβιος in Vatopedi.[45] Consequently, this epithet is not *ipso facto* sufficient to show that Ioannikios was dead at the time the *Deesis* mosaic was completed but needs to be combined with other evidence, which can be summarized as follows: firstly, the depiction of John the Forerunner in the *Deesis* reinforces the funerary implications of τρισόλβιος; secondly, the eschatological text in the Gospel of the enthroned Christ;[46] and thirdly, the death of Ioannikios is strengthened by the last verse, which is of crucial importance for understanding the text and the role of Sophronios.

The phrase ταῦτα … νῦν λέγει in the last line of the Vatopedi epigram and other similar expressions are very often used at the end of dedicatory epigrams, together with the name of the patron or the donor.[47] In contrast to the word πρίν at the beginning of the epigram, which refers to the period before the act of patronage, the word νῦν at the end of the epigram emphasizes the time of Sophronios' completion of it, which was occasioned by the execution of the mosaic.[48] In the Vatopedi epigram the word νῦν denotes the symbolic capture of the moment and the act of donation. Therefore, it is of particular significance for donor epigrams because it is a rare piece of evidence that the epigram was composed when it was clear what the actual mosaic would look like.[49] The monk Sophronios appears at the end of the inscription as another individual who addresses the readers. I would argue that Sophronios is an educated monk, possibly high up in the hierarchy of the Vatopedi community, who is responsible for the completion of the decoration and the composition of the epigram.[50] If he did not write the epigram himself, he commissioned another epigrammatist to

44 Steppan (1994: 100).

45 Τρισευτυχής, τρισεύδαιμον καὶ τρισολβία νύμφη ἐκ δεξιῶν σου τῷ καλῷ παράστηθι νυμφίῳ (*Historical Poem* 43d.1–2 ed. Hörandner [1974]); ἀλλ' ὦ μεγίστη γυναικῶν, ὦ τρισολβιωτάτη (*Historical Poem* 44.66 ed. Hörandner [1974]).

46 On the content of this text, see Kalopissi-Verti (2022: 1443).

47 Drpić (2016b: 85, 91, 291, 296, 368, 379). See also examples in Rhoby (2018: 132, n.119).

48 For the use of νῦν in dedicatory epigrams, see also Spingou (2012: 228–9).

49 In several cases it is not clear whether the syntax of donor epigrams is correlated with the place or the time of creation of the representations on which they comment, while in other cases inconsistency is observed between text and image. See Rhoby (2010b: 325) and (2011: 326) with examples.

50 I proposed this interpretation of the last verse in my paper presented at the X Meeting of Greek Byzantinists at Ioannina in 2019. See Zarras (2019: 20). This view is adopted by Kalopissi-Verti (2022: 1441, 1445).

do so. Whatever the case, the last line was added intentionally by Sophronios to state his name and make known his identity,[51] defining as νῦν his own present, which is temporally limited to the time of enunciation (νῦν λέγει). This close relation of Sophronios to the patronage of the abbot Ioannikios is declared in the last line of the epigram, which gives Sophronios the status of the second patron, who successfully accomplished the dedicatory composition that had started under Ioannikios. Sophronios praises Abbot Ioannikios as patron and seeks his salvation, using the eschatological symbolism of the *Deesis*. The iconographic scheme is described within the epigram and the praised abbot is included in the visual narrative together with the figures of the Virgin and John the Forerunner. On the basis of what has been said, the completion of the dedicatory composition as text and image in the *Mesonyktikon* of Vatopedi can be dated to the last years of the eleventh century and after 1094, the year in which there is the last mention of Ioannikios.[52]

Just as in the case of Vytoumas, this epigram is inspired by the painting and the patron, who projects his personality through the sophisticated coexistence of the arts of poetry and painting. I think it is obvious that the phrase ταῖς ἱκεσίαις πανάγνου καὶ Προδρόμου is linked directly with the *Deesis* scene, which also influenced the vocabulary of the epigram. The depiction of the *Deesis* confirms the relationship between epigram and image and strengthens the argumentation that has been presented with regard to the Vytoumas epigram for the interdependence of image and text. Consequently, it seems that in several epigrams one of the ways of projecting the patron is to connect him with the representation accompanying the text. The epigram places the patron within the soteriological character of the representation by frequently using an iconographic vocabulary that adds to the poem elements of descriptive epigrams. These poems can be considered as a particular subcategory of the literary genre of *ekphrasis*. However, I would argue that dedicatory epigrams should not be considered *ekphraseis per se*.[53] Rather, as texts closely connected with the depiction of *ktetors* in wider compositions, they include iconographic elements that are frequently described exactly, as is the case here. Due to the description of the iconographic elements that correspond to reality, it can be argued that elements of *ekphrasis* are included in the Vatopedi epigram,

51 In the problematical case of the Melbourne Gospels (second quarter of twelfth century), again in the last line Theophanes stresses his close relationship with the donation. See Ševčenko (2006: 334–43, esp. 335–7).

52 Tsigaridas (1996: 226–7, 230) dates the mosaic to the early twelfth century.

53 See Paul (2008: 65–6).

as has been maintained for other cases of donor epigrams.[54] The direct association of text and image within the donor composition creates a dynamic relationship in which the text describes the image and the image animates the text. The epigrams in Vytoumas and Vatopedi place the patron in the representation and demonstrate that these texts can reveal the donor portraits or contribute to the restoration of the destroyed images.[55] By reading an epigram that accompanies a destroyed representation we may not be able to reconstruct the iconographic details of the lost artwork, but we do have the possibility of reconstructing its general iconographic scheme. This artistic aspect of the epigrams was known in Byzantine times and it is to this that they owe their importance, because they are able to reveal iconographic elements, as is pointed out by Maximos Planoudes, occasioned by his epigram for Theodora Raoulaina Palaiologina.[56]

Epigram, Piety, Painting and Space

The role of the dedicatory text and image in projecting the person of the *ktetor* attains one of its strongest expressions in the metrical inscriptions in the church of the *Agioi Anargyroi* at Kastoria, which was founded by Theodore Lemniotes and his family in the last quarter of the twelfth century.[57] The church and Theodore Lemniotes articulate a rare and fascinating history of the relationship between founder and foundation, which has received little scholarly attention. For years now, the epigraphic material in the *Agioi Anargyroi* has raised critical questions about the presence and the role of the *ktetor* in the inscriptions, which call for further interpretation.[58]

The two long dedicatory inscriptions in the north aisle and the narthex of the church are among the most characteristic in Middle Byzantine monumental painting and survive almost intact *in situ*. They have been examined from a philological standpoint,[59] but there are still several other issues that should be addressed, such as the relation of the epigrams to the

54 Agapitos (2018: 94).

55 For a different view, see Lauxtermann (2003: 160).

56 Rhoby (2011: 318, n. 10) with bibliography.

57 On the *Agioi Anargyroi*, see primarily Hadermann-Misguich (1979: 262–4), Mouriki (1981: 108–9), Pelekanidis and Chatzidakis (1992: 22–49), Drakopoulou (1997: 44–56, figs. 25–31) with bibliography. On Theodore Lemniotes, see Kyriakoudis (1980/1) and Panayotidi (2006: 159–61) with bibliography.

58 Research on patronage in the church of the Saints Anargyroi has concentrated mainly on the donor representation of the Lemniotes family, on the south wall of the north aisle. I mention indicatively Drakopoulou (1997: 28–31) and Panayotidi (2006: 157–67) with bibliography.

59 Rhoby (2009: 162–8) and (2010b: 316–18, 320).

space and the iconographic programme, and the projection of Theodore Lemniotes and his family in the context of the ideology of patronage in the period. The epigraphic material in *Agioi Anargyroi* is important also for eliciting the deeper reasons why the patrons chose dedicatory epigrams.

I shall focus on the inscription on the west wall of the north aisle, above the door leading into the narthex, while I will comment on the epigram on the east wall of the narthex only briefly. The two inscriptions make up one of the most important groups of Byzantine dedicatory epigrams.[60] They offer valuable information about the interrelation between the founder and his foundation, and, by extension, the interaction of patron, poet and painter. The inscription in the north aisle runs as follows (Figure 10.2):

Ἔφθασα μὲν γράψαι σε πρὶν ἐν καρδίᾳ,
πολύτλα μάρτυ, μυστικαῖς β[αφαῖς] πόθου·
τανῦν δὲ καὶ [χρώμασιν ὑλι]κωτέ[ροις]
τῶν θαυμάτων σου ζωγραφῶ τὰς εἰκόνας,
δι᾽ ὧν με πολλ(ῶν) ἐρρύσω σ[υγκυρ]μάτ(ων)
πολύν φερόντ(ων) τῶ[ν κ]ακῶν μοι τον σ[άλον]·
ἐκεῖθεν αὐτῶν ἐκ βρεφικῶν σπαργάν(ων)
σε προστάτην ἔσχηκα φύλακ[α .....]
ῥύστην βοηθὸν [ἐν ζάλαις ταῖς] τοῦ βίου·
σύ μοι, Γεώ[ργιε], τῶν λαθῶν εὑρέθης·
σύ μοι παρέσχες χαρμονῆς ἀντλεῖν βί(ον)·
σύ μοι [............................] μέχρι·
ἀνθ᾽ [ὧν τὰ σεπτὰ στηλιτεύω] σου πάθη
ἐ[πί] τε ναοῦ [καὶ] Θ(εο)ῦ θείου τόπου
ζητῶν κακεῖσε σὴν ἀρωγὴν ἐν κρίσει
Θεόδωρος σὸς οἰκέτης Λημ[νιώ]της.

Earlier I depicted you in my heart,
much-enduring martyr, with the mystical dyes of affection.
But now, I also paint with more material colours
the images of your miracles,
through which you rescued me from many vicissitudes of fate,
which brought me the severe storm of evils.
Ever since I was still in my swaddling clothes
I have had you as my protector, guardian […]
eager saviour [in the turmoils] of life.
You, George, you proved to be saviour from my sins.
You granted me the opportunity to make the most of a life of joy.
You to me [.....................] until.
In return [I make a visual record] of your holy sufferings

60 Rhoby (2009: 161–7) and (2010b: 324–5) with bibliography.

Fig 10.2 Kastoria, Sts. Anargyroi, inscription in the north aisle (Nektarios Zarras)

in the church and the divine space of God,
asking for your help in the hereafter on the Day of Judgement.
Your servant, Theodore Lemniotes.

In the first line Lemniotes, with a terse yet touching declaration, voices the intensity of his relationship with Saint George, which led him to love the saint so deeply that, as he says, he painted him in his heart. This expression of love sparked the founder's desire to depict the life of the saint, who in the second verse is characterized as πολύτλα. This is a Homeric word that translates as 'much enduring' and is used of Odysseus,[61] denoting the one who suffers and is tortured, but who endures and triumphs in the end. The function of the specific word is nodal, because in the continuation of the text its meaning is transferred to the founder himself.

The narrativity of the text is based on the similarities between the life of Saint George and that of Lemniotes. The epigram, in the voice of the patron and addressed to Saint George, continues with a brief autobiographical introduction in which the founder justifies his patronage through the difficulties of his personal life.[62] The retrospection in the first part of the

61 E.g. *Iliad* 8.97, 9.676; *Odyssey* 5.171, 6.1, 7.1.

62 Drpić (2016b: 93–6). This is a common motif in epigrams, which is related to the same notion as is found in the *ktetorika typika* of monastic foundations. See Mullet (2004: 129–33).

epigram to Lemniotes' past life, from an early age, functions through recollection, which is particularly important as a concept of time in dedicatory epigrams. The reference to the *ketor*'s life, as well as to the protection he has found in his patron saint, gives the epigram the form of a prayer.

These elements in the inscription of the north aisle are quite common in several dedicatory epigrams of the eleventh and twelfth centuries. Characteristic is the similarity of the Kastoria epigram to an epigram in the *Anthologia Marciana*, which was composed to commemorate the dedication of a triple lamp in the church of the Virgin Kosmosoteira by a certain *protonotarios*, whose name is not specified.[63] In this epigram, the patron addresses a prayer to his tutelary saint. The name of the saint is not mentioned in the text, but he has been identified as Saint Nicholas,[64] because there is an emphasis on the many benefactions he received from him ἀπ᾽ ἀρχῆς μέχρι καὶ νῦν ('from the beginning until now', v. 1). The similarity between the two epigrams is apparent in both the structure and the general notion of protection that is developed by the *ktetors* in the text and which is expressed with specific phrases. In the Marciana epigram, the phrase φύλαξ ἄγρυπνος εὑρέθης βίου ('you have proven to be a watchful guardian', v. 3)[65] resembles, in terms of meaning and vocabulary, the phrase βοηθὸν ... τοῦ βίου ... τῶν λαθῶν εὑρέθης in the *Agioi Anargyroi* epigram. The difference is that in the latter the relationship between *ktetor* and patron saint is even more personal and the lives of the two are intertwined in both the text and the image. At the end of both texts the poets express the patrons' deep desire for their own salvation and the salvation of the members of their family.[66] It is clear that in the Kastoria epigram Saint George is introduced as the personal intercessor of Lemniotes for his salvation before the supreme court of God, as is the case in many dedicatory epigrams.[67] The plea for salvation on the Day of Judgement is projected through typical formulae of Komnenian dedicatory epigrams, which include rhetoric, personal devotion and imagery.

In the church of the *Agioi Anargyroi* the images of Saint George's *vita* on the south and north walls (Figure 10.3) became a life-guide for the patron. And the patron represents this life-guide in the church, which is his personal space. Consequently, the saint becomes the model for Lemniotes'

63 Full text and discussion of this epigram in Spingou (2012: 93, 165–7). See also Drpić (2016b: 96–8).
64 On the reasons for this identification, see Spingou (2012: 165).
65 Spingou (2012: 93).
66 Drpić (2016b: 94).
67 The introduction of saints as personal intercessors is a topos in epigrams. See Lauxtermann (2003: 161), Drpić (2016b: 45–6).

Fig 10.3 Kastoria, Sts. Anargyroi, north aisle: images of Saint George's *vita* (Nektarios Zarras)

personal lived experiences and his *alter ego*, while the inscription becomes the agent of Lemniotes' life. It is interesting to note that the justification of patronage through the difficulties of the patron's personal life is a usual motif in epigrams, which is related to the same notion as is found in the *ktetorika typika* of monastic foundations.[68] The parallelism between saint and patron, as conveyed through the text of the inscription, is also presented visually. The four representative scenes from the Passion of Saint George[69] are correlated with pivotal moments in the life of Lemniotes, with his wife and child on the south wall of the north aisle, and with his wife and himself as the monk Theophilos next to the large figure of Christ on the west wall of the south aisle. Consequently, the patron himself essentially stages his own life with the help of text and image; the founder portraits acquire dimensions of personal autobiography.[70] Four further scenes from the miracles of Saint George, on the north wall, complement those of his martyrdom and compose an integrated *vita* cycle of the saint, taking into account the small dimensions of the aisle. All the elements in the

68 See Mullet (2004: 129–33).

69 These are scenes from the martyrdom of Saint George, which are depicted on the south wall, below the donor representation of the Lemniotes family. For the scenes of this small martyrdom cycle of the saint, see Pelekanidis and Chatzidakis (1984: 23–5, nos 84–6), Drakopoulou (1997: 49).

70 It has been argued that founders disclosed autobiographical data in their foundations. See Angold (1998); see also Drpić (2016b: 95–8).

north aisle, both the 'biographical' disposition of the inscriptional text and the *vita* cycle of Saint George, lead to the conclusion that the space was in effect a *parekklesion*.[71]

The coexistence of the lives of Lemniotes and the saint in this space, through text and image, is the most important factor for arguing that the decision for the specific function of the aisle was taken by the *ktetor*. The aisle must have functioned as a *parekklesion* even before the death of Lemniotes, in the period when he assumed the monastic habit with the name of Theophilos.[72] The content of the inscription next to the scenes of Saint George and Lemniotes becomes the common reference point between the dedicator and his patron saint, patronage and faith, offering and divine reciprocation to the petition for personal salvation. The text reveals that the founder intervened in the iconographic programme by selecting specific scenes, the content of which was connected with his personal life. The life of Theodore Lemniotes and mainly of Saint George are narrated in the type of a personal invocation-prayer, which is the dominant form of the dedicatory inscription.[73] So, the choice of the metrical text in Kastoria is due to the fact that it was the ideal type of prayer-inscription that the founder deeply desired. At the end, Lemniotes alone, without any reference to other members of his family, asks for salvation on the Day of Judgement.

Lemniotes' prayer continues in the second metrical inscription on the east wall of the narthex (Figure 10.4).[74] Here, the poet carries on the narrative structure of the inscription in the north aisle with the patron's voice, bringing the dramatization to a climax with direct reflections of Lemniotes' life. Just as in the epigram in the north aisle, past events and experiences of the *ktetor* become the connecting link with the present and the construction of the church, so the epigram in the narthex refers to the present situation of the *ktetor* and of the building.[75] After the fifth verse, the text dramatizes Lemniotes' present life, as indicated by the phrase νῦν

71 Drakopoulou (1997: 49) rightly supposes that the north aisle would have been dedicated to Saint George.

72 The decision that this space would function as a *parekklesion* carries the personal stamp of Lemniotes, not only because of his close relationship with the space, but also because of his rights as *ktetor*, which entitled him to make changes in both the decoration and the use of spaces in his private foundation. Specifically, in the case of the Saints Anargyroi, the patron's long-standing and particular relationship with the church further reinforced his role in and responsibility for making decisions of this kind, which promoted his views. For the rights of patrons in their private foundations in this period, see Thomas (1987: 171–238).

73 On this form of dedicatory epigrams, see Spingou (2012: 226–8), Drpić (2016b: 80–9, esp. 82).

74 Rhoby (2009: 161–4) with bibliography.

75 Drakopoulou (1997: 44–6), Rhoby (2009: 161–4).

Fig 10.4 Kastoria, Sts. Anargyroi, east wall of the narthex: the epigram in the scene of the Ascension (Nektarios Zarras)

δὲ ῥῶσιν σαρκὸς ἠσθενημένης ('the recovery of my ailing flesh'),[76] and in the end turns to the future with the invocation for the salvation of the patron's family. This temporal sequence of past, present and future is typical of the structure of Middle Byzantine dedicatory epigrams.[77]

The two inscriptions in the *Agioi Anargyroi* are examples of patronal *ethopoiia*. Their narrative discourse includes some typical traits of *ethopoietic* dedicatory epigrams, the ultimate aim of which is to project the patron's persona.[78] The epigrams recall in temporal sequence past events, critical experiences and incidents directly associated with the life of the patron saint, moments of Lemniotes' life, the portrayal of his emotions, his obligation (πρέπον) and sacred desire (πόθος) for the renovation and the decoration of the church,[79] and finally his personal prayer for the salvation of his soul. This last characteristic is essential because it relates to the faith, the personal devotion and the piety of the patron. Rhetorical

76 See the English translation of the inscription in Gerstel (1999: 89).

77 Drpić (2016b: 82, 88–9).

78 For the meaning of this term and its relevance for understanding the role of the *ktetor* in dedicatory epigrams, see Lauxtermann (2003: 61), Drpić (2014: 907–11) and (2016a: 87–117, esp. 89–96) with examples from the Komnenian period. See also Zarras (2023: 109–11).

79 This complex activity of the patron with regard to his material donation to his foundation is stated using a rich vocabulary. See Spingou (2012: 191).

ethopoiia of *ktetors* is particularly common in this period; there are several dedicatory epigrams, in which the personal nature of patronage is intensified through the promotion of the patron's character.[80] Moreover, the two epigrams in the *Agioi Anargyroi* are important for understanding one of the basic problems that dedicatory inscriptions pose, namely the nature of the patron's involvement in the creation of an epigram, as well as the painter's relationship to the patron. These texts highlight dominant traits of the patron's personality, revealing his motivations[81] and his innermost beliefs, and consequently are directly connected to the ideology of patronage. The patron's involvement in the composition of the epigram, in the sense that Lemniotes supplied the poet with details about his life or a general idea of what he wanted the texts to project, in accordance with his conceptions and life experiences, should be considered certain. As is frequently the case with dedicatory epigrams, the poet may have presented to Lemniotes different types of epigrams, revolving around basic aspects of his life, from which he could choose.[82] The references to Lemniotes' patron saint, the uncertainty and turbulence in his life, his failing health and his wish for eternal salvation could be the basic narrative elements that the poet had available for composing the epigram. These pieces of information about Lemniotes' life, in the epigrams, are not born of the poet's imagination, nor are they texts of standardized structure which were offered indiscriminately to clients commissioning epigrams.[83] On the contrary, they are personal facets of the patron's life, which he himself reveals to the epigrammatist, because Lemniotes is not a passing patron, he is in the service of the *Agioi Anargyroi* and Saint George and has dedicated a large part of his life to the monument. This is also the basic difference between a donor, who benefacts a church or a monastery at one specific moment in his life, and a patron, who dedicates his life to his foundation and aids it in many ways.[84] When a profound personal relationship exists between the founder and his foundation, as is the case in the church of the *Agioi Anargyroi*, this relationship plays a decisive role in the composition of the epigram and should be given due consideration by research.[85]

80 Drpić (2016b: 89–92).

81 Lauxtermann (2003: 160, 164–6).

82 For this practice, see Maguire (1996: 8–9), Lauxtermann (2003: 42–4), Drpić (2016b: 37–9).

83 See Zarras (2023: 100–1, 106–9).

84 This deeper and more personal relationship between patrons and their endowments is very common in the Palaiologan period, as seen in the case of Theodore Metochites and the Chora monastery. See recently Zarras (2021).

85 The example of Lemniotes answers the questions asked by Lauxtermann (2003: 159) with regard to the relationship between patron and epigrammatist.

Lemniotes' collaboration with the painter in the *Agioi Anargyroi* church should be considered certain, because the *ktetor* is enhanced almost throughout the iconographic programme, through portraits of himself and his family. As in the case of the scenes of Saint George in the north aisle, the painter's consultation with the patron is surmised from the transfer of the Ascension from its typical space, the barrel-vault of the bema, to the narthex, the place of the patron's burial and eternal salvation.[86] The outcome of the collaboration of patron and painter was probably the joint decision to paint the dedicatory inscription close to the Ascension.[87] The inscription is very carefully incorporated in the upper part of the east wall, so that it is consonant with the hierarchic and symbolic arrangement of the iconography. The soteriological and eschatological character of the Ascension as the visual expression of Salvation, and the inscription as text and image, fully correspond to Lemniotes' petition for the eternal rest of his family in Paradise. The Virgin of the Ascension (Figure 10.5) is also perceived as intercessor for the salvation of the members of the Lemniotes family, as she raises her hands and symbolically transfers the patron's voice to the angels who 'step' on the inscription and point directly above to

Fig 10.5 Kastoria, Sts. Anargyroi, east wall of the narthex: the Virgin orans of the Ascension (Nektarios Zarras)

86 On the scene of the Ascension in the narthex of Saints Anargyroi, see Pelekanidis and Chatzidakis (1992: 49, figs. 28–30), Drakopoulou (1997: fig. 45).

87 Analogous correlations of the funerary role of the space and the Ascension are observed in other monuments of this period. Among the most characteristic examples is the Virgin Chalkeon in Thessalonike. See Tsitouridou (1982), Paissidou (2015: 129–30).

the ascended Christ.[88] In a similar way, the inscription frames the Virgin Arakiotissa καὶ κεχαριτωμένη ('and full of grace') in Cyprus, where the inscription-supplication of Leo ascends as an entreaty to the Virgin and to Christ.[89] Consequently, the iconography adds a metaphysical dimension to the epigram, because the supplication is written in the celestial zone of the decoration, away from human eyes.[90]

Conclusions

In concluding this chapter, the now-lost representation of Tarchaneiotes with his wife Zoe and the *sebastos* Andronikos in the Vytoumas monastery, in a probably patronal *Deesis* composition, is reconstructed for the first time in research, so pointing out the decisive contribution of epigrams to reconstructing the now-destroyed iconography of *ktetoric* compositions. The inscription from Vytoumas attests in characteristic manner that the members of the military aristocracy, in a period in which they enjoyed particular prominence in society, did not confine themselves to fulfilling patronage relationships and personal salvation, but through the patronage are presented as all-rounded personalities who combine high state office, education, aesthetic sensitivity and spiritual concerns. Consequently, *ktetoric* epigrams of this kind are not only useful for their relation to the iconography, but also for their ideological appeal, because they propagandize in such important spaces for society as churches and monasteries, the ideal model of the *ktetor*. The reference to iconographic elements of the image in the epigram accompanying it, as in the Vytoumas monastery, points to the relationship of these texts to the literary genre of *ekphrasis*. Thanks to the narrative epigram in Vatopedi, the chapter reinstates the relationship between the hegumen Ioannikios and the important personage for the monastery Sophronios, in relation to the *ktetoric* inscription. It is clear from the examples discussed here that patron, painter and poet collaborated to create a poetic dedicatory text which projects the faith, the ideology and the life of the *ktetor*. This synergy of the arts transforms the patron's supplication into an epigram of high artistic quality, in which the textual and the visual vocabulary, the poetry and the painting, serve both the founder and his foundation. The self-presentation of Tarchaneiotes and the image of Sophronios in the Vytoumas and Vatopedi monasteries, respectively,

88 Zarras (2023: 109, 111).
89 See Agapitos (2018: 93–4), Konstantinidi (2018: esp. 67–72) with bibliography.
90 For inscriptions written in the upper part of the naos, see recently Pallis (2022: 195–6).

are projected through their multifarious roles as poets or narrators of the descriptive epigrams and creators of the patronal compositions. This ideological underpinning in Komnenian patronage was to develop and reach its peak in Palaiologan times, with several state officials presented also as highly educated and cultured, as is clearly the case with Theodore Metochites. Thus, the systematic examination of the monumental iconography in relation to the epigrams is a promising avenue for future research.[91]

In contrast to this more usual type of presentation of the patron, the donor epigrams in the church of the *Agioi Anargyroi* have a narrative style that derives from the correlation of the lives of the founder and his patron saint. In the Kastoria church, the iconographic programme in combination with the space enhances the epigrams' spiritual character, to the extent that the epigram in the north aisle becomes a prayer of Lemniotes, with autobiographical details combined iconographically with the *vita* of his tutelary saint, Saint George. In the case of the narthex, the epigram loses its material substance and is transformed into a metaphysical medium of the founders' salvation, articulated through the content of the theophany that it accompanies. The narthex inscription clearly demonstrates that some dedicatory inscriptions were not written to be read, because the patron desired his personal supplication to be transferred through the Virgin and the angels to Paradise. The two epigrams from Kastoria, in combination with the image, have all the traits of a typology of patronal self-portraiture, which was the basis for the construction of the patron's identity, not only in Constantinople but also in the peripheries of the Empire.

Bibliography

Agapitos, P. A. (2000) 'Poets and Painters: Theodoros Prodromos' Dedicatory Verses of his Novel to an Anonymous Caesar', *JÖByz* 50: 173–85.

(2018) 'The Word as Animated Image: Inscribed Texts in the Frescoes of the Church of the Virgin Mary at Lagouderá Cyprus (AD 1192)', in *The Church of Panagia tou Arakos*, ed. A. Papagheorgiou, C. Bakirtzis and C. Hadjichristodoulou, 89–96. Nicosia.

Angold, M. (1998) 'The Autobiographical Impulse in Byzantium', *DOP* 52: 240–51.

Avraméa, A., and D. Feissel (1987) 'Inventaires en vue d'un recueil des inscriptions historiques de Byzance, IV: Inscriptions de Thessalie (à l' exception des Météores)', *T&MByz* 10: 357–98.

91 The Vytoumas epigram is a characteristic example of the interdependence between the metrical inscription and the image it accompanies. On this research direction, see Drpić and Rhoby (2019: 449).

Bernardini, L. (1992) 'Les donateurs des églises de Cappadoce', *Byzantion* 62: 118–40.

Bompaire, J., J. Lefort, V. Kravari and C. Giros (eds.) (2001) *Actes de Vatopedi*, vol. 1. Paris.

Djordjević, I., and M. Marković (2000–1) 'On the Dialogue Relationship between the Virgin and Child in East Christian Art: A propos of the Discovery of the Figures of the Virgin Mediatrix and Christ in the Naos of Lesnovo', *Zograf* 28: 13–48.

Drakopoulou, E. (1997) *Η πόλη της Καστοριάς τη Βυζαντινή και Μεταβυζαντινή εποχή (12ος–16ος αι.): Ιστορία – Τέχνη – Επιγραφές*. Athens.

Drpić, I. (2014) 'The Patron's "I": Art, Selfhood, and the Later Byzantine Dedicatory Epigram', *Speculum* 89.4: 895–935.

(2016a) '*Chrysepes Stichourgia*: The Byzantine Epigram as Aesthetic Object', in *Sign as Design: Script as Image in Cross-Cultural Perspective (300–1600 CE)*, ed. B. M. Bedos-Rezak and J. F. Hamburger, 51–69. Washington, DC.

(2016b) *Epigram, Art, and Devotion in Later Byzantium*. Cambridge.

Drpić, I., and A. Rhoby (2019) 'Byzantine Verses as Inscriptions: The Interaction of Text, Object and Beholder', in *A Companion to Byzantine Poetry*, ed. W. Hörandner, A. Rhoby and N. Zagklas, 430–55. Brill's Companions to the Byzantine World 4. Leiden.

Gerstel, J. E. S. (1999) *Beholding the Sacred Mysteries: Programs of the Byzantine Sanctuary*. Seattle.

Hadermann-Misguich, L. (1979) 'La peinture monumentale tardo-comnène et ses prolongements au XIIIe siècle', *Actes du XVe Congrès International d'Études Byzantines, Athènes 1976*, 255–84. Athens.

Hörandner, W. (ed.) (1974) *Theodoros Prodromos, Historische Gedichte*. Wiener Byzantinistische Studien 11. Vienna.

(2001) 'Epigrams on Icons and Sacred Objects: The Collection of Cod. Marc. gr. 524 once again', in *La poesia tardoantica e medievale. Atti del I Convegno Internazionale di Studi (Marcerata, 4–5 maggio 1998)*, ed. M. Salvatore, 117–24. Alessandria.

Jeffreys, E. M. (2012) *Four Byzantine Novels: Theodore Prodromos, Rhodanthe and Dosikles; Eumathios Makrembolites, Hysmine and Hysminias; Constantine Manasses, Aristandros and Kallithea; Niketas Eugenianos, Drosilla and Charikles. Translated with Introductions and Notes*. Translated Texts for Byzantinists 1. Liverpool.

Jolivet-Lévy, C. (1998) 'Carikli kilise. L'église de la Précieuse Croix à Göreme (Korama), Cappadoce: une fondation des Mélissènoi?', in *Ευψυχία: Mélanges offerts à Hélène Ahrweiler*, vol. 1, 301–11. Byzantina Sorbonensia 16. Paris.

(2001) *La Cappacoce médiévale: Images et spiritualité*. Paris.

Kalopissi-Verti, S. (2022) 'Epigram on a Deesis Mosaic', in *Sources for Byzantine Art History*, vol. 3.2: *The Visual Culture of Later Byzantium (1081–c. 1350)*, ed. F. Spingou, 1140–7. Cambridge.

Konstantinidi, C. (2018) 'Byzantine Painting in the Church of the Panagia tou Arakos', in *The Church of Panagia tou Arakos*, ed. A. Papagheorgiou, C. Bakirtzis and C. Hadjichristodoulou, 49–88. Nicosia.

Kyriakoudis, E. (1981) 'Ο κτίτορας Θεόδωρος (Θεόφιλος) Λημνιώτης', *Βαλκανικά Σύμμεικτα* 1: 3–23.

Lampsides, O. (1991) 'Der vollständige Text der Ἔκφρασις γῆς des Konstantinos Manasses', *JÖByz* 41: 189–205.

Lauxtermann, M. D. (2003) *Byzantine Poetry from Pisides to Geometres: Texts and Contexts*, vol. 1. Wiener Byzantinistische Studien 24/1. Vienna.

Leontiades, I. (1998) *Die Tarchaneiotai: Eine prosopographisch-sigillographische Studie*. Thessalonike.

Maguire, H. (1996) *Image and Imagination: The Byzantine Epigram as Evidence for Viewer Response*. Toronto.

Mamaloukos, B. S. (1996) 'The Buildings of the Vatopedi and Their Patrons', in *Mount Athos and Byzantine Monasticism: Papers from the Twenty-Eighth Spring Symposium of Byzantine Studies, Birmingham, March 1994*, ed. A. Bryer and M. Cunningham, 113–25. Birmingham.

Mamaloukos, B. S. (2001) *Το καθολικό της μονής Βατοπεδίου: Ιστορία και Αρχιτεκτονική*. Athens.

Mango, C., and W. J. E. Hawkins (1966) 'The Hermitage of St. Neophytos and its Wall-paintings', *DOP* 20: 119–206.

Millet, G., J. Pargoire and L. Petit (1904) *Inscriptions chrétiennes de l'Athos*. Paris.

Mouriki, D. (1980/1) 'Stylistic Trends in Monumental Painting of Greece during the Eleventh and Twelfth Centuries', *DOP* 34/35: 77–124.

Müller, E. A. (2005) *Berg Athos: Geschichte einer Mönchsrepublik*. Munich.

Mullett, M. (2004) 'Constructing Identities in Twelfth-Century Byzantium', in *Byzantium Matures: Choices, Sensitivities, and Modes of Expression (Eleventh to Fifteenth Centuries)*, ed. C. Angelidi, 129–44. Athens.

Ousterhout, R. (1999) 'The Aziözü Churches near Çeltek in Western Cappadocia', *CArch* 47: 67–76.

Paissidou, M. (2015) 'The Church "Panagia ton Chalkeon in Thessaloniki": A Different Approach to a Monastic Institution and its Founder', in *Studi e ricerche della scuola di specializzazione in Beni archeologici di matera. Siris* 15: 121–33.

Pallis, G. (2022) 'Texts and Their Audiences: Some Thoughts on the Addressees of Inscriptions in Middle Byzantine Churches in Greece', in *Studies in Byzantine Epigraphy* 1, ed. A. Rhoby and I. Toth, 191–201. Turnhout.

Panayotidi, M. (2006) 'Η προσωπικότητα δύο αρχόντων της Καστοριάς και ο χαρακτήρας της πόλης στο δεύτερο μισό του 12ου αιώνα', in *ΔΩΡΟΝ: Τιμητικός Τόμος στον καθηγητή Νίκο Νικονάνο*, 156–67. Thessalonike.

Papamastorakis, T. (1996) 'Εικαστικές εκφάνσεις της πολιτικής ιδεολογίας του Στέφανου Dušan σε μνημεία της εποχής του και τα βυζαντινά πρότυπά τους', in *Βυζάντιο και Σερβία κατά τον ΙΔ' αιώνα*, ed. E. Papadopoulou and D. Dialete, 140–57. Athens.

Paul, A. (2008) 'Beobachtungen zu 'Εκφράσεις in Epigrammen auf Objekten: Lassen wir Epigramme Sprechen!', in *Die Kulturhistorische Bedeutung byzantinischer Epigramme: Akten des internationalen Workshop (Wien 1–2 Dezember 2006)*, ed. W. Hörandner and A. Rhoby, 61–73. Vienna.

Pelekanidis, S., and M. Chatzidakis (1992) *Καστοριά*. Athens.

Rhoby, A. (2009) *Byzantinische Epigramme auf Fresken und Mosaiken*. Vienna.

(2010a) *Byzantinische Epigramme auf Ikonen und Objekten der Kleinkunst. Nebst Addenda zu Band 1 'Byzantinische Epigramme auf Fresken und Mosaiken'*. Vienna.

(2010b) 'The Structure of Inscriptional Dedicatory Epigrams in Byzantium', in *La poesia tardoantica e medievale. IV Convegno internazionale di studi, Perugia, 15–17 novembre 2007, Atti in onore di Antonino Isola per il suo 70° genetliaco*, ed. C. Burini De Lorenzi and M. De Gaetano, 309–22. Alessandria.

(2011) 'Interactive Inscriptions: Byzantine Works of Art and Their Beholders', in *Spatial Icons: Performativity in Byzantium and Medieval Russia*, ed. A. M. Lidov, 317–33. Moscow.

(2014) *Byzantinische Epigramme auf Stein. Nebst Addenda zu den Bänden 1 und 2*. Vienna.

(2018) 'The Poetry of Theodore Balsamon: Form and Function', in *Middle and Late Byzantine Poetry: Texts and Contexts*, ed. A. Rhoby and N. Zagklas, 111–45. Byzantios: Studies in Byzantine History and Civilization 14. Turnhout.

Ševčenko, P. N. (2006) 'Spiritual Progression in the Canon Tables of the Melbourne Gospels', in *Byzantine Narrative: Papers in Honour of Roger Scott*, ed. J. Burke, 334–43. Byzantina Australiensia 16. Melbourne.

(2012) 'Metrical Inscriptions in the Murals of the Panagia Phorbiotissa', in *Asinou across Time: Studies in the Architecture and Murals of the Panagia Phorbiotissa, Cyprus*, ed. A. Weyl Carr and A. Nicolaidès, 69–90. Washington, DC.

Spingou, F. (2012) 'Works and Artworks in the Twelfth Century and Beyond: The Thirteenth-Century Manuscript Marcianus gr. 524 and the Twelfth-Century Dedicatory Epigrams on Works of Art', PhD thesis, University of Oxford.

Steppan, T. (1994) 'Die Mosaiken des Athosklosters Vatopaidi: Stilkritische und ikonographische Überlegungen', *CArch* 42: 87–122.

Thomas, J. P. (1987) *Private Religious Foundations in the Byzantine Empire*. Washington, DC.

Thomas, J. P., and A. Constantinides Hero (2000) *Byzantine Monastic Foundation Documents*. Washington, DC.

Toth, I. (2015) 'Epigraphic Traditions in Eleventh-Century Byzantium', in *Insciptions in Byzantium and Beyond: Methods – Projects – Case Studies*, ed. A. Rhoby, 203–26. Vienna.

Tsigaridas, E. (1996) 'Τα ψηφιδωτά και οι βυζαντινές τοιχογραφίες', in *Ιερά Μεγίστη Μονή Βατοπαιδίου: Παράδοση – Ιστορία – Τέχνη*, vol. 1: 220–84. Athos.

Tsitouridou, A. (1982) 'Die Grabkonzeption des ikonographischen Programms der Kirche Panagia Chalkeon in Thessaloniki', *JÖByz* 32.5: 435–41.

Voyadjis, S. (1998) 'Η μονή Βυτουμά στα Τρίκαλα Θεσσαλίας', in *Εκκλησίες στην Ελλάδα μετά την Άλωση*, vol. 5: 37–52. Athens.
Zarras, N. (2019) 'Νεώτερα στοιχεία από την έρευνα αθωνικών επιγραφών της Μεσοβυζαντινής περιόδου: οι περιπτώσεις των μονών Μεγίστης Λαύρας και Βατοπεδίου', in *Ι' Συνάντηση Ελλήνων Βυζαντινολόγων 27–30 Νοεμβρίου 2019 (Ιωάννινα)*. Περιλήψεις Ανακοινώσεων 20. Ioannina.
(2021) 'Illness and Healing: The Ministry Cycle in the Chora Monastery and the Literary Oeuvre of Theodore Metochites', *DOP* 75: 85–119.
(2023) *Ideology and Patronage in Byzantium: Dedicatory Inscriptions and Patron Images from Middle Byzantine Macedonia and Thrace*. Turnhout.

CHAPTER 11

David as Model for the Emperor and his Poet
*Theodore Prodromos and John II Komnenos**

Rachele Ricceri

Δαυὶδ προφήτου καὶ βασιλέως μέλος ('Song of David, prophet and king'):[1] in over fifty Medieval Greek manuscripts, this dodecasyllabic verse introduces the first Psalm and serves as an overarching metrical title to the Book of Psalms. This implies that a single dodecasyllabic verse is sufficient to encapsulate David's essential features as recorded in Byzantium: he is a prophet and a king who sings chants, so he is also a poet. The kingship and the poetic art of this Old Testament figure are at the centre of the present considerations. This chapter studies how David's figure was received in the twelfth century by Theodore Prodromos and how David can be considered as a paradigm to better understand some of Prodromos' poetic choices. By reflecting on the depiction of David as an alter ego to both the emperor and the poet, I will shed new light on the exemplary role played by this biblical figure in the construction of the self-representation adopted by Prodromos. At the same time, this chapter contributes to a new understanding of the creative reception of the Psalms in twelfth-century poetry.

The analysis will be conducted using two complementary approaches. Firstly, the references to David will be used to investigate the construction and representation of the relationship between the poet and the emperor in one of Prodromos' historical poems, namely poem 17, dedicated to Emperor John II Komnenos.[2] Secondly, on a literary level, it will be shown

* I wish to express my sincere gratitude to the organizers of the conference in Vienna, Andreas Rhoby, Baukje van den Berg and Nikos Zagklas, for their hard work to give life to an invaluable opportunity for exchange and fruitful discussions, and to all the participants. I am also enormously indebted to Ilias Nesseris, who provided a response to this chapter at the conference, for the accurate reading of the text, his acute remarks and his insightful ideas on how to improve this contribution. This chapter has been written within the framework of the research projects *The Legacy of the Psalms in Byzantine Poetry: Book Epigrams and Metrical Paraphrases* (FWO-FWF, Project nr. G0E3918N) and *David, our Orpheus: Reception, Rewritings and Adaptations of the Psalms in Byzantine Poetry* (FWO, Project nr. G009618N). All translations are mine unless otherwise stated.

1 'Chant of David, prophet and king'. DBBE, Type 1912, www.dbbe.ugent.be/types/1912 (accessed 15 February 2023); Rhoby (2018: GR25, 204).

2 Ed. Hörandner (1974: 286–300).

how David's poetry (i.e. the Psalms) directly influences the construction of Prodromos' poetry and how the biblical hypotext informs the text of a poem written by one of the most celebrated and prolific Byzantine poets of the twelfth century. I argue that the biblical text, as a literary source on which Prodromos draws to compose his poems, justifies and elevates the court poems written in the twelfth century, and constitutes a secure foundation upon which the poet can construct the representation of his relationship with the emperor. The present chapter will show how important David's poetic nature is for Prodromos: of equal if not greater importance than his kingship.

The Emperor as a New David

The centrality of David as an unavoidable model of kingship in Byzantium has been fruitfully emphasized in several studies on Byzantine imperial ideology.[3] Claudia Rapp in particular has systematically investigated David's important role among Old Testament figures for Byzantine imperial ideology and has pointed out that early Byzantine emperors, already from the fifth century onwards, were often portrayed as a 'new David'.[4]

The validity of this identification continued into later centuries and the *mimesis* of David became a standardized element of imperial representation.[5] It can be traced in artistic representations as well, as for instance is testified by some of the miniatures of the Paris Psalter (Paris, Bibliothèque nationale de France, gr. 139 [Diktyon 49706], second half of the tenth century), in which the exaltation of David can be considered a product of Macedonian imperial ideology. It is interesting to note that in the Paris Psalter the representation of David evolves in subsequent full-page miniatures to be found in the front of the manuscript: on fol. 1v his qualities of poet and musician are highlighted as he is playing the lyre in a typically classicizing garb, which is similar to Orpheus' iconography; on fol. 6v the young David is represented in a coronation scene, wearing his chiton; on fol. 7v the mature David is dressed as an emperor, standing between *Sophia* and *Prophetia*. In manuscript miniatures the representation of King David acquires a universal value and sometimes even transcends the

3 It is noteworthy that the contributions collected in Magdalino's edited volume on *New Constantines* (1994), which addresses the representation of Byzantine emperors throughout the centuries, consistently refer to the comparison with David as a standard element that contributes to the legitimation of imperial power.

4 See Rapp (2010: *passim*).

5 See Zahnd (2008: 74).

identification with a specific emperor.[6] By the eleventh century the identification of David and the emperor had become a commonplace and was even part of court ceremonial.[7]

The reading of twelfth-century poetry as proposed in the present chapter can indeed benefit from a comparison with the contemporary visual representation of David in Byzantine art, and especially in manuscript illuminations. The peculiar nature of David, an Old Testament king who is remembered for his poetic skills, is remarkably significant in the iconographic representations of the prophet. Miniatures of King David playing the lyre are to be found in a significant number of Psalters. Anthony Cutler has collected such depictions, as they constitute a typical feature of the so-called aristocratic psalters.[8] Interestingly enough, in some twelfth-century manuscripts David is represented either as a musician (see Florence, Biblioteca Medicea Laurenziana, Plut. 6.36 [Diktyon 16023], fol. 275r), or as a king holding a Psalter book (see Vatican City, Biblioteca Apostolica Vaticana, Barb. gr. 320 [Diktyon 64863], fol. 1 bis v), or as an emperor composing or playing music (see Athos, Mone Batopediou 851 [Diktyon 18995], fol. 123v). This multifaceted depiction accounts for the complex and ubiquitous reception of this prominent biblical figure in Byzantine visual culture.

The life of David is paradigmatic of the moral qualities that a good emperor should possess and is a reference point for shaping praise of the Byzantine ruler, both for artists and for poets.[9] The image is indeed one of the most common literary epithets for the emperor.[10] The typological relationship between David and the emperors is thus widely attested in Byzantine literature, whether or not accompanying iconographic representation of the Old Testament king.[11] Two examples will help to sketch the cultural processes to which Prodromos' *Historical Poems* can be compared.

An anonymous dodecasyllabic encomium bestowed on Basil I and perhaps dating to 872–3 is constructed as a *basilikos logos* and consecrates the emperor as a new David, with whom he shares humble origins

6 See Dagron (2003: 119).

7 See Kalavrezou, Trahoulia and Sabar (1993: 199).

8 See Cutler (1984: *passim*).

9 See Maguire (1988: 91–3).

10 See Treitinger (1956: 129–31) and Hörandner (1972: 95). Hörandner edits the epitaph by George Akropolites for Irene Komnene, where a passage strikingly refers to the emperor as τὸν ἀνδρικὸν καὶ πρᾶον Δαυὶδ νέον ('the brave and mild new David', v. 40).

11 On the importance of this typological relationship as expressed in Byzantine literature, see Hörandner (2009: 104–8).

(v. 70: Δαυῒδ νέος, 'new David').[12] In this poem the identification with David precedes that with Christ and is a fundamental step towards exalting the Macedonian dynasty.[13] Another poem that illustrates the identification of the emperor as a new David is an epigram to be found in the Barberini psalter (Vatican City, Biblioteca Apostolica Vaticana, Barb. gr. 372 [Diktyon 64915], *c.* 1060). On fol. 4v an eighteen-line dedicatory epigram precedes a miniature depicting a coronation scene.[14] Remarkably, this epigram, where the emperor is addressed as 'simply another David' (v. 5: Δαυὶδ ἀτεχνῶς ἄλλον), was added at a later stage, possibly in the fourteenth or fifteenth century, to dedicate the book to a different emperor.[15] This topos is therefore a long-standing one and crosses chronological boundaries while retaining its original validity.

In twelfth-century literary production the comparison of the emperor and David has also been highlighted by many famous authors. It appears in different kinds of prose works, including panegyrics,[16] orations (such as a passage in which Michael Choniates extensively compares the images of David and Isaac Komnenos, also drawing a physical parallel),[17] and indeed poetry. Nicholas Kallikles, for instance, in his funerary poem for John Komnenos, turns to the metaphor of the new David, along with the image of the shepherd.[18] Remarkably, a third figure can be taken into

12 On the structure of the poem, see Agapitos (1989: 289–97). The text of the poem, as to be found in the manuscript Florence, Biblioteca Medicea Laurenziana, Plut. 9.23 [Diktyon 16111], is edited in Markopoulos (1992: 230–2). Recently the text has been analysed by Marc Lauxtermann (2003–19: 2:23–9) as an example of poetic encomium, rather rare in Byzantine literature.

13 See Markopoulos (1992: 228). On a general level, the figure of David was frequently evoked in the framework of imperial propaganda; see Angelov (2006: 203 with n. 45).

14 For the text of the epigram, see DBBE, Type 3677, https://www.dbbe.ugent.be/types/3677 (accessed 15/02/2023); Rhoby (2018: VAT81, 462–5); Spatharakis (1976: 34–5). On the connection of the miniature of this marginal Psalter with the Komnenian dynasty, see de Wald (1944: *passim*).

15 See Tsamakda (2010: 40–1).

16 As pointed out in Angelov (2007: 127–31). A particularly meaningful case is the encomium of Manuel I Komnenos composed by Michael Italikos, in which the emperor is attributed all the elements of David's sacral kingship in order to legitimize his power (see Magdalino [1993: 435–7]).

17 *Or.* 14, 1:215.15–26 ed. Lampros (1879–80): Δικαιοσύνης δ' αὖ καὶ πραότητος καὶ ἀνδρείας μέχρι μὲν καὶ ἐς δεῦρο μόνον τὸν Δαυῒδ σαφὲς εἶχον παράδειγμα, τοῦ λοιποῦ δὲ μετὰ Δαυῒδ ἔχω καὶ τὸν θεοειδέστατον Ἰσαάκιον. Μᾶλλον δὲ καὶ τἄλλα μικροῦ πάντα, ὅσα μὴ ψυχὴν μόνον, ἀλλὰ καὶ σῶμα κοσμοῦσι τῷ Δαυῒδ ὁ βασιλεὺς προσωμοίωται .... Εἰ γοῦν τῇ εἰκόνι Δαυῒδ ἐμφερὴς ὁ βασιλεὺς παραδειχθείη, δῆλον ὡς καὶ αὐτῷ τῷ Δαυῒδ ὁ βασιλεὺς πάντη προσόμοιος ('I used to see David merely as a clear model of justice, mildness and braveness up to this point, but hereafter, after David, I consider the utterly godlike Isaac. Rather, as for almost all other things that embellish not only the soul but also the body, the king is like David .... If then the king, resembling David, was compared to David's image, it would be clear that also the king is in every way similar to David himself').

18 *Carm.* 31.91 ed. Romano (1980): Ποιμὴν κραταιέ, Δαβὶδ ἄντικρυς νέε ('O mighty shepherd, openly new David'). For Kallikles, see also Gerbi in this volume. Manganeios Prodromos presents Emperor Manuel I Komnenos as a new David in the poem edited by E. M. Jeffreys and M. J. Jeffreys in this volume.

consideration when analysing the image of the Byzantine emperor seen as the new David. In Byzantium, the Old Testament king was actually 'treated as a prefiguration of Christ'.[19] This perception was clear in Byzantine poetry as well, as is testified, for instance, by a Pseudo-Psellian verse: ὁ γὰρ Χριστὸς ἐν ταῖς γραφαῖς Δαυὶδ καλεῖται νέος ('For Christ is called a new David in the Scriptures').[20] Therefore, the definition of the emperor as the new David is a complex one, as it bears multilayered meanings and is to be read in both directions: the emperor's usual identification as the new Christ is enriched by this image of David, who is the 'old Christ'.

The Psalms Reused in a Twelfth-Century Poem: Theodore Prodromos' *Historical Poem* 17

Within the massive corpus of Theodore Prodromos' *Historical Poems*, a close reading of poem 17 sheds some light on the reception of the figure of David in twelfth-century literature.[21] This is a 410-line composition written in decapentasyllables which was addressed to John II Komnenos (1118–43) on the occasion of a campaign against the 'Persians' (meaning the Seljuks). The metrical choice is not surprising, as Prodromos uses this 'political verse' – a metrical pattern largely attested in twelfth-century court poems and firmly embedded in the tradition of didactic poetry – in most of his long historical poems.[22] Intriguingly enough, the political verse serves a double purpose. Firstly, it fits the need to compose a eulogy, being a widespread metre used for court poetry in the twelfth century. Secondly, this metrical form is particularly suitable to a parenetic scope and is used by the poet to evoke biblical exempla.[23]

It is interesting to note that Prodromos deliberately shapes this poem using elements typical of the didactic tradition, such as indeed the metre, as well as formal features that resemble the structure of a hymn. This poem is clearly arranged in forty-one strophes of ten lines each. The *decastichon* is a typical form used for hymns sung by the representatives of the demes during ceremonies in the twelfth century and also recurs in *Historical Poems* 4 and 5.[24] These latter poems in particular are included in a group of

19 *ODB*, s.v. David.
20 (Pseudo-)Psellos, *Poem* 53.318 ed. Westerink (1992).
21 See Hörandner (1974: 286–300).
22 See Hörandner (1974: 123), Hörandner and Rhoby (2021: 413–16).
23 On the importance of the metrical choice to convey didactic elements, see Lauxtermann (2009).
24 On the formal features of deme hymns, see Hörandner (2003: 82). For Prodromos' poetry for the demes, see also Agapitos in this volume and Magdalino in this volume.

poems (*Historical Poems* 3–6) composed in various metres to celebrate John II Komnenos' campaign against Kastamon in the year 1131.[25] The praise of the deeds of the emperor in these occasional poems has been fruitfully compared to the hymnic tradition starting with the Homeric hymns.[26] Prodromos' decision to celebrate John's victories in the shape of a hymn is therefore not surprising and is applicable to the reading of *Historical Poem* 17 as well.[27]

In the opening lines of *Historical Poem* 17 the poet declares himself too weak to join the military expedition and decides therefore to accompany the emperor by means of his prayers (vv. 1–10).[28] He gives his physical weakness as the excuse for relying upon the prophets' words (vv. 11–18), which constitute the core of the poem. The thirty-seven central strophes of the poem, the overwhelming majority in terms of number of lines, form an actualization of biblical episodes, which functions as a model for talking about contemporary historical events. In vv. 19–390 Prodromos consistently relies on Old Testament passages comparing the emperor to several prophets, whose experiences are perceived as re-lived and embodied by those of the emperor. Among the prophets quoted, David has a prominent position (vv. 19–20, see below): two remarkably long sections of *Historical Poem* 17, of five strophes each (no less than 100 verses in total), are in fact a rewriting of some passages taken from the Psalms (vv. 21–70 and 341–90). Twenty-seven groups of verses, the ones that follow and precede the two Davidic sections, are devoted to the four major prophets and ten of the fourteen minor prophets,[29] whose words are borrowed by Prodromos to build the eulogy of the emperor (vv. 71–340). The last two strophes of the poem contain respectively a personal reference to Prodromos himself (vv. 391–400) and a final allusion to the defeat of the enemies and the desired triumph of the emperor (vv. 401–10).[30]

25 On the significance of the metrical *poikilia* in these poems, see Zagklas (2018: 64–5).

26 See Faulkner (2016: 262–3).

27 The similarity of *Historical Poem* 17 to the deme hymns is already mentioned in Hörandner (1974: 88). I use Hörandner's edition for all references to and quotations from the *Historical Poems*.

28 The idea of compensating for physical incapability by a suitable use of words is present also in other passages by Prodromos, such as *Historical Poem* 38.15–44; see Beaton (1987: 5). On the meaning of the good wishes towards the emperor formulated by Prodromos in this stanza, see Hörandner (1996: 108), with further parallels.

29 Habakkuk, Micah, Amos, Joel, Zephaniah, Malachi, Nahum, Obadiah, Haggai, Jonah, Jeremiah, Isaiah, Ezekiel, Daniel.

30 This very same *decastichon* also occurs in *Historical Poem* 19.192–201. The textual status of the end of the poem poses some philological challenges, as pointed out by Hörandner (1974: 301). Recently, Papagiannis (2012: 103–4) has hypothesized that the *decastichon* vv. 401–10 replaced the original ending of the poem.

The peculiar structure of this poem, together with its specific content, provides the opportunity to tackle some questions about the complex relationship between the poet and the emperor, who is directly addressed.[31] Moreover, this long poem is an interesting example of poetic reuse of biblical material. The close reading that follows is therefore divided into two parts. Firstly, the focus will lie on the persons mentioned in the poem, that is, on the characters that appear in the poem and that give life to the narrative structure of the work. Secondly, a more technical analysis of the biblical references will aim to detect the adaptation techniques used by Prodromos to refer to the psalmic passages he quotes and, more generally, to study the poet's use of this particular book of the Bible.

Personal Dynamics: David, the Poet, the Ruler

The structure of *Historical Poem* 17 is quite fixed and repetitive. As has been said, Theodore Prodromos devotes several *decasticha* of the poem to the words taken from the books of various prophets, which he quotes almost literally. However, some verses of each *decastichon*, usually two or three per strophe, are devoted to poignant references to contemporary events. In this way, the occasional character of the composition is made palpable by Prodromos. The poet mostly reserves the first two or three verses of the strophes to insert his own voice and to evoke several addressees, namely John II Komnenos, David and fourteen other prophets, the enemies, called the 'Persians' (v. 51), the New Rome (vv. 121, 271), the Byzantine people (v. 321). The biblical quotations are in this manner actualized and framed within a historical context close to the poet's personal experience. The biblical passages reused in the poem are significant in two complementary ways. On the one hand, the poet builds up his own verses drawing on the biblical heritage, which enhances the importance of the deeds of the emperor and is used as an *exemplum*. On the other hand, the Old Testament episodes are brought to life and vividly depicted in the present tense (e.g. v. 215: Ναοὺμ ὁ μέγας ἐκβοᾷ καὶ πάλιν προφητεύων, 'the great Nahum cries aloud and again prophesies'), so they acquire an additional meaning because of their relevance to the events contemporary to the poet.

Both the emperor and David in particular are frequent addressees of Prodromos' verses. Reading the poem, one cannot overlook the specific context in which Prodromos' activity was situated. He wrote his poems

31 For more general reflections on the relationship between poet and emperor in Prodromos' historical poems, see Bazzani (2007a).

in his capacity as court poet and did not miss any opportunity to ingratiate himself with the patron, using a well-known and widespread topos of twelfth-century literature, which was not immune from a certain degree of fictionality.[32] In vv. 16–20 the poet, addressing John Komnenos, announces why and how he will rely on David's words as a spiritual complement to the military campaign:[33]

> ἐπεὶ δὲ συγγινώσκω μου πᾶν ῥυπαρὸν τῷ βίῳ,
> ἀπ' ἐμαυτοῦ μὲν οὐ θαρρῶ τὰ τῆς εὐχῆς σοι δοῦναι,
> ἐκ τῶν σοφῶν δὲ προφητῶν δανείζομαι καὶ λέγω
> καὶ μάλιστα τῆς τοῦ Δαυὶδ πνευματοκρούστου λύρας
> καὶ τούτοις χρῶμαι συνεργοῖς ἄρτι καὶ συνευχέταις.
> (Prodromos, *Historical Poem* 17.16–20)

> Since I acknowledge the whole wretchedness of my life,
> I do not dare to offer you words of prayer from myself,[34]
> but I speak, borrowing from the wise prophets
> and above all from David's lyre, played by the Holy Spirit,
> and I use them just as helpers and fellow suppliants.

Prodromos acknowledges here the role of David as an unavoidable poetic model and source of inspiration in the composition of his verses. The image of the lyre of David, moved by the Spirit, seems to be a reference point for Byzantine poets. It is telling that an epigram written by George of Pisidia (seventh century), where the divinely inspired lyre is mentioned, was reused to accompany the text of the Psalms, and that this image was commonly employed in book epigrams that featured in Middle Byzantine Psalters.[35] Moreover, the invocation of David as a poetic 'muse' is also to be found elsewhere in Prodromos' poetic corpus, for example in *Historical Poem* 4.71–2, where John II Komnenos is also addressed: 'Give me, O David who plays the lyre, a few words from your songs, or be present and

32 For a general orientation on begging poetry in twelfth-century Byzantium, see Beaton (1987: 3–8). On the relevance of this attitude for Prodromic poetry (and the attribution problems posed by these compositions), see Alexiou (1986: *passim*).

33 For a similar passage, see *Historical Poem* 11.146–50: ἐπεὶ δὲ νοῦν ἀνθρώπινον αἱ νῖκαι σου νικῶσιν, | ἐκ τοῦ Δαβὶδ δανείζομαι τοῦ μουσικοῦ προφήτου | τοὺς ἐπαινέτας, βασιλεῦ, τῶν σῶν ἀριστευμάτων | καὶ συγκαλῶ τὸν οὐρανὸν καὶ τὰς ἀψύχους φύσεις | ὑμνῆσαι σε κατὰ θεὸν εὐλόγοις ἀλαλήτοις ('But since your victories surpass the human mind, I borrow praises from David, the musical prophet. O emperor, I convene the heaven and the inanimate natures to sing your praise in a godly manner, with unutterable eulogies').

34 In this verse Prodromos refers to his own poetry.

35 See DBBE, Type 4583, www.dbbe.ugent.be/types/4583 (accessed 15 February 2023). On the interpretation of this image, see Lauxtermann (2003–19: 1:202–4).

sing these things loudly for my king' (Δός μοι, Δαυὶδ κιθαρῳδέ, μικρά σου τῶν ᾀσμάτων, | ἢ σὺ παρὼν ἀλάλαζε ταῦτα τῷ βασιλεῖ μου).[36]

The figure of David is also particularly important at the beginning of another *decastichon* of *Historical Poem* 17, that is in vv. 41–3, in which John II Komnenos is again addressed and the identification of the emperor with David is explicitly expressed in a striking juxtaposition of the old David with the new one: 'Listen, divine king, bright bearer of trophies, to the words that the old David prophetically utters for you, the new David, as if from the divine voice' (Ἄκουσον, θεῖε βασιλεῦ, λαμπρὲ τροπαιοφόρε, | ἅπερ Δαυὶδ ὁ παλαιὸς σοί, τῷ Δαυὶδ τῷ νέῳ, | ὡς ἐκ φωνῆς τῆς θεϊκῆς προφητικῶς προλέγει).

The reading of these two passages of the poem makes clear the role of David, whose importance as a model is crucial both to the poet and to the emperor. Prodromos absolutely needs David's words to compose his poems and appropriates the Psalms skilfully, while John II is defined as a new David, and his kingship is dignified by the straightforward comparison with the Old Testament king.[37] In this respect, the presence of David in the poem is stronger and more meaningful than the reference to other prophets. The emperor is invited to listen to Prodromos' words as if he were listening to David. Another aspect that cannot be overlooked when analysing the relationship between Theodore and John is indeed the didactic one. Prodromos praises the ruler while instructing him.[38]

The presence of quotations from several books of the prophets besides the recurrent citations from the Psalms can indeed be explained as a didactic element, besides its function as a literary variation within the poem.[39] In twelfth-century Byzantium, the interest in biblical exegesis was particularly evident and widely testified.[40] The long-standing Byzantine tradition of learning the Psalms from a very early age onward was institutionalized by the decree issued in 1107 by Alexios I Komnenos, which possibly instituted the office of the *didaskalos tou Psalteriou*, along with the *didaskalos*

36 On Prodromos' habit of evoking David's lyre to praise the Komnenian emperors, see Zagklas (2023: 302).
37 Prodromos consistently stresses the divine element when portraying John throughout his oeuvre; see Magdalino (1993: 424).
38 See Zagklas (2019: 246).
39 I am grateful to Ilias Nesseris for raising this point at the conference.
40 Among other works, it is important to remember that in the late eleventh/early twelfth century Theophylaktos of Ohrid produced commentaries on Old Testament and New Testament books. Moreover, Nikephoros Basilakes composed *progymnasmata* on David. It is noteworthy, moreover, that the long prologue to the *Commentary on the Psalms* (*PG* 128, 41–1325) composed by Euthymios Zigabenos at the beginning of the twelfth century opens with an extensive account of David's life and deeds (*PG* 128, 41–8).

tou evangeliou and the *didaskalos tou apostolou*, all active in Hagia Sophia.[41] Theodore Prodromos could easily draw from his own experience as a teacher to compose a eulogy in verse with a manifest didactic character (provided both by the metrical choice and by the systematic borrowings from Old Testament passages used to instruct his addressee). His marked interest in the Psalms, and in the Old Testament in general, as found in *Historical Poem* 17, is furthermore expressed in the numerous tetrastichs he composed on episodes taken from the Old and New Testaments.[42] In our poem, Prodromos skilfully mixes episodes taken from the Old Testament and contemporary events. In doing so, he crosses the boundaries of panegyric poetry and proposes an idealized portrait of an emperor, depicted as a model to achieve. The ceremonial purposes and the didactic ones are not mutually exclusive but are complementary aspects that derive from Prodromos' identity and position of both court poet and private teacher.[43] The use of parenetic and didactic elements in such a poem, which is deliberately linked to a specific occasion, is thus not surprising.[44]

The intricate personal dynamics represented in *Historical Poem* 17 are also present in other occasional poems by Prodromos, composed to celebrate imperial splendour, such as in *Historical Poem* 1.39–44 (written in decapentasyllables for the coronation of Alexios I Komnenos), where the inspirational figure of David is also evoked so as to help celebrate the emperor:

> [...] Ὦ ἄνδρες, ὦ Ῥωμαῖοι,
> ἀθροίζεσθε μετὰ σπουδῆς, δεῦτε συνευφρανθῶμεν,
> δεῦτε πανηγυρίσωμεν ἄρδην ὁμοῦ καὶ πάντες
> χοροστατοῦντος τοῦ Δαυὶδ καὶ προκαταρχομένου
> μετὰ κιθάρας τῆς καλῆς τῆς πνευματοκινήτου
> καλὸν καὶ μέγα σήμερον προαναβαλλομένου.
> (Prodromos, *Historical Poem* 1.39–44)

> O people, O Romans,
> gather together quickly, come and let us rejoice,
> come you all immediately and let us exclaim together,

41 On the historiographical problems connected to the identification and the functions of the *didaskaloi*, see Gautier (1973: 172).

42 Ed. Papagiannis (1997). It is noticeable, however, that no epigrams specifically on David are preserved in this corpus, in spite of the fact that the Old Testament king was very often the subject of (book) epigrams commonly found in Byzantine manuscripts.

43 On the significance of this dual identity of Prodromos, see Zagklas (2023: 42).

44 See Lauxtermann (2003–19: 2:201).

as David leads and initiates a choir
with a beautiful lyre that is moved by the Holy Spirit,
singing a prelude on this beautiful and great day.

Towards the end of *Historical Poem* 17, the penultimate strophe interestingly reveals some more details about the personality of Prodromos, and especially about his attitude and role with respect to the emperor, as well as the importance of the poet's words compared with the biblical ones:

Οἱ μὲν λοιποὶ τῶν προφητῶν, ἄναξ, ἐπηύξαντό σοι,
ἡ τοῦ βοῶντος δὲ φωνὴ[45] λοιπὸν ἐκλαλησάτω,
ἐμὲ φημὶ τὸν Πρόδρομον τὸν ἐκ τῆς πανερήμου.
ἰσχύσαι τοίνυν, ὕψιστε, τὰ φῦλα τῶν βαρβάρων
καὶ τῆς Περσίδος ὁ λαός, ὅσον αὐτὸς ἰσχύω, 395
οὕτω τὸ βέλος πέμψειεν, ὥσπερ αὐτὸς ἐκπέμπω,
οὕτω τὸ δόρυ τείνειεν, ὥσπερ αὐτὸς ἐντείνω.
εἴπω τὰ πάντα συνελὼν καὶ παύσω μου τὸν λόγον·
γένοιτο τούτοις στόμαχος ὡς στόμαχος Προδρόμου
καίτοι μετὰ τὸν σίδηρον καὶ μετὰ τὸν καυτῆρα. 400
(Prodromos, *Historical Poem* 17.391–400)

The other prophets, lord, prayed for you,
but may the voice of one crying aloud divulge the rest.
I declare I am the Prodromos from the desert.
O highest, may the barbarian tribes
and the Persian people therefore be strong, as much as I am strong; 395
may they shoot the arrow, just like as I myself shoot it,
may they throw the spear, just like as I throw it.
Let me speak summarizing everything, and then I will cease to talk.
Let their stomach become like Prodromos' stomach,
indeed after the iron and after the branding iron.[46] 400

These verses highlight what Prodromos means by fighting together with the emperor (v. 5: ἤθελον συστρατεῦσαι σοι, 'I wanted to fight alongside you'). He depicts himself as John the Baptist, in Greek the Prodromos,

45 John 1:23.
46 Prodromos possibly refers in this passage to a surgery he had to undergo. His poor health condition is a recurrent topic in his poems, on which see Hörandner (1974: 30–2), Bazzani (2007b: *passim*). References to his stomach problems are also to be found elsewhere in his oeuvre, such as in *Historical Poem* 78.48–9: [Χριστέ,] σὺ σκέδασον στομάχοιο καὶ ἥπατος ἡμετέροιο | δῆριν ὀκρυόεσσαν, '[O Christ,] dispel the horrible battle from my stomach and my liver'. I am particularly grateful to Panagiotis Agapitos and Paul Magdalino for the opportunity to discuss the interpretation of this passage at the conference.

using a wordplay that is quite common in his writings. By wishing the enemies to be as strong as he is, Theodore actually means that they will hopefully be as weak as he is (in v. 7 he had complained about his own ἀσθένεια, 'weakness'). The depiction of his own fragility, however, is accompanied by a clear affirmation of the role and the value of his words in the war fought by the emperor. Prodromos puts his words on the same level as the prophets' words and declares that he will proclaim 'the rest' (λοιπόν, v. 392). If the emperor is customarily depicted as the new Christ, the poet is the new John the Baptist, whose presence is crucial in preparing and announcing Christ's parousia.

Adaptation of the Psalms

A survey of the literary features of *Historical Poem* 17 can lead to a deeper analysis of the use of biblical quotation in Prodromos' poetry. Besides its historical value, this poem is particularly interesting also because it contains a clear rewriting of some passages of the Bible in Byzantine decapentasyllables and therefore constitutes a conscious adaptation of an earlier hypotext.[47] Prodromos adapts the biblical text to the style of his time by using political verse. To modern eyes, the composition technique of the poem shows remarkable similarities with metaphrastic texts and can be considered a form of rewriting.[48] Taking the word *metaphrasis* in a broad sense, and meaning by it a technique rather than a literary genre,[49] we can indeed notice some parallels between the central strophes of the poem and actual *metaphraseis*, which denote rewritings of earlier texts where the same content is kept but is reshaped in a different style and presented in a new form.[50]

Within *Historical Poem* 17, two *decasticha* in the last part of the composition are a perfect example of the metaphrastic operation carried out by the poet. After the long list of quotations from the prophets that shape the

47 On the crucial distinction between an intertextual relationship and rewriting, see Efthymiadis (2021: 349).

48 The Psalms themselves were a privileged corpus of texts to be rewritten, as testified by the late antique hexametric metaphrasis attributed to Apollinaris of Laodicea (Faulkner [2020]) and the rewriting in political verses written by Manuel Philes (Gioffreda and Rhoby [2020]). For a comparison among these two metaphraseis, see Ricceri (2020).

49 See Lauxtermann (2003–19: 2:227).

50 For theoretical background on the forms of rewriting in premodern literature and relevant terminology, I refer to the recent introduction by Constantinou (2021: 10–18), with references to earlier literature on the topic (especially to Genette's theorization). The terminology used in this section of the chapter is also based on Signes Codoñer (2014).

core of the poem, vv. 341–60 open the second of the two long sections of the poem devoted to David:

Τῶν σῶν δέ, μέγιστε Δαυίδ, κόρον οὐκ ἔχω λόγων,
ἀλλὰ καλῶ καὶ πάλιν σου τὴν ἱερὰν κιθάραν
κιθαρῳδῆσαι τὰ χρηστὰ τῷ Κομνηνῷ δεσπότῃ.
παμβασιλεῦ, τὸ κρῖμα σου τῷ βασιλεῖ μου δίδου
καὶ τὴν δικαιοσύνην σου τῷ βασιλέως τέκνῳ. 345
ἐν ταῖς ἡμέραις γὰρ αὐτοῦ πλῆθος ἐστὶν εἰρήνης,
σώσει πτωχοὺς καὶ πένητας καὶ θραύσει συκοφάντας,
πασῶν κρατήσει θαλασσῶν, ἄρξει πασῶν ἠπείρων,
ἔμπροσθεν τούτου πέσωσιν ἄρχοντες Αἰθιόπων,
ἐχθροὶ δὲ τούτου λείξουσι κατὰ τοὺς ὄφεις χῶμα. 350
Ζητῶ τὸ λεῖπον τῆς εὐχῆς τῆς εἰς τὸν βασιλέα,
οὐ γὰρ ἐξετελέσθη σοι, προφῆτα μουσηγέτα.
Θαρσεῖς οἱ βασιλεύοντες, Ἀρράβων οἱ κρατοῦντες,
οἱ κυριεύοντες Σαβᾶ, νήσων οἱ τυραννοῦντες
δῶρα προσοίσουσιν αὐτῷ καὶ φόρους κομιοῦσι, 355
καὶ σύμπαν ἀλαζονικὸν ἔθνος αὐτῷ δουλεύσει,
ἀρθῶσιν ὑπὲρ Λίβανον οἱ τούτου θεῖοι κλάδοι,
καὶ ζήσεται μακραίωνα πανευτυχῶς τὸν βίον,
κἀκ τοῦ χρυσοῦ κομίσουσιν αὐτῷ τῆς Ἀρραβίας.
γένοιτο ταῦτα, γένοιτο τῷ βασιλεῖ, παντάναξ. 360
(Prodromos, *Historical Poem* 17.341–60)

Utterly great David, I cannot get enough of your words,
but I call again your holy lyre
to sing best wishes to the Komnenian ruler.
King of all, give your judgment to my emperor
and your righteousness to the emperor's son. 345
For in his days there will be an abundance of peace:
he will save the poor and the needy ones and will shatter the false accusers,
he will rule over all the seas, he will govern all the lands,
whereas the Ethiopian rulers will fall before him,
his enemies will lick the dust like the snakes. 350
I request whatever is missing from the prayer for the emperor,
for it has not been completed by you, prophet conductor of the choir.
The kings of Tharsis, the rulers of the Arabs, the lords of Saba and
the tyrants of the isles
shall offer gifts to him and shall bring tributes,
and all the arrogant barbaric nations shall serve him. 355
His divine offspring has been exalted to a higher point than Lebanon,
and he shall live a very happy long-lasting life.
And they will bring some of the gold of Arabia to him.
So be it, so be it for the emperor, O Lord of all. 360

The stanza opens with a clear reference to the Komnenian dynasty, to which the poet is connected with a tie of devotion (vv. 341–3). The poem becomes an occasion to praise the dynasty, as already noted above.[51] After three lines (vv. 344–6) in which Prodromos addresses David and declares his affection for the words of the Psalms, the poet quotes extensively from Psalm 71. The reference to the Psalms makes perfect sense in the context of a panegyric poem and contributes to the shaping of the image of John as a good sovereign.[52] These quotations are interrupted by the beginning of a new strophe, which opens with the clear distinction between the emperor and David, the prophet (vv. 351–2). This opening distich of the strophe emphasizes that the victory achieved by the emperor will be fuller than the achievements of the biblical king. The remaining lines of the strophe (vv. 353–60) again paraphrase the second part of Psalm 71, until the very end of the Psalm.

A synoptic reading of Prodromos' poem and the biblical text, as provided in Table 11.1, shows that the poet makes use of these two *decasticha* to paraphrase and summarize the text of Psalm 71. The general impression that one gets from reading these two strophes is indeed that Prodromos presents in this passage an abridged version of Psalm 71 rewritten in decapentasyllables.

In order to put Psalm 71 in political verse, Prodromos adopts the strategies of abbreviation, transposition and amplification, traditionally understood to have been employed for literary imitation.[53] Prodromos imitates his biblical hypotext and at the same time appropriates it.[54] This aspect of Prodromos' way of composing a long occasional poem is particularly meaningful in light of the observation that Byzantine rewritings are a prime example of how earlier texts were received and circulated.[55] The use of literary imitation does not affect the innovative character of Prodromos' composition, but represents for the poet a solid foundation on which he can build his very poetic eulogy, embedded in a specific occasion.[56] In doing so, Prodromos mixes different adaptation techniques and plays with the

51 See *supra*, p. 290–1.

52 On this topic, see Hörandner (2009: 111–12) with more parallels from Prodromos' poetic production.

53 See Genette (1982), Roberts (1985: 3). A thorough overview of the terminology formulated to discuss rewriting is to be found in Constantinou (2021: 10–18).

54 On the concept of appropriation applied to Byzantine metrical *metaphraseis*, see Ricceri (2020: 224–6), with further bibliography.

55 See Efthymiadis (2020: 359).

56 On the relationship between imitation and creativity, see Hunger (1969/70: 17) and, more recently, Nilsson (2010: 196).

Table 11.1 Comparison of Prodromos, *Historical Poem* 17 and Psalm 71

Historical Poem 17.344–60	Psalm 71 (selected passages)[a]
παμβασιλεῦ, τὸ κρῖμα σου τῷ βασιλεῖ μου δίδου	(1) Ὁ θεός, τὸ κρίμα σου τῷ βασιλεῖ δὸς
καὶ τὴν δικαιοσύνην σου τῷ βασιλέως τέκνῳ. (345)	καὶ τὴν δικαιοσύνην σου τῷ υἱῷ τοῦ βασιλέως
ἐν ταῖς ἡμέραις γὰρ αὐτοῦ πλῆθος ἐστὶν εἰρήνης,	(7) ἀνατελεῖ ἐν ταῖς ἡμέραις αὐτοῦ δικαιοσύνη καὶ πλῆθος εἰρήνης ἕως οὗ ἀνταναιρεθῇ ἡ σελήνη.
σώσει πτωχοὺς καὶ πένητας καὶ θραύσει συκοφάντας,	(4) κρινεῖ τοὺς πτωχοὺς τοῦ λαοῦ καὶ σώσει τοὺς υἱοὺς τῶν πενήτων καὶ ταπεινώσει συκοφάντην
πασῶν κρατήσει θαλασσῶν, ἄρξει πασῶν ἠπείρων,	(8) καὶ κατακυριεύσει ἀπὸ θαλάσσης ἕως θαλάσσης καὶ ἀπὸ ποταμοῦ ἕως περάτων τῆς οἰκουμένης.
ἔμπροσθεν τούτου πέσωσιν ἄρχοντες Αἰθιόπων,	(9) ἐνώπιον αὐτοῦ προπεσοῦνται Αἰθίοπες, καὶ οἱ ἐχθροὶ αὐτοῦ χοῦν λείξουσιν·
ἐχθροὶ δὲ τούτου λείξουσι κατὰ τοὺς ὄφεις χῶμα. (350)	
Ζητῶ τὸ λεῖπον τῆς εὐχῆς τῆς εἰς τὸν βασιλέα,	...
οὐ γὰρ ἐξετελέσθη σοι, προφῆτα μουσηγέτα.	
Θαρσεῖς οἱ βασιλεύοντες, Ἀρράβων οἱ κρατοῦντες,	(10) βασιλεῖς Θαρσις καὶ αἱ νῆσοι δῶρα προσοίσουσιν, βασιλεῖς Ἀράβων καὶ Σαβα δῶρα προσάξουσιν·
οἱ κυριεύοντες Σαβᾶ, νήσων οἱ τυραννοῦντες	(11) καὶ προσκυνήσουσιν αὐτῷ πάντες οἱ βασιλεῖς, πάντα τὰ ἔθνη δουλεύσουσιν αὐτῷ.
δῶρα προσοίσουσιν αὐτῷ καὶ φόρους κομιοῦσι, (355)	
καὶ σύμπαν ἀλαζονικὸν ἔθνος αὐτῷ δουλεύσει,	
ἀρθῶσιν ὑπὲρ Λίβανον οἱ τούτου θεῖοι κλάδοι,	(16) ... ὑπεραρθήσεται ὑπὲρ τὸν Λίβανον ὁ καρπὸς αὐτοῦ, καὶ ἐξανθήσουσιν ἐκ πόλεως ὡσεὶ χόρτος τῆς γῆς.
καὶ ζήσεται μακραίωνα πανευτυχῶς τὸν βίον,	(15) καὶ ζήσεται, καὶ δοθήσεται αὐτῷ ἐκ τοῦ χρυσίου τῆς Ἀραβίας, καὶ προσεύξονται περὶ αὐτοῦ διὰ παντός, ὅλην τὴν ἡμέραν εὐλογήσουσιν αὐτόν.
κἀκ τοῦ χρυσοῦ κομίσουσιν αὐτῷ τῆς Ἀρραβίας.	(19) καὶ εὐλογητὸν τὸ ὄνομα τῆς δόξης αὐτοῦ εἰς τὸν αἰῶνα καὶ εἰς τὸν αἰῶνα τοῦ αἰῶνος, καὶ πληρωθήσεται τῆς δόξης αὐτοῦ πᾶσα ἡ γῆ. γένοιτο γένοιτο.
γένοιτο ταῦτα, γένοιτο τῷ βασιλεῖ, παντάναξ. (360)	

[a] (1) O God, give the King your judgment and your justice to his son, to judge your people with justice and the poor in right judgment. (7) In his days the righteous one will grow, as will the abundance of peace until the moon is no more. (4) He will judge the poor of the people and save the sons of the needy and humble the extortioner. (8) And he shall exercise dominion from sea to sea and from rivers to the world's limits. (9) Before him Ethiopians will fall down, and his enemies will lick dust. (10) The kings of Tharsis and the islands will offer tribute; the kings of Arabia and Saba will bring gifts; (11) all the kings of the earth will adore him, all nations will serve him. (16) ... its fruit will surpass Lebanon, and they will blossom forth from a city like the grass of the field. (15) And he shall live long, and there will be given to him of the gold of Arabia. And they will pray for him continually; all day long they will bless him. (19) And blessed be the name of his glory for ever and ever, and the whole earth will be filled with his glory. May it be; may it be. (trans. after Pietersma 2000)

different possibilities offered by the practice of literary imitation.[57] In some passages, the poet chooses to adhere faithfully to the biblical text, as in vv. 347–8, which reproduce Ps. 71.1 almost verbatim. It is not a coincidence that the incipit of the quotation sticks to the incipit of the hypotext, so that the allusion is unmistakably recognizable from the very beginning of the citation, and in a way legitimizes Prodromos' text. However, the verses that follow do not entirely reflect the order of the biblical verses quoted, which Prodromos also handles quite freely in terms of their meaning,[58] so that what we are dealing with here is an example of literary transposition.

In the passage under consideration some verses of the Psalms are lacking, in rhetorical terms an abbreviation of the source. More specifically, the poet skips some portions of the biblical verses he quotes, as in v. 349, based on Ps. 71.7, in which Prodromos omits the reference to the moon. It is noteworthy, finally, that in some specific contexts the poet expands the text of the Psalm, using so-called amplification. This is the case with vv. 353–5, which have Ps. 71.10 as source text. In the biblical verses, the reference to the foreign rulers who will honour the king is only expressed by means of the repetition of βασιλεῖς ('kings') twice. Prodromos elaborates on the hypotext by using four synonyms (vv. 533–4: βασιλεύοντες, 'kings'; κρατοῦντες, 'rulers'; κυριεύοντες, 'lords'; τυραννοῦντες, 'tyrants'). Not only is this stylistic choice an elegant example of *variatio*, but it also underlines the vastness of the triumph of the emperor, who will defeat powerful and diverse enemies. By playing with different techniques, the poet cleverly chooses to underline the elements of the source text that are most suitable to mark the occasion of the poem.

Conclusions

The close reading of *Historical Poem* 17 has been particularly enlightening for at least two reasons, which shed light on typically twelfth-century poetic strategies related to the particular ways in which biblical exempla were used to depict the relationship between emperors and poets. It is by now clear how Prodromos in this long composition combines his background as a teacher and the typical features of an occasional poem (related to his function as a court poet).[59] The figure of David, in this example of twelfth-cen-

57 On the intellectual value of literary imitation in Byzantine literature, see Nilsson (2010: 198–201).

58 See Hörandner (1974: 286).

59 The interesting compresence of these two aspects in Prodromos' poetry has been pointed out by Zagklas (2023: 42).

tury learned poetry, is a model both for the emperor and for the poet. The eulogy of the ruler is intertwined with the systematic reuse of biblical material in a poetic shape. The imperial ideology is conveyed by the allusion to suitable Old Testament *exempla*, but at the same time the emperor and Constantinople itself are asked to learn from these prophets (by means of the verb εὐαγγελίζομαι, 'to preach the gospel', in vv. 82 and 123).

The poem's didactic thrust ties in with a general revival of interest in biblical exegesis in twelfth-century Constantinople. Moreover, *Historical Poem* 17 highlights the prominent role of Prodromos as a court poet, and is a convenient case study that reflects personal dynamics in the twelfth-century intellectual context. Prodromos customarily presents himself as the one who gives voice to the emperor's victories and explicitly links his poem to present events. However, it is noteworthy that the core of the poem is built as a literary play. Theodore Prodromos complies with his function of court poet by praising and teaching, and he presents himself as the one who has to serve his patron. At the same time, by describing himself as the new Forerunner, mirroring John the Baptist, he presents himself as opening the way to the new David and new Christ.

Besides the humility that the poet is accustomed to profess and the panegyric character necessary to this kind of composition, the centrality of David in *Historical Poem* 17 results in an interesting insight into the personality of the poet and his relationship with the emperor. The biblical poet-king, thanks to his twofold nature, is not only an inspiration in different ways both for Theodore and for John, but he also represents a perfect *alter ego* for both of them, depending on the level on which the text is read. The figure of David is depicted as a node that interconnects the emperor and the poet, who need each other as complementary parts of a broader picture.

The refined choice of Prodromos to arrange this poem as a metaphrastic patchwork, a poetic rewriting of selected passages of biblical poetry, gives us a glimpse into a specific aspect of the reception of the biblical text, which is an inevitable reference point for both the poet and the emperor. The former holds the Bible as a literary model and can creatively handle it; the latter is contrasted to prominent biblical models and is dignified by means of these comparisons. The analysis of the biblical hypotext as a literary source, moreover, has provided new insight into the role that the biblical text could possibly play within Byzantine authors' canonical reference system. The study of the Bible as a stylistic and literary model is a promising field of investigation to advance our understanding of intertextuality in Byzantine texts, beyond the boundaries of classical models.

The constant presence of David, in his double nature of king and poet, assures the achievement of a balanced composition: John II Komnenos indeed receives the ample and articulate eulogy that is expected to be delivered, while Prodromos at the same time highlights his own role by means of the identification with one of the most iconic archetypes of the poet that Byzantine writers could evoke.

Bibliography

Agapitos, P. A. (1989) 'Η εικόνα του αυτοκράτορα Βασιλείου Α' στη φιλομακεδονική γραμματεία 867–959', *Ἑλληνικά* 40: 285–322.
Alexiou, M. (1986) 'The Poverty of Écriture and the Craft of Writing: Towards a Reappraisal of the Prodromic Poems', *BMGS* 10.1: 1–40.
Angelov, D. A. (2006) 'The Confession of Michael VIII Palaiologos and King David: On a Little Known Work by Manuel Holobolos', *JÖByz* 56: 193–204.
(2007) *Imperial Ideology and Political Thought in Byzantium, 1204–1330*. Cambridge.
Bazzani, M. (2007a) 'The Historical Poems of Theodore Prodromos, the Epic-Homeric Revival and the Crisis of Intellectuals in the Twelfth Century', *ByzSlav* 65: 211–28.
(2007b) 'Theodore Prodromos' Poem LXXVII', *ByzZ* 100.1: 1–12.
Beaton, R. (1987) 'The Rhetoric of Poverty: The Lives and Opinions of Theodore Prodromos', *BMGS* 11.1: 1–28.
Constantinou, S. (2021) 'Metaphrasis: Mapping Premodern Rewriting', in *Metaphrasis: A Byzantine Concept of Rewriting and its Hagiographical Products*, ed. S. Constantinou and C. Høgel, 3–60. Leiden.
Cutler, A. (1984) *The Aristocratic Psalters in Byzantium*. Paris.
Dagron, G. (2003) *Emperor and Priest: The Imperial Office in Byzantium*. Cambridge.
DBBE: Database of Byzantine Book Epigrams, www.dbbe.ugent.be.
de Wald, E. (1944) 'The Comnenian Portraits in the Barberini Psalter', *Hesperia* 13.1: 78–86.
Efthymiadis, S. (2021) 'Rewriting', in *The Oxford Handbook of Byzantine Literature*, ed. S. Papaioannou, 348–64. Oxford.
Faulkner, A. (2016) 'Theodore Prodromos' Historical Poems: A Hymnic Celebration of John II Komnenos', in *The Reception of the Homeric Hymns*, ed. A. Faulkner, A. Vergados and A. Schwab, 261–74. Oxford.
(2020) *Apollinaris of Laodicea, Metaphrasis Psalmorum*. Oxford.
Gautier, P. (1973) 'L'édit d'Alexis Ier Comnène sur la réforme du clergé', *RÉB* 31: 165–201.
Genette, G. (1982) *Palimpsestes: La littérature au second degré*. Paris.
Gioffreda, A., and A. Rhoby (2020) 'Die metrische Psalmenmetaphrase des Manuel Philes: Präliminarien zu einer kritischen Edition', *MEG* 20: 119–41.

Hörandner, W. (1972) 'Prodromos-Reminiszenzen bei Dichtern der Nikänischen Zeit', *ByzF* 4: 98–104.

(ed.) (1974) *Theodoros Prodromos: Historische Gedichte*. Wiener Byzantinistische Studien 11. Vienna.

(1996) 'Nugae epigrammaticae', in *Philellēn: Studies in Honour of Robert Browning*, ed. C. N. Constantinides, N. M. Panagiotakes, E. M. Jeffreys and A. D. Angelou, 107–16. Venice.

(2003) 'Court Poetry: Questions of Motifs, Structure and Function', in *Rhetoric in Byzantium: Papers from the Thirty-Fifth Spring Symposium of Byzantine Studies, University of Oxford, March 2001*, ed. E. M. Jeffreys, 75–85. Society for the Promotion of Byzantine Studies Publications 11. Aldershot.

(2009) 'Les conceptions du bon souverain dans la poésie byzantine', in '*L'éducation au gouvernement et à la vie': La tradition des 'règles de vie' de l'antiquité au moyen-âge. Colloque international – Pise, 18 et 19 mars 2005*, ed. P. Odorico, 103–14. Autour de Byzance 1. Paris.

Hörandner, W., and A. Rhoby (2021) 'Metrics and Prose Rhythm', in *The Oxford Handbook of Byzantine Literature*, ed. S. Papaioannou, 407–29. Oxford.

Hunger, H. (1969/70) 'On the Imitation (ΜΙΜΗΣΙΣ) of Antiquity in Byzantine Literature', *DOP* 23/24: 15–38.

Kalavrezou, I., N. Trahoulia and S. Sabar (1993) 'Critique of the Emperor in the Vatican Psalter Gr. 752', *DOP* 47: 195–219.

Lampros, S. P. 1879–80. *Μιχαὴλ Ἀκομινάτου τοῦ Χωνιάτου τὰ σωζόμενα*, 2. vols. Athens.

Lauxtermann, M. D. (2003–19) *Byzantine Poetry from Pisides to Geometres: Texts and Contexts*, 2 vols. Wiener Byzantinistische Studien 24. Vienna.

(2009) 'Byzantine Didactic Poetry and the Question of Poeticality', in *'Doux remède…': Poésie et poétique à Byzance. Actes du IVe Colloque International Philologique 'ΕΡΜΗΝΕΙΑ', Paris, 23–24–25 février 2006, organisé par l'E.H.E.S.S. et l'Université de Chypre*, ed. P. Odorico, M. Hinterberger and P. A. Agapitos, 37–46. Dossiers byzantins 9. Paris.

Maguire, H. (1988) 'The Art of Comparing in Byzantium', *ABull* 70.1: 88–103.

Magdalino, P. (1993) *The Empire of Manuel I Komnenos, 1143–1180*. Cambridge.

(ed.) (1994) *New Constantines: The Rhythm of Imperial Renewal in Byzantium, 4th–13th Centuries. Papers from the Twenty-Sixth Spring Symposium of Byzantine Studies, St Andrews, March 1992*. Aldershot.

Markopoulos, A. (1992) 'An Anonymous Laudatory Poem in Honor of Basil I', *DOP* 46: 225–32.

Nilsson, I. (2010) 'The Same Story but Another: A Reappraisal of Literary Imitation in Byzantium', in *Imitatio–Aemulatio–Variatio: Akten des internationalen wissenschaftlichen Symposions zur byzantinischen Sprache und Literatur (Wien, 22.–25. Oktober 2008)*, ed. A. Rhoby and E. Schiffer, 195–208. Vienna.

Papagiannis, G. (ed.) (1997) *Theodoros Prodromos: Jambische und hexametrische Tetrasticha auf die Haupterzaehlungen des Alten und Neuen Testaments,* 2 vols. Vienna.

(2012) *Philoprodromica: Beiträge zur Textkonstitution und Quellenforschung der historischen Gedichte des Theodoros Prodromos*. Vienna.

Pietersma, A. (2000) *A New English Translation of the Septuagint: The Psalms*. New York.

Rapp, C. (2010) 'Old Testament Models for Emperors in Early Byzantium', in *The Old Testament in Byzantium*, ed. P. Magdalino and R. S. Nelson, 175–97. Washington, DC.

Rhoby, A. (2018) *Ausgewählte byzantinische Epigramme in illuminierten Handschriften: Verse und ihre 'inschriftliche' Verwendung in Codices des 9. bis 15. Jahrhunderts*. Vienna.

Ricceri, R. (2020) 'Two Metrical Rewritings of the Greek Psalms: Pseudo-Apollinaris of Laodicea and Manuel Philes', in *Poetry, Bible and Theology from Late Antiquity to the Middle Ages*, ed. M. Cutino, 223–36. Berlin.

Roberts, M. (1985) *Biblical Epic and Rhetorical Paraphrase in Late Antiquity*. Liverpool.

Romano, R. (ed.) (1980) *Nicola Callicle: Carmi. Testo critico, introduzione, traduzione, commentario e lessico*. Byzantina et Neo-Hellenica Neapolitana 8. Naples.

Signes Codoñer, J. (2014) 'Towards a Vocabulary for Rewriting in Byzantium', in *Textual Transmission in Byzantium: Between Textual Criticism and Quellenforschung*, ed. J. Signes Codoñer and I. Pérez Martín, 61–90. Turnhout.

Spatharakis, I. (1976) *The Portrait in Byzantine Illuminated Manuscripts*. Leiden.

Treitinger, O. (1956) *Die oströmische Kaiser- und Reichsidee nach ihrer Gestaltung im höfischen Zeremoniell: Vom oströmischen Staats- und Reichsgedanken*. Darmstadt.

Tsamakda, V. (2010) 'König David als Typos des byzantinischen Kaisers', in *Byzanz: Das Römerreich im Mittelalter*, ed. F. Daim and J. Drauschke, 24–54. Mainz.

Westerink, L. G. (ed.) (1992) *Michaelis Pselli Poemata*. Stuttgart.

Zagklas, N. (2018) 'Metrical *Polyeideia* and Generic Innovation in the Twelfth Century: The Multimetric Cycles of Occasional Poetry', in *Middle and Late Byzantine Poetry: Texts and Contexts*, ed. A. Rhoby and N. Zagklas, 43–70. Byzantios: Studies in Byzantine History and Civilization 14. Turnhout.

(2019) '"How Many Verses Shall I Write and Say?" Poetry in the Komnenian Period (1081–1204)', in *A Companion to Byzantine Poetry*, ed. W. Hörandner, A. Rhoby and N. Zagklas, 237–63. Brill's Companions to the Byzantine World 4. Leiden.

(2023) *Theodore Prodromos, Miscellaneous Poems: An Edition and Literary Study*. Oxford.

Zahnd, U. (2008) 'Novus David – Νεος Δαυιδ: Zur Frage nach byzantinischen Vorläufern eines abendländischen Topos', *FMS* 42.1: 71–88.

PART IV

New Texts, New Interpretations

CHAPTER 12

Manganeios Prodromos
His Life and Writings

†Elizabeth Jeffreys and Michael Jeffreys

The work of 'Manganeios Prodromos', perhaps the last significant poet from the twelfth century whose work still remains to be fully edited,[1] was for long subsumed within that of Theodore Prodromos. Since the early twentieth century, however, his verse has been ascribed to an otherwise unidentified poet from mid-twelfth-century Constantinople who wrote for the emperor Manuel and members of the aristocracy, in particular for the *sebastokratorissa* Irene and her children.[2] Most of his surviving poetry is more or less datable between 1142 and 1159. Nothing composed in prose has yet been attributed to him. This chapter offers a survey of some basic information on this poet's life and writings and concludes with an annotated edition of MP 15 as an example of how his verse might be presented to readers today.[3]

Name

In the manuscripts an authorial name is barely mentioned: the poems are regularly ascribed 'To the same' or preserved anonymously. In two manuscripts, however, the poet is named in the heading to MP 1 as 'kyr Theodore Prodromos'. But, although there are similarities in their careers and their lifetimes largely coincide, it has long been clear that this poet cannot

1 The long-promised edition by Elizabeth and Michael Jeffreys proceeds, albeit slowly. This contribution to the present volume is an earnest of the Jeffreys' good intentions.

2 Papademetriou (1903), who successfully argued against the thought that the corpus was produced by more than one poet. The question of poets named Prodromos, hotly debated *c.* 1900 by e.g. Chatzidakis (1897) and Kurtz (1901), (1907), and revived in the 1970s and 1980s by e.g. Bernardinello (1972), Kazhdan and Franklin (1984: 87–114) and Alexiou (1986), currently focuses on the authorship of the Prochoprodromic poems; see Zagklas (2023: 3–5).

3 In A and V; for details on the manuscripts, see below. Poems are cited in this chapter by the abbreviation MP followed by poem and line number; the poem numbering, which is that of the forthcoming edition, follows the catalogue entry to Venice, Biblioteca Nazionale Marciana, gr. XI. 22 [Diktyon 70658; hereafter M] in Mioni (1970: 116–31).

be Theodore Prodromos, not least because of the reference in MP 37.27–47 to Theodore as a recently dead colleague.[4] More generally Theodore Prodromos had a career as a teacher while there is no sign of this in Manganeios' work; Manganeios was deeply involved with the *sebastokratorissa* Irene and her family while Theodore's connection was limited; Theodore was a versatile writer who explored many styles and subjects in both prose and verse while there is no evidence that Manganeios ventured beyond 'occasional' verse and epigrams, using two metres only (though the hazards of transmission may be to blame for this). However, it is possible that Manganeios' family name was Prodromos: the title to MP 61 in Venice, Biblioteca Nazionale Marciana, gr. XI.22 exceptionally refers to the author as 'Prodromos', a name supported in MP 12.26 where the poet, one of several celebrating the imminent birth of Manuel's first child, claims to 'cry out with my Prodromic voice'.[5] There is no indication in the poems of his baptismal name. For convenience he has come to be known as Manganeios Prodromos, because of his persistent quest in later life for admission to the Mangana *adelphaton*, as indicated below.[6]

Manuscripts and Manuscript Relationships

There are five manuscript witnesses to Manganeios' corpus, referred to in the forthcoming edition with the sigla M, V, A, D, P (in chronological order).

M: Venice, Biblioteca Nazionale Marciana, gr. XI.22 (coll. 1235) [Diktyon 70658]; late thirteenth century.[7] This contains a collection of rhetorical texts from the twelfth century compiled almost certainly in Constantinople. Water-stained throughout but remaining legible, 144 of Manganeios' 148 surviving poems appear on fols 1–87 in a small, neat but as yet unidentified hand (Giacomelli's Scribe A); the lack of annotations in this section makes it unlikely to have been used in teaching. From Miller's transcription in P (see below) it is clear that by the mid-nineteenth century M had already lost folios after fols. 29v, 76v and 82v; fol. 68 was lost subsequently. Mid-page lacunas on fols. 21r and 61r and the lack of poem titles

4 Papademetriou (1903: 112–19, 147); Hörandner (1967), (1974: 21–2) and (1975); Magdalino (1993: 440).

5 MP 12.26: καὶ τῇ προδρόμῳ μου φωνῇ κἀγὼ συνανακράξω.

6 Papademetriou (1903: 151), Bernardinello (1972).

7 The description in Mioni (1970: 116–31) and the supplementary bibliography of editions in Magdalino (1993: 494–500) are now superseded by the comprehensive account in Giacomelli (2020); cf. Zorzi (2020).

on fols. 44, 59 and 63 suggest that M's exemplar was defective. Manganeios' texts are presented in two groups: texts in fifteen-syllable verse followed by those in twelve-syllables; exceptionally MP 20, a long narrative poem in twelve-syllables, appears on fol. 30r amidst the fifteen-syllables. The poems are loosely arranged hierarchically by addressee and topic (emperor followed by members of the aristocracy, then by secular ceremony and religious dedications). The scribe's orthography and syntax are usually correct.[8] The second half of the manuscript, fols. 91r–189v, contains a rich collection of twelfth-century rhetorical texts, copied for the most part by the scribe (Giacomelli's Scribe C) who is also responsible for much of Vienna, Österreichische Nationalbibliothek, phil. gr. 321, that is, ms V for Manganeios.

V: Vienna, Österreichische Nationalbibliothek, phil. gr. 321 [Diktyon 71435]; late thirteenth-century.[9] Like M, this is a collection of rhetorical texts, in this case arguably compiled for teaching purposes. Agapitos and Angelov have argued that the compiler and scribe was Manuel Holobolos, working on the manuscript between 1267 and 1273:[10] the case is tempting but palaeographically unconvincing. Acquired by Augerius von Busbeck when in Constantinople between 1555 and 1562,[11] it was already then bound in its present form. MP 1 and 2, and the title only of MP 21, are found on fols. 306r–308v, attributed to Theodore Prodromos; an indeterminate number of folios are missing after 308v. As noted above, the main scribe of this manuscript was also involved with the copying of Marcianus graecus XI.22, though not the section covering Manganeios Prodromos.

A: Milan, Biblioteca Ambrosiana, gr. O 94 (592) [Diktyon 43068]; before 1440.[12] Eighteen of Manganeios' poems are found on fols. 1r–38v, all in fifteen-syllable verse, riddled with iotacisms and attributed to Theodore Prodromos; four (MP 145–8), apart from a few lines in manuscript D (see below), are not found in any other manuscript. The sequence of poems in A does not correspond to that in M and many passages are omitted in comparison with M. The rest of the manuscript is taken up with extracts from the *Oneirocriticon*.[13]

8 Sideras (2010: 63) concludes, after a comparison of texts by Gregory Antiochos in M and El Escorial, Real Biblioteca, Y-II-10 [Diktyon 15478], that, while the scribes were both competent, the scribe of M produced a greater number of erratic forms.

9 Hunger (1961: 409–18). Digitized image: http://data.onb.ac.at/rec/AL00116655. We would like to acknowledge with gratitude that the late Wolfram Hörandner very kindly many years ago sent us an excellent photocopy of this manuscript.

10 Agapitos and Angelov (2019: 60).

11 Gastgeber (2020: 153–4).

12 Martini and Bassi (1906: 682–5).

13 Mavroudi (2002: 109).

D: Athos, Dionysiou 263 (3797) [Diktyon 20231]; late seventeenth century.[14] This varied collection of patristic and ecclesiastical material was probably created to restock the monastery library following a fire. On fols. 184r–186r it includes unattributed extracts from Manganeios Prodromos: all of MP 44, and MP 129, 130, 133, 137 taken from the sequence of MP 129–44, and also MP 147.2–23 (found only in A, in a fuller version).[15]

P: Paris, Bibliothèque nationale de France, Suppl. gr. 1219, fols. 1–567 [Diktyon 53884]; mid-nineteenth century.[16] This contains a transcription of M made by the Academician E. Miller (1810–86) for the volumes on the Greek historians in the *Recueil des historiens des Croisades* (1881) and provides the basis for Miller's extensive quotations from Manganeios in his annotations. P is the sole witness to MP 57–9 which were on M's now lost fol. 68 and is a useful witness to M in areas where that manuscript is now less legible than in the mid-nineteenth century.

To sum up, of the 148 poems and 17,236 lines that make up the surviving corpus of Manganeios' work, all but 4 poems and 141 lines are preserved in M. Eighteen poems (including the four not in M) and 1,844 lines are to be found in A;[17] 480 lines, two poems and a title in V; 208 lines in one poem and extracts from five others in D. However, no poem is found in all four witnesses and only two are in three (MP 1 in AMV and MP 44 in ADM). P is Miller's apograph of M, and as such (as noted above) is worth consulting. M, which preserves the bulk of MP's surviving corpus, is inevitably the foundation for any critical edition of these poems.

There are regrettably few points on which to draw conclusions about the stemmatic relationship of these manuscripts since so few poems are preserved in more than one manuscript and most items that could be recorded in the textual apparatus are due to A's loose scribal practices. That AMV derive from a common archetype[18] is suggested by a two-line lacuna in MP 1 in the stanza beginning at MP 1.171 where the stanza, regularly consisting of ten lines in this poem, here consists of only eight. The clearest indication that M's antecedents may be distinct from those of AV comes in MP 1.195 where M's μηδεύματα is contextually stronger than AV's βουλεύματα. There is however no other case of agreement of AV against M and no case in MP 1 where a reading of AM or MV is to be corrected from the third

14 Lampros (1895: 387–9).
15 Van Deun (2000: xxxvi), Kenens and Van Deun (2014: 115–18). We thank Professor Van Deun for generously providing us with images of this manuscript.
16 Astruc and Concasty (1960: 381–2).
17 MP 1, 14, 22, 27, 28, 30, 40, 43, 44, 45, 47, 61, 62, 64, 145, 146, 147, 148.
18 Hörandner (1967: 94) and (1975: 96 n. 4).

witness.[19] The fact that A preserves four poems not found in M, portions of one of which are to be found in D, suggests that more than one exemplar of the corpus was originally in circulation.

D is part of a large late anthology of mainly theological material; the small number of verses taken from MP focusses selectively on moral issues. Independence from M is shown by the lack of M's titles to MP 129, 130, 133 and 137 but more significantly by lines from MP 147, a poem present in A but not M, raising the unprovable possibility of D's connection with a manuscript descended from A or an antecedent of A. None of D's readings have independent value.

The overall agreement in wording in the four manuscripts A, D, M and V and the lack of a consistent pattern of errors indicate that they derive independently from a common archetype. The ordering of poems by dedicatee and subject in M suggests that this may have been a collected 'edition', whether authorially planned or not, which subsequently lost its title page.

Transmission

As a result of recent work by Zorzi and Giacomelli a tortuous, but not unprecedented, trajectory can be traced for Marcianus graecus XI.22 (= manuscript M for Manganeios), or for an apograph of its distinctive contents of which there is otherwise no trace yet discovered.[20] A manuscript with contents corresponding to Marcianus graecus XI.22 is recorded in Italy in the library of Pico della Mirandola (1463–94), then in that of Cardinal Grimani (1461–1523), who bequeathed his books to the monastery of S. Antonio di Castello. At some point in the seventeenth century the holdings of this library were dispersed following a fire. Marcianus graecus XI.22 made its way to Crete and the *metochion* in Candia of St Catherine's of Sinai, whose possession mark is on fol. 1r.[21] It was subsequently acquired by Bernardo Nani (1712–61) and Giacomo Nani (1725–97), possibly in the Ionian islands.[22] The books collected by the Nani brothers were left to the San Marco library in 1797.[23]

19 At MP 1.78, *contra* Hörandner (1975: 96 n. 4), the article is to be resolved in V as well as in A and M as τῆς, and then corrected to τὰς.
20 Zorzi (2020), Giacomelli (2020).
21 Zorzi (2020: 328–32); St Catherine's also had a *metochion* on Zakynthos, discussed at length in Zorzi (2020).
22 Zorzi (2020: 316–17).
23 Zorzi (2020: 328, n. 82) and especially Giacomelli (2020: 'Provenienz').

The other surviving witnesses to MP's text offer fewer excitements. The moralizing excerpts from Manganeios' work in Athos, Dionysiou 263 (= D), however, suggest – as indicated above – that other copies of the texts, whether complete or partial, were in circulation. Intriguingly *Poem* 7 of George Amiroutzes (d. after 1469), which celebrates Mehmed II's military triumphs, uses lines derived from MP 24. Given that Amiroutzes' poem is known only from Istanbul, Topkapi Sarayi, G. 1. 39 [Diktyon 33985], a possible source for Amiroutzes' awareness of MP's work could be the now defective Vienna, phil. gr. 321 (i.e. manuscript V for Manganeios) which was in Constantinople until 1562.[24]

Previous Editions

The writings of Theodore Prodromos were admired in his lifetime and during the Palaiologan literary revival; they also received much attention when Western scholars explored later writings in Greek as can be seen in the prominence given him by Allatius (1586–1669),[25] Du Cange (1610–88),[26] Fabricius (1668–1736)[27] or La Porte du Theil (1742–1815),[28] as well as in the early printing of some of his religious epigrams.[29] Theodore had also acquired in the manuscripts an extra element to his persona with the frequently used epithet 'Ptochoprodomos'.[30] However, Manganeios' poems had languished unnoticed – unsurprisingly since the main manuscript in which they are preserved, and in which they are attributed to Theodore, followed a circuitous and unobtrusive route round Italian and Ottoman territories before coming to rest in Venice as part of the Nani family's collection of antiquities. The Greek manuscripts from this collection were bequeathed to the Marciana Library in 1797. Mingarelli's catalogue of the Nani manuscripts had been published in 1784, with a full description. There Mingarelli queried whether the anonymous author of the poems on fols. 1–87 of what became Marcianus graecus XI.22 (but at that time was Nanianus 281) might be John Italos.[31]

24 On the date and context of Istanbul, Topkapi Sarayi, G. 1. 39 (containing Aristotle's *Parva naturalia*) and Amiroutzes' involvement with Mehmed, see Reinsch (1985) and (2020: 112–13); on Amiroutzes' *Poem* 7, see Janssens and Van Deun (2004: 319–24).

25 Migne (1864: 1003–16).

26 Ducange (1688: *passim*).

27 Fabricius (1705–28: 6:799–803).

28 Migne (1864: 1015).

29 Guntius (1536).

30 Hörandner (1993: 318).

31 Mingarelli (1784: 462, 477).

By the time texts had been collected and published for the volumes on the Greek historians in the monumental *Receuil des historiens des Croisades*[32] this anonymous author had been subsumed definitively into the name of Theodore Prodromos and was quoted copiously by Miller in the volume of notes to the Greek historians as Theodore Prodromos 'in the Venetian manuscript' ('cod. Ven.').[33] While many of Manganeios' poems are quoted in full, especially in the Appendix to the volume,[34] most were shorn of their rhetorical elaborations and often cited only for brief items of lexical or syntactical interest. Miller also published several groups of shorter texts, selected mainly for their historical interest.[35] As a result, much of Manganeios' work was made available but in a piecemeal fashion and with no literary context. More of Manganeios' writings were put into the public domain by Papademetriou, with several purposes:[36] to demonstrate that Manganeios is to be distinguished from Theodore Prodromos and cannot be identified with any other poet known from the twelfth century,[37] and also to put more material before the scholarly public, this time with a focus on the events surrounding the *sebastokratorissa* Irene. It is to Papademetriou, who drew attention to the emphasis on the Mangana *adelphaton* in the anonymous corpus, that this Prodromos owes his soubriquet of Manganeios.[38] Varzos subsequently reprinted in his prosopographical studies of the Komnenian elite much of the material published by Miller and Papademetriou.[39] In recent years clusters of poems on definable topics have been published,[40] or studied.[41] The extracts from Manganeios' poems in these works, though more reliably edited than in Miller's transcription, are rarely well dated or contextualized: an edition of the entire corpus remains to be completed.

MP's Life and Career

Manganeios' dossier as found in M offers tempting possibilities for the reconstruction of the temporal and physical circumstances of his life. This

32 The complete series was published by the Académie des inscriptions et belles lettres in 5 series and 16 volumes between 1841 and 1906, with the two volumes on the Greek historians appearing in 1875 and 1881.
33 Miller (1881: *passim*).
34 Miller (1881: 741–74).
35 Miller (1873), (1883).
36 Papademetriou (1898), (1899) and, most importantly, (1903).
37 See n. 2 above on this controversy.
38 Papademetriou (1903: 151).
39 Varzos (1984).
40 Racz (1941), Bernardinello (1972), E. M. Jeffreys and M. J. Jeffreys (2015).
41 Nunn (1986), E. M. Jeffreys and M. J. Jeffreys (2001), Antonopoulou (2010).

is, however, dangerous: Manganeios was a practised rhetorician and offers his work through a variety of *personae* – obsequious imperial encomiast, devoted servant of a persecuted princess, the persecuted princess herself, a rational adviser to obstinate adolescents, reliable purveyor of funerary commemorations and devotional epigrams, and artful seeker after his own well-being. Nevertheless, enough of his work can be meshed in with the record from twelfth-century historical resources to justify the following paragraphs.[42]

From scattered comments a shadowy picture emerges of Manganeios' life and circumstances. He was born in Constantinople, which he regarded as his homeland (πατρίς) (MP 61, 62). In 1152 or 1153 he declares that he had been in the service of the *sebastokratorissa* Irene for twelve years (MP 61.8) and grumbles that his body is collapsing under his advanced age. His latest poem that can be securely dated is MP 23, recording the wedding in August 1159 of the *sebastokratorissa*'s younger son Alexios.[43] This suggests that Manganeios would have been born *c.* 1100, and would have been a (probably) slightly younger contemporary of Theodore Prodromos, who was dead by 1158 (MP 37.27–32).[44]

There is little indication in his poems of Manganeios' social status. In his middle age he makes a puzzling claim, that he had fallen 'into the *sebastokratorissa*'s hands from my mother's womb' (MP 61.55) and that he was an illegally registered bastard who became a citizen (MP 61.9). Did this imply that he was the orphaned child of a member of Irene's household? Or was he a young prisoner of war brought up by her? The case of John Axouch, former Turkish playmate of the emperor John II and ultimately *domestikos* of West and East, would provide an illustrious parallel.[45] The phrasing makes it less likely that he was an aristocrat's child sent to Irene for some sort of training, as had been the experience of a grandson of Anna Komnene.[46] However, there are also suggestions that he had at one time been in prosperous circumstances but lost his fortune (MP 3.39–42, 14.18–19, 18.105). His complaints about his physical decrepitude brought on by age may be genuine, even if exaggerated to tug his sponsor's heartstrings, but his claims to have a speech impediment (MP 6.133, 20.271) are likely to be a modesty topos of literary inadequacy, based on Isaiah 35.6.

42 See e.g. Miller (1881), Papademetriou (1903), Chalandon (1912), Varzos (1984).
43 Varzos (1984: 2:189, no. 132); E. M. Jeffreys and M. J. Jeffreys (2015: 144–50).
44 Hörandner (1974: 32), E. M. Jeffreys (2012: 6, n. 29).
45 Brand (1989: 4–6, 14–15).
46 Magdalino (1993: 348–9).

Manganeios indicates that his education followed the standard path taken in the twelfth century by those hoping for advancement.[47] Under his parents' guidance, he began 'in the midst of the springs of holy letters | … watered like a plant with drinkable lessons' (MP 19.67–8), that is, the usual elementary classes based on the Psalms, but he was later led astray by the delights of secular literature, especially by Homer (MP 19.73–8); subsequently he developed rhetorical skills (MP 2.41–4). However, as indicated by his rapid assimilation in public memory to his illustrious putative namesake, he was not in the forefront of the writers of the mid-twelfth-century.

As no poem from Manganeios' surviving corpus can be dated before 1142 (cf. MP 89, 90, 91, 92, 102), everything we know from his work comes from the last twenty years of his life. There are no indications how he had used his literary training previously, whether in teaching (like Theodore Prodromos)[48] or in a bureaucratic position (like John Tzetzes).[49] It would seem that it was only when his patrons were from the highest echelons of the imperial aristocracy that his writings became worth preserving, though this may be due to the vagaries of transmission. Members of the *sebastokratorissa*'s family could well have had an active role here, as they arguably did for the lavish manuscripts for the letters and homilies of her spiritual father James of Kokkinobaphos,[50] and for the *Grammar* that Theodore Prodromos dedicated to her.[51] A twelfth-century manuscript, lavish or otherwise, lies behind Manganeios' collected poems in the thirteenth-century Marcianus graecus XI.22. That Manganeios apparently sprang into poetic activity only in his maturity, and that he wrote only verse, is surely an accident of textual transmission.

Manganeios does not rail against the folly of attempting a life supported by literary activity as do Theodore Prodromos and John Tzetzes, though this must be an element in the poems from his angry and dissatisfied later years (e.g. MP 18 and 37). He was once fourth in line to present an oration on a festive occasion held in the emperor's presence (MP 49.177–202) and he complained that the emperor ignored his literary efforts (MP 8.211–17, 11.100–3, 15.137–40).

Manganeios was in contact with his literary contemporaries: Michael Italikos is referred to by name (MP 50.340) while Manganeios shares

47 Markopoulos (2008) offers a useful survey of the standard Byzantine education.
48 Agapitos (2015), Zagklas (2023: 32–42).
49 Nesseris (2014: 1:159–60).
50 Linardou (2018).
51 Spatharakis (1985).

common themes with Michael Anchialou, Michael the Rhetor and Euthymios Malakes;[52] he sympathizes with an unfortunate but unidentifiable *grammatikos* (MP 109). His awareness of Theodore Prodromos and his work is much more obvious: they both wrote for the celebrations at Christmas 1149 (MP 26, cf. ThPr 30), they both wrote laments for Stephanos Kontostephanos (MP 60, cf. ThPr 48–51), Manuel Anemas (MP 42, cf. ThPr 54) and Constantine Kamytzes (MP 63, cf. ThPr 64); however, the soldierly monk Ioannikios Logaras of MP 115–18 cannot be the learned recipient of ThPr 61–2. Manganeios frequently followed the genre patterns and even detailed subjects set by Theodore though inaccuracies in his references to classical literature indicate that Manganeios was the lesser scholar.[53]

From parallels between Manganeios' verse and other contemporary accounts, notably that of Kinnamos, Manganeios had access to official versions of striking episodes in military campaigns.[54] These episodes include Manuel's wounded heel in the retreat from Ikonion in 1146 (MP 25.23–36, cf. Kinn. p. 62), his single-handed combat against the Turks (MP 25.35, cf. Kinn. pp. 49, 50–1) and at the river Tara in 1150 (MP 27, Kinn. pp. 111–12), Manuel crossing the Danube in a small boat (MP 1.81–100 and 2.11–20, Kinn. p. 117), the humiliation of Rainauld of Chatillon (MP 9, Kinn. pp. 181–3). Though no match for Tzetzes in vehemence,[55] Manganeios could be pugnaciously defensive over his work, as in his spat with a certain Leo (MP 38, 39) on Manganeios' use of the word *thermourgos* in an encomium on Manuel's campaigns of 1150 (MP 2.19).

MP's Work and Patrons

The bulk of Manganeios' work was directed to two patrons, the emperor Manuel (*c.* 7,590 lines of verse) and the *sebastokratorissa* Irene with members of her family (*c.* 6,850 lines); the remaining *c.* 2,640 lines have a variety of originating causes. Almost everything that Manganeios wrote can be classed as 'occasional' poetry, that is, poetry written to celebrate or commemorate a particular occasion or event.[56] The poems would have been written either in response to a commission or in the hope of gaining one or some other advantage.

52 Magdalino (1993: 470, n. 207).
53 See MP 1.131 and 161, 4.736, 8.429, 13.83, 24.151.
54 M. J. Jeffreys (2010).
55 M. J. Jeffreys (1974: 149–50), Agapitos (2017).
56 Baldick (2008: s.v. occasional verse), Nilsson (2021: 4–15).

Manganeios' poems for Manuel range from brief insults hurled at defeated enemies (e.g. MP 26, 31) through narratives of campaigns (e.g. MP 1, 2, 20) to lengthy encomia of the virtues exhibited by the victorious emperor (e.g. MP 4). Material of this sort during the reign of John II had largely been written by Theodore Prodromos. After the accession of Manuel, Theodore's contributions stopped, whether as a result of illness or because he had lost favour; meanwhile Manganeios was writing for his second patron, Irene. The earliest indication that Manganeios had attracted Manuel's official attention comes in his celebration of the campaign against Ikonion in 1146 (MP 25). There followed poems marking the drama of the passage of the Second Crusade, especially the German contingent (1147–9) (MP 20, 22, 24, 47, 55, 72). Manuel's frenetic military activities in Serbia and Hungary in 1149 and 1150 brought a sequence of long congratulatory poems from Manganeios (MP 1, 2, 3, 5, 6, 7, 26, 28, 31), which were probably presented in the company of several other orators. In 1149 this series of poems by MP was suddenly broken by a celebratory poem from Theodore put in the mouths of the 'demes', a regular pattern from Theodore's past under John II.[57] Events after 1150 are confused with Manganeios recording enthusiastically two mysterious sea-battles against Sicilian forces (MP 4, 6, 28). Manganeios' last set of formal encomia for a military campaign comes in connection with Manuel's Cilician expedition of 1158–9 (MP 8, 9, 10, 34, 35). Several earlier poems welcome the birth of Manuel's daughter in 1152/3 (MP 12, 13, 17, 29). A further set, starting *c.* 1152, initiates the series which has led to Manganeios' current name as he implored both his major patrons, initially the *sebatokratorissa* and then the emperor, to implement his attachment to the *adelphaton* at the Mangana monastery (MP 4, 5, 11, 14, 16, 18, 19, 30, 36, 37, 40, 61, 62); this narrative sequence, often treated as an easy entry into dating issues for the corpus, is probably among the most difficult to put in order.

Mingled with the grandiloquent rhetoric of imperial ideology are occasional skittish references to Manuel's amatory reputation (MP 4.535–99, 790–804, 30.49–56). Using the full panoply of imperial panegyric employed by Theodore for John II, Manganeios adds fulsome praise of Manuel as young, innovative, and a second David. The whole programme of imperial encomia is well discussed by Magdalino.[58]

57 Hörandner (1974: no. 30, and shorter hymns, nos. 31–3).

58 Magdalino (1993: 413–54). On both emperor and poet as a new David in the work of Theodore Prodromos, see also Ricceri in this volume.

Writers at this time made themselves known by presenting their work in a *theatron*, that is, to an interested audience of fellow-practitioners and potential patrons. In MP's case the *theatron* would have been that of his other major patron, the *sebastokratorissa* Irene;[59] from effusive compliments for her learning and generosity, this is generally assumed to have attracted writers such as Theodore Prodromos, John Tzetzes and Constantine Manasses.[60] However, while this group produced extensive narratives and semi-scholarly compositions for Irene, Manganeios' poems for her, written between her widowhood in 1142 and her death in *c.* 1153, are instigated by aspects of her family and domestic circumstances which had led to a perceived need for advice and support. Outright praise of her qualities – as in MP 102 – is the smallest element in Manganeios' verse for her; rather he presents her circumstances to earthly and celestial authorities, on both private or public occasions, in order to generate sympathetic responses to her claims of ill-treatment. His poems offer a frustratingly piecemeal, though at times intimate, personal narrative of Irene's numerous problems in the turbulent 1140s.[61]

There are several threads. Manganeios offers consolation as she faces the emperor's hostility (e.g. MP 43, 47, 50, 58, 66, 71, 74). He exhorts her to trust in the Theotokos when he composes verse to accompany the votive offerings made on behalf of herself or family members (e.g. MP 93, 94 when her son John was severely wounded in a tournament); most of these poems are brief epigrams intended for inscription on the votive objects themselves. Other reflective verses, frequently accompanying offerings of incense and candles, are to be read out during a service (as 'metrical prefaces' to a scriptural reading) in churches dedicated to the Theotokos (MP 67–74).

Some poems connected with Irene's family members are cheerful, such as MP 21 on the wedding of her son John (although it is apparent that Irene herself is not part of the scene) and MP 24, which celebrates her daughter Theodora's diplomatic marriage to the Austrian Heinrich. Many are tense, with an extreme in Irene's desperation at the removal of her youngest child for military training (MP 47) and her revelation that Theodora's marriage had caused her mother great personal grief.

Though Manganeios can address Irene as a philological Muse (MP 51.166, cf. 147.28), there is very little sign that under the welter of tribulations

59 Magdalino (1993: 348–53).
60 E. M. Jeffreys (2011–12: 191–3), Nilsson (2021: 13–20).
61 Papademetriou (1903), Varzos (1984: 1:361–79).

afflicting her Irene has any time for literary interests: the reading that Manganeios recommends to her is scriptural (e.g. MP 66.258–9). This suggests that the peak of Irene's literary patronage and participation in literary competitions referred to by the monk Jacob[62] may have taken place before her widowhood in 1142.

Despite the mass of words poured out for Irene, Manganeios' position in Irene's household is not clear. Did he survive on occasional handouts of food and clothing, as hinted at in MP 56 or in the anonymous encomium in Venice, Biblioteca Nazionale Marciana, gr. Z. 524 [Diktyon 69995]?[63] Was he one of the *grammatikoi* in her employment with whom Tzetzes exchanged acerbic letters?[64] Was he a steward with responsibility for managing her estates? Towards the end of her life Manganeios' relations with Irene were strained: MP 58 is an impassioned defence against accusations of his financial incompetence and in MP 62 he wishes to be released from Irene's service, situations which were presumably factors in his pursuit of the Mangana *adelphaton*. MP 58 and 61, datable to 1152/3, were probably among the last poems Manganeios addressed to Irene before, it must be assumed, her stormy life came to an end: no poem mourning her overtly survives.

Dates, with varying degrees of conviction, can be suggested on internal evidence for a large proportion of the poems written by Manganeios for the emperor and the *sebastokratorissa*. In the case of those written for members of the Constantinopolitan elite recourse must be had to external historical evidence: poems in this group include funerary laments (e.g. MP 42 (Manuel Anemas), 60 (Stephanos Kontostephanos), 65 (Antiochos), 63 (Kamytzes), 122 (Romanos Straboromanos). Largely undatable are devotional epigrams: for example, MP 75–82 (on the Theotokos for the *hegoumenos* of Petra), 83–4 (for the *hegoumenos* of Philanthropinos), 85–8 (for John Komnenos [Varzos no. 23] and his church of Christ Euergetes), MP 115–18 (for the monk Ioannikios).

A few poems have no apparent sponsor: for example, MP 44 (On Life), 45 (On Eros), 129–44 (On the marriage of an old man with a young girl). Others indicate that Manganeios was not impervious to the literary quarrels of the time: for example, MP 63–4 and 65 (on composing laments) and 109 (on an unlucky *grammatikos*).

62 E. M. Jeffreys and M. J. Jeffreys (2009: xxvi).

63 Lampros (1911: no. 57). On the relationship between poets and their patrons, see also Pizzone in this volume; on patronage and literature, see also Agapitos in this volume.

64 Tzetzes, *ep*. 43.12 ed. Leone (1972).

Form

Manganeios uses the two Byzantine metres most commonly employed in twelfth-century poetry – the twelve-syllable line (also known as the dodecasyllable or iambic) and the fifteen-syllable line (the decapentasyllable or *politikos stichos*). The twelve-syllable line had developed over a long period from the ancient iambic trimeter, gradually acquiring special Byzantine characteristics.[65] The fifteen-syllable line was a much newer and more original construct based on syllable numbers and stress; this had arisen as a result of the increasing inability of the average Byzantine to follow metres based on ancient syllable quantity. The first fifteen-syllable poems which showed the form in sequences of consecutive verses were from the tenth century. The metre grew in popularity for special purposes in the eleventh century and became very widespread in the twelfth. In ms. M the poems in the two metres are presented separately, apart from the twelve-syllable MP 20 which appears amidst the fifteen-syllables. MP 6 in fifteen-syllables includes a passage in twelve-syllables (MP 6.152–202),[66] which is marked in the manuscript with the punctuation that elsewhere indicates a separate stanza. In this case there are also ornamental capitals at lines 152 and 203 which normally signify a separate poem.

The twelve-syllable line (found in ms. M from fol. 77r = MP 66 onwards) is used for the most part for epigrams and other poems chiefly on religious themes, and usually observes the metrical conventions. The fifteen-syllable line is used for the ceremonial poems as well as more personal topics.

There is little enjambment in Manganeios' verse, in either metre. Most of the poems are constructed in sense units of a single line, usually ending with a punctuation mark,[67] combined into large blocks – paragraphs, as it were – of varying length, which are normally indicated in ms. M with the colon and dash symbol. MP 1 and 2, written in 1150/1 to celebrate Manuel's Balkan victories, are composed as alphabetic acrostics in ten-line stanzas marked off by the same symbol. Many other fifteen-syllable poems are marked with stanzas of irregular length.

In both twelve-syllable but especially fifteen-syllable verse Manganeios' texts employ a large number of devices, both verbal and metrical, which

65 See the chapters by Lauxtermann, Hinterberger and M. J. Jeffreys collected in the first part of Hörandner, Rhoby and Zagklas (2019: 19–91); Lauxtermann (2019: 267–383). See also Bernard (2018).

66 On implications of this mixture, see Zagklas (2018: 63–4).

67 The most frequent mark is a middle or low dot; the forthcoming edition has adopted a pragmatic approach to the much-debated issue of punctuation.

ornament their fabric. Most of these may be labelled according to the standard rhetorical repertoire, valid from antiquity to the present day, such as alliteration, anaphora (e.g. MP 15.43 Ἀλλ' ὅμως οὕτω καχεκτῶν, ἀλλ' ὅμως οὕτω πάσχων), asyndeton, chiasmus (e.g. MP 15.12 ἐπίσταμαι τὰς ἀρετάς, τὴν φρόνησιν γινώσκω) and polysyndeton.[68] Others are more particular to medieval fifteen-syllable verse, and even to modern Greek folk song, where this line with its caesura after the eighth syllable lends itself to the formation of balanced half-lines (hemistichs) and other types of rhythmic patterning.[69] It is puzzling that ornamentation reminiscent of learned antiquity can be almost indistinguishable from lines which seem to look forward to early Modern Greek developments. This is an area which demands further investigation. We hope that the pattern of codes about to be described will be helpful in this project.

Wordplay of various types is a frequent element in the patterning of this verse. There is frequent punning use of similar forms with or without regard for sense or relevance (e.g. MP 15.33 ῥυτῆρας … ῥυτίδας = code W01,[70] MP 15.146 κερδῷος ἀκερδής, … κερδῴου = code W02). The need for similar initial syllables and balance gives rise to idiosyncratic use of prefixes and suffixes (e.g. MP 15.92 παράθες εἰς παραψυχὴν … = W01); many of the numerous *hapax legomena* in Manganeios result directly or indirectly from this practice (e.g. MP 21.46 ἡ παμπρεπὴς καὶ παγκαλλὴς καὶ πανευγενεστάτη, MP 24.267 Ὡς ἀγλαής, ὡς φωταυγής, ὡς πυραυγὴς ἐφάνης). The rhetorical patterns are so numerous that it would be impossible to list and explain them all in separate notes, as the late Wolfram Hörandner has commented for Theodore Prodromos.[71] We have decided to use a code. In the edition of MP 15 that follows, patterns are indicated by a verse number at the foot of the translation (but referring to the Greek text) through an alphabetical code: e.g. anaphora: J 15.43 Ἀλλ' ὅμως οὕτω καχεκτῶν, ἀλλ' ὅμως οὕτω πάσχων; chiasmus: E 15.12 ἐπίσταμαι τὰς ἀρετάς, τὴν φρόνησιν γινώσκω. The code is elucidated briefly under 'Pattern Codes' in the Appendix.

A further feature to be noted in connection with Manganeios' poetic technique is that he was writing as an insider for insiders, not for people outside the linguistic and historical framework of his immediate audience. He used special twelfth-century phrases and references intelligible only

68 Hörandner (1974: 111–18), Lausberg (1960: §600–754).
69 Sifakis (1988), M. J. Jeffreys (2014).
70 See the Appendix ('Pattern Codes') for explanations of the terms.
71 Hörandner (1974: 113).

to an audience of his contemporaries. The allusive nature of much of his text can be compared to that in a modern popular newspaper writing for its regular readers. Prominent Byzantines and Byzantine enemies are frequently referenced by allusion, which sometimes would be understood by most twelfth-century readers and hearers, but in other cases comprehension would be restricted to those following a more limited story. A further problem for modern readers is the wide variety of Manganeios' subject matter, which makes it unlikely that the poems will be consulted sequentially. With these exceptions, the language of Manganeios is fairly straightforward, and will tempt even inexperienced readers of Greek to explore the texts in the original.

To assist and encourage such attempts, since no extant dictionary will be of help in many instances, we have drawn up a list of 'Key Words', phrases and topics which we feel may give rise to puzzlement and confusion. This list will be of little or no help to those who are expert in Greek, but we hope it may assist those whose expertise lies in other historical periods and geographical areas.

Thus, at the foot of the pages with the translation there are two layers of apparatus. The first, headed 'Pattern Codes', is experimental and designed to warn readers that the poet may be writing to produce a verbal pattern rather than convey precise meaning. The second, headed 'Key Words', is a fairly elementary aid to comprehension. In both cases there is a line reference and a word or code which sends the reader to further, brief information in the Appendix. In both cases this feature is designed to be helpful over the whole of Manganeios' huge corpus but is less effective when analysing this short poem.

Manganeios Prodromos, *Poem* 15[72]

Summary

1–27 The poet respects the emperor and realizes that he wishes the poet to write a verse text for him, but the poet is old and ill: will his writings have any effect when presented to the great emperor? 28–56 However, despite his great physical discomfort, the poet will make an attempt, unclear whether he is more impressed by the magnitude of Manuel's problems or

72 Mss. M: Marcianus graecus XI.22, fols. 26r–27r; P: Paris, Suppl. gr. 1219, pp. 155–60. Previous editions: Miller 1881: 676 (lines 22–4), 214 (lines 31–2), 596 (lines 43–5), 586 (lines 52–4), 595 (lines 74–7, 155–7); Papademetriou (1903): 141–2 (lines 8–13, 31–6, 43–5, 65–88, 132–41, 146–57).

the resolution with which he confronts them. 57–73 Indeed, inspired by Manuel, the poet will rise above his feeble health to the best of his ability. 74–102 The recent incident is merely a setback from which Manuel will soon recover: he should remember the disasters which have overtaken rulers in the past. 103–23 Even the founder of Constantinople was once in danger of being sacrificed to the Persian sun-god. 124–31 Manuel should think of this story as a reminder of God's benevolence. 132–54 The poet was hesitant to write for Manuel as many of his previous efforts had been ignored, but he is willing to try again if this is the emperor's wish. 155–7 May he reign long and confound his enemies.

Text

Εἰς τὸν αὐτὸν αὐτοκράτορα στιχουργῆσαι προστάξαντα[73]

Οἶδα, πορφυροβλάστητε, τὰ προτερήματά σου· fol. 26r
ἐπίσταμαι τὰς ἀρετάς, τὴν φρόνησιν γινώσκω,
τὴν ὑπερτέραν τῶν λοιπῶν, τὴν ἀρχικὴν ἀνδρείαν,
ἥνπερ καὶ πρώτην λέγουσιν ὡς κρείττονα τῆς ἄλλης
5 τῆς φαινομένης ἐν ἀλκῇ κρατίστων βραχιόνων,
ὁποίαν ὑπὲρ ἅπαντας ηὐτύχησας, μονάρχα·
οὐκ ἀγνοῶ τὸ συνετὸν οὐδὲ τὸ φιλολόγον·
οἶδα ποθεῖς τὸ στιχουργεῖν, ποθεῖς ἐμμέτρους λόγους·
τὸ γὰρ ἐπιπονώτερον προκρίνεις τοῦ ῥᾳδίου.
10 Κἀγὼ πρὸς τοῦτο νύσσομαι, κἂν ἐπιπόνως ἔχῃ,
ἀλλὰ τὸ γῆρας ἔφθασεν, ἀλλ᾽ ἤγγισε τὸ θέρος,
ἀλλ᾽ ἦλθεν ὥρα παρακμῆς, ἀλλ᾽ ἔκλινεν ὁ στάχυς,
κἂν καὶ τὸ πνεῦμα πρόθυμον, ἀλλ᾽ ἀσθενὴς ὁ ῥήτωρ,
κἂν ὁ κινῶν τὴν μουσικὴν ἔτι τὸ πλῆκτρον ἔχῃ,
15 ἀλλ᾽ αἱ χορδαὶ τῆς μουσικῆς οὐκ ἔχουσι τὴν τάσιν·
ἐκλυθεισῶν δὲ τῶν χορδῶν ποῦ χρήσιμον τὸ πλῆκτρον,
ἢ ποῖον ἀνακρούσεται τὸ μέλος ὁ τεχνίτης;
Εἰ δὲ καὶ μέλος ᾄσεται, τίνι μελήσει τούτου;
Ἂν δὲ καὶ πρὸς ἀνίσχοντα καὶ γίγαντα φωσφόρον
20 ἀναβαλεῖται χαλαρόν, ἰσχνόν, ἠσθενημένον,
πρὸς τόσον ὕψος γίγαντος ἀναδραμεῖται πότε;
Πότε τὸν δίφρον φθάσει σου καὶ σὲ τὸν διφρηλάτην,
οὕτω τελοῦντα ταχινὴν τὴν ἁρματηλασίαν,
καὶ πᾶσαν γῆν Αὐσονικὴν κατακτινοβολοῦντα;
25 Ἔχεις γὰρ ἵππους πτερωτοὺς ἀνέμων ταχυτέρους,
τὰς γενικὰς τῶν ἀρετῶν ἐν αἷς προσεπιβαίνεις,
καὶ σωστικὴν ἀποτελεῖς ἡμῖν τὴν ἱππασίαν.
Ὁρᾷς ὁπόσα τὴν ἐμὴν ὁρμὴν ἀναχαιτίζει,
ὁρᾷς, Αὐσόνων ἥλιε, τὰ προσιστάμενά μοι,
30 ἐξ ὧν ἀναχαιτίζομαι, κἂν προθυμῶ, κἂν σπεύδω.
Οὐχ οὕτως ἵππον ταχινὸν κημὸς ἀνασειράζει
ὁπόσον μοι τὸ πρόθυμον ἡ νόσος περικόπτει·

73 The only textual note we wish to make in this poem occurs in the title, where P reads προστάξαντα and M probably reads the impossible πρόσταξαντα. All other points (ignored in this edition) would involve our rejection of classical normalization of orthography by Miller and Papademetriou.

Translation

To the same emperor, who had ordered him to compose verse

I know, *porphyrogennetos*, your excellent qualities,
I perceive your virtues, I recognize your good sense,
which is superior to other qualities, the courage of command,
which they call the first since it is better than the other courage,
which becomes apparent through the might of powerful arms: 5
in possessing this you are more fortunate than all other men, monarch.
I am not unaware of your intellectual qualities, nor of your love of literature;
I know you desire verse composition, you desire metrical speeches,
for you prefer the more laborious to the easy.
I too am spurred on towards this, though it is hard work, 10
but old age has come, but harvest time is near,
but the time of decline is at hand, but the corn has drooped,
and though the spirit be willing, yet the rhetor is weak;
though he who plays the music still has his plectrum,
yet the strings of the instrument no longer have their tension; 15
and when the strings are slack, what use is the plectrum,
or what song will the performer strike up?
And if he does sing a melody, who will show interest?
If he sings to a rising celestial light of giant size
a song that is languid, thin and weakened, 20
will it ever reach such gigantic height?
When will it reach your chariot and you the charioteer
as you drive your chariot so swiftly,
and overwhelm with your rays the whole Ausonian land?
For you have winged horses swifter than the winds, 25
the chief virtues on which you mount
and perform for us the horsemanship of salvation.
You see how many things rein in my enthusiasm,
you see, sun of the Ausonians, the task that confronts me,
the restraints by which I am held back, though keen and eager. 30
No bit slows down a swift horse as much
as my enthusiasm is cut off by sickness;

ἔχω ῥυτῆρας χαλινοῦ τοῦ γήρους τὰς ῥυτίδας,
καὶ τῆς ταλαιπωρίας μου τὴν ψυχροτάτην νάρκην·
35 ἔχω χειμῶνος κρύσταλον τὸν καταψύχοντά με,
τοῦ φλέγματος τὴν κάκωσιν τὴν νῦν ἐπικρατοῦσαν·
τοῦτο δεσμεῖ τὰ γόνατα, ξηραίνει τὰς ἰγνύας,
ἰσχίων ἴσχει σύνδεσμον, οὐ φείδεται τραχήλου,
κακοποιεῖ καὶ τὰς πλευράς, τὴν πτέρναν ἐξορύττει,
40 πτέρναν πολλοὺς πτερνίσασαν καὶ τῶν ὑψηλοτέρων,
καὶ τῶν ἐν κάλλει θαυμαστῶν καὶ τῶν ἀρειμανίων·
κἂν δάκνῃ γὰρ λεγόμενον, οὐκ ἀπαρνοῦμαι τοῦτο.
Ἀλλ᾽ ὅμως οὕτω καχεκτῶν, ἀλλ᾽ ὅμως οὕτω πάσχων, fol. 26v
ἀλλ᾽ οὕτω προσταλαιπωρῶν, ἀλλὰ πυκτεύων οὕτως,
45 πρὸς χάριν σὴν ἐπείγομαι λόγους ἐμμέτρους πλέκειν.
Ἀλλ᾽ ὅταν στρέψω κατὰ νοῦν, ἀλλ᾽ ὅταν ἀποβλέψω
πρὸς τὸ τοσοῦτον πέλαγος τῶν κοσμικῶν φροντίδων
καὶ τὸ περιστοιχίσαν σε τῆς τρικυμίας νέφος,
καὶ τοὺς προβάντας κλύδωνας καὶ τοὺς περισπασμούς σου,
50 ἀποναρκῶ καὶ ψύχομαι καὶ ῥίπτω τὴν γραφίδα.
Εἰ γὰρ ἁρμόζει τἀληθὲς καὶ λέγειν τε καὶ γράφειν,
ὅταν συλλέξω καθ᾽ αὑτόν, ὅταν ἀθρήσω σύμπαν
τὸ συνεχὲς τῶν μεριμνῶν καὶ τὴν ἀλληλουχίαν,
καὶ πρὸς ἀντιπαράθεσιν ἐγγύθεν ἀντιθήσω
55 τὸ πεπηγὸς καὶ σταθηρὸν καὶ μεγαλόψυχόν σου,
ἀμηχανῶν ἐπαπορῶ ποῖον θαυμάσω πλέον.
Ἀλλὰ νικᾷ με, νικητὰ τοσούτων κλυδωνίων,
τὸ βεβηκὸς τοῦ τρόπου σου καὶ τὸ μὴ καταπίπτον·
οὐ μόνον γὰρ τετράγωνον ἐμφαίνεις τὴν ἀρχήν σου,
60 ὡς στερροτάτην πάντοθεν καὶ γύρωθεν ἑδραίαν·
ἀλλὰ καὶ τρίγωνον αὐτὴν πολλάκις ὑπεμφαίνεις,
ὡς καὶ πεσοῦσαν ἵστασθαι καὶ πάλιν ἀντιπίπτειν,
καὶ τοὺς δοκοῦντας μὴ πεσεῖν ἐκπλήττειν ὡς πεσόντας.
Τοῦτο σου τὸ προτέρημα πάλιν ἀνέρρωσέ με,
65 τοῦτο τὸ μεγαλαύχημα πάλιν ἐπτέρωσέ με,
τοῦ σθένους σου τὸ στάσιμον πάλιν ἐστήριξέ με,
καὶ πάλιν φέρω κάλαμον καὶ κάμπτω σκυταλίδας,
καὶ σύμμετρον τὸν ἔμμετρον ἀπόλογον ποιοῦμαι
πρὸς τὴν ἰσχύν μου τὴν σαθράν, ἣν ἤμβλυνεν ὁ χρόνος,
70 καὶ νόσος ἐταπείνωσε καὶ σὺν τῇ νόσῳ σπάνις.
Ἀλλὰ γὰρ πρόσχες τι μικρὸν τῷ δούλῳ ῥήτορί σου,

I have as reins for the bridle the wrinkles of old age,
and the icy cold numbness of my affliction;
I have the ice of winter that freezes me, 35
the distress of phlegm which now dominates me.
This binds my knees, it dries out my thighs,
it constrains my hips, it does not spare my throat,
it damages my ribs too, it destroys my heel,
the heel that has tripped up many, even of the more eminent, 40
both those admired for beauty and those frenzied for war;
for even if the comment stings, I will not deny it.
But yet despite being in such a bad state, despite suffering in this way,
despite being in great distress, despite struggling like this,
I make an effort for your sake to compose metrical speeches. 45
But when I contemplate this in my mind, but when I gaze
at this great ocean of universal concerns
and the storm-cloud which surrounds you,
and the rough water that besets you, and your distractions,
I grow numb and am frozen and I throw down my pen. 50
For if it is right both to speak and to write the truth,
when I contemplate the situation, when I consider as a whole
the constant succession of your anxieties,
and for comparison I set beside these
your fixity, firmness and generosity, 55
I am helpless and at a loss which to admire more.

But you vanquish me, you who have vanquished so many storms,
through the steadfastness of your character which does not yield;
for you not only demonstrate that your rule is foursquare,
being firm on all sides and steadfast all around; 60
but you also often prove that it is triangular,
because, when it falls, you stand it up and it still resists
and surprises by the fall of those who thought it would not fall.
This virtue of yours has again restored me,
this great boast has again given me wings, 65
the steadfastness of your strength has again supported me,
and again I pick up my pen and bend my fingers,
and I make a metrical response in proportion
to my feeble strength, which time has blunted
and sickness has humbled, and, with sickness, privation. 70
But pay attention for a moment to your servant and rhetor,

ναί, πρόσχες, αὐτοκράτορ μου, ναί, πρόσχες μοι, σκηπτοῦχε·
οὐ γὰρ σαθρόν τι λέξει σοι, κἂν καὶ σαθρὸς ὁ ῥήτωρ.
Τὸ πρὸ μικροῦ συνάντημα τὸ προλαβὸν ἐκεῖνο
75 οὐκ ἔδοξε κατόρθωμα τῶν ἀντιτεταγμένων,
οὐδὲ καταστρατήγημα τῶν μηδὲ συμβαλόντων
(χωρὶς γὰρ μάχης καὶ πληγῶν οὐδεὶς κατατροποῦται)
ἀλλὰ τὸ πᾶν ἀπότευγμα παράλογον, τυχαῖον.
Μὴ γοῦν ἐκεῖ πεμπέτωσαν οἱ φλήναφοι τὰς γλώσσας·
80 εἰ γὰρ ἀντισυμβέβληκε τὸ στῖφος τῶν Λατίνων
μετὰ τῆς μοίρας τῆς μικρᾶς τῶν ἀντιταξαμένων,
οὐδὲ τὴν πρώτην εἰσβολὴν ἤνεγκαν ἂν ἐκεῖνοι,
οὐδ᾽ ἀντωπεῖν ἐξίσχυσαν πρὸς τὴν αὐγὴν τοῦ ξίφους,
ἀλλ᾽ οὐδὲ στῆναι κἂν βραχὺ πρὸς τὴν κραυγὴν καὶ μόνην,
85 μή τί γε πρὸς τὴν προσβολὴν ἐκείνων ἀντιστῆναι.
Θάρσει λοιπὸν καὶ πρόβλεπε καὶ σύναγε τὸ μέλλον,
ἀτρύτα μου κατάκοπε, λυχνίτα μου, φωστήρ μου·
κἂν τὸ προφθάσαν νύττῃ σε, κἂν σε λυπῇ τὸ τραῦμα,
ἀλλ᾽ ὅρα καὶ τοὺς μώλωπας τῶν προκεκρατηκότων,
90 καὶ γνῶθι πῶς προσώζεσαν αὐτῶν αἱ σηπεδόνες.
Ἄνοιγε δέλτους παλαιὰς ἀρχαίων συγγραφέων,
παράθες εἰς παραψυχὴν ἱστορικὰς πυκτίδας,
ἐν αἷς εὑρήσεις συμφορῶν πυρίνων Ἰλιάδας,
ἃς δυστυχῶς ὑπήνεγκαν πολλοὶ τῶν στεφηφόρων,
95 καὶ μᾶλλον ὅσοι πρότερον τοῖς πλήθεσιν ἐθάρρουν,
καὶ μυριάδας ἤλαυνον παντοίων στρατευμάτων,
καὶ γῆν ὁμοῦ καὶ θάλατταν καινῶς ἐκαινοτόμουν,
ὑπείκειν θέλοντες αὐτοῖς καὶ τὰ στερρὰ στοιχεῖα·
Δαρεῖος ταῦτα πρότερον καὶ Ξέρξης μετ᾽ ἐκεῖνον,
100 ἐν Θερμοπύλαις ἡττηθείς, ὁ μέγας, ὁ τοσοῦτος
παρ᾽ ἐλαχίστου στρατηγοῦ βελτίστου Λεωνίδου·
ἔτι πρὸς τούτοις ἕτεροι μεγάλοι καὶ δυνάσται.
Ἀλλὰ γὰρ τί τῶν θύραθεν τὰς τύχας ὑπογράφω,
ἀφεὶς τὸν μέγαν πολιστὴν ταύτης τῆς νέας Ῥώμης;
105 Ἔγνως ὁποῖα πέπονθεν ἐκεῖνος, αὐτοκράτωρ,
ἐκεῖνος ὁ περίφημος τῆς Βύζαντος δομήτωρ;
Ἔγνως εἰς ὅσον ἔφθασε τῆς ἀτυχίας λόφον;
Ἔγνως εἰς οἵαν πέπτωκεν ἐσχατιὰν ὀλέθρου;
Οὐκ ἤκουσας τὴν συμφορὰν καὶ τὸν βωμὸν ἐκεῖνον;
110 Εἶδες παρ᾽ ὅσον ἤγγισε ταῖς πύλαις τοῦ θανάτου;

yes, pay attention, my emperor, yes, heed me, sceptred ruler:
For, though the rhetor is feeble, he will tell you nothing feeble.
That notable incident which occurred recently
should not be considered an achievement of your adversaries, 75
nor a great stratagem, for they did not even join battle
(for nobody is routed without a battle and wounds)
but the whole failure was beyond reason and accidental.
So the babblers should not waste their talk on that;
for if the band of Latins had engaged 80
the small detachment drawn up against them,
they would not have withstood even the first onslaught,
they would not have been able to face the gleaming sword,
nor even to stand for a moment against the battle-cry alone,
much less to withstand their opponents' attack. 85
So be heartened and foresee and infer the future,
my indefatigable yet exhausted emperor, my jewel, my celestial light;
though the event annoys you, though the wound gives you pain,
consider the bruisings that befell those who ruled before you,
and learn how they festered and stank. 90
Open the old books of ancient writers,
provide for your consolation codices of history,
in which you will find *Iliads* of fiery disasters
which many crowned heads had to endure,
especially those who earlier had confidence in multitudes, 95
and drove on countless men in disparate armies,
and made novel innovations on land and sea,
desiring that even the sturdy elements yield to them.
Darius did this first, and after him Xerxes,
the great, the powerful, who was defeated at Thermopylae 100
by an insignificant general, the excellent Leonidas;
other great rulers as well as these met the same fate.
But why should I write of the fates of heathen rulers,
forgetting the great founder of this New Rome?
Do you know, emperor, what suffering he endured, 105
that famous founder of the city of Byzas?
Do you know to what peak of misfortune he reached?
Do you know into what depths of disaster he plunged?
Have you not heard of the disaster and the famous altar?
Did you see how close he came to the gates of death? 110

Οὐκ ἔμαθες ὡς ἔμελλεν ἐν μέσῃ τῇ Περσίδι
θῦμα γενέσθαι προσδεκτὸν θεῷ Περσῶν ἡλίῳ;
Ἀλλ᾽ εἶδες καὶ τὸν ἥλιον τὸν τῆς δικαιοσύνης
ὅπως ἐπέλαμψεν αὐτῷ καὶ λέλυκε τὸν γνόφον,
115 καὶ πῶς αὐτὸν ἐξείλετο καὶ παρὰ προσδοκίαν
ἐξ ἐπαράτου καὶ φρικτοῦ καὶ χαλεποῦ θανάτου;
Ναί, νέας Ῥώμης ἥλιε, τὴν ἱστορίαν οἶδας,
τῆς συμφορᾶς τὸ μέγεθος ἐπέγνως ἀπὸ ταύτης,
τὸ μεγαλεῖον ἔμαθες τῆς παναλκοῦς ἰσχύος.
120 Ὁ δέσμιος ἐλέλυτο καὶ τῶν Περσῶν ἐκράτει·
ὁ μέλλων δὲ πυρίκαυστος παρὰ μικρὸν γενέσθαι
τοὺς πυρσολάτρας παγγενεὶ κατέκτεινεν ἐν ξίφει,
καὶ πῦρ Περσῶν κατέσβεσεν ἐν τελετῆς ἡμέρᾳ.
Ἀναλογίζου μοι λοιπὸν τὴν ἱστορίαν ταύτην,
125 καὶ φάρμακον λογίζου μοι καὶ τὸ λυποῦν ἐκκένου,
καὶ τὸ προφθάσαν λυπηρὸν ὑπόμνησιν ἡγοῦ μοι,
ἐντεῦθεν ἐπανάγουσαν ἐπὶ τὸν εὐεργέτην,
τὸν χρίσαντά σε πρὸς ἀρχὴν ἀπὸ γαστρὸς μητρός σου.
Τοιαύτην ὑποτίθημι τὴν ὑποθήκην ταύτην,
130 ἀπὸ πολλῶν ἱστοριῶν ἐκτεμμαχίσας μίαν,
παρηγορίας κύλικα τῷ κρατεῖ σου κιρνῶσαν.
Εἰ δὲ κατώκνουν τὴν γραφὴν ἄχρι τῆς νῦν ἡμέρας,
οὐ χρὴ θαυμάζειν οὐδαμῶς· ὡς ἀσθενὴς γὰρ ὤκνουν,
καὶ τὸν καιρὸν ἐμποδιστὴν τῆς στιχουργίας εἶχον,
135 πολλὰ καινοτομήσαντα τῶν μὴ προσδοκωμένων, fol. 27r
καὶ τὸ μοχθεῖν ἐπὶ κενοῖς καὶ τὸ κενοῦν ἱδρῶτας,
ἐφ᾽ οἷς αὐτὸς ἐμόγησα ῥητορικοῖς μου πόνοις,
τὰ σὰ μεγαλουργήματα τὰ πρὶν ὑφηγουμένοις,
ὧν οὐδενὸς μετέσχηκας, οὐ γέγονας εἰδήμων·
140 ἐλογιζόμην δυσαχθὲς καὶ μάταιον φορτίον.
Τί γάρ μοι κόπος ἄχαρις καὶ πόνος, μόνον πόνος;
Κερδῷον λέγει τὸν Ἑρμῆν ὁ μῦθος ἁρμοζόντως·
ἔχει γὰρ κέρδος λογικὸν ὁ συντιθεὶς τοὺς λόγους,
καὶ τοῦ φιλοπονήματος τὴν χάριν οἰκειοῦται,
145 ὅταν καὶ τὰ πονήματα κωφεύοντα μὴ κεῖται·
ἂν δ᾽ ὁ κερδῷος ἀκερδής, τίς χάρις τοῦ κερδῴου
ὅταν ὁ γράφων ἄγνωστος ἐν παραβύστῳ μένῃ,
κἀκεῖνος πᾶσαν ἄγνοιαν τῶν γεγραμμένων ἔχοι

Did you not learn that, in the middle of Persia, he was about
to become an acceptable victim to the sun-god of the Persians?
But you have also seen the sun of righteousness,
how it shone on him and dispelled the gloom,
and how it rescued him, though unexpectedly, 115
from an accursed, terrifying and cruel death?
Yes, sun of New Rome, you know the story,
you realized from it the greatness of the disaster,
you learned the magnificence of the almighty strength.
The prisoner was set free and defeated the Persians; 120
he who was all but sacrificed in the fire
slaughtered with the sword the whole race of fire-worshippers,
and quenched the Persians' fire on a day of ceremony.
So ponder, please, on this story,
and consider it, please, a remedy and drain the painful wound, 125
and regard, please, the painful event as a reminder,
leading back from it to the benefactor
who anointed you for rule from your mother's womb.
It is counsel of this kind I set before you here,
having sliced up out of many stories one 130
which mixes for your majesty a cup of consolation.
If I have shrunk from writing till this day,
this is no reason at all for wonder; for I delayed out of sickness,
and I had the crisis to hinder my writing of verse,
a crisis which has seen many unexpected innovations, 135
and the fact that I struggled and wasted my sweat fruitlessly
on the rhetorical efforts at which I laboured,
which narrated your previous great achievements,
in none of which you shared, or took close interest;
I regarded this as a grievous and vain burden. 140
For what use to me is thankless labour and pain that is just pain?
The myth rightly calls Hermes Kerdoös (the bringer of gain):
for he who composes speeches has a rhetorical gain,
and receives the thanks for his industry,
when the products of his labours do not lie dumb; 145
but what thanks are due to the Kerdoös if the writer has no gain,
when he lurks ignored in a corner,
and he for whom he struggles and endures industriously

δι᾿ ὃν πονεῖ καὶ καρτερεῖ, φιλοπονῶν πρὸς χάριν;
150 Ἐγὼ μὲν τούτων ἕνεκα τὸ στιχουργεῖν κατώκνουν·
εἰ δὲ καὶ πάλιν ὁρισθῶ καὶ πάλιν στιχουργήσω,
καὶ πάλιν ξέσω κάλαμον, πάλιν ὀξυγραφήσω,
καὶ πάλιν, ὅσον δυνατόν, ἐμμέτρως ῥητορεύσω,
ἂν τὸ δοκοῦν τῷ κράτει σου τῷ δούλῳ σου γνωσθῇ μοι.
155 Θεός σοι πολυχρόνιον τὸ κράτος ταμιεύσοι,
καὶ τράχηλον ὑπέρογκον ὡς κρίκον κατακάμψοι,
τιθεὶς ὑπὸ τοὺς πόδας σου τὴν ἐπηρμένην δέρην.

Pattern Codes

2 E | 8 R | 11 E | 12 B | 13–14 B/C | 18 Wo1 | 19–21 Wo1 | 20 A | 22 Wo2 | 25 Fo2 | 28–9 J | 30 S | 33 Wo1 | 37 C | 38 Wo1 | 39 E | 40 Wo2 | 43 B | 44 E | 46 B | 50 P | 52 B | 55 P | 57 Wo2 | 60 E | 62–3 Wo2 | 64–5 Mo1 | 68 Wo2 | 70 Wo2 | 71–2 R | 73 R | 82–4 J | 86 P | 87 R | 88 B, E | 92 Wo1 | 97 Wo2 | 98 Wo1 | 101 Wo1 | 105–6 R | 107–8 J | 112–13 R | 114–15 K | 116 P | 121–3 Wo2 | 124–5 Wo2 | 129 Wo2 | 132–3 Wo2 | 135 Wo1 | 136 Wo2 | 141 R | 142–3 Wo2 | 146 Wo2 | 149 Wo2 | 151–3 R

Key Words

1 Porphyrogennetos | 13 Rhetor | 19 Giant; Light (heavenly) | 21 Giant | 22 Chariot | 24 Ray; Ausonian | 29 Sun; Ausonian | 33 Wrinkle | 49 Rough water | 71 Rhetor | 72 Emperor | 80 Latins | 87 Jewel; Light (heavenly) | 95 Multitude | 97 Innovate | 104 New Rome | 105 Emperor | 106 Byzas' city | 112 Persian | 117 Sun; New Rome | 120 Persian | 131 Majesty | 135 Innovate | 154 Majesty

as a favour, is completely oblivious of what has been written?
I shrank from writing verses for these reasons; 150
but if I am commissioned again and write verses again,
I will again sharpen my pen, and again write in shorthand,
and again make rhetoric in verse as best I can,
if your majesty's wish is transmitted to me, your servant.
May God grant you rule for many years, 155
and bend the haughty neck down like a reed,
having placed his proud throat beneath your feet.

Notes

The historical context of this poem is clear, though it is not explained in detail. The Byzantine expedition to take revenge on Roger II of Sicily by conquering part of southern Italy, having been successful for some time, was brought to an abrupt halt in a battle in the harbour of Brindisi in the early summer of 1156. This serious setback has led to a request from Manuel I to Manganeios to write an appropriate poem. His reluctance, apparently due to his age and sickness, must in part be the result of the fact that the battle at Brindisi cannot possibly be presented as anything other than a Byzantine disaster. The poem would have been composed in May–June 1156 (see note to v. 74ff.).

3–5 courage of command: cf. Aristotle, *Politics* 1260a (ed. Becker, trans. Rackham), on relative virtues apparent in master and slave, men and women, giving pride of place to the ability to command.

8 metrical speeches: i.e. in quantitative prosodic metres (iambics) not using the stress accents of the fifteen-syllable line, which however Manganeios – for whatever reason – is using in

this poem. It is unclear whether στιχουργῆσαι in the title is making the same distinction.

13 Matthew 26.41.

27 Habakkuk 8.3 (Ode 4.8 = Prayer of Habakkuk).

46–56 An acknowledgement that Manuel is currently in a difficult position, but the poet finds Manuel's fortitude positive.

59–62 On the stability of quadrilaterals and triangles, cf. Plato, *Timaeus* 55d–e (ed. Burnet) and Aristotle, *De anima* 414b (ed. Becker) on the way in which the triangle is contained in a quadrilateral.

74ff. The collapse of Manuel's Italian campaign of spring 1156 is recorded most fully in Kinn. 4.13; cf. Nik. Chon. 94.6–95.9; see Chalandon (1912: 366–70), Magdalino (1993: 60–1, 442, n. 78), Stephenson (2000: 237–8).

78 the whole failure: the failure of Manuel's forces.

80–81 small detachment: Kinn. 4.13 (p. 168) comments that the Byzantine contingent available at the crucial moment was small.

89–90 Psalm 37/38.6.

99 Darius' invasion of Greece culminated in a Persian defeat at Marathon in 490 BC (Herodotus 6.93–120). Xerxes' expedition of 480 BC began with the construction of a pontoon bridge over the Hellespont and a canal through the Athos peninsula (Herodotus 7.22–5) and led to a Persian victory at Thermopylae, despite a heroic defence by the Spartan king Leonidas (Herodotus 7.201–33); Leonidas' heroism seems to have become a victory for Manganeios. However, Xerxes' forces were ultimately repulsed at the subsequent battle of Salamis (Herodotus 7.209).

101 It is difficult, but not impossible, to extract meaning from this oxymoron (ἐλαχίστου … βελτίστου); for the wording but not the meaning, cf. Plato, *Gorgias* 490c.

104–23 great founder of this New Rome (cf. v. 106 city of Byzas): Constantine I (273/4–337). The allusion is to Constantine's legendary capture by the Persians recounted in the Patmos *Life of Constantine* and the *Passion of Eusignios*; see Halkin (1959: ch. 9), Devos (1982: ch. 11), Kazhdan (1987: 234–5).

113 sun of righteousness: a reference to Constantine's role in the Christianization of the Roman empire, the sun being Christ.

117 sun of New Rome: Manuel.
128 benefactor: i.e. Christ.
132 There has been an interval between the disaster and Manganeios' composition.
142, 146: Kerdoös: a standard epithet for Hermes.
156 haughty neck: William I of Sicily (1120–66).
Like a reed: Isaiah 58.5.

Appendix

Pattern Codes: Definitions

A Asyndeton; a sequence of related nouns, verbs or adjectives without καί or other expected conjunctions.
B Full line, halved and balanced by metrical shapes and word patterns.
C Full line, halved and balanced to a lesser extent than in B.
E Chiasmus; four elements in the line in groups of two with the order of elements reversed in the second group.
F02 Halved first hemistich balanced with rhyme.
J Anaphora; repeated words or phrases at the beginning of lines or half-lines.
K A looser form of anaphora.
M01 Neighbouring lines with strikingly similar syntax over the whole line.
P Polysyndeton; sequence of words all linked by similar conjunctions.
R Significant words repeated in different sections of the line.
S Second hemistich divided in two with balanced syntax.
W01 Wordplay involving similar sounds, including alliteration.
W02 Wordplay involving the same root.

Key Words: Definitions

Ausonian (Αὔσονες) An Italian people, early absorbed into Rome, so a lofty and metrically useful synonym for Byzantines in their Roman dimension.
Chariot (δίφρος) Sometimes a real vehicle, sometimes an abstract to be driven, like the chariot of imperial power.
City of Byzas (ἡ Βύζαντος, Βυζάντιον, Βυζαντίς) The city of Constantinople and its inhabitants, named Byzantion before Constantine's refoundation; the name is difficult to translate without implying that it includes the whole empire.
Emperor (αὐτοκράτωρ, βασιλεύς) See also ἀετός, ἄναξ, αὔγουστος, γίγας, δεσπότης, (ὁ) κρατῶν, λέων, μονοκράτωρ, σκηπτοῦχος, σκηπτοκράτωρ.

Giant (γίγας) The astronomical giant sun or its earthly analogue the emperor; viewed positively in ceremonial and symbolism, though a few negative Goliaths also appear.

Innovate (καινουργῶ) Key term in Manuel's policy of renewal, used in many parts of speech.

Jewel (λυχνίτης) Apparently a general word for jewel, but often a particular red jewel (cornelian?).

Latin (Λατίνος) Usually a noun, a Western European (or an easterner originally from the West); more likely from Latin than Germanic areas.

Light, heavenly (φωστήρ, φωσφόρος) In astronomical images a body giving unreflected light, thus often the sun, moon, emperor or major aristocrat; φωσφόρος can mean 'sun', but usually represents a star or lesser noble.

Majesty (κράτος) Power and Victory, often imperial; sometimes an alternative address to the powerful, i.e. 'your majesty'.

Multitude (πλῆθος) Huge numbers, especially of armies hostile to Byzantium and Manuel; those relying on numbers alone tend to fail.

New Rome (Νέα Ῥώμη) Constantinople or Byzantium; curiously, Manuel's policies mean that New Rome is often described as elderly and in need of renewal.

Persian (Πέρσης) Literally 'Persian' in Persian contexts, but used more generally for the Turks, Byzantium's main opponents in the East; the Turks themselves felt a complex affinity with the Persians.

Porphyrogennetos (πορφυρογέννητος) alternative forms include πεπορφυρωμένος, πορφυρανθής, πορφυραυγής, πορφυροβλάστητος, πορφυρόβλαστος; a high dignity; born in the Porphyra (imperial birthing chamber), child of a reigning emperor and empress.

Ray (ἀκτίς) The basic word, including compounds, to accentuate objects illuminated by the light-show of Manganeios' poems; sometimes given a spiritual dimension.

Rhetor (ῥήτωρ) A literary man trained in public speaking, with a regular Byzantine secondary education.

Rough water (κλύδων) Almost always used metaphorically, of the troubles of the *sebastokratorissa* or of the emperor Manuel.

Sun (ἥλιος) Heavenly body, but, just as often, its equivalent on earth, the emperor.

Wrinkle (ῥυτίς) Sign of old age, usually of Rome as Constantinople needing renewal or of Manganeios himself.

Abbreviations

Kinn.	John Kinnamos, *Deeds of John and Manuel Komnenos* ed. Meineke (1836)
Nik. Chon.	Niketas Choniates, *History* ed. Van Dieten (1975)
ThPr	Theodore Prodromos, *Historische Gedichte* ed. Hörandner (1974)

Bibliography

Agapitos, P. A. (2015) 'New Genres in the Twelfth Century: The *schedourgia* of Theodore Prodromos', *MEG* 15: 1–41.

(2017) 'John Tzetzes and the Blemish Examiners: A Byzantine Teacher on Schedography, Everyday Language and Writerly Disposition', *MEG* 17: 1–57.

Agapitos, P. A., and D. Angelov (2019) 'Six Essays by Theodore II Lascaris in Vindobonensis Phil. Gr. 321: Edition, Translation, Analysis', *JÖByz* 68: 39–75.

Alexiou, M. (1986) 'The Poverty of Écriture and the Craft of Writing: Towards a Re-appraisal of the Prodromic Poems', *BMGS* 10.1: 1–40.

Antonopoulou, T. (2010) 'On the Reception of Homilies and Hagiography in Byzantium: The Recited Metrical Prefaces', in *Imitatio–Aemulatio–Variatio: Akten des internationalen wissenschaftlichen Symposions zur byzantinischen Sprache und Literatur (Wien, 22.–25. Oktober 2008)*, ed. A. Rhoby and E. Schiffer, 57–80. Vienna.

Astruc, C., and M.-L. Concasty (1960) *Le supplement grec*, Tome III, *Nos. 901–1371*. Paris.

Baldick, C. (2008) *The Oxford Dictionary of Literary Terms*. Oxford.

Bernard, F. (2018) 'Rhythm in the Byzantine Dodekasyllable: Practices and Perceptions', in *Middle and Late Byzantine Poetry: Texts and Contexts*, ed. A. Rhoby and N. Zagklas, 13–42. Turnhout.

Bernardinello, S. (ed.) (1972) *Theodori Prodromi De Manganis*. Padua.

Brand, C. (1989) 'The Turkish Element in Byzantium, Eleventh–Twelfth Centuries', *DOP* 43: 1–25.

Chalandon, F. (1912) *Jean II Comnène (1118–1143) et Manuel I Comnène (1143–1180)*. Paris.

Chatzidakis, G. (1897) 'Περὶ τῶν Προδρόμων Θεοδώρου καὶ Ἱλαρίωνος', *Vizantijskij Vremennik* 4: 100–27.

Devos, P. (1982) 'Une recension nouvelle de la passion grecque BHG 369 de S. Eusignios', *AB* 100: 213–38.

Du Cange, C. du Fresne (1688) *Glossarium ad scriptores mediae et infimae graecitatis*. Lyons.

Fabricius, J. A. (1705–28) *Bibliotheca Graeca*, 14 vols. Hamburg.

Gastgeber, C. (2020) 'Ogier Gislain de Busbecq und seine griechischen Handschriften', in *Bibliothèques grecques dans l'Empire ottoman*, ed. A. Binggeli, M. Cassin and M. Detoraki, 145–81. Turnhout.

Giacomelli, C. (2020) 'Marc. Gr. XI.22', in *Commentaria in Aristotelem Graeca et Byzantina*, https://cagb-db.bbaw.de (accessed 12 October 2020).

Guntius, H. (1536) *Κύρου Θεοδώρου τοῦ Προδρόμου ἐπιγράμματα*. Basel.

Halkin, F. (1959) 'Une nouvelle vie de Constantin dans un legendier de Patmos', *AB* 77: 62–106.

Hörandner, W. (1967) 'Theodoros Prodromos und die Gedichtsammlung des cod. Marc. X. 22', *JÖByz* 16: 91–9.

(ed.) (1974) *Theodoros Prodromos: Historische Gedichte*. Wiener Byzantinistische Studien 11. Vienna.

(1975) 'Marginalien zum "Manganeios Prodromos"', *JÖByz* 24: 95–106.

(1993) 'Autor oder Genus? Diskussionsbeiträge zur "Prodromischen Frage" aus gegebenen Anlass', *ByzSlav* 54: 314–24.
Hörandner, W., A. Rhoby and N. Zagklas (eds.) (2019) *A Companion to Byzantine Poetry*. Brill's Companions to the Byzantine World 4. Leiden.
Hunger, H. (1961) *Katalog der griechischen Handschriften der Österreichischen Nationalbibliothek*, vol. 1: *Codices historici, codices philosophici et philologici*. Vienna.
Janssens, B., and P. Van Deun (2004) 'George Amiroutzes and his Poetical Oeuvre', in *Philomathestatos: Studies in Greek and Byzantine Texts, Presented to Jacques Noret for his Sixty-Fifth Birthday*, ed. B. Janssens, B. Roosen and P. Van Deun, 297–324. Leuven.
Jeffreys, E. M. (2011–12) 'The *Sebastokratorissa* Irene as Patron', in *Female Founders in Byzantium and Beyond*, ed. L. Theis, M. Mullett and M. Grünbart, with G. Fingarova and M. Savage, 177–94. Wiener Jahrbuch für Kunstgeschichte 60–1. Vienna.
(2012) *Four Byzantine Novels: Theodore Prodromos, Rhodanthe and Dosikles; Eumathios Makrembolites, Hysmine and Hysminias; Constantine Manasses, Aristandros and Kallithea; Niketas Eugenianos, Drosilla and Charikles. Translated with Introductions and Notes*. Translated Texts for Byzantinists 1. Liverpool.
Jeffreys, E. M., and M. J. Jeffreys (2001) 'The "Wild Beast from the West": Immediate Literary Reactions in Byzantium to the Second Crusade', in *The Crusades from the Perspective of Byzantium and the Muslim World*, ed. A. Laiou and R. Mottahedeh, 101–16. Washington, DC.
(eds.) (2009) *Iacobi Monachi Epistulae*. Turnhout.
(eds.) (2015) 'A Constantinopolitan Poet Views Frankish Antioch', *Crusades* 14: 48–151.
Jeffreys, M. J. (1974) 'The Nature and Origins of the Political Verse', *DOP* 28: 141–95.
(2010) 'Versified Press Releases on the Role of the Komnenian Emperor: The Public Poems of Manganeios', in *Imperium and Culture*, ed. G. Nathan and L. Garland, 27–38. Sydney.
(2014) 'Written Dekapentasyllables and Their Oral Provenance: A Skeleton History and a Suggested New Line of Research', in *Medieval Greek Storytelling: Fictionality and Narrative in Byzantium*, ed. P. Roilos, 201–30. Mainzer Veröffentlichungen zur Byzantinistik 12. Wiesbaden.
Kazhdan, A. (1987) '"Constantin imaginaire": Byzantine Legends of the Ninth Century about Constantine the Great', *Byzantion* 57: 196–250.
Kazhdan, A., and S. Franklin (1984) *Studies on Byzantine Literature of the Eleventh and Twelfth Centuries*. Cambridge.
Kenens, U., and P. Van Deun (2014) 'Some Unknown Byzantine Poems Preserved in a Manuscript of the Holy Mountain', *MEG* 14: 111–18.
Kurtz, E. (1901) Review of Papadimitriou (1899), *ByzZ* 10.1: 234–8.

(1907) Review of S. Papadimitriou, *Theodoros Prodromos* (Odessa, 1905), *ByzZ* 16.1: 289–300.
Lampros, S. P. (1895) *Catalogue of the Greek Manuscripts on Mount Athos*, vol. 1. Cambridge.
(1911) 'Ὁ Μαρκιανὸς κῶδιξ 523', *Νέος Ἑλληνομνήμων* 8: 3–192.
Leone, P. L. M. (ed.) (1972) *Ioannis Tzetzae Epistulae*. Leipzig.
Lausberg, H. (1960) *Handbuch der literarischen Rhetorik*. Munich.
Lauxtermann, M. D. (2019) *Byzantine Poetry from Pisides to Geometres: Texts and Contexts*, vol. 2. Wiener Byzantinistische Studien 24/2. Vienna.
Linardou, K. (2018) 'The Homilies of Iakovos of the Kokkinoubaphou Monastery', in *A Companion to Byzantine Illustrated Manuscripts*, ed. V. Tsakmada, 382–94. Brill's Companions to the Byzantine World 2. Leiden.
Magdalino, P. (1993) *The Empire of Manuel I Komnenos, 1143–1180*. Cambridge.
Markopoulos, A. (2008) 'Education', in *The Oxford Handbook of Byzantine Studies*, ed. E. M. Jeffreys, J. Haldon and R. Cormack, 785–95. Oxford.
Martini, A., and D. Bassi (1906) *Catalogus codicum graecorum bibliothecae Ambrosianae*, vol. 1. Milan.
Mavroudi, M. (ed.) (2002) *A Byzantine Book of Dream Interpretation: The Oneirokritikon of Ahmet and its Arabic Sources*. Leiden.
Meineke, A. (ed.) (1836) *Ἐπιτομὴ τῶν κατορθωμάτων τῷ μακαρίτῳ βασιλεῖ καὶ πορφυρογεννήτῳ κυρίῳ Ἰωάννῃ τῷ Κομνηνῷ καὶ ἀφήγησις τῶν πραχθέντων τῷ ἀοιδίμῳ υἱῷ αὐτοῦ τῷ βασιλεῖ καὶ πορφυρογεννήτῳ κύρῳ Μανουὴλ τῷ Κομνήνῳ*. Bonn.
Migne, J.-P. (ed.) (1864) *Patrologia graeca*, vol. 133. Paris.
Miller, E. (1873) 'Poèmes historiques de Théodore Prodrome', *Revue archéologique* 25: 251–5, 344–8, 415–19; 26: 23–4, 153–7.
(ed.) (1881) *Recueil des historiens des Croisades. Historiens grecs*, vol. 2. Paris.
(1883) 'Poésies inédites de Théodore Prodrome', *Association pour l'encouragement des études grecques* 17: 18–64.
Mingarelli, J. (1784) *Graeci codices manu scripti apud Nanios patricios venetos asservati*. Bologna.
Mioni, E. (1970) *Biblioteca Divi Marci Venetiarum codices graeci manuscripti*, vol. 3. Venice.
Nesseris, I. C. (2014) 'Η παιδεία στην Κωνσταντινούπολη κατά τον 12ο αιώνα', 2 vols. PhD thesis, University of Ioannina.
Nilsson, I. (2021) *Writer and Occasion in Twelfth-Century Byzantium: The Authorial Voice of Constantine Manasses*. Cambridge.
Nunn, V. (1986) 'The Encheirion as Adjunct to the Icon in the Middle Byzantine Period', *BMGS* 10.1: 73–102.
Papademetriou, S. (1898) 'Οἱ Πρόδρομοι', *Vizantijskij Vremennik* 5: 91–130.
(1899) 'Θεοδώρου τοῦ Πτωχοπροδρόμου τα Μαγγάνεια', *Odessa Universit. Istoriko-filolog. otet. Letopis, Viz. Slac. Ot.* 7.4: 1–48.
(1903) 'Ὁ Πρόδρομος τοῦ Μαρκιανοῦ κώδικος XI 22', *Vizantijskij Vremennik* 10: 102–63.

Rácz, I. (1941) *Bizánci Költemények Mánuel Császár Magyar Hadjárataíról* (=Βυζαντινὰ ποιήματα περὶ τῶν Οὐγγρικῶν ἐκστρατειῶν τοῦ αὐτοκράτορος Μανουήλ). Budapest.

Reinsch, D. R. (1985) 'Byzantinisches Herrscherlob für den türkischen Sultan: Ein bisher unbekanntes Gedicht des Georgios Amirutzes auf Mehmed den Eroberer', in *Cupido Legum*, ed. L. Burgmann, M.-T. Fögen and A. Schminck, 195–210. Frankfurt am Main.

(2020) 'Greek Manuscripts in the Sultan's Library', in *Bibliothèques grecques dans l'empire ottoman*, ed. A. Binggeli, M. Cassin and M. Detoraki, 105–18. Turnhout.

Sifakis, G. (1988) *Γιὰ μιὰ ποιητικὴ τοῦ ἑλληνικοῦ δημοτικοῦ τραγουδιοῦ.* Thessalonike.

Sideras, A. (2010) 'Die codices Escur. 265 (Y II 10) und Marc. XI 22 als Überlieferungszeugen der Lobrede des Gregorios Antiochos an den Patriarchen Basileios Kamateros', *RHT* 5: 43–64.

Spatharakis, I. (1985) 'An Illuminated Greek Grammar Manuscript in Jerusalem: A Contribution to the Study of Comnenian Illuminated Ornament', *JÖByz* 35: 232–44.

Stephenson, P. (2000) *Byzantium's Balkan Frontier: A Political Study of the Northern Balkans, 900–1204.* Cambridge.

Van Deun, P. (ed.) (2000) *Maximi confessoris liber asceticus.* Turnhout.

van Dieten, J. L. (ed.) (1975) *Nicetae Choniatae historia.* Corpus Fontium Historiae Byzantinae 11. Berlin.

Varzos, K. (1984) *Ἡ γενεαλογία τῶν Κομνηνῶν*, 2 vols. Thessalonike.

Zagklas, N. (2018) 'Metrical *Polyeideia* and Generic Innovation in the Twelfth Century', in *Middle and Late Byzantine Poetry: Texts and Contexts*, ed. A. Rhoby and N. Zagklas, 43–72. Byzantios: Studies in Byzantine History and Civilization 14. Turnhout.

(2023) *Theodore Prodromos, Miscellaneous Poems: An Edition and Literary Study.* Oxford.

Zorzi, N. (2020) 'Da Creta a Venezia passando der le isole Ionie: per la storia del fondo di manoscritti greci della famiglia Nani ora alla Biblioteca Nazionale Marciana di Venezia', in *Bibliothèques grecques dans l'Empire ottoman*, ed. A. Binggeli, M. Cassin and M. Detoraki, 311–38. Turnhout.

CHAPTER 13

*An Unedited Cycle of Byzantine Verse Scholia on Herodotus in the Light of Twelfth-Century Verse Scholia on Ancient Historians**

Julián Bértola

In this chapter, I will present a cycle of verse scholia preserved in the margins of a number of manuscripts of Herodotus' *Histories*. Verse scholia are book epigrams that comment on specific passages of the main text and appear next to the sections to which they react in the margins of the folios.[1] Verse scholia also constitute a special case of scholia, precisely because they are written in verse.[2] In Byzantium, writing in verse implies the observance of a certain metre and the repetition of a rhythm, often visually expressed (e.g. by means of punctuation, accentuation and line breaks), which entails a modulation in syntax and vocabulary.[3] All this enhances expressivity and underscores the literariness of verse scholia, thus challenging the views on marginalia as superfluous scribblings or exegetical tools at most. Marginal annotations in general attest to the practices of reading in Byzantium, which could be combined with utilitarian and creative writing.[4] Our verse

* This chapter was written during my PhD studies at Ghent University, and thus parts of it are included in my dissertation 'Using Poetry to Read the Past: Unedited Byzantine Verse Scholia on Historians in the Margins of Medieval Manuscripts' (2021). This study is complementary to Bértola (2022a), which offers the first critical edition of the cycle of verse scholia from ten manuscripts of Herodotus. In the appendix to the present chapter, I print the text of the poems from this edition. I would like to thank Floris Bernard, Kristoffel Demoen, Baukje van den Berg and Nikos Zagklas for their valuable comments that improved this chapter. All remaining mistakes are mine.

1 On book epigrams, see primarily Lauxtermann (2003: 26–34, 132, 197–212), Bernard and Demoen (2019) and the Database of Byzantine Book Epigrams (DBBE, www.dbbe.ugent.be). On book epigrams by Tzetzes, see also Pizzone in this volume.

2 The designation 'verse scholia' is taken from Kaldellis (2015: 65). I follow the conventional practice of calling scholia the commentaries found in the margins of the manuscripts next to the passages concerned: see e.g. Browning (1991), Dyck (2008). However, the reduction of scholia to only these cases is a modern conception; see Lundon (1997), Dickey (2007: 11 n. 25), Montana (2011: 105–10).

3 For what verse means in Byzantine literature, see e.g. Jeffreys (2009), Lauxtermann (2009), Magdalino (2012: 30–3), Bernard (2014: 31–57), Drpić (2016: 21–5), Bernard and Demoen (2021).

4 See especially Cavallo (2006: 67–82, 133–7). Smith (1996) calls for a better study of Byzantine scholia in their own right, not as a mere repository of older material. Many valuable endeavours have been made to understand how specific sets of Byzantine marginalia function in their sociocultural context with due attention to the materiality of the manuscripts: see e.g. Webb (1997), Zorzi (2004), Mondrain (2005) and now also the papers collected in van den Berg, Manolova and Marciniak (2022).

scholia are motivated by the reading of Herodotus, but embedded in their own historical and material reality. In this chapter, a cycle of poems on Herodotus will be contrasted with other cycles of verse scholia on ancient historians by authors of the long twelfth century in order to investigate the circumstances in which it was produced.[5] As a result, I will look into Byzantine perceptions of the past and the medieval reception of ancient Greek literature in general.[6]

The topic of the present chapter is a cycle of verse scholia composed of eleven poems in forty-nine dodecasyllables inscribed in the margins of Herodotus' *Histories* 2.172–3.37. The earliest version of these epigrams is found in the manuscript Florence, Biblioteca Medicea Laurenziana, Plut. 70.6 [Diktyon 16571].[7] The verse scholia are written by the same hand as the main text, the scribe Nicholas Triklines, who copied the manuscript in 1318.[8] They also occur in some apographs of the Laurentianus and have only recently been edited.[9] But let us begin by showing some examples of

5 The scholia on Herodotus are incompletely edited and have been studied only partially; see Stein (1869–71: 2:429–40), Rosén (1987–97), Luzzatto (2000), De Gregorio (2002), Mazzucchi (2002), Corcella (2003: 261–8), Dickey (2007: 54), Cantore (2012) and (2013), as well as Bértola (2022a) and (2022b), Bianconi (2022). Colonna (1953: 16 n. 1) edits a scholion from fol. 39r of Vatican City, Biblioteca Apostolica Vaticana, gr. 2369 [Diktyon 69000], which Vassis (2005: 740) identifies as two dodecasyllabic verses (see Cantore [2013: 136–8]). Rapp (2008: 129–32) offers a survey of the reception of Herodotus in Byzantium; see now also Jeffreys (2019). On the reception of ancient historians in Byzantium, see e.g. Pérez Martín (2002: 133–47), Kaldellis (2012) and (2015).

6 The reception of ancient Greek literature is a recurrent theme throughout the present volume: see esp. the chapters by Agapitos, Bourbouhakis, van den Berg and Pizzone.

7 Manuscript T for Rosén (1987–97: 1:xxxiv–xxxv) and most of the editors, N for Hemmerdinger (1981: 106–21), d for Stein (1869–71: 1:xi–xii). See also Bandini (1768: 665), Colonna (1945: 47) and (1953: 23–4), Alberti (1960: 342–5), (1999: 3–5) and (2007), Turyn (1972: 132–3), Cantore (2013: 35), Wilson (2015: xx), Bértola (2022a: 65–7), Bianconi (2022: 86–9). Laur. Plut. 70.6 occupies a particular place in Herodotus' textual tradition, straddling its two main branches. Until *Histories* 2.123 it seems to belong to the Roman family and from that point onwards to the Florentine one; see Alberti (1960: 342–5) and (1999: 3–5), Hemmerdinger (1981: 110), Cantore (2013: 6 n. 17).

8 A colophon placed in fol. 340v gives the information. The manuscript was probably copied in Thessalonike, since Nicholas' last name, common palaeographic features and many collaborations suggest kinship with Demetrios Triklinios and a connection with his milieu. See Vogel and Gardthausen (1909: 360), Turyn (1957: 229–33), *PLP* 29315, Smith (1993: 188–9), *RGK* III 519, Pérez Martín (2000: 315–20) and (2002: 144–5), Bianconi (2005: 122–41), Kaldellis (2014: 259).

9 Bértola (2022a). On the fate of Laur. Plut. 70.6 and on the manuscripts related to it, see also Alberti (1959), Hemmerdinger (1981: 109–21), Rosén (1987–97: 1:xxxv), De Gregorio (2002: 47–9 n. 49), Bianconi (2005: 138–41), (2018: 125–8) and (2022), Kaldellis (2014: 45–8, 259–62), Akışık-Karakullukçu (2019: 1–3, 23–4). Among these manuscripts, the cycle of verse scholia (or part of it) was copied in Paris, Bibliothèque nationale de France, gr. 1634 [Diktyon 51257]; Milan, Biblioteca Ambrosiana, L 115 sup. [Diktyon 42974]; Vatican City, Biblioteca Apostolica Vaticana, Urb. gr. 88 [Diktyon 66555]; Naples, Biblioteca Nazionale 'Vittorio Emanuele III', III B 1 [Diktyon 46241]; Venice, Biblioteca Nazionale Marciana, gr. Z. 364 [Diktyon 69835]; Paris, Bibliothèque nationale de France, gr. 2933 [Diktyon 52572]; Vatican City, Biblioteca Apostolica Vaticana, gr. 1359 [Diktyon 67991]; Oxford, Bodleian Library, Barocci 114 [Diktyon 47401]; and Naples, Biblioteca Nazionale 'Vittorio Emanuele III', III B 2 [Diktyon 46242].

such verse scholia on Herodotus. On fol. 93v of Laur. Plut. 70.6, Herodotus' *Histories* 3.14.2–10 is copied and three poems in the left and lower margins comment on the passage. Herodotus tells here an anecdote about how the Persian king Cambyses after the conquest of Egypt seeks to humiliate his defeated Egyptian peer Psammenitus by mistreating his daughter and threatening to kill his son. These two scenes are set in a theatrical way in front of Psammenitus' eyes. However, his reaction is anything but dramatic: he remains imperturbable, looking down. At this point (*Histories* 3.14.3) the first verse scholion of this folio is found:[10]

3. Verses
How brave you say Psammenitus was,
acting so bravely in the face of painful misfortunes
that he suffered no disgraceful suffering at all,
as he refrained even from mere sighs
in sufferings that demanded many tears. 5

Then, by chance, Psammenitus encounters an old companion, now a beggar. Only then does he show the signs of sorrow he did not reveal to his family. Here (*Histories* 3.14.7) we find the following monostich:

4. Verse
You were admirable not only when you kept silence but also when you spoke.

Shortly afterwards, Cambyses is informed about Psammenitus' behaviour and in turn asks him the reason for it. Psammenitus replies that the misfortunes of his family were beyond lament, whereas the situation of his friend was worth tears. At Psammenitus' response (*Histories* 3.14.10) another epigram is found:

5. Verses
I am not only amazed at Psammenitus' silence
but I also esteem his speech more than his silence,
for his silence has an unfathomable purpose,
while his speech also reveals the grace of his wise mind
that embellishes both his silence and his words. 5

10 The poems are numbered from 1 to 11, following the order in which they appear in the manuscript. In the appendix to this chapter, I reproduce the Greek text of the cycle from my recent edition (Bértola [2022a]). Unless otherwise indicated, all translations in this chapter are mine.

Poems 3 to 5 focus on the positive moral content of the anecdotes told by Herodotus, playing with the complementary actions of silence and speech. In poem 3 Psammenitus' fortitude is praised as honourable. The surprise expressed in poem 4 is echoed in poem 5, where the poet stresses the obscurity of Psammenitus' behaviour and the respect provoked by his explanation of it. Another feature of these epigrams is the strong use of the first and second person. Poem 3 addresses the author and poem 4 the protagonist. In poem 5 the poet's figure occupies a prominent position instead. By these means some of the characteristic functions of verse scholia are revealed: they often enter into dialogue with the oeuvre or its author and leave room for personal reflections.

Poems 6 and 7 also comment on the events following the Persian conquest of Egypt (fol. 94rv). Poem 6 reacts to the desecration of the mummy of Amasis, the former pharaoh of Egypt (*Histories* 3.16.1). Through a rhetorical question, the Persian king is characterized as crazy, an element that will come up again in the last poem of the series:

> 6. Verses
> And who could be found crazier than he
> who commands a dead body to be whipped?

The subject of poem 7 will also reappear in the last two poems of the cycle. Cambyses instructs that the body of Amasis should be cremated (*Histories* 3.16.2–4) and Herodotus relates that this was against the Egyptian custom and against the Persian religion. The Persians believed that fire was a god and that the corpse of a man should not be offered to a god (*Histories* 3.16.3). Poem 7 reacts once again with a rhetorical question to the passage:

> 7. Verses
> Fire-worshipper, are you not ashamed of being impious,
> as you pollute the object of your devotion with dead bodies?

The epigram addresses the Persian with an epithet coined by George of Pisidia.[11] The infidel is scorned adding blame to his error, as he behaves impiously with respect to his already impious beliefs.

These verse scholia on Herodotus have received little attention until now. In the catalogue of the Biblioteca Medicea Laurenziana, Angelo

11 See e.g. *Heraclias* 1.14, 181 ed. Pertusi (1959).

Maria Bandini already noted the presence of marginalia in Laur. Plut. 70.6, but only Heinrich Stein in his description of this manuscript specified the versified nature of some of them.[12] Stein even published our poem 2 in a footnote and detailed the passages of Herodotus next to which some verses are placed. The next scholar to refer, albeit misleadingly, to the epigrams in Laur. Plut. 70.6 was Bertrand Hemmerdinger. In fact, he pointed to the presence of verses in some folios, such as fol. 93v, but he understood them to be by John Tzetzes and thus referred to Florence, Biblioteca Medicea Laurenziana, Plut. 70.3 [Diktyon 16568].[13] While describing this ancient and authoritative manuscript of Herodotus' textual tradition, Hemmerdinger noted that fourteen 'political verses' by Tzetzes comment on *Histories* 1.94.[14] This poem in Laur. Plut. 70.3 is indeed by Tzetzes and forms part of a larger cycle present in this manuscript. However, the verse scholia in Laur. Plut. 70.6 adopt different tones and viewpoints. In the next section, I will consider Tzetzes' poems on Herodotus from Laur. Plut. 70.3. After a brief analysis of Tzetzes' verse scholia on Herodotus, it will be evident that Hemmerdinger's statement regarding the authorship of the poems in Laur. Plut. 70.6 is not correct.

Tzetzes' Verse Scholia

John Tzetzes was a prolific scholar from the twelfth century known to have composed numerous commentaries on ancient authors. His own literary production is also full of references to ancient literature.[15] He wrote verse scholia on several authors, including himself, Hesiod, Pindar, Aeschylus, Sophocles, Aristophanes, Oppian, Lycophron, Thucydides and Herodotus.[16] Tzetzes' verse scholia on Herodotus were edited for the first time by

12 Bandini (1768: 665), Stein (1869–71: 1:xii).

13 Hemmerdinger (1981: 106).

14 Hemmerdinger (1981: 88), who makes the same mistake as Stein (1869–71: 1:xii) with regard to the metre of our poems. Both Tzetzes' poem in fol. 26r of Laur. Plut. 70.3 and the poems in Laur. Plut. 70.6 are dodecasyllables. The confusion may go back to the way unprosodic dodecasyllables were called 'political' by Maas and others; see Rhoby (2011: 138–9, n. 123).

15 For an overview of Tzetzes' life and works, see Wendel (1948). For Tzetzes' works on ancient literature, see Kazhdan and Epstein (1985: 133–8), Budelmann (2002), Kaldellis (2007: 301–7) and (2009), Pontani (2015: 378–85). See now also the contributions in Prodi (2022), van den Berg, Manolova and Marciniak (2022), Pizzone in this volume and van den Berg in this volume.

16 There are verses scattered in Tzetzes' scholia on his own *Allegories of the Iliad* (ed. Cramer [1836: 376–84]; Matranga [1850: 599–618]), *Letters* (ed. Leone [1972: 158–74]), *Carmina Iliaca* (ed. Leone [1995: 102–243]), *Histories* (ed. Leone [2007: 529–69]), *Theogony* (ed. Leone [2019: 65–70]) and *Exegesis of the Iliad* (ed. Papathomopoulos [2007: 417–60]). Significantly, Tzetzes' *Histories* are themselves conceived as an extensive commentary in verse on his *Letters*; see Pizzone (2017). Other poems appear in Tzetzes' scholia on Hesiod (ed. Gaisford [1823: 23–459]), Oppian (ed. Bussemaker

Maria Jagoda Luzzatto from the aforementioned Laur. Plut. 70.3.[17] The first folios of this manuscript, dated to the tenth century, are enriched with scholia written by a *manus posterior* of the Palaiologan era.[18] Some of them are composed in verse and have been ascribed to Tzetzes by Luzzatto on the basis of their form and content. It has already been shown that there is a considerable volume of verse scholia against which the authorship of these poems can be assessed. However, the natural point of comparison for this brief – and possibly fragmentary[19] – cycle is a large corpus of verse scholia by Tzetzes on the other major classical historian, Thucydides.[20]

Fifty verse scholia of Tzetzes can be read in the margins of a manuscript from the tenth century containing Thucydides' *Histories* (Heidelberg, Universitätsbibliothek, Pal. gr. 252 [Diktyon 32467]).[21] In general, these versified notes on Thucydides are devoted to textual elements that should be noted, modified or removed, and are often directly linked with an actual intervention that corrects the text in question. These verse scholia deal

[1849: 260–375]), Lycophron (ed. Scheer [1908]), Aristophanes (ed. Massa Positano [1960], Holwerda [1960], Koster [1962]). On the verse scholion on Pindar, see Drachmann (1927: 205) and Luzzatto (1998: 84–6). On Aeschylus and Sophocles, see Allegrini (1971–2), Bevilacqua (1973–4). On Thucydides and Herodotus, see now Bértola (2022b).

17 Luzzatto (2000); see Cantore (2012) and (2013: 82–93).

18 Luzzatto (2000) limits her analysis to the first twenty-six folios, where the verse scholia by Tzetzes occur, but Cantore ([2012], [2013: 70]) points out that the second hand adds other scholia until fol. 34r. In fact, there seem to be many later hands annotating the manuscript, such as the Planoudean one in fols. 1r and 376v or Nikephoros Gregoras in fol. 218v; see Mazzucchi (1999: 385), Luzzatto (2000: 651–2, 654). The issue of the marginalia is connected with a major discussion about the stratigraphy of this manuscript; see Bandini (1768: 657–8), Stein (1869–71: 1:v–vii), Colonna (1945: 43), Hemmerdinger (1981: 86–93), Rosén (1987–97: 1:xxv–xxvi), Agati (1992: 153, 250–1, 289–90) and (2001: 53–6), Alberti (2002: 3), De Gregorio (2002: 37–8 n. 19), Pérez Martín (2002: 136), Wilson (2015: xiv–xv), Bianconi (2018: 73 n. 127).

19 See Luzzatto (2000: 649–50), Cantore (2012: 20–2) and (2013: 79, 83–9). There are two other verse scholia in Laur. Plut. 70.3 not edited by Luzzatto. Two dodecasyllables are written in the lower margin of fol. 2v, which have been printed in Cantore (2012: 22) and (2013: 84) and comment on *Histories* 1.8.3. In the right margin of fol. 8r another verse scholion is found, which comments on *Histories* 1.32.1 (ed. and trans. Bértola [2022b: 350]): Συμμαρτυρεῖς, Ἡρόδοτε, τὸ θεῖον τῶν Ἑλλήνων | καὶ ταραχῶδες, φθονερόν, ἀνάμεστον κακίας· | εἶπας καὶ γὰρ ὡς ἔχουσι τὰ πράγματα πανσόφως ('You testify, Herodotus, to the deity of the Greeks | as troubling, envious and full of evil. | In fact you also say wisely how things are'). This last epigram seems to belong to a different yet contemporary hand and features an unusual metre for verse scholia, the political verse. The Tzetzean authorship of these two compositions is less evident, since they do not seem to pursue the typical goals of Tzetzes' interventions. However, some elements support Tzetzes' authorship, especially for the new verse scholion in political verse; see Bértola (2022b).

20 Tzetzes' verse scholia on Thucydides were edited and analysed by Luzzatto (1999); see also Hude (1927), Scott (1981), Baldwin (1982), Maltese (1995: 370–1), Reinsch (2006: 757–8), Kaldellis (2015: 65–79), Pontani (2015: 384–5), Kennedy and Kaldellis (2023: 257–8).

21 Manuscript E for the editors of Thucydides; see e.g. Alberti (1972: 12), Kleinlogel (2019: 13–16). Luzzatto (1999) argues that the notes are autograph, which seems to be confirmed by the discovery of the same hand in the margins of another manuscript connected with Tzetzes (Leiden, Bibliotheek der Rijksuniversiteit, Voss. gr. Q. 1 [Diktyon 38108]); see Pizzone (2020) and in this volume.

with orthography, accentuation and punctuation and exhibit great knowledge of the grammar of Greek dialects. They display erudition on syntax, rhetoric and style, but also on geography and chronology, with occasional allusions to mythology and other ancient authors. Some typical Tzetzean features appear frequently, such as a polemical attitude, a humour that varies from subtle to coarse, and an almost obsessive self-referentiality.[22]

Tzetzes' verse scholia on Herodotus in Laur. Plut. 70.3 follow these trends closely.[23] Luzzatto edits six epigrams. The first occurs in fol. 5v and is attached to *Histories* 1.23.[24] An orthographic problem is here intermingled with a dialectal one. The instructions to the reader, who could also be a student or a scribe, are followed by a polemic finale addressed to adversaries, all sealed with Tzetzean stylistic hallmarks.[25] The four epigrams in fol. 10r, corresponding to *Histories* 1.39–41, have a similar tenor.[26] Grammar, orthography and accentuation occupy centre stage here. Tzetzes teaches the reader how to write properly in these verses, which reveal his usual concerns.[27] I quote the first poem of the series:

(a) Τὸ φῇς περισπῶν, προσγραφὴν τίθει κάτω·
εἰ δ᾽ αὖ βαρύνῃς, προσγραφὴν μή μοι γράφε.

(a) If you put the circumflex over φῇς, put the iota *subscriptum*.
However, if you put the grave accent, do not put the iota *subscriptum*.

It is not until fol. 26r, however, that the force of Tzetzes' figure fully irrupts into the cycle. At *Histories* 1.94.3, where Herodotus talks about the alleged Lydian invention of certain games, the longest poem of the series was writ-

22 See a summarized typology of the verse scholia in Luzzatto (1999: 85).
23 See a summarized typology in Luzzatto (2000: 642, 649).
24 Text and translation in Luzzatto (2000: 642–3). See Luzzatto (1998: 74–6) and (1999: 95–102), Cantore (2002: 29–30) and (2013: 91), Agapitos (2017: 10–11).
25 Ed. Luzzatto (2000: 643), with minor spelling changes; trans. Agapitos (2017: 10): Ἀρίονα γίνωσκε μικρόν μοι γράφειν | Ἰωνικῶς τὲ καὶ κατ᾽ Ἀτθίδος λόγους· | ληρεῖν λόγους ἔα δε πρωξιμοπλόκους ('Know that Ἀρίονα is to be written with an omicron, | both in Ionic and according to Attic diction; | but let the teacher-intertwined speeches tell fooleries'). The same issue is found again in Tzetzes' scholion to his own *Histories* 1.396 ed. Leone (2007: 533.3–9).
26 Text and translation in Luzzatto (2000: 643–5). See Cantore (2012: 12–14) and (2013: 90–1).
27 For example, the subject of the first verse scholion in fol. 10r has parallels in Tzetzes' verse scholia to Aristophanes' *Wealth* 82 ed. Massa Positano (1960: 28.1–10) and *Frogs* 1137 ed. Koster (1962: 1033.15–20). On grammatical lessons in Tzetzes' scholia to his own *Carmina Iliaca*, see van den Berg in this volume; for orthography and the didactic poetry of Niketas of Herakleia, see Bernard in this volume.

ten in five columns in the lower margin.[28] Despite some relevant lexical and stylistic parallels, there is no more potent proof of the authorship of this poem than Tzetzes' use of his own name in the first verse (Τζέτζης κρατεῖ σε· πρόσσχες οἷς τὰ νῦν γράφεις, 'Tzetzes got you: pay attention to what you write now!'). With the second person, moreover, he establishes a discussion between himself, a proud scholar, and the content of Herodotus' narrative.[29] Through Homeric quotations, Tzetzes contests the truth of what the main text states, seeks errors and incoherencies, and tries to correct them.[30]

This kind of erudition, let alone the grammatical expertise, is not found anywhere in the anonymous verse scholia on Herodotus in Laur. Plut. 70.6. A single attempt to display some sort of erudition can be observed in the right margin of fol. 96r in Laur. Plut. 70.6, in an epigram that comments on *Histories* 3.23.2–3. Herodotus narrates at this point the longevity of the Ethiopians, allegedly derived from their diet and their familiarity with a spring of extraordinary light water that rendered them sleek:

> 8. Verses
> You report the prodigious nature of the water
> that flows I do not know from where or from which source.
> In any case, if it carries the unctuosity from metals,
> what would cause it to have the porousness or even the lightness?

Unlike Tzetzes, the author of this verse scholion does not give any explicit learned reference, nor does he argue with Herodotus. He shows curiosity and essays a rational explanation for the viscosity of the water, but the whole commentary is an exhibition of conjectures, halfway between a sense of bewilderment and mere incredulity.[31] The poet also establishes a dialogue with the author by means of the second person, but he does not confute Herodotus' report. The interests of Tzetzes are thus not reflected in

28 Text and translation in Luzzatto (2000: 646–8). See also Hemmerdinger (1981: 88), Luzzatto (1998: 70–2) and (1999: 158–9), Cantore (2002: 28–9) and (2012: 16–20). The passage commented on is actually in the previous folio (fol. 25v).

29 Cantore (2012: 16–20), however, argues that here Tzetzes reacts to a variant of the Roman family. Accordingly, the second person would refer to the copyist of that text.

30 On Tzetzes' scholarly programme of correcting the style and grammar and controlling the truth and consistency of the text he commented on, see the scholion to Aristophanes' *Frogs* 1328 ed. Koster (1962: 1077.49–1079.89); Luzzatto (1998: 72) and (1999: 159–61).

31 However, some of the terms employed appear to be technical. A quick search in *TLG* (*Thesaurus Linguae Graecae*) shows the co-occurrence of χαῦνον and κοῦφον (8.4) in scientific literature, such as the works of Theophrastus, Dioscorides, Galen, Oribasios and Ps.-Alexander of Aphrodisias.

the anonymous epigrams of Laur. Plut. 70.6; no trace whatsoever is found of orthography, grammar, stylistic or textual remarks, nor even many hints of erudition in terms of historical facts, chronology or topography. And, above all, Tzetzes' pervasive self-representation is not in sight anywhere. Therefore, the cycle in Laur. Plut. 70.6 and the poems in Laur. Plut. 70.3 should be clearly distinguished from each other and any identification of Tzetzes as the author of the former seems speculative at most, if not a simple mistake.

Verse Scholia Attributed to Niketas Choniates

The verse scholia found in the margins of another manuscript show more similarities with the cycle of poems in Laur. Plut. 70.6. Vatican City, Biblioteca Apostolica Vaticana, gr. 130 [Diktyon 66761] contains the first five books of Diodorus Siculus' *Bibliotheke* and was copied in the second half of the tenth century.[32] Carlo Maria Mazzucchi has identified eleven different later hands that annotated and corrected the manuscript, some of which wrote epigrams.[33] Despite the presence of Nikephoros Gregoras among the annotators of this manuscript,[34] the most prominent scholiast is by far hand 3: not only did he write seventeen verse scholia, but Mazzucchi also proposes Niketas Choniates as the author who composed these epigrams on the eve of the sack of Constantinople in 1204.[35]

The reasons Mazzucchi adduces to assert that Niketas Choniates wrote these verse scholia regard the style and content of the notes.[36] As for the content, apart from some more or less direct allusions to biographical details,[37] several contemporary issues are referred to in these epigrams, authentic instances of 'poetic journalism'.[38] In this regard, especially significant is the profusion of expressions in the poems that connect the main text with the present from which the poet is writing.[39] Besides some enigmatic

32 See Mazzucchi (1994: 165–76).

33 Mazzucchi (1994) and (1995). Hands 2, 5 and 9 wrote verse scholia; see Mazzucchi (1994: 181, 202, 218), Kaldellis (2015: 83, 95).

34 Hand 6; see Mazzucchi (1994: 202–11).

35 Edition, translation and analysis in Mazzucchi (1995); see also Kaldellis (2015: 80–97).

36 The reasons are suggested in Mazzucchi (1994: 188–97), thoroughly developed in Mazzucchi (1995) and summarized in Mazzucchi (1995: 254–6).

37 Poems II and XII, for example, describe the author as an old man and other elements allow us to imagine his familiar (see poem XIII) or professional profile (see poem I).

38 For the concept, see Magdalino (2012); it has now been called 'public diary-keeping' by Lauxtermann (2019: 32–3).

39 E.g. νῦν II.1, III.2, VII.1, IX.1, X.1, XVI.2; τῆς παρούσης ἡμέρας I.1; καθ' ἡμᾶς V.1, XII.2; see Mazzucchi (1995: 235 n. 152).

references to a war situation,[40] Italian invaders are explicitly named in these verse scholia, as for example in the right margin of fol. 298r (poem XVI).[41] This epigram reacts to *Bibliotheke* 5.67.4, where Diodorus talks about the mythical figure of Themis. Some terms in the main text are elaborated in the verse scholion, which reflects on the catastrophic present in contrast to a brighter past.[42] A practical lesson is drawn from history, which is conceived as *archetypia*.[43] The same principle runs through other poems. In the right margin of *Bibliotheke* 5.40.4–5 (fol. 281r), which recounts the luxurious customs of the Tyrrhenians, our commentator adds four verses (poem XV).[44] The epigram, which largely reuses the words of Diodorus, picks up again the motif of ancient glory gone to waste. The author advises a reader-soldier to avoid the errors of previous peoples, here crystallized in the abuse of alcohol.[45]

These poems have several points in common with the cycle in Laur. Plut. 70.6, such as the allusion to current affairs and the censure of drunkenness. The first two poems of the series in Laur. Plut. 70.6, which occur together in the left margin of fol. 87v, display these coincidences most clearly. The first poem comments on Herodotus' *Histories* 2.172.4–5, the end of the ingenious strategy designed by the Egyptian pharaoh Amasis to gain the favour of his subjects:

> 1. Verses
> How paternally you admonish the Egyptians
> to pay the token of honour suitable for you!
> Another ruler would admonish them by whipping.

40 See poems X, XIII, XVII.

41 Ed. Mazzucchi (1995: 213); trans. after Kaldellis (2015: 94): καὶ θεσμοθέτας εἴπερ ἠυτύχει πόλις: | πόλις κράτους πρὶν νῦν δε μεστὴ δακρύων: | πάρεργον οὐκ ἂν Ἰταλῶν ἦν ἀσπίδος: | οἱ θεσμοφυλακεῖν γαρ ἐξευρημένοι: | δίχα παρασπίζοντος, ἠσθενημένοι: ('If the city was fortunate enough to have legislators, | a city formerly of strength, but now full of tears, | it would not be subjected by Italian arms. | For those who are supposed to guard the law | become weak without someone to defend them'). The Italians are also mentioned in poems III (see below) and XVII.

42 This is a productive rhetorical device in descriptions of the decline of cities; see Demoen (2001).

43 See poem I.3.

44 Ed. Mazzucchi (1995: 213); trans. after Kaldellis (2015: 93): τοιαῦτα τὰ σπέρματα τῶν μακρῶν πότων: | τὸ πατρόθεν σβέννυσιν ἡ τρυφὴ κλέος: | ῥαθυμίαν ἄνανδρον ὁπλίτα φύγε: | εὔκλειαν οἶδε καὶ παλαιὰν ὀλλύειν: ('Such is the fruit of heavy drinking: | luxurious easy living extinguishes ancestral glory. | Soldier, avoid this unmanly indolence, | which knows how to destroy even an ancient glory.')

45 Drunkenness is also condemned in poem VIII, whereas the state of the army is criticized in poem VII. Our poet is keen on complaining about the contemporary parallels of subjects discussed by Diodorus: see e.g. poem V against astrologers and poem IX against doctors. Even the motif of rural bliss in poem VI can be taken as a complaint about life at the court.

The ancient ruler, addressed in the second person, is compared with what might be a contemporary counterpart in the last verse. Right after this epigram, a new set of verses reacts to the routine of Amasis described in *Histories* 2.173. The pharaoh spent only part of the day dealing with government affairs and the rest drinking and joking with friends. The poet compares this with the behaviour of more or less contemporary rulers:

2. Verses
Amasis was bearable, as he devoted to serious issues
one third of the short time of the day,
since those who ruled excessively as tyrants among us
devoted themselves all night and all day long
to amusements or to drunkenness, 5
living a life enslaved to passion.
Because of them, the beauty of the new Rome
was suddenly affected by a wrinkle of old age
and the capital superior to all
became the abode of hostile robbers. 10

These first two poems reuse some of Herodotus' words and show a number of interesting parallels to other Byzantine authors.[46] Moreover, the situation portrayed in poem 2 corresponds to the account of the causes and consequences of the Fourth Crusade given by Niketas Choniates. The last four verses (2.7–10) strongly evoke passages of Niketas Choniates' oeuvre, where the glorious past of Constantinople, queen of cities, is contrasted with the calamitous results of the invasion and compared with a wrinkled old lady.[47] The city that was once home to every beautiful thing was turned

46 The verb νουθετέω (1.3) is used by Herodotus in *Histories* 2.173.2 and νέμω (2.1) is the last word of Amasis in 2.173.4. The wording of poem 1, on the one hand, recalls some verses in Michael Choniates' *Schedos* (ed. Lampros [1879–80: 2.363.18–20]). The parallels of poem 2, on the other, are more evident. Verse 2.4 is identical to verse 90 of the *Epitaph of Empress Irene Komnene* (daughter of Theodore I Laskaris and wife of John III Vatatzes) dated to 1239 and wrongly attributed to George Akropolites (ed. Heisenberg [1978: 2.5.90]). The poem was re-edited by Hörandner (1972); Macrides (2007: 20, 78) rejects Akropolites' authorship. Note that verses 18 and 54 of this poem show further similarities with verses from our cycle (2.7, 5.5). Verse 2.5 is very similar to verse 8550 of Ephraim of Ainos' *Chronicle* (ed. Lampsidis [1990]). Verse 2.7 is almost identical to verse 889 of Constantine Stilbes' *Fire Poem* (ed. Diethart and Hörandner [2005]).

47 See Niketas Choniates, *Orations* 7, 9, 14, 15 ed. van Dieten (1972: 57.4–7, 85.22–4, 146.30–2, 160.6–21) and *History* 576.1–577.19; cf. 591.21–592.49 ed. van Dieten (1975). The epithets of Constantinople in verses 2.7 and 2.9 are paralleled elsewhere in Niketas Choniates (e.g. *History* 569.7–8, 609.86, 617.90, 627.87–9, 629.59–60), although they are not exclusive to him; cf. Demoen (2001: 119). Elsewhere we also find the comparison of the city with a woman, frequently young in relation to

into the residence of pirates.[48] In fact, the Fourth Crusade is characterized in the *History* as a pillaging excursion.[49] The spirit of poem 2 also coincides with the well-known *Kaiserkritik* of Niketas Choniates, who partly ascribes the capture of Constantinople to the corruption of Byzantine emperors.[50] In particular, the behaviour described in verses 2.3–6 brings to mind the western perception of a weak Byzantium subject to drunkenness and earthly pleasures, or the demeaning scene of Emperor Alexios IV Angelos sharing games and drinks with the Latins.[51] In Niketas Choniates' *History*, however, the title of tyrant (2.3) is not applied to legitimate emperors, but mainly reserved for usurpers of the imperial throne, especially Andronikos I Komnenos, and despots of limited realms, such as Cyprus or Sicily, former parts of the empire.[52] Yet the description of 'those tyrants from the Romans' (οἱ ἐκ Ῥωμαίων τύραννοι), who ruled the western regions of the empire after the fall of Constantinople 'like enslaved men, corrupted with luxurious pleasures and other indecencies' (ἀνδραποδώδεις ἄνθρωποι, τρυφῇ καὶ ταῖς ἄλλαις ἀπονοίαις διεφθαρμένοι), is not far from the portrait of the tyrants 'among us' in poem 2.[53]

The context of composition in this verse scholion is therefore less ambiguous than in any other of the epigrams in Laur. Plut. 70.6 and so are the similarities with the poems attributed to Niketas Choniates in Vat. gr. 130. In addition to the already mentioned censure of drunkenness and other dissolute behaviour (2.5–6), there is also the topic of the decay of Constantinople (2.7–8) and the reference to invaders (2.9–10). The picture seems to

the old Rome: cf. e.g. verses 4419–52 of Constantine Manasses' *Synopsis Chronike* (ed. Lampsidis [1996]) and Theodore Prodromos' *Historical Poem* 18.97–108 (ed. Hörandner [1974]). In our poems, verse 2.8 sounds like a tragic and ironic echo of verse 2321 of Manasses' *Synopsis Chronike* (cf. Theodore Prodromos, *Historical Poem* 4.41–50). Notably, the image of the old wrinkle in our poem 2 goes back to *Anthologia Palatina* 5.129.6 and 6.18.2.

48 Niketas Choniates, *History* 576.3 ed. van Dieten (1975; cf. *Oration* 15, 160.8–9 ed. van Dieten [1972]) and *Letter* 4, 204.22–6 ed. van Dieten (1972).

49 Niketas Choniates, *History* 539.5–15, 585.58–586.69; cf. 618.9–13, 621.95–2 ed. van Dieten (1975).

50 See Tinnefeld (1971: 158–79), Magdalino (1983), Harris (2000) and (2001). For *Kaiserkritik* in historiography after 1204, see Angelov (2007: 253–85).

51 Niketas Choniates, *History* 541.54–6, 557.13–21; cf. 549.9–13 ed. van Dieten (1975).

52 For Andronikos, see e.g. *History* 50.58, 101.68, 141.10, 147.68, 225.59–60, 227.5–6, 228.41, 245.74–9, 247.45, 259.37–8, 262.19–263.20, 270.31–4, 279.88, 279.5, 281.62–3, 292.64, 314.43, 321.18, 467.83, 639.70–1 ed. van Dieten (1975); cf. Michael Choniates, *Monody on his Brother* 1.349.17–350.9 ed. Lampros (1879–80). For Isaac Komnenos, tyrant of Cyprus, see *History* 291.39, 340.39, 369.74, 418.76, 464.13. For the kings of Sicily, *History* 296.75, 296.87, 370.93–4, 481.93. On the figure of the tyrant in historiography from the tenth–twelfth centuries, see Cresci (1990), Cheynet (1990: 177–84). On Andronikos, see Simpson (2013: 164–70).

53 See Niketas Choniates, *History* 637.34–40, 638.52–5 ed. van Dieten (1975). The rulers in the East are also accused of tyranny (cf. *History* 639.77–83). On Theodore II Laskaris' conception of tyranny, see Angelov (2007: 245–50).

match the fall of Constantinople during the Fourth Crusade and its aftermath. However, it remains uncertain how contemporary these events are, since the *νῦν* present everywhere in the epigrams in Vat. gr. 130 is absent from the cycle in Laur. Plut. 70.6.[54] The poet seems not to be describing things going on simultaneously outside the reading room, but seems rather to be referring to a recent past.

Both cycles furthermore share a moralizing trend in some of their poems. The poems attributed to Niketas Choniates and the poems in Laur. Plut. 70.6 agree not only on the condemnation of drunkenness but also on the censure of greed for gold and silver.[55] However, the edifying efforts of the cycle in Laur. Plut. 70.6 target religious elements, which are not found in the cycle on Diodorus Siculus by hand 3 of Vat. gr. 130. The consideration of ancient customs and deeds may reveal the Christian scruples of the poet of Laur. Plut. 70.6. An example of this can be observed in the last two poems of the cycle.[56] In the left and lower margin of fol. 97v the following verses are written, reacting to *Histories* 3.29.1, where Herodotus describes how the Persian Cambyses wounded a calf worshipped by the Egyptians as the deity Apis:

> 10. Verses
> In this way Cambyses showed himself to be full of intelligence
> as he welcomed the ox-like god with a sword
> to scrape off its thick flesh.

From then on, Herodotus tells of how Cambyses gradually sank into madness, committing several murders and sacrileges. Towards the end of this narration, he describes how Cambyses mocked and profaned Egyptian gods and concludes that the king was utterly mad. In the left margin of fol. 100v, the last poem of the series can be found next to *Histories* 3.37.3–38.1:

> 11. Verses
> Even if Cambyses has been mad regarding other actions,
> here at least he proves to be wiser than you
> as he laughs at those who deserve laughter.

54 Whereas the expression παρ' ἡμῖν (2.3) evokes καθ' ἡμᾶς from the cycle in Vat. gr. 130 (V.1, XII.2).

55 Cf. poems XI, XIV from Vat. gr. 130 and poem 9 from Laur. Plut. 70.6 (see below).

56 The religious topic first appeared in poem 7; see above. Poem 6 also anticipated the issue of Cambyses' madness, which is ironically turned into wisdom in poems 10 and 11.

The same idea pervades both poems: Cambyses is praised for despising pagan cults, despite being pagan himself.[57] The king's controversial figure is overlooked and his profanities are deemed almost an intuition of truth from a Christian perspective. At the same time, Herodotus, addressed in the second person (11.2), is questioned and receives criticism for disapproving of Cambyses' behaviour. The defiance of the authority of the main text occurs only with regard to this kind of topic in the verse scholia of Laur. Plut. 70.6. It is not the historical or grammatical accuracy that triggers the author's response, as in the case of Tzetzes, but the pagan stories of Herodotus.[58]

The poems by hand 3 in Vat. gr. 130 do not react polemically to pagan elements in the main text. This cycle was produced in a secular context by a person evidently belonging to the imperial administration.[59] The only time that hand 3 contests the information given by Diodorus Siculus is at *Bibliotheke* 2.5.6, which refers to the number of warships in only one harbour of Syracuse in the time of the tyrant Dionysius. The left margin of fol. 82v in Vat. gr. 130, which contains this passage, was annotated first by hand 2: 'Note what this historian says about the longships that came out of a single harbour of Sicily: it does indeed seem unbelievable to me' (σημείωσαι τί φησὶν ὁ παρὼν ἱστορικὸς περὶ τῶν μακρῶν νηῶν τῶν ἐξελθουσῶν ἀπὸ λιμένος ἑνὸς τῆς Σικελίας· ὅπερ τέως ἐμοὶ δοκεῖ ἄπιστον).[60] Under this note, hand 3 wrote a verse scholion to endorse the incredulity expressed by hand 2 (poem 111):

καλῶς ἀπιστεῖς· μᾶλλον εἰς νοῦν εἰ λάβης,
Βυζαντίων ναύσταθμον ὡς νῦν εὑρέθη.
πρὸς δυσάριθμα· καὶ δυσέμβολα σκάφη,
τὰ τῶν Ἰταλῶν, μὴ δὲ δὶς δέκα φέρων:

You are right to disbelieve this, especially if you consider
what the current state of the harbour of Byzantium is:

57 Note that poem 11 precedes the famous relativistic excursus on the equal power of custom in different societies (Herodotus, *Histories* 3.38). The poet of our epigrams appears less liberal than Herodotus.

58 See, however, the new verse scholion in Laur. Plut. 70.3, possibly by Tzetzes, commenting on *Histories* 1.32.1 (quoted above, ed. Bértola [2022b]).

59 See Mazzucchi (1995: 254).

60 Trans. after Kaldellis (2015: 88). See Mazzucchi (1994: 180) and (1995: 208). What has not been noticed by Mazzucchi or Kaldellis is that the text of Diodorus in Vat. gr. 130 reads ναῦς δὲ μακρὰς ἐξ ἑνὸς λιμένος ιβʹ μυριάδας (120,000) and not τετρακοσίας (400), as the modern editions. This makes it sound even less believable.

against the innumerable and invulnerable ships
of the Italians, it can barely muster twenty ships.[61]

The poet addresses the previous commentator in the second person and refers to what is happening simultaneously in the outer world. From the scene described in this poem, Mazzucchi infers that the author was in Constantinople in May 1203. The coincidence of the number of ships (twenty) with Niketas Choniates' report is one of Mazzucchi's strongest arguments for attributing the epigrams to Niketas Choniates.[62] Mazzucchi's study is a monumental philological work, well grounded in palaeographic and codicological analysis, which brings in references from an impressive variety of sources other than Niketas Choniates. However, one must remain cautious, since Niketas is also our most important Greek source for the period in which hand 3 certainly composed the poems in Vat. gr. 130. The arguments for identifying Niketas Choniates as the author of the poems run the risk of being circular. Nothing invites the rejection of the postulated authorship, but there is not enough evidence either to accept it without prudent hesitation.[63] Similarly, I refrain from attributing the new poems in Laur. Plut. 70.6 to Niketas Choniates, even if many elements would match his ideology and find parallels in his oeuvre.

Conclusions

This first presentation of the cycle of verse scholia in Laur. Plut. 70.6 has pinpointed numerous instances of dialogue with the main text and its author as well as with contemporary issues. Poems 1 to 5 praise the Egyptian rulers. Poems 1 and 2 compare them favourably with their Byzantine counterparts; poem 9 seems also to tacitly refer to the current decadence (see below). Poems 6 and 7 turn against the Persian Cambyses and introduce a point of criticism on ancient religion, which will reappear in poems 10 and 11. Poem 11 contains the most direct attack on Herodotus; before,

61 Ed. Mazzucchi (1995: 208); trans. after Kaldellis (2015: 88).

62 See Niketas Choniates, *History* 541.47–50 ed. van Dieten (1975) and Mazzucchi (1995: 224–7). Other parallels include the use of the word Τυνδαρίς in poem XII.7 and in Niketas Choniates' *De signis* 652.75 ed. van Dieten (1975); on this text, see now Spingou (2022: 211–12). Poem XVI quoted above would be self-referential and apologetic too, according to Mazzucchi, an attempt to free the author from any responsibility in the fall of Constantinople.

63 In a recent article, Kuttner-Homs (2020) addresses the literary aspects of the cycle in Vat. gr. 130 and its internal consistency. He accepts Mazzucchi's attribution to Niketas Choniates without adding any new evidence, but in fact his analysis of the poet's 'masks' rather undermines the biographical arguments offered by Mazzucchi.

only in poem 8 is Herodotus' narrative slightly called into question. The comparison of the epigrams in Laur. Plut. 70.6 on Herodotus with other cycles of verse scholia on ancient historians from the twelfth century has also shown that our cycle shares some interests with the one attributed to Niketas Choniates by Mazzucchi, but no connection at all with Tzetzes' scholarly programme. Our poems seem to react in a rather spontaneous and emotional way to Herodotus' text. However, spontaneous does not mean unprepared. On the contrary, these more or less refined divertissements betray an obvious educated background, as the moral and political overtones reveal. In fact, the improvisation of poetry while reading Herodotus should be understood as a sign of advanced rhetorical training and high social status.

Now that we have dispelled the confusion of the author of the cycle in Laur. Plut. 70.6 with Tzetzes, it may be possible to better delimit the circumstances of production of these verse scholia. The time of composition surely follows the capture of Constantinople in 1204, if we take into account the nature of the events depicted in poem 2. We have also observed that the historical indications seem to refer to a recent past. Linguistic and stylistic features, such as the aforementioned *loci similes et paralleli*, point to the same period.[64] A certain degree of familiarity with Niketas Choniates' oeuvre can be inferred from the treatment of the Fourth Crusade and the situation of Constantinople thereafter. However, some images (e.g. the city as a wrinkled old woman) are standardized motifs that do not belong to any single author.

The *terminus ante quem* of our poems is 1318, the date of the earliest manuscript that contains them. As stated before, the poems are written by the same hand responsible for the main text, the scribe Nicholas Triklines. The question is, thus, whether the epigrams are autograph and were composed by Nicholas Triklines as he was copying the *Histories*, or if they belong to an earlier author and were just copied together with Herodotus' text. Autography represents an important issue both for the Tzetzean verse scholia and for the ones attributed to Niketas Choniates. Both Luzzatto and Mazzucchi comment on the textual marks that attest to the process of composition of these verse scholia. Erasures, corrections, rewritings and empty spaces would reveal that the epigrams were jotted down while the

64 Cf. e.g. the *Epitaph* by Ps.-George Akropolites quoted above (ed. Heisenberg [1978], Hörandner [1972]), dated to 1239. Verses 65–75 of this poem also express a yearning for Constantinople redolent of our poem 2.

poet was reading the main text.[65] These kinds of traces can be useful to determine whether or not the poems in Laur. Plut. 70.6 are autograph.

Now, there is no palaeographic evidence indicating that the reading of Herodotus inspired Nicholas Triklines to compose the verse scholia while he was copying Laur. Plut. 70.6. At first sight, the fact that the same hand also copied Herodotus' text and other marginalia already undermines this idea.[66] But, even if no erasure or correction is found in the epigrams, a lacuna in poem 9 poses a major question. Like poem 8, poem 9 comments on an episode of the Ethiopian digression in the third book of the *Histories*. The Ethiopians, Herodotus recounts in *Histories* 3.23.4, used gold to chain up their prisoners, since it was less scarce than other metals in the region. The legend, which enjoyed some popularity in later literature,[67] paves the way for a moralizing condemnation of greed in the longest verse scholion of the cycle in Laur. Plut. 70.6 (fol. 96v):

9. Verses
Sweet is this bond for the gold-lovers.
If it had oppressed their feet as a burden for the feet,
it would have gladdened even more their hearts as it is made of gold.
Oh, who will bring these fetters for them
and thus render all of them prisoners, 5
those who breathe in gold more ...?
For none of them would have escaped the binding,
nor would have been content with receiving one single fetter,
but they would have been eager that together hands and neck and feet
and every part of their bodies 10
were tied up with golden fetters.

The epigram is well structured, with repetitions and variations of words and concepts,[68] including a rhetorical question full of pathos (9.4–6) and

65 See e.g. Luzzatto (1999: 51 n. 26), Mazzucchi (1995: 236, 244, 255 n. 296) and the critical apparatus of poems III, VIII, X, XIII, XIV and XV. Besides, both Luzzatto and Mazzucchi adduce the meticulous use of punctuation, accentuation and – in the case of Tzetzes – the indications of the length of the *dichrona* over the line to support the autography. Note that Tzetzes' poems in Laur. Plut. 70.3, on the other hand, were copied by a later hand.

66 Note that the other cycles of verse scholia discussed in this chapter were all added in an ancient manuscript by a *manus posterior*.

67 See e.g. Heliodorus, *Aethiopica* 9.1.5–2.1.

68 See e.g. δεσμὸς 9.1, δεσμίους 9.5, δέσιν 9.7; πόδας ... ποδῶν 9.2, πόδας 9.9; φιλοχρύσους 9.1, χρυσοῦς 9.3, χρυσὸν 9.6, χρυσίναις 9.11; πέδας 9.4, πέδην 9.8, πέδαις 9.11.

a climax (9.7–11) with an overall humorous effect: greedy people would willingly accept being seized and fastened with shackles made of gold, and everyone would benefit from the result.[69] In verse 9.6 a space is left blank at the beginning of the second hemistich in the manuscript, where three more syllables are needed to complete the dodecasyllable.[70] The phenomenon can be simply understood as a case of the scribe not being able to read the passage in the manuscript from which he copied the poem.[71] However, if we want to regard the scribe as the author of these epigrams, the particular layout of this verse could also be explained as follows: Triklines left an empty space until he could find a proper set of words to fit metre and meaning. In the meantime, he had already decided the ending of the verse, recurrent in our cycle.[72]

The last word still remains to be said on this matter. In general, the evidence points to a date of composition earlier than 1318, but it should be remembered that Nicholas Triklines' milieu may also have been favourable to the production of such verse scholia. To my knowledge, no scholion is ascribed to Nicholas himself. However, Nicholas was more than a mere copyist, as he shows philological skills. In addition, his supposed brother Demetrios Triklinios is known to have undertaken a huge editorial enterprise and produced a varied corpus of scholia that mainly deals with poetry.[73]

69 One could think that the same characters of poem 2 are targeted here, either the decadent tyrants (2.3–6) or the plunderers (2.11). This is, in fact, how Niketas Choniates' *History* and *De signis* depict the Angeloi emperors and, above all, the Latin invaders (cf. van Dieten [1975: 537.49–58, 539.1–15, 551.61–3, 559.77–80, 576.80–1, 602.4–7, 647.19–21, 652.83–7]). However, greed for gold was part of a fruitful literary motif attested elsewhere; see e.g. Rhoby (2019: 9–10).

70 Triklines' awareness of the versified nature of these scholia is expressed visually, as every verse is written in two lines when the poems occur in the external margin. Similarly, a space is left blank between verses when they are written in the lower margin (poems 5 and 10). Note that the partition of the verses into two lines does not necessarily coincide with the caesura, as it does in 9.6.

71 The syntax of the line could need a genitive to complete the meaning of πλέον (cf. e.g. our poems 5.2 and 6.1). The comparison with other passages where analogous turns of phrase are used seems to support the supplementation of ἀέρος ('than air'); see e.g. Michael Italikos, *Letter* 1 64.1–2 ed. Gautier (1972) and George Tornikes, *Letter* 10, 128.10 ed. Darrouzès (1970). This conjecture also conforms to the metre in completing the dodecasyllable. See now Bértola (2022a).

72 See 5.2, 6.1, 9.3, 9.6. Cf. a similar case in Pizzone (2020: 679 n. 87). Of course, this could have already happened in the model of Laur. 70.6: the author left the empty space and Triklines copied the verse as he found it. In Laur. Plut. 70.6, every epigram is preceded by the abbreviation for στίχος/-οι, except for poem 8. Likewise, one may wonder whether this omission should be attributed to the author or rather to an error of the copyist. The apographs of Laur. Plut. 70.6 show various solutions to emend the lacuna in poem 9 and some add the lemma in poem 8. See now Bértola (2022a).

73 Bianconi (2005: 130–6) gives an outline of the philological activity of Nicholas Triklines. He seems to have copied more prose (including some folios of Herodotus in his restauration of Rome, Biblioteca Angelica, gr. 83 [Diktyon 55990]), whereas he collaborated with Demetrios Triklinios

Without ruling out the possibility of Triklines' authorship, I am inclined to think that the poems were copied in the manuscript that served as model for Laur. Plut. 70.6 at some point between the years 1204 and 1318. In Laur. Plut. 70.6, Triklines copied Herodotus' *Histories* and all the marginalia with the same script and colour, thus erasing the visibly different layers of marginal interventions in the model. The author seems to be at least familiar with Niketas Choniates' account of the sack of Constantinople in 1204, but does not seem to have experienced the tragedy of the Latin occupation only through books. The incident seems to be fresh in the author's memory, if not still part of the author's reality. I am alluding here to the possibility that our verse scholia were composed before 1261, when Michael VIII Palaiologos recaptured Constantinople. It is indeed more reasonable to assume that the poet would refer to the disaster of the Fourth Crusade when the wound was still open.

Appendix

The text of the poems is taken from my recent edition (Bértola [2022a]).

1. On Herodotus' *Histories* 2.172.4–5
   Στίχοι
   Ὡς πατρικῶς σὺ νουθετεῖς Αἰγυπτίους·
   τὸ σοὶ πρέπον πρόσχημα τῆς τιμῆς νέμειν·
   ἄλλος δ' ἂν αὐτοὺς μαστιγῶν ἐνουθέτει.

2. On Herodotus' *Histories* 2.173
   Στίχοι
   Ἀνεκτὸς ἦν Ἄμασις τῇ σπουδῇ νέμων
   μικροῦ τριτημόριον ἡμέρας χρόνου·
   οἱ γὰρ παρ' ἡμῖν τυραννοῦντες ἐκτόπως,
   πάννυχον ἅμα καὶ πανήμερον χρόνον
   ταῖς παιδιαῖς προσεῖχον ἢ καὶ ταῖς μέθαις· 5
   ἀνδραπόδων βιοῦντες ἐμπαθῆ βίον·
   ἐξ ὧν τὸ κάλλος τῆς νέας Ῥωμαΐδος
   γηραλέα συνέσχε ῥυτὶς ἀθρόον·
   ἡ βασιλὶς δὲ καὶ πασῶν ὑπερτάτη,
   ληστῶν ὑπῆρξε δυσμενῶν κατοικία. 10

for poetry; see Smith (1993: 188–9), Pérez Martín (2000: 317–8), Bianconi (2005: 128) and (2018: 51–3), Pontani (2015: 427). On Nicholas' metrical training, see especially Turyn (1957: 232–3). For the figure of Demetrios Triklinios, see e.g. Mergiali (1996: 54–7), Fryde (2000: 268–94), Bianconi (2005: 91–118), Pontani (2015: 424–8).

3. On Herodotus' *Histories* 3.14.3
Στίχοι
Ὡς ἀνδρικὸν σὺ τὸν Ψαμμήνιτον λέγεις·
πρὸς λυπρὰς οὕτως ἀνδρισάμενον τύχας·
ὡς μηδαμῶς παθεῖν τι δυσγενὲς πάθος·
φεισάμενον δὲ καὶ ψιλῶν στεναγμάτων·
ἐν πάθεσι χρήζουσι πολλῶν δακρύων. 5

4. On Herodotus' *Histories* 3.14.7
Στίχος
Θαυμαστὸς ἦσθα καὶ σιγῶν σὺ καὶ λέγων.

5. On Herodotus' *Histories* 3.14.10
Στίχοι
Καὶ τὴν σιγὴν τέθηπα τὴν Ψαμμηνίτου·
καὶ τὴν λαλιὰν τῆς σιγῆς τιμῶ πλέον·
ἡ μὲν γὰρ ἀτέκμαρτον ἴσχει τὸ τέλος·
ἥ δ' ἐκκαλύπτει καὶ σοφῆς φρενὸς χάριν·
κοσμοῦσαν ἄμφω καὶ σιγὴν καὶ τὸν λόγον. 5

6. On Herodotus' *Histories* 3.16.1
Στίχοι
Καὶ τίς μεμηνὼς εὑρεθῇ τούτου πλέον,
ὅς σῶμα νεκρὸν μαστιγοῦν ἐπιτρέπει;

7. On Herodotus' *Histories* 3.16.2–4
Στίχοι
Ὁ πυρσολάτρης, ἀνομῶν οὐκ αἰσχύνῃ·
σώμασι νεκρῶν ἐκμιαίνων τὸ σέβας;

8. On Herodotus' *Histories* 3.23.2–3
Στίχοι
Τεραστίαν ὕδατος ἐξηγῇ φύσιν·
οὐκ οἶδ' ὅθεν ῥέουσαν ἢ πηγῆς τίνος·
τὸ γοῦν λιπαρὸν ἐκ μετάλων ἂν φέρῃ·
τὸ χαῦνον ἢ καὶ κοῦφον ἔσχεν ἐκ τίνος;

9. On Herodotus' *Histories* 3.23.4
Στίχοι
Γλυκὺς ὁ δεσμὸς οὗτος εἰς φιλοχρύσους·
ἂν τοὺς πόδας ἔθλιψεν ὡς ποδῶν βάρη,
τὰς καρδίας ηὔφρανεν ὡς χρυσοῦς πλέον·
ὢ τίς κομίσει ταύτας αὐτοῖς τὰς πέδας·

καὶ πάντας ἔνθεν ἀποφήνῃ δεσμίους· 5
τοὺς χρυσὸν ἐμπνέοντας <ἀέρος> πλέον;
οὐδεὶς γὰρ αὐτῶν ἐξέφυγε τὴν δέσιν·
οὐδ᾽ αὖ μίαν ἔστερξεν εἰληφὼς πέδην·
ὁμοῦ δὲ χεῖρας καὶ τράχηλον καὶ πόδας,
καὶ σωματικὴν σύμπασαν διαρτίαν, 10
ταῖς χρυσίναις ἔσπευσε ληφθῆναι πέδαις.

10. On Herodotus' *Histories* 3.29.1
Στίχοι
Ὧδε φρενῶν ἔδειξε Καμβύσης γέμειν·
θεὸν βόειον δεξιούμενος ξίφει·
ὡς πάχος αὐτοῦ σαρκικὸν ἀποξέσῃ.

11. On Herodotus' *Histories* 3.37.3–38.1
Στίχοι
Κἂν εἰς ἄλλα μέμηνεν ἔργα Καμβύσης,
ἐνταῦθα γε σοῦ σωφρονέστερος φθάνει·
γέλωτα τιθεὶς τοὺς γελώτων ἀξίους.

Bibliography

Agapitos, P. A. (2017) 'John Tzetzes and the Blemish Examiners: A Byzantine Teacher on Schedography, Everyday Language and Writerly Disposition', *MEG* 17: 1–57.

Agati, M. L. (1992) *La minuscola 'bouletée'*. Littera Antiqua 9.1. Vatican City.

(2001) '"Digrafismo" a Bisanzio: Note e riflessioni sul X secolo', *Scriptorium* 55: 34–56.

Akışık-Karakullukçu, A. (2019) 'A Question of Audience: Laonikos Chalkokondyles' Hellenism', *ByzZ* 112.1: 1–30.

Alberti, G. B. (1959) 'Il codice Laurenziano greco LXX, 6 e la traduzione latina di Erodoto di Lorenzo Valla', *Maia* 11: 315–19.

(1960) 'Note ad alcuni manoscritti di Erodoto', *Maia* 12: 331–45.

(ed.) (1972) *Thucydidis Historiae*, vol. 1: *Libri I–II*. Rome.

(1999) 'Alcuni *recentiores* di Erodoto', *BollClass* 20: 3–9.

(2002) 'Noterelle erodotee', *BollClass* 23: 3–7.

(2007) '*Retractationes* erodotee (con qualche precisazione)', *Prometheus* 33: 115–16.

Allegrini, S. (1971–2) 'Note di Giovanni Tzetzes ad Eschilo', *AFLPer* 9: 219–33.

Angelov, D. (2007) *Imperial Ideology and Political Thought in Byzantium, 1204–1330*. Cambridge.

Baldwin, B. (1982) 'Tzetzes on Thucydides', *ByzZ* 75.2: 313–16.

Bandini, A. M. (1768) *Catalogus codicum Graecorum Bibliothecae Laurentianae*, vol. 2. Florence.

Bernard, F. (2014) *Writing and Reading Byzantine Secular Poetry, 1025–1081*. Oxford.

Bernard, F., and K. Demoen (2019) 'Byzantine Book Epigrams', in *A Companion to Byzantine Poetry*, ed. W. Hörandner, A. Rhoby and N. Zagklas, 404–29. Brill's Companions to the Byzantine World 4. Leiden.

Bernard, F., and K. Demoen (2021) 'Poetry?', in *The Oxford Handbook of Byzantine Literature*, ed. S. Papaioannou, 365–80. Oxford.

Bértola, J. (2022a) 'A First Critical Edition of the Cycle of Epigrams on Herodotus in the Margins of Manuscript Florence, Biblioteca Medicea Laurenziana, Plut. 70.6 and Some of its *Apographa*', *JÖByz* 72: 63–96.

(2022b) 'Tzetzes' Verse Scholia on Thucydides and Herodotus: A Survey with New Evidence from *Laur. Plut.* 70,3', in *Τζετζικαὶ ἔρευναι*, ed. E. E. Prodi, 335–57. Eikasmos Studi Online 4. Bologna.

Bevilacqua, F. (1973–4) 'Il commento di Giovanni Tzetzes a Sofocle', *AFLPer* 11: 557–70.

Bianconi, D. (2005) *Tessalonica nell'età dei Paleologi: Le pratiche intellettuali nel riflesso della cultura scritta*. Dossiers byzantins 5. Paris.

(2018) *Cura et studio: Il restauro del libro a Bisanzio*. Hellenica 66. Alessandria.

(2022) 'L'Erodoto di Nicola Tricline, Giorgio Gemisto Pletone e Demetrio Raoul Cabace. Il Laur. Plut. 70.6 da Tessalonica a Roma, passando per Mistrà', *BollClass* 43: 61–110.

Browning, R. (1991) 'Scholia', in *The Oxford Dictionary of Byzantium*, vol. 3, ed. A. P. Kazhdan, A.-M. Talbot, A. Cutler, T. E. Gregory and N. P. Ševčenko, 1852–3. New York.

Budelmann, F. (2002) 'Classical Commentary in Byzantium: John Tzetzes on Ancient Greek Literature', in *The Classical Commentary: Histories, Practices, Theory*, ed. R. K. Gibson and C. S. Kraus, 141–69. Leiden.

Bussemaker, U. C. (ed.) (1849) *Scholia et paraphrases in Nicandrum et Oppianum*. Paris.

Cantore, R. (2002) 'Citazioni erodotee nei commentari omerici di Eustazio', *BollClass* 23: 9–30.

(2012) 'I *marginalia* dei primi trentaquattro fogli del Laur. Plut. 70.3 (A) di Erodoto', *BollClass* 33: 3–32.

(2013) *Per la storia del testo di Erodoto: Studi sulla famiglia romana*. Eikasmos Studi 22. Bologna.

Cavallo, G. (2006) *Lire à Byzance*. Séminaires byzantins 1. Paris.

Cheynet, J.-C. (1990) *Pouvoir et contestations à Byzance (963–1210)*. Byzantina sorbonensia 9. Paris.

Colonna, A. (1945) 'De Herodoti memoria', *BPEC* 1: 41–83.

(1953) 'Note alla tradizione manoscritta di Erodoto', *BPEC* 2: 13–25.

Corcella, A. (2003) 'Qualche nota in margine alla tradizione manoscritta erodotea', in *Studi di filologia e tradizione greca in memoria di Aristide Colonna*, ed. F. Benedetti and S. Grandolini, 253–68. Naples.

Cramer, J. A. (1836) *Anecdota Graeca e codd. manuscriptis bibliothecarum Oxoniensium*, vol. 3. Oxford.

Cresci, L. R. (1990) 'Appunti per una tipologia del *TYPANNOΣ*', *Byzantion* 60: 90–129.
Darrouzès, J. (ed.) (1970) *Georges et Dèmètrios Tornikès, Lettres et discours*. Paris.
De Gregorio, G. (2002) 'L'Erodoto di Palla Strozzi (cod. Vat. Urb. gr. 88)', *BollClass* 23: 31–130.
Demoen, K. (2001) '"Où est ta beauté qu'admireraient tous les yeux?" La ville détruite dans les traditions poétique et rhétorique', in *The Greek City from Antiquity to the Present: Historical Reality, Ideological Construction, Literary Representation*, ed. K. Demoen, 103–25. Louvain.
Dickey, E. (2007) *Ancient Greek Scholarship: A Guide to Finding, Reading, and Understanding Scholia, Commentaries, Lexica, and Grammatical Treatises, from their Beginnings to the Byzantine Period.* New York.
Diethart, J., and W. Hörandner (eds.) (2005) *Constantinus Stilbes: Poemata.* Munich.
Drachmann, A. B. (ed.) (1927) *Scholia vetera in Pindari carmina*, vol. 3. Leipzig.
Drpić, I. (2016) *Epigram, Art, and Devotion in Later Byzantium*. Cambridge.
Dyck, A. (2008) 'Scholia', in *Brill's New Pauly. Antiquity*, vol. 13, ed. H. Cancik, H. Schneider and C. F. Salazar, 69–74. Leiden.
Fryde, E. (2000) *The Early Palaeologan Renaissance (1261–c. 1360)*. The Medieval Mediterranean 27. Leiden.
Gaisford, T. (ed.) (1823) *Poetae Minores Graeci*, vol. 2. Leipzig.
Gautier, P. (ed.) (1972) *Michel Italikos: Lettres et discours*. Archives de l'Orient Chrétien 14. Paris.
Harris, J. (2000) 'Distortion, Divine Providence and Genre in Nicetas Choniates's Account of the Collapse of Byzantium 1180–1204', *Journal of Medieval History* 26: 19–31.
(2001) 'Looking back on 1204: Nicetas Choniates in Nicaea', *Mésogeios* 12: 117–24.
Heisenberg, A. (ed.) (1978) *Georgii Acropolitae opera. Editionem anni MCMIII correctiorem curavit Peter Wirth*, 2 vols. Stuttgart.
Hemmerdinger, B. (1981) *Les manuscrits d'Hérodote et la critique verbale*. Genoa.
Holwerda, D. (ed.) (1960) *Jo. Tzetzae commentarii in Aristophanem, Fasc. II continens commentarium in Nubes*. Groningen.
Hörandner, W. (1972) 'Prodromos-Reminiszenzen bei Dichtern der Nikänischen Zeit', *ByzF* 4: 88–104.
(ed.) (1974) *Theodoros Prodromos: Historische Gedichte*. Wiener Byzantinistische Studien 11. Vienna.
Hude, K. (ed.) (1927) *Scholia in Thucydidem ad optimos codices collata*. Leipzig.
Jeffreys, E. M. (2009) 'Why Produce Verse in Twelfth-Century Constantinople?', in *'Doux remède...': Poésie et poétique à Byzance. Actes du IVe Colloque International Philologique 'EPMHNEIA', Paris, 23–24–25 février 2006, organisé par l'E.H.E.S.S. et l'Université de Chypre*, ed. P. Odorico, P. A. Agapitos and M. Hinterberger, 219–28. Dossiers byzantins 9. Paris.
(2019) 'The Byzantine Reception of Herodotus and Thucydides', in *The Afterlife of Herodotus and Thucydides*, ed. J. North and P. Mack, 15–25. London.

Kaldellis, A. (2007) *Hellenism in Byzantium: The Transformations of Greek Identity and the Reception of the Classical Tradition*. Cambridge.

(2009) 'Classical Scholarship in Twelfth-Century Byzantium', in *Medieval Greek Commentaries on the Nicomachean Ethics*, ed. C. Barber and D. Jenkins, 1–43. Studien und Texte zur Geistesgeschichte des Mittelalters 101. Leiden.

(2012) 'The Byzantine Role in the Making of the Corpus of Classical Greek Historiography: A Preliminary Investigation', *JHS* 132: 71–85.

(2014) *A New Herodotos: Laonikos Chalkokondyles on the Ottoman Empire, the Fall of Byzantium, and the Emergence of the West*. Washington, DC.

(2015) *Byzantine Readings of Ancient Historians*. Abingdon.

Kazhdan, A. P., and A. Wharton Epstein (1985) *Change in Byzantine Culture in the Eleventh and Twelfth Centuries*. Berkeley.

Kennedy, S., and A. Kaldellis (2023) 'Thucydides in Byzantium', in *The Cambridge Companion to Thucydides*, ed. P. A. Low, 249–64. Cambridge.

Kleinlogel, A. (ed.) (2019) *Scholia Graeca in Thucydidem: Scholia vetustiora et Lexicon Thucydideum Patmense. Aus dem Nachlaß unter Mitarbeit von Stefano Valente herausgegeben von Klaus Alpers*. Berlin.

Koster, W. J. W. (ed.) (1962) *Jo. Tzetzae commentarii in Aristophanem, Fasc. III continens commentarium in Ranas et in Aves, argumentum Equitum*. Groningen.

Kuttner-Homs, S. (2020) 'Les poèmes-scholies de Nicétas Chôniatès: les masques de l'auteur', *ByzSlav* 78: 262–90.

Lampros, S. P. (ed.) (1879–80) *Μιχαὴλ Ἀκομινάτου τοῦ Χωνιάτου τὰ σωζόμενα*, 2 vols. Athens.

Lampsidis, O. (ed.) (1990) *Ephraem Aenii Historia Chronica*. Corpus Fontium Historiae Byzantinae 27. Athens.

(ed.) (1996) *Constantini Manassis Breviarium Chronicum*. Corpus Fontium Historiae Byzantinae 36. Athens.

Lauxtermann, M. D. (2003) *Byzantine Poetry from Pisides to Geometres: Texts and Contexts*, vol. 1. Wiener Byzantinistische Studien 24/1. Vienna.

(2009) 'Byzantine Didactic Poetry and the Question of Poeticality', in *'Doux remède…': Poésie et poétique à Byzance. Actes du IVe Colloque International Philologique 'ΕΡΜΗΝΕΙΑ', Paris, 23–24–25 février 2006, organisé par l'E.H.E.S.S. et l'Université de Chypre*, ed. P. Odorico, P. A. Agapitos and M. Hinterberger, 37–46. Dossiers byzantins 9. Paris.

(2019) 'Texts and Contexts', in *A Companion to Byzantine Poetry*, ed. W. Hörandner, A. Rhoby and N. Zagklas, 19–37. Brill's Companions to the Byzantine World 4. Leiden.

Leone, P. L. M. (ed.) (1972) *Ioannis Tzetzae Epistulae*. Leipzig.

(ed.) (1995) *Ioannis Tzetzae Carmina Iliaca*. Catania.

(ed.) (2007) *Ioannis Tzetzae Historiae*, 2nd ed. Galatina.

(ed.) (2019) *Ioannis Tzetzae Theogonia*. Lecce.

Lundon, J. (1997) 'Σχόλια: Una questione non marginale', in *Discentibus obvius: Omaggio degli allievi a Domenico Magnino*, 73–86. Como.

Luzzatto, M. J. (1998) 'Leggere i classici nella biblioteca imperiale: Note tzetziane su antichi codici', *QS* 48: 69–86.

(1999) *Tzetzes lettore di Tucidide: note autografe sul Codice Heidelberg Palatino Greco 252*. Bari.

(2000) 'Note inedite di Giovanni Tzetzes e restauro di antichi codici alla fine del XIII secolo: Il problema del Laur. 70,3 di Erodoto', in *I manoscritti greci tra riflessione e dibattito. Atti del V Colloquio Internazionale di Paleografia Greca (Cremona, 4–10 ottobre 1998)*, ed. G. Prato, 633–54. Florence.

Macrides, R. (2007) *George Akropolites: The History*. Oxford.

Magdalino, P. (1983) 'Aspects of Twelfth-Century Byzantine *Kaiserkritik*', *Speculum* 58: 326–46.

(2012) 'Cultural Change? The Context of Byzantine Poetry from Geometres to Prodromos', in *Poetry and its Contexts in Eleventh-Century Byzantium*, ed. F. Bernard and K. Demoen, 19–36. Farnham.

Maltese, E. V. (1995) 'La storiografia', in *Lo spazio letterario della Grecia antica*, vol. 2: *La ricezione e l'attualizzazione del testo*, ed. G. Cambiano, L. Canfora and D. Lanza, 355–88. Rome.

Massa Positano, L. (ed.) (1960) *Jo. Tzetzae commentarii in Aristophanem, Fasc. I continens prolegomena et commentarium in Plutum*. Groningen.

Matranga, P. (ed.) (1850) *Anecdota Graeca*, vol. 2. Rome.

Mazzucchi, C. M. (1994) 'Leggere i classici durante la catastrofe (Costantinopoli, maggio-agosto 1203): Le note marginali al Diodoro Siculo Vaticano gr. 130', *Aevum* 68: 164–218.

(1995) 'Leggere i classici durante la catastrofe (Costantinopoli, maggio–agosto 1203): Le note marginali al Diodoro Siculo Vaticano gr. 130', *Aevum* 69: 200–58.

(1999) 'Diodoro Siculo fra Bisanzio e Otranto (cod. Par. gr. 1665)', *Aevum* 73: 385–421.

(2002) 'Passato e presente nei *marginalia* bizantini', in *Talking to the Text: Marginalia from Papyri to Print*, vol. 1, ed. V. Fera, G. Ferraù and S. Rizzo, 153–66. Messina.

Mergiali, S. (1996) *L'enseignement et les lettrés pendant l'époque des Paléologues (1261–1453)*. Athens.

Mondrain, B. (2005) 'Traces et mémoire de la lecture des textes: Les *marginalia* dans les manuscrits scientifiques byzantins', in *Scientia in margine: Études sur les marginalia dans les manuscrits scientifiques du Moyen Âge à la Renaissance*, ed. D. Jacquart and C. Burnett, 1–25. Paris.

Montana, F. (2011) 'The Making of Greek Scholiastic *Corpora*', in *From Scholars to Scholia: Chapters in the History of Ancient Greek Scholarship*, ed. F. Montanari and L. Pagani, 105–61. Berlin.

Pérez Martín, I. (2000) 'El "estilo salonicense": un modo de escribir en la Salónica del siglo XIV', in *I manoscritti greci tra riflessione e dibattito. Atti del V Colloquio Internazionale di Paleografia Greca (Cremona, 4–10 ottobre 1998)*, ed. G. Prato, 311–31. Florence.

(2002) 'Lectores y público de la historiografía griega', *EClás* 121: 125–47.

Pertusi, A. (ed.) (1959) *Giorgio di Pisidia, Poemi*, vol. 1: *Panegirici epici*. Ettal.

Pizzone, A. (2017) 'The *Historiai* of John Tzetzes: A Byzantine "Book of Memory"?', *BMGS* 41.2: 182–207.

(2020) 'Self-authorization and Strategies of Autography in John Tzetzes: The *Logismoi* Rediscovered', *GRBS* 60: 652–90.
PLP = E. Trapp et al. (1976–96) *Prosopographisches Lexikon der Palaiologenzeit.* Vienna.
Papathomopoulos, M. (ed.) (2007) *Ἐξήγησις Ἰωάννου γραμματικοῦ τοῦ Τζέτζου εἰς τὴν Ὁμήρου Ἰλιάδα*. Athens.
Pontani, F. (2015) 'Scholarship in the Byzantine Empire (529–1453)', in *Brill's Companion to Ancient Greek Scholarship*, vol. 1: *History; Disciplinary Profiles*, ed. F. Montanari, S. Matthaios and A. Rengakos, 297–455. Leiden.
Prodi, E. E. (ed.) (2022) *Τζετζικαὶ ἔρευναι*. Eikasmos Studi Online 4. Bologna.
Rapp, C. (2008) 'Hellenic Identity, *Romanitas*, and Christianity in Byzantium', in *Hellenisms: Culture, Identity and Ethnicity from Antiquity to Modernity*, ed. K. Zacharia, 127–47. Aldershot.
Reinsch, D. R. (2006) 'Byzantine Adaptations of Thucydides', in *Brill's Companion to Thucydides*, ed. A. Rengakos and A. Tsakmakis, 755–78. Leiden.
Rhoby, A. (2011) 'Vom jambischen Trimeter zum byzantinischen Zwölfsilber: Beobachtung zur Metrik des spätantiken und byzantinischen Epigramms', *WS* 124: 117–42.
(2019) 'Gold, Goldsmiths and Goldsmithing in Byzantium', in *New Research on Late Byzantine Goldsmiths' Works (13th–15th Centuries) = Neue Forschungen zur spätbyzantinischen Goldschmiedekunst (13.–15. Jahrhundert)*, ed. A. Bosselmann-Ruickbie, 9–20. Mainz.
RGK III = E. Gamillscheg, D. Harlfinger and P. Eleuteri (1997) *Repertorium der griechischen Kopisten 800–1600*, vol. 3. Vienna.
Rosén, H. B. (ed.) (1987–97) *Herodoti Historiae*, 2 vols. Leipzig.
Scheer, E. (ed.) (1908) *Lycophronis Alexandra*, vol. 2. Berlin.
Scott, R. (1981) 'The Classical Tradition in Byzantine Historiography', in *Byzantium and the Classical Tradition*, ed. M. Mullet and R. Scott, 60–74. Birmingham.
Simpson, A. J. (2013) *Niketas Choniates: A Historiographical Study*. Oxford.
Smith, O. L. (1993) 'Tricliniana II', *C&M* 43: 187–229.
(1996) 'Medieval and Renaissance Commentaries in Greek on Classical Greek Texts', *C&M* 47: 391–405.
Spingou, F. (2022) 'Classicizing Visions of Constantinople after 1204: Niketas Choniates' *De signis* Reconsidered', *DOP* 76: 181–220.
Stein, H. (ed.) (1869–71) *Herodoti Historiae*, 2 vols. Berlin.
Tinnefeld, F. H. (1971) *Kategorien der Kaiserkritik in der byzantinischen Historiographie von Prokop bis Niketas Choniates*. Munich.
Turyn, A. (1957) *The Byzantine Manuscript Tradition of the Tragedies of Euripides.* Urbana.
(1972) *Dated Greek Manuscripts of the Thirteenth and Fourteenth Centuries in the Libraries of Italy*, vol. 1. Urbana.
van den Berg, B., D. Manolova and P. Marciniak (eds.) (2022) *Byzantine Commentaries on Ancient Greek Texts, 12th–15th Centuries*. Cambridge.
van Dieten, J. L. (ed.) (1972) *Nicetae Choniatae orationes et epistulae*. Corpus Fontium Historiae Byzantinae 3. Berlin.

(ed.) (1975) *Nicetae Choniatae historia*. Corpus Fontium Historiae Byzantinae 11. Berlin.

Vassis, I. (2005) *Initia carminum Byzantinorum*. Supplementa Byzantina 8. Berlin.

Vogel, M., and V. Gardthausen (1909) *Die griechischen Schreiber des Mittelalters und der Renaissance*. Leipzig.

Webb, R. (1997) 'Greek Grammatical Glosses and Scholia: The Form and Function of a Late Byzantine Commentary', in *Medieval and Renaissance Scholarship*, ed. N. Mann and B. Munk Olsen, 1–17. Leiden.

Wendel, C. (1948) 'Tzetzes', in *Paulys Real-Encyclopädie der classischen Altertumswissenschaft*, vol. 7, 1959–2011. Stuttgart.

Wilson, N. G. (2015) *Herodotea: Studies on the Text of Herodotus*. Oxford.

Zorzi, N. (2004) 'Lettori Bizantini della "Bibliotheca" di Fozio: *Marginalia* del Marc. gr. 450', in *Atti del VI Congresso Nazionale dell'Associazione Italiana di Studi Bizantini*, ed. T. Creazzo and G. Strano = *SicGymn* 57: 829–44.

CHAPTER 14

Constantine Manasses' Astrological Poem

Editorial Problems, Quellenforschung *and Cultural Context*

Konstantinos Chryssogelos

In 1905, Constantine Cavafy wrote a poem entitled 'Manuel Comnenus', which he published some ten years later. In what turns out to be the sole poem of the poet's canon pertaining to Manuel's reign, astrologers make a brief, yet significant appearance.[1] Cavafy must have drawn inspiration from Niketas Choniates' *History*, where the emperor's final moments are narrated in detail, including astrological predictions of longevity and prosperity for the dying monarch.[2] By reading the rest of Choniates' historical work, the poet must have realized that astrologers were an integral part of Manuel's court throughout his forty-year reign. Apparently, Choniates thought that Manuel's obsession with astrology was a symptom of a decadent empire on the verge of destruction.[3]

However, despite the fact that Manuel did indeed try to raise the discipline's status during his reign, astrology seems to have been a *sine qua non* component of the Greek and Graeco-Roman mentality from the Hellenistic period onwards.[4] The Byzantine court in particular had always been more or less receptive to it.[5] The difference is that before the twelfth century astrology was practised and used discreetly (with the exception of the seventh-century court of Herakleios),[6] due to the Church's hostile attitude towards it.[7] Conversely, Manuel was an outspoken advocate of astrology, and this attitude is attested by a variety of texts composed by both court literati and dignitaries, not to mention the emperor himself. In fact, astrology was such a prominent feature of Manuel's reign that his aunt, Anna

1 Two translations in English (by J. C. Cavafy and by E. Keely and P. Sherrard) can be found at the official website of the Cavafy archive (www.Cavafy.com).
2 Van Dieten (1975: 221). On Choniates as a source for Cavafy's poem, see Agapitos (1994: 14).
3 See Magdalino (2006b: 111) and (2015: 166).
4 Astrology was introduced to Greece around the third century AD. See Barton (1994: 23).
5 See Magdalino (2002: 37) and Papathanassiou (2006: 167–9).
6 See Papathanassiou (2006) and Magdalino (2006b: 33–54).
7 See Magdalino (2006b: 109).

Komnene, writing her celebrated *Alexiad* in the late 1140s or early 1150s,[8] felt compelled to consider the issue. However, her stance is ambivalent and it has been suggested that it is best understood as a reaction to her nephew's policy in this field.[9]

Among the texts pertaining directly or indirectly to astrology that were produced at Manuel's court, we find the *Astrological Poem*,[10] a didactic fifteen-syllable poem by Constantine Manasses, which until recently was attributed to Theodore Prodromos (more on the authorship in the next section).[11] The poem, which was commissioned by the well-known patroness *sebastokratorissa* Irene, constitutes an introductory course on the basic elements of astrology. In the only edition of the poem by Miller (1872), it numbers 593 verses and is structured as follows. First, it opens with an encomiastic address to the *sebastokratorissa* (vv. 1–15). Then the poet explains how the position and the configuration of the planets at the time of one's birth shape one's personality and affect one's health (vv. 16–357). The next section deals with the zodiac circle and the attributes of each sign (vv. 358–482). This is followed by further information on the configuration of the planets and their impact on everyday life (vv. 483–508). The penultimate section is dedicated to the twelve 'places' on the zodiac, which govern several aspects of the life cycle, such as death, marriage and friendship (vv. 511–64).[12] The poem concludes with an epilogue, in which the poet justifies his engagement with astrology, arguing that the planets and their effects are subject to God's will; therefore, he could not be accused of dealing with controversial topics (vv. 565–93).

Even though the *Astrological Poem* has attracted some attention in recent years, we still lack a modern edition based on all six manuscripts (Miller used only two). Moreover, there are still several issues that need to be addressed, such as the placing of the poem within the cultural context of Manuel's reign, when the discipline of astrology was popular. With these desiderata in mind, the purpose of the chapter is threefold: first, to discuss some editorial problems, in the light of Miller's edition and also by taking into consideration all six manuscripts that transmit the text, thus laying the groundwork for a future critical edition; second, to attempt to identify

8 See Magdalino (2000) and (2003: 28).

9 See Magdalino (2000: 29–30), (2003: 28–31), (2006a: 142) and (2015: 167).

10 It was edited, along with John Kamateros' astrological poem, under the title *Poèmes astronomiques* by Miller (1872). Modern scholarship refers to Manasses' poem as *Astrological Poem* (see e.g. Nilsson [2021: 117]).

11 References to the poem follow Miller (1872: 8–39). On didactic poetry, see also Bernard in this volume.

12 On the 'places' on the zodiac, see Barton (1994: 98).

some of the poem's possible sources; third, to delineate the way in which the poem interacts with the cultural milieu in which it was composed. The last section then offers some concluding remarks.

Editorial Problems

The only edition of the *Astrological Poem* is that published by Emmanuel Miller in 1872. The editor had at his disposal two manuscripts. The Paris manuscript (Paris, Bibliothèque nationale de France, Suppl. gr. 501 [Diktyon 53245], fols. 1r–11r; hereafter P) transmits the poem anonymously, while the Vienna manuscript (Vienna, Österreichische Nationalbibliothek, phil. gr. 110 [Diktyon 71224], fols. 533r–538r; hereafter W) attributes it to Theodore Prodromos. In the P manuscript the poem is untitled, but the titles of the works (Prodromos' historical poems) that immediately follow it suggest that they were written 'by the same author'. At present, we know of four more manuscripts that preserve the text.[13] In the Vienna, Österreichische Nationalbibliothek, hist. gr. 86 [Diktyon 70963] (fols. 175v–179v; hereafter W_1), the earliest testimony, dating to the thirteenth century, the poem is again ascribed to Prodromos, whereas in the Vatican manuscript (Vatican City, Biblioteca Apostolica Vaticana, gr. 677 [Diktyon 67308], fols. 99r–111r; hereafter V) the name of the poet is not mentioned. On the other hand, the other two manuscripts, both dating to the fourteenth century (Vienna, Österreichische Nationalbibliothek, phil. gr. 149 [Diktyon 71263], fols. 158r–168v = W_2; Istanbul, Bibliotheke tou Oikoumenikou Patriarcheiou, Kamariotissa 151 [Diktyon 33796], fols. 106r–116r = K), ascribe it to Manasses. Without knowledge of these two manuscripts, Miller accepted the explicit attribution to Prodromos in the W manuscript and the indirect attribution to the same author in the P manuscript.[14]

A first reading of all six manuscripts has shown that there are some interesting differences between them. Four manuscripts (W_1, V, P and W) form a more or less homogeneous group, which applies roughly to Miller's edition, although W_1 and V lack some verses that are present in the other two. However, all four manuscripts perpetuate the same mistakes. This suggests that already in the thirteenth century a manuscript or a group of manuscripts containing the astrological poem had corrupted the text. The false attribution to Prodromos is hardly surprising, since Prodromos was highly respected and venerated by generations of Byzantines.[15] In Hörandner's

13 The manuscript tradition of the poem is discussed briefly by Rhoby (2009: 321–2).
14 See Miller (1872: 2 and 7).

list of the author's literary production, there are no fewer than thirty-five entries with spurious works.[16] In addition, there is strong textual evidence that Prodromos exerted a profound influence on contemporary and later authors.[17] Also, in Ps.-Gregory of Corinth's treatise *On the Four Parts of a Complete Speech*, which dates to the mid- or late thirteenth century,[18] Prodromos is among the exemplars for the composition of iambs.[19] Furthermore, the same author had dedicated a grammar treatise to the *sebastokratorissa*, in which he calls her φιλολογωτάτη ('most learned'), which corresponds to the second verse of the astrological poem.[20]

On the other hand, the two manuscripts that ascribe the poem to Manasses (hereafter: the Manasses manuscripts) contain versions that are slightly different from that of the other four.[21] Both manuscripts omit several verses (not always the same ones), add some of their own, and occasionally offer alternative formulations. Therefore, the six manuscripts contain no fewer than three similar, but not identical, versions of the poem. How is this to be explained? With regard to the *Synopsis Chronike*, Lampsidis has proposed, although with caution, that verses added to the poem and which obviously do not form part of the original composition should be viewed as later insertions by scribes.[22] On the other hand, Horna has convincingly argued that the two different versions of Manasses' *Itinerary* are due to a reworking of the poem by the author himself.[23] Perhaps it could be argued that Manasses had done the same thing with his *Astrological Poem*, although it should be taken into account that in the *Itinerary* there were obvious reasons for the exclusion of specific parts in the second version of the first *Logos*. For instance, the *ekphrasis* of the princess who was initially selected as Manuel's prospective second wife was naturally dropped in the second version, when a new spouse for the emperor had been found.[24] If the different versions of the *Astrological*

15 The vocabulary and style of the poem show that it is by Manasses. See Rhoby (2009: 321–9); cf. Nilsson (2021: 118). Hörandner already questioned its attribution to Prodromos in his edition of the author's historical poems (see Hörandner [1974: 49, n. 76a]). See also Rhoby and Zagklas (2011: 177) for a similar case, where a poem that may have been composed by Manasses is attributed to Prodromos in the oldest testimonies.

16 See Hörandner (1974: 68–72, n. 216–50).

17 See Hörandner (2009: 210–12).

18 See Hörandner (2012: 117).

19 Hörandner (2012: 108), as 'Ptochoprodromos'.

20 See Zagklas (2011: 84). Cf. Rhoby (2010: 167–8).

21 The *variae lectiones* of W_2 were first transcribed by Lampros and published posthumously in Lampros (1922).

22 See Lampsidis (1996: lxv–lxxvi).

23 See Horna (1904: 318–19); cf. Chryssogelos (2017: 93–5).

24 See Horna (1904: 318–19); cf. Chryssogelos (2017: 93–5).

Poem are likewise the outcome of authorial revisions, it would still be difficult to say whether there were political reasons that obliged Manasses to rework his poem. To begin with, it is hard to tell which version is the oldest. A close reading and a comparison between the three versions will solve some of these problems, but for now, it is important to bear in mind that a new critical edition will alter our perception of the poem significantly.

For instance, Table 14.1 shows how the part relating to the effects of the planet Saturn is transmitted in the three versions. If we are inclined to read between the lines, there could be an extra-textual explanation for what we see. Saturn is a harmful planet and verses that refer to fathers dying early (vv. 99–100) are missing from both W_2 and K, while others about women committing adultery (vv. 106–10) are missing from K. It is tempting to assume that such verses were omitted by Manasses because someone at court felt offended by or took issue with them. It is also worth noting that only in the part concerning Saturn (and not the other planets) are so many verses missing in W_2 and K. Another suggestion would be to ascribe these omissions to a later editor, who wanted to use the poem as teaching material.[25] However, this would not explain the steady presence of the encomiastic verses addressed to the *sebastokratorissa* in all manuscripts, not to mention that such a speculation should be made after specifying which version came first. Needless to say, all these issues should be discussed thoroughly in a new critical edition of the poem.

Let us focus now on Miller's edition. As far as the reading of the manuscripts is concerned, the editor's conjectures are most often on the right track, although occasionally he appears reluctant to discuss readings that seem spurious (we shall deal with one such case later). On other occasions, he accepts readings that are obviously not correct (ὕπατος instead of ἥπατος [v. 307]; ὅλων [v. 267] is problematic, since we need a word with a stress on the ultimate or the antepenultimate

Table 14.1 The effects of the planet Saturn in the three versions of Manasses' poem

Miller (= version 1)	W_2 (= version 2)	K (= version 3)
vv. 26–134	vv. 35–104 desunt post v. 34, add. 2 vv.	vv. 44–134 desunt post v. 33, add. 2 vv. post v. 34, alt. v. add.

25 Cf. Nilsson (2021: 123), who also aptly stresses the poem's literary merits.

syllable; v. 197 lacks one syllable; v. 233 has an external hiatus). Last, there are some obvious errors, with readings that are not supported by the two manuscripts either. These may be regarded as simple misprints (διενεκῶς [v. 354] instead of διηνεκῶς, γίνεται πάλι τῶν ὥρων [v. 445] instead of ὡρῶν).

The two versions of the Manasses manuscripts can be helpful in emending verses that are or may be corrupted in Miller's edition (it should be noted, though, that they do not always offer satisfactory readings). Some examples of corrupted verses:

Ἑρμῆς συγχαίρει ταύτῃ δὲ στωμύλος τῇ Προιτίδι (v. 301 ed. Miller)

Loquacious Hermes rejoices with her [= Venus], the daughter of Proetus

The two manuscripts of Miller's edition read ποτρίδι and παιστρίδι, two words that do not make sense. The latter is also the reading of the other two manuscripts of this version, namely W_1 and V. Neither of these readings, not even Miller's suggestion, which draws from Greek mythology, is satisfactory. Ultimately, the best *varia lectio* is offered by W_2, which reads παιστρίᾳ (162v). According to *LBG*, the adjective, which means 'a female player', appears only in this manuscript and Manasses' *Synopsis Chronike*. In the latter it reads as follows:

ἔχαιρε δὲ [= Nero] κιθαρωδοῖς καὶ γυναιξὶ παιστρίαις (v. 2019 ed. Lampsidis 1996)

Nero rejoiced with cithara-players and female players

The *lectio* makes even more sense in the light of the *Synopsis Chronike*, when read together with the next line in the astrological poem that refers to Venus as a cithara-player:

Ἑρμῆς συγχαίρει ταύτῃ δὲ στωμύλος τῇ παιστρίᾳ
ὁ λάλος φιλοπαίγμονι μουσικοκιθαριστρίᾳ

Loquacious Hermes rejoices with this female (instrument) player,
namely the talkative (god) with the cithara-player, who is fond of playing

Another case that is emended by the Manasses manuscripts pertains to v. 540 in Miller's edition. The editor rightly argued that there is a lacuna there, although this was not indicated in his manuscripts. Miller is justified by both Manasses manuscripts, which confirm the loss of one verse, which reads as follows:

> ἕβδομος τόπος γυναικῶν καὶ γάμων καὶ τῶν γάμου (W2, 167v; K, 115r)
>
> the seventh place concerns wives, marriages and everything associated with weddings

Finally, there is the case of v. 592, which in Miller's edition reads καὶ τοίνυν εἰς λυκάβαντας ὡς ἀειρεῖσθαι πλέον. All four manuscripts related to Miller's edition give either ἀπειρῆσθαι or ἀειρῆσθαι. Neither is satisfactory. Rhoby proposed ἀπειρεῖσθαι, on analogy with Manasses' dedicatory epigram to the *sebastokratorissa* Irene, which precedes (or follows) the *Synopsis Chronike*, where we read:

> εἰς τοίνυν λυκάβαντας ἀπειρεσίους ἐλάσειας (v. 9 ed. Lampsidis 1996)[26]
>
> and this I say now: May you live for many years to come

Rhoby's conjecture is better than Miller's, yet the syntax still remains problematic. The verse is missing from W_2, but it is included in the K manuscript. It offers a slightly different *lectio*, which is the best so far and also strongly reminiscent of the aforementioned verse in the dedicatory epigram:

> <κα>ὶ τοίνυν ε<ἰ>ς λυκάβαντας ζήσ<α>ις ἀπειραρίθμους (K, 116r)
>
> and may you live for many years to come

The above cases make clear that we need a new critical edition. Despite some errors, Miller did a fine job with the manuscripts available to him. Today we are fortunate to possess four more testimonies which open up new possibilities in terms of editing, understanding and interpreting the poem.

Quellenforschung

Having explored some of the editorial problems that the modern editor of the poem has to face, we move on now to the detection of its sources,

26 See Rhoby (2009: 325).

yet another field where much work needs to be done. Miller had already indicated some of Manasses' possible sources in the *apparatus fontium* of his edition, such as the second book of Ps.-Manetho's *Apotelesmatica* (which is the first in Koechly's edition),[27] Paul of Alexandria's *Introduction to Astrology* (*Εἰσαγωγικά*) and excerpts from the then-unedited treatise of Rhetorius of Egypt. Ps.-Manetho is given as a parallel for the effects of the interaction of the planets on human behaviour; Paul of Alexandria is cited as a possible source for the information regarding the twelve signs of the zodiac; Rhetorius serves as a parallel for the part dealing with the 'places' of the zodiac. As regards the 'places', Miller also cites an anonymous astrological text that is preserved in Paris, Bibliothèque nationale de France, gr. 2506 [Diktyon 52138].

Of these texts, I shall focus first on Paul of Alexandria, whose treatise is indeed very close to Manasses' poem. However, it appears that the Byzantine poet had one more source, namely Vettius Valens' *Anthologia*. In using it, he describes the nature of the zodiac signs with some adjectives that are absent from Paul, but present in Vettius Valens. Table 14.2 shows the adjectives concerning the first two signs. As can be seen, the adjectives πυρῶδες ('fiery') and γεῶδες ('earthy') are not found in Paul of Alexandria. Therefore, it is quite possible that Manasses drew also on Vettius Valens, who, in turn, does not use the adjective ἐαρινόν. Moreover, Valens' treatise can be of great use on other occasions, as, for instance, in the part where Manasses elaborates on the effects of the Moon on human behaviour, as can be seen in Table 14.3.

Table 14.2 The nature of the zodiac signs in Manasses, Vettius Valens and Paul of Alexandria

Manasses (ed. Miller 1872)	Vettius Valens, *Anthologia* (ed. Pingree 1986)	Paul of Alexandria, *Apotelesmatica* (ed. Boer 1958)
Ζῶον Κριὸς ἀρσενικόν, ἐαρινόν, **πυρῶδες** (v. 380)	<Κ>ριός ἐστιν … ζῴδιον ἀρρενικόν, … **πυρῶδες** (p. 5.21–2)	Κριός, ἀρσενικόν, … ἐαρινόν (p. 2.10–11)
Ὁ Ταῦρος θῆλυ, στερεόν, ἐαρινόν, **γεῶδες** (v. 384)	Ταῦρός ἐστι θηλυκόν, στερεόν (p. 6.16) Ἔστι δὲ τὸ ζῴδιον … **γεῶδες** (p. 7.3)	Ταῦρος, θηλυκόν, στερεόν, ἐαρινόν (p. 3.9)

27 For the correct order of the books, see De Stefani (2017: 22–8).

Table 14.3 The effects of the Moon in Manasses and Vettius Valens

<table>
<tr><th>Manasses (ed. Miller 1872, vv. 351–4)</th><th>Vettius Valens, Anthologia (ed. Pingree 1986, pp. 1.14–15; 1.18 and 1.19)</th></tr>
<tr><td>ὄχλων δηλοῖ δὲ συστροφὰς καὶ ξενιτείας πλάνας,
οἷς οἶμαι τὸ πυκνότερον αὐξομοιώσεις τρέχειν.
οὐδὲ γὰρ ἔχει τὴν αὐτὴν ἀεὶ φωτοχυσίαν.
διενεκῶς δ᾽ ἀλλάττεται τὸ φῶς δανειζομένη.</td><td><῾Η> δὲ Σελήνη γενομένη μὲν ἐκ τῆς ἀντανακλάσεως τοῦ ἡλιακοῦ φωτὸς καὶ νόθον φῶς κεκτημένη σημαίνει ... ὄχλων συστροφήν, ... ξενιτείας, πλάνας.</td></tr>
</table>

Table 14.4 The effects of Saturn in Manasses and Claudius Ptolemy

<table>
<tr><th>Manasses (ed. Miller 1872)</th><th>Claudius Ptolemy, Apotelesmatica (ed. Hübner 1998)</th></tr>
<tr><td>(Κρόνος)</td><td>(ὁ Κρόνος ποιεῖ)</td></tr>
<tr><td>ποιητικὸς φθόνου καὶ βασκανίας (v. 32)</td><td>φθονερούς (p. 255.1232) | βασκάνους (1234)</td></tr>
<tr><td>ὑποκρίσεως, μονογνωμοσύνης (v. 33)</td><td>μονογνώμονας (1230) | ὑποκριτικούς (p. 256.1246)</td></tr>
<tr><td>βαθυφροσύνης σκοτεινῆς (v. 35)</td><td>βαθύφρονας (p. 255.1229)</td></tr>
<tr><td>(αἴτιός ἐστιν) (v. 39)</td><td>(ποιεῖ) τεταρταϊκὰς ἐπισημασίας (p. 136.708–9)</td></tr>
<tr><td>τεταρταίων (v. 46)</td><td>φθορᾶς τῆς κατὰ ψύξιν ἐστιν αἴτιος (p. 136.705–6)</td></tr>
<tr><td>πάντων τῶν ἐκ ψύξεως (v. 47)</td><td>πρὸς δὲ τοὺς τῆς γῆς καρποὺς ἔνδειαν καὶ</td></tr>
<tr><td>ἀπόλλυσι τοὺς καρποὺς ὑδάτων ἐπικλύσει (v. 51)</td><td>σπάνιν καὶ ἀπώλειαν [...] ὑπὸ [...] κατακλυσμῶν ὀμβρίων</td></tr>
<tr><td>ἢ χαλαζῶν σφαιρώμασιν (v. 52)</td><td>ἐπιφορᾶς ἢ χαλάζης (p. 137.723–6)</td></tr>
</table>

There are several issues in Miller's edition: πλάνας (here as a noun, meaning 'wandering', not an adjective) should be separated from ξενιτείας ('living abroad') by a comma, the second verse needs an emendation (perhaps αἷς instead of οἷς and πάσχειν, which is the reading of the K manuscript) and διενεκῶς should be written with an η (διηνεκῶς = perpetually). But even so, the two passages say the exact same thing: moonlight is a reflection of sunlight, for which reason the power of the moon may cause the gathering of crowds, travelling abroad and wandering in general.

Another text that was probably used by Manasses, especially in the first part of his poem that deals with the effects of the planets on a person's character and health from birth (vv. 16–357), is Claudius Ptolemy's *Apotelesmatica*. Table 14.4 shows how this is reflected in the case of the planet

Saturn and its effects on human character (vv. 32, 33, 35) and health (vv. 46–7), as well as on climatic conditions (vv. 51–2).

The influence of Rhetorius' astrological treatise on Manasses is certainly not restricted to the part of the poem that pertains to the 'places' of the zodiac.[28] For instance, the information that Saturn causes gout (ποδάγρα, v. 46) derives from Rhetorius, not Ptolemy.[29] Later on, Manasses says that the sun 'dominates' (δεσπόζει) the right eye and the heart (v. 263). This is reminiscent of Ptolemy's assertion that the sun 'is the lord of eyesight ... the heart ... and the parts of the human body on the right',[30] but again it is Rhetorius who stands closer to Manasses in making a specific reference to the right eye.[31] The same applies to the moon, which in Manasses governs 'the left pupil of the eye' (v. 357). This corresponds to Rhetorius' reference to the 'left eye', whereas Ptolemy speaks of 'the parts of the body on the left' in general.[32]

Moreover, it is important to observe and explore the way in which the poet treats the material that derives from his primary sources. Does he simply quote ancient astrologers or does he update the information they provide? For instance, according to all three versions Venus brings great fortune deriving from 'noble ladies (and) honourable queens' (vv. 293–4). There are relevant passages in Ps.-Manetho and Claudius Ptolemy that were possibly among Manasses' sources,[33] but the specific references to εὐγενεῖς γυναῖκας and βασιλίδας as generators of affluence and bliss seem to be his own. It is impossible not to discern here Manasses' attempt to praise further the generosity of his prominent patroness the *sebastokratorissa*[34] – this virtue of hers is stressed time and again both in this poem and in the *Synopsis Chronike*.[35] Ultimately, such references, no matter how implicit they are, remind us that the most important aspect of the astrological poem is first and foremost the relationship between the twelfth-century court poet and his rich and powerful patroness.

28 There are several problems regarding the transmission of Rhetorius' astrological writings, as well as the question of when exactly he was active, which I will not tackle in this chapter. For a recent discussion of these issues, see László (2020). Rhetorius' influence on Manasses' poem has also been stressed by Caudano (2012: 60).

29 See *CCAG* 7, p. 214.

30 Hübner (1998: 234).

31 *CCAG* 7, p. 219.

32 *CCAG* 7, p. 222 and Hübner (1998: 234), respectively.

33 De Stefani (2017: 66) and Hübner (1998: 140), respectively.

34 I owe this observation to Paul Magdalino.

35 On the praise of Irene's generosity by several authors who frequented her literary salon, see Jeffreys (2011–12: 182).

Literary Milieu and Cultural Context of Manasses' Poem

The last remark in the previous section can serve as the starting point for the study of the cultural context of the *Astrological Poem*. This literary piece was commissioned by the *sebastokratorissa* Irene, to whom Manasses had also dedicated his *Synopsis Chronike*.[36] Both poems are similar in form and style, and thus it could be argued that they were composed around the same time. However, the exact dating of the *Synopsis* is still debated, whereas less research has been done with regard to the *Astrological Poem*. Certainly, the *terminus ante quem* for these two poems is the date of Irene's death, in 1152 or 1153.[37] As regards the *Synopsis*, Lampsidis has argued in favour of a dating before the ascent of Manuel Komnenos to the throne (1143),[38] whereas recent scholarship surmises that the poem was written and edited over a span of several years, with its first sections perhaps composed as early as the late 1130s.[39] If the *Synopsis* was more or less completed during the reign of John Komnenos, namely in the early 1140s, it would mean that the few laudatory verses to Manuel included in the poem are later additions.[40]

Things are further complicated by the material relating to astrology, which can be traced in the *Synopsis* in the part pertaining to the fourth day of Creation (vv. 100–38 ed. Lampsidis 1996), which naturally suggests that there is a connection between this work and the *Astrological Poem*. This is reflected both in the shared vocabulary of the two poems,[41] as well as in some of the planets' attributes that are mentioned in passing in the *Synopsis* but treated in a more detailed manner in the *Astrological Poem*. However, in the *Synopsis* the planets are dealt with in such a way that knowledge of astrology is not really required in order for the relevant verses to be construed. Even v. 109, where the poet says that the sun is οἶκος πυρὸς ἀξύλου ('house of a woodless fire'),[42] a formulation that points towards

36 On the relationship between Irene and Manasses, see Rhoby (2009: 321–9). On the *sebastokratorissa* as patroness, see Rhoby (2010: 166–8) and Jeffreys (2011–12); on the *sebastokratorissa* as the patroness of Manganeios Prodromos, see E. M. Jeffreys and M. J. Jeffreys in this volume.

37 See Chryssogelos (2017: 13–14), Jeffreys (2011–12: 189–90) and (2012: 273–4).

38 Lampsidis (1996: xix); Lampsides dates it to 1142 but argues that it was published after 1143.

39 For the discussion, see Nilsson (2021: 147, 163 and 187).

40 See Lampsidis (1996: xix) and Nilsson (2021: 147).

41 For instance, in the *Synopsis Chronike* the moon is called γλαυκόφωτος and λιπαραυγής (vv. 111–12 ed. Lampsidis [1996]), in the same way as in the *Astrological Poem* (v. 282).

42 Cf. *Astrological Poem*, vv. 474–5: Τῷ γοῦν θαλάμῳ τοῦ πυρὸς Ἡλίου τὸν ἀέρα | πυροῦντι καὶ θερμαίνοντι ταχείαις εὐδρομίαις … ('to the chamber of the Sun's fire, which burns and heats the air most rapidly…'). These two verses appear in the section that deals with the 'zodiacal houses' of the planets.

the 'zodiacal houses',[43] could be well understood figuratively (i.e. 'the sun burns like fire').

Practically, all this means that it is not easy to say which poem came first, although it could be argued tentatively that when this section of the *Synopsis* was delivered to Irene, she was not yet familiar with astrological knowledge. If so, it would not be implausible to assume that Manasses introduced in the *Synopsis* themes, words and concepts associated with astrology, in a way that would not confuse the *sebastokratorissa*, perhaps even in preparation for her imminent acquaintance with the discipline via the *Astrological Poem*. It is useful to note that in the epilogue of the latter, the poet declares that this work is a gift to his patroness, as a token of appreciation for her previous generosity.[44] Does this 'generosity' refer to the poet's lavish remuneration for the composition of the *Synopsis Chronike*, or is some other commissioned work implied here?[45] The case must remain open for now.

In addition, we should consider the possibility that the verses in the *Synopsis* that concern the planets are also later additions, perhaps to one of the last 'versions' of the poem, just when Manuel had succeeded to the throne; we have already seen that the encomiastic verses to this emperor in the *Synopsis* could have been added at a later stage. Indeed, these hints at the discipline of astrology, as well as other instances where astrology is seen in a positive light,[46] within a long poem composed for a distinguished member of the court, fit better the reign of Manuel, a time when astrology, although all but absent in the time of the previous Komnenoi,[47] had become particularly fashionable, due to the emperor's own fascination with it.[48] As we shall see later on, the *Astrological Poem* relates to the astrological literature produced during the reign of this emperor in particular. Be that as it may, neither the aforementioned passage in the *Synopsis* nor

43 See Barton (1994: 96).

44 Vv. 587–8: Πολλῶν γὰρ ἀπολαύσας σου τῶν εὐεργετημάτων | δῶρον προσάγω σοι βραχύ, τοῦτό σε δεξιοῦμαι ('Since I have benefited greatly from your generosity, I bring to you now this small gift, as a token of my gratitude').

45 Jeffreys (2011–12: 181–2) relates this reference to the *Synopsis Chronike*. Nilsson (2021: 187) argues that these verses could well refer to other works, such as Manasses' erotic novel or a literary piece that is now lost.

46 See, for instance, in the edition of Lampsidis, vv. 2035–8 (astrologers predict the death of emperor Vitellius), 2083–2115 (a 'wise astrologer' foresees the passing of Emperor Domitian; the former is then subjected to torture but miraculously remains unharmed) and 2954–60 (an astrologer foretells, apparently with the aid of Divine Providence, the demise of Emperor Zeno). That astrological predictions in the *Synopsis* are proven mostly right is noted also by Magdalino (2006b: 112, n. 21).

47 See Magdalino (2003: 28–9) and (2006b: 101 and 106–7). For a general survey of astrology at the court of Manuel, with brief notes on the authors and their texts, see Magdalino (2021).

48 See Magdalino (2006b: 111).

the *Astrological Poem* as a whole should necessarily be viewed as solid proof of Manasses' own attraction to astrology,[49] for these texts function on multiple levels and are associated with a complex network of patrons, recipients and authors, but also with the authorial persona of the poet, which obviously is not identical to the historical figure of Manasses.[50]

Turning to the poetics of the *Astrological Poem*, we may start by noting that, thanks to the protective wing of the *sebastokratorissa* (we need look no further than the enthusiastic praise of her in the prologue of the *Synopsis Chronike*, as well as the accompanying dedicatory epigram, and likewise the prologue and epilogue of the astrological poem, all of them similar in tone),[51] Manasses was confident enough to elaborate freely on the subject of astrology without having to worry about the controversy this might cause. But he was also prudent enough to add some twenty verses at the end of the poem (vv. 565–84), where he argues that he had not lost his mind in claiming that the planets have a will of their own. On the contrary, he knows that it was God who granted them the power to affect human life, in the same way as He had given power to earthly things, such as stones, plants, trees and roots.

Of particular interest is the fact that Manasses turned to the Old Testament for help in order to seal his argument (vv. 583–4), and more specifically to the following verses from the book of Genesis (1:14), which, it should be stressed, are the source of the section in the *Synopsis* that pertains to the planets as well:

> Καὶ εἶπεν ὁ Θεός· γενηθήτωσαν φωστῆρες ἐν τῷ στερεώματι τοῦ οὐρανοῦ εἰς φαῦσιν ἐπὶ τῆς γῆς, τοῦ διαχωρίζειν ἀνὰ μέσον τῆς ἡμέρας καὶ ἀνὰ μέσον τῆς νυκτός· καὶ ἔστωσαν εἰς σημεῖα καὶ εἰς καιροὺς καὶ εἰς ἡμέρας καὶ εἰς ἐνιαυτούς.[52]
>
> And God said, Let there be lights in the firmament of the heaven to divide the day from the night; and let them be for signs, and for seasons, and for days, and years. (King James Version)

This passage was somewhat controversial throughout the Byzantine period, as the meaning of the word 'signs' is obscure. It appears that some

49 See Magdalino (2006b: 112, n. 21).

50 Cf. Nilsson (2021: 156–9 and 166–9), who regards the frequent appearance of the motif of slander in Manasses' work as a recycled literary motif rather than an autobiographical self-reference.

51 See Rhoby (2009: 323–7).

52 *Ἡ Παλαιὰ Διαθήκη κατὰ τοὺς Ἑβδομήκοντα, ἐγκρίσει τῆς Δ. Ἱερᾶς Συνόδου τῆς Ἐκκλησίας τῆς Ἑλλάδος* (6th ed.; Athens, 1969), p. 1.

Christians in early Byzantine times believed that this mention, along with others in the New Testament,[53] meant that the Holy Bible approved of astrology. In response to these views and with regard to the Genesis reference in particular, the fourth-century Church Father Basil the Great, a prominent authority in his time and beyond, composed a fierce invective against astrology, which was incorporated in his sixth homily on the Creation.[54] In spite of this background, the Genesis reference was deemed sufficient justification of astrology by Manasses. In any case, future events prove that his career was not affected in the slightest by such choices. Quite the opposite: during the 1160s Manasses was close to Manuel's court, a fact that is evidenced by his *Itinerary*,[55] as well as his oration to Michael Hagiotheodorites, the powerful *logothetes tou dromou*.[56]

Manasses' poem can be correlated with several other contemporary prose and verse texts that relate to the reign, or even to the court in particular, of Manuel. Those that deal directly with astrology are Manuel's treatise in defence of the discipline and John Kamateros' astrological poem. In his apology, Manuel argues that Christians are obliged to believe in astrology, on the grounds that the movements of the planets are God's creation and therefore subject to His will. Manuel's attempt to justify astrology with the aid of the Christian faith is one of the boldest efforts to defend the discipline in Byzantine history. But this attempt had consequences, for his text generated a response from Michael Glykas.[57]

It has been suggested that Manuel's treatise was written after 1164, the year Glykas became a monk, since it is in this capacity that the latter endeavours to refute it.[58] This would mean that Manuel's apology postdates Manasses' poem, the *terminus ante quem* of which, as already mentioned,

53 As, for instance, the story of the Magi and the rising star, which foretold the birth of Jesus (Mt. 2:1–2). For the astrological connotations of this narrative, see Barton (1994: 71) and Magdalino (2002: 39).

54 Giet (1968: 348–62). Cf. Magdalino (2002: 33, n. 1). On various early Christian attitudes towards astrology, both positive and negative, see Barton (1994: 71–80). It is worth mentioning that Michael Glykas, who, as we shall see, composed a critical response to Manuel's treatise in defence of astrology, emphasizes the passage from Genesis in his refutation, although Manuel only makes a brief mention. For the Greek text, see Eustratiades (1906: 494 and οδ', respectively).

55 On the association of this poem with the court of Manuel Komnenos, see Chryssogelos (2017: 73–6).

56 Horna (1906: 173–84); cf. Nilsson (2021: 188). It has also been argued that a verse *ekphrasis* of a chariot race composed by Hagiotheodorites was addressed to Manasses. On this, see Marciniak and Warcaba (2014: 109–12).

57 Edition: Eustratiades (1906: ξθ'–πθ', Manuel's treatise; 476–500, Glykas' response). Cf. Magdalino (1993: 377–8) and (2006b: 114). On satire against astrology in the twelfth and early thirteenth centuries, see Magdalino (2015: 167–75); cf. Zagklas (2016: 896–901).

58 On the dating of the refutation, see Magdalino (2006b: 114). Cf. George (2001: 29–30).

is 1152 or 1153. In addition, there is at least one passage suggesting that each author was aware of the other's text. Specifically, Manasses' brief defence of astrology from a Christian Orthodox perspective (vv. 573–82) is close, both verbally and semantically, to Manuel's assertion at the beginning of his apology that if God has given power to stones, plants and roots, then the study of the planets and the stars (and consequently the belief in their powers) is justified, as they too form part, and a rather magnificent one, of Creation.[59] The two passages are not identical, for Manasses focuses on the power (ἰσχύν) of earthly and celestial things, and Manuel on their usefulness (εὔχρηστον), but essentially they both express the same idea by using similar vocabulary – they both speak about λίθοι, βοτάναι and ῥίζαι. Yet, it is noteworthy that Manuel cleverly avoids discussing the passage from Genesis (Manasses' sole intertextual reference to the Bible), except for a passing mention. Instead, it is the New Testament that provides the emperor with a vast array of arguments.[60] We may assume that once Manuel decided to stand up publicly for the discipline's rights, he had perhaps to choose his words carefully.

John Kamateros' astrological poem is interesting in its own right.[61] The identification of its author as John Kamateros *epi tou kanikleiou*, which is supported by the manuscript, is not conclusive, as there was another person with the same name around this time, who was *logothetes tou dromou*. The former appears for the first time in official documents in 1166 and one may wonder whether Manuel, to whom the poem is addressed, was truly in need of an introductory poem to astrology more than twenty years after he ascended to the throne.[62]

A comparison between this poem and the one by Manasses highlights the different approaches taken by the two authors. Despite its rather loose structure, Manasses' poem is easy to follow. The author's obvious goal was to introduce the *sebastokratorissa* to the basic elements of astrology – although the poem's literary merits should not be overlooked either.[63] On

59 See Eustratiades (1906: ξη').
60 See Magdalino (2006b: 116).
61 References follow the edition of Miller (1872: 53–111).
62 See Magdalino (2006b: 113) for all these matters. It should be noted that there is another poem attributed to Kamateros, written in fifteen-syllable verse (ed. Weigl [1908]). The two poems by Kamateros are not variations on the same theme but two completely different works. In this chapter I shall leave the fifteen-syllable poem aside, which is written in a rather peculiar learned-cum-vernacular idiom and also contains elements that, as noted by Magdalino (2006b: 111–12), make it relevant to an eleventh-century cultural milieu. The two poems are also briefly discussed by Caudano (2012: 57–9).
63 See Nilsson (2021: 119–21).

the other hand, Kamateros' poem is much more elaborate and deep in meaning, a fact that is further underlined by the choice of the twelve-syllable verse instead of the more agreeable and playful fifteen-syllable.[64] Furthermore, the absence of references to God or Christian Orthodox theology in Kamateros is striking,[65] as is the emphatic statement at the beginning of the poem that it is impossible for one to live life without knowledge of astrology (vv. 15–18). Perhaps then his purpose was not to teach Manuel after all; his poem could be viewed as a piece of imperial propaganda, as a sophisticated political statement which could have been composed around the time Manuel wrote his apology, in order to consolidate the emperor's status within the court just when he was about to take things outside the palace.

This argument places Kamateros' poem in the mid-1160s or later, when the *epi tou kanikleiou* had already made his first official appearance. But for now this has to remain speculative, since neither this poem nor Manuel's treatise can be dated with certainty. As regards the relation between Kamateros' poem and that of Manasses, however, there is a hint that each was aware of the other's poem. Both use the compound θερμόυγρος ('warm and humid') to describe the 'temperament' (κρᾶσις) of the planet Zeus (v. 140 in Manasses; v. 172 in Kamateros, also in v. 176, in relation to Aphrodite). According to the *LBG*, this adjective is found solely in the two poems in question, while *TLG* offers one more instance, in Glykas' aforementioned refutation. Given that such compounds are otherwise absent from Kamateros' poem, whereas they appear elsewhere in Manasses' poem (after all, neologisms of this kind are an important feature of the latter's literary idiom),[66] it would be natural to assume that Kamateros took the adjective from Manasses rather than the other way around. While certainly one word does not constitute solid proof, not to mention that this particular adjective may derive from a common source that is now lost, such details may prove useful in future research. Nevertheless, if, for the sake of argument, we postulate that there is a deeper connection between the astrological texts

64 On Kamateros' more elaborate style in comparison to Manasses' poem, cf. Nilsson (2021: 124). On the flexible and playful character of fifteen-syllable verse in relation to didactic poetry, see Lauxtermann (2009: 45–6).

65 Miller (1872: 111, n. 4) aptly notes that vv. 1352–4, which constitute the sole Christian reference in the poem, were composed by the scribe of one of the manuscripts that preserve it. Caudano (2012: 60) also notes the absence of Christian references in both of Kamateros' poems.

66 It is noteworthy that θερμόυγρος appears two more times in Manasses (vv. 391 and 393). Other neologisms in the *Astrological Poem* include similar epithets, such as ξερόψυχρον (v. 416) and ὑδρόψυχρος (v. 424). That neologisms are an important feature of Manasses' craft has already been noted by Horna (1906: 173).

of Manasses, Kamateros and Manuel, we should take into account that each serves a different purpose – namely, to teach in a pleasant way, to validate (as it seems) the emperor's interest in astrology, and to prove that the discipline is not incompatible with Orthodoxy, respectively. This could explain why they do not share more elements in terms of content and poetic language.

As far as the use of θερμόυργος is concerned, Glykas uses the adjective in order to describe the temperament of Zeus,[67] in response to a relevant passage in Manuel's treatise.[68] However, Glykas deals also with the temperament of other planets, such as Mars and Saturn, whereas Manuel does not refer to other planets by name. With the exception of Zeus, the temperaments of the planets are described by Glykas with two adjectives (Zeus is θερμόυγρος, but Saturn is ψυχρὸς καὶ ξηρός, and Mars θερμὸς καὶ ξηρός). Interestingly enough, this corresponds to the vocabulary used by Kamateros in the part of his poem pertaining to the temperaments of these three planets.[69] Could it be surmised that in this instance Glykas had Kamateros' poem specifically in mind?[70] In any case, if there is indeed a connection between the two texts, it seems to me unlikely that Kamateros would want to quote the man who had derided his emperor.

Of course, astrological literature during the reign of Manuel was not restricted to didactic (or political) poetry and imperial treatises. Several poems by Manganeios Prodromos dating from the early 1150s testify to the emperor's interest in astrology early on.[71] However, it is John Tzetzes' *Allegories of the Iliad* and *Allegories of the Odyssey* that provide us with some intriguing textual data. Allegorical interpretation couched in astrological terms is employed frequently by Tzetzes in these poems.[72] First and foremost, this is related to the author's own interest in the occult sciences.[73] On a deeper level, we can assume that Tzetzes was trying to ingratiate himself with Manuel via his wife, Irene (née Bertha von Sulzbach), who had commissioned the *Allegories of the Iliad*. Tzetzes' references to 'Zeus, that king and great astrologer' and 'Zeus the astrologer and king' lure us into

67 See Eustratiades (1906: 497).

68 See Eustratiades (1906: 495–7 in Glykas and οα′ in Manuel).

69 Miller (1872: 61, vv. 171–3): Κρᾶσιν κακός, ξηρός τε καὶ ψυχρὸς Κρόνος, | ὁ Ζεὺς ἀγαθός, θερμόυγρος τυγχάνων, | κακὸς δ' Ἄρης, ξηρός τε καὶ θερμὸς μένων ('The temperament of Saturn is dry and cold, therefore harmful; Zeus is beneficent, for his temperament is both hot and wet; Mars, who is always dry and hot, is harmful').

70 Glykas uses the adjective θερμόυγρος in reference to Claudius Ptolemy (ed. Eustratiades 1906: 497), but the ancient astrologer does not employ such compounds.

71 See Magdalino (1992: 202). On the poetry of Manganeios Prodromos, see also E. M. Jeffreys and M. J. Jeffreys in this volume.

72 See Goldwyn (2017: 164–7); cf. Magdalino (2021: 166).

73 See Mavroudi (2006: 77–9).

assuming that he is implicitly praising Manuel's astrological skills.[74] There is at least one similar expression in the *Allegories of the Odyssey*.[75]

However, things are not that simple when it comes to dating Tzetzes' two poems. The *Allegories of the Iliad* are usually dated to the early or mid-1140s, but the aforementioned references to Zeus appear in the last nine books, which were written when Tzetzes had switched patrons. If the reason for him changing patrons was Irene's death, then we are dealing with a post-1159 dating. Yet, in the *Allegories of the Iliad* Tzetzes makes no mention of his patroness' passing (the title of Book 16, the first with a new patron, vaguely implies a lack of funding), whereas he does so, although again not explicitly, in the *Allegories of the Odyssey*, a work written entirely for his new patron Constantine Kotertzes.[76] It is tempting to assume that the verses in question were all composed in the early 1160s, when Manuel was planning to speak up for astrology. If so, the pen of the court literati and high-ranking officials would have offered the emperor a helping hand. But again, lack of concrete evidence with regard to dating the relevant texts does not allow us to draw any definite conclusions yet.

Before we close this section, we should remind ourselves that in the last twenty years of his reign Manuel strove to impose himself, in a rather authoritarian way, as a great theologian and a master of dialectic simultaneously – the prologue of Andronikos Kamateros' *Sacred Arsenal* (around 1170), in which Manuel's extraordinary intelligence and eloquence is attributed to the emperor's dialectic prowess, as well as to the grace of the Holy Spirit, speaks volumes.[77] Since it was arguably more difficult to establish himself as an astrologer too, Manuel may have thought it was more prudent to compose a treatise that combined argumentation in favour of astrology with profound knowledge of theology. In this respect, his astrological treatise could be viewed as a component of the complex agenda he was pursuing in the last two decades of his reign, thus providing further arguments in support of a post-1160 dating.[78]

74 The references to Zeus are in 19.62 and 18.179, respectively, in the edition of Boissonade (1851), here after the translation of Goldwyn and Kokkini (2015). Cf. Mavroudi (2006: 73).

75 Book 21.17–18 ed. Hunger (1955).

76 On the dating of the *Allegories of Iliad* and the problems surrounding it, see Goldwyn and Kokkini (2015: viii–ix); cf. Ravani (2022: 284, n. 68). On a possible post-1159 dating for the *Allegories of the Odyssey*, see Rhoby (2010: 161). In the latter's prologue (v. 16 ed. Hunger [1956]), Irene is referred to in the past tense.

77 Bucossi (2014: 13–14); cf. Magdalino (1993: 290–2) and Cameron (2016: 73–4 and 80–2).

78 Manuel's autocratic style with regard to theological matters during the last fifteen years of his reign is also seen as an argument for a post-1160 dating of his treatise by Magdalino (2006b: 114). Magdalino (2003: 30–1) has further argued that Manuel's strong interest could be also viewed as a reaction to the rising popularity of astrology in the West around this time.

Manasses' poem is not associated with this development. When the *sebastokratorissa* passed away (1152/3), Manuel was a young emperor. Manganeios' references to astrology notwithstanding, Manuel was in need of other symbols in order to overcome the obstacle of his young age and to win over the court (Eros, Alexander and David, to name but a few).[79] Despite adopting the title of ἐπιστημονάρχης with regard to Church affairs already in the late 1140s,[80] the emperor was not ready to promote himself either as a sophist or as an astrologer (better: an advocate of astrology) in an effective way. As regards the first quality in the early years of his reign, we need look no further than the pseudo-proceedings of Nicholas Mouzalon's resignation, which were probably written shortly after the event in 1151. In this slightly ironic dialogue between Manuel and the outgoing patriarch, the disgruntled emperor is unable to conquer his opponent with his successive pseudo-philosophical arguments, and this in a debate that had strong theological connotations.[81]

In this context, Manasses' astrological poem makes sense within the frame of the imperial court's private fascination with astrology during the first decade of Manuel's reign. The first fifteen books of Tzetzes' *Allegories of the Iliad* and several hints in Manganeios Prodromos' poetry apply to the same milieu. Moreover, and perhaps more importantly, Manasses' poem serves as further proof of the author's affiliation with his patroness, the *sebastokratorissa* Irene.

Final Remarks

Manasses' astrological poem constitutes an interesting if somewhat neglected example of twelfth-century poetry. Indeed, over the last two decades only a handful of relevant studies have been published, whereas we still lack a comprehensive study of the text that appears in Miller's edition or a comparative study between Manasses' and Kamateros' two poems. Yet, in order to comprehend and appreciate Manasses' poem in full, we need

79 See Magdalino (1992: 201–3). On David and John II, see also Ricceri in this volume.

80 See Stanković (2007: 22, n. 39) and Magdalino (1993: 281).

81 On the theological aspect of the dialogue, see Darrouzès (1966: 69–74). See also the emperor's angry reaction to Mouzalon's constant counterarguments on p. 320. Magdalino (1993: 278) regards the text as a reliable primary source ('possibly an exact transcript'), but this could be disputed, as the redactor's objective seems to be to criticize the emperor, at least to some extent. Therefore, this dialogue and Kamateros' *Sacred Arsenal* (the latter a product of official propaganda) are far from showcasing the same thing, namely Manuel's outstanding performance in dialectic and syllogisms, as Cameron (2016: 73–4) argues. For a recent analysis of the dialogue, see Chryssogelos (2020) and Zharkaya and Lukhovitskiy (2020).

a new critical edition that will highlight the differences between the three versions that are preserved in the six manuscripts. Hopefully this will pave the way for a reassessment of the poem, along with a concise analysis of its metrical, linguistic and aesthetic features. Naturally, the *Quellenforschung* will benefit equally from a new edition.

From a historical viewpoint, Manasses' astrological poem bears witness not only to a twelfth-century learned man's liaison with the court, but also to the fascination of an era with astrology. This fascination is most probably part of Manuel Komnenos' conscious effort to defend his firm belief in astrology, by arguing that the discipline was not incompatible with Orthodoxy. Apparently, several court literati were on his side, either directly (Kamateros) or indirectly (Tzetzes, Manasses), but his decision to express his support of astrology openly was met with contempt by at least one of his subjects. Even worse, Manuel's deep interest in astrology had a harmful impact on his posthumous reputation, as attested in the account of the final moments of his life in the *History* of Niketas Choniates.

Manasses did not have to worry about such things. In a way, his poem, having been composed in all probability in the early days of Manuel's reign and in the safety of the literary salon of the *sebastokratorissa* Irene, is an unrestricted celebration of ancient knowledge and literature itself. But this celebration had its limitations; if anything, Manasses' attempt to reconcile astrology and Orthodoxy in the epilogue of the poem, after more than 500 verses in the presence of the ancient gods and the absence of the Christian God, demonstrates the complexity and diversity of Byzantium's Greco-Judean heritage in all its glory.

Bibliography

Agapitos, P. A. (1994) 'Byzantium in the Poetry of Kostis Palamas and C. P. Cavafy', *Κάμπος: Cambridge Papers in Modern Greek* 2: 1–20.

Barton, T. (1994) *Ancient Astrology*. London.

Boer, A. (ed.) (1958) *Pauli Alexandrini Elementa Apotelesmatica*. Leipzig.

Boissonade, J. F. (ed.) (1851) *Tzetzae allegoriae Iliadis accedunt Pselli allegoriae*. Paris (repr. Hildesheim 1967).

Bucossi, A. (ed.) (2014) *Andronici Camateri Sacrum Armamentarium Pars prima*. CCSG 75. Turnhout.

Cameron, A. (2016) *Arguing it Out: Discussion in Twelfth-Century Byzantium*. The Natalie Zemon Davis Lecture Series 9. Budapest.

Caudano, A.-L. (2012) 'An Astrological Handbook from the Reign of Manuel I Komnenos', *Almagest* 3/2: 47–65.

CCAG = *Corpus codicum astrologorum graecorum*, 12 vols. Brussels 1898–1936.

Chryssogelos, K. (ed.) (2017) *Κωνσταντίνου Μανασσῆ Ὁδοιπορικόν: Κριτική έκδοση, μετάφραση, σχόλια*. Athens.
(2020) 'Nikolaos Mouzalon's Resignation from the Patriarchal Throne and Manuel Komnenos as the New Socrates', *Parekbolai* 10: 43–63.
Darrouzès, J. (ed.) (1966) *Documents inédits d'ecclésiologie byzantine*. Paris.
De Stefani, C. (ed.) (2017) *Ps.-Manethonis Apotelesmatica*. Wiesbaden.
Eustratiades, S. (ed.) (1906) *Μιχαὴλ τοῦ Γλυκᾶ εἰς τὰς ἀπορίας τῆς Θείας Γραφῆς Κεφάλαια Τόμος Πρῶτος*. Athens.
George, D. (2001) 'Manuel I Komnenos and Michael Glycas: A Twelfth-Century Defence and Refutation of Astrology', *Culture and Cosmos* 5.1: 3–47.
Giet, S. (ed.) (1968) *Basile de Césarée Homélies sur l'Hexaéméron*. SC 26.2. Paris.
Goldwyn, A. J., and D. Kokkini (trans.) (2015) *John Tzetzes: Allegories of the Iliad*. Dumbarton Oaks Medieval Library 37. Cambridge, MA.
Goldwyn, A. J. (2017) 'Theory and Method in John Tzetzes' *Allegories of the* Iliad and *Allegories of the* Odyssey', *Scandinavian Journal of Byzantine and Modern Greek Studies* 3: 141–71.
Hörandner, W. (ed.) (1974) *Theodoros Prodromos: Historische Gedichte*. Wiener Byzantinistische Studien 11. Vienna.
(2009) 'Musterautoren und ihre Nachahmer: Indizien für Elemente einer byzantinischen Poetik', in Odorico, Agapitos and Hinterberger, 201–17.
(2012) 'Pseudo-Gregorios Korinthios, *Über die vier Teile der perfekten Rede*', *MEG* 12: 87–131.
Horna, K. (1904) 'Das Hodoiporikon des Konstantin Manasses', *ByzZ* 13.2: 313–55.
(1906) 'Eine unedierte Rede des Konstantin Manasses', *WS* 28: 171–204.
Hübner, W. (ed.) (1998) *Claudii Ptolemaei Opera quae exstant omnia*, vol. 3.1: *Ἀποτελεσματικά*. Stuttgart.
Hunger, H. (1955) 'Johannes Tzetzes, Allegorien zur Odyssee, Buch 13–24', *ByzZ* 48.1: 4–48.
(1956) 'Johannes Tzetzes, Allegorien zur Odyssee, Buch 1–12', *ByzZ* 49.2: 249–310.
Jeffreys, E. M. (2011–12) 'The *Sebastokratorissa* Irene as Patron', in *Female Founders in Byzantium and Beyond*, ed. L. Theis, M. Mullett and M. Grünbart, with G. Fingarova and M. Savage, 177–94. Wiener Jahrbuch für Kunstgeschichte 60–1. Vienna.
(2012) *Four Byzantine Novels: Theodore Prodromos, Rhodanthe and Dosikles; Eumathios Makrembolites, Hysmine and Hysminias; Constantine Manasses, Aristandros and Kallithea; Niketas Eugenianos, Drosilla and Charikles. Translated with Introductions and Notes*. Translated Texts for Byzantinists 1. Liverpool.
Lampros, S. (1922) 'Κωνσταντίνου Μανασσῆ, Στίχοι συνοψίζοντες τὰ προχειρότερα περὶ τῶν ἀστέρων', *Νέος Ἑλληνομνήμων* 16.1: 60–6.
Lampsidis, O. (ed.) (1996) *Constantini Manassis Breviarium Chronicum*. Corpus Fontium Historiae Byzantinae 36. Athens.
Lauxtermann, M. D. (2009) 'Byzantine Didactic Poetry and the Question of Poeticality', in Odorico, Agapitos and Hinterberger, 37–46.

László, L. (2020) 'Rhetorius, Zeno's Astrologer, and a Sixth-Century Astrological Compendium', *DOP* 74: 329–50.

Magdalino, P. (1992) 'Eros the King and the King of Amours: Some Observations on *Hysmine and Hysminias*', *DOP* 46: 197–204.

(1993) *The Empire of Manuel I Komnenos, 1143–1180*. Cambridge.

(2000) 'The Pen of the Aunt: Echoes of the Mid-Twelfth Century in the *Alexiad*', in *Anna Komnene and her Times*, ed. T. Gouma-Peterson, 15–43. New York.

(2002) 'The Byzantine Reception of Classical Astrology', in *Literacy, Education and Manuscript Transmission in Byzantium and Beyond*, ed. C. Holmes and J. Waring, 33–57. Leiden.

(2003) 'The Porphyrogenita and the Astrologers: A Commentary on *Alexiad* VI.7.1–7', in *Porphyrogenita: Essays on the History and Literature of Byzantium and the Latin East in Honour of Julian Chrysostomides*, ed. C. Dendrinos, J. Harris, E. Harvalia-Crook and J. Herrin, 15–31. Aldershot.

(2006a) 'Occult Science and Imperial Power in Byzantine History and Historiography (9th–12th Centuries)', in Magdalino and Mavroudi, 119–62.

(2006b) *L'Orthodoxie des astrologues*. Paris.

(2015) 'Debunking Astrology in Twelfth-Century Constantinople', in *Pour une poétique de Byzance: Hommage à Vassilis Katsaros*, ed. S. Efthymiadis, C. Messis, P. Odorico and I. Polemis, 165–75. Dossiers byzantins 16. Paris.

(2021) 'Astrology at the Court of Manuel I Komnenos (1143–1180)', in *Unterstützung bei herrscherlichem Entscheiden: Experten und Ihr Wissen in transkultureller und komparativer Perspektive*, ed. M. Grünbart, 160–70. Göttingen.

Magdalino, P., and M. Mavroudi (eds.) (2006) *The Occult Sciences in Byzantium*. Geneva.

Marciniak, P., and K. Warcaba (2014) 'Racing with Rhetoric: A Byzantine *Ekphrasis* of a Chariot Race', *ByzZ* 107.1: 97–112.

Mavroudi, M. (2006) 'Occult Science and Society in Byzantium: Considerations for Future Research', in Magdalino and Mavroudi, 39–95.

Miller, E. (1872) 'Poèmes astronomiques de Théodore Prodrome et de Jean Camatère d'après les manuscrits de la Bibliothèque nationale de Paris', *Notices et extraits des mss. de la Bibliothèque nationale et autres bibliothèques* 23.2: 1–112.

Nilsson, I. (2021) *Writer and Occasion in Twelfth-Century Byzantium: The Authorial Voice of Constantine Manasses*. Cambridge.

Odorico, P., P. A. Agapitos and M. Hinterberger (eds.) (2009) *'Doux remède...': Poésie et poétique à Byzance. Actes du IVe Colloque International Philologique 'EPMHNEIA', Paris, 23–24–25 février 2006, organisé par l'E.H.E.S.S. et l'Université de Chypre.* Dossiers byzantins 9. Paris.

Papathanassiou, M. (2006) 'Stephanos of Alexandria: A Famous Byzantine Scholar, Alchemist and Astrologer', in Magdalino and Mavroudi, 163–203.

Pingree, D. (ed.) (1986) *Vettii Valentis Antiocheni Anthologiarum libri novem*. Leipzig.

Ravani, A. (2022) '"And Wishes also a Paraphrase of Homer's Verses": Structure and Composition of the *Prolegomena* to the *Allegories of the Iliad*', in *Τζετζικαὶ ἔρευναι*, ed. E. E. Prodi, 261–89. Eikasmos Studi Online 4. Bologna.

Rhoby, A. (2009) 'Verschiedene Bemerkungen zur Sebastokratorissa Eirene und zu Autoren in ihrem Umfeld', *Nea Rhome* 6: 305–36.

(2010) 'Ioannes Tzetzes als Auftragsdichter', *Graeco-Latina Brunensia* 15.2: 155–70.

Rhoby, A., and N. Zagklas (2011) 'Zu einer möglichen Deutung von Πανιώτης', *JÖByz* 61: 171–7.

Stanković, V. (2007) 'A Generation Gap or Political Enmity? Emperor Manuel Komnenos, Byzantine Intellectuals and the Struggle for Domination in Twelfth Century Byzantium', *Recueil des travaux de l'Institut d'études byzantines* 44: 209–27.

van Dieten, J. L. (ed.) (1975) *Nicetae Choniatae historia*. Corpus Fontium Historiae Byzantinae 11. Berlin.

Weigl, L. (ed.) (1908) *Johannes Kamateros, Εἰσαγωγὴ ἀστρονομίας: Ein Kompendium griechischer Astronomie und Astrologie, Meteorologie und Ethnographie in politischen Versen*. Leipzig.

Zagklas, N. (2011) 'A Byzantine Grammar Treatise Attributed to Theodoros Prodromos', *Graeco-Latina Brunensia* 16.1: 77–86.

(2016) 'Astrology, Piety and Poverty: Seven Anonymous Poems in Vaticanus gr. 743', *ByzZ* 109.2: 895–918.

Zharkaya, V., and L. Lukhovitskiy (2020) 'Socrates the Judge: A Not So-Platonizing Dialogue on the Deposition of Patriarch Nicholas IV Mouzalon', *ByzZ* 113.1: 219–48.

CHAPTER 15

The Learned Bishop and the Unicorn
Michael Choniates, Poem *5 Lampros*

Ugo Mondini

Michael Choniates (*c.* 1138–1222) was a prominent figure between the end of the twelfth and the first two decades of the thirteenth century.[1] Born around 1138, he spent his early years in Constantinople. In 1182, he was appointed as the metropolitan bishop of the city of Athens. Michael went into exile in 1204, when Boniface of Montferrat took Athens. In the following years, he lived on Keos until 1217,[2] and then he moved to the Monastery of Saint John the Forerunner in Boudonitsa. There he died in February 1222.[3]

Fourteen poems by Michael Choniates (eight in hexameters, six in dodecasyllables) are preserved.[4] Two poems were surely composed during his Athenian period: a satirical poem in hexameters[5] and his renowned poem in dodecasyllables on the current miserable conditions of the city of Athens if compared with its glorious past.[6] Three poems were written after 1204. The first, the *Theano*, was composed during Choniates' stay on Keos.[7] After a sophisticated praise of the fig tree, Choniates glorifies the victory of Keos against a failed invasion attempt by Latins; he also asks Jesus to grant his people the recovery of Constantinople.[8] The second is a

1 For the biography of Michael Choniates, see Stadtmüller (1934), Orlandos (1951), Kolovou (1993: 37–51) and (2001: 3–8).
2 The islands of Keos and Thermiai composed a suffragan bishopric under the jurisdiction of the metropolis of Athens. See Malamut (1988: 1:99–104).
3 Katsaros (1981).
4 Moscow, Gosudarstvennyj Istoričeskij Musej, Sinod. gr. 437 (Vladimir 302) [Diktyon 44062] falsely ascribes the poem *To Saint Mary of Egypt* to Choniates (text in Gregorovius and Lampros [1904: 726]), but it is actually by John Geometres; see Lauxtermann (2003–19: 1:289).
5 Text: Horna (1905: 29–30) and Gregorovius and Lampros (1904: 726–7); see also Zagklas (2019: 249).
6 Text: Lampros (1880: 397–8).
7 Text: Lampros (1880: 375–90).
8 On Homeric quotes, see Tziatzi (2015); see also Zagklas (2019: 249 n. 76). Choniates somehow knew part of the poetic production of the Hellenistic poet Callimachus, at least some verses from the *Aitia* and the *Hecale*; see Reitzenstein (1898) and, more recently, Kennedy (2016: 299–302).

short hexametric poem (*To the Mother of God*), in which Choniates asks the Mother of God to keep providing him with her protection after the fall of Athens into the hands of the Latins.[9] Since Choniates is searching for a protection that is apparently not certain at the moment of composition, he possibly wrote the poem before his arrival on Keos. In a dodecasyllabic poem, Michael gently reminds the Mother of God of his deeds in Athens and asks her for a quiet place to spend the last period of his life.[10] These verses could have been composed in the same period as their hexametric counterpart, but could also belong to the period after 1217, when Choniates was looking for a quiet place to spend the last part of his life.

It is very difficult to date Choniates' remaining poems because of their content and the complete absence of references to the context of their production both in the title and within the verses. They are the following:

- *On the Dormition of the Mother of God* (hexameters)[11]
- *On the Second Coming of Christ* (hexameters)[12]
- *On the Image of the Unicorn* (hexameters)[13]
- *On the Crucifixion* (dodecasyllables)[14]
- *On the Three-Formed God* (dodecasyllables)[15]
- *On the Angels* (dodecasyllables)[16]
- *On the Same Topic* [i.e. angels] (dodecasyllables)[17]
- *On the Ladder Described in John the Ascetic* (hexameters)[18]
- *On the Beheading of Saint Pantaleon* (hexameters)[19]

Michael Choniates' oeuvre still awaits an extensive study. This chapter offers a first study of the poem *On the Image of the Unicorn.*

Choniates' Poem and *The Man in the Well*

Two manuscripts preserve this poem: Florence, Biblioteca Medicea Laurenziana, Plut. 59.12 [Diktyon 16463], fol. 186v and Vatican City, Biblioteca

9 Text: Lampros (1880: 392–3).
10 Text: Gregorovius and Lampros (1904: 727–8) and Papadopoulos-Kerameus (1913: 246–7).
11 Text: Lampros (1880: 390).
12 Text: Lampros (1880: 391–2).
13 Text: Lampros (1880: 393).
14 Text: Lampros (1880: 393–4).
15 Text: Lampros (1880: 394–5).
16 Text: Lampros (1880: 395–6).
17 Text: Lampros (1880: 396).
18 Text: Horna (1905: 30) and Gregorovius and Lampros (1904: 727–8).
19 Text: Horna (1905: 30) and Gregorovius and Lampros (1904: 728).

Apostolica Vaticana, Ott. gr. 59 [Diktyon 65300], fol. 33v. I present the text of the poem with the readings of the Ottobonianus.[20]

Εἰς τὴν εἰκόνα τοῦ μονοκέρωτος

Τλῆμον ἐφήμερε οἷ᾽ ἀπατώμενος οὐκ ἀλεγίζεις,
ἀλλὰ κλεψινόου βιότοιο ἴυγξιν ἀπαχθείς
τῷδ᾽ ἐν δενδρέῳ ἀμφιβέβηκας ὄναρ κομόωντι,
ἀμφαγαπάζων ἣν μέλιτος γλυκεροῖο ἀπορρώξ
5 χείλεα τέγγῃ καί τοι ἄφρονα θυμὸν ἰαίνῃ.
Αὐτὰρ ὄπισθεν ἐλάᾳ διώκων οἰόκερως θήρ –
εἴδωλον τόδε δεινὸν ἀνεκφύκτου θανάτοιο,
κέντρον ἀλιτροσύνης προβεβληκότος ὡς κέρας ὀξύ.
Νέρθεν δ᾽ ἦμαρ ἰδὲ κνέφας ἠΰτε μῦες ἀναιδεῖς
10 αἰὲν ἔδουσι φίλης βιοτῆς πρέμνον ταχύποτμον,
ἐξ ἐρέβους δ᾽ Ἀΐδης ὥς τις δράκων ἀμφικέχηνε·
τοῖα σε δείματ᾽ ἄλλοθεν ἄλλα περισταδὸν ἄγχει.
Σοί γε μήν – ὤλεσε γὰρ φρένας ἡδονή – οὔ τι μέμηλεν
ὄφρα κε νήπιος ὑστατίοισι κακοῖς ἐπικύρσας
15 γνώσεαι οἷα σεαυτὸν ἔοργας ἄτῃσι νόοιο.

On the Image of the Unicorn

Poor mortal, since you are cheated you do not fret!
Instead, misguided by the charms of a deceitful life,
you embrace this tree that has dream as his own foliage.
You take great pleasure if a dripping of sweet honey
5 wets your lips and warms your foolish heart.
But a one-horned beast is chasing you from behind and pursuing you
– this is a fearful image of inescapable death,
sting of sinfulness pitched forward as its sharp horn.
From beneath, day and night, two shameless mice
10 are always gnawing at the short-lived trunk of your life.
From the darkness, Hades opens its mouth wide, like a snake.
Such frightful beasts of various kinds surround you from different sides.
Pleasure ruined your mind. You did not care,
until, a fool, you have fallen into the utter worst of evils
15 and noticed how much you wasted yourself for the blindness of your mind.

20 Cf. Gregorovius and Lampros (1904: 664–5). I disagree on two points with Lampros' edition: the reading of both manuscripts ἐλάα (transcribed by Lampros) is to be considered ἐλάᾳ (from ἐλάω); I do not classicize τοῖα σε into τοῖά σε as Lampros did; see Lauxtermann (2003–19: 2:316–17).

The poem is based on a famous moral tale known by the titles *The Man in the Well* or *The Sweetness of the World*.[21] This tale had non-Greek origins[22] and eventually was spread through two rather similar versions within Greek literature: the first in *Barlaam and Josaphat* (*HBJ*),[23] the second in the so-called third *prolegomenon* of *Stephanites and Ichnelates* (*SI prol.* Γ).[24] The individual tales of *Barlaam and Josaphat* and *Stephanites and Ichnelates* were also highly appreciated independently, and they had likely already been anthologized by the twelfth–thirteenth centuries.[25] For instance, tales from *Barlaam and Josaphat* appear in a collection of *apophthegmata* preserved by the mid-thirteenth-century miscellaneous manuscript Venice, Biblioteca Nazionale Marciana, gr. Z. 494 (= 331) [Diktyon 69965].[26] In ms. Messina, Biblioteca Regionale Universitaria 'Giacomo Longo', S. Salv. 161 [Diktyon 40822] the scribe copied two tales from *Stephanites and Ichnelates*.[27] Both the manuscripts contain *The Man in the Well*. The same tale was often marked by marginal notes that testify to its appreciation by both copyists and readers,[28] and it appears in illuminations next to the text of *Barlaam and Josaphat*.[29] Because of its popularity, its depiction featured as illumination in a wide range of manuscripts[30] as well as on other types of material;[31]

21 The traditional title of the parable is taken from *HBJ* 12.241–6; see Volk (2003: 128) and (2009: 104).

22 On the eastern provenance and the original meaning of the tale, see Kuhn (1888), Odenius (1972–3) and Volk (2009: 105–14).

23 Text: Volk (2006b: 127–30).

24 Text: Puntoni (1889: 45–7); see Krönung (2016) and Lauxtermann (2018).

25 On *Stephanites and Ichnelates* in relation to the *Katomyomachia*, see Lauxtermann in this volume.

26 On this manuscript, see Volk (2009: 475–6). The fortune of these anthologies spanned many centuries. Apart from the Marcianus, ms. Paris, Bibliothèque nationale de France, gr. 1313 [Diktyon 50922], written during the fifteenth century, contains three tales from *Barlaam and Josaphat*. Athos, Skete Hagias Annes, Gero Damianou 20 (Kourilas 630) [Diktyon 31319] was written on Mount Athos in 1642; from this testimony, dating to between the second part of the seventeenth century and the eighteenth century, two other manuscripts were copied: Athos, Mone Dionysiou, 256 (Lampros 3790) [Diktyon 20224] and 363 (Lampros 3897) [Diktyon 20331]; see Volk (2009: 255–6 and 263–4).

27 The first is *The Man in the Well* (*SI prol.* Γ X, 45.16–47.11 ed. Puntoni), the second is a fable on the lion and the hare (*SI* 1.29, pp. 170.2–171.4 ed. Sjöberg = pp. 90.12–92.2 ed. Puntoni). The two tales are linked by the presence of a well.

28 Thanks to Volk's work, I can offer much more data on *Barlaam*'s textual tradition than on *Stephanites*'. On Athos, Mone Iberon, cod. 462 (Lampros 4582) [Diktyon 24059], fol. 83v a secondary hand, more recent than that of the main scribe, marked the presence of the tale with 'behold and marvel!' (ὅρα καὶ θαύμασον); Istanbul, Bibliotheke tou Oikoumenikou Patriarcheiou, 89 (olim Mone Hagias Triados Chalkes cod. 97) [Diktyon 33595], fol. 46v: '<this text> is entirely beautiful and fearful' (ὡραῖον φοβερὸν ὅλον). The tale is often highlighted through *marginalia*; cf. e.g. Cambridge, King's College, gr. 45 (olim 338) [Diktyon 11885], fol. 42r.

29 For other examples, see Pitman and Scattergood (1977). For the textual tradition and the content of *Barlaam*'s cycles of illuminations, see Volk (2009: 525–81). For *Barlaam*'s illuminated manuscripts, see Der Nersessian (1937) and Toumpouri (2015).

30 See pp. 398–402.

31 Volk (2003: 128–30 n. 4).

contemporary drawings also attest to a rather widespread knowledge of the iconography of this image, and therefore of the tale.[32]

In the version in *Barlaam and Josaphat*, the tale appears after a section in which Barlaam explains to Josaphat that the example of apostles, ascetics and monks has to be followed to keep the purity of baptism throughout life (*HBJ* 12.1–174). After illustrating the ephemeral pleasures of life (*HBJ* 12.174–215), Barlaam tells a short moral tale (*HBJ* 12.215–41). While running away from a unicorn, a man stumbles into a well, but he manages to grasp a tree without falling in and he calms down.[33] Suddenly, an enormous snake with gaping maws appears under him, waiting for him to fall. The man also sees a pair of mice gnawing at the roots of the tree and four asps encircling the tree.[34] However, he sees also some honey streaming from the branches higher up on the tree and, savouring this sweet nectar, he completely forgets about the danger. Barlaam gives Josaphat a thorough elucidation of each passage of the tale (*HBJ* 12.241–56): the unicorn represents death;[35] the tree is life, which gets shorter day after day; the four asps are the four different unstable elements of the human body; the snake is Hell, waiting for the fall of the man, who neglects the dangers surrounding him because of the sweetness of worldly delights.

In *Stephanites and Ichnelates*, the tale closes the account of the life of Borzōē, the first translator of the text into Persian. The context and the content of the tale are very similar to the version in *Barlaam*. After a description of the propensity of human nature towards worldly pleasures and possessions, the tale is introduced as a parable (*SI prol.* Γ X, 45.15 ed. Puntoni: ὅμοιός ἐστι ὁ ἄνθρωπος ἀνδρί τινι κτλ.). The tale has the same agents as in *Barlaam*, but there are some minor differences in the Greek vocabulary used and the order of the agents in the vision.[36] For example, at the beginning of the tale, the man has already run away from a vague

32 See Mytilene, Mone tou Leimonos, 62 [Diktyon 45384] (hereafter: Mytil. Leim.), fol. 57v. Cf. p. 400.

33 In the early eastern versions of the text, as well as the Georgian *Balavariani*, the pursuing beast is an elephant, not a unicorn. Within Greek tradition, unicorns are traditionally held to be hostile towards elephants (see *Physiologus*, *Redactio tertia* 2, pp. 263.10–264.9 ed. Sbordone 1936). See Volk (2006a: 171–6) and, for the meaning of the unicorn in eastern and Arabic tradition, Ettinghausen (1950). The link between unicorns and elephants – and perhaps rhinoceros – could have been caused by the fact that these animals have a bulge in the middle of their head (the unicorn a horn, the elephant a trunk).

34 The dream, the mice and the dragon are all *Leitmotive* of Byzantine eschatological descriptions; see e.g. Bzinkowski (2015: 134–7, 142).

35 Einhorn (1972).

36 Volk (2006a: 174–6).

'terrible fear' (*SI prol.* Γ X, 45.15–16 ἔφυγε ἀπὸ φόβου δεινοῦ) which is then specified to be a unicorn (*SI prol.* Γ X, 46.7–11). As Lauxtermann has proved, this is only a later addition as the unicorn was not present in the most ancient manuscripts of *Stephanites and Ichnelates*,[37] in the antigraph of Bε and in the Greek text translated into Latin. Later, the unicorn was added following the example of *Barlaam and Josaphat*.[38]

In comparison to the tale as preserved both by *Barlaam and Josaphat* and by *Stephanites and Ichnelates*, the poem by Choniates rearranges the content: at the beginning, the man is already clinging to the tree, and he savours the honey; unexpectedly, the unicorn appears; then, other elements (two mice, the snake) emerge; the four asps do not appear. While the original tale discloses its meaning only at the end, in Choniates' poem the unicorn is directly identified with death (εἴδωλον τόδε δεινὸν ἀνεκφύκτου θανάτοιο, l. 7).[39]

The unicorn is the most important narrative agent of the poem. While the poem opens with the description of the pitiful condition of man, the introduction of the unicorn within the three central lines allows a shift of perspective. The animal arrives to chase the man who hangs on the tree – the symbol of human life. Thus, it introduces the eschatological vision: only the abrupt appearance of the unicorn/death interrupts the transient sweetness of worldly pleasures and displays the deadly dangers that are awaiting the sinner at the end of his life. But it is too late, and the man falls into Hell. Since the unicorn stands for death and its horn for the sting of sin, the entire description hints at 1 Cor. 15:56.[40]

Interestingly enough, Choniates rewrites the tale with an imagery and a lexicon that resembles what can be found in the tale from *Stephanites and Ichnelates*; nevertheless, he cannot have had access to this version, where the unicorn was originally absent.[41] In Choniates the unicorn is described as 'a fearful image of inescapable death' (εἴδωλον τόδε δεινὸν ἀνεκφύκτου θανάτοιο, l. 7): after the tale, the unicorn is explained in *Stephanites* as a symbol of death that always chases and is always pursuing and close to

37 Paris, Bibliothèque nationale de France, gr. 2231 [Diktyon 51860], fol. 51r–57v and Messina, S. Salv. 161, fol. 18v. In the latter, the unicorn is also absent in the illumination.

38 Lauxtermann (2023). I sincerely thank Marc Lauxtermann for providing me with the drafts of his article.

39 For the relation to death in Byzantium, see *DOP* 55, in particular Dennis (2001) and Wortley (2001); see also Marinis (2017).

40 1 Cor. 15:56: 'the sting of death is sin' (τὸ δὲ κέντρον τοῦ θανάτου ἡ ἁμαρτία). The rare term ἀλιτροσύνη is glossed with ἁμαρτία in Hesych. α 3072 ed. Latte (1953–66) Cf. the use of the tale's illumination as a complement to Ps. 143: 4–5 in London, British Library, Add. 19352 [Diktyon 38960], f. 182v.

41 Lauxtermann (2023). The first attested appearance of the unicorn in this version of the tale dates to the fifteenth century and depends on *HBJ*.

humans, who cannot escape from it (καὶ οὐ δύναταί τις ἐκφυγεῖν).[42] The explanation of the tale in *Stephanites* also says that the two mice gradually eat away the 'life of man, fated to die soon' (πρὸς μικρὸν διαφθείρουσι τὴν ὠκύμορον ζωὴν τοῦ ἀνθρώπου);[43] while talking about the action of mice, Choniates says that they 'are always gnawing at the short-lived trunk of your life' (αἰὲν ἔδουσι φίλης βιοτῆς πρέμνον ταχύποτμον, l. 10). The phrase is also very similar to the passage in *Stephanites* with the adjective ταχύποτμον that appears in grammatical sources together with ὠκύμορον because of their similar derivation from ταχύς and ὠκύς.[44] At the end of the tale in *Stephanites* the man dies while he is preoccupied only with the sweetness of the honey. Choniates' poem also ends with the death of the man, but here the character does eventually realize his sins.

Choniates and Other Medieval and Early Modern Greek Poems on the Parable

Choniates' poem on the unicorn is not the only poem based on *The Man in the Well*. Six dodecasyllabic poems by Manuel Philes deal with the same topic. In these poems, there is no trace of the unicorn, which is replaced with the figure of death.

Poem E246[45] is entitled *On the Image of Life* (εἰς εἰκόνα τοῦ βίου) and opens with the verse 'the sweetness from above, the death below' (l. 1: ἡ γλυκύτης ἄνωθεν, ἡ φθορὰ κάτω) and a reproach of human nature (l. 2); it ends with a comment on the nature of sin (ll. 8–9). The other five poems form a monothematic dossier (Poems E248–52). As often happens, the title of the dossier coincides with the title of its first poem: the Escorialensis preserves the reading 'On the image of life. It showed a tree, on which a man is gaping upwards and eats honey from above; but from below he is deprived of the support by mice',[46] while the Parisinus simply names the dossier as *On the Depiction of Life*.[47] The titles of this cycle only confirm that they belong to the same theme (εἰς τὸ αὐτό): however, these poems

42 *SI prol.* Γ X, 46.10 ed. Puntoni (1889).

43 *SI prol.* Γ X, 47.1–2 ed. Puntoni (1889).

44 Herodian, *Peri pathon*, Gr. Gr. 3.2, p. 261.17 ed. Lentz (1870). Choniates' use of the adjective probably depends on Pindar, *Olympian Ode* 1.65–6, cf. also Tzetzes, *Histories* 5.10.466–8 ed. Leone (2007).

45 Text: Miller (1855: 126). Miller's edition is based on El Escorial, Real Biblioteca, X.IV.20 (Andrés 415) [Diktyon 15031], fol. 76v, while the readings of Paris, Bibliothèque nationale de France, gr. 2876 [Diktyon 52514], fol. 231r are in *apparatus*. For Philes, I follow the abbreviations of Kubina (2020: ix–x).

46 Poem E248 (I p. 127 Miller): εἰς τὴν εἰκόνα τοῦ βίου ἥτις εἶχε δένδρον· ἐν ᾧ ἦν ἄνθρωπος χαίνων ἄνω, καὶ μέλι ἄνωθεν ἐπισπώμενος, κάτωθεν δὲ ὑπὸ μυῶν τὰς βάσεις τρυγώμενος.

47 Miller (1855: 127 n. 5): εἰς τὸν ἐζωγραφήμενον βίον.

are too similar for them to have been all used together,[48] within a cycle of epigrams for a depiction of *The Man in the Well*.[49] They are, rather, different realizations of the same given theme.

The first sixty-six verses of Bergades' *Apokopos* are also based on *The Man in the Well*.[50] Unlike Choniates and Philes, Bergades rephrased the tale's opening chase scene: in his text, a fearful animal does not chase the protagonist, but the latter dreams that they are hunting a deer at sunrise. Then, he finds the tree and sees a hive full of honey. Despite his initial fear of the queen bee, the man starts eating the honey and never stops even when the queen bee continues her attacks. Suddenly, the tree moves and the man stops eating and sees two mice who have gnawed the roots of the tree; then, he falls into the jaws of a dragon.

These occurrences of *The Man in the Well* are very similar to the contents of Choniates' poem. The following synopsis lists the main features of each poem (Table 15.1).

While the *Apokopos* is a first-person narrative, all the other poems are written as a direct reproach against the man on the tree; Man.Phil. E251 begins with two verses of direct speech in the first person, followed by four lines of reproach. In five poems out of seven (Mi.Chon.; Man.Phil. E246, E248, E250, E251) there is a vocative form that explicitly refers to the man.

The poem by Choniates and the four poems in Philes' corpus usually retain some images of the tale with their meaning, implicit or not (most of all honey/worldly sweetness, tree/human life, dragon/Hell), while some other agents are replaced with their explicit referent (unicorn/death in Philes) or avoided (the four snakes). Bergades keeps the images without explicit explanations.

In the great majority of the poems, there is no trace of the initial chase nor of the fall; Bergades' *Apokopos* turns the scene into a deer hunt by the main character. Most notably, any reference to the well is avoided. After all, even the original text of the tale deals with the human propensity to sin.[51] The poem by Choniates and the six by Philes begin with a man who is already eating the tree's honey, and then there is the vision. Four poems preserve some traces of the presence of the unicorn, both in depicting death as an animal (Man.Phil. E250) and in talking about its sting

48 See Table 15.1.

49 Text: Miller (1855: 127–9), based on Escor. X.IV.20, fols. 77v–79r (text) and Par. gr. 2876, fols. 193v–194r (*apparatus*).

50 Text: Vejleskov (2005: 184–9). Commentary: Matta (2017: 36–41). See also Bzinkowski (2015: 137–45).

51 Messina, S. Salv. 161, fol. 18v copies the version of *Stephanites and Ichnelates* from the point in which the man has already fallen into the pond without the initial chase, although its meaning is explained a few lines after.

Table 15.1 *The Man in the Well*: comparison between Michael Choniates, Manuel Philes and *Apokopos*

Mi.Chon. [II pers.]	Man.Phil. E246 [II pers.]	Man.Phil. E248 [II pers.]	Man.Phil. E249 [II pers.]
- No initial chase - No well - Tree - Honey - **Unicorn / Death** - Two mice - Dragon/Hades - *While falling into Hell, the character becomes aware he was deceived*	- No initial chase - No well - Synopsis - Man and honey - The character should help himself - Only one mouse - Dragon/Hades - *Nature of man's error*	- No initial chase - No well - Vanity of the world - Honey - Dragon	- No initial chase - No well - Man and Honey - **Upcoming death with its sting** - Dragon/Hades - Time destroys the tree
(no four snakes)	(no four snakes)	(no mice, no four snakes, no unicorn)	(no mice, no four snakes)
Man.Phil. E250 [II pers.]	Man.Phil. E251 [ll. 1–2, I pers.; ll. 3–6, II pers.]	Man.Phil. E252 [II pers.]	*Apokopos* [I pers.]
- No initial chase - No well - Man and honey - **Upcoming death / animal** As a generic violent fiend, death is both the dragon and the unicorn of the tale	- No initial chase - No well - Honey - Tree of life / Time - Dragon / Hades - **Death and its sting** - The character is still deceived	- No initial chase - No well - Honey - Tree of life - The character should help himself - **Death and its sting** - Dragon / Hades - *Final plea to the character*	- Deer Hunt - Tree of life - Honey - Bees and the Queen Bee - Fall of the tree - Mice - Dragon - *While falling into Hell, the character becomes aware he was deceived*
(no mice, no four snakes)	(no four snakes)	(no four snakes)	(**no well,** no four snakes)

Abbreviations: Mi.Chon.: Michael Choniates, *On the Image of the Unicorn*; Man.Phil.: Manuel Philes; *Apokopos*: Bergades, *Apokopos*, ll. 1–66.

(Man.Phil. E248, 251–2); in Man.Phil. E249, 251–2 the description of the sting closely resembles Mi.Chon. l. 8.[52] Finally, Bergades' *Apokopos* has the same content after the deer hunt: the man is deceived by honey, and the queen bee (which replaces the unicorn) stings him.[53] Man.Phil. E251 ends with the man deceived by honey despite the vision of death; Man.Phil. E246 and E252 present a rather similar, but not tragic ending. Mi.Chon. and the *Apokopos* end with the final fall of the man into Hell, when he realizes that he is lost.[54]

The synopsis makes clear that Choniates' rearrangement of the original tale is not isolated within the *corpus* of Byzantine literary works relating to *The Man in the Well*. Death (in its various forms: as a unicorn, as a generic violent animal, as its sting) appears usually when the character has already been deceived by the honey; its arrival opens the vision of the dangers that loom over him. At the same time, the poem by Choniates is rather exceptional for the language, the metre and the narrative effectiveness of the reproach against the sinner; but the selection of contents, their order and other inner features can be understood as belonging within a well-established set of literary approaches to *The Man in the Well* in Byzantine poetry.

Imagining the Tale: Poems, Images and Captions

As preserved by the Ottobonianus manuscript, the title *On the Image of the Unicorn* (εἰς τὴν εἰκόνα τοῦ μονοκέρωτος) is very similar to the titles of Man.Phil. E246 and E248 *On the Image of Life* (εἰς τὴν εἰκόνα τοῦ βίου). In particular, the two versions of the title of E248 leave no doubt about their function: in ms. Par. gr. 2876, the participle ἐζωγραφήμενον clearly refers to an image; the verb ἔχω of ms. Escor. X.IV.20 is frequently used to describe the content of images.[55]

The depiction of *The Man in the Well* is one of the most widespread images across Eurasian cultures and appears frequently in Byzantine art.[56] The testimonies can be divided into three groups: depictions that are part of the illumination cycles of *Barlaam and Josaphat*; single depictions in

52 Man.Phil. E249.2: 'the sting of death' (τὸ τῆς φθορᾶς … κέρας); E251.4 'the sting of death' (τὸ τῆς φθορᾶς … κέρας); E252.6–7: 'death, the destroyer of things, stretches its sharp horn' (ὁ θάνατος γὰρ ὁ φθορεὺς τῶν πραγμάτων | τὸ πικρὸν ἐξέτεινε τοῦ τέλους κέρας). Cf. n. 37 above.

53 For the bee as a symbol of death, see Matta (2017: 36–41).

54 See the following section.

55 The use of the imperfect tense (εἶχε, 'had', 'contained') is very interesting. Probably, the dossier never had an image attached, but the collector knew that these epigrams were composed for an image he describes through the title.

56 For an overview of the depictions of *The Man in the Well* across cultures, see Zin (2011).

manuscripts and elsewhere;[57] depictions that are related to *Stephanites and Ichnelates*.[58]

Four illumination cycles are known for *Barlaam and Josaphat*.[59] Each cycle has its own set of captions that are meant to clarify the content of the images; of the twelve manuscripts that preserve these captions, only five of them were eventually illuminated.[60]

As these illuminations were intended to be attached to the text of the parable, they usually follow the narrative and, consequently, two out of the four cycles have features that cannot agree with the contents of the poems. Both in ms. Paris, Bibliothèque nationale de France, gr. 1128 [Diktyon 50726],[61] fol. 68r and ms. Cambridge, King's College, gr. 45 [Diktyon 11885], fol. 41v, the depiction is divided into two distinct moments in which only the figure of the man is repeated: first, he is chased by the unicorn; secondly, he is above the tree (in Cambridge, King's College, gr. 45) or he is going to climb it (in Par. gr. 1128). The same type of 'narrative depiction' can be seen in ms. London, British Library, Add. 19352 [Diktyon 38960], fol. 182v and ms. Vatican City, Biblioteca Apostolica Vaticana, Barb. gr. 372 [Diktyon 64915], fol. 237v; the post-Byzantine illumination to the version of *Stephanites and Ichnelates* in Barb. gr. 172, fol. 15v also displays a narrative development. Although no illumination was eventually made in the two preserved manuscripts of the so-called 'Cycle 1',[62] their captions prove that the image of *The Man in the Well* would have been very similar to the ones in Par. gr. 1128 and Cambridge, King's College, gr. 45.[63]

An epigram to this kind of image could hardly describe the sudden appearance of unicorn/death when the man is on the tree, as the depiction

57 Volk (2003: 128–30 n. 4).

58 Some chapters of *Stephanites and Ichnelates* are preserved by New York, The Morgan Library and Museum, M.397 [Diktyon 46625] (the most ancient manuscript of its textual tradition) and they are accompanied by several images; on the manuscript and its contents, see Husselman (1938) and Lauxtermann (2018: 76). The Eugenian version was originally illuminated, see Lauxtermann (2018: 75–6). Both Leiden, Bibliotheek der Rijksuniversiteit, Vulc. 93 [Diktyon 38266] and Messina, S. Salv. 161 have drawings next to the text of *Stephanites*, but the unicorn is absent both in the text and in the picture; Vatican City, Biblioteca Apostolica Vaticana, Barb. gr. 172 [Diktyon 64720] has post-Byzantine illuminations.

59 Der Nersessian (1937), Volk (2009: 525–81), Toumpouri (2015) and Hilsdale (2017).

60 Toumpouri (2015: 390–2).

61 It is the main manuscript of 'Cycle 3'; see Volk (2009: 536–86). For its caption to *The Man in the Well*, see Volk (2009: 561, no. 96).

62 Volk (2009: 525–36); for the captions to *The Man in the Well*, see Volk (2009: 530, no. 46).

63 As Toumpouri (2015) shows, the cycle of illuminations on Athos, Mone Iberon, 463 (Lampros 4583) [Diktyon 24060] should be considered a fourth typology. However, there is neither illumination nor caption for *The Man in the Well*.

represents the two moments separately. On the contrary, the selection and the disposition of the contents within the poems by Choniates and Philes imply that the image would have represented the tale without a narrative development. In this respect, the depiction of 'Cycle 2' would fit better than the other two.[64] Although the two known illuminations of this cycle are unfortunately very poorly preserved,[65] both of them occupy an entire folio and the disposition of the scene is vertical. In this version, the chase is over, and the man is already hanging on the tree, in the middle of the picture; the unicorn looks at him from above, at the edge of the well; the dragon, the mice and the snakes are underneath.

However, some issues remain. First, the absence of the four snakes. Although ms. Jerusalem, Patriarchike Bibliotheke, Timiou Staurou 42 has a specific caption that attests to their presence in the illumination, the snakes can be easily skipped as their meaning is rather complex and secondary to the general sense of the tale. For the same reason, their presence in depictions and narratives is anything but necessary: they disappear even within *Apokopos*' rewriting, which elsewhere follows the original tale in every other detail.[66]

Another issue is the role and the position of the unicorn/death. As has been said in the first section of this chapter, the use of the unicorn as a tool of revelation is very effective from a narrative point of view and, at the same time, does not affect the storytelling and its general meaning. This type of relocation could have had an iconographic parallel. As mentioned before, the four snakes were probably the element of the tale most unattractive to Byzantine readers, and they are often omitted. Nevertheless, in ms. Cambridge, King's College, gr. 45, fol. 41v, the asps are not under the tree but emerge from a wall in front of it. Thus, the depiction has a chiastic structure (chasing animal + human; human + snakes) and the asps become

64 The drawing in Mytil. Leim. 62, fol. 57v has great similarities with the depiction of 'Cycle' 2 of *Barlaam and Josaphat*.

65 Ioannina, Zosimaia Bibliotheke, cod. 1 [Diktyon 32798] was one of the three parts into which an original single codex had been divided: the other two are Cambridge, University Library, Add. 4491 [Diktyon 12129] and New York, Columbia University, Rare Book and Manuscript Library, Plimpton MS 9 [Diktyon 46599]. The section in Ioannina was lost during the Second World War (see Volk [2009: 309–12] and Toumpouri [2015: 390–1, nn. 8–9]), but Der Nersessian (1937: 63 fig. 24) contains a drawing of the illumination of *The Man in the Well* on fol. 54r, which was already very damaged around the 1930s. A very similar illumination – in a very similar state – also appears in Jerusalem, Patriarchike Bibliotheke, Timiou Staurou 42 [Diktyon 35938], fol. 75r.

66 They are present neither in Barb. gr. 372, fol. 237v, nor in Mytil. Leim. 62, fol. 57v, nor – if I see correctly from the digital reproduction – in Par. gr. 1128, fol. 68r. The drawing in Der Nersessian (1937: 63 fig. 24) does not report any caption to highlight the presence of the four snakes, but it could have disappeared before Der Nersessian's inspection of Ioannina, Zosimaia Bibliotheke, cod. 1.

much more similar to something that threatens the man than to the representation of the parts of his soul, as in the original tale.[67]

The relocation of the unicorn allows for a single narrative unit in both poetry and figurative art. In ms. Messina, S. Salv. 161, fol. 18v the drawing depicts the man already on the tree but without any unicorn, since the tale from *Stephanites* omits its presence.[68] The man is also on the tree in ms. Paris, Bibliothèque nationale de France, gr. 36 [Diktyon 49597], fol. 203v and two fearful animals (a lion and a unicorn) threaten him from both sides.[69] In contrast, the illumination of the so-called 'Cycle 2' of *Barlaam* does not easily allow this relocation. In fact, although the initial chase is avoided, the scene is split into three sections, which are rigidly divided and follow the chronological order of the tale from above to below. Furthermore, the Ierosolimitanus attests to the presence of a note (namely the word βόθρος, 'abyss', 'well') which confirms for the viewer this division between the first and the second section of the illumination. Consequently, the well occupies most of the scene in this type of illumination as it contains both the tree (with the man) and the fearful animals beneath.[70]

Finally, there is the amount of information. If the poems by Choniates and Philes were epigrams, they could have been written in a single place on the folio or within a frame all around the image, as they are quite short; otherwise, they could also have been split into several sections, each written next to the figure at which they are hinting.[71] Extensive captions to *The Man in the Well* are attested. The above-mentioned London, British Library, Add. 19352, fol. 182v, put the illumination of this tale between LXX Ps. 143:4–5.[72] In contrast to the 'twin' image and captions in ms. Barb. gr. 372, fol. 237v, every element of this illumination is explained through thorough captions.[73] Ms. Par. gr. 36, fol. 203v preserves an illumination of

67 This depiction is described by a note on fol. 42v of the same manuscript as θεωρεῖ τέσσαρας κεφαλὰς ἀσπίδων τοῦ τοίχου (post corr.; ante corr. τοῦ τεύχου) προβεβληκυίας.

68 On the absence of the unicorn, see Lauxtermann (2023).

69 The illumination seems to resemble the details that are included in *Stephanites and Ichnelates*: the man is hanging to two branches of the tree and stands on a base; cf. *SI prol.* Γ X, 45.17–19. At the same time, the presence of the lion depends on the second tale in *SI* (1.29). In both depictions, the tree has fruits, not honey; on the contrary, the presence of two different species of birds in the illumination of Par. gr. 36 still needs to be explained. In general, both for the fruits and the birds, the depiction recalls Bergades, *Apokopos*, 25–32.

70 The position of the tree within the well is very clear in *SI prol.* Γ X, 45.16, while it is only implicitly hinted in *HBJ* 12.224–5.

71 The poems by Philes are best suited to appear as such, as they can be easily divided into sections of one, two or three verses: each section addresses a single element of the image; consequently, they could have been attached to each section of the depiction within the layout of the page.

72 Ps. 143:4–5: 'man is like to vanity, | his days pass away as a shadow' (ἄνθρωπος ματαιότητι ὡμοιώθη, | αἱ ἡμέραι αὐτοῦ ὡσεὶ σκιὰ παράγουσιν).

73 Text: Der Nersessian (1970: 57 I, ad fol. 182v).

the tale, introduced by an epigram with the name of its artist;[74] four texts in prose are arranged next to every element of the image and explain their meaning: as in the Londinensis, these texts are quite long and detailed.[75] The absence of Barlaam's text does not necessarily cause the need for (long) captions to be added to the illumination of *The Man in the Well* (cf. e.g. ms. Barb. gr. 372); however, its presence makes unnecessary any extensive explanations on the plot.[76] If poems like Man.Phil. E248 and E250 could have been written for any type of image, the other poems by Philes and, above all, the poem by Choniates could be attached to an image only if the text of the tale was not nearby.

To sum up, if the poems by Philes and Choniates were epigrams or descriptions of an existing image, their composition would be linked to a non-narrative depiction of *The Man in the Well*, in which all the elements are placed within a single scene (cf. e.g. the one in Par. gr. 36). It is much more probable that the poem by Choniates and, at least, Man.Phil. E246, E249, E251, E252 were thought to give a thorough account; therefore they would have been unnecessary with the tale itself in their vicinity.

Choniates and his Source

But does the poem by Choniates depend on the text of the tale or is it just a learned description in hexameters of an image? Inner features and the structure of the narrative confirm the first hypothesis.

There are close similarities between the tale in *HBJ* and Choniates' poem (Mi.Chon.). The verb διώκω describes the chase of the unicorn (*HBJ* 12.244; Mi.Chon. l. 6) and the verb χάσκω the opening of dragon's mouth (*HBJ* 12.237–8: ὁ πικρὸς δράκων κέχηνε καταπιεῖν; Mi.Chon. l. 11 ὥς τις δράκων ἀμφικέχηνε). In *HBJ*, the perfect participle of verb προβάλλω describes the heads of the four asps that emerge from the tree (*HBJ* 12.233–4); in Mi.Chon. the horn that emerges from the unicorn's head (Mi.Chon. l. 7).

There is another piece of evidence to take into account. The following synopsis presents a comparison between the contents of two versions of the tale (*HBJ*, Mi.Chon.); to this synopsis I add the *Apokopos* as a benchmark because the text follows the tale strictly, in a manner very similar to Choniates. The entry of Mi.Chon. simply lines up with the

74 *BEiÜ* IV, FR1 in Rhoby (2019: 119–20 + 600, table XX).

75 Text: Antonopoulos (2007: 38–9).

76 In fact, it is hard to find epigrams that openly describe the objects on which they are inscribed; see Paul (2008) and Rhoby (2011).

Table 15.2 *The Man in the Well*: comparison between *HBJ*'s version, Michael Choniates and *Apokopos*

HBJ	Mi.Chon.	*Apokopos*
- Escape from the unicorn - Fall into the well - On the tree he feels safe		- Deer Hunt - The man is in the middle of a meadow. Here, he finds a tree and relaxes next to it.
- Vision (1) the two mice (2) the dragon (3) the four asps		
- Honey from above the tree - The man savours the honey - He forgets about: (1) the unicorn	- The man is deceived - Tree - Honey - Vision (1) unicorn	- The man notices the hive and climbs the tree - The man savours the honey - Bees and the Queen Bee attack but he is still eating
(2) **the dragon**	(2) **mice**	- *The tree moves* and the man stops eating. He sees the **mice**.
(3) *the precariousness of the tree* (= **the mice**)	(3) **dragon**	- **dragon**
- He forgets all these things - He only cares about the sweetness of the honey	- Many dangers - But he does not care because of the honey - *He will notice his foolishness only when he eventually falls*	- *While falling into Hell, the character becomes aware he had been deceived*
Explanation: general meaning; unicorn; well; **tree and mice**; four asps; **dragon**; honey		

correspondent narrative point in the other three texts. As has been said before, Mi.Chon. – as all the poems by Manuel Philes quoted above – begins with the man who is already in the tree (see Table 15.2).

The narrative structure of the poem confirms that Choniates follows the text of *HBJ*.[77] The poem mentions the unicorn, the mice and the dragon

77 This literary operation is very similar to the passage of the *Apokopos* by Bergades, as the synopsis shows. Most notably, the appearance of the bees and of the queen bee occurs precisely when, in *HBJ*, the name of the unicorn reappears. In both cases, the man does not bother about the animal because he is deceived by the honey.

but not the four asps. However, although Choniates follows the order of the account strictly, the order of appearance of the dragon and the mice is reversed. This shows that Choniates' order actually follows *HBJ* 12.241–56, which explains the mice before the dragon.

Consequently, Choniates did not describe an image of *The Man in the Well*, but he based his poem on the tale as it appears in *HBJ* and restructured the story on the basis of the order of its explanation in *HBJ* 12.241–56.[78] In this context, εἰκών and εἰκονίζειν are used to reveal the meaning of the moralistic account (*HBJ* 12.251–3). Since the unicorn is the most important agent of Choniates' poem and is the symbol of death, the title refers to the fact that the poem is 'on the symbol of the unicorn' more than simply 'on the image'. In this sense, the title *On the Image of the Unicorn* could have a specific meaning related to the text. In *Barlaam and Josaphat*, the section is called ὁμοίωσις ('similitude', *HBJ* 12.241) and παραβολή ('parable', *HBJ* 13.1). The first term is also used in *HBJ* 14.6–7 to introduce the parable *The City with Foreign Kings*; moreover, the adjective ὅμοιος appears at the beginning of *The Fowler and the Nightingale* (*HBJ* 10.30), *The Man in the Well* (*HBJ* 12.220) and *The Man and his Three Friends* (*HBJ* 13.5). The term παραβολή introduces the tale of *The Wise and Foolish Virgins* (*HBJ* 9.120). The same markers are used as titles in the anthologies.[79]

In fact, Choniates' knowledge of the tale does not imply that he had access to the complete *HBJ*. Ms. Venice, Biblioteca Nazionale Marciana, gr. Z. 494 is a complex miscellany which assembles a great variety of moral works, among them the *apophthegmata patrum* and other *kephalaia kai logoi psychopheleis*. *Barlaam*'s parables are at the beginning of the first *centuria* (fols. 208rv); an abridged account of the *Ladder* by John Klimax is found at the end of the fourth *centuria*, followed by some excerpts from Mark the Hermit (fols. 231rv). Perhaps Choniates had access to the tale through a similar anthology.

Short Hexametric Poems and Moral Tales

As was said at the beginning of this chapter, it is difficult to ascribe *On the Image of the Unicorn* to a specific moment of Choniates' biography as there is no reference to the context of composition. It is, however, interesting

78 Cf. also the use of ἀπατώμενος in l. 1 of the poem, which echoes *HBJ* 12.241 τῶν τῇ ἀπάτῃ τοῦ παρόντος βίου προστετηκότων.

79 Cf. e.g. Marc. gr. Z. 494 fol. 208v: 'parable of earthly life and on how humans take the wrong way because they are deceived; the sweetness of the world' (παρομοίωσις τοῦ ἐνθένδε βίου καὶ ὅπως πλανῶνται χλευαζόμενοι οἱ ἄνθρωποι, τὸ ἡδὺ τοῦ κόσμου).

to see how the author reshaped the tale to convey a different perspective on human life. While the tale is introduced by a chapter on the human propensity to earthly desires in *Barlaam and Josaphat*,[80] Choniates' poem lacks contextualization. The author transforms the content into a direct reproach in the second person and, in this way, his narrative assumes a far more tragic and universalistic tone; it describes all of humanity as tainted and deceived by sin and, more notably, unwilling to escape from its condition, until it is too late.

Choniates did the same with another moral tale. The Ottobonianus preserves *On the Ladder Described in John the Ascetic*, a poetical rewriting of the description of the ladder in John Klimax's *Ladder of Divine Ascent*. A brief comparison of the two poems demonstrates their affinities. Both poems are quite short (15 and 18 verses, respectively) and are written in hexameters and in Homeric language and style. Furthermore, they have a very similar structure: an allocution/a direct question at the beginning; a central section in which the poet describes the subject; and, at the end, a moral sentence. Just like *Barlaam and Josaphat*, several manuscripts of *The Ladder of Divine Ascent* are illuminated; the description of the ladder circulated within anthologies – at least in one case together with the text of *The Man in the Well*.[81]

The function of both poems is not certain: they could have been hexametrical epigrams meant to be copied in the proximity of a 'static' illumination of *The Man in the Well* and of the Heavenly Ladder,[82] but also a poetical rephrasing of their prose description. Choniates' interest in moral tales in prose could relate to his patronage – if so, in Constantinople or on Keos; it could also depend on manuscript production (the two poems could be book epigrams for illumination of the subjects), maybe in Athens where he prompted the copying of various texts. The use of hexameters and the subject of the poem could hint at a learned public. But what these poems certainly testify is that Choniates was strongly interested in this type of short text about life and the human condition, and similar reflections about life can be seen throughout his literary production.

80 *HBJ* 12.241–2: 'this parable deals with those who cling to the deceitfulness of present life' (αὕτη ἡ ὁμοίωσις τῶν τῇ ἀπάτῃ τοῦ παρόντος βίου προστετηκότων).

81 In Marc. gr. Z. 494 *Barlaam*'s parables are at the beginning of the first *centuria* (fols. 208rv) and the abridged account of Klimax's *Ladder* is at the end of the fourth *centuria*, followed by excerpts from Mark the Hermit (fols. 231rv).

82 Epigrams in hexameters are very rarely composed for supports other than manuscripts; see Rhoby (2019: 68–9).

Bibliography

Antonopoulos, E. (2007) 'Πάντα ἀτελῆ, καὶ ἄθλια καὶ ἄχρηστα: Κώδιξ Parisinus Graecus 36 (14ος–15ος αἰ.), γραφόμενα καὶ ζωγραφούμενα', *Ionios Logos* 1: 15–42.

Bzinkowski, M. (2015) 'Notes on Eschatological Patterns in a 12th Century Anonymous Satirical Dialogue: The *Timarion*', *Eos* 102: 129–48.

Dennis, G. T. (2001) 'Death in Byzantium', *DOP* 55: 1–7.

Der Nersessian, S. (1937) *L'illustration du Roman de Barlaam et Joasaph*. Paris.

(1970) *L'illustration des Psautiers Grecs du Moyen Age*, vol. 2: *Londre, Add. 19.352*. Paris.

Einhorn, J. W. (1972) 'Das Einhorn als Sinnzeichen des Todes: Die Parabel vom Mann im Abgrund', *FMS* 6: 381–417.

Ettinghausen, R. (1950) *Studies in Muslim Iconography I: The Unicorn*. Washington, DC.

Gregorovius, F., and S. Lampros (1904) *Ἱστορία τῆς πόλεως Ἀθηνῶν κατὰ τοὺς μέσους αἰώνας*. Athens.

Hilsdale, C. J. (2017) 'Worldliness in Byzantium and Beyond: Reassessing the Visual Networks of Barlaam and Ioasaph', *The Medieval Globe* 3.2: 57–96.

Horna, K. (1905) *Analekten zur byzantinischen Literatur*. Vienna.

Husselman, E. M. (1938) *A Fragment of Kalilah and Dimnah: From MS. 397 in the Pierpont Morgan Library*. London.

Katsaros, V. (1981) ''Η "κατὰ τὴν Ἑλλάδα" βυζαντινὴ Μονὴ τοῦ Προδρόμου τελευταῖος σταθμὸς τῆς ζωῆς τοῦ Μιχαὴλ Χωνιάτη', *Byzantiaka* 1: 101–37.

Kennedy, S. (2016) 'Callimachus in a Later Context: Michael Choniates', *Eikasmos* 27: 291–312.

Kolovou, F. (1993) *Μιχαήλ Χωνιάτης: Συμβολή στη μελέτη του βίου του και του επιστολογραφικού του έργο*. Ioannina.

(ed.) (2001) *Michaelis Choniatae Epistulae*. Berlin.

Krönung, B. (2016) 'The Wisdom of the Beasts: The Arabic *Book of Kalīla and Dimna* and the Byzantine *Book of Stephanites and Ichnelates*', in *Fictional Storytelling in the Medieval Eastern Mediterranean and Beyond*, ed. C. Cupane and B. Krönung, 427–60. Leiden.

Kubina, K. (2020) *Die enkomiastische Dichtung des Manuel Philes*. Berlin.

Kuhn, E. (1888) 'Der Mann im Brunnen: Geschichte eines indischen Gleichnisses', in *Festgruss an Otto von Böhtlingk zum Doktor-Jubiläum 3. Februar 1888 von seinen Freunden*, ed. R. von Roth, 68–76. Stuttgart.

Lampros, S. P. (ed.) (1880) *Μιχαὴλ Ἀκομινάτου τοῦ Χωνιάτου τὰ σωζόμενα*, vol. 2. Athens.

Latte, K. (ed.) (1953–66) *Hesychii Alexandrini lexicon*, 2 vols. Copenhagen.

Lauxtermann, M. D. (2003–19) *Byzantine Poetry from Pisides to Geometres: Texts and Contexts*, 2 vols. Wiener Byzantinistische Studien 24. Vienna.

(2018) 'The Eugenian Recension of Stephanites and Ichnelates: Prologue and Paratexts', *Nea Rhome* 15: 55–106.

(2023) 'Unicorn or No Unicorn: *Stephanites and Ichnelates*, Prol. III.10', in *Virtute vir tutus: Studi di letteratura greca, bizantina e umanistica offerti a Enrico V. Maltese*, ed. L. Silvano, A. M. Taragna and P. Varalda, 409–28. Ghent.

Lentz, A. (ed.) (1870) *Grammatici Graeci*, vol. 3.2. Leipzig (repr. Hildesheim 1965).

Leone, P. L. M. (ed.) (2007) *Ioannis Tzetzae Historiae*, 2nd ed. Galatina.

Malamut, E. (1988) *Les îles de l'empire byzantin, VIIIe–XIIe siècles*, 2 vols. Paris.

Marinis, V. (2017) *Death and the Afterlife in Byzantium: The Fate of the Soul in Theology, Liturgy, and Art*. Cambridge.

Matta, S. (2017) 'Απόκοπος: Ένας σχολιασμός', PhD Thesis, Thessaloniki.

Miller, E. (ed.) (1855) *Manuelis Philae Carmina*, vol. 1. Paris.

Odenius, O. (1972–3) 'Der Mann im Brunnen und der Mann im Baum: Ein ikonographischer Beitrag', *Schweizerisches Archiv für Volkskunde* 68.19: 477–86, tables 786–7.

Orlandos, A. (1951) 'Ἡ Προσωπογραφία Μιχαὴλ τοῦ Χωνιάτου', *Επετηρίς Εταιρείας Βυζαντινών Σπουδών* 21: 210–14.

Papadopoulos-Kerameus, A. (1913) *Noctes Petropolitanae: Sbornik vizantīĭskikh tekstov XII–XIII viekov*. St. Petersburg.

Paul, A. (2008) 'Beobachtungen zu ἐκφράσεις in Epigrammen auf Objekten: Lassen wir Epigramme sprechen!', in *Die kulturhistorische Bedeutung byzantinischer Epigramme*, ed. W. Hörandner and A. Rhoby, 61–74. Vienna.

Pitman, R., and J. Scattergood (1977) 'Some Illustrations of the Unicorn Apologue from Barlaam and Ioasaph', *Scriptorium* 31.1: 85–90.

Puntoni, V. (ed.) (1889) *Στεφανίτης καὶ Ἰχνηλάτης: Quattro recensioni della versione greca del Kitab Kalilah va-Dimnah*. Florence.

Reitzenstein, R. (1898) Rec. U. von Wilamowitz-Moellendorff, *Callimachi hymni et epigrammata*, Berolini 1897, *Deutsche Literaturzeitung* 19: 225–8.

Rhoby, A. (2011) 'Inscriptional Poetry: Ekphrasis in Byzantine Tomb Epigrams', *ByzSlav* 69.3: 193–204.

Rhoby, A. (ed.) (2019) *Byzantinische Epigramme in inschriftlicher Überlieferung*, vol. 4: *Ausgewählte byzantinische Epigramme in illuminierten Handschriften*. Vienna.

Sbordone, F. (ed.) (1936) *Physiologus*, 2nd ed. Rome.

Stadtmüller, G. (1934) *Michael Choniates, Metropolit von Athen (ca. 1138–ca. 1222)*. Rome.

Toumpouri, M. (2015) 'L'illustration du "Roman de Barlaam et Joasaph" reconsidérée: Le cas du Hagion Oros, Monè Ibèron, 463', in *Barlaam und Josaphat: Neue Perspektiven auf ein europäisches Phänomen*, ed. C. Cordoni and M. Meyer, 389–415. Berlin.

Tziatzi, M. (2015) 'Homerzitate im Gedicht Θεανώ des Michael Choniates', in *Beiträge zum Gedenken an Christos Theodoridis*, ed. M. M. Billerbeck, F. Montanari and K. Tsantsanoglou, 521–41. Berlin.

Vejleskov, P. (ed.) (2005) *Apokopos*, with an English translation by M. Alexiou. Cologne.

Volk, R. (2003) 'Das Fortwirken der Legende von Barlaam und Ioasaph in der byzantinischen Hagiographie, insbesondere in den Werken des Symeon Metaphrastes', *JÖByz* 53: 127–69.

(2006a) 'Medizinisches im Barlaam-Roman: Ein Streifzug durch den hochsprachlichen griechischen Text, seine Vorläufer, Parallelen und Nachdichtungen', *ByzZ* 99.1: 145–93.

(2006b) *Die Schriften des Johannes von Damaskos: Historia animae utilis de Barlaam et Ioasaph (spuria)*, vol. 2: *Text und zehn Appendices.* Berlin.

(2009) *Die Schriften des Johannes von Damaskos: Historia animae utilis de Barlaam et Ioasaph (spuria)*, vol. 1: *Einführung*. Berlin.

Wortley, J. (2001) 'Death, Judgment, Heaven, and Hell in Byzantine "Beneficial Tales"', *DOP* 55: 53–69.

Zagklas, N. (2019) '"How Many Verses Shall I Write and Say?": Poetry in the Komnenian Period (1081–1204)', in *A Companion to Byzantine Poetry*, ed. W. Hörandner, A. Rhoby and N. Zagklas, 237–63. Brill's Companions to the Byzantine World 4. Leiden.

Zin, M. (2011) 'The Parable of "The Man in the Well": Its Travels and its Pictorial Traditions from Amaravati to Today', *Warsaw Indological Studies* 4: 33–93.

General Index

For EU product safety concerns, contact us at Calle de José Abascal, 56–1°, 28003 Madrid, Spain or eugpsr@cambridge.org.

www.ingramcontent.com/pod-product-compliance
Lightning Source LLC
LaVergne TN
LVHW021602060925
820435LV00004B/52